LOUISIANA

A Narrative History

LOUISIANA

A Narrative History

By

EDWIN ADAMS DAVIS

Head of the Department of History, Louisiana State University
Founding member of the Southern Historical Association
Past President, Louisiana Historical Association

ILLUSTRATED

BATON ROUGE

CLAITOR'S BOOK STORE

1961

For
"Kiddo"
(La Verna Rowe Davis)
With Love

FOREWORD

THE STORY of Louisiana is one of the most fascinating and fabulous sagas in the history of the Americas. Many flags have flown over the land and under each have occurred courageous movements, tragic and joyous events, and commonplace but interesting incidents of everyday living. Here is no ordinary state story.

Frenchmen from Normandy and Brittany and the vicinity of Paris first settled Louisiana during the last year of the seventeenth century, led by intrepid Pierre le Moyne, Sieur d'Iberville, who was the first governor of the colony. French, German, Swiss, and other immigrants slowly and painfully learned the ways of colony planting during the years of the next six decades. During the French colonial era, Louisiana was first a royal colony, then a proprietary colony under Antoine Crozat, a proprietary colony under the noted (perhaps infamous or notorious would be better words) John Law, and after 1732 a royal colony again.

The Spanish acquired Louisiana in 1762 and sent scientist Don Antonio de Ulloa to be its first governor, but Ulloa was expelled by irate French colonials. General Alejandro O'Reilly punished the rebel leaders and forcibly established Spanish authority. O'Reilly was succeeded by a series of strong and well-liked governors who actively promoted the welfare of the people and of the colony, including the brilliant Bernardo de Gálvez and the fun-loving, though serious and competent Baron de Carondelet. The Spanish welcomed Acadians, *Isleños* from the Canary Islands, American loyalists prior to and during the American Revolution, British inhabitants of the Floridas, and Americans after 1783. Louisiana rapidly developed into a successful colony.

The United States took possession of Louisiana on December 20, 1803, when William C. C. Claiborne and his little army watched the French tricolor hauled down and the starred flag of the young American republic raised at the old Place d' Armes in New Orleans. Louisiana only spent nine years as a territory and in 1812 was admitted into the United States as the eighteenth state. Meanwhile, the citizens of the Florida Parishes, at that time a part of Spanish West Florida, revolted, captured Baton Rouge, and organized the independent Republic of West Florida, which was soon joined to Louisiana.

The War of 1812 began soon after Louisiana's admission to the Union and in December, 1814, General Andrew Jackson and his small army arrived at New Orleans to help defend the state against a British invasion. Aided by white and Free Negro state militiamen and by Jean Laffite's "Barataria Pirates," Jackson defeated the British at Chalmette on January 8, 1815, in what was perhaps the most decisive victory ever won on American soil.

The period from 1815 to 1860 was the golden age of the plantation regime. New settlers arrived from the older states and from European nations. The plantation area was extended along Bayou Lafourche and Bayou Teche, up the Red River, throughout the prairies of southwest Louisiana, in the rich bottom lands west of the Mississippi, and in the rolling hill country of north and northwest Louisiana. By 1860 New Orleans was one of the major ports of the United States and Louisiana one of its richest commonwealths. Its combination of French and Spanish Creoles, Americans, Europeans, and other peoples had produced the most unusual civilization in America.

Louisiana seceded from the Union in January, 1861, joined the Confederate States of America, and mobilized for war. Military units marched off to join Confederate Armies in other sections of the South. The war which followed reached the state in 1862, when New Orleans was occupied. Baton Rouge fell, and Port Hudson, and campaigns along Bayou Teche and Bayou Lafourche gained those sections for Abraham Lincoln and his government. But Confederate armies in the rest of Louisiana held fast and General Richard Taylor repulsed General Nathaniel P. Banks during his Red River campaign at Mansfield and Pleasant Hill. By the winter of 1864-65 the economically ruined and war-weary people lost heart, General Robert E. Lee surrendered in April, 1865, and on June 2, 1865, General Kirby Smith surrendered the last of the Confederate armies. The South had lost its War for Independence.

Louisiana's so-called Period of Reconstruction began in 1862 with the occupation of New Orleans. It was, however, a period of "military occupation" rather than "reconstruction," for little rebuilding of the war-torn state was accomplished. Carpet-baggers, scalawags, and newly-freed Negroes began systematically to legally, extra-legally, and illegally strip cities, towns, farms, and plantations of the state and to wax fat upon a conquered land. The tragic drama finally ended in the spring of 1877, when President Rutherford B. Hayes withdrew Federal troops and Louisiana once again became mistress of her own destiny.

Louisianians "reconstructed" their exhausted state during the next generation, and the wasted land slowly recovered from the ravages of war and military occupation. It was not until after 1900 that Louisiana began to emerge into the modern era. By the coming of World War I the state was ready to furnish its full contribution to the war effort.

A New Louisiana began to develop during the early 1920's. Governor John M. Parker inaugurated road-building, educational, and economic programs. Huey P. Long became governor in 1928 and under his dynamic and frequently termed "dictatorial" leadership, Louisiana became a progressive state. Public improvements of all types appeared overnight, the educational system was overhauled, the revitalized State University made gigantic strides, as Long proclaimed that every man was entitled to every opportunity in a benevolent and somewhat socialized commonwealth. The state fulfilled its obligations during World War II, and since 1945 has enjoyed a period of general economic and industrial progress and expansion.

The romantic past, the dynamic present, and the limitless future are happily combined in Modern Louisiana. Its islands of nationalistic cultures—French, Spanish, English, Portuguese, Negro, Italian, Hungarian, German, Dalmatian, Indian, Slavonian, and numerous others—have largely disappeared, but these nationalities have given vivid color to the well-mixed and sometimes highly spiced "gumbo" that is present-day Louisiana, a state which is at once a combination of the old and the new. The native Louisianian, recently joined by newcomers from other states, faces the future with pride in his state's romantic heritage and with surging, sometimes roistering, confidence.

The story of Louisiana is all this—and much, much more. There has been no need to embellish the events and personalities of Louisiana's past; therefore the author has attempted to present the Louisiana story simply and without literary or historical subterfuge. It is his hope that Louisianians of the present and of the future will from this book gain some knowledge of their state's history and an appreciation of those men and women who have so diligently worked to make Louisiana a great commonwealth.

While the factual material in this book has generally been gleaned from primary and secondary historical works, newspapers, personal and family manuscripts, state, local, and business archival records, and other historical materials, the interest in, the affection for, and the understanding of the complex civilization of romantic and kaleidoscopic Louisiana has largely come from the many native Louisianians with whom, during the past twenty-eight years, it has been the author's privilege to have been acquainted. To each of them he owes a debt of gratitude for having given of themselves toward his gradual development as an adopted son of Louisiana, and toward the making of this book.

He sat at the feet of "Colonel Billy" Prescott, onetime professor of government at Louisiana State University, a grand gentleman of a past generation, and from him first gained that emotional loyalty to the state which is a part of the heritage of every Louisianian. "Miss Cammie" Henry of "Melrose" plantation near Natchitoches continued the teaching process, as did "Mister Bob" and "Miss Louise" Butler of "The Cottage" plantation in West Feliciana Parish, "Miss Eva" Scott of "The Shades" plantation in East Feliciana Parish, Andre Olivier of St. Martinville, Henry Lastrapes of Opelousas, and Trist Wood of New Orleans. "Miss Mary" Conner and Mary and Margaret Merrill of Natchez recounted tales and legends of the swamp and plantation country beyond the Mississippi.

From G. P. Whittington of Alexandria, J. Fair Hardin of Shreveport, Fred Williamson of Monroe, Robert Dabney Calhoun of Vidalia, Elrie Robinson of St. Francisville, Sidney Marchand of Donaldsonville, and Albert L. Grace of Plaquemine, each an authority on the life of his respective section, he received information which space limitations did not permit them to include in their published works.

Albert Dupont of Houma, Wade O. Martin, Sr., of St. Martinville, Roy Theriot of Abbeville, and numerous others recounted incidents of bygone and more recent political occurrences which were significant contributions. Dr. Hewitt L. Ballowe, the noted doctor-author-folklorist of the lower river below New Orleans gave of his mind, heart, and soul, and took the author up and down the river road to meet and become acquainted with men and women of a dozen nationalities. It was the author's privilege to have been a personal friend of Lyle Saxon, Roark Bradford, Robert Tallant, Weeks Hall, and other literary, artistic, and historical *habitants* of the state and of New Orleans, without whose tutorship in matters Louisianian this book would never have been written.

The author learned from many other men and women in various sections of the state—a ferryboatman at Melville, an ex-rumrunner at Buras, an old hunter of the Catahoula swamps, a retired woman journalist in northwest Louisiana, a planter of East Carroll Parish, an aged priest of Covington, members of the Ellis family of Amite, fishermen of Grand Isle, trappers of the coastal marshes, a centenarian Civil War veteran of Jackson, and others. His Louisiana experience was enriched by state and local governmental officials, members of the Legislature, and students in his Louisiana history and other courses at the State University.

Professor Raleigh A. Suarez, Head of the Department of Social Sciences at McNeese State College, Lake Charles, Professor F. Jay Taylor, Head of the Department of History at Louisiana College, Pineville, and A. Otis Hebert, Jr., associate editor of *Louisiana History* and the author's former colleague in the teaching of Louisiana history at Louisiana State University, read the entire manuscript and were uninhibited critics in noting errors of commission and omission.

John A. Hunter, James J. Corbett, Dwight Greever Davis, R. C. Kemp, William R. McGehee, Wade O. Martin, Jr., John C. L. Andreassen, John L. Loos, C. C. Wood, Martin J. Broussard, Joseph G. Tregle, Rex Laney, Edwin A. Davis, Jr., A. Leon Hebert, John Ferguson, J. R. Nelson, Martin Hall, Sam H. Jones, Charles L. Dufour, Carl Maddox, and Dorris Joseph read specific chapters or gave general advice and information dealing with their specific fields of interest. Miss Jo Ann Carrigan, former Graduate Teaching Assistant in the Department of History and presently senior Gottlieb Scholar, Louisiana State University, prepared the index.

Mrs. Sam P. Mistretta typed the several drafts of the manuscript and did a not insignificant amount of editing. Mrs. Mary McMinn, of Charleston, West Virginia, formerly a member of the staff of the Louisiana State University Press and well acquainted with Louisiana history, edited the manuscript. The author's wife, La Verna Rowe Davis, was an active collaborator and critic at all stages of the research and writing process.

To each of the above persons the author owes his thanks and his appreciation.

E.A.D.

Baton Rouge, 1960

TABLE OF CONTENTS

PART ONE

An Introduction
to Louisiana History

CHAPTER 1

THE LAND OF
LOUISIANA

INTRODUCTION. Let us begin by discussing the land of Louisiana—its location, size, and shape; its climate and general topography; its soils, rivers, lakes, and vegetation. Its native animal life must not be overlooked, for animals, birds, reptiles, and insects have played significant roles in Louisiana life since the first Indian set foot within the territory. These geographic factors determined where the Indian lived, and later where the white man settled, developed farms and plantations, built trading posts, towns, and cities. Together with the location of underground resources, they have been determining elements in the agricultural, industrial, commercial, and general economic life of present-day Louisiana.

Louisiana's geographic features have been the subject of praise since the first French settlers came during the last year of the seventeenth century. André Pénicaut, one of the early pioneers, wrote that if the forests could only be cleared "the country of Louisiana would be a terrestrial paradise with the agriculture that would be developed there. . . . In this country there is an astonishing abundance of game of every kind of species and fish in the rivers just as plentiful. There are fruits in great quantity and of a better taste than the fruits in France, the climate in Louisiana being a little bit warmer."

A hundred years later, James Brackenridge wrote of the lower Mississippi River section: "I could have believed that I was witnessing those paradisiacal scenes of which I have sometimes dreamed." About the same time geographer William Darby wrote of Louisiana's swamps: "Natural beauty is not wanting, the varied windings, and intricate bendings of the lakes, relieve the sameness, whilst the rich green of the luxuriant growth of forest trees, the long line of woods melting into the distant sky, the multifarious tints of the willow, cotton, and other fluviatic trees, rendered venerable by the long train of waving moss, amuse the fancy. The imagination fleets back towards the birth of nature, when a new creation started from the deep, with all the freshness of mundane youth."

After statehood Louisianians wrote just as enthusiastically of their land. The St. Francisville *Louisiana Journal* of June 9, 1825, editorialized that permanent residence in Louisiana was more inviting than in "any other section of the republic." During the War for Southern Independence, Union General Nathaniel P. Banks rhapsodized on the land he had invaded: "When we consider its natural resources, and the advantages it possesses from its climate, soil, and location, it is simply impossible to speak of it in terms of praise too strong." Some years after the war an Illinois farmer, who had successfully established himself and his family in southwest Louisiana, wrote to a friend: "I find I can raise everything in Louisiana that I can raise in Illinois, and that I can raise a hundred things there which cannot be raised in Illinois. I find the lands easier worked in Louisiana, infinitely richer than ours,

[3]

and yielding far more, with the finest climate on earth, and no trouble to get to market."

It was French author François René, Viscount de Chateaubriand, however, who wrote in the most extravagant terms of Louisiana's primeval, pristine grandeur. In his romantic and highly impressionistic *Atala*, he described "the waves of verdure on the limitless savannas" gradually rising "into the azure sky," how "trees of every form, of every color, and of every perfume throng and grow together, stretching up into the air to heights that weary the eye to follow." Animal life intrigued him, for the "multitude of animals spread about life and enchantment . . . bears, intoxicated with the grape, staggering upon the branches of the elm-trees; caribous bathe in the lakes; black squirrels play among the thick foliage; mocking-birds, and Virginian pigeons not bigger than sparrows, fly down upon the turf, reddened with strawberries; green parrots with yellow heads, purple woodpeckers, cardinals red as fire, clamber up to the very tops of the cypress-trees; humming-birds sparkle upon the jessamine of the Floridas." He continued his fanciful but inaccurate descriptions of Louisiana's natural assets, finally concluding that he "should in vain endeavor to describe them to those who have never visited these primitive fields of nature."

While some of these early writers greatly exaggerated Louisiana's geographic advantages, they merely intended to contrast or compare her physical features with those of their homelands or states.

LOCATION AND SIZE. Louisiana lies at the south end of the Mississippi River Valley, and with the exception of Florida and Texas, extends farther south than any other continental state in the Union. The state is bounded on the north by Arkansas on the thirty-third parallel and Mississippi on the thirty-first parallel, on the east by the Mississippi and Pearl rivers and the state of Mississippi, on the west by the Sabine River and Texas, and on the south by the Gulf of Mexico.

Louisiana is not a large state, for it has only 48,523 square miles of land and water area and ranks thirty-first among the fifty states. Of this total area, over 4,000 square miles are water—nearly 3,500 square miles in lakes and almost 650 square miles in rivers, bayous, and streams. It ranks sixth among the states with its 769 miles of coastline, being exceeded only by Alaska, California, Florida, Hawaii, and Maine. The state measures nearly 300 miles, at its widest part, from east to west, and about 275 miles from north to south. Diagonally, from the northwestern corner of Caddo Parish to the mouth of the Mississippi, the distance is slightly over 400 airline miles.

CLIMATE. Most of Louisiana has a semitropical climate, remarkably the same over most of the state, even though there are significant temperature changes and ranges in different sections in the different seasons of the year. Average annual temperatures range from about 60° F. in the north to nearly 71° F. at the mouth of the Mississippi River. The variations in daily temperature are largely caused by the differences in altitude and by the distance from the Gulf of Mexico. Summers are temperate, the thermometer seldom rising as high as in many northern states.

July and August are the warmest months, when the temperatures average approximately 82° F. The days are hotter and the nights cooler in the northern sections, the maximum of 100° being recorded during most summers, particularly in Shreveport in July. In New Orleans and the southern areas this temperature is rarely reached. On the other hand it sometimes falls below 20° along the northern border, although it seldom goes below freezing in the southern sections. The lowest recorded temperature of 16° below zero was at Minden, while the highest was 114° at Plain Dealing. In 1784 the inhabitants of Avoyelles Post observed floes of ice drifting down the Mississippi, as did the citizens of the Donaldsonville area during the 1890's and again in the 1930's.

Snow is rarely seen in the southern part of Louisiana, and when it does fall, generally only a few flakes reach and remain on the ground. Farther north there are only a few snowfalls each year, which total approximately one inch in the central regions and slightly over three inches in the northwestern section near the Arkansas line. In the northern parishes the first frost generally occurs early in November and cold weather lingers until the latter part of March, whereas frosts do not reach the truck-garden areas at the mouth of the Mississippi until near the end of December, winter weather lasting until about the middle of January. Temperatures are seldom severe enough in the southern parishes to freeze vegetation, and over the entire state there are delightful winter days when houses need not be closed for comfort.

The Louisiana growing season exceeds that of most other states, ranging from 220 days in the extreme northwestern and northeastern corners to 350 days near the outlet of the Mississippi. Certain types of hardy crops and vegetables grow even during winter months in the northern sections and at no time of the year is the ground too frozen for cultivation, for at most, freezes affect only an inch or so of the topsoil.

One of the wettest of the states, Louisiana has frequent rains, usually gentle showers or steady, heavy downpours unaccompanied by high winds. The average yearly rainfall is slightly over 57.0 inches, with the highest precipitation of nearly 60.5 inches in the vicinity of Franklinton and the lowest of about 41.5 inches in the Shreveport area. While rainfall is fairly well distributed over the entire year, February marks the beginning of the rainy season, and during the spring and early summer, rains and thundershowers are sometimes accompanied by vivid lightning and heavy peals of thunder. The dry season begins in July, continuing through the late summer and fall. During the fall, according to one traveler who visited the state nearly 150 years ago, "the atmosphere is of that mild and delightful blue, peculiar to a southern sky." But despite its rainfall, Louisiana is a "sunshine" state, and in New Orleans sunshiny days total from 45 per cent in December to nearly 70 per cent in October.

Sometimes high winds blow into the state from the northwest. These winds move in a clockwise direction, and as their centers usually pass to the north, their general directions gradually shift from south to west and then to northwest. When accompanied by fast drops in temperature, they are called "northwesters." The centers of occasional tropical storms which originate in the Gulf of Mexico usually miss Louisiana by passing eastward of the mouth of the Mississippi River, with the southeastern coast being generally in the weakened areas of these storms. Hurricanes occasionally hit the coastal areas and carry for some distance inland, as for example the tragic Last Island storm of 1856 and the Cameron hurricane of 1957. Sudden tornadoes sometimes sweep through the northern section and the Florida Parishes, but, compared with the devastating tornadoes of the eastern Plains states, are of little consequence.

The atmosphere of the southern half of Louisiana is extremely humid during most months of the year—a fact which has given rise to considerable criticism of Louisiana's climate. Traveler Josiah Gregg wrote in 1839 that "it is no wonder that the air of New Orleans should be generally so unhealthy, and in autumn quite pestilential, for the town is built in a complete swamp . . . never intended by nature for the abode of man." He continued that it was "the natural abode for alligators, frogs and mosquitoes. It is the churchyard of the United States." Louisianians have since proved him wrong.

Louisianians have always bragged and told stories about their weather, particularly about their fogs. In early February, 1838, during a bad fog period, the New Orleans *Picayune* indulged in a little "tall-tale telling" for the benefit of northern readers. The fog was the greatest which had "occurred here within the recollection of the oldest inhabitants." It completely blanketed the river, and at the wharf, where the *Columbia* was preparing to sail for Texas, "some fifty laborers were busy with spades, axes, crowbars, &c. &c. endeavoring to open a pathway through the fog; but its density was so great, that nothing but gunpowder would affect it." A few blasts did loosen it a little, but at two o'clock in the afternoon the *Columbia* was still "jammed up against the pier."

A postscript attached to the above account read: "The butchers at Slaughter

House Point being unable to force their pirogues through the fog, climbed up about 40 feet, and finding the air sufficiently thin at that height, they hauled their beef up after them, and trundled it across the city on top of the fog, by means of wheelbarrows." New Orleanians chuckled over the account for several days.

TOPOGRAPHY. The southern section of the state makes up an immense lowland which averages less than fifty feet above sea level, the eastern two-thirds of this section once being a part of the great flood area of the Mississippi River. This entire region is comparatively level and is cut by rivers, streams, and bayous, and dotted here and there with lakes.

The rocks and rock formations of the northern sections are of several types, most of them being loose and without form. Some sedimentary rock is found, such as shale, limestone, and sandstone, as are small amounts of granite, an igneous rock form, and marble, a metamorphic rock made by heat and pressure. Few rocks are found in the southern part of the state.

All of the state lies within a general southern area known as the Gulf Coastal Plain, which may be divided into two subregions—the upland districts and the lowland districts.

There are three sections of Louisiana uplands, which range in altitude from lower levels of one hundred to two hundred feet to higher levels of two hundred to over five hundred feet.

The Florida Parishes Uplands, which lie east of the Mississippi River and north of Lake Pontchartrain, include most of the parishes of East Feliciana, West Feliciana, St. Helena, and Washington, the northern half of Tangipahoa, and the northern edges of East Baton Rouge and St. Tammany. This section slopes from north to south, averages about two hundred feet in altitude, and is marked by several deep gorges of which the most scenic are Fluker's Cave and Fricke's Cave in St. Helena and Washington parishes. The Tunica Hills of West Feliciana Parish rise to altitudes of over three hundred feet, and one early traveler in Louisiana inaccurately compared "their wild grandeur" to the Alps of Switzerland.

The North Louisiana Uplands in the north and northwest sections of the state lie roughly between the Red and the Ouachita river valleys, and here again the land generally slopes from north to south. The Driskill Mountains, in Claiborne, Lincoln, and Bienville parishes, rise at their highest points to over five hundred feet. East of this region are the Bastrop Hills, the Macon Ridge, a low, flat ridge which runs from Franklin Parish northeast into southeast Arkansas, and Sicily Island, which has a core of Catahoula Sandstone rock older than the Ice Age.

The West Louisiana Uplands lie west of the Red River and north and northeast of the Calcasieu River. These uplands are approximately the same height as those in north Louisiana, and the Kisatchie Hills, on the border of Vernon and Natchitoches parishes, compare favorably with the Driskill Mountains. The entire area is crisscrossed with bluffs and ravines, most notable of which is the Grand Écore Bluff in Natchitoches Parish.

The lowlands of Louisiana, which average only about fifty feet above sea level, may also be divided into three sections.

The Mississippi River Plain is narrow in the north, along the west side of the river, but widens to more than a hundred miles south of Baton Rouge. The higher portions of this plain, leveelike ridges built up by the waterways, are called "front lands" because they generally front the great river, one of its tributaries, or another river, stream, or bayou. Behind the front lands are the "backlands," and behind them the swamps. In general, the front lands do not drain into the rivers or bayous but back toward the swamps, which therefore serve as a sort of catchall for rainfall and for the overflow river waters. Throughout the section are numerous lakes, lagoons, and marshes.

The Gulf Coastal Plain lies west of the Atchafalaya River, and the land is much like that of the Mississippi River Plain, except that it slopes gradually from north to south. The coastal marshes are protected from the Gulf of Mexico by barrier beaches, composed of fine sand with a little soil held together by sometimes matted undergrowth and occasional groves of trees. Sand and shell ridges, called *chénières* (because of the numerous oaks growing on them) and "land islands," are scattered throughout the marshes. Some of the inland sand ridges are old barrier beaches, as for example, Grand Chénière. A line of the largest and most important land islands, a few of which are over 100 feet in height, begins a few miles west of New Iberia, runs in a generally southeast line toward the mouth of the Atchafalaya River, and includes Jefferson Island, Avery Island, Weeks Island, Côte Blanche Island, and Belle Isle.

The third lowland region is the prairie section of southwest Louisiana, some sixty miles in width, extending roughly from the vicinity of Opelousas to Lake Charles. This section is comparatively level, sparsely timbered, and cut by numerous streams and bayous. In the past it was divided into several specifically-named prairies, known as the Atakapas Prairie, the Mamou Prairie, or the Opelousas Prairie.

SOIL. The extremely fertile soil of Louisiana is its basic resource, for in addition to having an unusual abundance of plant food, most of it is porous and warm. It is extremely deep in most sections of the state, so that after years of cultivation only subsoil plowing is needed to restore much of its original fertility. The soil is generally divided into two broad classifications, the lowland alluvial and silt deposits found along the Mississippi and other streams and in the southern part of the state, and the sands, sandy loams, and many-colored clays of the upland regions. The clay soils were brought into Louisiana by prehistoric rivers or were deposited by muddy, shallow seas or bays of the Gulf of Mexico. The lowland alluvial and silt soils were deposited by the overflowing of the large Louisiana rivers and by the many bayous in the southern sections. Few regions in the world have as much alluvial soil as Louisiana, since roughly one-third of the state is covered with this type.

While Louisiana soils may be subdivided into over a dozen divisions, the most important in extent are dark-brown to gray Mississippi River alluvials, reddish-brown Red River bottom soil, sandy clays found in the hill or rolling regions of the southeastern, west central, and north central parts of the state, gray to black soils of the southwestern prairies, and the water-laden lands of the tidal marshes that border the Gulf of Mexico. Soils of minor importance include Mississippi bluff and terrace loess deposits just west of Bayou Macon in northeast Louisiana and in the western section of the Florida Parishes and the so-called "flatwoods" soils found chiefly along the upper Red River and in Beauregard and Allen parishes.

RIVERS AND LAKES. The Mississippi is Louisiana's most important river, and from the viewpoint of political history is the most important river of the Western Hemisphere. From the early 1700's to 1803 the control of this river was very important to Great Britain, France, and Spain, and since 1803 has been of equal importance to the United States. Until the coming of railroads the river and its tributaries —with their 15,000 miles of inland waterways—carried much of the inland commerce of the entire central portion of the United States.

No river has been called by so many names as the Mississippi. The Indians called it the *Malbrancia, Misisipi, Michi Sepe, Chucagua, Tamalisieu, Tapatu, ad Mico, Ochechiton,* as well as variations of these words. A hundred years ago T. B. Thorpe wrote that the name finally chosen came from two Choctaw Indian words, *missah,* meaning "old big," and *sippah,* meaning "strong," thus the "old-big-strong" river. T. P. Thompson, who wrote nearly a century later, credits the present name's ancestor word to Spanish Governor of New Mexico Diego de Penalosa, who first wrote the Algonquin Indian name *Mischipi* into the records. Father Claude Jean Allouez, an early French missionary in the Great Lakes region, is credited by Ruben Gold Thwaites with having first used the word *Mississippi.* Another authority claims that the word *Mississippi* does not mean "father of waters" at all, but rather "river of meadows and grass." Summarizing all the explanations and arguments, and there are many more of them, it can be generalized that the present name for the river was derived from an Indian word or words.

The Spanish and French gave it other names. At various times the Spanish called it the *Palisado,* the *Río Grande,* the *Río del Espíritu Santo* (river of the Holy Spirit), the *Río de Flores* (river of flowers), *Río Grande de la Vega,* as well as others. The French used such names as *St. Louis, Colbert, Buade, Louis,* and several other names from prominent Frenchmen. When Pierre le Moyne, Sieur d'Iberville, sailed from France to settle the colony of Louisiana, he was looking for "La Salle's River."

To the Indian the Mississippi was a place to fish and a river upon which to travel. To Hernando de Soto and his followers it was a great river to be crossed, a hazard. To the French it was an important artery connecting the settlements of upper Louisiana and the Great Lakes country with the lower country and New Orleans. To the Spanish it was an international boundary line with Great Britain and later with the United States, and a river of commerce. To Americans it has been the great commercial waterway of the nation, for it drains over twenty-five states with a total area greater than the combined areas of Great Britain, Ireland, France, Germany, Spain, Italy, and a few other smaller European nations. During the early years, the Mississippi and the rivers which flow into it determined the paths of Louisiana settlement, and until the arrival of the railroad and the hard-surface highway, they dictated the routes of Louisiana commerce.

The Mississippi is a strange river. Mark Twain said that it was the "crookedest river" in the world, for it traveled "one thousand three hundred miles to cover the same ground that a crow would fly over in six hundred and seventy-five." A scientist once estimated that it carries into the Gulf of Mexico every year over 400,000,000 tons of sediment, equal to a pile of earth 2 miles square and nearly 150 feet in height, and that it has the strength of over 60,000,000 horses. It discharges more water than all European rivers combined, an annual discharge which would fill a tank 159 miles long, 1 mile wide, and 1 mile high.

With the exception of the Red River, no streams flow into the Mississippi from the west in Louisiana and the same is true south of Baton Rouge on the east side. The reason is that the front lands built up by the river have caused the streams to flow away from it to the lower lands behind, and the levees which have been constructed along the entire west bank and along the east bank south of Baton Rouge have blocked off the bayous. It has no islands or shoals south of Pointe Coupée Parish. At the present time the Mississippi is trying to change its course and drain into the Gulf of Mexico by way of the Atchafalaya River, which now carries about 20 per cent of the great river's flow. This runoff is increasing about one per cent annually, and unless prevented by locks, gates, and other engineering measures, will reach about 40 per cent by 1965. After 40 per cent is reached the change will grow swiftly and soon reach proportions disastrous for the ports of Baton Rouge and New Orleans.

The Mississippi has been the subject of many unkind comments. French writer Alexis de Tocqueville was being only mildly critical when he compared it to a god of antiquity dispensing both "good and evil." British traveler Frederick Marryat wrote that "there are no pleasing associations connected with the great common sewer of the Western America, which pours out its mud into the Mexican Gulf, polluting the clear blue sea for many miles beyond its mouth. It is a river of desolation." Frances Milton Trollope, another British traveler, wrote after arriving in New Orleans: "I never beheld a scene so utterly desolate as this entrance of the Mississippi. Had Dante seen it, he might have drawn images of another Bolgia from its horrors."

One of the most derogatory descriptions came from the pen of young Lieutenant Richard Butler, who left Pittsburgh in a small boat, in April, 1798, with military messages to the Commandant at Natchez. He wrote in his diary: "The Mississippi, I believe, is the last river God Almighty made, the bottom all quicksand, the water something the color and thickness of lime and water when mixed for white-washing." He wrote that there were no springs, the low banks permitted overflows for countless miles, and the river was "extremely dangerous owing to millions of sawyers, alias old trees, fast in the bottom." He frequently encountered rough water. A sawyer ripped a hole in his boat, his sail blew away, the crew were drunk and useless, so he had to bail with one hand and paddle through the half-submerged trees with the other. After finally landing, he stood on the low bank "and here I cursed for half an hour." But he later moved to the Feliciana country, learned to love the river, and lost much of his former ability at profanity.

The Red River is the second most important Louisiana waterway. Rising in northwestern Texas, it divides Texas and Oklahoma, then Texas and Arkansas for a short distance, and enters Louisiana near the northwestern corner of the state. Flowing in a generally southeasterly direction, past Shreveport and Alexandria, it enters the Mississippi and the Atchafalaya just below the northwestern corner of West Feliciana Parish. It was an important water highway during the colonial period, and after the clearing of its great "raft" greatly contributed to the commercial and economic life of the state.

There are other important Louisiana rivers and streams. In the northeastern section of the state is the Ouachita-Black river system, so-called because the Ouachita and other streams join to form Black River. In southwest Louisiana are the Sabine, Calcasieu, Mermentau, and Vermilion, all of which flow into the Gulf of Mexico. Farther to the east are Bayou Teche, the Atchafalaya River, Bayou Plaquemine, and Bayou Lafourche. Pearl River serves as part of the Louisiana boundary on the east side of the Florida Parishes.

While the words "bayou" and "river" are used interchangeably in Louisiana, the word "bayou" really means a sluggish inlet, the outlet of a lake or bay, or one of several deltas of a river. Therefore, if one follows the definitions, Bayou Teche is not a bayou but a river and the Atchafalaya River is not a river but a bayou, for it is one of the delta outlets of the Mississippi. From 1904 until recently Bayou Lafourche was cut off from the Mississippi by a levee and was a river, but it is now a bayou again due to the construction of a large pumping station at Donaldsonville which pumps in water from the Mississippi.

Another commonly used but frequently misunderstood Louisiana geographical name is the "Isle of Orleans," which is not an isle at all. The land that makes up the Isle of Orleans is bounded by the Mississippi River on the south and west and the Gulf of Mexico on the east. Going from west to east, its northern boundary is Bayou Manchac, the Amite River, Lake Maurepas, Lake Pontchartrain, Lake Borgne, and Mississippi Sound. This area, however, has been called the "Isle of Orleans" since long before Louisiana was purchased from France in 1803.

Louisiana's lakes are of four types. Coastal lakes, sometimes called lagoonal or deltaic lakes, only slightly above sea level, include Lakes Pontchartrain, Maurepas, Borgne, Grand, Calcasieu, and others in south Louisiana. The lakes of this group were caused by the growth of barrier beaches, the sinking of the land, or by the Gulf beating openings in a weakened section of the shore line. Depression lakes were formed, principally in the northern and central portions of the state, when rivers overflowed and the water filled the lower-leveled areas. If the areas were large enough, permanent lakes were formed, such as Catahoula, Caddo, Bistineau, Wallace, and several others. The third class was formed when a river, particularly the Mississippi, cut across one of its big bends. The front land then built up and the water in the old river bed continued to live as a lake. There are many of these half-moon-shaped, oxbow lakes along the west side of the Mississippi north of Baton Rouge. The last group of lakes are man-made and were built to prevent floods, furnish urban water supplies, offer sportsmen hunting and fishing waters, or to create refuges for migratory wild fowl.

[9]

VEGETATION. In Louisiana the plant and forest areas achieve striking contrasts which together with the luxuriant growth of all types of vegetation give the state much of its beauty. Over 150 species of trees are native to the state, and shrubs, vines, and small plants grow in profusion owing to the richness of the soil, extremely mild and temperate climate, and abundant rainfall.

The live oak is perhaps Louisiana's most spectacular tree, for, clad in its drapery of Spanish moss, it is a sight not easily forgotten. It is native to the coastal regions and grows naturally as far north as the Red River, and may be transplanted successfully farther north. The cypress tree, which grows best in swamp and lowland areas, is distinguished by feathery green foliage and wide, cone-shaped base. The roots frequently grow above the surface of the water or swampland for air and are called "knees." Because of its durability, cypress makes a very valuable lumber, but is rapidly being exhausted, for it takes the cypress over a century to reach maturity. The magnolia, another native tree which grows best in south Louisiana, produces large, fragrant flowers and is transplanted in all parts of the state. Other important trees include beeches, pines, cedar, walnut, pecan, elms, laurels, willows, hollys, maples, and mulberrys.

At the present time slightly over 55 per cent of the land area of the state is timberland, a large percentage of which is in the process of regrowth. Louisiana forests may be divided into several regional groups. In the southern marshlands grow cypress, live oak, marsh elder, and hackberry; the uplands of the Florida Parishes are noted for ash, hickory, beech, red gum, and white oak; and in the Mississippi River flood plain and delta regions are found ash, red maple, and tupelo gum. Longleaf-pine forests are concentrated in the central sections, while shortleaf pine, oak, and hickory flourish in the northern and northwestern areas.

Many ornamental trees are native to or have been imported to Louisiana—pride of China, tallow trees, bananas, bitter oranges, sweet olives, palms, camphor trees, mimosas, and numerous others. Shrubs and flowers grow in great profusion during the entire year, particularly in the southern half of the state, and include honeysuckle, clematis, spirea, camellia, azalea, crape myrtle, jasmine, and hyacinth. Lilies, irises, and other bulbed flowers are found in many varieties. When Alexander Campbell, the noted Protestant minister, visited Louisiana in 1839, he described one of the planter's homes and wrote: "He literally resides in the midst of gardens . . . with flowers that bloom in January."

ANIMAL LIFE. Louisiana offers an attractive home for many forms of animal life. Quadrupeds of numerous species inhabit all sections, and the rivers, lakes, and Gulf waters teem with fresh-water and salt-water fish. The southern coastal region is probably the most important winter resort in North America for wild geese and ducks and is also the year-round abode of numerous varieties of sea and fresh-water birds.

Louisiana animals are classified in three general categories, game animals, commercial fur-bearing animals, and outlaw animals. Few large quadrupeds of the game class survive in the state, for the buffalo disappeared years ago and only a few black bears still inhabit the swamp and bottom lands of the southern section and along the Mississippi and Tensas rivers. Deer in sizable numbers inhabit the timber and wooded swamp areas. The water hare, the marsh rabbit, and the southern cottontail are found in all sections of the state. Commercial fur-bearing animals of most importance include muskrat, nutria (introduced a few years ago from South America), mink, otter, raccoon, skunk, opossum, and fox. In commercial value the muskrat ranks first, followed in order by the nutria, mink, and raccoon. The marketing of the skins of these four animals alone makes Louisiana one of the leading fur-producing states of the Union. The important outlaw animals are cougars or panthers (sometimes also called "catamounts"), wildcats, foxes, and wolves. Unprotected by conservation laws, these animals are hunted at any time of the year for sport and to prevent their destruction of farm animals and fowls.

The state has an unusually wide variety of birds. Due to its geographical position, the Mississippi River, and the semitropical climate, migratory birds offer sport for hunters during the hunting season. These include several varieties of geese and ducks, many of which remain in the state throughout the entire year. The Eastern Brown Pelican, which appears on the state emblem of Louisiana, nests in the salt marshes of the Gulf Coast and the Mississippi Delta. These sections are also the homes of many smaller birds, including gulls, terns, sandpipers, black skimmers, herons, bald eagles, marsh wrens, seaside sparrows, egrets, and wood ducks. The wooded uplands and the less swampy lowlands have many forms of bird life: woodpeckers, warblers, cardinals, southern whippoorwills, Baltimore orioles, sparrows, redbirds, snipe, and numerous others. Wild turkeys are sometimes found along the rivers and in the swamps and pine-wooded uplands.

Fish and other forms of water life may be divided into two categories, those of the Gulf and those of the freshwater rivers, streams, and lakes. Gulf game fish include tarpon, jackfish, king mackerel, sharks, giant rays, and jewfish. Flounder, pompano, Spanish mackerel, redfish, trout, croaker, and sheepshead are the most important food varieties. Turtles, shrimp, crabs, and oysters are also of great commercial importance and are shipped in large numbers to all parts of the nation. Commercial fishing is most important from Atchafalaya Bay eastward, past Terrebonne Bay, Barataria Bay, the long peninsula above the mouth of the Mississippi, and northward to Mississippi Sound. The most important fresh-water game fish are the several species of bass, trout, crappie ("perch" to many Louisianians), and sunfish. The Mississippi catfish and the yellow catfish lead all other freshwater commercial varieties. Louisiana bullfrogs thrive in such numbers and are of such size as to make the state the national leader in the production of this table delicacy. Crawfish are found in great numbers along the bayous and streams and in the lakes in the southern sections of the state.

The adjacent Gulf waters have several varieties of unusual fish. The manta, or devilfish, grows to tremendous size, occasionally weighing over a ton, and commercial and sports fishermen have learned to respect it highly. The stingaree is a threat to swimmers and bathers. Electric rays, southern stargazers, and torpedo fish all have the ability to deliver electric shocks of several volts. One of the most unusual of Louisiana fish is the choupique, sometimes called the "grindle" or "bowfin," which lives in the sluggish bayous and streams or lakes and ponds of southern Louisiana. The choupique's family tree runs back to the days of the dinosaur, and it is the only surviving member of its family. Because of the peculiar construction of its breathing apparatus, it is able to exist for long periods in mud or even in slightly dampened earth, and some have been plowed up in fields long after overflows have passed.

Louisiana's reptiles are numerous, though few are harmful. The most commonly found poisonous snake is the water moccasin, or water viper, a dark-colored, blotched, venomous reptile. A relative of his is called the "highland moccasin," copperhead, or sometimes the "copperhead moccasin." Even more poisonous is the rattlesnake, of which there are three varieties, the diamond-back, the ground or pigmy, and the timber rattlesnake, which is frequently found in timber or canebrake areas. The most poisonous reptile is the coral snake, a first cousin to the Indian cobra, which does not strike as other snakes do but chews into the flesh. The several families of nonpoisonous snakes are beneficial to Louisiana farmers, for they live largely on insects, mice, rats, and other rodents. They include king snakes, blue runners, black snakes, bull snakes, rat snakes, coachwhips, and ribbon snakes.

Louisiana's most spectacular reptile is of course the alligator, which like the choupique fish traces his ancestry back for hundreds of thousands of years. Many of the early travelers in Louisiana wrote fantastic descriptions of the prehistoric-appearing monster, but Father Jacques Gravier, who was a missionary during the early French period, wrote without embellishment of pen or imagination: "This is an animal of the color of a Toad, shaped like a Lizard. It is often found on land, and, although it walks very slowly, no one approaches it unless he is well armed. The scales with which it is covered are proof against small shot, and a ball is needed to pierce them. I know not how the savages do so who have only arrows, unless it be that these slip under the scales from the rear. Its mouth is very large, and is armed with two rows of teeth, longer than those of a Bear. To see it, and hear it gnash its teeth, frightens one. It is said that the tongue is good to eat, but I have never had the curiosity to taste any of it, or any other part of the body, which most of the Savages consider a great treat. From time to time, some of them lose their lives by risking themselves in diving to catch it after it is wounded." While presently protected throughout the rest of the state because of its commercial value, the alligator is classed as an outlaw in St. James Parish and may be hunted at any time of the year and killed in any number.

Throughout Louisiana history the most talked-about form of insect life has been the mosquito. It would seem that every traveler who has visited the state and every author who has written about Louisiana had something to say about the *maringouins,* as the French called them.

Father Paul du Poisson, a Jesuit priest, left a memorable comment: "Since the French have been on the Mississippi, this little beast has caused more cursing than has been done in the rest of the world up to this time." Sir Charles Lyell, a British traveler who visited the state about the middle of the nineteenth century, once asked an Irishman about Louisiana's summers. After commenting on the hot weather, the Irishman referred to mosquitoes: "There is one set of musquitoes who sting you all day, and when they go in toward dusk, another kind comes out and bites you all night." T. B. Thorpe, the northerner who lived for a time during the ante bellum period in Baton Rouge and the Feliciana country, wrote that they were not so large in that section, but down the river they "torment alligators to death, and sting mules right through their hoofs." Mark Twain had much to say about them, and once wrote of "those Lake Providence colossi," of which two could whip a dog and four could hold down a man. People did not "kill" them in the Lake Providence country, they "butchered" them. The only life insurance necessary there was the "mosquito policy." A friend of his had seen them try to vote, certainly he had seen them around the polls "canvassing."

UNDERGROUND RESOURCES. Louisiana is one of the richest states in the Union in natural underground resources. Except for iron and coal, the combined products of their agricultural and forest lands, fishing waters, and underground resources would enable Louisianans to live very well on what they produce within their own state. The state Department of Conservation is primarily concerned with the exploration, production, storage, transportation, processing, marketing, and conservation of these underground resources, while the state Geological Survey is concerned with their development through research, the publication of maps and bulletins, and the general diffusion of knowledge.

The most important underground resources include oil, natural gas, natural-gas liquids, stone for the production of cement, and lime, gypsum, clays, salt, sand and gravel, stone for quarrying, and sulphur. Offshore or tidelands oil-well drilling began during the late 1940's off the coast of Terrebonne Parish, but full-scale production of the tidelands area has been considerably curtailed because of the controversy between Louisiana and the Federal government over the ownership of the offshore Gulf bottom. The supply of ground water and the flow of raw water within the state has become increasingly important in recent years due to its extensive use in manufacturing, particularly in the field of chemicals.

CHAPTER 2

INDIANS AND THEIR
CIVILIZATION

PREHISTORIC BACKGROUND. While it is impossible to fix the date when the first Indians came to Louisiana, it is the general opinion that they entered the present limits of the state over two thousand years ago. These extremely primitive people were hunters and fishermen who settled along the Gulf Coast and the inland waterways where sea food and game were most plentiful. They used harpoons and spears and later developed the spear thrower, wove crude baskets and other articles out of reeds, grasses, and bark, and constructed simple habitations by bending small saplings over at the top toward a center then covering the tepeelike framework with grass, moss, and leaves. They used fire for burning out logs for boats and for cooking food by the stone-boiling method, which was the dropping of heated stones into the depression of a large skin or hide, the edges of which were held up by stakes. The Indians who lived along the Gulf Coast gradually built up large shell middens, the oldest remains of these primitive people existing today.

These Indians eventually invented bows and arrows or acquired them from other tribes, learned to make a crude form of pottery, and domesticated dogs for protection, hunting, and food. Still later, they learned to make stone axes and knives, tube pipes, a few everyday tools and utensils, to do some farming, and began to build burial mounds for their dead. During the last thousand years before the explorations of Europeans they began to build more-or-less permanent houses grouped together in villages, some of them with earthen walls and ditches for protection, and started to work the softer metals. A few hundred years prior to the settlement of Louisiana in 1699 they greatly improved their pottery and built a few stockaded villages and large temple mounds.

Except in the western areas, numerous prehistoric Indian village sites have been found in all sections of Louisiana. These sites have yielded large amounts of physical remains in the form of shells, animal bones, and fragments of pottery, tools, weapons, and personal or home decorations.

INTRODUCTION TO THE HISTORIC INDIANS. When the first Europeans visited Louisiana during the first half of the sixteenth century it is believed that about 15,000 Indians lived within the present boundaries of the state, but by the time of the settlement of the Louisiana colony a century and a half later the total had declined to an estimated 12,000 to 13,000. This was a very small population for an area so rich in natural resources and indicates that in general culture the Louisiana tribes belonged to the Eastern Maize Area, "that portion of the eastern United States where agriculture takes its place with hunting, fishing, and the gathering of wild fruits as a source of subsistence."

Over two-thirds of the Indians lived in the south and southeast sections of the

[13]

state, where wildlife was more plentiful and where grains, fruits, and vegetables could be grown more easily. The pine forest and swamp sections had the smallest populations.

A few of the tribes in 1699 were still living in the mound-building stage, and some authorities believe that many of the mounds were built during the eighteenth century, after the arrival of the French settlers. The mounds are of two classes, the older burial and temple mounds and those occupied in times of flood. During the Dunbar-Hunter exploring expedition up the Ouachita River in 1804, one of these mounds was found to measure over eighty feet in height, but a half century later had been reduced by erosion to only fifty feet. This mound was one of a dozen in the same area, collectively known as the Troyville group.

Our knowledge of the Louisiana Indians during the early years of French settlement is largely dependent upon the writings of French priests, civil officials, and military officers who explored the region and visited the various tribes. Their descriptions frequently differ, as some of them were given to exaggeration and others were not good observers. Many of these differences in description can be explained by the fact that the tribes differed from one another. The Natchez group appealed most strongly to the romantic natures of these early Frenchmen, who gave the Natchez a glamour out of all proportion to the true values of that group's level of civilization, and they became widely known in Europe after Chateaubriand wrote his noted novels *Atala* and *Les Natchez* during the early years of the nineteenth century.

The presentation of all tribal differences is an impossibility; therefore, the Louisiana Indians will be considered as a composite group, though occasional variations will be noted.

INDIAN GROUPS. The Louisiana tribes were divided into three basic linguistic groups, the Caddoan, the Muskhogean, and the Tunican, but there seems to have been considerable interchange of words and phrases among the groups. The Caddoan group occupied the entire northwestern section of the state, the Muskhogean the central eastern region and the area east of the lower Mississippi, and the Tunican the regions of northeast, southeast, and southwest Louisiana.

These basic groups may be further subdivided into six family groups, living in fairly definitely located areas and speaking languages so similar as to make communication between the tribes belonging to the individual families a not too serious problem. The family-group culture patterns were closely interwoven, so that the civilization of the individual tribes belonging to each group was essentially the same.

The *Caddo* occupied the northwestern one-fourth of the state and had considerably more contact with tribes farther north and west than they did with the other Louisiana tribes. They were a seminomadic, agricultural people and generally moved their villages from place to place with considerably more frequency than did other Louisiana Indians. American wild horses had originated with the Spanish horses in Mexico and had gradually moved northward, where they were caught and broken by the Plains Indians. The Caddos, therefore, were the first Louisiana Indians to use horses and thus were able to live considerably easier through the hunting of the buffalo ranging over northwestern and western Louisiana. The Caddo and the Ouachita were the most important tribes of the Caddo family; among those of lesser consequence were the Adai, Doustionis, Kakohadacho, Natchitoches, and Yatasi. The *Tunica* lived in northeastern Louisiana, generally east of the Ouachita River and north of the present city of Harrisonburg, and spread north and east into Arkansas and Mississippi. This family included the Tunica, Koroa, Grigra, Tioux, Yazoo, and perhaps a few other smaller tribes. The *Atakapa* family, which included the Atakapa, Akokisa, Opelousa, and perhaps the Bidai tribes, lived in southwest Louisiana, along the Calcasieu, Mermentau, Vermilion, and other rivers and streams. They occupied a lower cultural level than did the other tribes.

East and northeast of present-day Alexandria lived the *Natchez,* whose center of population was, however, across the Mississippi near the modern city of Natchez. The Natchez possessed a higher degree of civilization and culture than the other Louisiana families, which perhaps accounts for the tendency of many writers and historians to glamorize this group. By 1700 they were generally an agricultural people with fixed towns and villages, lived in considerable comfort, and had a rather well-defined social organization. The Natchez, Taensa, and Avoyel tribes were members of this family.

The *Muskhogeans* occupied practically all of southeast Louisiana east of the Mississippi and a rather narrow strip of land west of the Mississippi down to its mouth. The Muskhogean family had more tribes than any of the other groups and included the Quinipissa, Tangipahoa, Bayougoula, Acolapissa, Houma, and several others. The Tangipahoa, who had villages on the northern shores of Lake Pontchartrain, and the Acolapissa, who lived just east of Pearl River, were the most important tribes. The Houmas lived in the Felicianas, and the Bayougoulas had villages near the present village of Bayougoula in Iberville Parish. All of their villages were on streams or lakes; the least populated area was the pine section of the Florida Parishes.

The *Chitimacha* group lived east of Bayou Teche and west of the Mississippi. Along with the Muskhogeans, they were great fishermen, and remains of numerous shell mounds indicate that shellfish were consumed in great quantities. Most of their villages were located on the shores of the numerous lakes, rivers, and bayous of this region. The Chitimacha, Washa, and Chawasha were the most important tribes.

The total population of the various groups can only be estimated, as censuses were unknown to Indians and the early French visitors rarely paid much attention to population totals, although they frequently counted the inhabitants of specific villages. The Atakapa was probably the largest group during the early years of the eighteenth century and numbered about 4,200 members. The Muskhogean group was second with about 3,500 and the Chitimacha third with 3,000. The Caddo probably numbered 2,500, but this figure is indefinite, for the Caddos were a migratory people whose Louisiana population was constantly shifting. The two smallest groups were the Natchez with 1,200 and the Tunicas with only some 500 members.

The land occupied by each of these six family groups had no specific boundaries, though it was generally understood that one group should not settle or hunt or fish in an area already occupied by another group. Within a family group, however, there was some overlapping of occupied land by individual tribes, for tribes were at best loose political organizations and little attention was paid to land boundaries. In general the rivers did not mark the boundaries of tribes or family groups.

Several Choctaw tribes, who were related to the Louisiana Muskhogean family, migrated westward to the southern Florida Parishes area or just west of the Mississippi on the lower Red River during the 1760's because of their opposition to the British. Most of these tribes went under the group name of Choctaw, though a few of them, like the Pascagoulas and the Biloxis, were called by individual tribal names. The Coushatta tribe, now generally called the Koasati, who were not closely related to the Choctaws, settled west of Opelousas after the Louisiana Purchase.

PEACEFUL THOUGH CRUEL NATURE OF LOUISIANA TRIBES. Most of the Louisiana Indians were peaceful people who had little trouble with one another or with neighboring tribes. Their tribal governments were comparatively simple, and while there were few laws or regulations, a multitude of traditions and customs were followed in daily life. The Natchez probably had the highest order of government, while the Caddos, because of their migratory nature, usually followed the leadership of a chief called a "Caddi," who led them on hunting expeditions and war parties and who summoned council meetings for the discussion of important problems. Father Jesus Maria, who lived about fifteen months with one of the Caddo tribes, reported that he did not hear any quarrels during his entire stay.

The Tunicas were probably the most warlike group, and the Assinais, of the Atakapa group, were probably the most warlike individual tribe. Two important Indian

[15]

wars occurred soon after the arrival of the French. In 1700 the Quinipissas went to live with the Bayougoulas, and shortly thereafter the Bayougoulas massacred over two hundred of the men and adopted the women and children into their tribe. About half of the Houma tribe was killed when in 1706 war broke out between the Tunicas and the Houmas.

Most of the Louisiana tribes indulged in war dances before setting off on war expeditions. The Caddos, for example, usually sang and danced for about a week, offering to their gods such gifts as tobacco, corn, and bows and arrows. They threw tobacco and buffalo fat into their war fires, believing that the smoke strengthened them and brought the blessing of the gods. They then prayed that water would drown their enemies, fire would burn them, arrows would kill them, and that the wind would blow them away.

Most of the tribes tortured prisoners on occasion, but according to early French travelers the Koroas of the Tunica group were the most cruel. André Pénicaut has given one of the best descriptions of Koroa torture:

> When they have taken one of their enemies alive, they fasten him to a frame, which is composed of two poles 8 feet in height, 5 feet apart, the two hands being well bound above and the two feet below, in the form of a St. Andrew's cross. The poor wretch being fastened thus completely naked, the entire village collects around him. They have a fire lighted in this place, where they have placed pieces of iron such as old gun barrels, shovels, or the iron parts of axes and other similar things, to make them red hot, and when they are thoroughly reddened they rub them upon his back, arms, thighs, and legs; they then lay bare the skin all the way around his head as far as the ears, tearing it off from him by force. They fill this skin with burning coals, which they replace on his head; they put the ends of his fingers into their lighted pipes, which they smoke, and tear out his nails, tormenting him until he is dead.

While several French travelers who visited the Atakapa of southwestern Louisiana during the first quarter century of French settlement charged them with cannibalism, later authorities believe that in all probability only the Assinais were actually cannibalistic and then only for religious purposes. Pénicaut wrote of one instance of ritual cannibalism. Two war prisoners brought to the village were suspended from a pole laid across the tops of two nine-foot stakes set about four feet apart. The religious ceremonies began when the men were faced toward the rising sun, and that afternoon they were turned to face the setting sun. The next day incisions were made in the arms, thighs, and legs and the dripping blood was caught by Indian priests, who then cooked it in two kettles. After the cooked blood had been eaten, the bodies of the two dead men were cut up and distributed to the families of the village, and while the meat was being cooked more dances and ceremonies were performed, after which the flesh was eaten. Pénicaut concluded his description: "I was so sickened at seeing this execrable feasting that I was squeamish for three days, and neither my comrades nor I could eat until after we had quit those cruel cannibals."

ECONOMIC LIFE. Indian villages were generally built in the form of a large circle around an open space, usually not more than a hundred feet in diameter, which was used for dances, games, meetings, and religious ceremonies. While some of the tribes built a temple in the center of this open space, others placed the temples off to one side of the town common. The houses were scattered about in irregular circles or other patterns, the house of the chief being the largest and near the center of the village. There were generally no palisades or walls around Indian towns at the time of founding of the Louisiana colony.

The Indians of southern Louisiana built their homes of wood, canes, or reeds and thatched them with grass, moss, palmetto leaves, or cornhusks. They were usually round, about fifteen feet high, and had small doors but no windows. A large hole in the top of the roof let out the smoke from the cooking, mosquito, or heating fires and let in a little light, although Father Gravier reported that the houses of the Tunicas had no opening but the door and that it was as "hot in them as in a vapor bath."

Farther north homes were much more substantial, for those tribes, with the exception of the Caddos, moved about less and needed better houses because of the colder climate. Henri de Tonti described one of the larger Taensa houses as being forty feet square with mud walls twelve feet high and about two feet thick. The roof was dome-shaped, laced with canes, and covered with turf.

There was little house decoration, either inside or out, though some of the Koroas adorned their cabins with large round pieces of copper, "very shining, made like lids of kettles." Household furnishings were few and consisted of pottery cooking pots, water bottles and storage jars, small wooden mortars, red, black, or yellow baskets made of split canes, and woven mats and beds. Beds were made of canes or wooden posts permanently fixed in the ground, topped with a woven framework, and covered with reed mats and skins. Fires were lighted by rubbing pieces of mulberry wood and cedarwood against each other. Small fires were usually kept burning in the houses during winter months and were lighted in summer as needed to keep out mosquitoes. If the weather was mild only a torch made of dried canes was needed for warmth.

Most of the Louisiana Indians had storage buildings for corn, beans, sweet potatoes, squashes, pumpkins, and other food crops. They were built atop four large posts, some twelve to fifteen feet high, and polished "so that mice can not climb up, and in this way protect their corn and squashes."

They had few tools or weapons. Bows were made of acacia wood. Cane arrows had points that were fire hardened or tipped with bone splinters, deerhorn tines, garfish scales, or flints. Cane blowguns were used for hunting birds and small animals, and these had cane-splinter darts feathered with thistledown and tipped with fire-hardened points. They had stone knives and hatchets and sometimes stone-pointed spears. Crude hoes fashioned of wood were used for digging the ground of their small fields. Fish were caught in a variety of ways, with bone fishhooks, barbed fishing arrows, nets made of cedarwood strips, and funnel-shaped reed fish traps.

While there were a few elm-bark canoes, most boats were made by hollowing out large cypress logs. Pénicaut described the dugout-manufacturing process, writing that the Indians built a large fire at the foot of a tree and "kept it up until the tree fell to the ground. They then burned it off at the desired length. When they had burned the tree sufficiently for their purpose, they extinguished the fire with moist earth, and scraped out the tree with large thick shells. They then washed the canoes with water so as to give them a fine polish. In the burning out process they directed the fire with small blow canes." Some of their large pirogues were as much as thirty and even forty feet long and would carry forty to fifty men. Cane rafts were used for crossing streams or bayous and were pulled across with ropes made of woven strips of cypress bark.

The Caddo, and perhaps a few of the Atakapa, had horses. Wild horses were captured by the simple process of constantly trailing a single animal with a succession of riders until he was exhausted. In all probability the Caddos first secured their mounts through trading with Texas Indians. Bridles were made of crude rope or leather thongs, and saddles were simply a few folds of deerskin, sometimes with stirrups. By 1700 the Caddos possessed large horse herds, and one early visitor reported that there was "not a cabin that has not four or five of them."

The Louisiana Indians, with the exception of the Caddos, traveled little, and ordinarily for short distances. Longer trips were made for four purposes, to trade with other tribes, to secure salt, to follow herds of buffalo or deer, and to seek health by going to the Hot Springs of Arkansas. When traveling overland they followed well-defined animal trails, which usually skirted the hills, crossed streams at the shallowest fords, passed the richest pastures, and always stayed close to streams or lakes.

FOOD SUPPLY AND ITS PREPARATION. The problem of food supply was never a serious one for Louisiana Indians. Bear, deer, alligators, and various small animals roamed the forests, swamps, and prairies, and buffalo were found in large numbers in the northwest section. Ducks, geese, and other migratory birds were hunted during the entire year and particularly during the winter season. Corn, numerous kinds of roots, plant shoots, grains from native grasses, many varieties of beans, sweet potatoes, cabbages, pumpkins, watermelons, and other vegetables were found growing wild or were cultivated. Peaches, plums, mulberries, persimmons, grapes, and berries of many types grew over the entire region. There were numerous varieties of edible nuts. Bees furnished wild honey. Salt was made from sea water, from the water of saline springs, or was dug from near-surface deposits. De Soto had carried a considerable number of swine and chickens on his expedition, and many of these escaped or were captured by the Indians of northeast Louisiana and from that section spread to the various tribes.

Fresh, salted, dried, or smoked meats were boiled or roasted. Individual cooking pots were used for meats and fish, for the Louisiana Indians did not like to mix flavors. Fruits were dried and used in a variety of ways, such as with meats or vegetables, or in breads. Meals and flours were made from corn, beans, and various tubers and nuts, being ground with large wooden mortars and pestles. Grains were parched, cooked, or dried. The Chitimacha *ha sutopa,* for example, was a kind of corn meal made by parching corn, grinding it fine, and removing the hulls with a flat basket-like sifter. Hominy was made by soaking corn in water containing wood ashes and then cooking it. Fish and meats were sometimes seasoned with bear's fat, which was a congealed white in winter and like olive oil in summer, a custom soon adopted by early French settlers. Perhaps the most common Indian dish was the famed *sagamite,* a sort of porridge made of corn and beans, to which meats, nuts, and fruits were sometimes added. Bread was usually cooked by wrapping small loaves or cakes in corn shucks and baking them in hot ashes or in depressions hollowed out under the cooking fires.

Although general methods of food preparation were passed on to the early French settlers, few specific recipes were recorded; perhaps more is known of Choctaw cookery than about that of any other tribe. *Ahe* was a cake made from a root paste mixed with water and fried in bear's grease; *ahelosa,* a dish made of boiled and mashed roots; *okesok,* a broth or soup made of nut paste; *nuse,* a porridge made of acorns. Filé for thickening soups was called *kombo ashish* and was made from dried sassafras leaves pounded in a mortar to a fine powder and well sifted.

Most Louisiana Indians celebrated numerous religious, political and social festivals, always accompanied by feasts. Religious festivals were given as a token of thanksgiving for favors received; political festivities to honor chiefs, treaties, or the successful return of a war raiding party; and social celebrations simply to honor individuals or groups of individuals. Jean François Dumont de Montigny in his *Historical Memoirs of Louisiana* records a sacred corn feast of the Natchez at which "more than 350 dishes of all shapes and of all kinds, of wood, or earth, round, oval, filled with all kinds of viands" were served, and which lasted for several days.

DRESS AND PERSONAL DECORATION. Mode and manner of dress varied greatly among various tribes. Clothing was made from animal skins, from cloth woven from grass or wood fibers, or from various kinds of feathers. Some Indian men were fully clothed with shirt and pants, some with only pants, and still others with only a breechcloth. La Page du Pratz, however, disagreed with the generalization of pants wearing and maintained that "no savage in America wears breeches; they content themselves with a breechcloth, or with a piece of cloth or skin with which they conceal what ought to be concealed." A few tribes permitted their men to go entirely naked during the warm seasons of the year. Women usually wore long, fringed skirts and loose-fitting, long blouses, tied at the waist with a belt or cord, although the women of some south Louisiana tribes, as for example the Bayougoulas, occasionally wore only a breechcloth made of red and white tinted bark, about eight inches wide, from which was suspended a number of cords about a foot in length. Moccasins were worn by some tribes only in winter and by others during the entire year. Children were generally dressed like their parents, though frequently smaller youngsters wore no clothing at all, or at most " a little bundle of moss, held by a thread, which passes between their thighs and is knotted to a belt which they wear."

There was much variation in hairdressing, even among Indians of the same tribe. Chitimacha men, for example, sometimes wore the hair long, with a stone or piece of lead fastened at the end to hold the long tresses in place and to aid in holding the head erect; but others shaved the head at the sides and in front, leaving only a single ridge of hair extending from the middle of the head to the back of the neck, cut to a length of two or three inches, tied with strips of deerskin, and ornamented with colored feathers. While women generally wore their hair in plaits or tresses, ornamented with plumes, some of them cut the hair in the same fashion as the men or wound it in coils or in a tight bun on top of the head. Men did not wear beards and generally removed the hair from their faces, as Pénicaut described the process, with "shell ash and hot water as one would remove the hair from a suckling pig."

Both men and women painted their faces and exposed portions of their bodies on many occasions. Painting men for the warpath was an intricate business, frequently calling for the skill of a semiprofessional painter. Both sexes painted for social and religious occasions and liberally daubed their faces and bodies with blues, greens, yellows, and reds, which were favorite colors. One of the most commonly used designs was that of a half-moon painted in bright yellow on each cheek.

A few of the tribes flattened the heads of small children by the simple process of putting a flat piece of wood, which was sometimes cushioned, to the forehead and then binding it to the back of a rude cradle. The forehead and front portion of the head were thus flattened by the gradual tightening of the cords until, according to one French visitor, "when they grow up their faces are as big as a soup plate."

Tattooing was used by a few tribes as a method of personal ornamentation, without totemic significance. Faces, shoulders, and knees were favorite locations for crude and sometimes individualistic designs. There were two methods of preparing the skin for tattooing; it was either punctured with needlelike thorns or scraped with the jawbone of a small species of garfish. Pulverized yellow-pine soot or other colored substance was rubbed into the lacerated skin, which was then allowed to heal. Knee tattooing was a mark of distinction for famed warriors.

All Indians were especially fond of gaudy ornaments, such as necklaces, finger rings, bracelets, nose rings, earrings, metal disks, breastplates, ribbonlike decorations, pins, shells, and feathers; and economically successful individuals, chiefs, or priests wore necklaces or bracelets of pearls or semiprecious stones. Highly decorated leather or fiber-platted belts were worn by both men and women, as were fancy mulberry-cloth or feather capes. Festivals and feasts were times for dressing up in one's best, and early French visitors who witnessed these events usually wrote extravagantly of the elaborate costumes.

EDUCATION. Indian life was simple and centered around the family. Education for boys and girls was designed to prepare them for their duties in providing for a family when they reached adulthood; in addition, the boys were taught the arts of war. Both boys and girls were trained in physical fitness, and some of the exercises were so strenuous that the weaker ones died.

Beginning at the age of four or five, boys and girls were given regular training in running, tree climbing, swimming, jumping, and wrestling, and these fundamental exercises were continued until the age of fifteen or sixteen. During the interim years boys were taught to cultivate grain or garden crops, fish, hunt, and fight, and the

[19]

girls to cook, prepare skins, sew, grind grains, select edible wild grains, roots, nuts, fruits, berries, herbs, and shoots, and to do decorative work.

The old men and women of a village had general charge of education and they were hard taskmasters. Shaming and appeals to pride were used rather than whippings, though boys who could not get along with their fellows were sometimes exiled or were shut up in the temples for varying periods. All children were taught courtesy and politeness to all persons and respect for their elders, and Henri de Tonti once recorded that when he visited the Taensa one of the chief's sons "wishing to pass between the chief and the fire in order to go out, was withdrawn quickly by his mother and made to pass around." The importance of personal honor, honesty, forbearance, and stoicism were instilled in early youth, and in these qualities the Louisiana Indian will have to be placed above the white settlers who crowded him from his land.

SOCIAL LIFE. Indians have usually been thought of as serious and stoic people who had very little social life. On the contrary, they had many kinds of amusements, including all sorts of sports, games, dances, feasts, and other social gatherings.

In the Louisiana tribes were numerous subdivisions, each of which had a specific name. Each subdivision usually occupied a separate village, where the various families were related or bound together by particular ties of friendship. The Choctaws, for example, had many such subdivisions, including the *Kashapa ogla* or Half people, the *Shatje ogla* or Crawfish people, the *Inhulata ogla* or Prairie people, the *Chufaikas ogla* or Bunches-of-flies people, and others.

Social and governmental organization was highest among the Natchez. The leading chief was called the "Great Sun," and below him were numerous "Little Suns," various ranks of royalty, and social stratifications of different classes of citizens. Women were held in high esteem, owned most of the property, and usually married below their station as a means of protecting their rights and possessions.

Customs of social courtesy were generally rigid and were enforced and followed as if they were laws. Politeness was a great virtue, though specific customs varied from tribe to tribe and even from village to village. When the Bayougoulas, for example, met a friend they placed the hands over their own faces and breasts, then over the hands of their friends, then raised them upward with the palms outward in a kind of salute. It was a general custom among Louisiana Indians when meeting a Frenchman during the early colonial years to say, before stopping for a chat, "Is it you, my friend?"

While amusements varied considerably, dancing was universal and most villages had a dance house used for social as well as religious dances. The Choctaws had a series of seven different dances which were always danced in the same order, the Man Dance, the Tick Dance, the Drunken-Man Dance, the Ring Dance, the Duck Dance, the Go-And-Come Dance, and the Snake Dance, and both men and women participated in all of them. In dancing the Tick Dance the dancers locked arms and formed into straight lines. They first moved forward two or three steps, then backward a step, then forward again. When they took the forward steps they looked down upon the doomed little imaginary ticks they were crushing with their feet.

Circle dances were common, and Pénicaut wrote that twenty to thirty Pascagoulas whom he observed dancing one of these dances were extremely good; for "at a whistle they break their circle and mingle together, always keeping time. Then, on a second whistle, they reform their circle with astonishing accuracy." Snake dances were practically universal among the tribes. The dancers formed in a single line, placing one hand upon the shoulder of the dancer immediately in front, first men, then women, and finally children. Following the leader, the dancers moved in a serpentine course, gradually circling and tightening the coil, until the dancers were too tightly packed together to move.

Religious dances were sometimes highly formalized and were given in honor of one of the gods or one of the forces of nature. The Chitimacha *Kutnahansh,* or

Noon-Day Sun Dance, for example, was well described by Albert S. Gatschet: "The management was intrusted to leaders who were provided with long wands or poles. The men danced with the breechcloth on, the body painted red, and with feathers stuck in the ribbons encircling the head. Gourd rattles and the scratching of alligator skins furnished the music for the occasion. They fasted during the six days the dance lasted. When the ceremony was drawing to a close, they drank water in order to produce vomiting; and, after they had removed in this manner any impurities in their systems, they began to eat heartily."

There were numerous types of gambling games, though the Louisiana Indians generally seem not to have bet on them. In the hat game the leader placed a stone under one of seven hats, while chanting the game song, after which each player had three guesses at the hat under which the stone had been placed. The corn game was played with five or seven kernels of corn blackened on one side. The kernels were tossed on the ground, and the player getting the greatest number of black sides up won.

Ball games of many types were played. The Choctaw *tole,* similar to soccer football, was played on a large field about two hundred feet long which had a pole set in the ground at each end. Two rival teams each tried to touch the ball to the pole at the opposite end of the playing field. The Natchez ball game was somewhat different, for the ball must not be carried or allowed to contact the ground, and the objective was to touch the ball to either the house of the Great Sun or to that of his opponent, a lesser chief. The two teams wore feathered plumes of two different colors and at the beginning of the game mingled together in front of the Great Sun, who unexpectedly tossed the ball into the midst of the players. The ball went back and forth, side to side, in the mass of struggling contestants. Du Pratz wrote that "fear, disquietude, and vexation have their different cries. That of joy rises above all others. Ordinarily the game lasts two hours, and the warriors sweat great drops. Finally, the ball touching one of the cabins, the amusement is at an end."

Louisiana Indians had numerous kinds of musical instruments, generally used for keeping time rather than for producing harmonious sounds. Horns were made of canes, reeds, or wood; and rattles were fashioned of gourds filled with pebbles, peas, or beans. Drums of varying sizes and shapes were made of wood or earthenware over which skins were tightly stretched. One type of drum resembled a modern kettledrum, though the earthenware bodies were filled with varying amounts of water in order to produce differently pitched tones. Whistles were carved from wood or molded from clay. One of the favored instruments was made by exposing the body of an alligator to ants until they had eaten all of the flesh and the tender inner parts of the skin, after which the bones were carefully removed and the skin thoroughly dried. Sounds were produced by raking a stick across the rough, irregular top of the skin.

Most of the Louisiana Indians loved to tell stories, tales, and legends, narrating them in a kind of singsong voice. There was the tale of *Kwanokaska,* the little man-spirit about the size of a three-year-old child who lived in a cave under some large rocks. When Indian children were ill they frequently left their village and went off by themselves into the forest, where *Kwanokaska* took them to his cave. His three assistant spirits offered each child a knife, a bunch of poisonous herbs, and a bunch of curative herbs. If the child accepted the knife he would grow up to be an evil man, if he accepted the poisonous herbs he would never be able to assist others who were ill, but if he accepted the curative herbs he was destined to become a great medicine man and the spirits taught him the important medicinal secrets. The Indians said, however, that few children chose the bunch of curative herbs, hence the scarcity of good medicine men.

The tale of *Okwa Naholo* was about the "White People" who lived in the deep pools of the rivers and lakes and bayous. They were harmless spirits, but frequently enticed people to join them and become *okwa naholos. Kashehotapalo* was the neither-man-nor-beast spirit with the body of a man, a hideous and shriveled face, and cloven hoofs. Though harmless, he enjoyed frightening hunters with his woman-like cry.

One of the favorite Choctaw stories concerned the hunter and the alligator. The hunter had been unable to kill a deer for his family, although he had seen many in the forest. Finally he met an old alligator who was lost and weak from thirst. The alligator asked the hunter where he could find water nearby, for he was nearly exhausted. The water was far away, so the hunter carried the alligator to a deep pool. The alligator plunged into the pool, drank his fill, and then surfaced. Thanking the hunter, he ordered him to go into the forest where he would find two does and a young buck, but he must not kill these deer. Eventually he would find a very large, old buck and this deer he should kill. If he followed these instructions he would become a great hunter and his family would never go hungry. As David I. Bushnell ended his account of this legend, "The hunter did as the alligator told him, and never again was without venison in his camp."

Hundreds of these legends were told by Louisiana Indians, and many of them were collected by early French travelers and later-day folklorists. They indicate that the Indian had a vivid imagination, a sense of the dramatic, and a basic desire to see good triumph over evil.

MEDICINE. Medicine was generally considered a part of religion, and many medicine men were also priests or keepers of the temples. In their practice of medicine Louisiana Indians were more advanced than most American tribes and were not far behind the Europeans at the time the French came to Louisiana. The French reported numerous examples of Indian medicine men or women "snake doctors" who cured cases given up as lost by French physicians, some of them in miraculously short periods.

Louisiana Indians were ordinarily healthy. Cripples, hunchbacks, or other deformed persons were rarely seen, for such unfortunates were generally dispatched when small babies to the vague Indian hereafter. Boys and girls were given constant training in physical education and grew up to be healthy adults. Du Pratz graphically described how the children of one village were called out every morning by an old man to go to the nearby river for a swim "in order to strengthen the nerves, and harden them against cold and fatigue."

Few contagious diseases existed, although the Indians were plagued by a considerable amount of rheumatism, arthritis, and neuritis, caused probably by more-or-less constant exposure. In the treatment of disease there was much purging, vomiting, bleeding, and blistering, as was the European practice. Every village had sweat huts, and Captain Jean Bossu described what he called the "sweat stoves": "When they are tired and excessively fatigued, after returning from a war, or from a hunt, they use sweating in stoves as a restorative. In these baths they boil all sorts of medicinal and odoriferous herbs, whose essences and salts rising with the steam of the water, enter into the body of the afflicted person, and restores his lost forces." Surgery was practically unknown and according to Dumont de Montigny, if a tribal member suffered a broken limb or other incurable injury, his fellows simply "make a feast to the one who is thus crippled, and after some days of amusement they strangle him." The white man brought the Indians various infectious diseases, including smallpox, measles, diphtheria, and tuberculosis, and widely scattered the common venereal diseases. These diseases, when epidemic, carried off large numbers of Indians, for they had built up little resistance to them.

Authorities differ as to the exact number of medicinal herbs known to and used by the Indians of Louisiana. Noted historian of Louisiana Charles Étienne Arthur Gayarré states that the number exceeded three hundred, and modern Louisiana medical historian John Duffy agrees that the number was indeed large. Diron d'Artaguette, an early French colonist, reported that "there are large quantities of medicinal plants for all sorts of maladies, but very few Frenchmen have any knowledge of them. The savages who know their properties use them with success, but zealously guard the secret from the French." Ripe persimmon pulp and sumac seeds were used to treat dysentery or diarrhea; jalap, rhubarb, snakeroot, sarsaparilla, sassafras, and several other roots and herbs were given as a physic; acacia cured toothache; boiled elderberry roots reduced swellings. Snakebites were treated by blowing strong tobacco smoke into the wound, by passing the steam from boiling poplar leaves and bark over it, or by keeping the bitten limb for some hours in a hole in the ground filled with earth and water. But the universal panacea was a kind of tea, brewed from many herbs, plants, leaves, and roots, and sometimes only from the sweet gum; for, according to the Indians, it "gladdens the heart."

RELIGION AND MORALITY. Louisiana Indians were religious and worshiped many gods. The Tunicas, for example, had nine gods—the sun, thunder, fire, and the gods of the east, south, north, west, heaven, and earth. The Chitimachas had numerous gods representing plants, animals, or birds. Father Paul du Ru, who built a chapel among the Houmas in 1700, had little success in proselytizing these Indians to his faith; and twelve years later, when Father Gravier visited the tribe, they still refused to reveal any information regarding their gods. The same year, Father Gabriel Marest reported that "We must first make men of them and afterwards work to make them Christians."

The Yazoo idea of God was reported to Dumont de Montigny by an obscure abbé, who asked these Indians to tell him their belief regarding Him. One of them replied that He was "the great Spirit, Minguo-Chitou; that he was good and did harm to no one; that even if a man should be bad he would always pardon him." When the abbé asked about prayer, the Indian answered: "Well, why pray to him since he is goodness itself and gives us all that we have need of? The one whom it is necessary to pray to is the little spirit, Minguo-Pouscoulou, who is bad, since he can make us die, cause us to be sick, and destroy our goods by storms and tempests. It is that one that it is necessary to invoke in order that he do us no harm."

The religion of the Natchez was the most formalized and elaborate of all the Louisiana tribes; and though all of the French chroniclers of the early eighteenth century made some effort to explain their basic beliefs, none more than superficially described the temple customs and general ceremonies. The Natchez, like many of the other tribes, did not reveal their religious secrets to the unbelieving white man.

Temples were a characteristic feature of religious culture, and a few of them, especially those of the Natchez, were large, sometimes being nearly a hundred yards square. Some were elaborately furnished, while others were practically bare. Some had perpetual fires burning, some had fires only on special occasions, and others had no fires at all. One authority states that all the Louisiana tribes lighted their temple fires with fire from the Mobile Indians of Alabama, but his statement is questioned by other authorities.

All of the Indians seem to have had one major god, numerous lesser gods, and a host of good and evil spirits; and there were numerous religious myths, ceremonies, and customs. The Caddos recounted the legend of a flood which drowned all Indians except a few favored families led by the Great Spirit to an exceptionally high hill. All of the peoples of the world were descended from these few families.

Formal mourning of deaths of ordinary persons was not usually practiced, the body being interred with comparatively little ceremony; however, in the case of chiefs or other important personages there was considerable gift-giving, lying in state, and formal ceremony, the most intricate being among the Natchez. Personal belongings were usually buried with the deceased, and sometimes the husband or wife was strangled and buried with the spouse. An early writer reported the funeral of a Yazoo chief: "When their chief is dead they go into the woods to bury him, just as in the case of an ordinary man, some on one side, some on the other, the relatives of the deceased accompanying the convoy bearing in their hands a pine stick lighted like a torch. When the body is in the trench all those taking part throw their

[23]

lighted torches into it in the same way, after which it is covered with earth. That is what the entire ceremony is confined to."

The Natchitoches, like the Plains Indians, frequently buried their dead aboveground, the body being placed on a low platform and covered with mud and bark as a protection against animals and birds. A small jug filled with water, together with personal belongings and food, was placed under the platform and professional mourners were hired to weep beside the body. After about six weeks the body was uncovered, the flesh burned, and the bones placed in a small basket and deposited in the temple.

Moral customs were rigidly enforced, although they were strange to the European settlers. Men were generally held in tight rein, but women were permitted to do what pleased them, being allowed to discard husbands at will or to indulge in extramarital relations without permission of husbands or in spite of their protests. The Natchez and Taensa women were the most lascivious, and more than one French priest strongly protested against their indecent acts. Father François Xavier de Charlevoix wrote that he knew of "no nation on the continent where the sex is more disorderly than the Natchez. . . . If their husbands are unfaithful to them, they may cause them to be put to death but are not subject to the same laws themselves. On the contrary, they may entertain as many gallants as they please, without the husband's daring to take it amiss, this being a privilege attached to the blood of the sun."

The tribes had different types of marriage ceremonies, some of them long and elaborate, especially for important people. In one tribe, for example, the young man and a group of his male friends went to the house of his bride-to-be. Just before arriving at the house they would see the girl, protected by a group of her friends. The young man tried to capture his sweetheart, and after he had succeeded, everyone went into the house where the old men of the tribe were seated. The old men then asked the couple numerous questions, and when they were answered to their satisfaction, gave consent to the marriage, which was immediately performed. Then everyone attended a great feast and danced until daybreak.

French Catholic missionaries had little success in Christianizing Louisiana Indians, but it should be explained that far too few missionaries were sent to labor in Louisiana. Those who came worked diligently but had to cover too large a territory and to work with too great a number of persons. The Louisiana Indian's resistance to Biblical teaching was strong, for he had a tenacious belief in his own faith. Father Marest summed up the general situation very accurately: "Nothing is more difficult than the conversion of these savages. . . . But the more averse they are to the Kingdom of God, the more our zeal ought to be quickened to draw them near, and cause them to enter it."

LATER HISTORY OF LOUISIANA INDIANS. During the eighteenth century, tribal conflicts, wars against the French, and enforced migration north and westward constantly reduced the native population of Louisiana. The French seem to have had no recognizable Indian policy beyond furnishing a limited number of gifts and inferior-quality trading goods. The Spanish, on the other hand, tried to protect the Indian, made regular treaties with the tribes, and gave them large amounts of gift goods at regular intervals. But all of the tribes had been materially reduced in number by the time of the Louisiana Purchase and a few, including the Natchez, had been completely exterminated. The Avoyel tribe, for example, in 1698 was estimated at about 280, but by 1805 only a half-dozen were left; in 1698 the Tunicas were estimated at nearly 500, but in 1803 only a few over 50 were living in the northeastern section of the present state.

The decline in Indian population continued after the purchase of Louisiana. Their lands were gradually sold to white men, whole tribes moved out of the present state limits, white men's diseases carried off large numbers, and some intermarried with whites or Negroes and left their tribes. In 1880 only about 850 Indians were scattered through more than ten parishes, and a decade later the number had declined to 628. Chahta-Ima, Father Adrien Rouquette, the noted poet-missionary to the Choctaws, died in 1887, and with his death sympathy for the Louisiana Indian ceased. By 1950, the Indian population had declined to 409, comparatively few being of pure blood. About 125 Koasatis now live in Allen Parish, some 50 Chitimachas in St. Mary Parish, and a few others are scattered in Terrebonne, Calcasieu, and other parishes. Within a few years the Louisiana Indian will have disappeared as a racial group; he will have become an American.

The Indian left a great legacy. There are hundreds of geographic place names, and many of his words are now a part of Louisiana speech. The plants which he was cultivating when the French arrived have been further domesticated and contribute to the state's present-day economy. Many of his methods of food preparation have been refined into modern Louisiana dishes. Some of his legends and folk tales are still told.

In general, he was a peaceful member of a peaceful community when the French arrived, and he fought only to protect his hunting grounds and his fireside. He had honor and dignity and integrity. Witness the speech of the chief of the Choctaws, for whom Chef Menteur was named:

> I can neither read nor write. I am not learned as thou art, but simplicity is in my heart and truth is upon my lips. What the echo is to the voice, the mirror to the face, the perfume to the flower, my words are to my thoughts. It requires no long speeches to tell thee with clearness what I think, what I feel, what I want. Long speeches come from a false heart and a deceitful tongue. They make a great noise but they mean very little or nothing at all. . . . Tell me then, in a few words what thy mind thinks and thy heart feels. Speak to me clearly. My ears are open to listen to thee. Let simplicity be in thy heart and truth upon thy lips. A true and warm talk gladdens the heart as the light of the rising sun gladdens the earth. . . . Let thy talk be as clear as thy skin. Speak little and speak truly.

He faced the unknown intruders with friendship and with outstretched hands. The Chitimacha chief spoke with "wonderful grace of gesture and majesty of mien" to Bienville and his men:

> Formerly the sun was red, the ways were filled with briars and thorns, the clouds were black, the waters were troubled, and stained with our blood. Our women wept without ceasing, our children cried affrighted, the deer fled from us afar, our houses were abandoned, our fields were waste, we had nought to fill our stomachs, and our very bones began to appear. But to-day the sun is warm and bright, the sky is clear, the clouds have gone, the ways are pleasant to walk, the waters are so clear that we behold our images therein. The deer has returned to his haunts, our women dance until they forget to eat, our children leap about like young fawns, the heart of the whole nation laughs with joy to see that to-day, O Frenchmen, we shall walk along the same path, the same sun will shine upon us; our tongues will speak the same word, our hearts will beat as one; we shall break bread together like brothers. Will that not be pleasant to behold? What sayest thou, O chief of the pale faces?

CHAPTER 3

THE LOWER MISSISSIPPI
VALLEY IN EUROPEAN
COLONIAL DIPLOMACY, 1519-1803

EXPLANATION. From the early 1500's, when the first Europeans sighted Louisiana shores, until 1803, when Louisiana was purchased from France by the United States, the area was claimed and controlled by three western European nations. Its history then, until 1803, is a part of the history of the colonial empires of France, England, and Spain; not until after that date does it become a part of the history of the United States.

This was the empire-building period of Western Europe, when monarchs, urged by adventuresome and mercantilistic advisers, dreamed of establishing dynastic empires across the seas. Columbus and his immediate followers had opened a new area for the satisfaction of the personal ambitions of kings, and they rose eagerly to the occasion. For almost three hundred years Louisiana would be subject to the ambitions, intrigues, follies, and fashions of European courts.

Spain was first in the field and through a strong and driving vitality at home and the early winning of the riches of Mexico and Peru soon reached the zenith of world power. England began an almost constant naval war with the Spanish which did not cease until after the American Revolution. France, though somewhat slower to centralize her home government, entered the lists. The race toward the west had begun, and by 1700 the spheres of influence and settlement were fairly well outlined.

During the entire period the story of Louisiana may be organized into rather well-defined eras. First was the era of the early decades of the sixteenth century, when Spain explored a considerable portion of the southern part of the United States and charted fairly well the northern shores of the Gulf of Mexico. The Spanish, however, sought riches and immediate profits. Lured by the fabulous stories of captured and tortured Indians, they plunged deeper and deeper into the southern wildernesses, following their visions of a terrestrial paradise in the form of gold and silver but finding only bitter hardships, constant disappointments, dearly-won battles, and death. In the end Spain turned her attention to more attractive lands and, except for Florida, made no attempt to gain footholds in the South.

A century later the French from Canada began to explore the Great Lakes region in search of new sources of furs, finally reached the Mississippi, and followed it to its mouth in the 1680's. But nearly two decades passed before the French actually began occupation of the southern Mississippi Valley. France settled and controlled Louisiana for slightly over sixty years but never succeeded in building a populous and successful colony. The decadence of France had already begun, and that decadence is painfully manifest throughout the whole of French Louisiana history.

Spain acquired Louisiana in 1762, took possession a few years later, and immediately began to build a strong colony. About the same time, England acquired West Florida, of which the present-day Florida Parishes of Louisiana were a part, and began to actively settle the region. Spain won this section of Louisiana during the American Revolution, and from 1783 to 1803, under the guidance of a series of strong Spanish governors, the colony made such tremendous progress that within nine years after the United States acquired Louisiana the area which is now the present state was ready for admission to the Union on an equal basis with the other states. The Spanish, not the French, had been responsible for Louisiana's coming of age.

The French, however, succeeded in forcing their language, customs, and civilization upon other nationalistic groups in Louisiana. Their language was almost universally spoken and written, except officially by Spanish government officials and army and navy officers. The French member of a household dominated that household; the children became French Creoles rather than Spanish Creoles; and their descendants, to the present day, have continued to give praise to Mother France rather than to Mother Spain, to whom it should be given. Practically all of Louisiana's historians have given an extremely pro-French interpretation to their writings; to them the Spaniard is the villain of colonial Louisiana history.

EARLY SPANISH EXPLORATIONS. Within twenty years after the discovery of America, Spain explored and made settlements in the West Indies. During the next decade Vasco Núñez de Balboa pushed across the Isthmus of Panama and discovered the Pacific, Juan Díaz de Solis explored the eastern coast of South America, Francisco Hernandez de Córdoba and Anton de Alaminos skirted the shores of Yucatán, and Juan de Grijalva sailed along the eastern Mexican coast from Yucatán to the Panuco River, near the present city of Tampico. In 1519, Alonso Álvarez de Pineda was dispatched by the Governor of Jamaica on an exploring expedition along the northern shores of the Gulf of Mexico, and discovered the mouth of a great river which he called the Río del Espíritu Santo, which may have been the Mississippi or, as claimed by some scholars, the Mobile River.

Hernando Cortes completed his conquest of Mexico in 1521, and Spanish treasure ships soon began sailing home laden with gold and silver. The failures of Juan Ponce de León and Lucas Vásquez de Ayllon in Florida and the Carolinas did not deter Pánfilo de Narváez, a Spanish grandee living in Cuba, from returning to Spain and organizing an expedition of exploration and settlement. He left Spain with five ships and about six hundred men in 1527 to take possession of Florida and any other lands which he might desire. His claim to the region was explained simply to the Indians: "God has created Adam and Eve and through them the nations of the earth. All these God has placed in charge of one person, Saint Peter, who was commanded to place his seat in Rome. One of the successors of Saint Peter has given the American lands to the Spanish Sovereigns. In this Charles and Juana [the king of Spain and his mother] are the rulers of the natives of those countries."

Nearly 150 men deserted Narváez in Santo Domingo. He lost sixty more in a storm off the coast of Cuba. Landing on the southern coast of western Florida, he began a northward march, but ran into disaster after disaster. Somewhere along the west Florida coast he decided to abandon his explorations, built several small ships, and set sail for the Mexican settlements near the Panuco River. The little fleet passed the mouth of the Mississippi, and shortly ran into a storm which wrecked the vessels. The survivors continued westward by land. After nearly a decade of captivity and wandering, five men reached the Mexican settlements. One of them, Alvar Núñez Cabeza de Vaca, wrote a *Relacion*, a narrative of the expedition, which gave some description of the southern Louisiana coast line.

A few years later Hernando de Soto, a Spanish adventurer who had acquired immense wealth with Francisco Pizarro in Peru, hearing of the account of Cabeza de Vaca, organized another exploring expedition to seek the fabled riches of the Flor-

[27]

idas. He landed at Tampa Bay in May, 1539, with a force of 620 well-equipped and well-supplied men. Moving northward, he ranged for three years across Florida, Georgia, South and North Carolina; turned westward across Alabama, southern Tennessee, northern Mississippi; crossed the Mississippi into Arkansas; moved through portions of southwest Missouri and perhaps northeastern Oklahoma, and back to Arkansas again. He died in May, 1542, on the shores of the great river somewhere between Memphis and Baton Rouge, probably in southeastern Arkansas at a camp called Anilco, leaving a worldly estate of only "5 Indian slaves, 3 horses and a herd of swine."

After De Soto's death Luis de Moscoso de Alvarado commanded the expedition. He crossed northwest Louisiana into Texas, but returned to the river, built seven brigantines, floated down the river, fighting Indians almost constantly, and finally reached the Mexican settlements with about three hundred men. According to the old chronicler Garcilasso de la Vega: "The inhabitants of Panuco were all touched with pity at beholding this forlorn remnant of the gallant armament of the renowned Hernando de Soto. They were blackened, haggard, shriveled up, and half-naked, being clad only with skins of deer, buffalo, bears and other animals, and looking more like wild beasts than human beings." After this, Spain turned from the Lower Mississippi Valley, though she did establish settlements in Florida, principally for the purpose of helping protect the sea lane between Spain and Mexico.

The Spanish had acquired a little geographical knowledge of the area that is now Louisiana. They knew of the mouth of the Mississippi, were somewhat acquainted through Cabeza de Vaca with the southern coast, and had some knowledge of the northwestern section through the reports of Moscoso and his men. This information, however, was locked up in Spain and little of it reached France, England, or other European nations. For a century white men did not explore the lower lands of the great river. When they came they were not clad in the armor of Spain nor were they hunting for gold and silver, though they would have appreciated finding some; they were clad in the armor of France and they were hunting an outlet to the sea for the Indian trade of the upper valley and a site for a city which could protect the French American empire in the west as Montreal and Quebec did in the northeast.

FRENCH EXPLORATIONS. France had begun the settlement of eastern Canada during the early 1600's. Quebec was founded in 1608, and Samuel de Champlain began the establishment of the isolated settlements which made up New France. The Great Lakes region was explored by the 1660's, and in 1673, Father Jacques Marquette and Louis Joliet entered the Mississippi from the Wisconsin River and paddled down as far as the mouth of the Arkansas.

Meanwhile, René Robert Cavelier, the Sieur de la Salle, had been engaged in exploring, in trading activities, and in establishing posts in the Great Lakes area. La Salle had been recommended to French Minister Jean Baptiste Colbert by Canadian Governor Louis de Buade, Count de Frontenac, in 1674 as a "man of intelligence and ability, more capable than anybody else I know here to accomplish every kind of enterprise and discovery," and Father Louis Hennepin had reported that he was "a man of considerable merit, constant in adversities, fearless, . . . and capable of everything."

La Salle proposed to establish a colony on the Gulf of Mexico, as historian Herbert Eugene Bolton wrote, "not only as a means of controlling the Mississippi valley and the northern gulf shore, but also as a base of attack, in case of war, upon the Spanish treasure fleets and upon the northern provinces of Mexico." The time was near when Louisiana would begin to play a role in the drama of European colonial empire building, but first the southern section of the Mississippi River had to be explored and definitely located by the French, for the Spanish still kept secret their own information.

After organizing an expedition of twenty-three Frenchmen and eighteen Indians with ten squaws and three children, La Salle followed the course of the Illinois River and entered the Mississippi on February 13, 1682. In March the party reached northeast Louisiana, where La Salle visited the Koroa, Quinipissa, Taensa, Natchez, and other river tribes, and on April 6 reached the mouth of the river. That night, according to Nicolas de la Salle, a nephew of the explorer, they camped "some three leagues from the mouth of the river" and spent the next two days in exploring the several outlets.

On the morning of April 9 they erected a post and a cross, chanted the *Te Deum,* the *Exaudiat,* and the *Domine Salvun fac regem,* fired their guns, and shouted, "Long Live the King." Then La Salle, in "a loud and audible voice," took possession "of the country known as Louisiana, its seas, havens, ports, bays, adjacent straits and of all nations, peoples, provinces, cities, villages, settlements, mines and mineral deposits, fisheries, rivers and streams comprised within the territory and extent of the said Louisiana," in the name of the "all mighty, all powerful, invincible and victorious Prince, Louis the Great, by the grace of God, King of France and Navarre."

La Salle returned to France and organized an expedition of settlement. His small fleet, consisting of the ships *Joly* and *Aimable,* the brig *La Belle,* and the ketch *Saint-François,* sailed from France in July, 1684. On board were 280 indifferent settlers, including 50 soldiers, 12 immigrant families, 12 gentlemen, and 5 priests. The *Saint-François,* a slow sailer, was captured by Spanish privateers before reaching the Gulf of Mexico. The mouth of the Mississippi was missed, some authorities advancing, though without proof, the theory that La Salle purposely missed it in order to settle within closer striking distance of the riches of Mexico. A bay was found with a narrow entrance channel, which was staked in order that the ships might enter, though the *Aimable* grounded and was soon pounded to pieces. The settlement was made in Texas, not Louisiana. Misfortune beset the little colony from every hand. The captain of the *Joly* sailed away with most of the supplies. The *La Belle* was wrecked. In early January, 1687, La Salle started for Canada with nearly a score of men to secure aid for his colony, but after several weeks' march, was assassinated by some of his men.

Historians of Louisiana generally have given La Salle a place in Louisiana history far superior to that which he had earned. So far as Louisiana is concerned, La Salle was simply the leader of a French exploring expedition that reached the mouth of the Mississippi and visited several of the Indian tribes en route. He did not explore any territory beyond the immediate vicinity of the river. It was on his expedition, however, that France staked her claim to the territory, but Spain had perhaps a better claim through the discoveries and explorations of De Soto and Moscoso.

These writers have called La Salle "the Columbus of the Mississippi Valley," a "Don Quixote," or "the one who absolutely blazed the virgin trail in the Mississippi Valley." Gayarré wrote that "he who will write the life of that extraordinary man . . . will hardly be able to prevent the golden hues of poetry from overspreading the pages which he may pen, where history is so much like romance that, in many respects, it is likely to be classed as such by posterity." Alcée Fortier, who was one of Louisiana's most respected historians, called him "one of the most remarkable men that history presents to us."

La Salle was a great explorer and colonial leader, but most of his work was done in the Canadian and Great Lakes region. Within a few years after the expedition of Marquette and Joliet in 1673, French *coureurs de bois* became well enough acquainted with the lower Mississippi to know that it ran into the Gulf of Mexico. For his work farther north, La Salle deserves a place with the great French colonial explorers and settlers, with Jacques Cartier, Samuel de Champlain, and others, but for his expedition to the mouth of the Mississippi he should be placed as just another explorer along with his Spanish predecessors. In 1818, Spanish diplomat Luis de Onis, in a communication to the French government, perhaps best summarized the Louisiana phase of his career when he wrote: "I wish not to rob La Salle of the glory you are disposed to allow him. . . . But what I . . . can prove by the fullest evidence of which facts of this nature are susceptible, is that La Salle did nothing more than traverse . . . through territories which, although included in the dominions of the Crown of Spain, were still desert, and without forts or garrisons to check the incursions of that French adventurer; and that nothing resulted from them."

TRADERS AND TRAPPERS IN THE LOWER MISSISSIPPI VALLEY. Meanwhile, in Canada and the Great Lakes region, the French had developed the fur trade to sizable proportions. French *coureurs de bois* pushed ever westward, sometimes ahead, sometimes behind the Jesuit priests who traded for furs along with their saving of souls. Governors of Canada frequently beseeched the home government not to issue additional trading permits, but the number of men engaged in the business consistently increased.

By the 1670's the trading activities of the Jesuits had reached such proportions that Count Frontenac wrote back to France that the Jesuits "think as much about the conversion of beaver as of souls; for the majority of their missions are pure mockery." A little over two decades later an Englishman of New York charged that the "Jesuits at Canada are so cunning to have their share of whatever an Indian hunts, which are brought and laid before the image of the Virgin Mary in the Church, and this being done they have not only remission of their sins, but her prayers to the bargain for good luck when they go out a hunting next time." While the charges were probably too severe, they had some merit, for all Canada was interested in the Indian fur trade.

Naturally the French fur traders pushed southward in search of new sources of fur supply and between 1682 and 1699, when the colony of Louisiana was finally settled, many of them paddled over the waterways of Louisiana. Henri de Tonti was probably the most important of these explorer-traders. He was a romantic and fascinating character known to the Indians and French Canadians as "Bras-de-fer" (Iron Hand) because a hand he had lost in a Mediterranean war had been replaced by a metal one. The son of an Italian banker, Tonti came to Canada in 1678 with La Salle and was with him on the 1682 expedition to the mouth of the Mississippi. In the spring of 1686 he led an expedition down the river to join forces with La Salle, but not finding him, returned to the trading posts on the Illinois River. Two years later he was again in Louisiana, and in 1689 went up the Red River to the vicinity of present-day Shreveport in search of information regarding the Texas colony. There is reason to believe that he made other expeditions to Louisiana between the years 1690 and 1699. After the settlement of Louisiana he served Iberville and Bienville until his death at Fort Saint-Louis de la Mobile in 1704.

During these years, English traders from Virginia, Maryland, the Carolinas, and Pennsylvania were pushing farther westward. The Pennsylvania traders used the Ohio River, and some of them undoubtedly passed its mouth into the Mississippi. The Maryland traders frequently crossed over to the Ohio, where they made and floated their river boats. The Virginia and Carolina traders, however, depended upon pack trains for carrying trading goods and furs, and following old animal and Indian trails, pushed westward across Georgia, Alabama, Mississippi, and Tennessee. While it is not known exactly when these pack-horse traders reached the Mississippi, there is little doubt that some of them had reached it by 1700.

PLANS OF FRANCE, ENGLAND, AND SPAIN DURING THE LATE SEVENTEENTH CENTURY. By the late 1600's, then, Louisiana was becoming important to the colonial empires of France, England, and Spain. France wished to establish herself in the Lower Mississippi Valley in order to extend her Canadian and Great Lakes colony, to aid in keeping the English and Spanish out of the region, to further the national ambitions of Louis XIV, and to make profits in the fur trade. England was looking toward the mouth of the Mississippi, and there were reports of an English plan to drive down the Ohio to the Mississippi and then southward. William Penn of Pennsylvania and the southern colonial governors and proprietors had plans for a series of western settlements. Spain wanted to push her frontier line from Mexico into Texas and then to connect this area with her settlements in Florida.

During the early 1690's several reports were sent from Canada to France urging the planting of a settlement near the mouth of the Mississippi, but no action was taken by the ministers and advisers of Louis XIV. In October, 1697, Tonti forwarded a memoir to Paris urging the exploration of the lower Mississippi and the establishing of a colony near the mouth of the river; but his memoir was rejected, for the recently ended King William's War (War of the League of Augsburg) had been costly to the French. Late the same month the Canadian Louis la Porte, Sieur de Louvigny, petitioned for the right to plant a proprietary colony on the lower Mississippi, and the following December, the Chevalier de Remonville, who had been a close friend of La Salle and who had shared La Salle's enthusiasm for French colonial advancement, forwarded another memoir urging the establishment of a settlement in Louisiana. Remonville did not wish personal profit or gain, he was interested only in the glory of France. Louis Phélypaux, the Count de Pontchartrain, Minister of Marine, was at last aroused and began to push the plan for a Louisiana colony.

LOUISIANA DURING THE FRENCH REGIME. The Louisiana colony was established by Iberville in 1699 and France held the area until 1762. During those sixty-four years Louisiana played a not insignificant role in the American colonial rivalries of France, England, and Spain. The English pushed ever westward in their search of furs and hides and Indian markets for their goods, trampled the toes of the Spanish in the Floridas and the French in Louisiana, and finally established Georgia as a buffer colony against Spanish Florida during the 1730's.

Meantime, Great Britain and France fought Queen Anne's War (War of the Spanish Succession), during which the English were prevented by the Choctaw Indians from launching an attack upon the Louisiana settlements. Great Britain won Newfoundland, Acadia, and the Hudson Bay region; and the Louisiana French continued, with Spanish assistance, their intrigues against the British among the southern Indians. The Tuscarora Indian War was fought by the English settlers of the Carolinas in 1711-12 and was followed a few years later by the Yamassee Indian War, both wars costing the settlers heavily in lives and property. Spain and Great Britain fought a brief war in 1727-28 and the War of Jenkins' Ear from 1739 to 1742, and the French joined other European nations against Great Britain in King George's War (War of the Austrian Succession) from 1740 to 1748. The brief interim of peace was only a prelude to the French and Indian War (Seven Years' War), which actually began in the American colonies in May, 1754, and which continued in America and in Europe until 1763.

Thus, from the founding of Louisiana in 1699 to 1763 Great Britain and France were either fighting wars or getting ready for wars, and during the intervals of peace an undeclared war was going on between the French and Spanish traders of Louisiana and the Floridas on one side and British traders of Georgia and the Carolinas on the other. The colonial settlers of Great Britain, Spain, and France were playing an important role in European colonial diplomacy.

Spain had become involved in the French and Indian War and had lost Havana and Manila. Partially for the purpose of compensating Spain for her losses and for her aid, France, on November 3, 1762, by the Treaty of Fontainebleau, granted her the Louisiana colony. But Louisiana had been a sort of stepchild of France during the entire period of French control. The dissolute courts of Louis XIV and Louis XV had cared little for Louisiana. The colony had never been successful. After over sixty years of French settlement there were only about 7,500 people in the colony, a high percentage of whom were Negro slaves, for Frenchmen simply would not settle in Louisiana. The cost had been tremendous. The Louisiana colonial government had been loosely controlled and some of the governors and many of the officials had been more interested in filling their own pockets than in forwarding the French flag of empire. The colonists were lazy, drank more than was good for them, quarreled among themselves and with officials, and generally depended upon the Mother Country for supplies rather than developing a sound economy of their own. The Crown was glad finally to be rid of an expensive and unprofitable colonial luxury.

France had failed to establish a successful colony in the Lower Mississippi Valley. Would Spain be able to yank the colony up by its boot straps and make it successful and a strong buffer against the British?

LOUISIANA AS A PART OF THE SPANISH EMPIRE. For nearly forty years, from 1762 to 1800, Louisiana was one of Spain's American colonies. During that period, it developed into a strong Spanish colony which played an important role in the intrigues and wars of European nations. Great Britain secured the Floridas after the French and Indian War, the western boundary of West Florida being the Mississippi River north of the Isle of Orleans. That section of Louisiana now known as the Florida Parishes, therefore, was a part of the British Empire, and for the first time Louisianians faced the British at close quarters.

The diplomacy of Spain during this period was twofold. First, the colony had to be made secure against attack by the advancing British. To accomplish this forts were erected, militia units strengthened, and a Mississippi River fleet of small warships was built and kept in operation. Secondly, the settlers must be protected from a greater menace, British economic penetration; but Spain's trade laws were constantly violated, English businessmen established themselves in New Orleans, and English colonists settled on the rich farming and grazing lands of the Opelousas and other districts.

During the American Revolution, Spain won back the Floridas, then prepared to enjoy a period of peace. But this was not to be, for the Americans pushed westward with more energy than they had shown as Englishmen. Soon Spain was at odds with the United States over the navigation of the lower Mississippi and the boundaries. These problems were temporarily settled in 1795 by the Treaty of San Lorenzo, but within three years the two nations were again at loggerheads.

At the end of the century Louisiana had come of age and her citizens were listening to the arguments of French writers and revolutionaries. Napoleon had arisen in France and he wanted Louisiana again brought under the French flag. England, although having lost the American colonies, still possessed Canada and hoped that Louisiana could in some way be secured so that the two could be joined together into a strong buffer colony against the advancing Americans. Spain still held the Floridas and Mexico, of which Texas was a part, and Louisiana was an important connecting link between these two areas. A few Louisianians wanted to revolt against Spain and join the United States and a few wished to revolt and return to the French fold. A few others talked ambitiously of establishing an independent nation; after all, had not Louisianians captured Baton Rouge from the British during the American Revolution, and Mobile and Pensacola? But the great majority of the population cared little what part their colony played in international intrigue. Louisiana was economically prosperous, and revolutions or internal disturbance do not generally originate in prosperous areas. The Creole did not worry much about Louisiana's future.

GREAT BRITAIN AND THE UNITED STATES AFTER 1803. Napoleon browbeat unhappy Spain into ceding Louisiana back to France by the Treaty of San Ildefonso in October, 1800. For some strange reason, although Spain had shown much more interest in the colony than had the French and the colony had advanced to maturity during the Spanish period, some Louisiana French Creoles were overjoyed. The colony, however, was only a pawn to be used by Napoleon and he soon sold it to the United States.

The United States took possession of Louisiana in December, 1803, and began to prepare the colony, which had never known a working democracy, for statehood. Great Britain resumed its death struggle with Napoleon and rapidly swept the seas. A war broke out between England and the United States in 1812, and Great Britain began to plan the conquest of Louisiana, which failed when the Battle of New Orleans was lost. Less than four months later Louisiana celebrated its third anniversary as an American state.

SUMMARY. For nearly three hundred years, Louisiana had been one of the areas in the world most sought after by the three major powers of Europe. Spain had first explored it but had withdrawn in favor of richer lands farther south. France then settled the land, but a decaying monarchial government cared little for it, while the minds of the French statesmen who were interested seem never to have embraced the vast fields upon which their policies were to operate, did not comprehend the great extent of the country, and were entirely ignorant of the amount and character of the means necessary for the success of their lower Mississippi colony. Spain secured the colony and did a magnificent job of colony building, but was finally forced by Napoleon to relinquish control. France, still not heeding the cries of loyal French Creoles who had pleaded for a French Louisiana back in the 1760's, sold it for a figurative thirty pieces of silver to the United States. Great Britain held the Floridas for two decades but lost the opportunity to build an empire in the Mississippi Valley.

The struggle for Louisiana was finally won, not by one of the European nations which had intrigued and fought for its permanent control for so long, but by the infant nation which had arisen on the eastern shores of North America.

PART TWO

French

Colonial Louisiana

CHAPTER 4

THE FOUNDING OF
LOUISIANA

THE AGE OF LOUIS XIV. During the late years of the seventeenth century Louis XIV of France, *Le Grand Monarque,* or the "Sun King" as he loved to be called, sat complacently on his throne and surveyed western Europe. France was at the zenith of her power as a Continental nation. The comparatively weak countries of northern Europe caused no concern; Spain had the greatest colonial empire, but was a friendly ally; Great Britain was a small island kingdom which had been harassed for a hundred years with civil wars and other internal disturbances, and had a relatively unproductive group of colonies.

Louis fell heir to the French throne in 1643, when he was only five years of age, but until he reached manhood his government had been directed by the brilliant Cardinal Mazarin. After 1661, Louis fortunately selected such men as Jean Baptiste Colbert and the Marquis de Louvois to further industry and manufacturing and to head his war cabinet, generals like the Viscount de Turenne and Prince de Condé to command his armies, the Marquis de Vauban to plan his military fortifications, and Jules Hardouin Mansard to build state buildings and palaces and to lay out parks. These men did their work well, and by the ninth decade of the century Louis could relax at the Hôtel des Invalides or the Palais Royal or the Tuileries amidst the most brilliant court in all Europe.

He continually sought the gratification of a great vanity and pride, loved pageantry and all forms of pleasure, and thirsted for dominions and renown. Court favor became the major objective of all Frenchmen, and the adroit use of flattery was the surest and most rapid way to accomplish it. It was a venal age, and the personal rule of Louis, as one authority has written, "extinguished all civil freedom, sound morals and manly sentiments among his subjects."

But the last twenty-five years of his reign—he did not die until 1715—saw the beginning of the decline of France. His armies and navies suffered reverses. His revocation in 1685 of the Edict of Nantes, which had given French Protestants some measure of religious freedom since 1598, was as unjustifiable as it was impolitic, and his stern persecution of the Huguenots drove over a half million of his most useful and industrious subjects from his realm. His financial policies squeezed the purses of Frenchmen ever tighter and tighter. There was no room in France for individual initiative or self-expression, for Louis was the state. While he never uttered the words, *"L'état, c'est moi"* (I am the state), he did say, "It is God's will that whoever is born a subject should not reason, but obey," and during the last two decades of his reign what good ministers Louis had were not able to halt the forces of decay in his kingdom.

Louisiana had the unhappy fate to be born and to spend its years as a colony of France during this decadent period of French history. French officials cared little for the struggling colony on the northern shore of the Gulf of Mexico. At home France began with the English a series of wars ending in the complete loss of the French Empire in America. Louisiana had better been born under a King William or a Queen Anne of England, or a King Charles or a King Philip of Spain.

FRANCE PLANS TO SETTLE LOUISIANA. During the closing years of the seventeenth century Spain stood like a colossus in the Western Hemisphere. She controlled most of South America, many of the West Indies Islands, all of Central America and Mexico and the Floridas, and was pushing northward into what is now the southwestern sections of the United States. Her American culture was already old, and her vast trading activities in the Americas made the Gulf of Mexico a Spanish lake. She claimed the Lower Mississippi Valley area because of the explorations of Spaniards during the first half of the sixteenth century.

By the same period Great Britain had along the Atlantic seaboard from Maine to the Savannah River a string of colonies becoming self-sufficient. Although thin, the line of settlements was tightly grouped, and the colonials already were beginning to push westward toward the Appalachian highlands.

France's lone American colony was Canada, which, except for a small area in the vicinity of Montreal and Quebec, consisted largely of isolated villages and Indian trading stations stretched along the St. Lawrence River and the Great Lakes. If France was to continue successfully her colonial activities in North America, the English must be confined to the area east of the Appalachians.

René Robert Cavelier, the Sieur de la Salle, had claimed the Louisiana territory for France and had tried to plant a colony at the mouth of the Mississippi. However, unskilled navigation, shipwreck, desertion, dissension, disease, Indian hostility, and lack of colony-planting experience led to the failure of his Texas colony, and his own dictatorial imperiousness led to his assassination. If France, wished to prevent the great valley from falling into other hands, a colony must be planted and quickly. La Salle had especially feared the English, writing that "it is necessary to establish colonies . . . lest the English, who are our close neighbors in New York, Virginia, and Carolina, anticipate the French."

In 1690, Louis Phélypaux, the Count de Pontchartrain, became the French Minister of Marine, and he was ambitious to expand French possessions. Four years later, Henri de Tonti, who had been a friend and companion of La Salle, offered his services in establishing a Louisiana colony. In 1697, the Canadian Sieur de Remonville proposed organizing a company to send an expedition of settlement. The same year *La Salle's Last Discoveries in America*, based on Tonti's memoirs and describing the geography, the Indians, and the resources of the Mississippi Valley, was published in Paris under Tonti's name. The War of the League of Augsburg (King William's War) ended in 1697, and Louis's ministers turned their attention to expansion in America.

The news that Dr. Daniel Coxe, one of the New Jersey proprietors and a patentee of Carolina, had developed a scheme for establishing an extensive colony west of the Carolinas and that the English were listening sympathetically to Father Louis Hennepin, who had been deported from France for scandalously attacking La Salle, stirred the lethargic Louis to action. But the King would not approve the idea of a chartered company; the colony of Louisiana must be planted by royal effort. Before the French commissioners left to help draft the Treaty of Ryswick, which ended the War of the League of Augsburg, Louis ordered them not to discuss the title to the Mississippi, as he had decided to establish a colony there. Two problems remained to be solved. Would the expedition of settlement be sent from Canada or would it proceed directly from France? In either case, whom should be chosen to lead the expedition?

While the King's ministers were considering these problems, the English began to hear rumors of the project—Louis had set aside 300,000 livres for the colony, he had approved a proprietary colony, he had promised the use of a fleet and eight companies of troops. From May 28 to May 31, 1698, the *Post Boy* of London carried stories that Louis had decided "to erect a Colony on both sides of the River Mechisippi."

PIERRE le MOYNE, SIEUR d'IBERVILLE. The man chosen to lead the expedition of settlement was Pierre le Moyne, the Sieur d'Iberville. He was born in 1661, the third son of Charles le Moyne, a native of Dieppe who had emigrated to Canada when a young man. Charles le Moyne became a *coureur de bois,* learned Indian languages, went into trading for himself, made a fortune, and invested it in lands. One of his estates, Longueuil, was on an island opposite Montreal, and when the King raised him to the Canadian nobility he took the title of Sieur de Longueuil. Each of his eleven sons was given estates named for places in Normandy and adopted these names as titles. Thus Pierre le Moyne became the Sieur d'Iberville. Each son achieved renown in Canadian French colonial history, while two of them played important roles in the early history of Louisiana.

Iberville entered the French navy, rapidly rose to a command, and during the War of the League of Augsburg was one of the few French commanders who fought the English with success. With a fleet of five ships he defeated a small English fleet in Hudson Bay and removed the English menace from the waters of northern Canada. A later victory off the coast of Newfoundland enhanced his reputation, so that by the end of the war Iberville was the greatest hero in Canada. Becoming restless after the end of the war, he revived La Salle's old plans for establishing a colony on the lower Mississippi, and not long afterwards was called to France. The young Canadian, "the Cid of New France," was appointed to lead the expedition which was to found Louisiana.

THE VOYAGE. Iberville proceeded to La Rochelle to organize the expedition. Securing two frigates, the *Badine* and the *Marin,* and two small storeships, he collected supplies, assembled crews of Canadians and other experienced seamen, two companies of marines, and about 200 colonists. A few of the colonists were ex-soldiers, others were artisans, laborers, and down-and-out adventurers. There were a few wives and children.

The little fleet sailed from La Rochelle on September 24, 1698, and proceeded to Brest, where final preparations to cross the Atlantic were made. On October 24 the fleet put out from Brest and charted a course toward the southwest. Late in December, the expedition arrived at Cap François, Santo Domingo, where it was joined by the French ship of the line *François,* which was to escort the little fleet through West Indian waters filled with Spanish and English buccaneers. Here also, according to Alcée Fortier, Iberville picked up a pilot acquainted with Gulf Coast waters, Laurent de Graaf, "a celebrated buccaneer." On January 24, 1699, the fleet finally anchored off Santa Rosa Island, near the entrance of Pensacola Bay.

The Spanish had settled Pensacola only a short time before and had built a small fort. The Spanish Commandant received Iberville politely but refused him permission to enter the bay, so he sailed westward to Mobile Bay and anchored off an island lying just west of the bay entrance which he named the Isle de Massacre, because of the human bones found there, present-day Dauphin Island. Iberville soon moved southwestward past Petit Bois, Horn, Ship, and Cat Islands and then turned southward to the Chandeleur Islands, so named because they were reached on Candlemas Day. He then returned to Ship Island where good anchorage was found and built temporary huts.

On February 13, Iberville sent his brother Jean Baptiste le Moyne, the Sieur de Bienville, to explore the immediate coast line of the mainland. The party captured an Indian woman of the Biloxi tribe and the same evening encountered a war party of Bayagoulas on their way to attack the Mobiles. From the Bayagoulas they learned that about a hundred miles to the west was a large and deep river called the Malabouchia which emptied into the Gulf of Mexico. On February 21, the *François* sailed for the West Indies. Then, on February 27, accompanied by Bienville and about fifty Canadians and sailors, Iberville set off to locate the mouth of the Mississippi. Iberville planned to move upstream and choose a site for the new settlement. The little fleet was ordered to remain in the harbor at Ship Island, and if supplies should run short or Iberville did not return within six weeks, the *Marin* was to return to France for additional supplies and colonists.

EXPLORATION OF THE LOWER MISSISSIPPI. For four days the party pushed slowly southward through the numerous islands lying off the southeast coast of Louisiana south of Mississippi Sound. The wind was usually against them, so the pulling was hard. Fogs slowed the progress of the boats. The islands were low and marshy, offering little protection from the winter winds and rains. Firewood was scarce, and water could be had only by digging into the sands of the low beaches. One day it stormed, and that night the men had to build platforms on which to sleep, for the water covered the swampy island on which they were encamped.

The storm continued the next day, but the party pushed on. Late in the afternoon they rounded a sort of cape, and the wind drove them toward a series of jutting crags with calmer water between and beyond them. Iberville wrote in his journal: "As I neared the rocks, I perceived that there was a river." The "rocks" were not rocks at all, but driftwood and logs covered with mud. The river was the Mississippi. It was the second of March, 1699.

The next morning the party started up the Mississippi, after Father Anastase Douay had chanted a *Te Deum* in acknowledgment of its discovery. Iberville did not deem it necessary to take formal possession of the territory in the name of the King of France; but a day or two later he caused a large cross to be erected, probably somewhere in the vicinity of present-day Fort Jackson. No Indians were found for some distance from the mouth of the river, but eventually a hunting party of Bayagoulas and Mongoulachas were sighted. The Bayagoulas led Iberville to their village, where several Indians offered to guide the party upriver. Here, also, Iberville was shown a letter that Tonti had written to La Salle back in 1685.

The expedition continued upriver, passed Plaquemine, and finally arrived at a small Indian town on the riverbank with "many cabins covered with palmetto leaves, and a Maypole without branches, reddened with several heads of fish and of bears attached as a sacrifice," the site of the present city of Baton Rouge. The Frenchmen reached Pointe Coupée, where the Mississippi was just beginning to cut through the loop and isolate what is now False River. Here "Monsieur d'Iberville used this neck of land which is about a musket shot wide, as a portage for the canoes, sending the larger barges the long distance around." On March 20, the party reached the villages of the Houma Indians in the northwestern section of present-day West Feliciana Parish.

After being entertained several days by the Houmas, the party started on the return trip. At Bayou Manchac, Iberville turned eastward with a few men and returned to Cat Island by way of Bayou Manchac, the Amite River, and Lakes Maurepas, Pontchartrain, and Borgne, while Bienville and the rest of the party continued down the Mississippi to its mouth, then turned northward to Cat Island. The two brothers arrived at Cat Island within a few hours of each other.

FORT MAUREPAS, THE FIRST SETTLEMENT.* Iberville now determined to establish a settlement on the Gulf Coast instead of at some point on the lower Mississippi. There were several reasons for this decision; the banks of the river were low and the land behind them swampy, it was feared that larger ships would be

---

*The Fort Maurepas settlement became known as the "Fort du Biloxi" or "Biloxi" and declined after the founding of the first settlement at Mobile. In the fall of 1719 Fort Louis was built on the site of present-day Biloxi. Thereafter the names Old Biloxi and New Biloxi were rather generally used.

[40]

unable to cross the bars at the mouth of the river, and English traders were already operating as far west as the Mississippi—the forerunner perhaps of actual settlement —and a post was needed somewhat nearer their field of operations. Then, too, a fort on the coast would enable France to control the mouth of the river and perhaps even gain possession of the entire northern shore of the Gulf of Mexico.

Iberville explored the shores of the bays and inlets as far eastward as Mobile. He finally chose the projection of land on the eastern side of Biloxi Bay as the site for his settlement. Here springs would provide fresh water, and the bay was so shallow that large enemy ships could not get within cannon range; French vessels could, however, find safe anchorage behind Ship Island. On April 8 the men began the construction of a small fort which was completed by the first of May and named Fort Maurepas. It was a small, square fort built of logs, on each side of which was a deep ravine and at the back a deep trench to give additional protection against a land attack. It was armed with twelve cannon and a dozen swivel guns mounted at the bastions, was garrisoned by seventy men and six ship boys, and was provisioned for about six months.

Now that he had planted the settlement destined to grow into the French colony of Louisiana, Iberville was ready to return to France for additional colonists and supplies. He appointed the Sieur Sauvole de la Villantray Acting Governor of the little colony, with his brother Bienville second in command, and on May 4 set sail for France. Some Louisiana historians have confused this Sauvole de la Villantray with another of Iberville's brothers, François Marie le Moyne, Sieur de Sauvole.

THE EARLY YEARS. The majority of the Canadians and Frenchmen detested farming, much preferring to trade for furs and hides or to explore the region in search of gold and other precious metals. No crops were raised the first year, resulting in hardship and a heavy and constant drain upon the supplies brought from France.

Some weeks after the departure of Iberville, Bienville set off on another exploring trip up the Mississippi. He made his way upriver to the "fork on the Chetimachas," at the present site of Donaldsonville. On his return trip downstream he experienced an adventure which has become famous. About a dozen miles below present-day New Orleans, he rounded a bend in the river and to his amazement saw a twelve-gun British vessel anchored near the riverbank.

In October, 1698, Dr. Daniel Coxe and several other proprietors had dispatched an expedition from Great Britain to settle a colony on the lower Mississippi. The little fleet had wintered at Charles Town, South Carolina, and in the summer of 1699 a corvette under the command of Captain Lewis Banks was sent to explore the Mississippi and to choose a site for the settlement. It was this vessel which Bienville now saw.

Bienville boldly paddled his little fleet of two canoes up to the British ship and informed Banks that he was in French territory, that he (Bienville) had a fleet a short distance upriver, that this was not the Mississippi anyway, and that the English must leave immediately. Bienville had a secondhand knowledge of the character of Banks, for Iberville had captured a vessel commanded by him in Hudson Bay some years before and at that time had called him an obstinate fool. Bluffed by Bienville's bold action, Banks turned around and sailed back down the river, after uttering dire threats and promising to return in greater force to drive out the French. The place has since been called Detour des Anglais, or English Turn.

Iberville returned from France in early December, 1699, with supplies and new colonists. With him came a young Jesuit, Father Paul du Ru, who had been selected to found a mission in the colony, and a young uncle of Iberville's wife, Louis Antoine Juchereau de Saint-Denis, who was to become one of the most romantic figures in Louisiana history.

Told of Bienville's encounter with the British at English Turn, Iberville ordered his brother to build a fort on the Mississippi at the first high and solid ground.

Bienville selected a site about fifty miles upriver on the east bank, and here his men built a low stockade, a small blockhouse, armed with two eighteen-pound and four four-pound cannon, and a powder magazine. The name Fort de la Boulaye was given to the little fortification, perhaps because some birch trees were found in the vicinity.

The site of the fort had not been well chosen. The land sometimes flooded, and the undrained soil was so water laden that crops would not grow. Furthermore, mosquitoes thrived there. Father Jacques Gravier wrote that "after the month of March, these insects came in so prodigious a number that the air was obscured" and that the men "could not distinguish one another at a distance of ten paces." The post did not prosper. It was officially occupied until 1707, was used as a troop-gathering place until 1715, and was completely abandoned after the founding of New Orleans. Gradually all evidences of the fort disappeared and the site was finally lost. It was not until 1930 that a group of New Orleans historians who systematically searched for the site discovered its exact location.

Henri de Tonti arrived from Canada with ten canoes, fifty men, and cargoes of furs while Bienville was constructing Fort de la Boulaye. Tonti had made several trips to the lower river after La Salle's expedition and on one of them in 1686 had reached the mouth of the Mississippi. During this period he had covered a considerably larger area than had been explored by La Salle, and by 1700 his *coureurs de bois* were fairly well acquainted with the eastern and northern portions of modern Louisiana. His biographer has written that "he possessed qualities of patience, endurance, and leadership which La Salle manifestly lacked." He had, however, little to show for his nearly twenty years of exploration and fur trading, for about this time he wrote that "all the voyages I made for the success of this country have ruined me." He settled in the Louisiana colony, rendered signal service as an Indian diplomat and fighter, and later became the Commandant at Mobile. He died of yellow fever in September, 1704. He is remembered in American history as "the faithful lieutenant of La Salle" rather than as one of the great explorers of the Mississippi Valley, one of the intrepid pioneers of early French Louisiana, and one of the most chivalric leaders of American colonial history.

During this period Iberville was engaged in exploring the Mississippi River as far north as Natchez, for he expected to build settlements along the river. He sent his cousin Pierre le Sueur up the river in search of minerals. Le Sueur returned with some blue-and-green earth which he thought contained copper, but it contained no minerals, and one of the settlers later wrote that "we never had any news of it since."

While Iberville was away Fort Maurepas received an unexpected visit. The Governor of Spanish Pensacola sailed into the roadstead opposite the fort and informed the French that he was searching for English vessels which might be trespassing. He was royally entertained by the French, who strongly suspected his real motives. Shortly afterwards the Spaniards departed, only to have their fleet wrecked by a storm. The French rescued the survivors, supplied them, and sent the Governor "in a double Shallop—with all oars, and with Hats off—to his fort of Pensacolas." Villantray had carefully concealed the fact that he was extremely hard up for supplies and had fed the Spanish on pork, peas, beans, poultry, venison, Madeira wine, and French bread. The Spanish were convinced that the little colony was well supplied and prosperous.

In late May, 1700, Iberville again sailed for France, detouring on the voyage by way of New York. Picking up a Jersey pilot, he headed for the Narrows. Under the pretext that he was taking on wood and water, he remained for a month taking soundings between Sandy Hook and the Battery, though the British kept a day-and-night watch on him. Extremely suspicious of his real motives, they soon strengthened the fortifications of New York.

Upon his return to Louisiana in December, 1701, Iberville found only about 150 persons living in his colony. Over fifty colonists had died, including Acting Governor Villantray. Supplies had run short, and for some months the colonists had had only a little corn to eat. Some had gone to live with the Indians.

Iberville decided to move the colony to a better location and chose the area of Mobile Bay. He ordered a group of men to proceed to Massacre Island to establish headquarters until a fort could be built on the mainland. He remained at Biloxi, because since leaving Santo Domingo he had been bedridden with an abscessed side which had necessitated a six-inch incision across the stomach. It was not until the middle of February, 1702, that the convalescent Iberville finally arrived at Mobile Bay.

THE FOUNDING OF MOBILE. Bienville came from Fort de la Boulaye to Massacre Island and soon began construction of the new fort, the site for which Iberville had selected about "sixteen leagues from Massacre Island, at the second bluff" on the Mobile River. Fort Saint-Louis de la Mobile was much larger than Fort Maurepas, being some 375 feet square and armed with four batteries of six cannon each. Within the fort were a guardhouse, a storehouse, a residence for the commandant, a house for the officers, and a chapel. Outside the palisade, some fifty yards above, were barracks for the soldiers, and near the river was a powder magazine twenty-four feet square and ten feet deep. Homes for the settlers would be constructed farther upstream.

Iberville left Louisiana for the last time on April 27, 1702, shortly after he had given good colony-building advice to the French government in one of his dispatches. He hoped to plant several strong permanent settlements peopled by sturdy colonists along the Gulf of Mexico to better protect the entire area from the English and Spanish. He wrote that it was "necessary to send here honest tillers of the earth," not men who came primarily to make quick fortunes. Years would pass before his dream would be realized.

Shortly before his arrival in France, Queen Anne's War broke out between France and England and Iberville was sent with a strong fleet of eleven vessels to the West Indies. He occupied the English islands of St. Nevis and St. Christopher, captured an enormous treasure at the island of Martinique, but found the Barbados and other larger islands too strong for him to attack. He then sailed to join forces with the Spanish at Havana, where he was seized with yellow fever. On July 9, 1706, within two weeks of celebrating his forty-fifth birthday, he died on board his flagship, which was appropriately named the *Pelican*. He was buried in the Church of San Cristóbal. Some thirty-five years later the church was demolished and his remains lost. They repose today in some unknown place without a monument or even a marker.

Iberville "was unquestionably the greatest Canadian of his generation," yet in spite of his tremendous achievements as a soldier, ship captain, fleet commander, colonizer, statesman, and planner of empire, French historians have generally neglected him. Only in the French naval histories are his naval exploits given adequate treatment. Nellis M. Crouse has suggested that "he suffers from the cavalier treatment bestowed by French historians upon most of their Canadian heroes," and in addition perhaps because "his successors were not able to hold the conquests he made and the colonies he founded," but concludes that "in Canada and in Louisiana, at any rate, the name of Iberville is not entirely forgotten."

As far as Louisiana is concerned, Iberville had succeeded where La Salle had failed. He had planted a colony which, though small, was firmly rooted. He had given his colonists sound advice in urging the extension of agriculture, and had encouraged the coming of families and of young women to make homes for unmarried settlers. No French colonizer had made a better record of heroism, work, and self-sacrifice than this inspiring leader who finally gave his life for the Empire of France. He well deserves to be called the "Founder of Louisiana."

SLOW GROWTH OF THE COLONY, 1702-12. The little Louisiana colony grew slowly during the years after 1702. A few farms were established along the Gulf Coast and along the swampy, undrained banks of the lower Mississippi. Voyagers and fur traders arrived every year from the Great Lakes region or the upper Mississippi with furs, bear's fat, hides, and other goods; but since they brought no food with them, they lived off the poor colonists.

The colony faced many problems. Disease, particularly yellow fever, carried off many settlers. Storms destroyed what few crops were planted, blew down the ramshackle houses, and ruined food supplies received from France. The few farmers had difficulty clearing the land, for they constantly faced "the savage aspect of the almost universal forest." The home government kept men busy searching for mines and pearl fisheries, sent them off on expeditions "to catch bison-calves, tame them and take their wool," or directed them to raise silkworms. The colonists bickered among themselves, refused to obey orders, and simply would not plant sufficient food crops, preferring to depend upon the "paternal providence of Versailles."

The indefatigable Bienville and the priests pleaded for the establishment of homes. "With wives," Iberville had written, "I will anchor the roving *coureurs de bois* into sturdy colonists." "Send me wives for my Canadians," wrote Bienville. "Let us sanction with religion marriage with Indian girls," pleaded the priests, "or send wives of their own kind to the young men." Finally in the summer of 1704 twenty-three young women arrived, girls who "were reared in virtue and piety, and knew how to work." The same ship, the *Pelican*, also brought seventy-five soldiers, four families of artisans, a curate, and two Gray Sisters.

Colonists approaching the entrance of Mobile Bay looked over the sides of their vessels toward a land which they believed to be one of fabulous riches, where life would be easy and the work not too difficult. They were bitterly disappointed, for they were "dumped, like ballast," as Grace King wrote, "upon the arid glittering sands of Dauphin Island or Biloxi, ill from the voyage, without shelter, without food, without employment." Many of them, unaccustomed to the climate and the hardships, died within a short time.

The majority of the newcomers were lazy and shiftless and to some historians "a scurvy lot," representative of the lower and middle classes remaining in France after that nation drove out the Huguenots in 1685, totally unfit to plant a strong and economically sound colony. If Louis XIV had only had the foresight to permit the Huguenots to settle in Louisiana instead of "forcing them to swell the numbers of the English colonies on the Atlantic coast, and eventually assist them in taking the New France from which they had been barred!" But when four hundred Huguenots petitioned Bienville for permission to settle in Louisiana and there to have freedom of worship, the answer came back from France: "Have I expelled heretics from France in order that they should set up a republic in America?" The dancing and the coquetries continued in the Versailles halls of Abundance, Venus, Mars, and Apollo, while across the seas France was losing an empire on the Mississippi.

By late 1704 the colony had only 195 inhabitants, including 8 officers, 72 soldiers, 14 naval officers and sailors, 10 shipboys, 40 Canadians, 16 laborers, and 23 women or girls. The two families had a total of six persons. There were three priests. During this year Jean François le Camp was born to Jean le Camp and his wife. Most authorities claim that Jean was the first Creole child born in the Louisiana colony, a claim which must be challenged however, because in 1731, Claude Jousset de la Loire, supported by witnesses, won a New Orleans court decision that he had been the first child born at Mobile.

The Louisiana settlers were in a deplorable condition. They lived in rude huts and dressed in rags, while the soldiers wore skins rather than their completely worn-out uniforms. For food they had only the little corn which had been raised, acorns and roots, the wild game and fowl obtained by hunting, and the fish of the Gulf and nearby bays. Some small beginnings had been made, however, in raising chickens and livestock, for they had "14 cows; 4 bulls, of which 1 belongs to the King; 5

calves, 100 hogs, 3 goats, 400 chickens, which the commissary has preserved carefully for breeding."

By 1706 the colony had been reduced to 85 inhabitants. Two years later, owing to the arrival of several shiploads of settlers, the population increased to 279 persons, not including over 100 wandering Canadians and Indian slaves. But the census of 1710 listed only 178 persons, excluding soldiers, Canadians, and a few sailors.

Beginning in 1707, Mobile was visited by a series of floods which overflowed the low and marshy ground and destroyed the low stock of supplies and in 1710 it was decided to move the settlement to a site about eight leagues above the mouth of the bay, the present location of the city. The new Fort Saint-Louis de la Louisiane, which was completed in 1711, was considerably larger than the old fort, and within its walls were the governor's house, the magazine, the King's storehouse, and a guardhouse. Mobile, Biloxi, and Dauphin Island were to be the center of Louisiana life for the next several years, although new posts would be established on the Coosa, Tombigbee, and Red rivers, and a new town, New Orleans, founded on the banks of the Mississippi.

BEGINNINGS OF TRADE AND AGRICULTURE. The fur trade with the upper Mississippi and western Great Lakes region had begun in 1700, when Tonti brought a shipment of furs down the river in opposition to the orders of Canadian officials. During the years following, the fur and hide trade increased greatly in volume and value, as did the trade in bear's fat, corn, and smoked or cured meats. On several occasions when supplies from France were delayed, the Louisiana colonists depended upon the upper-river settlers in the general vicinity of later-day St. Louis and the other Illinois towns to supply practically all of their foodstuffs. The governors of Canada constantly protested to French officials, arguing that the trading goods frequently belonged to Canadian creditors and that "the rebels ought to be arrested."

When, shortly after the settlement at Fort Maurepas was established, Iberville suggested to the Commandant at Pensacola that trading relations be opened between the two colonies, the Spanish official accepted Iberville's offer. By 1704 the Louisiana-Florida trade was well established and supplies of flour, lard, and other goods were being furnished the Spanish from the French royal storehouse at Biloxi.

As early as 1701, Iberville began to investigate possibilities of trade with the West Indies and Mexico. Supplies for Louisiana were obtained in 1704 and 1706 from Havana, and finally in 1707 the Havana merchants sent a cargo of Canary Islands wine to Biloxi. The next year a small vessel arrived from Havana with brandy, lard, and tobacco. From this time the trade gradually improved, although Spanish officials steadily prevented the exportation of seed wheat and other items which would promote the economic development of the colony.

Requests of Louisiana officials for permission to open trade with the southern Atlantic coastal colonies of Great Britain received little consideration from the home government. In June, 1706, however, a British ship appeared in the Gulf of Mexico with food supplies and had little difficulty in selling its cargo, but the possibility of trade development was stopped by Queen Anne's War. At least one Louisiana ship was captured by the British, its cargo confiscated, and the crew landed unceremoniously at Havana. In 1710 an English ship sacked Dauphin Island. This event terminated the English trade until the end of the war.

The first cottonseed had been brought to Louisiana by Iberville in 1699, and by 1712, according to Louisiana's first general historian, François Xavier Martin, "trifling but successful essays had shown that indigo, tobacco, and cotton could be grown to great advantage but hands were wanting." The production of these staple crops had to await the day when the colony was producing enough food crops to satisfy annual needs. Throughout the period metallic currency was scarce, so the colonists traded and bartered or depended upon "bills of credit" issued by the Governor.

GOVERNMENT DURING THE EARLY YEARS. Until 1704 the Governor was the sole governing official in the Louisiana colony. In that year a Commissary-Commissioner (Commissaire Ordonnateur) was added. The Governor was the representative of the King and head of civil, military, and naval affairs, while the Commissary-Commissioner served as the auditor, treasurer, and chief storekeeper of the colony. There were no courts of law, so the officials at the various settlements decided disputes and sentenced criminals.

Acting Governor Villantray died during the summer of 1701 and was succeeded by Bienville. A few years later Nicolas de la Salle, the Commissary-Commissioner, encouraged by Henri Roulleaux de la Vente, the Curate of the colony, brought charges of official misconduct against Bienville. In 1707 the French government appointed a new governor, but he died before reaching Louisiana. Early in 1708, Diron d'Artaguette, who had been appointed Commissary-Commissioner, arrived at Dauphin Island. Although D'Artaguette apparently outranked him, Bienville continued to serve as Governor.

Within two weeks of his arrival D'Artaguette opened a formal inquiry into the charges against Bienville, who, however, was not permitted to be present at the hearings nor to be represented by counsel. In his report, D'Artaguette did not either acquit or convict Bienville, possibly because he had not been given complete judicial authority. The charges against Bienville were never reopened and the affair was generally forgotten in Louisiana. With the exception of the period of his trial in 1708, Bienville served as Governor until the summer of 1713.

LOUISIANA BECOMES A PROPRIETARY COLONY. Shortly after Diron d'Artaguette returned to France in 1711 he made a full report to the King on the condition and future prospects of the colony. It was a disheartening report. The Crown had maintained direct control over Louisiana for a dozen years, appointing officials, generally directing the activities of the colony, and providing supply ships, supplies of all types, and settlers. While the colony was now on a permanent footing, its few settlements scattered along the shores of the Gulf and the Mississippi had a total population of only about four hundred persons, including about a hundred troops and a score of Negro slaves. Only a small number of the colonists worked in agriculture. Some worked in a civilian capacity for the army, and still others were laborers, mechanics, tavern keepers and shopkeepers, or were engaged in trading with the Indians. A few Indians, mostly women and children, lived with the settlers and did menial tasks, while numbers of Indian men loafed around the little settlements, consuming large amounts of supplies but contributing nothing to the economic life or progress of the colony.

France had been unfortunate in her choice of locations for the settlements, a not unusual circumstance during the period of early European colony planting. The land in the vicinity of Mobile and Biloxi was sandy and generally sterile, while Dauphin and Ship Islands were only sandy spits rising out of the sea. Fort de la Boulaye was on ground subject to overflow, and the French had not yet learned the art of ditching and draining the land for crop planting. While wild game and fowl were plentiful, Martin writes of the "buz [sic] and sting of the musquitoes, the hissing of the snakes, the croaking of the frogs, and the cries of the alligators," deterrents to semitropical colony planting.

The little Louisiana colony during those first twelve years had cost the King considerable treasure which he would have much preferred to spend on his palaces and on courtiers, courtesans, and entertainment. Proprietary colonies had been successful for other countries, particularly Great Britain, and Louis finally found a man willing to gamble a fortune on the possibility of developing Louisiana into a profitable colony. On September 14, 1712, letters patent granted Louisiana to a wealthy merchant and recently created nobleman, Antoine Crozat, the Marquis de Chatel, and on the twenty-sixth the fifteen-year charter was signed.

Crozat was given the rights and privileges usually granted in a proprietary charter.

He acquired all the territory called "Louisiane" south of the Illinois country and all commercial rights hitherto possessed by the King, including the exclusive privilege of importing and exporting goods, in the area between Mexico and the Carolinas. He was given specific permission to open and work mines and to export ores, metals, precious stones, and pearls to France, and was to be granted title to all land he might personally occupy or cause to be occupied and the complete ownership of all manufactures he might establish. He was to have exclusive use of all colony buildings and property belonging to the King. Given complete control of all local trade in the colony, he was also granted the exclusive right to import slaves from Africa for his own profit.

Crozat in return was obligated to govern his colony under the laws, edicts, and ordinances of France. He must send yearly from France two supply ships, on which the King might send without charge twenty-five tons of military provisions and ammunition. The King would continue to pay the cost of maintaining the army units stationed in Louisiana, including 10,000 livres a year for officers' salaries, but Crozat was to assume this burden after nine years. One hundred quintals of powder were to be furnished annually to Crozat by the King at cost.

ANTOINE CROZAT. Comparatively little is known of the early life of the Marquis de Chatel, but apparently he was a peasant's son, born on one of the great landed estates. Noticing Crozat's acuteness of mind, the son of the feudal lord became his patron and financed at least a rudimentary education. When about fifteen, Crozat was apprenticed to a wealthy merchant and within twenty years gained a partnership in the firm, married the merchant's daughter, and on the death of his father-in-law came into possession of his property. Within a few years he had become one of the wealthiest men in Europe. He won royal recognition by loaning money to the government during several occasions of financial crisis. Rewarded by a grateful monarch with the title of "marquis," he became one of His Majesty's councilors and rose to the envied post of secretary of his household, where he was in the position to influence the King's decisions in matters of government and finance.

Crozat had become interested in colonies some years before, when he acquired stock in the Guinea Company which traded with Africa and in the Asiento Company which imported African slaves to the New World. He had made a profit from these investments. Might not profits be made in Louisiana? For as the land had been described to him, it abounded with splendid opportunities for trade and commerce, possessed potentially successful gold and silver mines, had pearl fisheries which could be easily developed, and contained boundless acres of raw land which might soon become fabulous estates. Undoubtedly there was another reason for his interest. If he could develop the hitherto unsuccessful and costly Louisiana colony it might be the means of his advancement to a dukedom. He was socially ambitious as well as patriotic.

Gayarré, on one of the numerous occasions when his pen wandered far afield from sober factual history, gives still another reason for Crozat's interest in Louisiana. His wife had long been dead and his life now centered around his daughter Andrea. She fell in love with a prince, but the prince's mother informed Crozat that the marriage was unthinkable unless Crozat attained a more noble rank. Suffering because of the hurt to his beloved child and the bitter blow to his pride, he resolved to develop a principality in the New World, the greatest of all French feudal estates. Then he would return to the duchess and say: "I give him a princess for his bride, and domains ten times broader than France, or any kingdom in Europe, for her dowry!" Gayarré gives no sources for the highly colorful story; it belongs to the romance of Louisiana, not to its history.

For whatever reasons, Crozat decided to invest 700,000 livres in the Louisiana project.

CADILLAC, THE NEW GOVERNOR. The colonists first learned that Louisiana had been granted to Crozat when a fifty-gun ship of the line arrived at Dauphin Island on May 17, 1713. On board were the new Governor, Antoine de la Mothe Cadillac, new Commissary-Commissioner Jean Baptiste du Bois du Clos, a comptroller, two men who would direct and protect the personal interests of the proprietor, twenty-five prospective brides from Brittany for the unmarried settlers, and large stores of supplies.

Cadillac had entered the French army as a youth and during the early 1680's, when in his early twenties, had settled in Canada. Upon retiring from the army he received a large grant in northern Maine, but lost it through the incursions of the English. Moving to Quebec, he re-entered the army and served as Commandant at Michilimackinac, where he won the friendship of the Indians but somehow attracted the violent hostility of the Jesuits, who accused him of "the most infamous debauchery."

In 1701 he established a post at the site of present-day Detroit, and here he succeeded in winning some little reputation as an outpost commandant. Evidently he got along little better with the Governor of Canada than he did with the Jesuits, for the Governor and the Intendant soon began to charge him with "looking to his own advantage in every thing," of being considerably more "interested in making money for himself than in the good of the establishment," and of "being equally hated by the troops, by the inhabitants, and by the savages." On the other hand, however, it was generally admitted that he was a man of courage and had tremendous drive and energy, and by some that he was personally moral and pious. An experienced frontier-outpost administrator, he brought with him to Louisiana a list of sound instructions from the Count de Pontchartrain for the government of his colony.

Cadillac got off to a bad start. Some of the twenty-five prospective brides whom he had brought with him were so ugly that no one could be enticed into marrying them, a personal affront to the proud Governor. The poor colony was a great disappointment, and he wrote back to France: "Believe me, this whole continent is not worth having, and our colonists are so dissatisfied that they are all disposed to run away." Dauphin Island he described as consisting of "a score of fig-trees, three wild pear-trees, and apple-trees of the same nature, a dwarfish plum-tree, three feet high, with seven bad-looking plums, thirty plants of vine, with nine bunches of half-rotten and half-dried-up grapes, forty stands of French melons, and some pumpkins." He did not approve of the character of the male settlers and said of the women: "If I send away all the loose females, there will be no women left here at all, and this would not suit the views of the King or the inclinations of the people." However, after reporting that "the colony is not worth a straw for the moment; but I shall endeavor to make something of it," he went to work with characteristic energy, not so much to advance the colony as to augment his personal fortune.

Following his instructions, Cadillac first reorganized the government and installed the officials who had come with him. He set up a court called the Superior Council and put into operation the various laws of France and the "Custom of Paris," which was simply the laws and legal customs of that section of France. Then he turned his attention to agriculture and offered plans for raising tobacco and indigo, although he predicted little success, writing that "this wretched country is good for nothing and is incapable of producing either tobacco, wheat or vegetables even as far north as Natchez." He attempted to promote the Indian fur trade, and encouraged trade with the Spanish in Mexico and the Floridas, with the English colonies, and with the islands of the Caribbean. He sent out parties to plant settlements. He tightened the distribution of warehouse supplies to the colonists and tried any sort of economic venture that might make the colony more self-sustaining and yield a personal profit to Crozat.

EXTENDING FRONTIERS AND PACIFYING INDIANS. Cadillac early complained of the army, writing: "What can I do with a force of forty soldiers, out of whom five or six are disabled? A pretty army this, and well calculated to make me respected by the inhabitants or by the Indians! As a climax to my vexation, they are badly fed, badly paid, badly clothed and without discipline. As to the officers, they are not much better." Despite this criticism, however, he called upon Saint-Denis in 1714 to establish a post on the Red River in northwest Louisiana. Saint-Denis, who had come to Louisiana as a young man in 1699 and had been engaged in exploration and the fur trade, was well qualified to lead such an expedition. He chose a site at the modern city of Natchitoches and began construction of the new post. It was well that the French arrived at this time, for a few Spanish were already settled near present-day Robeline and an expedition had been sent to plant a settlement and establish a mission near the same place.

The post completed, Saint-Denis loaded a pack train with trading goods and proceeded southwest to San Juan Bautista, a Spanish settlement on the Río Grande, where the Spanish Commandant held him prisoner until orders could be received from the Viceroy at the City of Mexico. During the passing weeks Saint-Denis fell in love with Commandant Don Diego Ramon's granddaughter, Señorita Manuela de Sanchez y Ramon. He was finally taken to the City of Mexico and offered the command of a company of cavalry with the rank of captain if he would enter Spanish service, but he refused and was later returned to San Juan Bautista. He continued his courtship of Manuela, until her father at last consented to their marriage.

For several years Saint-Denis traded with the Indians of western Louisiana and eastern Texas and in 1722 was appointed Commandant of Fort Saint Jean Baptiste at Natchitoches, where he lived until his death in 1744. Many of his contemporaries maintained that he deserved to have been made Governor of Louisiana; unquestionably for over twenty years he was the strongest force the French had in northwest Louisiana.

About the same time Saint-Denis led his expedition up the Red River, Cadillac decided to establish posts in the area north and northeast of Mobile; Fort Toulouse was built near the junction of the Coosa and Tallapoosa rivers, and Fort Tombecbe was established on the Tombigbee River. These posts were designed to help keep the English out of the region, for since the early 1700's they had been trading with the Indians as far west as the Mississippi and in 1713 a trader named Price Hughes had urged the Indians of the Natchez villages to ally with the English and to "break the heads of the French at Mobile"; shortly afterwards the Natchez had murdered several French traders.

The Governor soon called for Bienville. He had never liked the man, probably because of Bienville's popularity with the colonists, soldiers, and Indians, and recently his dislike had turned to hatred. According to Bienville, writing in one of his dispatches, "the cause of Cadillac's enmity to me, is my having refused to marry his daughter." Bienville might also have admitted that he held no love for the Governor, that they had frequently quarreled, and that he was intensely jealous of Cadillac for having replaced him in the governorship.

Cadillac ordered Bienville to take a detachment of thirty-odd men and to punish the Natchez for murdering the traders. Bienville proceeded up the Mississippi to an island opposite the Tunica village, built a strong stockade ringed with entrenchments, and invited the Natchez chiefs to smoke the calumet with him. Upon their arrival, he treacherously captured them and informed them that they would not be given their freedom until they had sworn to execute Chief Oyelape and his three accomplices, who had murdered the traders. In addition they must agree to have the Natchez cut 2,500 logs and gather a great store of bark in order that Bienville might build a fort on the banks of the Mississippi near their White Apple village.

The chiefs agreed to his terms, returned to the tribe, executed the guilty men, assembled the logs, and gathered the bark. Then Bienville, who in the meantime had been reinforced by some twenty Canadians on their way to Biloxi, moved upriver. In early August, 1716, he completed Fort Rosalie on the site of present-day Natchez. He had won without bloodshed what is usually called the First Natchez War. Even the strategies of Bienville, however, could not pacify the Natchez, for the hauteur of the Governor and his niggardly trading policies continued to alienate a majority of the tribe. Soon they began to send their goods to Charles Town, South Carolina, and to again welcome the English traders to their villages.

ECONOMIC LIFE OF THE COLONY. The colony made slow economic progress. Settlers had to be forced to plant food crops, for they much preferred to make more certain profits from tobacco and indigo; on few occasions was there a surplus of foodstuffs which could be sold. Many of the settlers still refused to work or at best worked indifferently. The majority of them were Canadian hunters and *coureurs de bois,* fortune seekers from France, or former inmates of jails and almshouses of the Mother Country.

Cadillac imported Negro slaves from Martinique, Guadeloupe, Santo Domingo, and other West Indies Islands in order to secure at least a partially adequate labor supply for the field. Five hundred were brought in during 1716 and about three thousand the following year. The West Indian Negroes were troublesome and rebellious, and the majority of them believed in voodooism, but there were not enough slave ships to furnish an adequate supply from Africa.

Commissary-Commissioner du Clos continued to prod the colonists to plant foodstuffs, particularly maize, or Indian corn, but with little success. In compliance with the King's order, he also strove to establish the cattle industry on the Louisiana prairies so as to increase the supply of meat and milk products for food, and hides and tallow for sale.

Cadillac's attempts to increase the small volume of trade with Mexico, the Floridas, the West Indies, and the English colonies ended in failure. Saint-Denis had seemed on the way to success, but the death of a friendly viceroy in the City of Mexico ended his plans, while the Spanish of the Floridas and West Indies, fearing that the French might encroach on their European trade, ceased sending their ships to the Louisiana colony. Another reason for the failure of trade was that Crozat, with a monopoly on the trade of the colony, refused to give a reasonable share of the profits to others.

Consumer goods became increasingly scarce. Prices soared, for only the monopoly goods supplied by Crozat were available. Credit could not be had, for the proprietor wanted cash, and even the drafts of army officers and civil officials were refused. Many colonials had to sell slaves, livestock, or personal belongings to secure necessities, and begged to be returned to France. A few escaped to Spanish Texas and Florida or to the southern English colonies. As French historian Georges Oudard wrote: "The breath of ruin and despair swept through the country."

RECALL OF GOVERNOR CADILLAC. Cadillac's temper steadily grew worse. He quarreled with the people and with the officials, particularly Du Clos, and with Bienville. When the soldiers complained that they had nothing to eat but corn, he replied that "the troops in Canada were satisfied with corn for their food," that they had "lived on it three years, and that I saw no reason why they should not continue." Du Clos defended the soldiers, for which Cadillac "gave him a good rapping on the knuckles."

The people met without Cadillac's permission and framed a petition demanding free trading privileges with all countries. But this was not all. After considering the drunkenness, quarrels, and duels which occurred daily, and the spirit of sedition and revolt, Cadillac prohibited all commoners from wearing swords or carrying other weapons and required all persons of noble birth to deposit proof of their nobility in the archives of the Superior Council. Whereupon the people fabricated all sorts of ludicrous mock papers and deposited them with the Superior Council, which in turn passed them on to Cadillac. The colonists, however, were only half finished with their Governor. The precious metals he had expected to find failed to materialize, so they derisively created a new order of chivalry called the Order of the Golden

Calf and made him the Grand Master, in recognition of his great achievements in his search for gold and silver, and sang a newly composed and scurrilous song about him. Stung to the quick, Cadillac wrote back to France, "Decidedly, this colony is a monster without head or tail," then prepared to put down the rebellion.

Meanwhile, Pontchartrain had informed Crozat and the King of the difficulties between Du Clos and Cadillac. Early in 1716, Crozat asked the King's permission to replace the Governor; and he wrote at the bottom of one of Cadillac's reports, "I am of opinion that all the disorder in the colony of which M. Lamothe-Cadillac complains is due to the bad administration of M. Lamothe-Cadillac himself." In March, 1716, the Governor received an official communication from Crozat, dismissing him and Du Clos from office. Du Clos was happy to be relieved of his Louisiana position and transferred to Santo Domingo, while Cadillac, according to Gayarré, "contemptuously shook off his feet the colonial dust which had there gathered, and bundling up his household goods, removed himself and them out of Louisiana, which he pronounced to be hell-doomed." The tried and loyal Bienville would act as Governor until the new Governor arrived.

Cadillac had accomplished some good for the little colony and had been constant in his efforts to make it profitable. He had more than one defender, the Curé at Mobile writing that he was a "very ordered and well-intentioned man. As for the colonists, they are demons." The caustic-penned Cadillac has been almost completely forgotten as a colonial Governor of Louisiana; today he is chiefly remembered for founding the post which grew into the city of Detroit, and for the automobile which bears his name. He hated the Louisiana colony and its people and after his return to France continued writing violent denunciations and accusations until, as Richebourg Gaillard McWilliams writes, "he was thrown in the Bastille for a period of cooling." He should at least be remembered for his letters and his reports from Louisiana, as they are, in the words of one writer on the Louisiana colonial period, "on a high level in the literature of invective."

END OF CROZAT'S COLONY. Bienville held his second governorship for less than a year. In March, 1717, Jean Michiele, Seigneur de Lepinay et de la Longueville, the new Governor, arrived. A former naval officer, he had served over twenty years in Canada. He brought with him a new Commissary-Commissioner, several other officials, three companies of infantry, and some fifty colonists; he also brought Bienville the Cross of St. Louis and title to Horn Island. Lepinay had hardly landed in Louisiana when he and Bienville began to quarrel, and soon the entire colony was involved, one group supporting the Governor and the other rallying behind the popular Bienville.

In France, Crozat's affairs had taken a turn for the worse. The regents of the new King, six-year-old Louis XV, had imposed a higher property tax, and Crozat's tax amounted to something over six and a half million livres. He began to reconsider his Louisiana venture, which had cost one and a quarter million livres and had returned only a little over three hundred thousand. Then he learned that Lepinay was doing no better than Cadillac had done. In early August, 1717, he petitioned the King for release from his agreement, and the ministers of the King acceded to his request.

Crozat had failed. French government officials worried, for the colony had not developed as it should have. France had recently lost Newfoundland and Acadia to Great Britain. The British must not be permitted to push west of the Appalachians; therefore, it was necessary "not only to maintain Louisiana, but to back it as much and as promptly as possible." A new proprietor or a company must be persuaded to inject new blood and new funds into Louisiana. At last a company was found, headed by one of the most unusual and daring financiers of all time. His name was John Law.

CHAPTER 5

JOHN LAW'S LOUISIANA

JOHN LAW. The story of Louisiana from 1717 to 1731 is the fabulous tale of a Scottish businessman and financier with grandiose ideas, of a company which he organized, and of another company which he for a time controlled. Next to Iberville and Bienville, he contributed more than anyone to Louisiana's development during the French colonial period.

Born in Edinburgh in 1671, John Law was the eldest son of a wealthy goldsmith and banker. He received a sound general education and early in his youth showed marked ability in mathematics, finance, and commerce. After his father died, Law developed into a flashily dressed dandy, became noted as a gambler and debauchee, killed a man in a duel, and finally fled to France to avoid prosecution. He soon lost much of his fortune gambling and moved on to Holland, where he began the serious study of finance in a Dutch banking house.

About 1700 he suddenly appeared in Edinburgh with new, and for that time fantastic, ideas of banking, which he presented in a published pamphlet. According to Law, a state or nation should establish a bank to serve as the fiscal agent of the country. Receiving all state monies and holding these funds as capital, it would then issue paper money, discounting them for the profit of the government. His plan was ridiculed by Scottish and English banking circles and tossed unceremoniously out of Parliament as the wild scheme of an idle dreamer.

Soon afterward he returned to Paris and laid his scheme before aged Louis XIV and his advisers, but they, too, rejected his proposals. For a time he became the most noted playboy and gambler of the French capital, but his methods and his enormous winnings prompted the police to order him to leave the city because he was "rather too skillful at the game which he had introduced." He roamed about Europe for some years, presenting his financial schemes to the governmental advisers of one country or another without success. The Duke of Savoy became much impressed with his ideas, but after careful and sober reflection, told Law, "I am not sufficiently powerful to ruin myself."

Shortly after the accession to the throne of the boy king Louis XV, Law again appeared in Paris with something over a half a million livres in cash and presented his plans to the reckless and extravagant Philippe, duc d'Orleans, the King's Regent. Philippe was fascinated. Law argued that his new methods would be the only salvation of a nearly bankrupt France. Despite the opposition of the ministry and higher officials, in May, 1716, Law and his brother organized a banking house of deposit, discount, and circulation. John Law became the Chief Director of the new company, which soon became known as the General Bank of France, and that same year the government announced that it would accept the paper money of the bank at face value. Two years afterward the bank was reorganized as the Royal Bank of France, with Law as Director-General.

THE COMPANY OF THE WEST. The Scotsman now conceived the idea of using some of the deposits of the bank to develop the Louisiana colony, which imaginative Frenchmen still envisioned as capable of producing fabulous riches if properly handled. The Company of the West, capitalized at 100,000,000 livres, was organized by Law, and 500-livre shares were offered to the public. France went wild with the idea of vast real and speculative gains, and as Joseph Wallace wrote: "Society was thus stirred to its very dregs, and people of the lowest order hurried to the stock market to invest their small savings. All honest, industrious pursuits, and moderate gains were now despised. The upper classes were as base in their venality as the lower. The highest nobles, abandoning all generous pursuits and lofty aims, engaged in the vile scuffle for gain. Even prelates and ecclesiastical bodies, forgetting their true objects of devotion, mingled among the votaries of Mammon." The selling price of shares climbed—to 1,000 livres, 2,000 livres, 4,000 livres, and even to 8,000 livres for a 500-livre share.

On September 12, 1717, the Company of the West was given proprietorship of the Louisiana colony on approximately the same terms that had been granted Crozat. The grant was to run twenty-five years. Officials in the colony were to be nominated by the Company and appointed by the King. The Company promised to send 6,000 colonists and 3,000 Negro slaves to Louisiana within 10 years, and children of Catholic European immigrants were to be considered as native-born Frenchmen. The citizens of the colony were to be exempt from "any tax or imposition."

The Company acquired all the lands of Louisiana as they had been held by Crozat, and in addition the Illinois country, as well as all forts, military and naval equipment and munitions, provisions, trading vessels, and all merchandise surrendered by the former proprietor. The colony was to remain a part of the Diocese of Quebec, and the Company promised to build churches and furnish clergymen for all parishes.

Two years afterward, all French trading and colonizing companies were merged into one large company called the Company of the Indies; and the Company of the West, or the Company of the Mississippi as it was popularly known, was included in this merger. The Company of the Indies announced even greater plans for the development of the Louisiana colony: the number of immigrants would be increased; agriculture would be promoted; new settlements would be established; and trade with the Spanish in the Floridas and Mexico, with the English in their southern colonies, and with the Illinois country northward would be expanded. Credit would be given to reputable colonials, and currency would be sent to the colony to replace the unsatisfactory paper money. The actual settlement of French Colonial Louisiana was about to begin; the early years and the era of Crozat had been but a prologue.

PROBLEMS OF GOVERNMENT AND ADMINISTRATION. Governmental offices were left largely as they had been under Crozat. Under the governor were two lieutenant governors, an attorney general, and a commissioner, who acted as treasurer, kept and distributed merchandise for the colonists and the Indians, and was in charge of the forts and posts, their equipment, and the upkeep of troops. These officials, together with two residents of the colony chosen from those best qualified, composed the Superior Council. The Council served as an advisory body, was the court of the colony, and registered public notices, all forms of land and mortgage records, contracts, marriages, and other permanent records. It was, in short, the general repository of all archives pertaining to personal rights and property. Membership on the Council was a coveted honor, so there was much wire-pulling and playing of politics to secure appointments. Each of the most important settlements—Biloxi, Dauphin Island, Mobile, Natchez, and Natchitoches—had a commandant, who acted as the chief civil and military official.

The headquarters of the colony was first at Dauphin Island, but in 1717 a storm formed a sand bar in front of the harbor, and in 1719 the capital was moved to Fort Maurepas. Shortly afterward a part of Fort Maurepas burned, and a company of "stout German soldiers" was sent to build a new town on the western side of the bay, the site of present-day Biloxi. They cleared land, built Fort Louis, barracks, a few houses, and dug a cistern. In December, 1720, the capital was moved to New Biloxi.

By 1721, the colony was divided into nine governmental districts, each under the charge of a commandant and a judge. The districts included New Orleans, Biloxi, Mobile, Alibamons, Natchez, Yazoo, Arkansas, Natchitoches, and Illinois. About the same time three large religious divisions were created. The section south of the Ohio River, north of the Isle of Orleans, and east of the Mississippi was given to the Carmelites; the Illinois country was given to the Jesuits; the third, which included the area west of the Mississippi and the Isle of Orleans, was given to the Capuchins.

In February, 1718, when Governor Lepinay was recalled to France, Bienville became Governor of Louisiana for the third time. The last years of his governorship were stormy, for Marc Antoine Hubert and after him Jacques de la Chaise, the King's commissioners, constantly disagreed with Bienville's policies, reporting that Louisiana was the finest country in the world and failed to prosper only because of the maladministration of the Governor. Bienville returned to France to report on his stewardship in 1725, and early the next year was deprived of his position and granted a pension of 3,000 livres.

Pierre Dugué de Boisbriant, one of the King's lieutenants and Major-Commandant of the Illinois country, a thoroughly capable, amiable, and extremely well-liked leader, was appointed Acting Governor until a new chief executive could be selected. He officially served until August, 1726, when Étienne Boucher de la Perier de Salvert was appointed Governor, and continued as an ad interim official until Perier arrived in March, 1727.

Perier was a former naval officer, who had distinguished himself during the War of the Spanish Succession. After that conflict he entered the service of the Company of the West, commanded several of the Company's ships, and won recognition for his loyalty to the Company's interests and for his ability as a practical psychologist in patching up disputes among company employees. The orders of the Company were specific. He was to reach a complete understanding with Commissioner de la Chaise, to eliminate the bickerings and rivalries and plottings of the Bienville–De la Chaise factionists, and to strip nonconformists of their offices and return them to France if necessary for official investigation.

Though Perier was not a man of strong personality, he was generous, broad-minded, and prudent. He completely disregarded his orders relating to the punishment of certain indiscreet though capable and diligent officials, writing the Company that it mattered little whether such and such a person was attached to his own person or not, "as long as that person is attached to his work and makes himself useful."

For some months the bickerings continued. But De la Chaise lost support of the Council, and as his star declined that of the new Governor rose. Soon De la Chaise realized that to retain his position he must co-operate with the Governor; thereafter there was little difficulty between them. Perier became "a marvellous success," as one contemporary wrote, because under his tactful peacemaking old animosities were put aside, the people began to sing his praises, and even the Directors of the Company in Paris forgot their former anxieties over Louisiana government and management.

But Perier had neither the ability nor the experience to successfully govern a pioneer colony. He lacked decisiveness, hesitated to require discipline, and attempted the impossible in trying to keep everyone happy at the same time. He also had ill luck, partly in having the last Natchez Indian War, which began with a massacre of French settlers, occur during his administration. For this there was no forgiveness. He was recalled in 1731, though he continued to serve as Governor until Bienville arrived for his last governorship in 1733.

BOUNDARY TROUBLES WITH SPAIN. The Louisiana colony played a significant role in the French-Spanish colonial rivalries of the period. In 1718, Bernard de la Harpe arrived in the colony with orders to prevent Spanish encroachment upon western Louisiana and eastern Texas, which France claimed through the discoveries of La Salle. La Harpe took a small force to Natchitoches, and from there went a short distance up the Red River, where he built a fort. Meanwhile the Spanish had established the post of Los Adaes a few miles west of Natchitoches. After considerable correspondence between the Spanish and French leaders, a rather indefinite boundary, somewhat east of the Sabine River, was accepted by both sides.

In 1720, La Harpe led an expedition to establish a settlement on the Texas mainland in the vicinity of Galveston, but the hostility of the Indians forced him to give up the attempt. He returned to New Orleans, and shortly thereafter, his health having failed, he sailed for France. There he wrote a historically valuable *Journal of the Establishment of the French in Louisiana.*

Meanwhile, in 1719 a rather insignificant war had broken out between France and Spain. Upon receiving the news in middle April, Governor Bienville immediately called a meeting of the Superior Council, at which it was decided to organize an expedition against Spanish Pensacola. Bienville moved against the town and captured it by surprise, for its commandant did not know that war had been declared. After garrisoning the place, Bienville returned to New Orleans.

But the French did not long hold Pensacola; in August two Spanish vessels bombarded the fort heavily, forcing the French to surrender. The Spanish then attacked Dauphin Island, but retreated upon the appearance of a French naval squadron. The French organized another expedition, recaptured Pensacola, and destroyed its fortifications. The place remained in French hands until it was returned to Spain by the peace treaty of 1722. Thereafter the Perdido River was generally considered by both nations as being the boundary between their colonies.

THE FOUNDING OF NEW ORLEANS. Bienville and Iberville differed over the location of the capital of Louisiana. Iberville insisted that it should be built on the Gulf of Mexico, while Bienville argued that the first high ground on the lower Mississippi was a much more strategic site. Bienville found a likely place at a point where the river was nearest Lake Pontchartrain, but it was some years before he had the opportunity to carry out his plans.

In the fall of 1717, Bienville wrote the Directors of the Company outlining his plans for building a town, enthusiastically but inaccurately describing the location as safe from high water, tidal waves, and hurricanes. On October 25, 1717, the Company authorized the founding of the new town, although its Directors did not get around to sending instructions favoring a site on Bayou Manchac to the colony's engineer until the next spring. By this time Bienville had already begun operations at the present site of the city.

Early in 1718, Bienville left Mobile with about fifty men, including a few indifferent carpenters. Arriving at the crescent bend in the Mississippi, he chose the site, and the men began to clear the ground of trees and brush and to build rude shelters. The work progressed slowly, for the men were inexperienced, had to be forced to their tasks, and the physical difficulties were many.

By the end of the year only a portion of the land had been cleared and only a few palmetto-thatched huts had been built. In 1719 a severe hurricane inundated the land, ruining some of the stores, so for some time the work practically ceased. That fall the Company ordered Le Blond de la Tour, the chief engineer, to look over the situation and decide whether the town should be moved to another site.

The engineer, apparently trusting the report of an assistant, decided against the location. Nevertheless Bienville continued the work.

An assistant engineer, Adrien de Pauger, arrived in the colony in 1720, and he directed the completion of the first four blocks. In March, 1721, Pauger drew up general plans for a town of eight blocks facing the river by five deep, and under his direction the town gradually began to take shape. Drainage ditches and canals were dug, a wharf was constructed, low levees were thrown up, a cemetery was located, and a small church and government buildings were built. But in September, 1721, a five-day storm destroyed most of the buildings, so the work had to be done all over again.

The Company records indicate that its officials named the proposed town for the Duc d'Orleans when they first discussed the project in October, 1717. The name, however, was spelled "Nouvelle" Orleans, and when Father Charlevoix visited the town late in 1721 he wrote: "Here I am in this famous city which they call *Nouvelle-Orleans*. Those who coined the name must have thought that Orleans was of the feminine gender. But what does that matter? The custom is established and custom is above the rules of grammar." Historian of New Orleans Stanley Arthur wrote that "the good priest had reason for raising the point as the general rule in France gives masculine preference to names of towns when derived from foreign names of masculine or neuter gender."

By the end of 1721, New Orleans had a population of slightly over 370 persons, including 147 men, 65 women, 38 children, 28 servants, 73 slaves, and 21 Indians. Disaster, however, came the next year, when two hurricanes hit the city. In March, for eight consecutive days the populace heard "a hollow noise, somewhat loud"; then a three-day storm struck, and while it did not pass directly over the town, destroyed several buildings. In September another hurricane swept the entire Lower Mississippi Valley, leaving New Orleans a pile of ruins.

The town was speedily rebuilt, this time with a few brick buildings. The central portion fronting the river was occupied by the church, with the rectory on the left and a guardhouse and prison on the right, and in front of the church was the Place d'Armes. Scattered about the river front were government warehouses. Bienville built his house on approximately the present site of the Custom House, and in front of it a powder magazine was erected. At the other extreme end of the town were the quarters of the soldiers. Today the area occupied by Pauger's plan, which had been enlarged to eleven by seven blocks, is called the "Vieux Carré," or Old Square.

Pauger had done his work well. The streets were properly lined in parallels and were for that day of excellent width. Each square was surrounded by a low drainage ditch and was divided into five lots with plenty of space for a yard and a garden. Father Charlevoix thought that Pauger's plan was "very handsome and very orderly; but it will not be as easy to carry it out as it was to put it on paper." The good Father, though he admitted that the town's buildings "would not adorn a poor village in France," was optimistic of the future, for he wrote: "I have the best grounded hopes for saying that this wild and deserted place, at present almost entirely covered over with canes and trees shall one day . . . become the capital of a large and rich colony. . . . Rome and Paris had not such considerable beginnings, were not built under such happy auspices, and their founders met not with the advantages on the Seine and the Tiber, which we have found on the Mississippi, in comparison of which, these two rivers are no more than brooks."

What is the actual date for the founding of New Orleans? In 1917 the Louisiana Historical Society passed a resolution that the official dates should be February 9, 10, 11, 1718, in keeping with the usual historical practice of dating a town when work was actually begun at the site. However, in 1917, the two-hundredth anniversary of the founding of the city was celebrated in Paris; a noted French historian writing that "the choice of 1718 seems quite indicated, but 1717, the date of the founding in Paris can equally well be adopted . . . a city with a pay master . . . can it not exist?" It must be remembered, however, that the Company had favored a site on Bayou Manchac, and not at New Orleans.

NEW COLONISTS FOR LOUISIANA. Although it had promised to send new colonists to Louisiana, the Company of the West soon faced the simple fact that Frenchmen did not want to leave France for a distant and unknown land. Arrangements were therefore made with the government for the release of inmates of certain prisons and houses of correction on their promise to emigrate to Louisiana. Convicts were offered their freedom if they would marry prostitutes and go with them to Louisiana. In 1719, one ship's passenger list of 189 included 7 tobacco smugglers, 53 dealers in contraband salt, 6 vagabonds from Orleans, 10 vagabonds from Lyon, 20 women and girls taken for fraud, and 16 women and girls from Rochefort by order of the Council.

In March, 1721, the Company contracted with La Salpêtrière, a house of correction in Paris, and brought over eighty-eight inmate girls; and on another occasion sixty vagrants, prostitutes, and criminals from the Hôpital-Général, another house of female detention and correction, were secured for the colony. The records of the Company for the years 1717 to 1721 reveal that more than 50 per cent of the women sent to Louisiana were prostitutes.

Soon the roads of France were filled with hundreds of these people being driven like herds of cattle. Clad in scanty clothing, fed only enough for bare subsistence, at night locked in barns or forced "to lie down in heaps at the bottom of ditches and holes," insulted and forced along as fast as possible by brutal soldiers, many of them died before reaching port, and "their unburied corpses, rotting above ground, struck with terror the inhabitants of the districts through which the woebegone caravan had passed."

Still, not enough colonists could be found, so orders were given to kidnap the poor and the unfortunate and send them to Louisiana. There was no time to select or examine or ask questions. In Paris the Company employed a regiment derisively called the "Bandoulliers de Mississippi" (Mississippi Bandits) to clean the city of its rabble, and each soldier received an additional fixed salary and 100 livres a head for every person secured.

Georges Oudard painted a terrible and fantastic word picture of the securing of Louisiana colonists: "Parents generously offered incorrigible children. A libertine had killed his mother. Send him out to the Mississippi! A day-laborer of port St. Paul has a dissolute daughter; an honest bourgeoise widow has another who roves the country with the first comer. Dry your tears, good people; they shall both be conducted immediately to Lorient." The "Mississippi Bandits" gathered them in, seized "the son of some wealthy grocer in the Rue St. Honore, heedless of his shrieks, or the daughter of a lieutenant of the watch, despite her father's protests."

As Grace King has written, "it was a dog-catcher's work; and dog-catchers performed it." Soon the word "Louisiana" became hated, for it meant a place of exile, far from France, to which criminals and prostitutes and other low-class persons, as well as those kidnapped from the decent classes of society, were being herded like animals.

These immigrants suffered indescribable hardships on the voyage to Louisiana. Paid according to the number of people they brought over, ship captains packed the greatest possible number into their vessels. The average voyage took from six to nine weeks, though if the weather were unfavorable it might last for four or five months. Hygenic conditions were almost nonexistent, food was moldy and often rotten, and water was stale and usually impure. Hundreds died. Out of 213 persons who sailed on one vessel, only 40 reached Louisiana.

Criminals and persons of bad character do not generally make good citizens, and when the Company finally realized its mistake in forcing these people to Louisiana as colonists, it adopted a new method of attracting settlers. Upon their promise to settle families on their grants, large grants of land called "concessions" were given to wealthy or noble Frenchmen or to other Europeans, and smaller tracts called "habitations" were given to the less wealthy. Yet these offers were not sufficient to attract enough settlers. Therefore another method was tried. The Company promised to pay the expenses of families of other nationalities who would migrate to Louisiana. In addition, each family would be given thirty arpents of land, horses and oxen for the cultivation of fields, pigs, sheep, and chickens, furniture and kitchen utensils, and food supplies until the first harvest.

Soon sections of Germany, the Low Countries, and Switzerland were flooded with pamphlets and handbills describing the wonderful land of Louisiana. The soil was described as "extremely pleasant" and capable of producing from four to six crops a year. There was plenty of game within easy gunshot. The land was "filled with gold, silver, copper, and lead mines." If one wished to search for medicinal herbs and plants, "the savages will make them known to us." It was simply impossible "to picture the abundance of this country." Many Europeans believed these descriptions and made plans to migrate to the French colony. Several thousand Germans came, as did many Swiss and smaller numbers of other nationalities. Since the channel of Dauphin Island had become clogged with sand and New Orleans was still under construction, it was decided in Paris over Bienville's strong protests to make New Biloxi the port of immigrant debarkation. Here immigrants were deposited on the beach and left to shift for themselves. Hundreds died within a few weeks from starvation and exposure.

By 1722, two years after Law's financial bubble had burst, the Company of the Indies was broke and in process of reorganization, and the French government had lost interest. Forced immigration had generally stopped. The colony was in a state of confusion, with quarreling factions, abandoned concessions, habitations, and farms, and an immoral and generally worthless French citizenry. Bienville was harassed on all sides as the cause of the disaster. There was only one ray of hope, and this was in the non-French population—the Germans, Swiss, and other Europeans. These people had not come to Louisiana to make quick riches and return home or because they had been shipped out as criminals or moral lepers, they had come of their own volition to build homes and to make a new life for themselves and their families. The Germans probably saved the Louisiana colony.

They concentrated their settlements at first along the Mississippi, a short distance above New Orleans, a general area which soon became known as "La Côte des Allemands" (the German Coast). Later they pushed upriver nearly to Baton Rouge, and many settled in the Lafourche country and in other more isolated sections. They were industrious and hard-working; soon farm lands began to appear where a wilderness had been.

Many of these Germans and Swiss changed their names to French equivalents; Trischl became Triche, Foltz became Folse, Wehrle became Verlay, and Milterberger became Mil de Bergue. Their towns became French towns in name. But they remembered their Germanic origin; even today their descendants say with truthful pride: "We are the descendants of those Germans who turned the wilderness into a paradise such as Louisiana never possessed before."

It is not known how many new settlers came to the colony between 1717 and 1722. Father Charlevoix gives the number of Germans alone at about 9,000; another French authority fixes their number at 10,000. In 1722, for example, nine ships arrived with a few over 4,000 settlers. In that year the total Louisiana population was estimated at about 6,000 persons, including some 600 Negro slaves. Three years later less than half of this total were still alive.

After 1722 the number of new settlers drastically declined, although the Company continued its efforts to arouse interest in France and in Europe. Men still outnumbered the women, and in 1727 the first group of *filles à la cassette*, or casket girls, arrived. Called "casket girls" because each had been given a sort of hope chest filled with personal belongings, they were young women of marriageable age and of good moral character. They were lodged in New Orleans under the care of the Ursulines, who had arrived earlier the same year. All of the girls were soon married, even the one who "looked more like a soldier on guard duty than like a young lady"—a duel over her was prevented only by intercession of the authorities.

NEGRO SLAVES SENT TO THE COLONY. There was only a comparatively small number of Negro slaves in the colony prior to 1717, and the Company soon made plans for supplying this type of labor. During the summer of 1719 the *Grand Duc du Maine* and the *Aurora* arrived from Africa with about five hundred slaves. That same year the Company built a slave corral, or prison, across the Mississippi from New Orleans, calling it the "Plantation of the Company," and here the slaves were distributed and sold to the colonists.

By 1724, slaves, Free Negroes, and persons of mixed blood had become so numerous that Bienville felt it necessary to enact special legislation for them, so the "Code Noir," or Black Code, was promulgated, its provisions being generally adapted from the slave code then in force in Santo Domingo. While the Black Code dealt mainly with slaves, it also restricted the activities of Free Negroes, ordered all Jews out of the colony, and forbade "the exercise of any other religion than Catholic." Many of the articles of the Code protected the slaves. They must be properly fed and clothed, cared for in sickness and old age, and must not be shackled or tortured in any way. On the other hand, they could not assemble if they belonged to different masters, were not permitted to carry weapons or marry whites, and could not sell goods without the permission of their owners.

African slaves caused little trouble, but about 1730 a West Indian slave named Samba organized a Negro uprising. He, together with seven men and one woman, plotted to kill as many settlers as possible and then sail away from Louisiana; but the plot was discovered, the woman was hanged, and the eight men were broken on the wheel.

THE NATCHEZ INDIAN WAR. On December 2, 1729, a ragged, half-starved, half-dead man staggered into New Orleans. He told the excited people that the Natchez Indians had massacred all but a few of the settlers of Fort Rosalie and the surrounding country. He had been away from the fort and had thus escaped.

The Natchez had been at peace for several years, during which some three hundred settlers had established farms among them. The two races had been friendly, and several of the Indians had visited France. Wishing to establish a large plantation near the Natchez village, Governor Perier sent a new commandant, a certain Captain Chepart, to Fort Rosalie and promised him an interest in the plantation if he could secure the Natchez lands. Chepart was an ironhanded commander who treated his soldiers and the Indians harshly. Because of this, he was ordered to appear before the Superior Council, which decided to dismiss him from the post. However, Perier, influenced by the advice of others or by his desire for the Indian lands, interceded and returned him to Fort Rosalie.

Chepart chose a large area on which was located the village of the White Apple, and ordered the Indians to vacate their lands just as soon as the harvest was completed. The Great Sun of the Natchez protested that there was much unoccupied land available, but Chepart was adamant. The Commandant was informed that the Indians were planning an uprising, but the brutal and overconfident fool ignored the warning. On November 26, the Natchez began their massacre and killed nearly three hundred colonists. Chepart hid in a garden but was found and clubbed to death.

Some of the Louisiana Indians joined in the uprising, and settlers were killed even in the southern and southeastern sections of the colony. One settler, however, on an island off the coast of the Terrebonne District, drove away the attacking Indians in a peculiar way. Upon seeing them, Sylvain Filiosa grabbed a kettledrum and banged it so loudly that the Indians stopped and gazed in alarm at the strange weapon. From this time Filiosa and his island were called "Le Timbalier," the Kettledrummer.

The French soon mobilized for an attack on the Natchez. A force of nearly seven hundred men routed the Natchez, who then withdrew to two strongly fortified forts. After an unsuccessful siege, the French withdrew upon the promise that the Indians would surrender their white captives. When the whites were not released, Perier ordered several of his Indian captives, including one woman, burned at the stake in New Orleans. In middle January, 1731, the French again attacked the Natchez and drove them from their forts and across the river.

The Indians were hunted down like animals. Several hundred were captured and sold as slaves in the West Indies, only a few escaping farther westward in Louisiana or joining the Choctaws. The Natchez ceased to exist as an organized nation. A few of them returned to their country in the 1730's but shortly afterward joined the Chickasaws and Cherokees.

GROWTH AND EXPANSION OF THE COLONY. Louisiana grew slowly after 1722. The pioneers faced many hardships. The land had to be cleared of trees and brush. They had to learn how to plant and grow crops in a climate which was diffrent from that of western Europe. Domestic animals were scarce. Good prices were not always received for farm products, because the Company generally fixed prices for its profit. Droughts, storms, and insects caused repeated crop losses.

New Orleans grew rapidly during the early 1720's, then settled down to slow progress, by 1728 having an estimated population of nearly a thousand persons. By 1729 a low levee protected the town from the river, and low dikes kept out high waters on the other three sides. A shallow, narrow canal had been built from the town to Lake Pontchartrain. Drainage ditches and banquettes, sometimes topped with wooden planks, bordered the streets. Stanch efforts were being made to rid the city of frogs, snakes, and alligators. A new church had been completed in 1727 and was considered a fine building, for it was constructed of brick and wood and stuccoed on the outside. Four small forts, St. Jean, St. Charles, St. Louis, and Bourgogne, had been built at the corners of the town.

One of the Ursulines, Marie Madeleine Hachard, Sister Saint Stanislas, described the town shortly after her arrival: "Our town is very handsome, well constructed and regularly built. . . . The streets are large and straight . . . the houses well built, with upright joists, filled with mortar between the interstices, and the exterior whitewashed with lime. In the interior they are wainscotted. . . . The colonists are very proud of their capital. Suffice it to say that there is a song currently sung here, which emphatically declares that New Orleans is as beautiful as Paris. Beyond that it is impossible to go."

Sometime prior to 1719 a large concession had been given to the D'Artaguette family, which had strong connections in France and which had had at least one member in the colony since the early years. On the east side of the Mississippi "some five leagues above le Manchac," the concession included a place called "Bluffs in that country, and in the savage tongue *Istrouma* which signifies *Baton Rouge,* because there is in this place a reddened post, which the savages have placed to mark the division of the lands of two nations." A younger member of the family, probably Captain Bernard Diron d'Artaguette, was entrusted with the establishment of a settlement. By 1722 it was reported that "the land there is very fine and good and there are many prairies. Half of this concession is burned over. They have tried to increase the fields. Last year rice and vegetables were harvested. There are in this concession thirty whites and twenty negroes and two Indian slaves." The family tried to change the name of their concession settlement to "Dironbourg," but the settlers continued to call it "Baton Rouge."

In 1723 a small detachment of soldiers was sent up the Red River to establish a post at the rapids, and the Poste du Rapides had its beginnings. A small stockade was built and later a chapel, and the place gradually grew into a sizable settlement, the modern Pineville.

By the early 1720's the post at Natchitoches had a population of about a hundred, including Negro and Indian slaves. Here the colonists raised wheat, corn, tobacco, beans, and numerous vegetables, and made considerable profits from the Indian trade. The Spanish post of Los Adaes lay only a few miles westward, and between it and the Sabine lived a few settlers, so there was some clandestine trade with the Spanish.

Of the older settlements, Mobile and New Biloxi were the most prosperous. But newer settlements had sprung up along the lower Mississippi above and below New Orleans and along the upper Lafourche. Here the Germans and Swiss were developing productive grain, livestock, and truck farms, which already provided New Orleans with most of its supplies. While the colony was not self-sustaining in regard to foodstuffs, the Company, during good crop years, was able to cut down on the amount of food sent to the colony.

THE COMPANY OF THE INDIES GIVES UP LOUISIANA. John Law's "Mississippi Bubble" had burst early in 1720. The news of the tremendous hardships of the settlers, the misery and poverty, the horrors of the voyage to the colony, the difficulties of clearing land and planting crops, the false rumors of rich gold and silver mines, the enormous amounts of money which the Company had been pouring into the Louisiana venture, the failure of the Spanish and English trade to develop—all these facts began to filter into France and to reach the ears of stockholders. For these and other reasons shrewd businessmen began to withdraw their deposits from the bank. Gold and silver disappeared, France was flooded with paper money, and although the government issued orders that paper money must be accepted, the orders were ignored. Individuals were ordered to turn in all silver and gold over the amount of 300 livres; these orders were likewise ignored.

In a final and desperate move the Prince Regent appointed Law Comptroller-General of France. By this time the paper money in circulation was estimated at over two and a quarter billion livres. In May the value of the paper money was reduced by 50 per cent, but a short time later it was restored to full value. On May 29, Law was dismissed as Comptroller-General, and a Swiss guard had to be stationed at his house to keep the mob away. In July the Company was given a complete monopoly of all French commerce on condition that it retire 600 millions of paper livres within the year.

Matters went from bad to worse. Law was stoned on the streets, and although he escaped serious injury, his carriage was destroyed. The run on the bank began. All was lost. On December 10, 1720, he slipped out of Paris to one of his estates about half a dozen miles distant and a few days later set out for the Belgian frontier under the protection of four soldiers furnished by the Regent. He had with him about 800 louis d'or, a considerable amount of jewelry, and a few personal effects.

The Company of the Indies reorganized after the bursting of the "Mississippi Bubble." New funds were secured, and money was poured into the Louisiana colony until about the middle of the decade. After that time the Company spent considerably less, and the colony suffered as a result. Immigration sharply declined, while more and more the colony was left to shift for itself. Confusion reigned in Louisiana. Officials quarreled, and Perier's bungling caused the Natchez Indian War.

When the Directors of the Company of the Indies received word of the Natchez Massacre and the Indian war, they agreed that they could no longer furnish the funds, supplies, and colonists necessary to rebuild the colony. They had understood some of the problems involved in making Louisiana a profitable commercial enterprise; others which had been encountered were beyond their experience.

In January, 1731, the Directors of the Company of the Indies asked the King to take back their charter. After lengthy negotiations the King assumed the Company's assets in Louisiana to a value of nearly half a million livres, and the Company paid the Crown something over a million livres to be released from its contract. It was some years, however, before a final settlement was made. Perier was retained as Governor until 1733, when Bienville returned for his fourth and last governorship.

As for John Law, in 1721 he went to Great Britain, was presented at court, and shortly thereafter returned to the Continent. He received a pension from the French government until 1723, then began to wander about Europe. He rapidly sank into complete obscurity, lost his health, and died, practically a pauper, in Venice in 1729.

WORK OF LAW AND THE COMPANIES. John Law, the Company of the West, and the Company of the Indies had accomplished much for the benefit of the Louisiana colony. Law found the colony with fewer than 1,000 inhabitants; in 1731 the population was estimated at as high as 7,500 persons, including Negro slaves. Huge amounts of goods and supplies had been furnished the settlers. New Orleans had been founded and the German Coast had been settled, as had other and more distant areas.

Law and his followers had done more in fourteen years than had been done by the Crown and Crozat during the preceeding eighteen years. The colony of Louisiana was at last firmly rooted.

"Of all the men who, under the old regime, were engaged in transforming this virgin soil into a true civilized country," wrote Oudard, "Law was perhaps, in his capacity as director of the Western Company and the Indian Company in turn, the one who did most to mould it." Despite his shortcomings and the impracticability of some of his ideas, Louisiana owes him a great debt of gratitude.

CHAPTER 6

THREE ROYAL
GOVERNORS

B IENVILLE'S FOURTH GOVERNORSHIP. From 1731 until France ceded Louisiana to Spain, the colony was a royal domain of Louis XV and its government was entrusted to his personally appointed ministers. Prior to the outbreak of the Seven Years' War in 1756, France enjoyed a few years of peace and should have developed Louisiana as the English were developing their colonies along the Atlantic seaboard, but the worthless Louis and his inept advisers did little to assist the Louisiana colonists. France lost the Seven Years' War and was forced to surrender practically all of her American empire by the Treaty of Paris of 1763.

The Chickasaw Indians, always enemies of the French, continued to be the cause of grave concern and not infrequent bloodshed. The colonists were discontented. The Natchez War had frightened those living on the frontiers, and many frontier settlers fled to New Orleans, where there was no employment and where they were dependent upon the government to furnish housing and food. Government officials were lax in their duties and took unfair advantage to make excessive profits at the people's expense. Members of the Superior Council often disagreed violently among themselves, and this constant disorder filtered through to the populace of New Orleans.

In 1732 the Superior Council was reorganized, and the same year the King exempted from duties all commerce between Louisiana and the Mother Country. Perier lost interest and begged to be recalled. Apparently a man of personal integrity, he had grown brusque and harsh, which resulted in strained relations with both the Indians and his subordinates. Late in July, 1732, the government recalled Bienville to the governorship, with the title of Commandant-General, gave him a completely free hand in the government of the colony, and ordered him to proceed to Louisiana as quickly as possible. After spending several months arranging his journey, he embarked at La Rochelle, with 150 fusiliers, on December 9.

Meantime, the news that Bienville would soon return had reached Louisiana, and the people were overjoyed; "Father" Bienville had his faults, but they had seen governors come and go and they felt that he was the only man who could resolve their present difficulties. As the weeks passed and Bienville failed to arrive, it was rumored that his ship had been sunk by a hurricane. Perhaps West Indian pirates had captured the vessel. Anxiety mounted. Ships were sent to range the Gulf in search of the missing Governor, to no avail. Finally in the spring of 1733 a French ship docked at the wharves of New Orleans. On its deck stood an old, somewhat yellow-complexioned man of nearly sixty. Bienville had at last returned.

REORGANIZATION AND THE CHICKASAW INDIAN WAR. Bienville found an apathetic, economically poor, and disorganized colony. Military equipment was obsolete and in disrepair; the 800 soldiers were living in dilapidated and unsanitary barracks, and two-thirds of them were on the sick list. Food was scarce, many buildings along the Gulf Coast showed hurricane damage, and the hospital at New Orleans was struggling with insufficient staff and funds to care for an overflow of patients. The Indian situation was alarming, for the Chickasaws and Alabamas had been won over by the British, the Illinois and Choctaws were ready to slip from French influence, and other tribes had lost much of their former regard for the French. The people were dispirited, and a large number, perhaps even a majority, wanted to return to France.

The battle- and frontier-scarred old leader faced a Herculean task, but with characteristic energy plunged into his work. Unable to get new arms and military and civilian supplies, he did the best he could with what he had. Soldiers rebuilt and renovated barracks, repaired arms and other military equipment. Citizens were drafted for work in the hospital. Food supplies were gathered and then rationed on a basis of actual need. Settlers who had been driven in from the frontiers were ordered to return to their settlements and farms. Soon order was established and some stability enforced upon the entire colony.

Bienville now turned his attention to the Indian problem. He pleaded for reinforcements from France, but when they arrived, he wrote his superiors that "there are but one or two men among them whose size is above five feet," and "out of fifty-two who have lately been sent here, more than one-half have already been whipped for larceny. In a word, these useless beings are not worth the food bestowed upon them; they are burdens to the colony, and from them no efficient military service is to be expected."

He sent word to the Chickasaw chiefs to bring in the heads of the Natchez warriors who had led the massacre of 1729 and who now lived with the Chickasaws, but the chiefs refused, replying that "the Natchez are now one nation with the Chickasaws and we cannot deliver their heads." Bienville had no recourse but to declare war against them. The Chickasaws had to be destroyed.

He ordered Pierre d'Artaguette, a commandant in the Illinois country, to organize an army and meet him at the Chickasaw villages in May, 1736. D'Artaguette gathered a little force of about fifty soldiers and marched for the Chickasaw country, but when he reached the meeting place on the day set for the joining of the two forces, Bienville was not there. After waiting for over a week, his Indian allies from the Ohio country became impatient for action, so D'Artaguette decided to attack the villages without waiting for Bienville.

The Chickasaws, assisted by Englishmen from the Carolinas, had built strong forts of heavy logs, roofed with poles and earth so as to be safe from fire arrows, with notched loopholes and firing pits not unlike modern foxholes. To take such fortifications was a job for cannon, but D'Artaguette had no cannon, so he outflanked one fort and forced its abandonment. Encouraged, his soldiers and Indian allies drove the Chickasaws from the second fort, but in this attack the leader was wounded and the Indian allies fled. D'Artaguette and about half of his men were cut off and forced to surrender.

The Indians first planned to demand ransom for the prisoners, but enraged by their own losses, finally decided to put most of them to death. They tied all except a few to large stakes, after stripping, reviling, and beating them, and lit the death fires. Mathurin le Petit, one of the survivors, reported that the doomed men knelt with Father Antoine Sénat and said their prayers, which the Indians called "the song to go above," "nor did they interrupt their singing amid the fire until they fell. . . . This sight won the admiration of the savages, so that those whom they had, on the very same day scornfully called 'women' they often proclaimed to be men and heroes."

Meanwhile, after considerable delay, Bienville had set out from Mobile with his army. He moved slowly, for the men were mutinous and heavy rains made the trail almost impassable. When he finally reached Lusser's Camp on the Tombigbee River, he was joined by a large band of Choctaws. After court-martialing and executing six mutineers, he reorganized his force and moved northward toward the Chickasaw forts. Not finding D'Artaguette at the appointed place and realizing he was late himself, he decided to attack.

Two assaults on the Indian fort failed. Over thirty French were killed and some sixty wounded. The dead were not recovered, and Bienville was forced to watch the Chickasaws quarter their bodies and hang them above the walls of their fort. Not knowing what had happened to D'Artaguette, Bienville could do nothing except retreat. The so-called Battle of Ackia was a defeat for the French.

Over a hundred soldiers had been killed in the campaign, yet the power of the Chickasaws remained unbroken. Joined as one force, the two armies could have won a decisive victory; separated, they had been defeated. Bienville accepted full responsibility for the defeat, from which he never fully recovered.

Anxious to avenge the deaths of D'Artaguette and the other men, to blot out the stain of defeat, and to regain prestige with the Indians, Bienville appealed to Canada and to France for assistance. France sent reinforcements, supplies, and equipment, and after organizing his new army, Bienville in the summer of 1739 built Fort Assumption near present-day Memphis. Here he was joined by a force of irregular militia from Canada and the Illinois country. For some reason, however, the march toward the Chickasaw towns was delayed, although by the end of 1739, Bienville had an army of nearly 3,200 men, including about 2,000 Indians hostile to the Chickasaws. Then sickness broke out, and the unacclimated soldiers from France suffered heavy casualties. Provisions failed. Heavy rains prevented movement of the artillery.

Early in 1740, Bienville decided to offer the Chickasaws peace, and sent a small force to treat with them. The Indians, believing that this was the advance guard of a large French army, themselves sued for peace, and a treaty was signed in April. Bienville rewarded his Indian allies, and after destroying Fort Assumption returned to New Orleans. The Chickasaws, never really conquered, from time to time throughout the French period committed depredations on outlying settlers.

BIENVILLE'S LAST YEARS AS GOVERNOR. Bienville spent the next three years engaged in routine matters of administration. He encouraged agriculture and trade, assisted in the establishment of the Charity Hospital endowed by the sailor Jean Louis, and aided in the relief of suffering when hurricanes, high water, drought, and an epidemic of mad dogs hit the Gulf Coast in 1740. He proposed the establishment in New Orleans of a school where boys could be taught geometry, geography, and other subjects; unfortunately his plea was curtly dismissed with a brief statement that New Orleans was too unimportant for such an institution. He helped establish settlers at points on the Ouachita and Red rivers, at St. Francisville, and at several places farther up the Mississippi. He struggled to remedy the scarce-currency situation but accomplished little, for this problem could only be solved through increased trade and vastly augmented supplies of hard money.

When he failed to subdue the Chickasaws, Bienville's star had begun its decline. For nearly forty of his sixty-five years he had battled the unceasing stupidities of two kings and their ministers, attempting to carve a successful colony out of the Louisiana wilderness. On March 26, 1742, he wrote the King's Minister: "If my success had always been in proportion to my devotion to the affairs of this government and my zeal in the King's service, I would willingly have consecrated to him the rest of my days. But a sort of fatality which for some time has attended my best concerted projects has often cost me the fruits of my labor and perhaps also a certain degree of Your Highness' confidence. I therefore believe it is my duty no longer to oppose myself rigidly to my ill fortune. I hope that the officer chosen to replace me will be happier than I. I shall devote all my attention during the remainder of my stay here to removing the difficulties attaching to the place that I resign to him, and I can flatter myself that I am leaving everything in better order than it has ever been." No higher sentiments have ever been uttered by a Louisiana official.

THE GRAND MARQUIS. Pierre François de Rigaud Cavagnal, the Marquis de Vaudreuil, the new Governor, arrived in New Orleans on May 10, 1743. Vaudreuil was the son of an arrogant and imperious, vain and jealous, weak and somewhat debonair former Governor of Canada. The son had certainly inherited some of the traits of his father, for he had elegant manners, enjoyed giving magnificent dinners and balls, and loved formal ceremonies and military displays. Throughout his governorship, he maintained in New Orleans a fashionable little court which attempted to copy the elegance and fashion of the French court at Versailles.

On the other hand, he had a somewhat genial and kind nature, well illustrated by one of the many stories that have been told about him. A servant who had lost or misplaced a valuable piece of silver was brought trembling before the Governor. Vaudreuil looked him over and then said to the butler, "Get a bottle of my best wine, and give it to this poor fellow to cure him of his fright."

On May 27, Bienville, who hated ostentation, gave Vaudreuil a simple inauguration and in middle August sailed for France.

VAUDREUIL'S INDIAN PROBLEMS. The Indians, particularly the Chickasaws, continued to cause trouble, for the Chickasaw peace with Bienville had been in reality only a truce. Since it was difficult for Vaudreuil to secure trading goods of good quality, the Indians played the French and English against each other and traded with whichever could supply the best goods at the cheapest prices. Several of the Chickasaw chiefs and Chief Soulier Rouge (Red Shoe) of the Choctaws went over to the English and caused the Governor considerable harassment.

In 1747 the Indians raided along the east bank of the Mississippi for some distance south of Baton Rouge, and the German and other settlers fled to the protection of New Orleans. The next year the Indians again moved down the river, killing and plundering as they went. Some of the settlers escaped by crossing to the west side, where they could be protected by the militia, but many were killed. The Governor did not endear himself to the colonists along the lower coast during the two raids, for he ordered the militia to try to cut off the retreat of the Indians instead of moving directly to protect the settlements.

In 1752 the Chickasaws again went on the warpath, and Vaudreuil sent a large force of some seven hundred men against them. The expedition burned several Indian villages and destroyed cornfields and vegetable gardens. The Chickasaws sued for peace, and caused little trouble during the remainder of the French period.

COLONIAL DEVELOPMENTS UNDER VAUDREUIL. Louisiana's economic life improved but little during the administration of Vaudreuil, although he attempted to encourage agriculture. Production of cotton, tobacco, indigo, and myrtle wax gradually increased, and while there was some improvement in the yields of corn, rice, and vegetables, the colony was still not self-sufficient in regard to foodstuffs.

The census of 1744 revealed that the colony had only slightly more than 3,000 white inhabitants, some 800 soldiers, and over 2,000 slaves, a decline in total population since the Company of the Indies turned it back to the Crown in 1731. New Orleans had about 1,100 inhabitants, including over 300 slaves. Only a few settlers were sent over during the 1740's, and the majority of these seem to have been convicted salt smugglers and other undesirables. In 1751 a ship from France delivered some sixty girls, the last Louisiana was to receive, and these were soon married to discharged soldiers who had decided to remain as settlers. The couples were given land, seed grain, a cow and calf, some chickens, and supplies for three years. However, there was little increase in total population from 1744 to the end of Vaudreuil's governorship.

Trade generally languished, for ships from France could not be depended upon and the closely watched trade with the Spanish colonies was at best irregular. At one time the Superior Council protested to French officials concerning the openness of British smuggling: "How mortifying is it for Frenchmen to suffer all the rigors to which their commerce is subjected, whilst a foreign nation their ambitious rival, openly carries on the trade of the colony." There was much criticism of the Illinois trade, for convoy and boat captains and government officials made huge profits at the expense of the government.

Military discipline steadily declined after the departure of Bienville, and by 1750, according to Oudard, "had never been so bad. Nearly every month some soldier was executed on a capital charge. The lack of discipline was general. . . . Every freedom was allowed these rogues as long as they spent their money at the canteen, which was run by an officer who shared the profits with the major and even, it was said, with the governor himself." Soldiers sold wine and brandy to Indians and slaves, contrary to regulations, and even sold goods from government warehouses. One official wrote back to France that the entire province was filled with drunkenness, brawls, duels, and other disorders. Army officers paid little attention to discipline and wandered about New Orleans out of uniform; both they and civil officials openly kept mistresses who were received and entertained at the Governor's palace.

The convicted criminals, prostitutes, and vagabonds who had been sent to the colony formed a disturbing minority of the total citizenry, and many of this class crowded New Orleans. According to Herbert Asbury "the capital city became more than ever the resort of the vicious and criminal elements of the population, who devoted themselves to stealing, brawling, and drinking in the many pot-houses, taverns, and gambling-dens which had made their appearance along the river front and the edges of the swamps." In 1751 governmental feuding ceased long enough for a series of police regulations to be adopted. Strict tavern rules were drawn up, soldiers were restricted to only two liquor shops, slave and Free Negro restrictions were tightened, and any white who violated slave or Free Negro regulations was to be "whipped by the public executioner, and, without mercy, be sentenced to end his life on the King's galleys." Insolent Negroes or slaves were to be "punished with fifty lashes, and shall be branded."

By the middle 1750's, however, after slightly over half a century of French control, Louisiana was a completely demoralized colony, without adequate agriculture, industry or commerce, without a large enough body of solid citizenry, open to Indian raids and the insults of the English, and generally without hope for the future.

END OF VAUDREUIL'S GOVERNORSHIP. Vaudreuil, because of his numerous balls, dinners, and various celebrations and holidays, was extremely popular with the favored and wealthy classes of New Orleans; he was not so popular among the less fortunate army officers and public officials and with the common people. These groups charged him with filling important posts with his own or his wife's relatives and with friends, with granting monopolies which allowed a favored few to gain wealth at the common people's expense, with selling army supplies and issuing the soldiers inferior goods in place of government issues, and with being personally interested in the clandestine Negro and Indian trade.

Much of the hatred of the common people was centered on Madame Vaudreuil. She held a regular court, gave fabulous and fantastic entertainments and carnivals, drove a four-horse carriage imported from Paris, and conducted a regular business from the Governor's palace. She forced merchants and other individuals, according to one protestant, "to take charge of her merchandise, and to sell it at the price which she fixes. She keeps in her own house every sort of drugs, which are sold by her steward. . . . The husband is not ignorant of this. He draws from it a handsome revenue, to obtain which is his sole wish and aim."

The protests of the more worthy citizens of the colony carried little weight in France, where the King's counselors were even more corrupt than were the King's representatives in Louisiana. Vaudreuil remained in favor with high government officials and in 1752 was promoted to the governorship of Canada, where he considerably hampered the work of the Marquis de Montcalm, the commanding general in Canada, during the French and Indian War. His administration in Louisiana, though not profitable to the Mother Country nor to the colonists, enhanced the prestige of vainglorious French officialdom. His governorship was long remembered in Louisiana for its splendor, luxury, and military display, for its grand balls, and for the refined and ostentatious manners of the upper-class society; during later years when hard times came many Louisianians enjoyed recalling the "good old days of the Grand Marquis."

GOVERNOR KERLEREC. Louis Billouart, Chevalier de Kerlerec, the man chosen to succeed Vaudreuil, was a bluff, hearty, honest naval captain with twenty-five years of service to his credit. He bore a number of wounds as mute testimony of his fighting prowess and his devotion to duty. He was accustomed to discipline, which he insisted should be rigidly enforced. He was not, however, a man of great administrative or financial ability and simply could not handle adequately the problems which arose during his term of office. The French and Indian War was fought during most of his governorship, and as a result he faced many grave difficulties. But he did the best that could have been done under the circumstances, and, what was more important, the citizens of Louisiana admiringly said that he had "qualities of heart very different from those of his predecessor."

Although Kerlerec's commission was dated April 1, 1752, he did not arrive in New Orleans until late in January of the following year. Vaudreuil, as would be expected, gave Kerlerec a pompous and ceremonious inaugural, topping it off with a magnificent banquet followed by an even more magnificent ball. Over two hundred guests were invited to the banquet and hundreds more to the ball. During the banquet the uninvited common folk outside crowded around two fountains of constantly flowing wine. The supper was followed by a fabulous fireworks display, begun when Madame de Vaudreuil and Madame de Kerlerec released two doves to carry the lighted matches some hundred feet to ignite the display.

KERLEREC'S GOVERNORSHIP. The new Governor first tackled the Indian problem. He held conferences with the chiefs, criticized them for their disloyalty to the French, and urged them to discontinue their trade with the English. When they replied that the English goods were better and their prices lower, Kerlerec promised to send them the best goods he had, and he kept his word. Soon he gained the confidence and respect of the Choctaws, who eventually bestowed on him the flattering title of "Father of the Choctaws," because he sent them better trading goods than had his predecessor.

He begged for well-trained and well-disciplined troops, argued that Swiss troops were better than those sent from France, and although he succeeded in getting a few Swiss soldiers, not enough were sent to do much good. He strengthened New Orleans by building a palisade around the city and by rebuilding the battery at English Turn. At the entrance of the Mississippi he anchored an old ship which could be sunk in case English ships attacked the colony.

But France seemed to have forgotten Louisiana, and after the French and Indian War began did little for the colony; indolent Louis XV continued to enjoy the pleasures of his fashionable court and seemingly worried little about the empire which was soon to be lost. One day, for example, while in a thoughtful mood, he murmured, "What would life be worth without coffee?" And then languidly added: "But then, what is it worth even with coffee?" One of his chief ministers, Étienne François, Duc de Choiseul, has been well described by French historian Jules Michelet: "vivacious, brilliant, keen, penetrating, believing nothing, fearing nothing, an easy moralist, an uncertain ally, a hater of priests, light minded, inconstant." The King said to him one day, "You will be damned, Choiseul." "And you, sire?" "I, oh, I am different; I am the anointed of God." How could hard-working, well-meaning Kerlerec expect assistance from such men? Conditions in Louisiana grew steadily worse.

The army dropped to about three hundred effective men, the rest having been sent to Canada, and these the settlers feared almost as much as they did the Indians, for the officers were either overbearing tyrants or without ability to enforce military discipline. When the Commandant at Cat Island forced his men to cultivate his private garden and traded army rations and other supplies to the settlers and Indians, a number of the soldiers revolted and killed him. The mutineers attempted to escape from Louisiana but were captured and court-martialed at New Orleans. Several of the French soldiers were broken on the wheel and one, a Swiss, was sentenced "to be placed in a coffin and be sawed alive through the middle of the body, according to the custom of the Swiss regiment." Soldier and officer discipline improved after this incident and after Kerlerec's decisive orders concerning officer conduct.

In 1759 a cabal was organized against the Governor by several military officers and civil officials. It took Kerlerec nearly four years to finally break it, and then only through an official letter from the Duc de Choiseul. The conspirators were sent to France and imprisoned for a time in the Bastille, but were soon liberated through the influence of friends high in court circles.

The thrifty Governor and the Commissary-Commissioner quarreled over the costs of government, which had risen during Vaudreuil's administration to over 800,000 livres a year. The militia could not be depended on, and the most important posts had to be garrisoned by the Swiss soldiers. The Jesuits and the Capuchins were engaged in what some of the people called a religious war, causing considerable dissatisfaction. The Commissary-Commissioner was replaced, but his successor soon began to send derogatory reports concerning Kerlerec. Many of the settlers and citizens criticized the Governor for the decline of agriculture and foreign trade.

By 1762, Kerlerec was ready to give up his unappreciated and unsupported governorship. However, he had achieved much in Louisiana and, among all French colonial governors, must be accorded second place to Bienville. He had held the southern Indians in allegiance to France and had so influenced those of the Old Northwest country that it took the English three years after 1763 to pacify them. Improving the fortifications of the colony, he had prevented English invasion. With little assistance from an unpatriotic and, according to some historians, a generally worthless citizenry, he had personally held the colony together.

Kerlerec returned to France in 1763 and found an ungrateful government awaiting him. He was rewarded for his years of faithfulness, honesty, and stanch devotion to duty with a felon's cell in the Bastille. He died a short time later, after generously having been released from prison through the influence of a few friends at court.

LOUISIANA CEDED TO SPAIN. The cession of Louisiana to Spain in 1762 has long been a subject of controversy by historians. Why did France, after holding the colony for over sixty years, suddenly give it away?

Theories of historians as to why France gave up the colony may be placed in several groups. There is the "generosity" theory, namely that Louis gave Louisiana to Spain out of the simple generosity of his heart to a brother King who had stood fast with him against Great Britain, a common enemy. But generosity was not a characteristic of Louis, particularly where his dynastic colonial empire was concerned. William R. Shepherd's "Gallic impulsiveness" theory can hardly be supported, for Louis and his advisers were not impulsive men; they ordinarily acted with rather cold calculation. Richard Stenberg's "family compact" theory likewise breaks down, for the members of the French-Spanish family compact were selfish men who would keep everything possible. The "peace bribe" theory of Arthur Scott Aiton and E. Wilson Lyon that France bribed Spain with Louisiana in order to get Spain's acceptance of the peace terms laid down by a victorious Great Britain after the French and Indian War also breaks down. Although the cession may have been "a calculated move of selfish national policy" on the part of France, that nation would have never made that move had she believed it possible to longer hold a desired colony.

The most logical theory, for which there is an overwhelming amount of evidence, is the "white elephant" theory. Louisiana had been a burden insofar as France was concerned. By 1760 that nation was ready to admit freely that she had failed in planting a successful and profitable colony. Pontchartrain had spent huge sums, Crozat had lost a fortune, the Company of the Indies had gone broke, and the French government had expended between 70,000,000 and 80,000,000 livres on the colony, with comparatively little return.

French leaders realized that Louisiana was a "white elephant" as early as the 1750's, for at that time the colony, after a half-century of settlement, could boast of a population of only between 6,000 and 7,000 persons. In 1757, Kerlerec wrote bitterly that he had not had even a letter from France for two years, and in 1761 the French Ambassador to Spain admitted that France had sent no supplies to Louisiana during the past four years. France had fought for and lost Canada, which she treasured much more than the colony on the Mississippi. Why try to hold a colony which had never been successful?

By the early 1760's France wanted peace. In September, 1762, the French Ambassador to Spain declared his government's views: "The King has decided in his Council that he would order the French to evacuate the whole of Louisiana rather than miss the opportunity for peace on account of discussion about a Colony with which we are unable to communicate by sea, which has not and can not have either a port or a roadstead into which an xebec of twelve guns could enter and which costs France eight hundred thousand livres a year, without yielding a sou in return." About the same time Choiseul admitted: "I offered Louisiana to the English in place of Florida, [but] they refused it."

Spain had become interested in acquiring Louisiana as early as 1760. The English captured Havana in August, 1762, and the Spanish wanted to regain possession of it and of Cuba. Perhaps Great Britain would trade Havana for Spanish Florida. In this case, Louisiana would be important to his Spanish Majesty. While the colony would be expensive, it might some day develop into a profitable venture.

The Spanish ministry drew up a list of reasons why Spain should gain Louisiana. The location of the Isle of Orleans and the city of New Orleans were important to the defense of the Spanish colonial empire bordering the Gulf of Mexico and the Caribbean Sea. Spain would acquire an excellent port. If Spain did not secure Louisiana it might fall into the hands of Great Britain, for France could no longer protect it.

Louis XV did not bother himself over the prospect of losing Louisiana. The Prime Minister, the Duc de Choiseul, did not worry about it either. In September, 1762, Choiseul wrote to a diplomat in Spain: "I warn you that we will not allow the negotiations to break up." France was much more interested in saving her West Indies islands than in saving Louisiana. Only a few Frenchmen protested, among them the philosopher Voltaire, who wrote that he could not conceive how Frenchmen could abandon "the most beautiful climate of the earth, from which one may have tobacco, silk, indigo, a thousand useful products." If he had not just built a new estate—even Voltaire had excuses—"I would go and establish myself in Louisiana."

On November 3, 1762, by a secret treaty signed at Fontainebleau, France ceded the Isle of Orleans and the rest of Louisiana west of the Mississippi River to Spain. The French Empire in North America had run its course. The Louisianians, however, knew nothing of these dynastic and diplomatic maneuverings. It was twenty-three months after the cession before they were informed that they were now Spaniards rather than Frenchmen.

CHAPTER 7

ECONOMIC LIFE AND GOVERNMENT IN FRENCH COLONIAL LOUISIANA

AGRICULTURE. The difficulties of the first Louisiana farmers were many. The climate of Louisiana was somewhat intermediate between that of temperate France and tropical Santo Domingo, areas familiar to the French. Some crops, such as wheat, could not profitably be raised because of wet summers, and occasional freezes limited the production of tropical or semitropical grains and fruits. Lack of knowledge and technical skills long delayed the production of special staples like silk, tobacco, and sugar. The restrictions on the export of seed grain, fruit stock, and domestic animals of all sorts from the Spanish and English colonies prevented Louisianians from acquiring acclimatized sources of production. The heavy, water-laden soils along the rivers and bayous, or the sandy, poor soils of the Gulf region in the area of Biloxi or Mobile needed careful and experienced handling for successful crop production. Louisiana was generally a land of upland forests and lowland forested swamps; clearing land took time and much hard work. It is, therefore, not surprising that French colonial agriculture never adequately met the demands of the colonists.

The first farms were generally located near the sites of former Indian villages, where already-cleared fields were available, and the practice of using Indian fields continued throughout the French period. It was not until these cleared lands were exhausted in the vicinity of the settlements that the colonists cleared lands of their own. Early agriculture was of a subsistence nature, providing only the food needs of individual farm operators; some years had passed before individual farmers began to produce small quantities of excess products for the markets of the towns and villages.

Louisiana agriculture really began when the Company of the Indies started sending Germans to the colony and settling them along the Mississippi above New Orleans, the upper Lafourche, and in smaller numbers in the vicinity of Biloxi and Mobile. Soon these thrifty and hard-working immigrants were producing truck crops for sale. Small markets were established in the villages and a large general market in New Orleans, and during good crop years were filled with corn, rice and wheat, staple vegetables, and some fruits including apples, peaches, pears, figs, oranges, and lemons.

Farmers crowded these emporiums with their produce on market and festival days. There was no advertising except by voice, so men cried out the names and quality of the various articles they had for sale. Money was scarce, and things were more frequently bartered than sold; a pig for so much grain, vegetables for fruits, articles of home manufacture for a chicken or a cow, trinkets, notions, tools, and other manufactured goods for poultry. Everything was labeled "Creole," which meant native to the colony or grown in the colony, and there were "Creole" pigs, "Creole" figs, and "Creole" rice. After all, many of the people were "Creoles," for they had been born in Louisiana of European parents or had European ancestors.

But farmers had many problems. Sometimes it rained too much and sometimes not enough. Heavy rains frequently caused streams and bayous to overflow, while storms and hurricanes destroyed crops. Insects, raccoons, opossums, and other animals ate the plants or the matured vegetables, grains, or fruits. The numerous weeds and shrub undergrowth often grew faster than the cultivated plants. Sometimes the brush or pole fences caught fire or were weakened, so that livestock raided neighboring fields. Witness a law suit in 1741, when a score of Madame Maieux de Lormaison's cattle broke into Monsieur Jean Robin's bean field and destroyed six acres of beans. The lady filed a countersuit to the effect that Robin's cattle had "wasted her entire crop of corn and beans last year."

By 1723 there was "an abundance" of all kinds of vegetables and other food-stuffs produced in the New Orleans area. The next year the corn, rice, and bean crop totaled more than 5,000 barrels, and the potato crop totaled almost 3,000 barrels. In 1725 the crops were even larger. Louisiana never reached complete self-sufficiency during the French period, however, and despite increased production and good crop years, some food supplies had to be imported more or less regularly from the Mother Country.

Owing to the general food scarcity during the first two decades of settlement, the French were forced to eat Indian corn. They did not like corn in any form, and constantly grumbled and pleaded for shipments of wheat flour from France. On one occasion the newly arrived women refused to eat corn bread and locked themselves in their houses until flour was distributed from the storehouse. But, like the English settlers of the Atlantic seaboard and the Spanish settlers of Mexico and other areas farther south, the Louisiana French colonials eventually came to depend heavily upon corn and corn meal. By 1710 corn was being cultivated in all the settlements, and its production constantly rose as the years passed.

Rice was first mentioned in 1712 by Diron d'Artaguette in a letter to the Count de Pontchartrain. He wrote that although he believed rice would grow in the colony he had been unable to get seed rice from the West Indies, for the people of the islands "regard this establishment with great jealousy." Du Pratz reported that rice was introduced from the Carolinas, apparently shortly after 1712, and in 1718 the Company of the West sent to Africa for slaves who "know how to cultivate rice." By 1720 rice was competing with corn as the staple grain crop. Rice mills, probably from the southern English colonies, were introduced shortly after 1740.

Legend credits the introduction of sugar cane to the Jesuits, who are supposed to have brought it from Santo Domingo about 1751, but in all probability it was first planted at some point along the Gulf Coast or the lower Mississippi by either Iberville or Bienville during the first years of settlement. It was certainly being grown in 1733, as Bienville mentions it in his report of that year. Until the late 1740's it was grown only in small amounts for the making of a poor-grade syrup or an even poorer alcoholic drink called "tafia." There is reason to believe that during the late 1740's Joseph Villars Dubreuil began to experiment with sugar cane and sometime before his death in 1757 built the first sugar mill in Louisiana. But the clarifying and granulating process could not be mastered, and the sodden mass called "sugar" leaked from the casks in shipment; the Louisiana sugar industry had to await the success of Étienne de Boré in perfecting the granulation process in 1795.

Nonedible agricultural products did not become important until the Company of the Indies acquired the colony. The company literally forced general subsistence agriculture upon the colonists, and once food production had reached substantial proportions, began to encourage the production of salable staple crops such as myrtle wax, silk, cotton, indigo, and tobacco.

Indians were growing tobacco when the French arrived in Louisiana, and the plant had been known in Europe for over a hundred years. As soon as the food problem became less acute, the settlers began to raise tobacco for export to France. Comparatively small amounts were produced, however, until after 1720.

The production of tobacco steadily increased as the settlers improved the quality of their plants and methods of curing. Du Pratz described a method which he developed for curing tobacco of a better-than-average quality. He hung the stalks in a drying-shed, bottom end upward in order that the sap would gradually flow down into the leaves. As the leaves dried and "assumed a bright chestnut colour," he stripped them, tied them into bundles, wrapped the bundles in cloth for a time, then tightened and rewrapped the bundles. Du Pratz wrote that "This tobacco turned black and so waxy, that it could not be rasped in less than a year; but then it had a substance and flavour so much the more agreeable, as it never affected the head; and so I sold it for double the price of the common." By 1760 the best tobacco-producing areas were the Natchez and Pointe Coupée districts, and the total crop had reached a value of 480,000 livres, the high point for the French period.

A wild indigo of poor quality grew on the highlands of Louisiana, so a domesticated variety of this plant was soon introduced from the West Indies. As it could be grown along with tobacco or cotton, many farmers and planters alternated their fields. The processing of the indigo, however, was a tedious and distasteful job. The three-vat, steeping system was used, the first vat being the "rotting" vat, the second the "beating" vat where the liquid was beaten with wooden paddles, and the third the "settling" vat. The product, of moist consistency which could be spread with a knife or paddle, was put in cloth bags and hung up to drain, after which it was packed in casks for shipment.

Indigo production varied considerably from year to year, since the price depended upon the East Indian supply and European wars frequently cut off that source. By 1756 the Louisiana export averaged something over 200,000 livres annually and reached its peak in 1762, when the amount exported was valued at slightly over one and a third millions.

Agricultural crops of minor importance included cotton, mulberry trees for silk culture, and candleberry trees for the making of candle wax. Cotton did not grow well in the heavy, strong soil of south Louisiana and had to await the settlement of lands in the Feliciana, Natchez, and Red River sections; it remained a crop of minor importance through the French period. The Company of the Indies urged colonists to plant mulberry trees along their boundary lines, raise silkworms, and produce silk for export. However, the project ended in complete failure. There was more success with the production of candle wax; the shrub grew well, the berries were easily harvested, and about eight pounds of berries yielded a pound of wax. Although it developed rapidly during the 1720's, by the late 1750's the industry had almost disappeared.

Livestock raising languished throughout the French period, and the colonists never produced enough meat to take care of their yearly needs. Hogs, cattle, and sheep were brought to the colony by Iberville, but by 1713 the total cattle in the colony numbered only about three hundred, and there were even fewer hogs and sheep. As late as the 1740's it was necessary for the government to issue regulations prohibiting the slaughtering of cattle. The Illinois country produced most of the meat consumed in early Louisiana, and pork, mutton, and beef was salted, smoked, dried, and shipped down the Mississippi during the winter and early spring. By the 1750's Louisiana was producing a fair percentage of its meat, and plantations and *vacheries*, or stock farms, were raising more meat animals than they needed and so had some for sale.

The raising of horses and oxen for field work progressed even more slowly. New Orleans had a total horse population in 1721 of only nine (even the Governor did not own a horse), and eleven years later had only fourteen. As late as 1731 most Germans along the lower river did not own a single work horse or ox. After 1735 horses were imported from Spanish Texas via the Natchitoches country.

The agricultural units of the French period may be divided into several categories. The subsistence farm operated by a single family was the smallest and most common. After securing a few slaves a more prosperous farmer enlarged his acreage and began to grow nonedible staples. Plantations were developed by successful farmers or by settlers who secured concessions and brought capital to the colony.

Land values rose steadily. During the early years land could be purchased for only a few livres per front arpent, with "the usual" or forty-arpent depth; by the end of the period good cleared land sold at from 60 livres to over 100 livres per front arpent.

Sizable plantations began to appear by the 1720's. They were frequently industrial as well as agricultural enterprises, producing brick, timber, lumber, and cordwood, tiles and other products. The larger planters sometimes rented portions of their lands for a share of the crop, and practically all of them employed one or more overseers or managers to direct various operations. In 1731 an inventory of the plantation of Petit de Livilliers totaled 34,134 livres; in 1758 the estate of Joseph Villars Dubreuil, including 188 Negro slaves and nearly 200 head of cattle, was inventoried at a little over 570,000 livres. French Louisiana's most noted estate was "Montplaisir," across the river from the Place d'Armes in New Orleans, owned by the Chevalier Jean Charles de Pradel. In 1754 the Chevalier completed a spacious château, modeled after one in France, and furnished it with the best silver, glassware, and furniture that could be secured in Europe. By this time Pradel had moved up the social ladder from gentleman to "grand Seigneur," and lived according to his position. This shrewd businessman operated a full-scale plantation, raising rice, indigo, corn, and vegetables, manufactured candle wax, brick, and various wood products, and had extensive business interests in New Orleans.

MANUFACTURING AND INDUSTRY. There was comparatively little industry or manufacturing in French colonial Louisiana. The major manufactured items included brick and tiles, sawed timber and lumber, pitch and tar, and barrels and casks. While most of the production was for local use, some of it was exported.

A few tradesmen and artisans appeared in the early years, and by the 1720's the colony could boast shopkeepers, bakers, armorers, carpenters, locksmiths, harness makers, turners, millwrights, barbers, coopers, stone masons, tanners, tailors, blacksmiths, shipbuilders, cabinetmakers, edge-tool makers, and at least one wigmaker and one pastry cook. Some of these artisans journeyed from village to village or from farm to farm, making or repairing the various items in general use. The first shoemaker apparently arrived in the early 1720's, and by the end of that decade the Chevalier de Pradel had conceived the idea of importing skilled *sabotiers* from his native Bas Limousin to make wooden shoes for the colonists.

Boys learned trades by being apprenticed to master artisans. Apprenticeships ordinarily ran for a period of from three to five years and cost the parent or guardian up to as much as 1,500 livres. The master artisan furnished the lad with food, lodging, clothing, and medicines, but extended the period of apprenticeship if time was lost due to "libertinism, debauchery or any other cause." Occasionally a clause in the contract obligated the master to teach the apprentice to read and write.

Wages were low, although there was constant scarcity of labor. Artisans and skilled laborers were sometimes contracted for by the year or season, and were usually given housing and board. River boatmen were hired by the trip; in 1740, for example, young Guillaume Potier was engaged in the Illinois country to make a voyage as ordinary boatman to New Orleans and return for 200 livres, 4 pots of brandy, and some tobacco. Day laborers generally made from 3 to 10 livres a day, the average in 1729 being about 5 livres.

TRADE WITHIN THE COLONY. The Gulf of Mexico, the Mississippi River and its tributaries, and the numerous connecting lakes, bayous, and streams were the arteries of commerce. As the period progressed, however, a considerable pack-train trade developed, generally following the old animal "traces" and Indian trails.

Numerous varieties of boats were used. Pirogues were small, but dugouts might be as large as forty to fifty feet long, carrying a crew of as many as thirty men and a cargo of several tons. *Bateaux plats* or *radeaux,* which had flat or slightly rounded bottoms, were of varying sizes but generally averaged about twenty tons capacity. Large and small broadhorns, longboats, shallops, feluccas, ketches, and numerous other boat types were used. The keelboat, which appeared after 1740, was sometimes sixty to seventy feet long, fifteen to twenty feet wide, drew four to five feet of water, and had a capacity of many tons. The river boats gradually grew larger, and by the end of the period some boats, called *traversiers,* were running between two points on a somewhat regular schedule.

The waterways in the vicinity of New Orleans were filled with boats of every description, many of which depended to some extent upon sails. In season farmers made weekly voyages down the Mississippi or across Lake Pontchartrain to sell farm produce or to purchase supplies. Lumber, timber, tar and pitch, hides, and other products were brought to New Orleans for local use or shipment beyond the colony. Mobile, Dauphin Island, and Biloxi were centers of the Gulf Coast trade.

River travel to the Illinois or Natchitoches country involved many hardships and some real danger. There were strong currents, swirling eddies, and the ever present danger of running into tree trunks called "planters," which were firmly fixed in the river bottom, or "sawyers," which had their upper ends moving up and down with the waves. Good camp sites were frequently difficult to find while rains and storms drenched the boatmen and sometimes their cargoes. Fevers and colds plagued them. Upriver voyages with a full cargo were slow and back-breaking work, frequently necessitating the use of tow ropes. Indians and renegade white men haunting the riverbanks pilfered night camps or openly attacked the boats; soon the French began to use the convoy system in Mississippi River travel. Convoys were commanded by an officer of the King's troops or by an experienced boatman and usually carried a few soldiers or armed guards. Discipline was rigidly enforced, while lookouts were stationed by day and guards posted by night.

The voyage upriver to the Illinois country took from two to four months, while the downriver trip could be made in from fifteen to thirty days. Convoys ordinarily left New Orleans sometime between August and October so as to reach their destination before winter set in, and left for New Orleans during the late winter when the boatmen could take advantage of the five- to seven-mile-per-hour flood current.

From the Illinois and Natchitoches country came furs and hides, flour, corn and corn meal, beef and pork, bear's oil, lard and tallow, tobacco, leather, lumber, beeswax, bacon, and hams. Lead came from the upper Mississippi north of the mouth of the Ohio. From the Natchez country and lower-Mississippi and Red river areas came tobacco, indigo, and cotton, along with some lumber, bear's oil, and truck products. To the upriver areas went manufactured goods of all types, including groceries, dry goods, spirituous liquors, furniture, notions, tools, household and farming equipment, and the articles especially needed in the Indian trade. These goods were first furnished from the King's storehouses, then by the agents of Crozat and the Company of the Indies, and after 1729 by agents of the King and by private merchants. Prices were always high, and upriver settlers were charged premium prices. Crozat and the Company of the Indies made huge profits from their sales, and after 1731 unscrupulous royal officials gouged even deeper.

Trade was normally carried on by means of barter, or what was called "semi-barter," in which commodities such as corn, tobacco, bear's oil, lead, liquors, tafia, and hides and furs were given standards of value which were used in determining the prices of other articles of trade. But the "standards" varied with supply and de-

[75]

mand, so the trader had to know the market demand of various commodities to avoid receiving less than the actual trading value of his goods at a given time. The "made beaver" or wampum of the English was occasionally used in trading with the southern Indian tribes east of the Mississippi.

FOREIGN TRADE. Trade with France presented many difficulties. Ships were slow and frequently so badly built that they sank during even slight storms. The voyage from the French ports of La Rochelle, Rochefort, Bordeaux, St. Malo, Le Havre, Marseilles, Bayonne, Nantes, and Dunkerque usually took from six weeks to two and a half months. Sailors were picked up wherever they might be found, and many were not sailors at all. The poor food and bad water aboard ship caused scurvy and other diseases, and epidemics were not infrequent. Goods were frequently of poorer quality than listed in the invoices.

There was much corruption and just plain stealing among ship captains and among Louisiana and French officials, and many cargoes were short when they arrived at New Orleans or Mobile. The Governor ordered the captain of one vessel to give the people an opportunity to buy the goods, but the captain sold the entire cargo to one of the officials for 250,000 livres; the official in turn retailed the goods at a profit of 150,000 livres. Colonial merchants enthusiastically connived or co-operated with officials, and not a few acquired sizable fortunes.

Supply ships from France were irregular. From the beginning of settlement until 1712 only a dozen ships arrived. Crozat, however, sent twenty-five vessels during the five years of his proprietorship, and from 1718 until 1732, the Company of the Indies dispatched over a hundred ships to Louisiana. During the royal period from 1732 to the outbreak of the French and Indian War, the Crown sent an average of six ships a year; after the war began the number declined, and none arrived during the last few years of the conflict.

Supply vessels from France brought cargoes of spices, cloth, cutlery, utensils, wines, flour and other foodstuffs, notions of all sorts, and after 1730 many types of luxury goods. The amount of luxury items imported was amazing, considering the general economic condition of the colony and the fact that it did not supply its own basic food needs. From Louisiana to France went tobacco, indigo, pitch and tar, lumber and mast timber, furs and hides, lead, a little cotton, rice, sassafras, and quinine of poor quality.

The West Indies trade did not become important until after 1720. Difficulties were many, for Spain frequently confiscated ships as well as cargoes, there was considerable danger from pirates, and Gulf and Caribbean storms took their toll. To the islands went lumber, dried or salted meats, brick, tiles, corn and beans, pitch and tar, tallow and a few other items, while from them came sugar, coffee, rum, rare woods, drugs, cocoa, tanned leather, spices, tortoise shell, syrup, and other goods. In times of food scarcity, Louisiana depended more upon the West Indies than upon France for supplies.

Saint-Denis was the founder of the Louisiana-Texas-Mexico trade, and he continued in this work until his death. Carried overland by way of Natchitoches in the early years, later most goods went by sea to the Mexican ports on the Gulf. During periods of war when Spain and France were allies against Great Britain, Spain permitted the trade, but during times of peace Spain tried to enforce her trade regulations. Texans, Mexicans, and Louisianians, however, needed goods, so both nationalities engaged in smuggling.

Louisiana carried on considerable trade with Spanish Florida, and Spanish vessels from Pensacola frequently arrived at Mobile, Biloxi, or New Orleans in search of flour, corn, rice, and meats. By the 1740's the Florida trade was annually yielding in excess of 14,000 livres.

Royal officials attempted to prevent trade with the English, but often Louisiana so desperately needed foodstuffs and manufactured goods that they were forced to wink at trade violations. British ship captains became adept at making excuses for putting into Louisiana ports. One captain in 1735 boldly sailed into Mobile Bay on the excuse that he had come to collect some debts which were owed him, and while the captain was collecting his debts, the ship was unloading its cargo and reloading with export goods from Louisiana. The Governor of South Carolina protested to the British Board of Trade in 1760 that Louisiana was securing its Indian trading goods from Rhode Island. This was no new development, for such commodities had been received from the North Atlantic coastal colonies since the early 1730's. Despite the watchfulness of British and French officials, the trade continued, even after the fighting began in 1754, for British traders had goods to sell and the French of Louisiana desperately needed them.

CURRENCY AND CREDIT. Gold, silver, or copper money was always scarce in French Louisiana; until 1740 all types of coins were extremely difficult to secure. Between 1740 and 1750 hard money was somewhat more plentiful, but after that time almost completely disappeared from circulation; what little could be secured generally came from Mexico or Cuba, and the Louisianians hoarded it.

Bills of credit, first issued by Iberville, were the first paper money used in Louisiana. Somewhat similar to modern checks, they continued to be issued until 1722, when they were called in at a depreciated rate. By this time other forms of paper money had come into general use. There were bills of exchange, French treasury notes and orders, storehouse receipts and orders, Company of the Indies contracts, and other forms of legal paper which could be passed from person to person and thus used as money. In 1732 *bons* came into existence, small-sized paper notes valued at from 10 sols to 200 livres. Meanwhile the use of milk, bread, or other kinds of tickets called "little *bons,*" and *écus en carte,* or card money, had become common.

By 1719 the Company of the Indies had issued 25,000,000 livres worth of paper money, and additional amounts were issued as the years passed; by 1731 paper money had depreciated 50 per cent in value and in 1746 a livre in hard money was worth 22 livres in any form of paper. Counterfeiting further depreciated the value of paper money after the 1730's. Despite the efforts of Kerlerec and his successor, Jean Jacques Blaise d'Abbadie, to reduce the amount of paper money in circulation and to give it a fixed value, it was not until after Spain took possession of the colony that the money problem was solved through the importation of silver.

In view of the money situation, Louisiana settlers generally bartered and traded or used personal notes and private contracts at face value as long as the financial reputation of the issuer was unquestioned. The sellers of goods for foreign shipment learned to demand money or goods in payment for their consignments, and many shrewd colonials mastered the art of sharp trading in various kinds of paper money, successfully engaged in money speculation, and invested their gains in durable goods or in land.

GOVERNMENT AND THE LAW. During the first period of colonization from 1699 to 1712, Louisiana was considered a military outpost of empire, and few officials beyond a governor and a commissary-commissioner were needed. During the Crozat period, France began to establish permanent principles of government which were to remain in force throughout the French regime.

The Superior Council, a court of original, exclusive, and final jurisdiction, was first established in 1712. In 1719 it was made a permanent institution and was further reorganized in 1732 when its membership was limited to the governor, commissary-commissioner or intendant, the lieutenant governor, and the attorney general. Additional members were later added, and by 1748 it had become an unwieldy body composed of the governor, intendant, acting procurer general, counselor, three counselor assessors, the Lieutenant of the King, the clerk of the Council, a sheriff, a deputy sheriff, the "Major" of New Orleans, the agent of the Company of the Indies, the commandant, the judge, and the notary at Pointe Coupée, the "surveyor of the King's Highways," the attorney of vacant estates, and an attorney.

The commissaire ordonnateur (commissary-commissioner or commissary general) was at first the custodian of the King's warehouse and the supplies furnished the colony, but in 1729 the office was enlarged to include all police, agriculture, commerce, and financial matters, and the new title of "intendant" was given to the official, a title, however, not frequently used. As might be expected, there were frequent clashes between the commissary-commissioner and the governor.

Lesser and local officials included the attorney general, judges, syndics (who performed the duties of justices of the peace), sheriffs in larger towns, notaries, and clerks. A notary collected debts, acted as coroner, supervised estates and actions of minors, drew up wills and testaments, registered gifts and donations, and witnessed business contracts, deeds, probate inventories and sales, marriages, and papers of apprenticeship.

Governmental officials acquired their offices through one of three methods, by appointment of the King or the governor, through military rank, or through purchase. The purchase of offices was common in both the French and Spanish colonial systems, and positions subject to sale or purchase were known as "venal offices." The applicants for such offices were investigated, sometimes with extreme care and sometimes with extreme laxness, and the reports were filed with the Superior Council.

The over-all quality of French officials seldom rose above mediocrity. Iberville, Bienville, Saint-Denis, La Harpe, Kerlerec, and a few others were men of real ability, sound judgment, and marked qualities of leadership; the majority, however, were very ordinary men engaged in the routine performance of their duties, and few possessed a strong desire for government service. Many secured appointments solely for the legal opportunities offered for making money, some violated the law or at least skirted it, and others were simply thieves. A decadent French government could hardly be expected to furnish good officials for its Louisiana colony.

The Catholic Church was a part of the state and was supported by governmental payments or through forced contributions by the citizens. All governmental edicts, ordinances, and announcements were posted "at the issue of the parochial Mass," in addition to "the usual places," in order that "none may pretend ignorance." When the Church of St. Louis needed repair in 1738, the Governor and the Intendant contributed prize money to the amount of over 9,000 livres obtained from the sale of the *La Marie* and placed a slave tax on slaveowners and a direct tax on all others to raise the necessary funds. As priests and religious orders commonly engaged in business or planting operations, they could sue or be sued in the courts.

The army played an important role in local government, since the commandants of posts were the chief governing officials of their districts and the army was the chief arm of the governor for the defense of his colony and the maintenance of his administration. Army officers were appointed by the King, sometimes upon the recommendation of the governor; and family connections in France, Canada, and Louisiana counted greatly in the applicant's favor.

During the early years of the Company of the Indies the colony was divided into nine military districts, each under a commandant, who was the representative of the governor and subject to his orders. A judge tried ordinary civil and criminal cases, and appeals from his decisions could be made to the Superior Council.

The number of soldiers stationed at various Louisiana posts was never large, the total in the colony seldom exceeding a thousand men. Governors consistently complained of the quality of the soldiers and appealed for Swiss rather than French troops. Military discipline was rigid, the privations many, the pay low, and the officer class generally venal. Rations and housing were poor. The net result was that insubordination and desertion were chronic problems, and in several instances entire detachments mutinied.

The functions and problems of the governing officials were varied and numerous. Police regulations and ordinances were drawn up and promulgated by the governor and were enforced by local and lesser officials, as were regulations concerning levees, roads, taverns, the sale of goods, markets, the sale of liquor, and numerous others. Land grants were confirmed, contracts for equipment and supplies were let, and the stationing and movement of troops supervised. Frontiers were closely watched, for the Spanish of Texas and Florida consistently attempted to settle on lands claimed by France. It should be realized that Louisiana was a colony of tremendous size and that communication was slow and precarious; governmental administration was not an easy task.

French Louisiana colonial law was composed of the ordinances and edicts of the King and the governor, the orders of the French Council of State, and after 1712 the Custom of Paris, which had been codified in the sixteenth century. Criminal and civil laws were all written laws. The practice, procedure, and forms of pleading closely followed those prevailing in the Châtelet of Paris, one of the oldest courts in France.

Perhaps the most unusual feature of French colonial Louisiana law was that it never had forced upon it any of the laws of primogeniture or others then existing in France which were a part of the old feudal system. There was equality in the distribution of estates, and lands were ordinarily granted in fee simple. The rights of the wife, the rigid restrictions on the disinheritance of children, the community of acquests and gains between husband and wife, and the restraints upon widows and widowers were carefully watched. That the general system was just and equitable is plainly evident in the great number of French characteristics in present-day Louisiana law.

Land titles, trespass, collection of debts, the settlement of estates, and contracts of various types gave opportunity for civil suits of varying degrees of importance; records of criminal cases are numerous, especially those involving personal injury. A few cases will serve to illustrate. In 1737, Louis Brouet, a wheelwright, charged that three men stood before his door and insulted him "continuously until 2 o'clock in the morning, evidently to make him come out to ill treat him." The next night they fell upon him "with a club, mutilating his right arm and giving him a black eye." In 1745, Jean Baptiste Provenche charged Monbrun Carrière with having killed one of his dogs. The next year Jean Pierre Hardy, called "La Vierge," charged that his wife and her son by a former marriage stole some of his property and beat him severely.

Torture and mutilation were used to obtain confessions, particularly in criminal cases, and the most commonly used methods included cutting off hands and ears, breaking arms, legs, thighs, and loins upon a scaffold, breaking on the wheel, and the use of the rack. In 1753 when André Baron, a soldier at Mobile, was accused of the crime of bestiality, he was ordered to be "put on the rack and that ordinary and extraordinary torture be applied in the usual manner" until a confession could be secured. Some years later a Negro slave accused of stealing chickens and clothing was placed on the rack, his legs were put into "torture boots," and he was tortured and questioned until he confessed and named his accomplices.

Punishments were severe and barbarous. Jacob Keha, who was convicted of theft, was sentenced to be keelhauled. A slave who struck a soldier had his right ear cut off and was sentenced to be whipped daily and to carry a six-pound ball on his foot for the rest of his life. In 1745 several soldiers who mutinied against "munition bread," charging that it was not fit for dogs to eat, were sentenced to be strangled to death. Several of the mutineers at Fort Toulouse above Mobile were executed by having their heads crushed. In 1747, René Meslier was sentenced "to the galleys for life for having dared to raise his hand against a sergeant of the King."

The government of the Louisiana colony was marked by extreme simplicity and centralization of power; there was no actual separation of powers except that between the governor and the intendant. The colony was supervised by the French Minister of Marine, to whom the governor and the secretary of the Superior Council submitted reports and from whom the governor and the intendant received their orders. Despite the claims of some Louisiana historians, democratic tendencies did not develop during the French regime. Popular ignorance of, and prejudice against, democratic institutions continued through the Spanish period and plagued the American territorial government after the purchase of Louisiana in 1803.

SLAVERY. Indian slavery was attempted as early as 1703, but Indians did not work well and found it difficult to understand the agricultural practices of the settlers. In 1708, Bienville proposed trading Indian slaves to the West Indian planters for Negroes, arguing that "the Indians once they are in the islands, will not be able to run away, the country being unknown to them; and the Negroes will not dare to become fugitives in Louisiana, because, if they do, the Indians will kill them." The government did not agree to his proposition. The comparatively small number of Indian slaves used during the French period were unprofitable, except in isolated cases, and few colonists wanted them.

It is believed that Negro slavery began in 1708, when Bienville imported two slaves from the West Indies, but the government did not give its official sanction to the institution until 1712, at which time there were ten slaves in the colony. At the end of the Crozat period the slave population was estimated at between ten and twenty. The Company of the West began importing slaves after 1717, and by 1731 had imported over 6,000, of whom about 2,000 were still alive. This number increased but slightly during the remaining years of the French regime.

Louisiana farmers and planters preferred African to West Indian slaves because the voodoo practices of the West Indian Negroes made them more difficult to control. The great majority of African slaves were secured in Senegal, though smaller numbers were brought from Gorée, Angola, Caye, and other sections. The mortality during the voyage from Africa was high, for there was severe overcrowding and almost complete violation of governmental regulations as to sanitation and food supply. Upon arrival in Louisiana, the *Africains bruts,* as they were called, were placed in slave pens, cleaned up, and the sick segregated from the healthy. Distribution was by lot. Private sales were handled as for any other form of property, and the slave was generally minutely examined by an "honest doctor," after having been stripped "as naked as the hand."

Slaves were taught something of the Catholic religion, the French language, how to use field tools, to cook, and to take care of their cabins. In winter they wore pants and shirts or dresses of rough, heavy cloth, had long blanket coats with a hood drawn over the head, and wore shoes of rawhide which laced over the foot and ankle. In summer they went barefooted and wore only a pair of short pants or a thin dress. Their cabins had only the barest necessities, and they usually prepared their simple food over fireplaces. In many cases, however, the smaller planters and the farmers treated the slaves as members of their families.

French colonial Louisiana slaves occupied a unique position in law, for they could legally marry, testify in court, and in some cases could hold property. They were protected by law against miscegenation, forced marriage or breeding, and marriages with slaves of different masters. Cruelty by slaveowners was condemned, as was the separation of families; but the whites controlled the courts, so slave justice depended generally upon the moral standards of individual owners.

Slave crime consisted chiefly of petty thievery and running away, which was called "marooning," and for these crimes slaves were punished by their masters or by the courts. The records of slave court cases are numerous, indicating that they were frequently given the right of trial. Punishment for minor offenses usually was a severe flogging, but for more serious crimes they received the same harsh punishments as whites. There were few threatened slave revolts or uprisings during the French period.

INDIAN PROBLEMS. Except for the three Natchez wars, Louisiana Indians caused little trouble; but the government faced a thorny problem with some of the southern tribes, particularly the Chickasaws, the Illinois tribes, and those living on the western borderlands between Louisiana and Spanish Texas. The persistent encroachment of the French upon the lands of the Indians, the agitation of the English and Spanish, and the general poor quality of French trading goods provoked most of the difficulties which arose.

During early years white occupation of already-cleared Indian fields invited discord, for the Indians seldom were completely satisfied with the prices they received for their lands. Occasionally the commandant of a district ordered lands to be occupied without compensation, and an Indian's appeals to the colonial government rarely brought him justice; in the end he was forced off his land to less desirable tracts where he could eke out only a bare existence.

The British and Spanish persistently encouraged Indians to war against the French, while the French in turn agitated them into opposing British or Spanish traders or into going on the warpath. Bienville held the southern tribes in check until 1725, but after his departure from the colony there was much trouble with the Natchez, and his Chickasaw campaigns during his last governorship ended in failure. On the other hand, Saint-Denis at Natchitoches held the western Louisiana and eastern Texas tribes as allies of the French until his death in 1744, and they caused little trouble after that time.

The British of the Carolinas were the chief competitors of the French for the southern Indian trade, as the British were already operating in the region when the French settled the Louisiana colony. English pack trains set out for the Indian country with each animal generally being loaded with three fifty-pound packs. Trading goods included cloth, blankets, brass kettles, hatchets, guns, knives, flints, powder and bullets, colored ribbon, plumes, brandy, razors, beads, wines, tobacco, rum, ready-made clothing, hats, paints of assorted colors, all types of notions, and other goods. In return the traders received furs, hides, bear's fat, small quantities of roots and herbs, and a few other items. Charleston and Baltimore were the centers of the British trade, while New Orleans, Mobile, Natchez, Natchitoches, and the settlements in the Illinois and Missouri country were centers of the French trade. The Spanish were forced to operate from small settlements in northeastern Mexico and southern and eastern Texas.

French officials made little effort to follow the royal regulations for Indian trade, for protests were few and generally came from the missionaries. In 1750, Father Louis Vivier eloquently protested against the selling of intoxicating liquors: "The brandy sold by the French . . . has ruined this mission, and has caused the majority of them to abandon our holy religion. The savages and especially the Illinois, who are the gentlest and most tractable of men, become, when intoxicated, madmen and wild beasts. Then they fall upon one another, stab with their knives, and tear one another. Many have lost their ears and some portion of their noses, in these tragic encounters." The good Father's protests, however, had little effect.

Even during periods of peace between their nations, British and French traders engaged in a bitter struggle for the Indian trade; English pack trains were ambushed, French trading boats were attacked, and Indian war parties were hired and equipped by both sides. Saint-Denis won the long struggle against the Spanish in western Louisiana and French commandants in the Illinois and Missouri countries had comparatively little trouble with the English.

During most of the French period, Louisiana governors complained of the scarcity, quality, or variety of the Indian trading goods sent them. In 1762, for example, Kerlerec informed his government that the ships "brought none of the articles we wanted most and hardly any of the things in the invoice. What they have brought is either not to the taste of the Indians, or is so inferior or bad quality, that it is without value. I am therefore under the shameful and humiliating necessity of not keeping my plighted faith to the savages. . . . How shall I keep them quiet? I am in a frightful position. Is the province of Louisiana destined to be the sport of cupidity and avarice?" The diplomacy of the French, however, was successful against superior British trading goods, and in 1762 their power over the Indians of the Lower Mississippi Valley could not be questioned.

CHAPTER 8

EVERYDAY LIFE IN FRENCH
COLONIAL LOUISIANA

COLONISTS AND SETTLERS. The composite portrait of the French colonists who settled Louisiana prior to 1762 generally has been painted by Louisiana historians in soft, rosy hues. While admitting that during the early years of the regime of the Company of the Indies rather sizable numbers of the criminal and low-moraled class were sent from the Mother Country, they dismiss this group as being of little consequence. It would seem, from reading the pages of these writers, that the colony was settled by a sturdy middle-class stock, with several handfuls of persons of wealth, an even larger number of younger sons of the French nobility, and only a sprinkling of peasants.

Travelers, sojourners, and residents in the colony during the period who later wrote of their experiences probably originated the legend, which was eagerly appropriated by those who began to write the Louisiana story during the third decade of the American period. Captain Jean Bossu of the "Troupes de la Marine" wrote from New Orleans in 1751 that the Creoles were in general "very brave, tall and well made; they have many dispositions for the arts and the sciences." This was a completely inaccurate description of the average Louisianian of that day.

The candid generalization must be made that no American colony was settled by colonists of poorer over-all quality than was French Louisiana. They simply do not measure up to the settlers of the English Atlantic seaboard colonies, the Dutch of New Amsterdam, the Swedes of Delaware, or the Spanish of Texas, California, and the Floridas. The one exception is the Germans, who have received far too little credit, for it was this group which gave the colony its stability.

The only significant years of French settlement were those between 1717 and 1731, when the colony was under the control of the Company of the West and the Company of the Indies. During this time the Company and the Crown closely cooperated in a forced colonization program, and at bayonet point shipped from France large numbers of undesirables, criminals, and those of such low morals as to be unacceptable to the low-moraled France of that day. The Acadians are not to be included, for they did not migrate to Louisiana until after the beginning of the Spanish period.

The character of the settlers during the last years of the Company of the Indies was graphically described in official reports sent back to France. About 1728, according to one of them, Louisiana's capital was inhabited by large numbers of people who "gambled, fought duels, lounged about, drank, wantoned, and caroused—'sans religion, sans justice, sans discipline, sans order, et sans police.'" Seven years later Bienville wrote: "I neglect nothing to turn the attention of the inhabitants to agricultural pursuits, but in general they are worthless, lazy, dissolute, and most of them recoil from the labours necessary to improve the lands."

[83]

One of the most remarkable features of Louisiana history is that these people, during the last three decades of the French period, made as much economic progress as they did and that their descendants, under Spanish governmental supervision and with the augmentation of new settlers, developed a strong colony.

By 1762, Louisiana society had become rather well stratified. At the top was a comparatively small number of high government officials, wealthy merchants, and planters. Middle-class farmers, professional men, small merchants and traders, and officers and officials of lesser grade made up the second group. At the bottom were poor farmers, day laborers, boatmen, hunters and trappers, peddlers, and a few other unclassifiable groups who possessed little property. A typical *coureur de bois* who died in 1737 owned only "two old shirts, a worn pair of breeches, a savagess, a jar of oil [probably bear's oil], and 40 pounds of tobacco." The *gens de couleur libres,* or free persons of color, descended from whites and either slaves or Free Negroes, stood at the top of the colored group. Beneath them were slaves, either Negroes or those of mixed Negro and white or Indian blood.

By 1762 the average *bourgeois* and *paysan* Louisianian was a person of "good spirits, physical elasticity, and exceeding animation," who lived his life with comparatively little enterprise and little inspration, who "danced on Sunday after mass, was passionately attached to faro and half a dozen other card games," who "gossiped long over a friendly pipe and a congenial mug of brandy in the half-dusk of his porch." He had little ambition for intellectual or cultural achievement and was generally satisfied with the small share of the world's goods which he had accumulated.

TOWNS, VILLAGES, AND FARMS. At the end of the French regime, there were no urban centers of consequence in the colony. New Orleans was the only important community and it had less than three thousand inhabitants, while Mobile, Biloxi, Baton Rouge, Natchez, Les Rapides, Natchitoches, Pointe Coupée, and Les Allemands were small towns or villages. There were only a few posts farther up the Mississippi in the northern section of the colony.

New Orleans did not extend beyond the limits of the present Vieux Carré, and not all of its blocks were filled with houses or other buildings. There were a few scattered houses along the river front above and below the town, as well as along Bayou St. John

The Place d'Armes, present-day Jackson Square, was the center of the capital. Behind and fronting the river was the St. Louis Church; to the left of the church was the house of the Capuchin Fathers and to the right was the town jail and the guardhouse. On each side of the square was a row of soldier's barracks. In front of the town was a low levee, cluttered with goods of all sorts, ship rigging, gear and ballast, agricultural products, rubbish, and garbage. Most houses, shops, and other buildings were constructed of wood, although there were a few brick houses. On the sides of the regularly-laid-out streets were small ditches, bridged at the street intersections with over a hundred small brick bridges. While the capital was a poorly drained, poorly policed, unimposing town, it was the governmental and commercial center of the colony and its inhabitants looked with disdain upon their rural countrymen. They had a few amusements not found elsewhere and even a rude semblance of a court.

The majority of the smaller towns had originally been founded as military or trading posts and by 1762 boasted only a few hundred inhabitants. Natchitoches, for example, had a barracks, a guardhouse, a store, a church, a powder house, a public oven, the commandant's house, the storekeeper's house, and several smaller buildings used as kitchens or as quarters for servants or slaves. The commandant's house was built of adobe, the church of logs and adobe, and the other structures of logs. The fort was surrounded by a palisade made of logs set nine feet above the ground. The houses of the villagers were scattered without pattern about the fort. The general layout of other towns followed a similar design, and they were located on rivers, large streams, or bayous, except in the case of Mobile and Biloxi, which were located on bays fronting the Gulf of Mexico.

French settlers, unlike British and later American settlers who preferred to establish scattered farms because of their desire to become landowners, generally settled in rather compact little villages on the banks of a stream or bayou. Houses were built close together for protection or to enable the villagers to converse with one another without difficulty. If possible, they were located close to both forested and open lands so that building material and firewood and ground for grazing and tillage would not be too far distant. Most villages had a "common" where livestock was penned at night and "common fields" allotted to the several families, both of which were regulated by the village. In many cases settlements were replicas of villages in France, and village life was much the same. Trading posts consisted of a small palisaded fort in which were storerooms and the quarters for the trader and a few men.

Most rural Louisianians lived on farms located near the lower Mississippi or other streams and bayous or along the Gulf of Mexico from present-day Bay St. Louis to Mobile. At night or during bad weather pole fences confined the livestock; during the day the animals grazed on pasture land or in the woods. Farms were separated by a double furrow, a ditch, or a low fence made of poles or brush.

CONDITIONS OF TRAVEL. Most travelers journeyed in various types of boats on the many waterways threading the colony. River or bayou travel was slow and difficult. Long river loops and bends so lengthened a journey that one traveler in describing a short trip wrote that "we boxed the compass in three hours travel, and went half around in going two leagues." Besides poor camp sites and landing places, scarcity of good drinking water, problems of carrying and preserving food, the excessive heat or the biting cold, and the constant annoyance of insects added to the hardships. "One day's journey" was a commonly used phrase meaning ten "post leagues," about twenty-four miles.

Father du Poisson graphically described a river voyage up the Mississippi from New Orleans in 1727. He wrote that the river had risen some forty feet higher than usual, and "we were exposed to the danger of finding no 'cabanage,' that is to say, no land where we could cook or sleep. When we find it, this is the way we spend the night. If the ground be still muddy, which happens when the water recedes, we begin by making a bed of boughs, so that the mattress may not sink into the mud; then we spread upon it a skin or a mattress and sheets, if we have them. We bend three or four canes in semi-circles, the two ends of which we fix into the ground and separate them from one another according to the length of the mattress or the skin. Across these we fasten three others; then we spread over this frail structure our bars, which is to say, a large canvas, the ends of which we carefully place beneath the mattress. In these tombs, stifling with heat, we are compelled to sleep. . . . We are much more to be pitied when we find no camping ground. Then we fasten the pirogue to a tree and if we find an 'embarras' of trees [a mass of floating trees], we prepare our meal on it; if we do not find one, we have no supper and we remain still in the same position that we kept during the day, exposed during the whole night to the fury of the mosquitoes. . . . The heat was intense and the height of the trees and the denseness of the woods did not permit us to enjoy the least breath of air, although the river is half a mile wide."

Wheeled vehicles did not come into prominence until the 1730's because of the great scarcity of horses and oxen and because of the lack of roads. By 1732, however, Governor Perier found it necessary to issue a new levee-road ordinance requiring all landowners along the lower Mississippi in the vicinity of New Orleans to build a six-foot-wide and two-foot-high levee, which also was to serve as a foot and bridle path, and those settlers between Gentilly and Bayou St. John were to build a road forty-eight feet wide. Additional road laws were promulgated in 1735, 1743, and 1749. The first carriage was brought to New Orleans from Havana in

1730; Bienville brought the second three years later. By mid-century the colony had many two-wheeled oxcarts and a few wagons. Almost all persons of means rode in a two-horse chaise, while a few even owned four-horse berlins and coaches. The average village dweller or farmer, however, ordinarily rode an ox or walked.

HOMES AND HOME FURNISHINGS. Unlike the English colonists who built their log houses by laying the logs one on top of the other, the early Louisiana settler stood his logs on end and called his home a *maison de poteaux en terre,* a house of posts in the ground. The spaces between the posts were filled with *bousillage,* a mixture of grass or moss and earth or clay. Later, when certain colonists could afford better houses, they placed bricks between square posts and called them *brique entre poteaux,* brick between posts. Gradually houses of sawed lumber and of brick began to make their appearance.

Houses had steep roofs of straw, grass, or wooden shingles, with low and projecting eaves, and floors of plain earth or roughhewn or rough-sawn boards. The great majority were equipped with wooden shutters called *contrevents* in the place of windows, though some had scraped skins or oiled papers nailed over the openings and a few had glass windows. Of plain battened boards, the doors were hung by leather straps or wooden hinges. Chimneys were on the outside of the house, were made of wood and clay, and had small fireplaces opening within.

Most dwellings were much alike, with only one or two rooms, but in the towns and on large plantations there were houses with three or even more rooms. In most cases the rooms were placed end-to-end with the front doors opening out upon a gallery, or porch, though frequently there was a gallery at the back of the house and occasionally galleries on all four sides.

The combined kitchen and living room was the most important room in the house and had a fireplace equipped with andirons, a pothook, and a spit for roasting meat. Nearby were the frying pan, an iron grill, and several copper or iron kettles and pots. In the center of the room was a large table surrounded by some straight chairs; along the walls were a few benches and large, heavy chests to hold the family's belongings and to serve as seats. The bedroom was sometimes partitioned into several smaller rooms. Frequently six or more feet square, beds held a straw mattress or a feather tick, were covered with buffalo hides, bearskins, or heavy woolen blankets, and were sometimes curtained with hangings of red or green serge or other heavy material. If the family did not have enough beds, the children slept on cots or on the floor on pallets.

Food was eaten from earthenware or pewter dishes, for glassware was too expensive to be widely used. Forks were usually of steel or iron, while spoons were made of pewter. When the fire in the fireplace was low or the weather warm, the family used crude iron lamps or candles. On the wall hung a picture of the Virgin, perhaps the parents' marriage certificate, and the father's musket, powder horn, and bullet pouch. The mantel held some of the family's prized ornaments and trinkets.

Behind and to the sides of country houses were stables, hen houses, pigpens, granaries, dovecotes, storehouses, and perhaps slave huts. Around the barn lots or in the stables or storehouses were scattered wooden plows, rakes, harrows, hand flails for threshing grain, wooden carts and ox yokes, rawhide harness, crude saddles, scythes and sickles, axes, hoes, spades, hammers, hatchets, and other implements, tools, and agricultural equipment.

The few mansions of the more affluent citizens were built with style and good taste, generally resembling homes of similar size in France. They had much hand-carved work, large and ornate fireplaces, glass windows, hand-sanded wooden floors, painted walls, and high ceilings. Their furnishings were the best that could be secured in France, including large gold-leaf-framed mirrors, carved mantlepieces, couches called *canapés* with mosquito curtains, costly hand-painted tapestries, chairs covered with red velvet, expensive clocks, crystal chandeliers, gold-leafed cellarettes with matching flasks, and great quantities of silver and silverware, glassware, and brassware. The age of elegance had already appeared for a fortunate few prior to 1762.

CLOTHING. Imported clothing was expensive, and only government officials, army officers, planters, and wealthy businessmen could afford it for themselves and their families. The average family's wearing apparel was made at home from imported wool, cotton, or other materials, for spinning wheels and looms were uncommon in French Louisiana. Home spinning and cloth manufacture had to await the coming of the Spanish regime and the Acadians.

Men and large boys wore loose-fitting shirts and knee-length pants of coarse blue cloth or deerskin, and in summer they went barefoot. Many of them owned a knee-length jacket, with a sash and hood, called a *capot*. Women and larger girls were dressed in ankle-length skirts and short-sleeved blouses made generally of coarse imported cloth. In winter they added shoes and stockings, a bodice over the blouse, and perhaps a heavy *capot*. For church or parties they put on bright-colored festive costumes—"bodices of red and blue stuffs, waists of flowered muslin, skirts of scarlet drugget and printed calico, and starched white caps." Smaller boys and girls were dressed like adults.

Luxury in clothing appeared in the Louisiana colony just as soon as the colonists could afford it. As early as 1727 one of the Ursuline Sisters of New Orleans wrote: "The women here are extremely ignorant as to the means of securing their salvation, but they are very expert in the art of displaying their beauty. There is so much luxury in this town that there is no distinction among the classes so far as dress goes. The magnificence of display is equal in all. Most of them reduce themselves and their family to the hard lot of living at home on nothing but sagamite, and flaunt abroad in robes of velvet and damask, ornamented with the most costly ribbons. They paint and rouge to hide the ravages of time, and wear on their faces, as embellishment, small black patches." The good Sister should have also explained that the men of the city dressed just as elegantly. Though in the rural areas the people had less money, they did the best they could; for the French were infatuated with fine clothing, as numerous inventories of estates amply prove. When one commandant died in 1737, the Governor wrote of him as a "poor man," yet his clothing inventory included eighty-five "new, trimmed men's shirts," thirty muslin shirts, twenty-five ordinary shirts, twelve pairs of silk and cotton stockings, numerous pairs of pants and dress coats, and one "great coat" trimmed with "gold lace and buttons."

By 1762 good-quality men's suitings cost 250 livres a yard; silk lining, 150 livres; shirt cloth of fair quality, 60 livres; shirt cloth of batiste, 200 livres; silk stockings, 150 livres; a beaver hat, 400 livres (with a gold band, 250 livres extra) ; ordinary muslin, 200 livres a yard; ordinary shoes, 45 livres a pair; powder for the face and hair, 15 livres a pound; and unperfumed imported soap, 25 livres a pound.

French colonists washed clothing as they did in France at that time, by dipping it in a stream or bayou or wooden tub, then scrubbing it with a coarse brush or pounding it with short-handled paddles. Soap was made at home of ashes and waste fats and was so strong and hard on the skin that women rubbed their faces and hands with bear or sheep fat to soften them. Only people of means could afford perfumed soaps, creams, and lotions.

FOOD AND FOOD SUPPLIES. During the early years as well as in many of the later years of the French regime, Louisiana depended upon imported food supplies from France, which consisted largely of salt meat, flour, rice, and beans. When supply ships did not arrive, the ordinary citizen had to subsist on meager supplies of corn, vegetables, wild nuts, fruits, and game. During periods of extreme scarcity the most common diet was *gru* and wild meats, or *sagamite*. *Gru* was boiled corn meal, perhaps seasoned with a little fat, while *sagamite* was corn meal, fat, and meat cooked together, sometimes with nuts, vegetables, or fruit added. Occasionally *sagamite* was made into patties in the same manner as corn cakes, and parched corn meal was mixed with beans and boiled, a dish Du Pratz called *cooëdlou*.

J. Hanno Deiler writes feelingly of how the poor early German settlers, when their work was done in the fields, had to grind the corn or rice for the evening meal with a *pilon,* hand mill, or pounding trough. There was no domesticated meat for their tables because they had no poultry, beef, or pork; their diet consisted mainly of rice, corn, and beans, in varying order and in different combinations. It was not long, however, before the Germans began to eat well, better than other colonists; for their gardens, orchards, fields, and grazing lands produced all sorts of foodstuffs.

The prosperous citizen's breakfast was a light meal at sunrise. Dinner, at noon, was the most important meal of the day; soups, various meats, vegetables, and fruits were served. For supper the family ate the leftovers from dinner or had a stew or soup.

Bread was baked out of doors in large, rounded clay ovens. Meats were salted, smoked, dried, or partially cooked and put into large jars and covered over with hot fat, which then cooled and preserved it. Butter was made by whipping the cream with a spoon or shaking it in a bottle, for there were few churns in French Louisiana. Wild honey instead of sugar was generally used for sweetening. Meats were boiled, roasted over open fires or in small ovens, or fried in hog lard or bear's fat. Cucumbers served raw in cream and roasted pumpkin topped with honey were favorite dishes.

The larger villages and towns had open-air markets. During good seasons all kinds of vegetables, fruits, meats, and fish were sold, most of the food supplies of New Orleans being furnished by the Germans from above the town. Although there was no meat inspection during the early years, regulations specified that it should be of sound quality and as advertised. In 1723, Robert Villeneuve was tried and convicted of having sold the cooked meat of dogs to patients of the hospital. He was sentenced to be paraded around the city on a wooden horse for two hours wearing a dead cat around his neck and bearing a sign reading "Master Eater of Dogs and Cats." By 1735 all game had to be inspected before sale in New Orleans, and two years later an ordinance required permits before slaughtering, inspection before selling, and fixed the prices of meats.

Weights were standardized in 1728. A hogshead of meat must weigh 360 pounds; a barrel or cask, 240 pounds; a *quintal,* 180 pounds; and an *ancre,* 90 pounds. From time to time, particularly during food scarcity, prices for staple items were fixed by the government; but although officials tried to enforce the ordinances, there were much profiteering and violation of regulations.

During good crop years, even as early as the 1720's, there was an astonishing variety of foodstuffs sold in New Orleans. One of the Ursuline Sisters in a letter listed geese, fowls, ducks, pheasants, partridges, wild beef, venison, swans, catfish, carp, bass, salmon, and other varieties of fish, peas, beans, rice, potatoes, eggplant, corn meal, flour, pecans, figs, bananas, pumpkins, watermelons, pineapples, and other fruits and vegetables.

The colonists consumed large quantities of wines and various liquors; drunkenness had become such a problem by 1726 that the Superior Council enacted the first of a series of ordinances regulating liquor sales and requiring all dramshops to be closed on Sundays while Mass was in progress. The following year another ordinance forbade the selling of liquor to slaves, and soon Indians were included on the prohibited list. But the liquor laws and regulations were never well enforced.

Cistern, well, or river water was the most common beverage. Lieutenant Philip Pittman of the British army reported on Mississippi River water during the 1760's: "I have filled a half-pint tumbler with it, and have found a sediment of two inches of slime. It is, notwithstanding, extremely wholesome and well tasted, and very cool in the hottest seasons of the year. . . . The inhabitants of New Orleans use no other water than that of the river, which, by keeping in a jar, becomes perfectly clear."

THE STATE OF PUBLIC HEALTH. Bad food, exposure, the almost complete lack of ordinary sanitation, impure drinking water, poor housing conditions, and the scarcity of good doctors led to an unusual amount of disease, which carried off hundreds and even thousands of the newly arrived immigrants. Diseases of the stomach or intestines and tuberculosis were the most common. From time to time some diseases, such as *la grippe*, smallpox, yellow fever, malaria, mumps, various fevers, and others, became epidemic and ravaged the entire colony.

The government made few regulations concerning public health. Perier was probably the first governor to issue what might be termed a sanitary ordinance for New Orleans. He decided that the prevailing sickness was caused by the dense forests; so in order to permit "proper ventilation of the city," he began the task of clearing the land between the town and Lake Pontchartrain, a project which was never completed. By 1732 an ordinance required the citizens to dig drainage ditches around their houses and a few years later another required the weeds to be cut. No regulations were issued, however, concerning wells, cisterns, or open privies.

While it was French government policy to provide a doctor for each post or sizable settlement, the faraway colony did not attract enough physicians to make this possible. Doctors were paid about 500 livres a year in Louisiana proper and 1,000 livres in the Illinois country, but they soon found that they could make more in private practice than in working for a proprietor or for the King. They were a temperamental lot, sometimes took advantage of their position, and often dressed as dandies, as did the post doctor at Natchitoches about 1730, who wore "colors to shame the cardinal."

Doctors charged a fixed price for each call or for each treatment or medication, or contracted by the year, usually at the rate of about 10 livres per year per person. Bleeding averaged 5 livres; dressings, 3 livres; pills, 1½ livres; purging, 2½ livres; and a good cordial, 4 livres. They carried in their bags a kitchen knife with case, surgeon's scissors in a small tin box, a syringe in a case, a razor or two, a dozen lancets, and a few other items. They seldom performed autopsies nor did they ordinarily handle obstetrical cases, which were left to midwives.

Used in treatment of disease were numerous drugs and alleged drugs, including sarsaparilla, manna, mercury, antimony, rhubarb, balm of Mecca, coral, crab's eyes, Landel lozenges, senna, brandy, Epsom salts, oil of sweet almonds, licorice syrup, ipecac, turpentine, chicory syrup, extract of hyacinth, maidenhair fern, and opiates for the repose of the patient "and his neighbors at night."

Having little respect for the doctors and their practice of medicine, priests treated diseases through prayer, novenas, and the application of reliquaries and relics. Father Gravier thus reported one successful fever cure: "I promised God, jointly with Pierre de bonne, who had a violent tertian fever for a long time, to recite for 9 days some prayers in honor of Father François Regis, whose relics I have." The man's paroxysms eventually ceased, and "he has had none since." On a later occasion he used a "small piece of Father François Regis's hat," which "is the most infallible remedy that I know of for curing all kinds of fever."

The first hospital was built in Mobile about 1713, and from that time hospitals were maintained at the larger towns and posts. New Orleans had a small military hospital sometime prior to 1722, and the Ursuline convent and hospital was built in 1734. A sailor named Jean Louis, who died in 1736, provided in his will that after the payment of his debts and personal bequests totaling 500 livres, the remainder of his estate should "be applied in founding an infirmary for the sick of New Orleans." The $2,500 bequest launched the charity-hospital movement in Louisiana.

RELIGION. Roman Catholicism was the only religion permitted in the Louisiana colony. The movement for religious freedom begun in the sixteenth century in France had won significant success with the Edict of Nantes, which granted some concessions, in 1598; but the Edict was revoked in 1685, and thereafter religious freedom made little if any progress. In the colony, as in the Mother Country, there was a close alliance between Church and state. The Louisiana church was supported by governmental subsidies and by forced assessments and contributions from each citizen, which at times were collected only after successful lawsuits brought by the Church and tried before the Superior Council. No dissenters of any faith were permitted to migrate to Louisiana during the entire French period; even the French Huguenots, who petitioned for official permission to migrate from France or from the Carolinas, where they had settled after the revocation of the Edict of Nantes, were rejected.

Priests accompanied Iberville on his voyage of settlement, and after that time came to the colony in comparatively small numbers. It is believed that the first mission was built in late 1699 or early 1700 by Father Paul du Ru near the junction of Bayou Goula and the Mississippi. Father Joseph de Limoges and Father Anthony Davion arrived from Canada in 1700, worked for a time with Father du Ru, and established missions among the Houmas, Tunica, Avoyel, and Natchez tribes. Soon small churches were built at Biloxi and Mobile.

Louisiana was under the ecclesiastical jurisdiction of the Bishop of Quebec, and after 1722 the Capuchins, Carmelites, and Jesuits were given charge of different areas in the Mississippi Valley. The Capuchins received the Isle of Orleans and the territory west of the Mississippi and northward to the mouth of the Ohio, the Carmelites the area east of the Mississippi and northward to the Ohio, and the Jesuits all of the country north of the Ohio. When the Carmelites failed to furnish a sufficient number of priests, their territory was turned over to the Jesuits. Soon the Jesuits and Capuchins began to disagree over jurisdictional matters and over the control of the Ursulines; by 1755 the quarrel had almost reached the stage of religious warfare. Meanwhile the Jesuits had lost favor in France, and by 1762 their colleges were closed. In July, 1763, the Superior Council banned the order; their chapels were razed, their sacred property was turned over to the Capuchins, and their extensive lands and other holdings were sold for the benefit of the King's treasury. In 1764 the Jesuit Fathers embarked for France.

Contrary to their excellent record in Canada and the Great Lakes region, the Church and the orders could not be proud of their achievements in Louisiana. Despite the notable efforts of many individual priests, little was done until the Company of the Indies acquired possession of the colony; after the 1720's the French Capuchins lost their aggressiveness, which was so well displayed by Spanish Fathers of various orders in Mexico and California. Neither did the Jesuits accomplish much in Louisiana compared to what they had done farther north. As late as 1738, Father Mathurin Le Petit wrote to Rome: "Here in New Orleans, the chief, or rather the only city of this vast region, we count two priests, living with two lay brothers." After the fight began between the Capuchins and the Jesuits, the colonists frequently became involved in the disputes, and as Henry P. Dart wrote, "the effect upon the white people of the Colony was disastrous." Although the Louisianians were practicing Catholics, they did not receive enough priests to care adequately for their spiritual needs, while many towns and villages had no church.

Daily services were held in the existing churches, and on Sundays High Mass was sung. During the harvest season, Sunday vespers were held right after Mass so that the men could return to the fields. Every family had its own pew or bench seat which was rented by the year, and the family's social position was indicated by its location in the church; important families sat directly in front of the sanctuary, near the altar.

More than twenty-five holy days of obligation were celebrated each year, and on these days the Blessed Sacrament was carried along the streets and roads. The parish priest was closer to the people than the district or post commandant, for he received their confessions, granted them absolution, officiated at their baptisms, announced their marriage banns and performed the ceremonies, administered extreme unction, presided at their religious festivals, took active part in their holiday functions and entertainments, and as Robert Dabney Calhoun wrote, "was counselor to the literate and adviser, accountant and scribe to the unlettered."

SOCIAL CUSTOMS. French-Indian marriages were common during the early years, particularly in the northern sections; they were not so prevalent along the lower Mississippi or in the southern sections of the colony. Mixed marriages had about ceased by the end of the French period, although many of the colonists by this time had Indian blood. In 1728 the Canadian Superior Council ordered that Indian widows be paid an annual pension from the income of the husband's property, and this order apparently was applied to Louisiana. The protest which followed resulted in a French edict prohibiting Indian-white marriages without the consent of the post commandant or a higher official. Father René Tartarin protested that this simply resulted in cohabitation without marriage, that there were many young Frenchmen who were openly living with their Indian slaves "to the scandal of the community," and that the "bastards" were left without education or any hope of an inheritance. There is no evidence that the edict was ever revoked.

Mixed marriages between whites and Negroes was forbidden, but there were numerous cases of owners cohabiting with female slaves. Frequently the women and the children were freed and inherited the man's property, although many of the women and their half-white children remained slaves, and at the father's death were sold along with the rest of his property.

Marriages occurred at an early age, and youthful widows and widowers were not unusual. Many of them, however, did not remain single long. In a few cases the official inventory of the dead spouse's estate and the new marriage contract were drawn up on the same day, the banns were dispensed with by an understanding priest, and the marriage was performed. Marriage contracts were a universal practice. A community property was established, which consisted of all the movable property owned by the two signers on the day of their marriage, to be managed by the husband, though the wife might renounce the agreement and take back her property along with her dowry at any time. The contract also included provisions regarding inheritance, especially of children by a former marriage.

Breach-of-promise suits were not uncommon. One of the suits for which there is a rather complete record was filed by Corentine Millon against Jacques Carrière de Maloze on August 28, 1730. The lady stated that she had signed a marriage contract with Maloze, that the banns had been published, but that Maloze "now refuses to fulfill his promises; let him be sentenced to fulfill the same." A week later she testified that Maloze's change of heart was due to "slanderous reports on her character," and she would have the charges proved or else he should "pay fine of 10,000 francs." The case dragged on until February 9, 1731, when Mademoiselle Millon finally won her suit.

Extant records of divorce suits leave no doubt that they were common in the colony and that they were at least tolerated by the Church. Some cases were settled to the satisfaction of both parties through the good offices of the Council members; others were fought to a decision. Françoise Richard Debat, for example, won separation by charging that her husband had, in a fury and without cause, "ill treated her with kicks and punches and bruised her body black as a hat, as well as her face, and damaged her eye."

When Madame de Membrede, wife of a captain of infantry (the record of the case does not give their full names), accused her husband of "appropriating her children's goods from their father's estate, of cruelty, and abuse towards her" the captain frankly answered the charges in open hearing. He asserted that "Mme. de Membrede entered into contract of marriage without wishing to bear its yoke, that she had no idea of the obedience a wife owes her husband. As to the marks on her face: The scratches were inflicted by herself and the lump came from her curiosity. Talking with a friend and not supposing that she had put her ear to the door, he opened it to go to his room and she was struck by the latch. He had treated her with all the gentleness and tenderness to be expected from a husband, remonstrating with her for extravagance; if her life was ever in danger, it was through illness, when he cared for her with assiduity, and not through any attacks by him, which can be proved by surgeons and physicians." The Council ruled that the plaintiff's proofs were "nonconclusive" and dismissed the suit.

Funeral costs varied with the social status and wealth of the deceased; and funeral details were all handled by a priest, who submitted an account to the Superior Council in New Orleans or to the post commandant for approval before payment. The priest sometimes fixed the payments to be made to the Church, but ordinarily the family made a gift in proportion to its ability to pay. Suicides and executed criminals were buried without religious services. In the suicide case of one Labarre, cited by Gayarré but which cannot now be found among the records, the body "was indicted, tried, convicted and sentenced to be deprived of Christian burial, and to lie rotting and blackening on the face of the earth among the offals, bones, and refuse of the butcher's stall."

CULTURE AND EDUCATION. As has been mentioned previously, during the early years many Louisiana colonists had no intention of making permanent homes; rather they meant to get rich as quickly as possible from fur trading or mining and then return to France. The forced immigrants of the Company of the Indies were "sentenced to Louisiana"; they did not come of their own free will nor were they the type to be interested in things educational or cultural. The German settlers were for the most part poor and illiterate, and were unable to rise above this status throughout the French period. The Louisianians in no way compared with the British settlers along the Atlantic seaboard in their ambition for education and culture.

The Church, which should have fostered education and culture, was never strong enough to accomplish much, for the orders quarreled, too few priests were sent to the colony, and most of those who came, at least after the first two decades, were far too complaisant to exert themselves beyond routine parish duties.

It has been claimed that the first Louisiana school was opened by Capuchin monk, Father Cecilius de Rochfort, at New Orleans about 1723, for the good Father taught the boys who lived in the immediate vicinity of his church, though it is not known for how long. In 1725, Capuchin Father Raphaël de Luxembourg wrote to his superior: "I have just made an establishment for a little school at New Orleans. To direct it I have found a man who knows Latin, mathematics, drawing and singing [and] whose handwriting is fairly good. . . . He is of our order and left it through a thoughtlessness of youth." It is barely possible that Father Raphaël was referring to Father Cecilius de Rochfort. However, the school did not grow, and in 1731, Father Raphaël admitted that the project had been a failure and asked to be relieved of its financial obligations.

After discussing the educational problem with Father Nicolas Ignatius de Beaubois, the Jesuit superior in Louisiana, Bienville presented a proposal to the Company of the Indies, and in 1726 an agreement was signed with the French Ursulines whereby they promised to send a group of Sisters to the colony. In August, 1727, twelve of the Ursulines, led by Mother Maria Tranchepain de Saint Augustine, arrived at New Orleans, were given Bienville's house, and immediately went to work. They established in this house the first girl's school in the present-day United States. Their new building was not completed until 1734, a short time after Mother Tranchepain's death. Here for the next ninety years the Ursulines ministered to the sick, reared orphans, and educated white, colored, and Indian girls.

There was little or no education outside of New Orleans, Mobile, Biloxi, and a few of the larger towns. For a time at least Jean François Richelme was a teacher at Dauphin Island, but the names and records of other teachers, if any, are as yet undiscovered. In most cases the parish priest taught the few children sent by their parents a little reading and perhaps some arithmetic. Most boys and girls, whose parents were unable to afford tutors, grew to adulthood unable to read or write. The New England or Virginia schoolhouse did not have a counterpart in French Louisiana.

Few books were imported into the colony, and the extant records would seem to indicate that only a small number of the colonists possessed many books; a few inventories of estates do however reveal that some of the more wealthy planters and city dwellers owned them. There were a few booksellers in New Orleans during the later years of the French period, but they apparently sold books only as a sideline. The first printer, although a Frenchman, did not establish his press until after the beginning of the Spanish period.

The first theatrical performance in the colony was supposedly given at Governor Kerlerec's residence in 1753, an amateur production titled *Le Père Indien* (The Indian Father). The play was later written in blank verse by Le Blanc de Ville-neuve, one of the military officers, and had subsequent performances. There were apparently several other amateur productions during the later years of Governor Kerlerec's administration.

Art was practically unknown, although map makers accompanied many of the early explorers of the colony. Legend has it that a Spanish artist named Miguel Garcia accompanied Iberville on one of his trips to the colony, but the first known artist signed his crude Indian sketches "A. de Batz." A few other Louisianians sketched or painted, but their work was of little consequence.

Practically all of the literature of the period is in the nature of chronicle writing, by men who either lived or traveled in the colony, and their writings, with very few exceptions, were not published until after 1762. Henri de Tonti, Henri Joutel, Father Louis Hennepin, André Pénicaut, Father Paul du Ru, Father Pierre François Charlevoix, Bernard de la Harpe, Diron d'Artaguette, Le Page du Pratz, Captain Jean Bossu, Dumont de Montigny, Sister Madeline Hachard, and several others were letter writers, diarists, keepers of journals, annalists, recorders of Indian customs, or writers of natural history and geographical descriptions.

Such music as there was in the colony was that of the Church and the old folk songs of France, many of which were given new words to make them fit the Louisiana scene. Amateur musicians played in the home and for rural or city dances on violins or other stringed instruments, blew a few types of horns, or beat on percussion instruments, many of which had been adopted from the Indians.

AMUSEMENTS. Most of the amusements centered around the Church and its many holy and fete days. Christmas was celebrated with much revelry, beginning with the Midnight Mass on Christmas Eve, after which the people went to different homes for *Le Réveillon,* the great Christmas breakfast. On Christmas morning there was another Mass, and afterwards dinners and parties in the evening. On New Year's Eve many of the people dressed in costume, put on masks, and headed by a man playing a violin, paraded through the village or along the streets of the larger towns. St. Nicolas *(Le Père Noël)* visited the children on the Twelfth Night and left gifts, and the following morning everyone enjoyed a holiday breakfast and then visited their friends and neighbors.

The Carnival season began on the eve of Epiphany, and in many villages the girls were hostesses to the boys at a pancake party. After this, party followed party until Ash Wednesday put a complete stop to the festivities. Mid-Lent, or *La Mi-Carême* as they called it, was a sort of "half-way station on the penitential journey," and then there were more parties. In August the colonists celebrated the feast of St. Louis and brought out their best wine with which to toast the King. Other days were opportunities for strenuous merrymaking.

The favorite French festivity was the party or ball, given at every opportunity and for any reason. The parties and balls were under the general direction of provosts, and some elderly and much respected grandsire or grandam had charge of the various ceremonials, while the village priest saw to it that the affair was conducted with dignity and propriety and that all went home at a decent hour. While the dancing was in progress, the slaves held their own ball nearby and the children played games in another room or in the yard—"Hide the ring," "In my hand I hold a rose tree," or "To whom shall we marry her?"—to the accompaniment of patter songs.

Some of the balls had more ceremonious beginnings. On New Year's Eve the young men of a village, costumed as beggars, paraded along the streets, entered the houses, petitioned their sweethearts for bread, and after being fed invited the girls to the New Year's Ball. The King Ball was held about a week after New Year. Cakes were baked into which four beans were deposited, and the four men who drew the slices with the beans became kings of the ball, each selecting his queen. The King Ball had many variations in the villages and communities of French Louisiana.

Organized sports were unknown, and athletic contests were few and of the ordinary rural varieties, but there was much hunting and fishing. These sports of course had the threefold purpose of providing meat and fish for the family larder, sport for the hunter or fisherman, and the excuse for game dinners and fish fries.

In the towns and villages there was a great deal of social drinking, a practice not so prevalent in rural districts. Taverns, where both food and drink were served, developed early in the colony; and by the 1720's cabarets, which sold only drinks, were operating in New Orleans. One of the first cabarets was opened by the Chevalier de Pradel and Nicolas Chauvin de la Frenière in 1729. By the next decade New Orleans was well supplied with taverns and cabarets and the Superior Council was receiving complaints of peace disturbances.

In 1746 the Council limited the number of taverns to six, not including the Swiss and French army canteens, and stipulated that licenses were to be sold to the highest bidder, the money paid in quarterly payments, and the proceeds given to the hospital for the poor of the city. Further, taverns were prohibiting from selling "any drink to the inhabitants or to the slaves under the penalty of Two Hundred Livres and confiscation of all drinks found in the premises." Five years later taverns were again permitted to sell liquors, but under comprehensive regulations. They were not to supply wine or spirits to soldiers, Indians, or Negroes, but were permitted to sell such items to "travellers, sick people, the inhabitants, and seafaring men; and this they must do with the requisite moderation." They must not "retail refreshments" on Sundays and other holidays during divine worship, must close at nine in the evening, and must pay 200 livres to the Church and 100 livres to the poor for the privilege of operating. The new regulations, however, were generally ignored, and New Orleans remained a wide-open town throughout the French period.

Throughout the colony the typical French colonist was a carefree, good-humored, and even a gay and spirited individual. He worried comparatively little about the future, for the future would take care of itself. He enjoyed life and within the limitations of his environment took advantage of every opportunity to enjoy social intercourse with his fellow men; in this aspect of his existence he achieved considerably more success than did the British colonist of the Atlantic seaboard.

PART THREE

Spanish
Colonial Louisiana

CHAPTER 9

EARLY YEARS OF SPANISH
LOUISIANA

FRENCH REMAIN IN POSSESSION OF LOUISIANA. Although the Isle of Orleans and that portion of Louisiana west of the Mississippi River had been transferred to Spain by the secret Treaty of Fontainebleau on November 3, 1762, the colony remained under French control until the arrival of Spanish Governor Don Antonio de Ulloa on March 5, 1766. Meanwhile, on February 10, 1763, by the Treaty of Paris, Great Britain had acquired from Spain both East and West Florida and from France that portion of Louisiana north of the Isle of Orleans and east of the Mississippi River.

Those were troubled days in Louisiana. The colony was still small, totaling perhaps between 6,000 and 7,500 persons, with its settlements scattered along the various waterways in a triangle from Natchitoches to Mobile to New Orleans. The years of French neglect showed in generally bad economic and other conditions. Trade and commerce had declined, while the paper money which had flooded the colony was practically worthless. Farmers and planters could not sell their products. The Capuchins and Jesuits were engaged in the struggle which soon ended in the expulsion of the Jesuits from the colony. Vincent de Rochemore, the Commissary-Commissioner, accused Kerlerec of stealing from the treasury and of being a dictator, and Kerlerec in turn charged Rochemore with theft and with neglecting his duties. The colonists had until the arrival of Kerlerec enjoyed almost complete freedom; now, under his tightening of governmental control, they had grown increasingly insubordinate and rebellious.

Finally, in the spring of 1763, Kerlerec was recalled to France and three officials were appointed to conduct Louisiana affairs until the Spanish took possession of their colony—Jean Jacques Blaise d'Abbadie, Comptroller General; Nicolas Chauvin de la Frenière, Attorney General; and Nicolas Denis Foucault, Intendant. The new Comptroller General, whom most Louisiana historians have by courtesy called "Governor," was the son of a French naval official and had seen long years of service in various departments of the French government. He described his colony in one of his reports as having been in a state of more-or-less-constant disorder since 1737, saying that its financial condition was deplorable, that the people were lazy, insubordinate, drank too much, and that about three-fourths of them were "in a state of insolvency." He was optimistic, however, for he wrote that "everything will again be set to right."

Although D'Abbadie had an army of only about three hundred men, he strengthened the defenses of the colony. He permitted English ships to go up the Mississippi to the English posts of Manchac (at the mouth of Bayou Manchac), Baton Rouge, St. Francisville, and Natchez, and closed his eyes to their trading activities. Soon economic conditions began to improve, for the colonists sold their products to the British for good prices.

Meanwhile, the French of Louisiana continued to live as if they were French rather than Spanish colonists, and the Fleur-de-Lis still floated over New Orleans and the towns, villages, and posts. The feast of St. Louis was celebrated in July, 1763, with the booming of 123 cannon shots, and the following year with 125. J. H. Schlarman writes that during this period Louisiana and the Illinois country constituted "a sort of No Man's Land, a Fools' Paradise, where no one really had authority," and that it was soon to become a land where "bold and arrogant men unwarrantedly forced to the front and became bastard heroes for the moment."

Then on September 9, 1764, D'Abbadie recorded in his diary: "By the departure of the ship *l'Angelique,* Captain Gariele going to the Cape, I rendered my account to the Minister of all that had transpired here . . . and sent my correspondence." The ship *Meder* arrived the following day, bringing to D'Abbadie from the French Minister a dispatch to which was "joined the Act of Cession to the King of Spain of all the part of Louisiana which remains to us and of the Island and the City of New Orleans." The dispatch ordered D'Abbadie to return to France immediately upon arrival of the Spanish representative, bringing all his records and the officials and soldiers who wished to leave Louisiana.

The next month the Governor informed the people of the cession and explained his orders for closing out French affairs in the colony. They received the news with dismay. They had lived under the flag of France for over sixty-five years and considered themselves just as much Frenchmen as if they had lived in Paris, La Rochelle, or Bordeaux. They had lived under pioneer conditions allowing them considerable personal freedom or in an atmosphere of general governmental laxity in more settled areas, but they had heard that Spain governed her colonies with a tight rein. They did not know that Spain had already decided not to include Louisiana in the Spanish colonial-empire organization or that the Spanish Ambassador at Versailles had consulted with former Governor Kerlerec as to the "population, products, abilities of the inhabitants, method of government, administration of justice, ecclesiastical organization, commerce, and troops," and various other matters pertaining to the Louisiana colony. There was no doubt, however, as to the genuineness of the treaty of cession or of the instructions to D'Abbadie for turning the colony over to the representative of the Spanish Crown when he should arrive.

JEAN MILHET SENT TO FRANCE. The colonists in New Orleans and the immediate vicinity held a mass meeting, attended by a number of prominent citizens, and La Frenière and others made stirring speeches which inflamed the New Orleans populace. Surely the King did not know what had been done. He must be informed, and quickly. Jean Milhet, a wealthy merchant, was selected to carry a petition to the King, urging him to regain possession of Louisiana.

The months passed. The Fleur-de-Lis still floated from the roof of the Governor's palace. The people of New Orleans continued to hold meetings, but as the days passed and the Spanish representative did not appear, many of them lost interest. D'Abbadie's health, considerably aggravated by the many problems of his office, began a rapid decline, and on February 4, 1765, he died. He had been a patriotic and just governor, and now the people began to appreciate his work and his true character. They held a mass meeting and paid tribute to his memory.

Governor D'Abbadie was succeeded by Captain Charles Philippe Aubry, the senior military officer in the colony. He had been a valiant soldier, had won the Cross of St. Louis, possessed some social graces, and had many friends in the colony among the wealthy and official classes; but he lacked strong character and real ability, and did not measure up to the situations he had to face. One of his contemporaries wrote graphically: "M. Aubry was a little, dry, lean, ugly man, without nobility, dignity, or carriage. His face would seem to announce a hypocrite, but in him this vice sprang from excessive goodness, which granted all rather than displease; always trembling for the consequences of the most indifferent action, a natural effect of a mind without resource of light, always allowing itself to be guided, and thus often swerving from rectitude; religious through weakness rather than from principle; incapable of wishing evil, but doing it through a charitable human weakness; destitute of magnanimity or reflection; a good soldier, but a bad leader; ambitious of honors and dignity, but possessing neither firmness nor capacity to bear the weight."

Aubry soon wrote to France that the government of the colony "in its present condition is a very thorny proposition; it is very difficult to find means of contenting at one and the same time the French, the English, and the savages. I am trying as far as it lies in me to maintain tranquillity between all and to prepare the way for the Spaniards. It is time, my lord, that the Spaniards arrive." He continued to vacillate and to try to please everyone.

Jean Milhet, meanwhile, had proceeded to Paris, where he immediately called on Bienville. Although the aged former Governor had not been in Louisiana since 1743, he still loved the colony. When he and Milhet went to see the King, Louis XV would not receive them. Finally they were granted an interview with the Duke de Choiseul, the Prime Minister, but despite Bienville's pathetic appeal, the Duke refused to alter his resolution concerning the colony. He said to them: "Is it not better, then, that Louisiana should be given away to a friend and faithful ally, than be wrenched from us by an hereditary foe? Farewell. You have my best wishes; I can do no more."

At first the people refused to believe Milhet when he said France would do nothing for them; then they became angry and the streets of New Orleans throbbed with the sounds of marching, shouting citizens. Mobs, however, do not retain their entity for long, and the marching and the shouting soon ceased. The average colonist soon forgot about the whole business; outside of those living in New Orleans and its immediate vicinity, none had been much excited anyway.

But a small group still plotted; La Frenière, Joseph Rouer de Villeré, Nicolas Foucault, Joseph Milhet, Pierre Caresse, Jean Noyan, and a few others. It is believed that they met near the corner of present-day Carondelet and Common streets at the elegant estate of the widow of the Chevalier Jean de Pradel, who, it was whispered, was secretly in love with Foucault. Here, according to Grace King, "after a luxurious supper, they would . . . discuss the situation, and prepare, point by point, the policy to be adopted."

GOVERNOR ULLOA AND THE REBELLION OF 1768. Late in the summer of 1765 a letter from Havana addressed to the Superior Council arrived at New Orleans. Don Antonio de Ulloa wrote that he had been appointed to take possession of Louisiana in the name of His Catholic Majesty and would soon arrive. But as the months passed and Ulloa did not appear, the conspirators gained confidence and boldly continued with their plans.

At last on March 5, 1766, the new Spanish Governor landed at New Orleans in the midst of a violent rainstorm, accompanied by several Capuchin friars, eighty soldiers, and a few officials, including Juan José de Loyola, Commissary of War; Esteban Gayarré, Comptroller; and Martin Navarro, Treasurer. The Governor brought his commission from the King, which stated specifically that "for the present, no change in the system of its government shall be undertaken" in the colony. Ulloa was received by an indifferent populace with superficial good will, respect, and courtesy, and by the French officials with the homage due his rank and position. He presented his papers to Aubry, and the cession of Louisiana to Spain was duly and officially registered by the Superior Council.

Ulloa was fifty years of age. He had been trained at the Royal Academy of Midshipmen, showing considerable ability in science. Upon graduation he was sent to South America, where he spent ten years organizing the naval defenses of Peru and Chile and assisting an expedition of the Paris Academy of Sciences in measuring an arc of the meridian at the equator. On his return voyage he was captured by the English, but English scientists secured his release and elected him to membership in the Royal Society of London. Back in Spain he did scientific research, founded a metallurgical laboratory and an observatory, and discovered the crater in the moon which bears his name. In addition, he planned the Castile Canal, supervised the drafting of an accurate map of the Iberian Peninsula, and fostered improvements in printing and clothmaking. By the time he completed these activities he was considered one of the greatest scientists of Europe.

Unfortunately, his appearance was against him, for he was a small, thin man, with an unpleasant voice, an almost "unbearable forced laugh," suspicious eyes and a hypocritical air, and an excitable and nervous temperament. He was absent-minded and at times forgot his diplomatic and courtly manners with the proper-mannered French officials. His Catholic Majesty could not have chosen a man worse fitted to inaugurate Spanish government in Louisiana.

Ulloa had a purse of about 150,000 pesos with which to pay an army enlisted from the Louisiana troops and citizens, his own soldiers, and other general expenses. Since the Spanish at the moment did not have troops readily available, French Prime Minister Choiseul generously offered to permit French soldiers to enlist in the Spanish service. The soldiers refused, however, despite the urgings of Aubry and Foucault.

After issuing orders regarding troop discipline which were much stricter than any the French had heretofore known in Louisiana, Ulloa left New Orleans on a tour of inspection. His subsequent report was not one to cheer the government that had only recently acquired the colony. There was not a building in the entire colony which did not "need repair," and many needed rebuilding. Many churches were in ruins, as were most government buildings and warehouses. It would be "necessary to rebuild the principal church of the city [New Orleans], as the present one is so threatened with ruin that it has been decided to remove the Holy Sacrament and place it in a guard house." A run-down stockade was the only defense of New Orleans. The post at the Balize must be rebuilt.

Don Antonio's inspection of his colony was so thorough that Governor George Johnstone of British West Florida wrote that "Mr. Ulloa has been Examining every Part of the Province as narrowly as a Jew does his Bride & still seems in doubt. He is undoubtedly a man of Indefatigable Genius & Industry tho there is something Piddling in the Mechanical Part."

Soon Ulloa wrote back to Spain that "without inhabitants there can be no commerce, and without commerce few inhabitants," and after consultation with Aubry proclaimed a new commercial ordinance. This ordinance, one of the principal causes of the later rebellion, fixed prices for the benefit of the consumer against the merchants, forced French ship captains to accept Louisiana money in payment for their goods, stipulated that returning ships should carry a cargo of Louisiana goods in proportion to the cargo brought in, and required French ships to secure passports at a Spanish port before coming to Louisiana. While the ordinance benefited the average colonist, it cut deeply into the excessive profits of merchants and conniving French ex-officials.

Ulloa parceled out his soldiers to the different posts of the colony. They were sent to build forts opposite the mouth of Bayou Manchac, at the site of present-day Vidalia, and at the mouth of the Missouri River. One detachment was sent to build Fort Real Catolica on an island near the Balize at the mouth of the Mississippi.

An affair of a personal nature which colored the Governor's behavior at social functions further increased his problems. His bride by proxy marriage, Francisca Ramírez de Laredo, the Marquesa d'Abrado, was to arrive shortly from Peru. As soon as his duties permitted he went to the Balize to await her arrival and there, according to the report, they were again married by the Governor's chaplain. The French Creoles of New Orleans society were outraged, for they had planned a formal state wedding in the capital, and when Ulloa brought his wife to New Orleans they proceeded to cut her cold. Whereupon, as Grace King writes, she "immured herself in her hotel, associated only with her own attendants, repulsed all advances from society, shunned the Creole ladies publicly, ignored them privately, and would not even worship in a common church with them, attending Mass only in her private chapel." The breach widened between the Governor and the French.

Meanwhile, according to historian James E. Winston, the "some dozen factionists" of New Orleans and the immediate vicinity, "blinded by passion, self-interest and the hope of re-establishing their fortunes by a revolution," continued their conspiracy. In March, 1768, another commercial ordinance, which had originated in Madrid, was proclaimed. The illegal trade with the British must be stopped, trade from France could come to Louisiana only via Spanish ports, and wine could be imported only from Spain—now Louisianians must drink the "vin abominable de Catalogne." Here was an opportunity to inflame the people, so the conspirators redoubled their efforts.

Ulloa tried to be a good colonial administrator, although he had not publicly assumed the governorship. While waiting at the Balize for his bride, Don Antonio had worked out an unusual governmental arrangement with Aubry. The French flag was to fly at New Orleans, but the Spanish colors would fly over all other towns and posts in the colony. Government orders would be given by Ulloa through Aubry or by Aubry in the name of the King of Spain. By his influence over Ulloa, Aubry thus became the most important governing official in the colony and remained so throughout Ulloa's regime.

Ulloa strove to help economic conditions by trying to raise the value of French money, then circulating at about 25 per cent of face value, permitting smuggling with the British to continue, making tours of inspection, assisting the Acadians by giving them land, livestock, tools, and supplies, and abrogating some of the harsh features of the slave code. Although he achieved success in these endeavors, on October 26, 1768, he wrote back to Spain that what the French Creoles wanted was "military or political employment according to the fancy of each, highly comfortable and lucrative at the expense of the King. They desire liberty in everything, and that the Sovereign be so only in expenditures but not in authority with the country said to belong to Spain, and the people to France."

The guns at the gates of New Orleans were spiked the night of October 27. A convention of merchants, tradesmen, and a few planters met the next day to draw up a petition demanding the expulsion of the Spanish and the restoration of their former freedom of trade. That afternoon a mob of about four hundred milled about the streets. Upon the advice of Aubry, Ulloa hurriedly set up headquarters aboard a Spanish frigate anchored at the wharf. He wrote to Spain that "the insurgents" planned to attack his house that night and "carry off everything of value." The mob demonstrated again on the morning of October 29, but the Superior Council refused to consider the convention's petition until the mob had dispersed. The defiant crowd scattered, and despite Aubry's formal protest, the Council passed a decree ordering Ulloa and the Spanish troops to leave the colony within three days.

Beyond making the formal protest to the Council, Aubry had done nothing to stop the rebellion. Ulloa requested the mobilization of the hundred-odd soldiers in the city, and Aubry actually ordered cartridges issued, then wavered and tried to settle the matter by arbitration. He conferred separately with La Frenière, Foucault, and Ulloa, but La Frenière would not alter his decision and Foucault answered questions ambiguously. Indecisive Aubry wrung his hands and did nothing.

For years loyal Frenchmen of Louisiana told this story of Ulloa's departure from New Orleans. It was on the night of either October 31 or November 1, and a group of citizens returning from a wedding went to the wharf where his ship was tied up. In their eagerness to see the last of the Spaniard, they sang French songs and yelled: "Long live the King! Long live Louis—the-Well-Beloved! Long live the wine of

Bordeaux! Down with the fish of Spain!" Then a man named Petit cut the mooring cables of Ulloa's ship, setting it adrift on the Mississippi. For a long time historians told the story as fact, but it is now thought to be only a legend. At any rate, after a short wait at the Balize, Ulloa sailed for Cuba on November 16.

Overly patriotic Louisiana historians and writers have attributed a significance beyond all justification to the little rebellion. These writers leave the impression that the entire colony was "up in arms" in "revolution" against Ulloa and Spain and that after a commission which had gone to France with a copy of the decree expelling Ulloa and a memorial of the "Inhabitants and Merchants of Louisiana," returned to Louisiana with the news that France would give them no assistance, the Louisianians seriously considered proclaiming a republic. If this idea ever existed at all it existed in the minds of only a few men primarily interested in protecting their own commercial and economic interests. Gayarré wrote that the Louisianians could claim "the merit of having been the first European colony that entertained the design of proclaiming her independence." Fortier stated that the colonists "were animated by the same spirit as the English colonists in 1776, and we are proud that our ancestors of 1768 should have been the first men on this continent to have thought of making themselves independent from the rule of a European monarch." This is good pro-French propaganda, but it is not history.

In judging Ulloa, most modern authorities agree that he was simply not a strong enough governor for the situation in which he found himself. One of them asserts that he "was the wisest and kindest well-wisher of Louisiana" and exercised a really mild and liberal rule. The British of West Florida believed that he had served Louisiana well, and one of the officials wrote: "To see the Fortifications, Churches, Hospitals and Public Buildings, which are every where erecting on the Spanish Dominions, since the arrival of Don Antonio de Ulloa, whilst nothing is undertaken on our part is extremely [sic] mortifying to those who consider the changeful State of European Powers."

THE INTERIM PERIOD. As Acting Governor, Aubry was now in a trying position. Should he support the rebels, who apparently had been successful? Or should he support Spain? It was more than possible that Spain might send another governor with sufficient forces to put down the rebellion and establish her power. Aubry began to carry water on each shoulder.

Before this he had written to France: "My position is most extraordinary. I command for the King of France and at the same time I govern the colony as if it belonged to the King of Spain." Now he tried to satisfy the French government and the rebels by placing the burden of the insurrection on Ulloa's shoulders, but admitted that "it is no pleasant mission to govern a colony which undergoes so many revolutions." He wrote to the Spanish Captain General at Havana that he "trusted" Ulloa had reported the services he had performed for Spain; for, as he said, "no one venerates the Spanish nation as I do. . . . This revolution dishonors the French in Louisiana. . . . The leaders should be punished."

The period between the departure of Ulloa and the arrival of Governor Alejandro O'Reilly on August 17, 1769, was one of confusion and disorder. Aubry reported to the Captain General that the leaders of the rebellion were animated by "fury and frenzy," by "dizziness and blindness," and that on at least twenty occasions the rebel group and the remnants of the Spanish force were on the verge of slaughtering each other. He reported recurrent disturbances in a subsequent series of communications and in his letter of August 20, 1769, to O'Reilly, stated that the colony was inflamed until that general's arrival. During the latter months he felt that everyone involved should be pardoned, except the leaders, who should be dealt just punishment.

O'REILLY ESTABLISHES SPANISH AUTHORITY. On August 17, 1769, a Spanish fleet of twenty-four ships, carrying detachments of cavalry, artillery, and infantry totaling slightly over two thousand men, arrived at New Orleans. The expedition was commanded by Lieutenant General Don Alejandro O'Reilly, the recently appointed Captain General and Governor of Louisiana.*

O'Reilly was totally unlike Ulloa. A native of Ireland, he migrated to Spain when a young man and entered the army. He served in Spain, France, Austria, Portugal, and other countries, advanced in rank, and at the close of the French and Indian War reorganized Spanish infantry tactics and rebuilt the fortifications of Havana. In 1765 he saved the life of Carlos III during a Madrid street riot, and the subsequent favor of the King created considerable jealousy against him. He was suave, courteous, and mild-mannered, but was withal a soldier and a man of iron.

O'Reilly carried orders to take formal possession of the colony and to establish the Spanish government, adapting Spain's laws to the welfare of the colony. In accordance, at five o'clock on the afternoon of August 18 a signal gun was fired, and with strict military precision the Spanish troops landed. The batteries of artillery and companies of infantry and cavalry marched the short distance to the Place d'Armes and took their posts about the square in front of the church.

Preceded by a specially uniformed guard of honor bearing the silver mace, symbol of the Captain General's authority, O'Reilly and his staff came ashore and with great pomp, made more impressive by the General's slight limp, marched to the square. Aubry awaited at the flagpole from which fluttered the flag of France. Down came the French flag and up went the Spanish emblem, to the roars of *"Viva el Rey"* and the booming of the ship's guns and the fifty cannon of the batteries. O'Reilly then entered the church to receive the blessing of the Vicar-General. Then the troops, with rigid bearing, disciplined precision, and glittering equipment, paraded through the town.

The abortive little Rebellion of 1768 had failed. What chance had a few hundred Frenchmen against the armed might of Spain? O'Reilly had taken the first step in establishing Spanish authority, for, wrote John Walton Caughey, he had "displayed most effectively the military force under his command, and through the pageantry of his dramatic entry had inspired the respect of the colonists."

TRIAL AND PUNISHMENT OF THE CONSPIRATORS. O'Reilly had been specifically instructed to prosecute and punish the leaders of the rebellion, and he proceeded immediately with this task. He consulted with Aubry and Aubry wasted no time in naming the leaders and charging that they had plotted "to send away the governor, and to free themselves from the Spanish domination." He informed a delegation of citizens that a careful investigation of the rebellion would be made and that they could expect "no ill that might not be very much justified, nor likewise very necessary." His actions were straightforward and direct; despite the assertions of older Louisiana historians, O'Reilly cannot be charged with duplicity.

On the morning of August 21 the leaders were quietly arrested. O'Reilly advised them that he had been ordered "to have arrested and tried, according to the laws of the kingdom, the authors of these excesses and of all these deeds of violence. . . . My earnest wish is, that you may prove your innocence, and that I may soon set you free again. . . . You will produce all your defenses before equitable judges who are before you, it will be they who will prepare your process and who will judge you."

On August 23, O'Reilly issued a proclamation of amnesty, stating that the majority of those who had participated in the rebellion had been "seduced by the intrigues of some ambitious, fanatic, and evil-minded men, who had the temerity to make a criminal use of the ignorance and excessive credulity of their fellow-citizens. These men alone will answer for their crimes, and will be judged in accordance with the laws." Three days later the people of New Orleans and vicinity were ordered to take the oath of "fidelity and obedience to His Catholic Majesty."

The trial of the conspirators began about the first of October and lasted a little

---

*O'Reilly's age at this time is a matter of controversy. Some authorities give the year of his birth as 1722, others 1725, and still others 1735.

over three weeks. The prisoners were charged with treason and rebellion. On this point Spanish law was clear: "He who labors by deed or word to induce any people, or any provinces, under the domination of the King, to rise against his Majesty, is a traitor." There was no question but that the leaders of the rebellion had tried to free Louisiana from Spanish rule and, if convicted by the court, would suffer the death penalty.

The sentence of the court was pronounced by the Governor on October 24. Five of the leaders (one had died in prison) were sentenced to death and were shot; six others were given prison terms, their property to be confiscated after the payment of all debts. Three days later the Governor stated in a report of the trial: "Everyone recognizes the necessity, justice, and clemency of the proceedings. . . . Henceforth, I shall receive without discrimination those who were seduced and signed the first representation to the council, and it will be the greatest consolation to the public to know that I shall not leave in the province any memory of that ill-considered act."

Aubry, the man who had permitted the little fiasco to develop, slipped aboard the ship *Père de Famille* in early January, 1770, and sailed for France, carrying, so it was said, a fortune. On February 18, when entering the mouth of the Garonne River, the ship encountered a storm. Failing to see the light at Cordian, she ran onto a reef and was broken in two. There were few survivors, and Aubry was not one of them. It is doubtful that many in Louisiana mourned his death.

O'REILLY'S REORGANIZATION OF THE COLONY. Even before the trial of the conspirators, O'Reilly set about reorganizing the colony. He fixed food and other prices and forced profiteering merchants to adopt them. Tension immediately eased somewhat in New Orleans and gradually was dispelled throughout the colony as his directives and regulations were received.

He wrote to Spain that the province needed "flour, wine, oil, tools, arms, munitions, and all kinds of cloth to make clothing, and can obtain them only by exporting its products." He recommended free commerce with Spain and Havana and encouraged the exportation of wood, indigo, cotton, peltries, corn, rice, and the development of sugar mills. Although he stopped smuggling, he winked at trade with the British when it was necessary for the good of the colony. Besides appointing a commission to study and recommend the best sea routes to Gulf of Mexico, Caribbean, and European ports, he temporarily abolished import and export duties at New Orleans. As trade increased, the general economic condition of the colony began to improve.

He convened an Indian council at New Orleans, smoked the calumet with the chiefs so as "not to depreciate their customs," presented them with medals, and then staged a spectacular sham battle for their entertainment and to impress upon them the power of Spanish arms. The Indians departed with "such manifestations of gratitude and admiration as the interpreters and the French officials still in the colony had never before seen."

He dispatched commissions throughout the colony to write descriptions of the country and survey the situation of the inhabitants, their crops, and livestock. The Governor himself went up the Mississippi as far as Pointe Coupée in order to "listen to all complaints which they may have, inform myself as to the conditions of the country and the number of inhabitants in these parts, establish companies of militia, and issue regulations by which they may be rapidly united for defense in case of Indian insults or in case this Governor should need them for any other purpose." He ordered the taking of a census, which showed that the population of New Orleans was 3,190 persons of all races, nationalities, sexes, and ages and that the population of the entire colony totaled slightly over 13,500 persons, more than double what it had been at the conclusion of Bienville's last term of office. Most of the new settlers had arrived during the latter years of the French and Indian War or soon afterward and included many Acadians.

While organizing twelve militia companies with a total of over a thousand men,

O'Reilly began to send his regular Spanish troops back to Havana. At the same time he improved the fortifications at the Balize, New Orleans, Pointe Coupée, and in the Arkansas, Missouri, and Illinois countries, for they had not been kept in repair. By the end of December this work was complete, and the colony had sufficient strength to make a noble effort in defending itself. He established a better system of land titles, particularly for agricultural lands, fixed requirements for homesteading, issued regulations for the Indian trade, stopped the stealing of livestock on the western frontier, and investigated the Church and recommended reforms.

In November, 1769, O'Reilly abolished the old French colonial government and established the province of Louisiana. He annulled the laws of France and substituted the laws of Spain and her colonies. So that the people might become acquainted with them, he had published in French the "Ordinances and Instructions of Don Alexandre O'Reilly," an abridgment of Spanish and Spanish colonial laws and his own regulations, which also contained a modification of the French Black Code of 1724.

O'Reilly reorganized the government of New Orleans according to the Spanish custom of making local officials responsive to local interests and of making the town support its own government. A *Cabildo,* or town council, was established to govern the city, though the previous decisions of the Superior Council were upheld and its regulations ordered to remain in force until abrogated by the *Cabildo.* The *Cabildo* met for its first session on December 1, 1769. Since the public buildings of New Orleans had fallen into disrepair, on December 11, 1769, O'Reilly signed a contract for the construction of a Casa Curial (a courthouse, town hall, or government building—generally called the "Cabildo" by Louisianians) to be "finished, perfected, and delivered by the end of the month of April, 1770"; the building, however, was not completed and accepted by Governor Unzaga until August 17.

O'Reilly had come to Louisiana with the title of Captain General and Governor, but he had brought his successor as Governor with him, Colonel of the Regiment of Havana Don Luis de Unzaga y Amézaga. He had authority to place Unzaga in the governorship as soon as the colony was ready for regular governmental administration, and he therefore installed Unzaga at the first session of the *Cabildo.* O'Reilly's subsequent work in Louisiana was in his capacity as Captain General, which outranked the Governor.

By the middle of February, 1770, O'Reilly's reorganization of the colony was complete, and early in March he sailed for Havana. He arrived at Cadiz, Spain, on May 31 and reported at court on June 9. The King, "finding himself entirely satisfied" with O'Reilly's "distinguished zeal, talent, and military skill, and also with the ability and perfections demonstrated in the repeated important commissions... especially in that which was just concluded in Louisiana," promoted him to Director-General of Spanish Infantry.

O'REILLY'S PLACE IN LOUISIANA HISTORY. Louisiana historians have almost universally condemned O'Reilly for executing the leaders of the Rebellion of 1768, and along with General Benjamin F. Butler's "Woman Order" of 1862 this incident has aroused the passions of more writers than any other in Louisiana history. These writers have excoriated the second Spanish Governor and have labeled him "Bloody O'Reilly."

François Xavier Martin set the pattern of the interpretation when he wrote: "Posterity, the judge of men in power, will doom this act to public execration. No necessity demanded it, no policy justified it." Gayarré, a descendant of one of O'Reilly's officers, devotes many pages to the incident and ends, after some justification, by calling it simply a "bloody execution." Alcée Fortier states that "nothing can excuse O'Reilly's cruelty" and calls those executed and imprisoned the "Martyrs of Louisiana." John R. Ficklen, Henry Rightor, Albert Phelps, George W. Cable, Grace King, and Henry E. Chambers deal briefly with the incident but generally take the same view. André Lafargue wrote that the leaders "were shot down in cold blooded murder."

It must be remembered that O'Reilly was a soldier, accustomed to a soldier's discipline, who had been ordered by his King to punish, "in strict conformity to the laws," the leaders of the rebellion. He followed his orders, but through a regular trial for high treason, which as Laura Porteous admits, "was carried out without passion or prejudice, as far as the records show, and was perfectly correct in all its formalities according to Spanish law."

By some modern standards, O'Reilly's action does seem harsh, but treason is still punished by the death penalty. The year prior to the Rebellion of 1768 in Louisiana, Viceroy Matias de Gálvez of Mexico faced a similar situation in the province of Guanajuato, and for this revolt he executed 85 persons, had 73 lashed, imprisoned 674, and banished 117 from the province. Bacon's Rebellion in the British Virginia colony nearly a century earlier had resulted in the execution of more than twenty prominent Virginians; the Leisler Rebellion in New York likewise resulted in the execution and imprisonment of its leaders. Certainly by eighteenth-century standards the execution of five men and the imprisonment of a half dozen more for organized rebellion was not only accepted, but light punishment, and under no circumstances could be called severe. Unquestionably the trial and execution of the leaders of the Louisiana Rebellion of 1768 was approved by universal governmental opinion in Europe.

It should be remembered that the Louisiana settlers had been notoriously insubordinate and rebellious for years, often causing the French government considerable concern. A certain element in the colony must be classed as continual troublemakers. Should not the critic also remember the army executions during the French regime; the soldiers who for revolting against cruel military officers had been broken on the wheel, and the Swiss who was placed in a coffin and then sawed to death? Was O'Reilly more brutal than Kerlerec? Was not treason a greater crime than the revolt of hungry, ill-treated soldiers?

James E. Winston perhaps best summarizes the case: "The revolt against Ulloa, his expulsion, the trial, condemnation and execution of the Creole leaders, were doubtless just another instance of merited punishment being meted out to those rebelling against constituted authority." The rebellion was against constituted authority, for the French monarch had made it clear that he had "abandoned to His Catholic Majesty all his rights, as well as those of ownership and possession over Louisiana." There is no question that under Ulloa the Spanish flag had been raised over the entire colony, with the exception of New Orleans, and that all commerce, finance, and government had been transacted under his direction.

Henry E. Chambers charges Aubry with venality and states that "much of the blame for cruelty subsequently ascribed to O'Reilly must be borne by Aubry" and that "Aubry, and Aubry alone, must shoulder the onus that otherwise would be borne by O'Reilly" for the execution of the conspirators. There is little doubt but that Aubry could have prevented the rebellion from developing; by his failure to do so he became the man responsible for one of the saddest pages in Louisiana history.

The French Creoles never forgave nor forgot O'Reilly. Years later Thomas Wharton Collens wrote a play called *The Martyr Patriots; or, Louisiana in 1769,* and Louisiana children memorized and recited the lines:

> What! sold like cattle?—treated with disdain?
> No! Louisiana's sons can never bear
> Such foul disgrace. And when I'll tell them all,
> Of every insult, and the shame which thus
> This reckless King would heap upon their heads,
> 'Twill put a burning fagot to their pride;
> 'Twill blow their indignation into flame;

And like the fire on our grass-grown plains,
By ravaging winds devouring driven,
'Twill spread, in blazing waves, e'en to the edge
And utmost limit of the land; and then,
Proud Kings, beware! lest e'en within the bounds
Of Europe's slave-trod vales the blaze would catch,
Sweep despots and their thrones away, and like
Unprofitable weeds consume them all.

It should also be remembered that just as Iberville was the founder of French Louisiana, so O'Reilly was the founder of Spanish Louisiana. As David K. Bjork wrote, "so thoroughly did he apply himself to this work that few changes were made during the thirty odd years that Spain ruled that colony." "In the last analysis, then," as John Walton Caughey states, "O'Reilly's administration is not to be regarded as coterminous with the proceedings against the insurgents but as beginning, in its full significance, after that ordeal." When all his accomplishments are considered, it becomes obvious that Alejandro O'Reilly should be ranked with Iberville, Bienville, Gálvez, and Carondelet as one of the really great governors of colonial Louisiana.

WORK OF GOVERNOR UNZAGA. Colonel Don Luis de Unzaga y Amézaga was a native Spaniard and had served in the army since 1735. He had campaigned in Spain, Italy, and Africa. Considerably older than O'Reilly, he was placid, mild, even-tempered, conciliatory, and possessed the ability to make friends and inspire confidence. Within a short while he won the respect and esteem of the Louisianians, and social intercourse between the Spanish and French completed the work of conciliation. The Governor soon married a St. Maxent, a relative of one of the executed rebels, and many of his officers followed his example. As Grace King wrote: "National and political differences became not only obliterated, but amalgamated (as we have more than once seen since) in a common Creolism."

Unzaga served as Acting Governor from December 1, 1769, until August 17, 1772, when the King formally approved his commission making him Governor in fact. The years were peaceful, and he devoted his attention to the betterment and progress of the colony. He became acquainted with the various districts, fostered education, proposed sound ordinances, completed the public building program begun by O'Reilly, and had the habit, of which the Louisianians approved, of being blind on occasion when the colonists openly traded with the British of West Florida or smuggled in European goods. He issued an ordinance requiring all carpenters and joiners of New Orleans and other towns to hasten to fires with axes, pickaxes, and other necessary equipment and ordered all citizens to keep ladders, buckets, axes, and other fire-fighting equipment in their homes at all times.

When Spanish Capuchin Father Cirilo de Barcelona came from Havana and penned violent tirades against lazy, ignorant, and sometimes corrupt Capuchins, and rather viciously attacked easygoing, shepherdlike old Vicar-General Père Dagobert de Longuory, who was reported to be "blissfully ignorant of the finer points of Catholic doctrine," the Governor stalled for time. Unzaga was finally censured by the Bishop of Havana, who protested to the King. The King eventually sided with the Bishop but did not worry the Governor about the matter, believing that the trouble would blow over. Unzaga wrote, probably with a twinkle in his eye: "I know how difficult it is to come to a correct appreciation of the true merits of men of that sacred calling, when they choose to quarrel among themselves." The patient Governor won in the end, for Father Cirilo became the auxiliary Vicar-General and additional French priests were sent to the colony.

As time passed, Unzaga found the heavy duties of his governorship more and more demanding upon his flagging energies. He was advanced in years, was in poor health, and his eyesight was failing. From time to time he wrote letters back to Spain asking permission to retire. He had been promoted to Brigadier General and was satisfied, wanting nothing more than to return to his native Malaga; but instead of being retired he was made Captain General of Caracas, one of the most important Spanish posts in South America. Unzaga vacated the governorship on January 1, 1777, and on March 22 sailed from New Orleans on board the frigate *La Luisiana*. He left a colony where, in the words of Gayarré, "he had won the esteem and affection of the population," a colony which was prosperous beyond all its experience.

CHAPTER 10

LOUISIANA AND THE
AMERICAN REVOLUTION

BERNARDO DE GÁLVEZ. The story of Louisiana during the American Revolutionary period is the fabulous saga of a young Spanish colonel whose brilliant civil and military achievements rate him as one of Louisiana's most noted colonial governors.

Bernardo de Gálvez, fourth Spanish Governor, was born in Spain in 1748, the son of Don Matias de Gálvez, who served Spain as Captain General of Guatemala and Viceroy of Mexico. Don José de Gálvez, an uncle who was a great favorite of Carlos III, was Secretary of State and President of the Council of the Indies. Young Bernardo entered the army at the age of sixteen, saw service in France, Portugal, and Mexico, fought under O'Reilly in Algiers, was ordered to Louisiana in 1776, became Colonel of the Louisiana Regiment, and was soon appointed second in command of the Louisiana forces. Subsequently he succeeded Unzaga as Governor on January 1, 1777, at the age of twenty-nine.

He was one of the most popular governors of colonial Louisiana, and was said by Gayarré to have had "that nobleness of mien, that gracefulness of manner, that dignified and at the same time easy affability for high and low, which, in persons of his rank, never fails to win the heart." Joseph Xavier Delfau, Baron de Pontalba, a contemporary, recorded that he was distinguished for "the sweetness of his temper, the frankness of his character, the kindness of his heart and his love of justice."

GÁLVEZ AS GOVERNOR. As was customary, Gálvez received an elaborate set of instructions from the King by which he was directed to take a census of Louisiana, prepare a statement of the yearly expenses of the colony, welcome foreign settlers on condition that they were, or would agree to become, Catholics and take the oath of allegiance to Spain, encourage agriculture, take especial care to see that slaves were humanely treated, and promote commerce, but was to act promptly and sternly against smuggling. The friendship of the Indians was to be cultivated. He was specifically ordered to watch the English of West Florida closely, reorganize and improve the discipline of the Louisiana militia, and make carefully prepared reports on practically everything—roads, money, the people, mines, the religious situation, commerce, etc.

The young Governor reduced the export duty and permitted trade with the British of West Florida. He called mass meetings of farmers and planters to discuss agricultural matters (the first agricultural conferences in Louisiana history), and as the labor supply was short, they recommended and he accepted a plan to again begin importing slaves. The census was completed in May, 1777. The population had more than doubled since Spain acquired the colony in 1762, for 17,926 persons now lived in Louisiana; 16,292 in the area occupied by the present state, and 1,634 in the Arkansas and Illinois districts. There were 8,381 whites, 536 free mulattoes and Negroes, and 9,009 mulatto and Negro slaves. New Orleans had a population of 3,206.

One of the Governor's chief interests was the encouragement of immigration. He promised each settler five arpents of land fronting a river or bayou and as far back from it as the man and his family would clear and cultivate or pasture the land. Each family was to receive supplies for a year and "an axe, a hoe, a scythe or a sickle, a spade, two hens, a cock, and a pig of two months, with which they may easily found and establish a household which will provide them a living." Soon Spanish pioneers began to arrive, as did *Isleños* from the Canary Islands, Britishers from West Florida, American loyalists from the Atlantic-seaboard colonies, Acadians, and even a few Frenchmen from France. The years of Gálvez' administration were boom years of settlement; by 1785 the population of Louisiana had again almost doubled.

While the majority of the new settlers settled on scattered farm lands, a few established small villages. One of these, Galveztown, located on "a site of high ground" near the confluence of the Amite River and Bayou Manchac, will serve as an example of villages established during this period. The place was probably settled in 1778 by a small group of British and American loyalists who had fled from their West Florida homes at the approach of an American expedition down the Mississippi led by Captain James Willing.

In January, 1779, Gálvez reported that he was sending additional settlers "as rapidly as possible in order that the planting season may not be over, and that the new settlers may have a harvest this year." Late in the spring the villagers had forty-two houses built, and by the end of the year eighty-seven British and Americans had taken the oath of allegiance to the King of Spain. The settlers, "in order to demonstrate the love and kindness which they feel for the Spanish nation," named their village "La Villa de Gálvez" (Galveztown), and begged Francisco Collell, the Commandant, to give a Spanish name to each house; so, for example, the house of Luis Deves became "La Carlota," in honor of the King. Names of persons were likewise changed—Davis became Deves, Riley became Reeli, and Morris became Moris.

Gálvez treated the Indians with respect and fairness, soon winning the loyalty of a majority of the tribes. On one occasion, however, the Choctaws threatened to raid Galveztown, but the raid never materialized. Thereafter the colony was seldom disturbed by Indian problems.

Despite their many duties, Gálvez and his officers and officials had ample time for social life, and more Spaniards succumbed to the charms of the French Creole girls. Don Esteban Miró, an army officer and future Governor of Louisiana, married Marie Céleste Elenore de Macarty; Jacinto Panis, another officer, won Margarethe Wiltz, widow of the Joseph Milhet executed by O'Reilly. Gálvez himself petitioned His Majesty for permission to marry Félicie de St. Maxent d'Estréhan, a young and beautiful widow. Their marriage was a happy one, and the Governor's wife greatly aided her husband's political career.

BRITISH IN POSSESSION OF WEST FLORIDA. While, after the Treaty of Paris of 1763, the Spanish did not attempt to take possession of Louisiana until 1766, the British occupied Pensacola and Mobile during the late summer and fall of 1763, appointed Captain George Johnstone of the Royal Navy Governor of West Florida, and immediately began to encourage settlers from Great Britain and from the English colonies to move to West Florida. Land grants of 5,000 acres were offered to field officers, 3,000 acres to captains, 2,000 acres to lower-grade officers, 200 acres to noncommissioned officers, 50 acres to privates, and 100 acres to civilian husbands and wives, and 50 acres for each slave or child. Civilians might be granted as much as 1,000 acres if they agreed to occupy and cultivate the additional land.

Under these generous terms, settlers poured into West Florida, and by the time Governor Johnstone resigned in 1766 the colony was well organized; had a legislative council and assembly functioning; was raising large crops of cotton, tobacco, corn, and rice, as well as other products; was producing sizable amounts of pitch, tar, masts, and lumber for export; had begun the building of fortifications at "Tanchipaho," at the mouth of Bayou Manchac, Baton Rouge, and Natchez; and had started clearing Bayou Manchac and the lower Amite River of obstructions. The British colony was in excellent condition, and the Natchez District was potentially "the most flourishing Country in his Majesty's dominions."

But the people of the western section of the colony depended upon the Mississippi River to carry their commerce, and the Spanish controlled the lower section of the river. They could take small ships from the Mississippi through Bayou Manchac and the lower Amite River into lakes Borgne and Pontchartrain only during times of high water. By the late 1760's the settlers had about given up their attempts to clear and deepen the river and bayou waterway and were beginning to hope for a British-Spanish war so that they might capture New Orleans and gain control of the lower Mississippi.

Governor O'Reilly and Governor Unzaga had carefully watched the British in West Florida, and although they had permitted considerable clandestine trade, they were fearful for Louisiana. This was the major factor in building the Louisiana militia into a comparatively strong military force by 1775. Gálvez was aware of the British threat, but fortunately for him the America Revolution broke out the same year.

LOUISIANA AND THE AMERICAN REVOLUTION. The Englishmen of West Florida did not join their kinsmen along the Atlantic seaboard; they remained loyal to the Mother Country and began to strengthen their defenses against possible attack by the Americans or the Spanish. The militia received equipment from Great Britain, the forts at Mobile and Pensacola were strengthened, and German mercenaries began to arrive. Military roads were surveyed from Pensacola to Mobile and from there to Baton Rouge and Natchez. Fort Panmure at Natchez, Fort New Richmond at Baton Rouge, Fort Bute at the mouth of Bayou Manchac, and smaller posts at the mouth of Thompson's Creek, near present-day Port Hudson, and at a point on the lower Amite River near modern French Settlement were strengthened.

Taking no chances, Gálvez began to strengthen the defenses of Louisiana. By summer of 1777 he had decided not to rebuild the palisade at New Orleans, as it could be carried by frontal attack, and recommended the building of several "lanchones," or small river boats, to be armed with heavy cannon. In December he repaired the old batteries and built some new ones at New Orleans, and established posts and watchtowers at some distance from the town in the general directions from which he might expect attack. By the end of the year, three of the boats were completed, each armed with eighteen- or twenty-four-pounders and propelled by either oars or sails.

Despite repeated requests, by the middle of 1778 he had only slightly over 400 regular troops and about 300 militia. Some reinforcements were received during the following months, but the majority were men "from the islands and Mexico who do not yet know either the handling of arms or the evolutions." Nevertheless, by early 1779 he had built up his militia to eighteen companies totaling nearly 1,550 men. At that time his regular troops totaled about 750 men, including 10 artillerymen. However, he wrote his uncle: "As to the militias, although I am certain of their good will, Your Excellency knows very well that one cannot count much on them, because as war is not their profession, they do not wage it with enthusiasm. Besides, they always have in mind, in view of the danger, the consideration of their families, and this increases the risks for them."

The American agent in Louisiana during this period was a businessman named Oliver Pollock who had come to Pennsylvania from Ireland in 1760, when he was twenty-three, and soon ventured into trade with the Spanish West Indies. In 1768 he moved to New Orleans, where he soon ingratiated himself with Governor O'Reilly during a food shortage by selling him a cargo of flour at practically cost price. By the beginning of the American Revolution he was a rich man with a large trading interests in Upper and Lower Louisiana and the West Indies.

Pollock espoused the American cause, became purchasing agent for the United States in Louisiana, and was soon sending much-needed supplies to the American armies; in large measure he was responsible for George Rogers Clark's success in the conquest of the Northwest. He could not secure reimbursement from the infant United States, so he used his own funds, and when they were exhausted, privately borrowed from the King of Spain and from certain citizens of New Orleans. When he was threatened with imprisonment for debt, Gálvez went his surety for nearly $135,000.

Prior to Spain's declaration of war against Great Britain in middle June, 1779, the young Louisiana Governor co-operated with Pollock in every possible way. He constantly and covertly skated on thin ice in his relations with the British, even though Spain and Great Britain were still at peace. Governor Peter Chester of British West Florida protested, and once upbraided him for his "every possible Countenance & Encouragement given to the Rebels in Louisiana." Pollock wrote to Congress in May, 1778, lauding Gálvez for his "noble Spirit & behavior" and later expressed the wish to have his portrait painted for Congress to perpetuate his memory "in the United States of America . . . with those that have been of Singular Service in the Glorious Contest of Liberty." Concerning himself Pollock later wrote: "I have laboured without ceasing. I have exhausted my all and plunged myself deeply in Debt, to support the cause of America." His claims were finally paid in part by the United States.

JAMES WILLING'S EXPEDITION. English and Spanish relations were further complicated by an American expedition against West Florida, led by James Willing, in 1778. Willing belonged to a prominent Philadelphia family, and his brother was a partner of banker and businessman Robert Morris and a member of the First Continental Congress. Shortly before the Revolution, he had moved to Natchez, where he established a store, but this was a poorly managed and profitless venture, since he spent his time in gambling and dissolute living. He became an ardent revolutionist, and when he failed to stir up the Natchez District to revolt against Governor Chester, returned to Philadelphia, hoping to organize an expedition to wrest West Florida from the British. After several conferences the Congressional Committee on Commerce agreed to his plans.

Willing was appointed to a captaincy in the Navy, proceeded to Fort Pitt, enlisted a volunteer force of about thirty men, and on the armed river boat *Rattletrap* set off down the Ohio River in early January, 1778. When the expedition reached the West Florida plantations above Natchez about the middle of February, Willing raided them, seized the leaders of the area and their property, and then moved against Natchez. He landed at Natchez, and according to one of the citizens, "early on the following morning sent orders to all parts for us to convene in order that at the same time that we should be made prisoners of war to the United States he might take possession in their name of this jurisdiction."

Continuing down the Mississippi, he raided the plantations along the river, captured the British sixteen-gun ship *Rebecca,* and ordered raids along Thompson's Creek and the Amite River. Subsequently, he sold the captured boat and his other booty in New Orleans, but instead of "applying the money to the purpose for which it was intended," according to one authority, he spent it "in riotous living and debauchery." Running out of cash, he reascended the river and pillaged the area in the vicinity of Baton Rouge, finally being driven off by a hastily collected group of citizens. He returned again to New Orleans, and soon Pollock was forced to support him and his party.

Willing was an unwelcome guest in New Orleans, and both Gálvez and Pollock were anxious to be rid of him. In early July, Pollock reported to the Continental

Congress: "The Small Party you sent here under the Command of Captn. James Willing without any order or subordinations has only thrown the whole river into Confusion and created a Number of Enemies and a heavy Expence." A month later he wrote that he was "determined to stop all Supplies in order to get him away." Willing finally sailed for Philadelphia, but the ship was captured by the British and he was taken to New York. He escaped, was recaptured, "loaded with irons for having resented an insult offered by a British officer," and finally exchanged.

Although Willing's Expedition had no positive effects on the Revolution, in general it damaged the American cause. At the time of his arrival in West Florida many of the settlers were seriously considering joining the patriots, but the conduct of Willing and his men and their plundering, estimated at as much as $1,500,000, shook their confidence in the integrity of the American War for Independence and caused the great majority to remain loyal to Great Britain. It is possible that another leader might have won West Florida as a fourteenth state.

The expedition contributed to the strengthening of the British forces in West Florida. A new commander was sent to the district with orders to "erect a fort on the Mississippi, at or near where Fort Bute stood . . . to protect the navigation of the river and to prevent any craft of the rebels descending to New Orleans." It also strained British-Spanish diplomatic relations.

Governor Gálvez took this opportunity to ingratiate himself with the British refugees pouring across the Mississippi; he not only cared for them, but also offered them lands, equipment, and supplies, and many remained in Spanish Louisiana. One letter to the Governor, signed with thirty-six names, offered him "very gratefull thanks for the Succor you have had the goodness to afford us."

GÁLVEZ AND THE CAPTURE OF BATON ROUGE. The Spanish government cautiously watched the progress of the American Revolution. If the United States won its independence it would be a calamitous example for Spanish colonies as well as a definite threat to Spanish possessions in Louisiana and even the West Indies, Mexico, and California. On the other hand, the defeat of Great Britain would greatly assist Spain in securing areas, particularly the Floridas, which she had lost to that country. During the first years of the war, Spain secretly aided the Americans, but it was not until April, 1779, that she signed a convention with France and prepared to declare war, which was formally done on June 16 of the same year. The principal Spanish war aim in America was to drive the British "from the Gulf of Mexico and the banks of the Mississippi, where their settlements are so prejudicial to our commerce, as well as to the security of our richest possessions."

The British of the Floridas were eager to attack Louisiana, because as one of their leaders wrote, "we are all firm and relishing the opportunity to strike a blow against the Dons." During the spring of 1779 rumors reached New Orleans that the British were planning to launch two attacks against the colony, one down the Mississippi from Canada and the other by sea from Pensacola.

Governor Gálvez did not receive the news of the declaration of war until the ninth of August, but by this time, knowing war was inevitable, he had completed plans to defend the colony and to invade British West Florida. His agents in British territory had kept him informed as to their strength, his kindness to the refugees from Willing raids had won many friends among the West Florida settlers, and his fair measures with the Choctaws had prevented them from allying with the British. Gálvez would be ready to move within a matter of days.

In late August, 1779, José de Gálvez relayed to Havana the King's orders regarding Louisiana's part in the war. His Majesty directed that an expedition be sent to attack Mobile and Pensacola, "the keys to the Gulf of Mexico," and either before or after these places were won to send detachments "to attack and clear the English from the banks of the Mississippi." Governor Gálvez of Louisiana would command these expeditions, for "he has had the foresight to map the area and acquire a practical knowledge of that country," and for this and other reasons was given preference "over other officials of greater experience and doubtless more suitable for any other enterprise than this one." But the enterprising and energetic Gálvez had left New Orleans for Baton Rouge two days before the order was written.

Gálvez had kept secret the news of the official declaration of war and of his recent promotion from Acting Governor to Governor. Advertising his work as preparing for the "defense" of New Orleans, he had begun to gather a fleet of river boats, gunboats, supplies, and munitions, and to equip and drill the regular army and militia units. The preparations had proceeded with amazing rapidity and success. Commandant Francisco Collell at Galveztown had kept him informed of the British movements at Baton Rouge. Gálvez' expedition was almost ready to leave New Orleans when, on August 18, a hurricane struck, sank several of his river boats, and destroyed much of his equipment and supplies.

On August 19 the Governor called the people of the capital together at the Plaza de Armas (the old French Place d'Armes), informed them of the serious results of the hurricane, of the official war declaration, and of his appointment as their Governor. He promised to "defend the province," but refused to accept the governorship unless they promised to help him in every way possible. According to one contemporary, he cried out: "What do you say? Shall I take the oath of Governor? Shall I swear to defend *Luisiana?*" The cheers drowned his words. He took the oath and continued his preparations.

The little army of about 650 men of all nationalities left New Orleans for Baton Rouge on the afternoon of August 27. There was no engineering officer, the artillery officer was ill, the men were without tents and other much-needed supplies, and the roads were almost impassable. The Governor had dispatched messengers ahead of his army to rally local militia units to the defense of Louisiana, and soon they began to join his force. Over 700 men answered the appeal, swelling his force to more than 1,400.

Meanwhile there had been a threat of British attack upon Galveztown, which was garrisoned by a handful of former British loyalists and *Isleños,* and Collell wrote the Governor that the place would be ably defended and that he was hurrying the fortifications. On the morning of August 27 he again wrote Gálvez: "The English have not executed the attack they had intended for last night. I don't know what reason has prevented them, but I think that it was due to their seeing with what speed we strengthened our position and placed ourselves in a state of defense." A few days later the Galveztown militia joined Gálvez.

But sickness and the hardships of the march from New Orleans so cut down the force that by the time it reached Fort Bute the afternoon of September 6, Gálvez had considerably less than 1,000 men. However, he knew that most of the Fort Bute troops had been withdrawn to Baton Rouge, so at dawn the next morning he assaulted and captured the fort, which he found had a garrison of only "a captain, a lieutenant, and eighteen men."

Gálvez rested nearly a week at the mouth of Bayou Manchac to reorganize his illness-ridden army, then moved on to Baton Rouge. He found it would be impossible to take the fort by assault "because it was well fortified with a ditch eighteen feet wide and nine feet deep; walls high and sloping, encompassed by a parapet adorned with Chevaux-de-frise, crowned with 13 cannons of a large caliber, and defended by more than 400 veteran and war-tried soldiers and 100 armed inhabitants."

Tricking the British into believing he was placing his batteries in a grove of fruit trees, so that they fired all night at the orchard, the young commander, under cover of darkness, placed his guns on the other side of the fort. On the morning of September 21 the British realized their mistake. The bombardment of the fort, directed by Don Julián Álvarez, began at sunrise and continued for three and a half hours, after which time "their fort was so dismantled that they sounded a call, sending forth two officers with proposals for capitulation."

The next day the British garrison marched out with banners flying and drums beating, saluted their flag, and formally surrendered. The surrender terms were generous. The British soldiers were to be conveyed to Pensacola as quickly as possible, the sick and wounded would be cared for by the Spanish until able to be sent to Pensacola, soldiers would retain their baggage and other effects, civilians in the fort would be treated as soldiers, inhabitants of the district would retain their British laws until peace was declared, all citizens would enjoy the "full and entire possession of all their effects and slaves, and in short of every thing that belongs to them, . . . there shall not be the least insult offered to the troops of the garrison," and "no papers, whether public or private, shall be seized, searched, or examined under any pretence whatever."

As the entire western section of West Florida had been surrendered, Infantry Captain Don Pedro Favrot was placed in command at Baton Rouge, a force was sent to occupy Fort Panmure at Natchez, and smaller units soon held other British posts on Thompson's Creek, the Amite River, and at Tangipahoa. Within a short time seven British ships on the Mississippi, the Amite, Bayou Manchac, or on Lakes Pontchartrain and Maurepas were captured, and others were forced to withdraw to Mobile or Pensacola.

Early the next year a supplement to *La Gazeta de Madrid* published a complete account of the Baton Rouge campaign and commended the "zeal, activity and constancy of the officers and troops." The militia "exercised themselves with indescribable zeal in all their work. . . . Especially deserving are the companies of Acadiaños, in whom burned the memory of the cruelties of the English and the past war when they obliged them to abandon their homes." The "companies of negroes and free mulattos who were continually occupied in the outposts, in false attacks, and discoveries [scouting]" conducted themselves with "valor and generosity." The Indians "gave for the first time a noble example of their humanity in not having done the slightest injury to the fugitive and disarmed English inhabitants . . . in spite of the general custom they have of treating their prisoners with the most horrible cruelty."

The Baton Rouge campaign had significant consequences. It proved the loyalty and unanimity of the Louisiana settlers, some of whom only eleven years previously had been involved in the Rebellion of 1768. On September 26, Commandant Collell at Galveztown wrote the Governor congratulating him on the victory, and in the letter said significantly: "This victory should be placed in history among those of the first rank. It is a phenomenon, because it has been said of other generals that they won various victories but have sacrificed many men, but Your Lordship with the loss of only one man has obtained the surrender of 400 and the advantageous result of the evacuation of Natchez." Collell expressed the sentiments of everyone in the colony. Gálvez had completely thwarted British plans for an invasion of Louisiana. Their defeat in West Florida cost the English much prestige with the northern Indians and immeasurably aided George Rogers Clark in consolidating his control of the Old Northwest.

THE CAPTURE OF MOBILE. Upon the outbreak of the American Revolution the Spanish government ordered administrative officials in Cuba and Louisiana to secure as much information as possible regarding British military strength in the Floridas, particularly at Mobile and Pensacola. Jacinto Panis, who was dispatched by Gálvez in 1778 to Mobile and Pensacola to confer with British officials regarding Spanish neutrality problems, was perhaps the most effective of the secret agents. He reported that the fort at Mobile was "built of brick, and flanked with breastworks, trench, and glacis, as before, situated very near the barracks and at the shore of the bay for defense by sea, as on land by Indians." But "its walls are going to ruin. Almost all of the artillery is dismounted, and the trenches in some places are choked up. The barracks are in equally bad repair."

After the capture of Baton Rouge, Gálvez returned to New Orleans with about fifty veterans, the New Orleans militia, and several hundred British prisoners whom he had placed on parole. The city was crowded to overflowing, for, in addition to the prisoners, Indians from many tribes came to pay homage to the victor and to offer assistance against the British. The Governor soon completed plans for an offensive against Mobile and Pensacola. The Captain General at Havana at first overruled the plans, but finally consented and promised to furnish ships and troops.

Louisiana militia units poured into New Orleans. Louisianians, still elated over the Baton Rouge campaign, hoped for greater honors at Mobile. In late January, 1780, Gálvez embarked about 750 regulars and militia in a dozen ships and dropped down the Mississippi to the Balize. Including the sailors, he had a total force of slightly under two thousand men. After about two weeks, when he got all his ships over the bar, he headed for Mobile, but a few days later a violent storm scattered the little fleet, crippled some of the ships, and forced him to land his troops just east of Mobile.

He had landed between Mobile and Pensacola and was in an unfavorable position between two British forces. General John Campbell at Pensacola immediately dispatched over 550 troops to the relief of Captain Elias Durnford at Mobile. Gálvez moved by forced marches, however, and within a few days had his army in front of Fort Charlotte and his eight eighteen-pounder guns in position. Meanwhile the relieving British force coming from Pensacola had run into bad weather. One of the soldiers wrote that the soil was very soft and heavy with water and that they marched through a country where there was "not a human dwelling, and at night surrounded by wild beasts." Supplies ran out and "in the morning we drink a glass of water and eat a piece of bread; at noon we have nothing to drink but water, and our supper consists of a pipe of tobacco and a glass of water." The force returned to Pensacola when its scouts reported that Gálvez was already in position at Mobile.

Gálvez bombarded the fort and laid plans for a grand assault as soon as a breach was made, but the Spanish artillery fire was so accurate that the attack was not necessary and Captain Durnford surrendered on March 14. The garrison totaled nearly two hundred regular troops and slightly over a hundred white and colored militia.

The following days were spent in rebuilding Fort Charlotte, repairing buildings, strengthening earthworks, remounting the fort's batteries, and receiving oaths of allegiance from the citizens of the area. Within a short time the occupation of the entire Gulf Coast area west of Pensacola was complete.

The Mobile campaign had tested the abilities of the young Louisiana Governor. He had succeeded in securing the consent of the Spanish officials at Havana to make the campaign, though they had given him but small reinforcements. He and his men had successfully battled the storm and had reorganized their strength without delay. They had won the race to Mobile while the relieving contingent had been floundering slowly along the muddy roads east of the town. The attack had been brilliantly planned and had been carried out by the Louisiana militia and regulars with steady efficiency. Louisianians received the news of Gálvez' victory with wild enthusiasm, while the King rewarded him for his achievement by making him Major General in command of the Spanish forces in America and giving him the title of "Governor of Louisiana and Mobile."

THE CAPTURE OF PENSACOLA. A week before the fall of Mobile an expedition sailed from Havana against Pensacola. The attack ended in complete and ignominious failure, for "it had not appeared possible to the commander of the squadron for the vessels of war to come near enough to silence the forts which defended the said port," and the expedition returned to Cuba.

Upon hearing of Gálvez' victory at Mobile the Louisianians urged him to immediately launch an attack against Pensacola. But the loss of equipment and supplies during the storm and the siege of Mobile, as well as the known strength of Pensacola, prompted Gálvez to use prudence and seek assistance from the Captain General at Havana. He refused to attack until he had a force sufficient for success.

The young Louisiana Governor checked closely the reports of Jacinto Panis and his other spies—the British had carefully strengthened Fort George at Pensacola with additional trenches, breastworks, and cannon, and at the foot of the fortifications, at intervals of about a foot and a half, they had "opened three rows of funnel-shaped pits, such as are called wolf traps, with sharpened stakes in the bottom." The garrison included 1,300 regular troops, 600 hunters and militia, 300 sailors, 300 armed Negroes, and a sizable force of Indian allies. The place could only be captured by a well-organized combined naval and military operation. Louisianians could not accomplish this alone; they must await aid from Havana.

But the days passed at Mobile and reinforcements did not arrive. Gálvez toyed with the idea of securing such reinforcements from Louisiana as he could and attacking without Spanish assistance. On April 10 he wrote to Havana: "I have been in possession of Mobile for nearly a month. . . . I am still inactive, but it is not my fault and I am yet unaware of whether I will go on to Pensacola. If I decide to attack, I shall advise Your Excellency and I will inform the Court only of its surrender, if it takes place." After carefully studying the British strength and the problems involved, however, Gálvez concluded he would need around five thousand men if the expedition was to have any chance of success, so he abandoned the project and wrote to Havana on May 5: ". . . finding myself with but few land resources and much fewer marine resources, I have decided to dissolve the expedition and order the troops to be withdrawn." He left a garrison at Mobile under the command of Don Josef de Ezpeleta and returned to New Orleans with the remainder of his army.

The victories of Gálvez at Baton Rouge and Mobile were hailed with enthusiasm in the United States as well as in Spain and her colonies, and George Washington wrote the young general a letter of congratulation. Spanish officials at Madrid promised assistance, so Gálvez went to Havana to speed up the organization of an expedition against Pensacola.

In early October, 1780, the expedition of fifteen armed ships and nearly fifty transports carrying nearly 4,000 men sailed from Havana, but again a violent storm struck and the ships were scattered, some of them landing at New Orleans, a few at Mobile, and the majority in Campeche, on the southern coast of Mexico. Gálvez reached Cuba about six weeks later, "not knowing the whereabouts of his convoy." Within three months he had another expedition organized and sailed from Havana on the last day of February, 1781. The fleet, under the command of Don José Calbo de Irazabal, arrived off Pensacola on March 9. Here Gálvez was met by a small fleet and force from Louisiana.

He landed a few troops on Santa Rosa Island at the entrance of the bay and made plans for the fleet to enter the bay and bombard Fort George, during which operation the army was to invest the fort from the land side. However, Irazabal refused to risk his ships in the shallow waters at the entrance of the bay and in vain Gálvez pleaded with him. A council of the naval officers unanimously agreed with Irazabal. Gálvez surveyed the situation and the forces under his direct command. He had a small Louisiana naval flotilla, 1,400 veteran troops from Havana, a sizable contingent of Louisiana troops and militia commanded by Colonel Don Esteban Miró, and a smaller force from Mobile under Josef de Ezpeleta. The captain of the Louisiana brig Galveztown had sounded the channel at night and reported that the bar could be crossed, so again Gálvez pleaded with Irazabal. Again he was refused. He consulted with his own commanders. It was decided that the Louisiana flotilla would cross the bar alone.

Gálvez dramatically lined up his troops in dress-parade formation to watch the attempt. Then he went aboard the Galveztown with his staff, raised the Spanish flag, and ordered the little fleet put under way. The guns of Fort Barrancas Coloradas near the bay entrance opened up as the ships came into range, but they crossed the bar unscathed, passed beyond the fort, moved up the bay, and anchored out of range of Fort George. Then Irazabal, realizing that he had been overly cautious, followed Gálvez into the bay.

The troops moved to the mainland, suffering some losses from Indian attacks, and invested the fort. The siege continued through the month of April. The Spanish fleet drew in and bombarded the fort, but was driven off. Gálvez tightened his lines, increased his artillery fire, and asked for the surrender of the fort. General Campbell refused. Then, on May 8 a shell from one of Gálvez' batteries pierced the magazine door in one of the advanced redoubts and the explosion killed and wounded over a hundred men. The Spanish immediately took the redoubt and began an intense cannonade of the main fort. At two o'clock in the afternoon a flag of truce was hoisted. The formal surrender of Pensacola and the entire British colony of West Florida took place on the afternoon of May 10, 1781.

The prisoners totaled only about 1,100 men; many had escaped from the fort before the lines were tightened, over 350 had deserted, and a considerable number had been killed. The captured British troops were sent to Havana, and later to New York. By the Treaty of Peace of 1783, East and West Florida were returned to Spain.

The King was pleased with Gálvez' capture of Baton Rouge and Mobile, but he was particularly gratified with the capture of Pensacola, where the young commander was twice wounded. He issued a Royal Proclamation thanking the Louisiana Governor for the "expulsion of the English from the entire Gulf of Mexico," and renamed Pensacola Bay "La Bahia de Santa Maria de Gálvez" (the Bay of St. Mary of Gálvez). He promoted Gálvez to Lieutenant General, raised him to the Spanish peerage with the title of Viscount of Galveztown, decorated him with the cross of Knight Pensioner, and made him Captain General of Louisiana and the Floridas. Perhaps most important of all to Gálvez, he authorized him to place on his coat of arms the motto "Yo Solo" (I alone), in recognition of his having led the fleet into Pensacola Bay.

The capture of Pensacola had significant results for the United States as well as for Louisiana. It closed forever the door of the Floridas to the British, and it further consolidated the peoples of Louisiana, giving them a strong feeling of military achievement which was not forgotten when Andrew Jackson faced the British on the Plains of Chalmette.

GÁLVEZ AND THE REBELLION OF 1781. The English living in the Natchez area had surrendered at the capture of Baton Rouge and had taken the oath of allegiance to Spain. Just before Pensacola fell they heard a rumor that Gálvez had been defeated, so without waiting for verification they laid siege to Fort Panmure and finally forced its surrender. Then they discovered that the rumor was false and that Gálvez had been victorious. Gálvez would certainly lead an army to Natchez and punish the rebels just as O'Reilly had punished those who had led the Rebellion of 1768. Some of the English decided to retain possession of the fort and fight, others decided upon surrender, while still others escaped to western Georgia.

Gálvez was furious, for the British of the Natchez area had revolted against fully constituted Spanish authority, had fired upon the Spanish flag, had captured a Spanish fort, and seized Spanish governmental property, and had killed Spanish soldiers. He wrote: "The conduct of the people of Natchez has been infamous, a reflection on all good Englishmen, and a scandal to other nations. Nevertheless, we who know the insignificant effects of the rebellion realize that punishment need not be made severer than to establish respect for the law, and ought not to extend to any innocent inhabitants."

Carlos de Grand Pré, Commandant of the Natchez–Baton Rouge District, sent a force of Atakapas militia under Esteban Roberto de la Morandière from Baton Rouge to recapture Fort Panmure. The fort soon capitulated, and the rebel leaders were sent to New Orleans for trial. The property of twenty-one of the leaders was confiscated and several were convicted of treason and sentenced to prison terms, but all were released within two years. Probably Gálvez was too lenient with the British of the Natchez area, for they continued to be troublemakers as long as Spain held the country north of the thirty-first parallel.

GÁLVEZ LEAVES LOUISIANA. Gálvez returned to Spain in 1783, in 1784 was appointed Captain General of Cuba, retaining his position as Governor of Louisiana and the Floridas, and returned to Havana in October of the same year. In the spring of 1785 he was made Viceroy of New Spain. He arrived in the City of Mexico early in 1786, and was received by the Mexicans with "the greatest pomp and jubilee." However, he did not live long to enjoy his new honors, for he contracted a fever and died November 30, 1786. The City of Mexico mourned his loss, for he had already instituted many reforms and had completed the construction of the Cathedral, which had been over a hundred years in the building. The Archbishop wrote that "all the kingdom of New Spain is filled with mourning and tears and overwhelmed by the deepest sadness because of the unlooked for death of its most beloved viceroy."

Louisianians mourned his death too, for, as Caughey states: "Gálvez' compelling personality, his youth, his warmth, his valor, not to mention his Louisiana wife, drew the creoles into ardent support of Spain. O'Reilly had imposed Spanish rule. Gálvez, by more subtle means, acquired dominion over the hearts of the Louisianians." Gálvez did a commendable job as a colonial civil administrator, working constantly and diligently for the welfare of the people. As a military leader he won brilliant success, and he generously shared that success with the Louisianians who had so steadfastly and enthusiastically aided and followed him. When the King of Spain offered him the title of "Viscount," Gálvez asked to be given the title of "Viscount of Galveztown" and to have a "gold fleur-de-lis on a field of blue" on his coat of arms. When the request was granted, he wrote to the people of Louisiana on July 15, 1783: "It will always be an incontestable proof of your love for me and a public testimony of my good conduct toward you."

CHAPTER 11

LAST YEARS OF THE
SPANISH REGIME

SPANISH PLANS AFTER THE AMERICAN REVOLUTION. Spain had wrested East and West Florida from Great Britain during the American Revolution and at its conclusion controlled the Floridas, Louisiana, and Texas. The treaties of 1783, however, had left the northern boundary of Florida in dispute. The British treaty with the United States fixed the boundary at the thirty-first parallel of latitude westward from the Chattahoochee River to the Mississippi, but Spain denied this boundary, claiming the old British line of 32 degrees and 28 minutes. Spanish objectives in the Louisiana-Florida area after 1783 became the possible enlarging of the Floridas to the northward, safeguarding of the entire Mississippi Valley, checking the westward expansion of the United States, and developing Louisiana into a strong, self-sufficient colony.

GOVERNORSHIP OF MIRÓ. Colonel Don Esteban Rodriguez Miró served as Acting Governor of Louisiana after the departure of Gálvez on the Mobile expedition early in 1780 until he was appointed Governor on July 14, 1785, in recognition "of his services as governor ad interim." He was a native Catalan, and while not as brilliant as Gálvez, was intelligent and mild-tempered, well educated, acquainted with several languages, and had a stout code of personal honor. He had come to Louisiana shortly after the beginning of the Spanish regime and had served as aide-de-camp to Gálvez and as commander of the Louisiana Regiment. Already well known for his tireless industry and strict standards of conduct, accepted by the French Creoles because of his marriage to Céleste de Macarty, daughter of a wealthy Creole planter, he had a quiet but progressive governorship which prompted many Louisianians to compare him to Governor Unzaga.

Gálvez had directed that a census be taken, and upon its completion in 1785, Miró found that the population of Louisiana had almost doubled during the preceding sixteen years; more people had settled in the colony during that period than during all the years of French control. The population of the Isle of Orleans and Louisiana west of the Mississippi now totaled more than 25,000, while the number of inhabitants of West Florida had grown to almost 7,000. New Orleans was a city of nearly 5,000, while the adjacent Tchoupitoulas District totaled just over 7,000. The population of the German and Acadian Coasts was 4,500; the Pointe Coupée and Natchez districts, more than 1,500 each; the Opelousas District, 1,200; the Atakapas country, over 1,000; and Baton Rouge and the nearby area, nearly 300.

To further increase the colony's population, Miró offered assistance to prospective settlers, and soon new immigrants began arriving from France, Spain, and the Canary Islands. Acadians continued to settle along the lower Teche, along Bayou Lafourche, in the Avoyelles District, and in more isolated areas in the southern sections, over 1,500, for example, arriving in 1786. Americans received land grants in the Florida Parishes, the Opelousas District, and other areas. After the outbreak of the slave insurrection in Santo Domingo in 1791, numerous white and some Free Negro planters migrated to Louisiana, many of them bringing slaves. The only conditions imposed on immigrants by the Louisiana government were that they swear allegiance to Spain and openly practice the Catholic religion.

As was usual with Spanish colonial governors, in 1786 Miró issued a *Bando de Buen Gobierno* (Proclamation of Good Government), in which he listed needed reforms and issued his civil and police regulations. He prohibited labor on Sundays and on religious festival days, ordered all shops and other places of business closed during the hours of Mass, forbade slave dances before the end of Sunday evening services, and tightened the regulations of the activities of slaves and Free Negroes. Inhabitants of New Orleans were forbidden to leave the city without a passport, and all persons arriving were to present themselves at the Government House. Regulations were issued regarding street drainage, maintenance of levees, taverns, sales of liquors, and even such items as hogs running at large, the keeping of dogs, and the removal of dead animals from the streets. Gambling and dueling were prohibited, as was the carrying of pistols, swords, or knives. Women of New Orleans were ordered not to pay "excessive attention to dress." Women of color were forbidden to wear plumes or jewelry and were required to cover their heads with *tignons,* handkerchiefs or turbans, to distinguish them from white women.

Shortly after the capture of Baton Rouge, the Spanish government had approved Gálvez' recommendations for the promotion of trade and commerce. The new regulations permitted Louisianians to trade with France and the French West Indies for a ten-year period, to purchase slaves free of duty for ten years, and to trade through duty-free ships for two years. Exports and imports were to be taxed at the rate of only 6 per cent, and plans were made to build a customhouse at New Orleans.

These regulations went into effect shortly before Miró became Governor and greatly aided him in the promotion of trade and commerce, particularly with western Americans. Before long all kinds of goods began coming down the Mississippi from the Upper Valley and from the Ohio country. As many as forty river boats at a time might be seen at the New Orleans landing. Agricultural and timber products began to arrive in increasing amounts, as well as hides and furs from the frontier trading posts.

Miró pursued a peaceful policy toward the southern Indians. He held congresses with the various tribes and invited individual chiefs to New Orleans, where he entertained them, distributed presents, and secured advantageous trading agreements. Occasionally a chief declined to make the journey to New Orleans. One of them wrote, through an uneducated interpreter: "i am willing to come and see you and take you by the hand if you will appoint to meat me at Mobile for if i was to set of[f] to come to Orleans with ten men i should not Get back with five of them alive upon the account of the sickley Cuntrey which i thing you will say that my talk is Verey Reasonable for you cant want to see me alone with a few of My warers for when i get presents for my self i would wish for all my Nation to Get there part as well as me which the Next talk i get from you i expect that it will be to meat you at Mobille that i may lay off my tiger skin to put on good Close." The spelling and grammar of the interpreter may have been poor, but the chief's message was clear.

Indian problems, however, were many. Tribes raided neighboring tribes; then appeals were made to the Governor for assistance and for replacement of plundered goods. The camps of white traders were occasionally attacked, traders killed, and trading goods stolen, as in the early summer of 1787, when Louis de Blanc, captain of the militia and Acting Commandant at Natchitoches, received a report that while traders Toutin, St. Pierre, and Salvadeau were out hunting, Indians raided their camp and decapitated the four watchmen. Tribes quarreled over hunting grounds, stole from white settlers, abandoned their own fields, and tried to occupy those cultivated by other Indians or by whites. Trading goods and gifts consigned to trading posts sometimes disappeared en route, but the blame, however, could not always be put on the Indians. In September, 1789, De Blanc reported that he had given Bicheda, a chief of the Caddoes, a "large medal of merit," a banner, and other gifts, including "thirty jugs of brandy which were consumed on the journey as a result of the bad character of the corporal."

By treaties signed at Pensacola, Mobile, and New Orleans, Spain gained alliances with most of the southern Indians in which the Indians agreed to join with the Spanish in case of war with the United States. Although the United States signed treaties with the Cherokees in 1785 and with the Choctaws and Chickasaws in 1786, little was gained, while the Creeks refused to negotiate at all. Throughout the Spanish period the Indians were generally hostile toward the western settlers of the South Atlantic states and, armed by the Spanish, continued their border warfare.

Another census completed in 1788 revealed that Louisiana's population had grown more than 10,000 during the preceding three years. The Atakapas, Opelousas, Iberville, Manchac, and Lafourche districts had increased by more than 50 per cent, probably due largely to the incoming Acadians. Louisiana, including West Florida, now boasted a population of 19,500 whites, 1,700 persons of color, and 21,500 slaves.

Early in 1788 the King of Spain prohibited the establishment of the Inquisition in Louisiana, and when Father Francisco Antonio Ildefonso Moreno y Arze (known at this time as Father Sedella because he was born in Sedella, Granada, Spain, and later as Father Antoine), Commissary of the Spanish Inquisition, attempted this in April, 1790, the Governor had the Capuchin arrested and returned to Spain.

THE FIRE OF 1788. About half past one o'clock on the afternoon of Good Friday, March 21, 1788, a lighted candle in a private chapel in the Chartres Street, New Orleans, home of the military treasurer of the colony, Vicente José Núñez, fell against the lace draperies of the altar, and in a few moments the house was in flames. A strong south wind effectively hindered the fire fighters, who were delayed, according to the French *Gazette des Deux-Ponts,* because it was Good Friday and "the priests refused to allow the alarm to be rung, because on that day all bells must be dumb." Also, the firemen frequently did not understand the commands of the officials, which were given in Spanish, not in French.

Within four or five hours, between eight and nine hundred buildings and their contents had been consumed, representing an estimated loss totaling about three million dollars. Four-fifths of the populated section of the city was burned; only a few structures near the levee, including the Government Building, the Royal Hospital, and the Ursuline Convent, and those in the southern and western sections, were saved. The parochial church, the Presbytery, the Casa Curial (Cabildo), the military barracks, the arsenal, the jail, most of the government warehouses, the quarters of the Capuchins, and numerous other public buildings were destroyed.

The conflagration was one of the greatest of that century, and newspapers in other countries carried lengthy accounts. The *Gaceta de Mexico,* published in the City of Mexico, reported that much of the confusion of the populace was caused "by the explosion of the powder, which some citizens had cautiously hidden in their houses in violation of government orders."

The *London Chronicle* praised the Governor, Intendant, and other officials and reported that on the morning after the fire the Governor issued a general order "to prevent raising the price of provisions of all sorts above their former value," dispatched couriers up and down the river in search of supplies, and stationed himself near the Government House, "where he, with his own hands, dealt out bags of money to those whom he thought the greatest objects of his charity." The *Chronicle,* in closing its account, spoke of the "destruction of the most regular, well-governed, small city in the western world."

In his report of April 1, the Governor wrote that "night momentarily removed the sight of so many misfortunes, but the dawn the following day brought a worse one, that of seeing along the road, crying and sobbing and in the most abject misery, so many families who, a few hours before, enjoyed considerable riches and conveniences. Their cries, weeping and pale faces told of the ruin of a city which in less than five hours had been transformed into an arid and horrible wilderness; the work of seventy years since its foundation."

The Governor distributed campaign tents and rations of rice "without distinction of person," thus caring for some seven hundred persons, lodged others in houses still standing, and dispatched three ships to Philadelphia for "provisions, supplies, medicines and other articles of first necessity," and with 24,000 pesos for the purchase of 3,000 barrels of flour. The clergy suspended parish dues, and private citizens gave food, shelter, and money to numerous unfortunates.

Miró immediately set about rebuilding the city, securing financial assistance from wealthy citizens, particularly Don Andrés Almonaster y Rojas. The Church of St. Louis was rebuilt, as was the Casa Curial, the arsenal, the military hospital, the customhouse, and other public buildings. A new governor's house was erected and, as Grace King wrote, "on the open levee space on the lower side of the Place d'Armes . . . a shed, a butcher's market, was put up, the beginning of the arcades of the French market of to-day." The new buildings were of Spanish rather than French architecture, with high-ceilinged rooms, arched windows and doorways, courtyards, and hand-made ironwork. A few of the buildings were constructed of brick and adobe instead of wood.

The destruction, however, was not without its good effects. It called attention, according to Henry Rightor, to "the utter deficiency of the city in the matter of preparations to fight fires. . . . The result of the great fire, which was felt in New Orleans for many years afterwards, was the organization of a fire department." Perhaps of even greater importance, the three ships dispatched to Philadelphia began commercial intercourse between the two cities in defiance of Spanish regulations, "countenanced," according to Minter Wood, "if not actually encouraged, by both Miró and Carondelet."

COMING OF CARONDELET. Miró had asked several times to be relieved of his governorship so he could retire to Spain, for he was tired from his labors in Louisiana. For some time the Americans of the Ohio River country had been causing considerable trouble; some even threatened to invade Louisiana. The growth of the colony had greatly increased the duties of the Governor. Miró was satisfied with his army rank, for in 1789 he had been promoted to Brigadier General. In October, 1791, he wrote the Council of the Indies that he had had "the honor of serving the King, always with distinguished zeal, for thirty years and three months," of which twenty-one years and eight months were in America, and that "the state of my health requires my return to Europe." His petition granted, he returned to Spain, where he later rose to the rank of *Mariscal de Campo* (Field Marshal). "He carried with him," according to Martin, "the good wishes and the regrets of the colonists."

On the last day of December, 1791, Don Francisco Luis Hector, Baron de Carondelet, de Noyelles, Seigneur d'Haine St. Pierre, Knight of St. John, Brigadier of His Majesty, and Governor of San Salvador, of the province of Guatemala in Central America, succeeded Miró to the governorship of Louisiana. A native of Flanders, he was a colonel in the royal army and had been promoted to a colonial governorship. He was described as a short, somewhat plump gentleman, of kindly nature and good heart, who was at times, however, of choleric and domineering disposition; active, prudent, and firm, with sound business and administrative judgment; and completely honest and honorable. He was moderate in his tastes and habits.

DOMESTIC AFFAIRS UNDER CARONDELET. The new Governor issued his inaugural proclamation less than a month after taking office. Among the new regulations was the division of New Orleans into four wards, each under the administration of an *Alcalde de Barrio,* a sort of police commissioner. The *Alcalde* kept the list of citizens of his ward, added the names of newcomers as they reported to him, was in charge of fire-fighting equipment, commanded the firemen and axmen when there was a conflagration, collected small debts, and preserved peace and order. Oil lamps (lanterns) were ordered hung from ropes suspended diagonally across each street corner, the expense to be met by a tax of $1.12½ on each chimney in the city. Importation of slaves from the French West Indies was prohibited for fear they would attempt to lead revolts in Louisiana.

The Governor also issued new police regulations because of "the frequent and almost inevitable robberies which are perpetrated in the city of six thousand souls by a multitude of vagabonds of every nation." The new *serenos,* or civil guardsmen, dressed in blue breeches and frock coats, wearing cocked hats, and armed with a flintlock musket, bayonet, and short sword, patrolled the city in squads of four or five.

By 1796, New Orleans was one of the most modern cities in the New World, had thirteen *serenos* who patrolled the streets from dusk to dawn, calling out the time and the state of the weather at every hour, and was lighted with eighty street lamps. A navigable canal, named the "Canal Carondelet" in honor of the energetic Governor and running from the city to Bayou St. John, had been completed by donated slave labor, and the fortifications had been repaired. To meet the cost of these improvements, additional taxes had been placed on wheat bread and meat.

In 1792, Carondelet issued a new series of regulations generally providing additional safeguards for slaves. About the same time, new directions were sent to the commandants of the various districts ordering them to be more careful in the administration of justice, more systematic and orderly in the keeping of records, and to make regular reports on conditions in their districts. A report from Louis de Blanc at Natchitoches, for example, stated that the fort was square, had a stockade but no moat, was armed with eighteen guns, "all almost useless, without carriages, powder, or ball," had a commandant's house, soldier's quarters, "an excellent magazine," two guardhouses, four sentry boxes, "one royal jail, and an oven." The post was garrisoned by only a corporal and two soldiers, but the Commandant could depend upon the militia of the district and "by sending around a drawing of a painted leg" would "instantly have" at his command all of the allied Indian tribes.

New Orleans suffered losses from two fires during the governorship of Carondelet. The fire of 1792 was not very destructive, for there was little wind and the fire-fighting companies performed their duties efficiently; but the fire of 1794, although it burned fewer buildings, caused a heavier finacial loss than had that of 1788. A strong north wind was blowing on December 8, 1794, when the Feast of the Immaculate Conception was being celebrated. Some children playing in a courtyard behind a hay store set fire to the hay, and within a few minutes the blaze was out of control. The fire companies performed their duties well, but most of the buildings were of wood, were tinder dry, and the wind was too strong. Within three hours over two hundred buildings were consumed, including the Calabozo and the Casa Curial, though the newly completed Church of St. Louis was miraculously spared. "The levee and the square," in the words of Cable, "again became the camping-ground of hundreds of inhabitants, and the destruction of provisions threatened a famine."

Upon the petition of Attorney General Miguel Fortier, Carondelet established a building code which provided that all future buildings of more than one story in the central portion of the city must be constructed of brick or adobe and roofed with tile. The rebuilding of the city immediately began, again aided by loans from Almonaster and other public-spirited citizens. As Grace King wrote: "As the town's central parts filled up again, it was with better structures, displaying many Spanish-American features—adobe or brick walls, arcades, inner courts, ponderous doors and windows, heavy iron bolts and gratings (for houses began to be worth breaking into), balconies, portes-cochères, and white and yellow lime-washed stucco, soon stained a hundred colors by sun and rain. Two-story dwellings took the place of one-story, and the general appearance, as well as public safety, was enhanced." The Cabildo, without its 1847 French mansard roof, and other buildings and houses date from this time and remind the modern Louisianian that the Vieux Carré is really Spanish and not French in style.

LOUISIANA AND THE FRENCH REVOLUTION. The French Revolution broke out in 1789, causing some French Creoles to hope for a revolt against Spanish control of the colony, but Spain was still a strong power and able to enforce her rule. An even more important deterrent to revolutionary ideas was that she had given the Louisianians many economic concessions; economic conditions were generally good, and Governor Miró had little trouble during the last years of his administration.

In 1793, however, two events occurred which inflamed the Creoles of Louisiana— the execution of Louis XVI and the declaration of war between France and Spain. Now they marched through the streets of New Orleans yelling "Liberty, Equality, and Fraternity" or "Hang the aristocrats," and singing the "Marseillaise," the "Ça Ira," and other French revolutionary songs. Carondelet issued a proclamation forbidding the reading of "public writings, printed matters or papers relating to the political affairs of France" and prohibited meetings, gatherings, or even conversations in which the French Revolution was discussed. Those who violated the proclamation were to be imprisoned at Havana or fined 200 pesos. Copies of the proclamation were to be distributed throughout the colony for all to read, and "anyone who finds the observance of this order too rigorous may withdraw from the colony with all his effects to where he pleases, as the government does not care to admit or retain any subjects other than those who come to enjoy the peace, union, immunities, and advantages that form the basis of its prosperity."

The Governor appealed to Don Manuel Gayoso de Lemos, Commandant of the Natchez District, for three hundred militia volunteers; so Gayoso dispatched a company of cavalry and a company of infantry to New Orleans, where they were of invaluable service in restoring order. James Padgett wrote that Carondelet, "by extreme vigilance, scouring and punishing, banishing, intercepting letters and documents, by prevaricating . . . succeeded better than he expected, and thus managed to keep the people quiet." To guard against new outbreaks and to better protect the colony in case of attack by either France or Great Britain, the Governor reconstructed the five forts at New Orleans and connected them by a system of wooden palisades.

Early in 1795 even greater disorder broke out. The populace of New Orleans compelled orchestras to play revolutionary songs, secured communications and revolutionary literature from France and from the French Jacobin Society of Philadelphia, which was urging rebellion in Louisiana, and sent a petition signed by 150 citizens to the American government asking annexation to the United States. Anonymous incendiary documents appeared, reviling government officials, and citizens began to discuss the possibilities of getting rid of them by use of the guillotine. Suspicion was everywhere; no one could be trusted. Mobs thronged the streets of the capital, destroying property, shrieking that Carondelet was a *Cochon de lait* (sucking pig), and promising him the first place on the guillotine. A slave conspiracy, believed to have been instigated by the more radical revolutionaries, was discovered at Pointe Coupée, and the black leaders were hanged and the inciting whites banished. Jean Delvaux, a parish priest at Natchitoches, led an open revolutionary movement. Louisiana was practically in open rebellion against the Governor and the Spanish regime.

Unable to get reinforcing troops at the moment, Carondelet placed general governmental responsibility in the hands of the landowning and more substantial citizenry. The regulations set forth in his decree of June 1, 1795, provided for the appointment of syndics, justices of the peace, "at a distance of every three Leagues," to serve under the commandants and to assist them in preserving public order; by the time two companies of Spanish dragoons arrived, order had been generally restored. To ensure the tranquillity of the colony, the Governor continued to strengthen its defenses and to reorganize the militia companies of the various districts. Perhaps of even more significance, he invited numerous members of the French nobility who had fled France to immigrate to Louisiana, and when they arrived aided them in acquiring lands. This conservative element did much to calm the excited people and to put down the spirit of revolt.

Fewer than a hundred Louisianians were expelled from the colony for their part in the disturbances of the early 1790's, and less than a dozen were sentenced to prison at El Moro in Havana, although Spain perhaps had even more justification for punishing them than it had for those who participated in the Rebellion of 1768.

THE LAST YEARS. In the late summer of 1797, Carondelet was appointed President of the Audiencia Real of the Province of Quito, South America, and he and his baroness left Louisiana the following fall for his new assignment. He had given the colony a strong and businesslike administration, had weathered the storms caused by the French Revolution, had to some extent checked the advancing Americans, had assisted greatly in the growth of population and wealth of Louisiana, and had been a well-respected governor. To some writers his years in Louisiana were the zenith of the Spanish regime.

From the summer of 1797 to the last day of November, 1803, three Spanish governors served Spain in Louisiana. Little of material importance to the colony occurred during that period, for the diplomatic relations of Spain, France, and the United States and the constant difficulties with the western American settlers prevented the Spanish government from continuing the active development of her colony.

Brigadier General Don Manuel Gayoso de Lemos was appointed Governor of Louisiana on August 1, 1797. Educated in England, after considerable military service he had been sent to the Natchez country. Gentlemanly, suave, and tactful, a sound judge of human nature, he rapidly rose in the esteem of his superiors and soon became almost independent in the command of the Natchez District. He won a reputation for honesty in office rare among European colonial officials of this era.

His brief governorship was almost completely occupied with problems of immigration, most of which concerned Americans. He permitted liberty of conscience, but formal worship must be that of the Catholic faith, in which all children must be reared. Land grants were liberal, and Gayoso continued Carondelet's policy of encouraging the *empressario* system, through which individuals received extensive grants of land upon their promise to settle large numbers of families, and confirmed the grants Carondelet had made to the Marquis de Maison Rouge, Delassus de St. Vrain, the Baron de Bastrop, and others in northeast Louisiana. Gayoso died of a fever, brought on according to some writers by overindulgence in entertaining General James Wilkinson, on July 18, 1799.

The Captain General of Cuba appointed Sebastian Calvo de la Puerta y O'Faril, Marquis de Casa Calvo, Acting Governor of Louisiana until the new Governor could be commissioned in Spain, and Casa Calvo arrived in New Orleans the middle of September, 1799; the new Governor was Brigadier General Don Juan Manuel de Salcedo, the King's Lieutenant on the island of Teneriffe, but he did not assume his duties in Louisiana until June 15, 1801. A connection of Governor O'Reilly's, Casa Calvo was not overly popular in the colony. During his period of service Louisiana was again acquired by France through the Treaty of San Ildefonso in 1800.

Salcedo, the last Spanish Governor, was a dull and superstitious, almost senile old man, whose son, an uneducated and greedy individual, did more governing than the father. The son was aided and abetted by underhanded and arrogant but tactful Andrés Lopez de Armesto, the Secretary; Maria Nicolas Vidal, the Auditor, who according to French historian Oudard was "a shameless roue with a face like a monkey"; and Juan Ventura de Morales, the Intendant. The Salcedos did such governing as was done until French Commissioner Pierre Clement de Laussat took possession of the colony on November 30, 1803.

THE AMERICAN PROBLEM. One of Spain's objectives in declaring war on Great Britain during the American Revolution was to wrest the trans-Appalachian west from that country. The Peace of 1783, however, gave to the young American republic the territory west to the Mississippi and south to West Florida. The treaty also gave the Americans the right of navigating the Mississippi River, a concession which the British had no right to make, since Spain controlled Louisiana and had conquered British West Florida. The problems resulting from the close proximity of Americans and Spanish—the disputed West Florida boundary, the navigation of the Mississippi, trade relations, land grants in the disputed area—vexed Spanish and American diplomats until the end of the Spanish regime in Louisiana.

By the spring of 1785, Georgia had completed plans to establish the so-called "Bourbon District" in the vicinity of Natchez and had sent three commissioners to claim the area. Spain thwarted the attempt and to check "the ambitious Views of the Americans" began to work more actively to "Secure the attachment & affections of all the Indian Nations." By the end of the year Alexander McGillivray, half-breed leader of the Creeks, had begun to carefully watch American movements and had reported that "a Numerous body of American banditti were Meditating an Invasion of the Spanish territorys on the Mississippi."

Spain soon met Americans from another quarter, the Kentucky and upper Ohio River region, whose settlers needed the outlet of the Ohio and Mississippi for their products. The Spanish seized an American river boat near Natchez, the Americans retaliated by seizing Spanish goods in the country north of the Ohio, and an undeclared economic war between Louisiana and the western country began. By 1788, Spain had established a system of "observation posts" along the Mississippi south of the mouth of the Ohio and a fleet of gunboats to guard against the Americans and to regulate river traffic. Militia units were reorganized at such river towns as Baton Rouge and Natchez. These measures for protecting Louisiana and the Mississippi River were continued until the end of the Spanish period.

The Mississippi River trade grew rapidly during the 1780's and early years of the 1790's, for the "Kaintocks," as the French Creoles called all western Americans, needed Louisiana markets and a place of deposit for the export of their flour, salt meat, corn, timber, furs and hides, and other products. Despite the needs of the Louisianians for western goods and although Spanish governors generally permitted the trade laws of Spain to be violated by the Americans, their craft were irregularly seized by Spanish officials; so "Kaintock" tempers were kept at boiling point, and Miró and Carondelet attempted to turn this discontent to the advantage of Spain.

Carondelet feared the Americans and their continuing westward movement and wrote that "the Americans will spread like a torrent [into] the Internal Provinces, which are very fertile, and would threaten even the Kingdom of Mexico." He favored granting them the free navigation of the Mississippi; otherwise, Kentucky might join with the other states and attack Louisiana or might separate from the United States, make an alliance with Great Britain, and thus become "a power more terrible to Spain than that of the United States." He sent agents to the Ohio country in an attempt to get the people of that area to secede from the United States and join Louisiana.

Meanwhile, there were plots and counterplots among the western Americans. Some entered the Spanish service; others intrigued for a separated west. The Spanish government, however, during the summer of 1794 switched to a policy of conciliation toward the United States, a conciliatory policy which became stronger after the signing of the Jay Treaty with Great Britain in November of the same year. The strong action of the Washington administration in putting down the Whiskey Insurrection had broken the back of western opposition to the Federal government; and separatist ambitions began to decline rapidly. In 1795 the United States and Spain signed the Treaty of San Lorenzo, frequently called the Pinckney Treaty, by which Spain reopened trade relations with the United States, agreed to the free navigation of the Mississippi with the right of deposit at New Orleans for a three-year period, and accepted the boundary claims of the United States.

Spain, however, was reluctant to withdraw from the Natchez District and held the area until Captain Isaac Guion, with a military force, arrived in 1798. On March 30, the Spanish garrison evacuated the fort and dropped downriver to Baton Rouge. The right of deposit at New Orleans expired in 1798, but was continued with the tacit agreement of Spain and the United States. However, on October 16, 1802, Intendant Morales withdrew this right, causing grave concern on the part of the United States. Jefferson now feared that France intended to become an aggressive power west of the Mississippi and would close the river to American trade. The United States laid plans to negotiate with France for a tract of land on the lower Mississippi to use as a port or to secure guarantees of the right of free navigation of the river and of deposit at New Orleans.

FRANCE REGAINS LOUISIANA. France began to cast acquisitive eyes at Louisiana shortly after the American Revolution; now that Great Britain was no longer immediately dangerous to French colonial possessions, Spain should return the colony which many Frenchmen believed she had only been holding in trust for the Mother Country. In 1789, Elenore François Moustier, former French representative in the United States, prepared a lengthy memoir describing Louisiana and urging its return to France. The publication of Jean Pierre Brissot de Warville's *Nouveau voyage dans les États-Unis* in 1791 called attention to the problem, and two years later French author Comte Constantin François de Volney was sent to Louisiana to secure information on the colony and the sentiments of its citizens.

The Louisianians had been making secret overtures to the French government since 1779. In 1790 a Louisiana petition was sent to the French government and two years later two petitions were received by its officials. Another petition was dispatched in 1794, signed by some 1,500 citizens and begging that Louisiana be returned to France, from which it had been "treacherously and shamefully wrenched by the abominable de Choiseul."

France and Spain had gone to war in 1793, and although Louisiana had played some part in the peace negotiations, France did not insist upon the return of the colony when the treaty was signed in 1795. The following year French General Victor Collot visited Louisiana and succeeded in securing considerable information concerning the colony and its fortifications before being expelled by Carondelet. But in 1797 an attempt to purchase failed. Success had to await the rise of the Corsican.

Napoleon Bonaparte, the First Consul of France, had put his house in order by the summer of 1800 and was ready with plans for an overseas empire. He ordered Foreign Minister Charles Maurice de Talleyrand-Périgord to begin negotiations for the retrocession of Louisiana with Mariano Luis de Urquijo, the chief minister in charge of Spanish foreign affairs. While negotiations were continuing, Napoleon received a somewhat lengthy report from Baron de Pontalba of New Orleans giving full description of Louisiana and a clear and succinct statement of its present relation to the United States and the states of the west.

By this time Spain had decided to give up Louisiana. Refusal might mean a war with both the United States and France, in which case Great Britain would go to war with France, while the American republic would be free to move against Louisiana. The colony was costing Spain over a quarter of a million dollars yearly in deficits. "Frankly," Urquijo wrote to the Spanish Ambassador in Paris, "it costs us more than it is worth," and continued that it would further serve as a barrier against the American plans of colonization and would be safe in the hands of France.

Louisiana was at last returned to France by the Treaty of San Ildefonso, signed on October 1, 1800. The reoccupation of the colony was a simple military matter, which Napoleon decided to postpone until he had regained control of Santo Domingo and had made peace with Great Britain. Spain would continue to govern Louisiana in the interim.

SPANISH ACCOMPLISHMENTS IN LOUISIANA. In 1762, Spain acquired Louisiana, a small and comparatively weak colony whose inhabitants were generally concentrated along the Mississippi in the vicinity of New Orleans or scattered in isolated settlements; at the end of the Spanish regime Louisiana was a well-populated and prosperous colony. Spain governed the colony with efficiency and with leniency. She humored the French Creoles, allowed them a large measure of control over local affairs, and, while Spanish was the official language, permitted the general use of French, even in the deliberations of the *Cabildo*. Her governors were of an over-all higher quality than those of France, generally hard-working, intelligent, and honest.

But the Spanish left few traces of their domination in Louisiana. Alcée Fortier listed them: "a high and chivalric spirit, a few geographical names and a remnant of their laws to be seen in our civil code." Nevertheless, the Creoles of Louisiana owed a greater debt to Mother Spain than they did to Mother France. In a memorial to French Commissioner Laussat, after his denouncement of the Spanish government, the planters of Louisiana perhaps best expressed Louisiana sentiments toward the Spanish and their regime. A section of the memorial read: "We have no cause of complaint against the Spanish Government. We have never groaned under the iron rod of an oppressive despotism. . . . Bonds of relationship and of friendship unite us with most of them. Let them still enjoy, in the soil of liberty, all they possess, and let them share with us the favors of our brothers."

After the ceremonies of transfer in 1803, Spanish Intendant Morales reported to his government: "On November 30, at 12 o'clock, took place the transfer of the province. There was not a single demonstration of joy when the French flag was raised, and there were many tears when the Spanish flag was taken down."

CHAPTER 12

ECONOMIC AND GOVERMENTAL
LIFE IN SPANISH LOUISIANA

IMMIGRATION. Although it is generally-accepted knowledge that the population of Louisiana increased more than sixfold during the Spanish regime, immigration during the period from 1762 to 1803 is one of the least-known phases of the Louisiana story and at the same time one of the most dramatic. Settlers came in a trickling though steady stream until the end of the American Revolution; their numbers materially increased during the early 1780's and became a mighty torrent during the last decade and a half of Spanish control, the first real boom migration era of Louisiana history.

At the end of the French period the French inhabitants, perhaps a majority of whom dreamed of being able to someday return to France, the contented, home-making Germans, and a few grateful Acadians and other nationalities totaled only about 7,500; by 1803, according to a careful estimate of the American Consul at New Orleans, the population of Louisiana was approximately 50,000. The Spanish policy of subsidizing immigration had been costly (over 128,500 pesos was spent in 1779, for example), but it had built a populous colony whose inhabitants were fairly well distributed throughout the area of modern Louisiana.

The movement began within a few weeks of the acquisition of West Florida by the British in 1763, when inhabitants of that section, not wishing to be "forced to remain under the yoke of the British," petitioned for lands in Louisiana. Governor Ulloa, shortly after his arrival in the spring of 1766, offered homesteads to German settlers dissatisfied with conditions in Maryland, and began granting lands and giving supplies to the Acadians, who had begun migrating to the colony during the middle 1750's.

Governor O'Reilly's Ordinance of 1770 set the official Spanish immigration policy, which was not fundamentally changed throughout the remainder of the Spanish period. The O'Reilly ordinance granted tracts of six to eight arpents fronting a river or bayou and forty arpents in depth, more or less, "according to the means of the cultivator," and required that a new settler "occupy" the land, "enclose, within three years, the whole front of his land which shall be cleared," and meet the requirements relative to roads and levees. Later governors and intendants added other stipulations.

Freedom of conscience was granted to all new colonists, although to quote Miró's offer to western Americans in 1789, "no other publick worship will be permitted to be publicky exercised than that of Roman Catholic Church," because government officials generally believed that the Protestant "will not exert any influence on the other older towns of the Colony, in which . . . the Catechism is the only thing that is accepted." A decidedly opposite view, however, was taken by Bishop Luis Ignacio Maria de Penalver y Cardenas. He called the Americans "a gang of adventurers who have no religion and acknowledge no God" and who "have made much worse the morals of our people." He was opposed to "permitting the slightest American settlement to be made" because the Louisianians were "losing their faith and their old customs."

Governor Miró, as did the other governors, promised that the immigrants "shall enjoy the same franchises & privileges as the other subjects of his most Catholic Majesty, under the condition they shall at the same time take the due oath of allegiance & bound themselves only to take up arms in defense of this Province against Whatsoever enemy who could attempt to invade it."

While most of the land grants were for comparatively small tracts, during the late 1780's was inaugurated the practice of giving extensive concessions to individuals upon their agreement to bring families and settle them on the land. Bryan Bruin and William Fitzgerald received such grants and settled Catholics from Virginia and New York on them in 1787. In 1795, German Baron de Bastrop received a grant in excess of a million acres northeast of Fort Miró; French Marquis de Maison Rouge, one of over two hundred thousand acres south of that post; and Spaniard Jacinto Mora, the Las Ormegas grant of over two hundred thousand acres east of the Sabine River. Two years later American Ed Murphy secured 144 square miles of land in present-day Sabine Parish.

Many nationalities immigrated to Louisiana during those years. Canary Islanders established settlements at Terre-aux-Boeufs, on the east side of the Mississippi below New Orleans, at Valenzuela on Bayou Lafourche, and along the southern banks of the Amite River. Francisco Bouligny conducted a group from Malaga to the lower Teche region and settled New Iberia. English, German, and other refugees from the American Revolution received lands, as did French colonials who had fled Santo Domingo during the 1790's.

Acadians began to arrive in large numbers during the middle 1760's, and with Spanish financial assistance, continued to come to Louisiana for the next twenty-five years. In 1769, O'Reilly wrote that "the settlement of these poor families is very costly to the exchequer." In 1785 a detailed agreement was drawn up between France and Spain whereby Spain was to transport Acadians who had returned to France to Louisiana, and the next year 375 families with a total of 1,574 persons were brought from one French port alone. The Acadians settled in small groups in the southern sections of the colony, where they became small farmers, herdsmen, and fishermen. Estimates as to the total number who migrated to Louisiana prior to 1790 vary greatly, from as few as 2,500 to as many as 10,000. Governor Miró's census of 1787 listed the number then living in the colony at 1,587, an obvious underestimate.

While Spain spent large sums in assisting other nationals to immigrate to Louisiana, land was the only inducement necessary to attract Americans, who began to arrive shortly after the Revolution. Some came by sea from New England and the Middle Atlantic states, others journeyed overland to Pittsburgh and then floated down the Ohio and Mississippi, as did settlers from Pennsylvania, Kentucky, and Tennessee. Those from the southern seaboard states migrated overland, as one of them wrote to Governor Miró, "thro' a howling Wilderness . . . infected by *hostile Hords* of Savages." Many settlers brought slaves and other movable property with them, while others, according to Carondelet, were "traders, hunters, and vagabonds" but withal a "hardy people who can live on a little maize." Merchants and other businessmen came from American cities, keen for new opportunities at quick fortunes. It was not long after 1783 before American names, as Grace King wrote, "queer and foreign," began to appear "among the French and Spanish, on signboards, in society, in families."

NEGROES, FREE AND SLAVE. In no other southern colonial city, except possibly Charleston, did Free Negroes constitute so important an element in relation to the total population as they did in New Orleans at the end of the Spanish regime. Their numbers had grown steadily, 98 in 1769; 353 in 1778; 1,355 in 1803, or roughly one-ninth of the total population of the city. While many lived in smaller towns, villages, and rural areas, their percentages were not so large as in the capital.

They were divided into two distinct groups, the *gens de couleur libres,* free people of color of mixed blood, and *nègres libres,* free persons of pure African ancestry. These and variant French terms were used to designate the two groups until as late as the 1850's. Both groups enjoyed a degree of governmental protection, had considerable freedom of movement, but were rather strictly regulated in their commercial activities. Their ancestors having been slaves, their status retained certain slave characteristics; they were required to carry certificates of freedom at all times, must obtain special permits to engage in business, and from time to time had imposed upon them regulations closely resembling those for slaves. The two groups were mostly small tradesmen, artisans, carpenters, tailors, or skilled workmen in mechanical trades. In rural areas many owned farms and a small number had plantations—a few of large acreage and with numbers of slaves—which had generally been inherited from white fathers.

The free people of color, as Charles Rousseve states, were "a hot-blooded, self-assertive class, militant and proud." Many of this group had emigrated to Louisiana from Santo Domingo, where they had owned plantations and slaves, and had brought some wealth with them. The Santo Domingans were generally a cultured class having "the customs and manners of a softer climate, a more luxurious society, and a different civilization." In the Church records these people and their descendants were listed as *Creoles de couleur,* just as slaves were referred to as *nègres creoles.*

Sensation- and sales-minded authors have emphasized the young girls of the mixed-blood group who "were placed by their mothers with white men at the age of fourteen or fifteen," have described how "white men, married and unmarried, lavished to a ruinous extent attentions upon these dusky beauties," and have generally given them numbers and an importance out of all historical proportion. They agree that there were at least 1,500 of these women in New Orleans in 1788, and leave the impression that by the 1790's practically every white man in the city maintained a separate house for his other and unmarried wife and her children. The houses were there, but *not* in significant numbers. Nevertheless, the women of this small, mixed-blood group dressed and acted the part of courtesans so effectively and aspired to white association so successfully as to make necessary special regulations regarding their dress and personal actions.

The importation of slaves had declined during the last decades of French control, and when agricultural operations increased after the depression of the 1760's, slavery became a more important economic institution. Slaves were imported from Africa and the West Indies in sizable numbers during the 1770's and 1780's, but the insurrection in 1791 stopped the slave trade with Santo Domingo. While the Spanish attempted a close regulation of the trade, there was considerable smuggling throughout the period.

Slaves were regulated with considerable leniency and caused little trouble during early years, the Spanish generally accepting the old French code of 1724, modified as necessity demanded; after 1791 there was a general tightening of control, caused by the Santo Domingo insurrection, the depression of prices, and the growth in the numbers of slaves on individual plantation units which changed slavery from a patriarchal to an economic institution. On July 11, 1792, Governor Carondelet issued a new series of regulations generally protecting slaves from excessively cruel treatment in that they stipulated maximum hours of labor, that Sundays were to be days of rest except in unusual circumstances when the slave should be compensated, that slaves should have a half-hour for lunch and two hours for dinner, that they should be given adequate clothing in summer and winter, and that "no master shall have the power to have more than thirty blows of the whip dealt to his slave; should he deserve more, he shall leave at least one day's interval between one punishment and the other." These regulations remained in effect, with later additions, throughout the rest of the Spanish period.

With the exception of the threatened Pointe Coupée insurrection of 1795, a plot headed by three white men, Louisiana slaves caused little trouble during the Spanish period. Many were freed by their masters or purchased their freedom. A number fought in the militia companies under Gálvez; and Santiago, who distinguished himself at the siege of Pensacola, was decorated by the Governor.

AGRICULTURE. Louisiana had not reached self-sufficiency in staple foods when Spain acquired the colony; it immediately became the Spanish policy to encourage the production of corn, wheat, meat, and other foodstuffs. In 1768, Governor Ulloa encouraged wheat growing by ordering six horse-drawn mills and six water-driven mills sent to Louisiana, reporting that there were only two horse-drawn mills in the entire colony, one at Opelousas and one at Natchitoches. Once the production of foodstuffs began to increase, the government encouraged the raising of indigo, tobacco, flax, hemp, and cotton in order to swell trade balances and to give Louisianians additional purchasing power.

During the 1770's the government started purchasing tobacco to meet the needs of the tobacco monopoly in Mexico and for export to Europe. In the early summer of 1777, Governor Gálvez called a meeting of tobacco planters to deliberate on a fair price. A price set, he agreed to purchase the entire crop, worked out problems of grading, packing, and shipping with the Viceroy of New Spain, and paid the planters more than 50,000 pesos. By 1790 the production of the Pointe Coupée District alone was nearly 75,000 pounds. Later in the decade, perique tobacco was introduced in the St. James Parish area, it is believed by an Acadian, Pierre Chenet, and soon became a staple product there. By the end of the Spanish period tobacco exports from Louisiana were averaging over 125,000 pounds annually.

Indigo production increased during the first two decades of Spanish control but began to decline because of unfavorable seasons, the attacks of insects, the fact that it produced a rust in wheat, the competition of the Far Eastern product for the European market, and because its manufacture was considered injurious to the health of slaves. It was charged that "on the average, it killed every negro employed in its culture in the short space of five years." By 1800 annual production had dropped to only a few thousand pounds.

Small quantities of wet, partially granulated sugar were exported during the 1760's, but it leaked from the casks so badly as to make production impractical. In 1790, Tahitian seed cane was introduced, and the following year two Spaniards from Santo Domingo began to experiment in Louisiana with the granulation process. One of them achieved partial success and produced a few barrels of sugar. Étienne de Boré, a planter living near New Orleans, purchased seed cane from him, imported an experienced West Indian sugar maker, and built a mill and a drying shed. His experiments achieved success in 1795, earning him the right, as Frederick W. Williamson wrote, "to be called the father of sugar making in Louisiana." By 1802 seventy-five plantations, many of which had sugar mills, were engaged in sugar-cane growing, and the colony boasted over a dozen sugar "refineries."

General agriculture, however, was more commonly practiced; and farmers produced corn, wheat, barley, rice, beans, vegetable crops, livestock, and poultry, while battling floods, insects, and the extremes of hot and cold. During the middle of February, 1784, for example, temperatures along the lower Mississippi fell to below zero, and ice floes, "12 to 30 feet in surface and two or three feet thick," floated past New Orleans. Ranches developed rapidly in the southwest, where the prairies were covered with grass reaching a height of "about 5 feet." The ranches produced horses, cattle averaging from seven hundred to eight hundred pounds, hogs, and numbers of poultry. Branding animals had become a common practice by the early 1770's.

Agricultural labor was scarce throughout the Spanish period, and planters could never secure enough slaves to meet their needs. White laborers, hired by the day or contracted by the month, received an average of about $12.00 per month and board, estimated at $6.00, and on smaller agricultural units lived in the homes of their employers. Girls were contracted for housework, as illustrated by the 1796 contract of Katherine Douberg, a German immigrant, whereby her daughter was "to do maid service in the home of the Manhaupecs for her board and upkeeping including instruction in reading and arithmetic, for twelve years, until she is of age." Boys were likewise contracted for farm work; in 1796, for example, Antonia la Montagne contracted her ten-year-old son to do farm work for ten years, the boy to be given a heifer and a mare and their increase and "to be lodged and fed and clothed; in a word, he is to be treated as a son."

Numerous descriptions of plantations and farms may be gleaned from estate inventories. The inventory of Cazelard Plantation, a comparatively small estate about three miles up the Mississippi from New Orleans, in 1771 listed twelve arpents of land fronting the river, a four-room house, a kitchen, a grange (sheepfold), a storeroom, a hen house, a dovecote, a shed, a warehouse, seven houses for Negroes, a wooden canoe, two worn-out pirogues "used to feed the animals," a small pirogue with four oars and a paddle, twenty-nine slaves, an undetermined number of which were leased rather than owned, twenty-six head of cattle (including oxen), thirty-seven sheep, sixteen hogs, nineteen turkeys, three hens and one rooster, and the usual implements and tools. Not all agriculturists, however, owned this much property. In 1792, Zacherous Routh, a farmer of the Avoyelles District, made his will: "I leave my body to earth, and my soul to God, who gave it to me. I bequeath to my wife the cow . . . [and] give to my son, Ben Routh, my house, 3 cows, and 2 calves, my horse, my tools, etc."

MANUFACTURING AND INDUSTRY. Although the production of manufactured goods increased during the Spanish period, it played but a minor role in the economic life of the colony. The number of timber mills and sawmills increased along the lower Mississippi and other waterways in the southeastern section, and by the end of the century more than $50,000 worth of lumber products were being exported annually. Many plantations produced lumber, tar, and pitch as a by-product to planting activities.

Indigo was processed; hides were tanned, although the quality of the work was poor; an increasing number of mills made flour and corn meal; candles were made from tallow and myrtle wax; bear's oil, lard, and butter, which were given the Spanish group name of *manteca,* were packed in outlying districts and sent to New Orleans for local consumption or for export; tobacco was processed and packed for shipment; syrup was boiled and considerable amounts went into the making of tafia, a spirit similar to New England rum; a rather large number of medicines were manufactured in the northwestern section from wild herbs; and several brickyards were located in the vicinity of New Orleans.

By the end of the century New Orleans had several manufacturing plants, including a cotton mill, a sugar refinery, a large ropewalk, two plants making small shot, one making starch and another producing hair powder, a "beer factory," and a dozen distilleries making large amounts of tafia. Most manufacturing, however, was done in the home to satisfy home and purely local needs and markets, and included furniture, leather shoes, harness and other goods, clothing, utensils, and various tools and other items made of iron.

LOCAL AND MISSISSIPPI RIVER TRADE. Local trading was still done in open-air markets or public squares, but within a few years after the arrival of the Spanish, villages and towns had a few shops carrying all sorts of basic commodities. By the end of the period most of the larger towns had small shops which stocked shoes, clothing, piece goods and notions, imported and domestic foodstuffs, or other specific types of items. Spanish Catalans soon took over the retail trade, but after the Revolutionary War, Americans thronged to New Orleans to go into business.

Goods distribution was in the hands of three types of merchants: first, the merchant who owned a shop; second, the peddler who traveled along the bayous and streams in a trading boat, stopping at every landing; and third, the peddler who roamed the country on foot, on horseback, or in a hack or carriage called a *carriole*. Most trading was done by barter, and there was much haggling over the value of the articles the villagers and country people wanted and the produce they had for trade.

Money gradually became more plentiful as the Spanish imported Mexican silver pesos, *reales de vellon* (especially designated to replace the old French livres), or piastres, which equaled about five livres. As soon as possible the government called in the over seven million French paper livres in circulation and redeemed them at 25 per cent with hard money.

Prices at New Orleans were not excessive, though the value of imported commodities increased as they were moved northward and reached a premium of about 50 per cent in the upper part of the colony. In 1769 fresh beef and pork cost about 6 cents a pound; fresh butter, 25 cents; a jar of milk, 12 cents; and a barrel of kidney beans, $3.75. By the last years of the century sugar was 30 cents a pound; meat, 7 to 10 cents; a hat or pair of shoes, $2.00; a cask of good rum or brandy, $15.00; and a barrel of tafia, $60.00.

Ordinarily goods were shipped by boat along one of the numerous waterways which threaded the entire area. There was no uncertainty on one of the major rivers or bayous, but the journey from New Orleans to Opelousas, for example, was slow and circuitous. The few cross-country land routes were merely traces, as both French and Spanish simply marked the trees and used them as guides through the wilderness; the royal roads fronting the rivers and streams of more populated sections were little more than cleared trails. The old Route de Bienville ran from present-day Vidalia westward through the lowlands and divided into two trails, each leading northwestward to Natchitoches. From Natchitoches the Camino Real passed through Los Adaes, Nacogdoches, and on through Texas to the City of Mexico. Northward from Natchitoches a trail wound its way to the thinly settled areas in north Louisiana and Arkansas, while a cattle-and-horse trail went southeasterly toward the southern reaches of the Teche, to join another trail from southern Texas and turn eastward to New Orleans. Not without reason has it been said that all early Louisiana roads led to Natchitoches. After 1795 the Natchez Trace was opened from Nashville southward and for several decades was the principal land route to Kentucky and Tennessee.

Settlements along the upper Mississippi, in Arkansas, and in northern and northwestern Louisiana shipped salt meat, hides and furs, bear's grease and buffalo suet, medicinal and other herbs, corn and corn meal, flour, and other goods to New Orleans on flatboats, keelboats, scows, broad horns, and other types of river craft. They generally came down during the winter or early spring when the water was high and returned in the summer, laden with manufactured goods and supplies of various sorts, when the water was low.

It is believed that the Ohio River settlers of western Pennsylvania, Virginia, and Kentucky first attempting to sell goods at New Orleans about 1770 were refused clearance by Spanish officials, and that the first successful trading voyage was made by Jacob Yoder, who left Fort Redstone on the Monongahela River in May, 1782, with a flatboat of produce. In 1784, Acting Governor Miró received instructions to stop American navigation of the Mississippi, which he did not do because the Spanish needed American products. Some boats were confiscated in 1786, but the following year royal orders opened the Mississippi to American commerce subject to a 25 per cent duty. The duty was lowered to 15 per cent in 1788, and for persons of importance, to only 6 per cent. The New Orleans fire of 1788 greatly stimulated trade, and by 1790 American flatboats were arriving in ever increasing numbers. The Treaty of 1795 further opened trading opportunities. Nearly 600 river boats landed at New Orleans in 1801, and the following year over 80,000 barrels of flour were sold there. During the entire period, however, the vexations, seizures, confiscations, imprisonments, and interferences were numerous, despite the need of Louisianians for many American commodities for local consumption and for export, goods which in 1802 were valued at nearly $5,000,000.

FOREIGN TRADE. Foreign trade presented as many difficulties to the Spanish government as it had to the French, for both nations believed in the mercantile system of commerce through which mother countries profited from the economic production of their colonies. The first regulations were issued by Governor Ulloa in 1766 and limited foreign trade to six peninsular ports, but the economic depression soon forced duty exemptions on Spanish merchandise and permission for two French vessels a year to trade at New Orleans. O'Reilly reported that "this province cannot live without commerce" and recommended free trade with Spain and Havana, then permitted the smuggling of British goods and the temporary duty-free use of the port of New Orleans. Unzaga secured the lowering of duties, and in 1778 Gálvez, "owing to the distress of the times," obtained freedom of trade with Cuba, Yucatán, France, and the United States, which "revived the industry and activity of the merchants and planters." The King's schedule of 1782 permitted direct trade with France and with all ports of allied and friendly nations, a policy more or less in effect until intercourse with France was stopped during the French Revolution in 1793.

A large contraband trade began with the British after they occupied West Florida in 1763 and continued until Gálvez conquered the area during the American Revolution. Although the trade was against Spanish commercial policy, Louisiana governors consistently closed their eyes to violations, for the colony desperately needed the goods the British had to sell. British vessels sailed directly to the mouth of the Mississippi and upriver past New Orleans, ostensibly on their way to the West Florida settlements of Manchac and Baton Rouge, but once past the city, "made fast to a tree . . . where the people of the city and neighbouring plantations came to trade with them." While Spanish officials did not object to the English purchase of planters' products, they disapproved of the English furnishing "the planters with what they need," to the detriment of Spanish traders; one official reported that "it would be necessary to place a guard in every house" to stop it and that the commerce of the colony amounted "annually to about $600,000, of which only $15,000 belongs to the Spanish commerce." After 1783 the British firm of Panton, Leslie and Company was granted a trade monopoly in the Floridas and soon won over the southern Indian trade, thus helping to hold the friendship of the Indians for Spain.

Spain continued to prohibit the Louisiana-Texas trade after she gained possession of the Louisiana colony. The Texans were eager to exchange their horses, mules, and cattle for Louisiana's manufactured goods and for products such as sugar and tobacco, but New Spain opposed the trade because it cut heavily into the profits of Mexican merchants and of the government tobacco monopoly. Spanish policy was indecisive until 1788, when upon the specific orders of Governor Miró, Louis de Blanc, Commandant at Natchitoches, proclaimed: "We are expressly forbidden to give any passport to the provinces of Texas, or to allow the entry of any merchandise whatsoever into the kingdom of New Spain since it is contraband." The trade continued, nevertheless, until the end of the Spanish period.

At the beginning of the Spanish regime Louisiana exports were comparatively few and in order of importance included indigo, deerskins, lumber, naval stores, rice, peas and beans, and tallow, to a total value of about $250,000. By 1770 the value of exports was estimated at over $600,000, and by 1802, augmented by goods received from western Americans for reshipment, had multiplied several times. In 1802 exports included: over 2,000,000 pounds of cotton, nearly 2,500,000 pounds of sugar, 225,000 pounds of deer hides, 167,000 pounds of lead, 2,000 hogsheads of tobacco, 50,000 barrels of flour, 3,000 barrels of salt beef and pork, 800 hogsheads of molasses, and such unusual items as 350,000 flints, 34,500 pounds of raisins, 38,500 pounds of cheese, 6,100 reams of letter paper and 6,300 pieces of "paper hangings," 11,000 pounds of paints, and 10,000 pounds of "hair powder." Among the more unusual exports were 54 snuff bottles, 31 pairs of pistols, 4 hand organs, 3 pairs of ready-made sheets, 1 ship anchor, and 1 grandfather clock.

In 1788, Martin Navarro, treasurer of the colony, reported that one-third of all Louisiana imports consisted of wines and liquors, one-third manufactured goods primarily from France, and one-third flour which came chiefly from Philadelphia. By 1802 the chief imports included steel, fish, coffee, hemp, meats, nails, cloth, hardware and tools, tile, corks, cordage, soap and other sundries, shoes and clothing, empty bottles (over 100,000), whiskey, wines, and other liquors, flour, beans, and other foodstuffs, in general the necessary goods of a rapidly growing agricultural economy. Among the more unusual items were over 5,000 fishing lines, 26 telescopes, 6 woolen carpets, 6 sets of brass-mounted harness, 2 mahogany bookcases, 2 fire engines, and one "riding chair."

The foreign trade grew rapidly during the 1790's. Only 31 ships cleared the port of New Orleans in 1794, but the number increased to 78 in 1799, slightly over 200 in 1801, and 265 in 1802, of which 158 were American, 104 Spanish, and only 3 French; 74 of them sailed for American ports in 1802. Spanish Louisiana, however, never had a favorable trade balance, and the government annually paid a *situado*, a cash payment to make up the difference, which in one year amounted to over 500,000 pesos.

GOVERNMENT AND THE LAW. Many Spanish governmental records are still extant in Louisiana, reposing in their boxes or on the shelves in the Cabildo, in offices of clerks of court in parish courthouses, or in other repositories. Many of them are ill housed and all of them ill cared for. They are not "dead documents" but are filled with life, for with the Spanish, as Henry P. Dart once wrote, "it was the rule to spare neither ink nor paper in their composition." These records, on folio sheets and numbered only on one side, were meticulously written and all corrections were carefully attested. Signatures were classified, and all were followed by a paraph, a sort of flourish somewhat in the nature of a trademark, which further identified the official.

On December 10, 1769, General O'Reilly, acting in his capacity as the ranking Spanish official in Louisiana, reported that he "had established in that province the Laws of the Indies and the political government prescribed by them." The Louisiana government differed from some other Spanish colonies in that its *Governor* was appointed by the King, yet it was under the Captain General of Cuba, and through him under the Viceroy of New Spain in the City of Mexico. Within these limits, the Governor's authority was practically supreme; he issued instructions and regulations which had the effect of laws, had complete civil and military powers, represented the King, and had much to do with the appointment of minor officials.

O'Reilly organized a municipal council for New Orleans called the *Cabildo*, a quaisi-deliberative, -administrative, and -judicial body, which advised the Governor, suggested policies concerning the public welfare, sat as a court of appeals for the colony in civil cases, and in its administrative capacity governed the city.

The Governor installed major officials in their offices. The *Intendant* administered revenues and controlled the commercial and naval departments. His office was separate and independent of the governorship, which frequently caused difficulties. A *collector* collected taxes and other monies due the government and turned the sums over to a treasurer, a *Contador* kept account of all receipts and disbursements, and an *Interventor* superintended purchases and sales. An *auditor of war* advised the Governor in legal matters, while an *auditor of the intendancy* advised the Intendant. A *Procurador*, or attorney general, proposed measures beneficial to the people and defended their rights, rather than acting as a prosecutor. The *Administrador* managed customhouse matters, assisted by a harbor master, a collector, and a special notary. A *Lieutenant Governor* was stationed at St. Louis and another at Natchitoches to assist the Governor in general administrative problems. There were French-, English-, and Indian-language interpreters and several notaries public. A *judge of residence* acted as the censor of all officials, investigated their official conduct when they left office, and made a complete report to the Council of the Indies, the official agency governing Spanish colonies. Several minor officials administered lesser details of government.

The *Cabildo,* whose members must all be landowners, was composed of *regidores,* which included the *alferez real* (royal standard bearer), *alcalde mayor provincial* (a sort of combined city judge and chief of police), *alguazil mayor* (high constable and keeper of the prison), *depositar general* (treasurer of the city for a 3 per cent commission), *pena de camara* (a keeper of fines, who kept a 10 per cent commission), a *mayordomo de propios* (mayor, commissioner of public works, and tax collector combined, who also kept a small percentage of the tax money), two *alcaldes* (city judges), a *syndic procurador general* (a sort of city attorney), and an *escribano* (the clerk of the body).

The *regidores,* who purchased their positions, were jealous of their importance and carried heavily ornamented walking sticks as emblems of authority (in 1787 they protested that their canes were "very shabby and the golden handles were worn out" and a horrified *Cabildo* immediately ordered the purchase of new *bastons*). The *regidores* elected the other members of the *Cabildo* for varying terms.

The *Cabildo* met every Friday, and the Governor had authority to convene it at any time. The Governor presided, and in his absence one of the *alcaldes,* in which case two of the *regidores* immediately after a session went to the Governor's house and informed him of what had taken place. Salaries of *Cabildo* members ranged from 100 pesos to 800 pesos a year, depending upon the importance of the respective position, though some of the members had their salaries lowered later. The Governor and the *Cabildo* regulated every phase of city life.

Outside New Orleans, O'Reilly divided the colony into twelve districts, including New Orleans, for the purpose of local government, and this number was later increased as the population grew. District government was in charge of a *Commandant,* a combination military, administrative, and judicial official who also acted as Indian agent. He registered titles to lands, witnessed contracts, performed marriage ceremonies, took inventories of property, acted as sheriff of his district, and judged all cases involving not more than $20.00. He received his regular army salary, legal fees allowed him by law, and a small allowance for supplies. *Syndics* (justices of the peace), who generally governed parish or subdistrict units, had charge of levees and roads, controlled travelers and Negroes, and heard less-important civil cases. Citizens paid no taxes but were forced to keep roads, levees, bridges, and ferries in good condition.

Governor O'Reilly officially abolished French laws and legal practices in 1769 and issued two ordinances generally known as O'Reilly's Code, which presented in abstract form the laws of Spain and those for the government of Spain's colonies which would be used in Louisiana. Other regulations were issued from time to time. Legal practice stemmed not only from Spanish regulations but from the French Code Louis of 1667.

Ordinary court cases in the districts began with the Syndics and the Commandants and were then appealed to the Governor, who referred them to one of several courts into which the *Cabildo* was divided. There was no appeal from the *Alcalde mayor provincial,* and not even the Governor could pardon criminals. Civil cases involving more than $330.00 might be appealed after 1781 to the *Audiencia* at Havana, and from that court to the Council of the Indies in Spain. The charge has been made that Spanish justice "reeked with graft" and was "controlled and swayed according to the power or the wealth of the litigant." However, Henry P. Dart wrote that "what time and fire and water and theft have left to us is enough to prove that the

[138]

legal end of government under Spain was handled with care and skill and on the whole with a justice which is very pleasant to contemplate," and John Walton Caughey tersely observed that "by comparison with the administration of justice in the preceding French regime, that of the Spanish period was highly efficient."

Justice was rapid and there was apparently little if any favoritism. Civil suits were settled, divorces granted, marriage contracts witnessed, land titles legalized, and criminals convicted and punished. Torture was permitted as it had been under the French. In 1778, for example, the Negro Jacob, who was charged with murder, was "placed upon a gun carriage at a distance from the fire, because there was no other machine for roasting (*maquina de las asadas*) in the prison and having applied it in a manner that he felt the heat, he cried out denying the act;" three additional attempts to wring a confession failed, and Jacob was acquitted.

Punishments were still harsh and barbarous. In 1771 two slaves convicted of murder were hanged and their heads and hands cut off and nailed to a post on the public road. In 1778 the sentence of Negro slave Clement, convicted of having murdered his brother, read: "Clement has been condemned to the ordinary penalty of death on the gallows, after having been lashed at the foot of the gallows, after death his body put in a leather sack with a dog, a monkey, a viper, and a cock and the sack sewed up at the mouth will be dragged along and pitched into the river." In 1780, Molly Glass, a murderess, was sentenced to be hanged, "and when cutt down, her head to be severed from the body and stuck up upon a pole at her former place of residence at Browns Cliffs and her right hand to be nailed to the same Post."

Even the bodies of those already dead were sometimes punished. The body of the Indian slave Jean Baptiste, who had "hung himself with a rope to a peach tree," was sentenced to be tied to the back of a cart "head downwards and face to the ground, and to be thus dragged through the streets of this City to the place where he will be hung by the feet to a scaffold for that purpose erected at said place, and after having remained there twenty-four hours to be thrown into the public sewer."

But not all court cases were horrible, nor the punishments barbaric. In 1781, Miguel Homes brought charges against Santiago Dupre, Pedro Guerin, and accomplices for having beaten him up in a row following a game of "eleven" at a Sunday night dance at Guerin's house which did not break up until 7 o'clock Monday morning. The judge closed the case by jailing Dupre and fining the others, including the plaintiff Homes, for "the judge was the only man who could recall . . . the Sunday night dance at Pedro Guerin's place on January 14, 1781."

The costs of Spanish administration in Louisiana were high. By 1785, Spain was spending an average of $16.55 per capita in that colony, while Great Britain was spending only about 15 cents per capita in North Carolina. The colony never met expenses, and in 1797 the deficit was nearly $260,000; salaries, maintenance of troops, establishment and upkeep of fortifications and public buildings, gifts and other Indian expenses, expenses of the Church, agricultural, industrial and commercial subsidies, all items had gradually risen over the years. At the beginning of October, 1800, the Intendant had only 8,000 pesos and owed 200,000; the King had forbidden the issuance of paper money, but the Intendant threatened to do so unless someone relieved his distress. The Louisiana colony was given back to France the same month, but Spain had to foot its bills for two more years.

INDIAN AFFAIRS. The Spanish pursued an honorable Indian policy and through a system of councils, regular gifts, and efficient trading methods generally kept the tribes at peace and allied to themselves rather than to the Americans. They showed proper respect to individual chiefs, furnished goods at "the ordinary trade price," attempted to keep unlicensed traders and "rovers" from trespassing, gave medals to chiefs for "distinguished services," and attempted to prevent whites from settling on Indian lands. Indian slavery was forbidden by O'Reilly, the prohibition was rather efficiently enforced by succeeding governors, and the Indian was given justice in the courts.

Complaints against Indians were generally over the theft of supplies and animals. In June, 1782, Antonio Maxent wrote from Galveztown that a "great number" of Indians were "wandering about the neighborhood" and "doing injury to the poor inhabitants, for there is not an animal belonging to them that they do not kill." Six months later he complained that 400 Choctaws were encamped nearby and that 1,500 more were expected to arrive on their way to New Orleans. He had to feed the Indians, and they were stealing from the settlers; they had broken into his warehouse and stolen twenty barrels of corn and forty barrels of potatoes. Another report from the Sabine area complained that the Indians had eaten all the corn crop and almost all the beans, pumpkins, and watermelons, and that sugar was getting short because they found it "most pleasing to their appetites."

The Indian trade was an important source of revenue for the outlying settlements, and the governors constantly attempted to regulate it through a system of licensed traders. After 1783 the trade east of the Mississippi was generally carried on through the British firm of Panton, Leslie and Company; west of the river it was done through individually licensed traders. The Texas Indian trade presented unusual difficulties. While Texas was under the jurisdiction of Mexico, those sections near Louisiana were 1,500 miles from the capital and it was easier for the Indians there to do business with traders operating from Natchitoches. More than one viceroy of New Spain complained that the east Texas Indians, and even the Apaches, were being supplied from Louisiana.

Indians traded skins, hides, medicinal herbs, and a few other items for muskets, powder, lead, knives, clothing, tobacco, and such miscellaneous goods and notions as mirrors, beads, lace, ribbons, needles, combs, bells, scissors, dyes, buckles, and fancy foodstuffs. The trading in rum, tafia, and other liquors was closely watched at the trading posts, and their sale was prohibited by several governors, though unlicensed traders continued to ply the streams of the northwestern country in boats loaded with intoxicants.

Governors and commandants carried on a more or less regular and friendly correspondence with the chiefs. In 1794, for example, Franchmastabbia (which was spelled in a half-dozen ways), chief of the Choctaws, wrote to Commandant Gayoso de Lemos at Natchez:

OLD FRIEND AND BROTHER

This Comes to Let you no that I am well and hope this will find you in the Same

This is to Let you no that I am a man of a Strate hart and one talk and don want to tell you lyes nor to hid any talk from you—

I Believe in you and you Believe in me   Our Acquaincence is Small but the Chaine of our Frindship is Grate   We are bound to hid no bad talks from Each other

The Silver wair that was Sent from the Stats to me I did not Send for it   for that reason your hart will tell you what Sattisfaction you will make for it

Old Friend I have not for Got your Talk but I shall for Bare Beging   I am old and Is a Red man   I Cant Make nothing But Children   For that Reason I shall Leave it to your one hart to Send Me Just what you Please   I think Its is too hard for me to Send for what is not Mine and to Beg I never did   I shall Leave ite to your one hart to Scend By my Nephefew what you think is Best for an ole Red man

You have Seen and heard Everything there is Pasing and My Nephfew will in form you of the talk that we hav now—

I have nothing to Inform you of More that you will heare—

So no more But Remaine With Esteem your Sincere Friend and Brother

Franchmastabbia

To His Excellency DON MANUEL GAYOSO DE LEMOUS

[140]

CHAPTER 13

SOCIAL AND CULTURAL LIFE
IN SPANISH LOUISIANA

FRENCH CREOLES NEVER BECOME SPANISH. Spanish colonial Louisiana began with a rebellion against Governor Ulloa, and the execution of the French Creole rebel leaders by Governor O'Reilly created intense and lasting animosity toward Spain and the Spanish. O'Reilly and the succeeding governors, however, went to unusual extremes to placate the French and promote an acceptance of the Spanish regime; even O'Reilly on more than one occasion signed his name "Alexandre" instead of the spanish form "Alejandro." They appointed French Creoles to high positions in the army and in the colonial government, permitted them to hold the great majority of the local offices and generally to govern themselves, and allowed them to continue speaking French.

The Spanish faced a difficult task, for the average French Creole was a highly individualistic and in some ways a most peculiar person. He made little attempt to adjust himself to the new government. In the larger towns, particularly in New Orleans, he frequently refused to obey the laws; and the Spanish, vainly trying to gain acceptance of their regime, seldom prosecuted or punished him. His relationships with his neighbors, according to modern historian Minter Wood, "were marked by abuse, sarcasm, gossiping and quarreling." Berquin du Vallon, a French author who wrote during the last years of the Spanish period, stated flatly that the French Creole had "more simplicity than kindness, more conceit than pride, more slyness than penetration," and that he lied about everything, "sometimes about nothing, just for the pleasure of it." While Du Vallon may have gone too far in his condemnation, it certainly carried some elements of truth.

French hatred of the Spanish slowly declined in intensity as time passed and the Louisianians observed the benefits of the Spanish government. They were flattered when they were appointed to local offices, and they took justifiable pride in the roles they played during the campaigns of Gálvez against the British. Furthermore, they received enormous satisfaction from filling their money chests much more rapidly and easily than was possible only a few short years previously. The French colonials who came to Louisiana from Santo Domingo after the Negro insurrection of 1791 brought no hatreds against the Spanish, and as many were wealthy and cultured, they immediately gained a high position in the society of the Louisiana colony.

The French Louisianians, however, would not speak Spanish nor would they accept Spanish social customs. French was the language of the people. French was the language even in the homes of Spaniards who had married French Creole women and few of their offspring were taught Spanish. At social functions the language was French, the food was French, the wines and liquors were French, the formalities were those of Paris, and even the cotillions were patterned after Versailles rather than the courts of Iberian rulers.

The French Creole regarded the bloodlettings of the French Revolution distantly, but the creation of the new Republic in France fired his long-suppressed enthusiasms. By 1793, when Spain's foe was republican France, Carondelet found he was only holding a town of the enemy. The Creole could no longer restrain himself. He defiantly shrieked, *"Ça ira, ça ira, les aristocrates à la lanterne,"* though there was not a lamppost in New Orleans until three years later. Carondelet sent comparatively few to exile in Cuba.

Seldom in history has a dominant power been so lenient with colonials of another nationality, and seldom has the ruling nationality been so quickly and so completely dominated and assimilated by that held under control. The Spanish, therefore, left comparatively few traces of their colonial rule in Louisiana. Many of the French, however, did not forget that their life under the Spanish had been peaceful and happy.

TOWNS, VILLAGES, AND FARMS. By the end of the Spanish regime the population of the colony had increased more than 500 per cent. New Orleans had grown rapidly and Natchitoches, Baton Rouge, Les Rapides (Pineville), Opelousas, Atakapas (St. Martinville), and the various suburbs of New Orleans had developed from tiny villages into small but thriving towns. Farms and plantations lined the Mississippi and most of the bayous and streams in the southeastern section of the colony, the Red River section was settled as far as Natchitoches, most of the land in the Florida Parishes had been occupied, the Ouachita River area was rapidly being filled, and Fort Miró (Monroe) had become a small town.

Only in the southwestern, western, and northern sections were the settlers few and widely scattered.

Whereas the population had been predominantly French at the beginning of the period, the descendants of French from the Mother Country was now a minority; for there were many Acadians, Creoles from Santo Domingo, Spaniards and Canary Islanders, additional Germans and Swiss, and a few Scandinavians and Gypsies. Englishmen, Scots, and Irishmen had settled in the Florida Parishes prior to 1775, while British colonials and Americans had established themselves in the Florida Parishes, the central area around Opelousas, and in towns and villages after that date. The Spanish policy of opening their colony to settlement had paid handsomely in population increase.

New Orleans, when O'Reilly arrived, was only a small and unimposing town. Of its total of sixty-six squares, eleven squares fronting the river and six squares in depth, only about thirty had been laid off into lots and had houses or other buildings on them. The majority of the buildings were of wood, though some were built with timber frames filled in with brick or *bousillage*. The Church of St. Louis, backing the Place d'Armes, was described in 1768 by British Lieutenant Philip Pittman as "in so ruinous a condition that divine service has not been performed in it since the year 1766." According to Pittman the house of the Capuchins, on the left hand side of the church, was "totally deserted and gone to ruin." On the right side of the church were the prison and the guardhouse, which were in good condition. The barracks, formerly located on both sides of the plaza, were "entirely destroyed." The town had no public lighting, no drainage system, no fire-fighting equipment or fire companies, and no night watch or city guard. Its fortifications, which consisted principally of a poor stockade fronted by a small ditch, according to Pittman could be of no use except against Indians or slaves.

New Orleans was rebuilt following the fires of 1788 and 1794; thus by 1803 it was a comparatively new city with well-built houses and other buildings constructed in the Spanish style. The town was surrounded by an earthwork and palisaded walls, and five redoubts, or bastions, called "forts," offered additional protection. Fort San Luis faced the river upstream and directly behind it was Fort San José; facing the river downstream was Fort San Carlos and behind it stood Fort San Juan. Fort San Fernando stood in the center of the land side of the town. As John Pintard wrote, after visiting New Orleans in 1801, "the city is encircled by Saints alth[ough] it may be filled with Heretics & sinners."

Pintard also noted that public buildings were numerous and that the Cathedral was "a handsome square building of brick coated with white plaister [*sic*] that resembles stone. . . . The Town House is a very beautiful building of 2 stories forming a wing to the Cathedral, with wh[ich] the Bishops Palace is to correspond, & when finished will make a very elegant appearance." The Cabildo housed public auction rooms, the town prison, and "the public Hall—where the council assembles to regulate the town affairs, and where Concerts are sometimes performed." On either side of the square fronting the Cathedral were soldiers' barracks, adjoined by the military hospital on the downriver side. The Charity Hospital was at the rear of the town and was "not much used," while the market adjoined the levee at the lower corner. The visitor, however, was extremely critical of the market, for the market, "of all places of the kind is the most filthy I have ever seen—whether it be ever hoed out or not I cannot say—."

He was graphic in his description of the cemetery, which was just outside the city: "Everyone who dies here must literally find a watery grave—This being consecrated ground—Heretics are not allowed to be interred within its pale—The poor Americans are of course deposited indiscriminately without the Burial place—It is of little consequence whether ones carcass is given a prey to crayfish on land—or the catfish of the Mississipi [*sic*] . . . a body is speedily devoured & transmigrated in crayfish or catfish dressed by a French cook & feasted upon by a greasy Monk—a fair lady—a petit maitre or a savage who in their turn supply some future banquet—Heavens what luxury! Mon Dieu, quelle sort! Give my bones terra firma I pray."

William Johnson, who visited New Orleans the same year, was more complimentary of the city in his diary entries: "New Orleans is a large and beautiful town, containing about 1,600 houses and about 11,000 souls. The streets are narrow but regular; the houses have principally flat roofs and are mostly elegantly built. The whole city is inclosed in either walls or pickets, at every convenient part of which are iron gates through which all persons or carriages must pass to go in or out of town. Sentinels are kept night and day. . . . A garrison is continually kept in the city and contains three regiments of Mexican and Havana troops. A governor and attendant [*sic*] are the principal officers of justice before whom all causes of whatsoever nature must inevitably come."

Within the wooden and earth fortifications lay a town whose streets were straight, even though they were unpaved, and filled with mud, garbage, and crawfish holes. The narrow plank walks and small bridges over the gutters at the corners were in bad repair. The streets were impassable seas of mud during rainy seasons, and at such times, according to Minter Wood, "the lack of drainage made veritable cesspools in the town's center, for refuse of all sorts and the dung of horses and cows which was never carted away presented a sea of filth and slime a foot deep to separate neighbors and produce a stench when half dry." On the other hand, the town had a regular night watch, fire-fighting and axmen companies, and street lights.

Its total population was estimated at from about 8,000 to as high as 13,000. From two-thirds to three-fifths of the people were whites, the rest being Negro or mixed-blood freedmen and slaves. About half of the white population were French Creoles, some 25 per cent were Spanish, and the rest were Americans, British, Germans, and persons of other nationalities.

French historian Georges Oudard admits that although the population of the city had grown over 300 per cent, the character of its French Creole inhabitants "had not changed. They were still the sons of those bold adventurers, gamblers and debauches who had founded Louisiana. . . . Devoted to every form of pleasure, they were usually ignorant, indifferent to education and even to reading." The Frenchman might have added that perhaps a majority of the newcomers were adventurers, out to make their fortunes. New Orleans, at the end of the Spanish regime, was not unlike an overgrown frontier boom town in many ways.

A traveler up the Mississippi passed first the Tchoupitoulas Coast, then the First German Coast, the Second German Coast, the First Acadian Coast (called "Cabanose" or "Cabahanose" in some of the documents), the Second Acadian Coast, the Iberville Coast, the Baton Rouge Coast, the Punta Cortada or Pointe Coupée Coast, and on the east bank the Thompson's Creek and Bayou Sara communities. Eastward from the mouth of Bayou Manchac was Galveztown. If the traveler journeyed up the Red River he first passed Les Rapides (called "El Rapido" by the Spanish) before arriving at the old French town of Natchitoches. If he journeyed up the Ouachita, he eventually arrived at Fort Miró, center of the Ouachita community. Southward from Les Rapides were Opelousas, market town of a large area rapidly being filled by Americans, and Atakapas, the old capital of the Atakapas District.

Farther down the Teche was the growing Spanish settlement of New Iberia. There were no sizable villages on bayous or streams in this section, but along all the waterways were farms and plantations, ranches, truck farms, and the homes of hunters and fishermen.

These settlements were small villages in 1769, but by the end of the century a few had grown into sizable towns. As late as 1788, for example, the entire Ouachita District had only about two hundred inhabitants, of whom Don Juan Filhiol, Captain of Militia and Commandant of the post, wrote: "These men are composed of the scum of all sorts of nations, several fugitives from their native countries. . . . They excel in all the vices, and their life is a veritable scandal. The savages . . . hold them in contempt." By the end of the Spanish period the population of Fort Miró had grown to 450 whites and 50 to 60 slaves, its citizens being "Canadians, Spanish from Mexico, some Irish, some Americans, a small number of French born in France, some from Santo Domingo," according to the French traveler Abbé Charles Robin.

CONDITIONS OF TRAVEL. Conditions of travel improved but little during the forty years of Spanish control and continued to be slow and hazardous. Most journeys were still made over the various waterways in boats, but the same dangers and discomforts existed as during French times. However, boats were improved during the period, and many were outfitted with crudely built wooden shelters or tents. In 1790, when Julian Poydras traveled along the Mississippi, his flatboat was "covered with a tent, but he had with him six oarsmen, a cook and a servant, and lived in regal fashion."

Chaises, berlins, and coaches became fashionable with the more affluent in the towns and villages, but farmers and ordinary townspeople traveled by wagon, oxcart, or on horseback. By the last years of the period a few stagecoaches were running irregularly between the more important towns, although discomforts were many and progress was extremely slow, thirty-five to forty miles in fifteen or sixteen hours being considered good time. Frequently the driver had to leave the road and find a route across open fields, checking the ruts and marking a path "by guiding stakes which he cut from the underbrush with his hatchet." Fence rails were sometimes used to pry the coach out of mud holes, and when deep streams were forded, the ladies stood on the seats to avoid the water which frequently flooded the floor of the vehicle.

HOMES AND HOME FURNISHINGS. The homes of New Orleans greatly increased in size, comfort, and ostentation during the last forty years of the eighteenth century. City housebuilding regulations, first issued after the fire of 1788 and strengthened after the fire of 1794, required that all houses of more than one story should be constructed of brick. Lumber used for one-story houses and for all finishing work should be cypress cut during specific periods of the year and even during certain phases of the moon. Such lumber was believed to better resist decay and the attacks of insects. Half-round red French tiles or flat green Spanish tiles should be used rather than wooden shingles. Many of the new houses were flat roofed according to the Spanish custom in order that the family might enjoy the late afternoon and early evening breezes. The houses were built flush with the banquette and behind them were typical Spanish courtyards.

Wrought-iron decorations began to appear on the balconies and at the windows during the early 1790's. Contrary to popular belief, most of this ironwork was Castilian and was manufactured in Spain rather than being hammered out by skilled slaves in New Orleans. Spanish ironwork was grained somewhat like wood and did not rust, being of the puddled and slag-bearing variety. Balcony railings and other decorative work of wrought-iron were popular until about 1830, when it was largely replaced by cast iron, highly susceptive to rust and requiring frequent painting.

Country and village residents continued to live in *poteaux en terre* or *brique entre poteaux* houses built after the French fashion or in hand-sawed lumber houses or log cabins constructed according to American methods.

The larger homes of New Orleans and the country districts began to be furnished better during the last two decades of the century, and while the best furniture came from France and Spain, several furniture makers of New Orleans gained considerable reputation with their products. Spanish officialdom set the styles in cabinets, tables, sofas, chairs, chests, bureaus, and other pieces, although it was some years before the older and more conservative French Creole families would accept them. The home furnishings of the common people remained much as they had been during French years.

In 1785 the household furnishings of Antonio Morin, who lived in New Orleans, was appraised at only 133 pesos, and included an old walnut armoire, 2 small walnut tables, 12 chairs "good and bad," a pair of chimney irons, a large kettle, a gridiron, a large earthen jar, a cypress bed "together with 1 straw, 1 feather and 1 moss mattress, 1 pillow, 1 striped mosquito bar and 1 woolen blanket," and a large cypress chest. Fourteen years later the home of farmer Gidgeon Walker of the Avoyelles District contained only a bed, a chest, a mirror, a pressing iron, a pair of scissors, a large bucket, 2 knives, 3 chairs, a table, a blanket and spread, a few dishes, and cooking utensils.

Nowhere in the Spanish Judicial Records is listed a stove, a churn, a carpet, or a spinning wheel, and only a few Dutch ovens were among the possessions of French Creoles. These items were first introduced by American colonials, British, or Acadians prior to the American Revolution, but the French Creoles were extremely slow in adopting them. Containers for liquids, particularly bottles, were scarce. Among the curiosities of Creole homes was the *rondin,* a large wooden roller used to smooth out the sheets before retiring. Other Creole household items were "chocolate pots," clocks, framed pictures, watches, religious objects, various types of "night vessels," and musical instruments.

CLOTHING. Imported clothing became more common after the arrival of the Spanish, for the colonists had considerably more money to spend, and by 1800 the shops of New Orleans and the larger towns carried stocks from Spain, France, Great Britain, and the United States. In 1797 the average cost of a man's coat of ordinary material and quality was $3.00; a pair of trousers, $2.00; a hat, $2.00; and a pair of shoes, $2.00. Women's skirts, blouses, petticoats, stockings, and shoes were about the same price.

All classes frequently dressed beyond their means, as the inventories of the property of deceased persons reveal, although the French and Spanish were more inclined to do so than Americans, British, or Germans. Government officials, ship captains, planters, doctors, and businessmen almost without exception kept themselves and their wives at the height of fashion. When ship captain Edward Jenkins (which was spelled by the Spanish Eduardo Juan Kins) died in 1777, his clothing inventory included shirts, stocks, cotton and silk stockings, waistcoats, cravats, handkerchiefs, silk sashes, vests, a dark-blue "Bergot" rain coat, a "suit of white cloth with blue silk vest trimmed with lace," several pairs of trousers one of which was of "black silk with holes bored in the leather trimming," and a suit "of Queens velvet with vest and two pairs of trousers, manufactured in Peru." Seven years later Santiago Lemelle's clothing inventory included 30 shirts, 42 vests, 13 handkerchiefs, 14 caps, 10 pairs of drawers, 27 pairs of trousers, and several coats and suits.

Men's accessories were numerous and were frequently of considerable value. Included were such items as toothbrushes and tooth powders, "iron pincers to cut the nails," lace ruffles, ornamental patches or plasters for the face, fancy nightcaps, gold and silver cravats, belts, and shoe buckles, gold and silver buttons, gold-lace-trimmed smoking jackets, walking sticks with ornamented heads and gold trimmings, silk shoes, and "Indian silk" jackets.

Women dressed just as extravagantly and elaborately in silks, *mousselines,* velvets, laces, taffetas, and rich embroideries; wore plumed, beaded, or gemmed aigrettes and quantities of jewelry; and creamed, powdered, and painted their faces. When Antonia del Castillo, the wife of Lieutenant Francisco Godoy, died in 1783 she left clothing and jewelry valued at over 500 pesos, including point-lace veils; "one pair of flower of thistle corsets"; fans, one with "gold sticks"; pearls; rings; ornamental buttons; a "little dove, made of stones, for the neck"; a pair of earrings with "stones from Thrace"; and a "gold enchased rosary with its cross and beads intact" valued at 50 pesos.

Inventories and accounts of shops and stores reveal that cosmetics, perfumes, fancy soap, pomades, hair powders, and other such items were much in demand by both sexes and were carried in quantity. Residents of New Orleans dressed more elegantly than citizens of American cities and held their own with those of Havana, the City of Mexico, and other Latin-American capitals.

FOOD AND FOOD SUPPLIES. Louisiana became self-sufficient in basic and staple food supplies within a few years after Spain acquired the colony, and needed to import only luxury foods. More than enough meat, grains, vegetables, and fruits were produced for home needs, and often there was a surplus for export. The rough diet of French days passed; it was seldom necessary for even the poorest farmers to subsist on *gru* or *sagamite.* Only in the frontier districts was there a lack of food variety. Methods of food distribution improved, for Spanish regulations were specific and were enforced. Weights and measures were standardized according to Spanish laws, and prices were fixed during periods of food scarcity. These regulations extended not only to the large open-air market of New Orleans but to the selling of foodstuffs in the smaller towns and villages.

The market at New Orleans established after the fire of 1788 was in full operation by 1791, and although sanitary conditions would not have met modern standards, an attempt was made to meet the standards of that day. John Pintard, while extremely critical of the market's cleanliness and the quality of its meats, gives a long list of foodstuffs for sale. The fish were abundant and of excellent quality as were shrimp, crawfish, crabs, oysters, chickens, eggs, ducks, geese, snipes, rabbits, squirrels, beef, milk, and vegetables. Female domestics "seem to be the chief buyers & sellers of the place" and "are very expert at selling—wait upon the ladies with their wares and are very honest & faithful to their employers." The New Orleans market at that time would have compared favorably with any large food-distribution center in the world.

Methods of food preservation and preparation had changed little. Bread was still baked out of doors in large, rounded clay ovens. Meats were still salted, smoked, dried, or partially cooked, placed in jars and then covered with hot fat. Creole butter was still made by shaking cream in a bottle or whipping it with a spoon. Meats and vegetables were still boiled, roasted over open fires or in small ovens, or fried, though now in lard instead of in bears' fat. Food-preparation customs of the French and Spanish were generally similar, although the Spanish added more hot seasonings. While all incoming nationalities contributed to establishing a Louisiana cuisine, generally speaking French and Spanish culinary art predominated south of the Red River, while American customs gained the upper hand north of the river.

Thus, North Louisiana, by 1803, had already become "southern" in its cooking habits, while South Louisiana kept the old French and Spanish Creole methods.

The French and Spanish preferred coffee and wine to all other drinks. Coffee was dark roasted, made very strong, and served either alone, with sugar, or as *café au lait*. Favorite French Creole wines came from Bordeaux or Provence, while the Spanish preferred the wine of Catalonia. French brandy, sometimes called *eau-de-vie*, and West Indian brandy from Cuba or Martinique, called *aguardiente*, rum, or tafia ("taffy," by Americans), was imported. Shortly after the American Revolution quantities of cider royal, much more potent than applejack, and rye whiskey were sent down the Mississippi. Later in the century Kentucky and Pennsylvania began to produce what Stanley Faye called "distilled nectar from Indian corn" and to introduce Louisianians to its potentialities.

THE STATE OF PUBLIC HEALTH. The Spanish colony was plagued by the same diseases that had wrought havoc among the French. Pleurisy, pneumonia, skin diseases, dental troubles, children's diseases, epilepsy, dysentery and other diseases of the stomach or intestines, mumps, mange, and malaria were the most common. Tuberculosis declined, probably owing to better housing and dietary conditions. Smallpox was the most feared epidemic malady until late in the period, when yellow fever was identified as an epidemic disease. While some authorities give 1796 as the date for the appearance of yellow fever, there seems little doubt that a calenture first appearing in 1769 and reaching epidemic proportions in 1779, 1791, and from 1793 to 1795 was in reality the same disease. Yellow fever, however, was late arriving in Louisiana, for it had appeared in 1668 in New York, in 1691 in Boston, and in 1693 in Philadelphia.

The problem of securing doctors was a serious one, particularly since French Creoles preferred physicians from France. French doctors remained in the majority for the first twenty years of the Spanish regime, but after this time doctors from all countries came in greater numbers. One of the most noted doctors of the period was a Scotsman, Dr. Robert Dow, who left a rather large number of treatment records and bills. He was apparently a genial, kindly man and it has been written that "no member of his profession ever acquired more popularity." A few persons practiced medicine without requisite degrees, as for example Negro James Derham (or "Derum"), who had "the right only to cure throat disease and no other." Physicians generally dressed well, possessed numerour pairs of stockings and satin trousers, waistcoats, and even cravat buckles "set with stones."

The first decree relating to the practice of medicine was issued by Governor O'Reilly in 1770, and divided medicine into three disciplines: medicine proper, surgery, and pharmacy, which was concerned with the preparation of remedies. This was the first legal recognition of pharmacy as a distinct branch of the medical arts in America. In order to practice medicine and surgery, doctors must furnish records of study, certificates of good character and of belief in the Catholic faith, show their books and instruments, and submit to an examination before the King's physician. In addition, those practicing medicine must keep their remedies open to inspection, while those "who shall sell suspected drugs and such as can be abused by others than persons of honor, and without having received therefor a certificate in writing, shall personally answer for all evils which shall result and shall be adjudged an accomplice."

According to medical testimony, leprosy was brought to Louisiana in 1756 by the Acadians. Whether or not this was true, the disease had reached serious proportions by the early 1780's; and in 1785 the *Cabildo*, upon Miró's recommendation, built a leper hospital on Metairie Ridge behind New Orleans. The area, rather wild and primitive and covered with palmetto, soon became known as "La Terre des Lepreux," Lepers' Land. The disease had almost completely disappeared by the end of the Spanish period.

A new charity hospital costing over 100,000 pesos was completed through the

[147]

munificence of Don Andres Almonaster in 1786 and named the Charity Hospital of St. Charles in honor of the King. The superintendent of the institution was to be appointed by Almonaster, who endowed it with property, rents, and slaves, one of whom, a mulatto named Domingo, a "phlebotonist, instructed in surgery," was to be head surgeon. The benefactor drew up a rather long list of hospital regulations, which were extremely advanced for that day.

The institution's doctors must have studied at the colleges of Cadiz, Madrid, or Barcelona and have the same qualifications as those required for the Royal Navy. Special attention was to be given to "the poor in real distress." Incurable or infectious patients were not to be admitted. No religious distinction was to be made. All patients were to be supplied with a wooden bed, a table, bed clothing, and garments for hospital wear. Almonaster prepared a complete list of menus, which included a "ration of meat." The hospital operated under these regulations during the rest of the Spanish period.

The doctors of that day believed in humors, the most important being blood, phlegm, black bile, and yellow bile. Treatment of disease, therefore, was designed to rid the body of corruption and to restore the humors to their proper balance, and depended largely upon bleeding, sweating, blistering, purging, and vomiting. Drugs and remedies were many, and as John Duffy states, "the idea that the efficacy of a remedy bore a direct relationship to its loathsomeness still influenced prescriptions." Crabs' eyes, dried toads, urine, Bezoar stones, and excreta were prescribed along with mercury, arsenic, antimony, camphor, opium, tartar emetic, ammonia, cream of tartar, alum, calomel, quinine, ipecac, vitriol, hemlock, and numerous other remedies whose names are meaningless today. Much wine and brandy was used, as were cordials, aloes, rhubarb, licorice, syrup of absinthe, "honey of roses," myrrh, sarsaparilla, and such strange-sounding remedies as "marsh-mallow camphire salve," "basilicum salve," "citrine pomade," "antispasmodic," "antivenereal emetic," and "Extract of Diabotanum."

Medical charges averaged a little lower than those of the French period. Bleeding cost 50 cents; purging, $1.00; ordinary pills, 50 cents; liquid medicines, from 25 cents to $1.00; dressing a wound, 50 cents; "assisting" at a miscarriage, $4.00. On March 13, 1779, Doctor Le Duc "assisted at the miscarriage of the Mulatress, Magdelon," and treated her until May 9. His treatments included one purging, five bleedings, the application of one blister (which probably became infected, for he had to treat it on six occasions), and the prescribing of wild red poppy, Spanish licorice, basilicum salve, arcanum, Swiss vulnerary, marsh-mallow and camphire salve, and sarsaparilla. Eventually restored to health, on July 14 she fell off an ox, an accident which necessitated a good bleeding.

Sanitary and health conditions were generally unsatisfactory, particularly in New Orleans, despite the constant efforts of officials. In 1800 one of them listed the most important problems: general lack of cleanliness in the city, its streets and alleys, water closets, drainpipes, and stables; filth and rubbish thrown on the batture, making the "stenches and corruption" particularly bad in warm weather; trash and garbage being dumped too near the city; the cemeteries, where coffins received insufficient lime to properly consume the bodies, and the burial places of those "who have the misfortune to die in other beliefs than that of Our Holy Catholic Religion," whose bodies were literally dumped on open ground to become "the food for birds and carnivorous beasts"; and sailors and immigrants who brought epidemic diseases.

RELIGION. The Spanish were Roman Catholics just as the French, but to them religion was a much more serious and austere matter. The French practiced their faith in easygoing fashion; if they lived near one of the few churches in the colony, they went to Mass on Sunday and kept the Holy Days, and that sufficed. The Spanish attempted to remedy this lackadaisical attitude. With the Jesuits already gone, Governor O'Reilly, immediately upon his arrival in Louisiana, proceeded to straighten out the Capuchins and religion in general. He first removed the Louisiana

Church from the jurisdiction of the Bishop of Quebec and placed it under the Bishop of Santiago de Cuba, then divided the colony into twenty-one parishes. There were not enough priests to go around, but he did the best he could, and soon the religious situation showed signs of improvement.

The Spanish watched the French Capuchins closely. Spanish Father Cirilo de Barcelona criticized them in reports to his diocesan at Havana; they wore a "watch in a fob," had a clock in the refectory which cost $270, had silver spoons and "smaller ones to take coffee with." They also ruled teal duck as fish and ate it on fast days. Father Hilaire de Genevaux, a French Capuchin who had lived in the colony for some years and who had twice been expelled for making trouble, joined the Spanish in denouncing Father Dagobert de Longuory: He "rises at six o'clock in the morning, says, or does not say, mass . . . takes his three-cornered hat, a very superfluous and unworthy appendage for a Capuchin, and goes to a somewhat suspicious house, where he plays until dinner,—that meal over, he resumes his occupations until suppertime."

Father Genevaux also criticized the Ursuline nuns: "They live as they always have done, without being cloistered, and as if they were not nuns at all." That the Ursulines later proved their loyalty to the Church is a matter of record. They did not approve of the French Revolution nor of Napoleon, and when Louisiana was given back to France sixteen of the twenty-five nuns refused to live under what they considered to be a Godless France. On Whitsunday in 1803 these sixteen boarded a ship for Havana.

It will be remembered that when Father Antonio de Sedella made the attempt to establish the Holy Inquisition, Miró quickly sent him out of the colony. In his official dispatch to the Spanish government Miró commented on Sedella and his activities: "When I read the communication of that Capuchin, I shuddered. . . . The mere name of the Inquisition uttered in New Orleans not only would be sufficient to check immigration, which is successfully progressing, but would also be capable of driving away those who have recently come, and I fear that, in spite of my having sent out of the country Father Sedella, the most fatal consequences may ensue from the mere suspicion of the cause of his dismissal." In 1795, Father Sedella, who now called himself "Padre Antonio" or "Pere Antoine," returned and spent the rest of his life in New Orleans. He became one of the most beloved priests in Louisiana history, and when he died in 1829 at the age of eighty-one Protestant and Catholic alike mourned him.

The Louisiana Church remained under the Bishop of Santiago de Cuba until 1790, when it was placed under the jurisdiction of the Bishop of Havana. In 1793, Louisiana and the two Floridas were formed into a new diocese, with headquarters at New Orleans. On July 24, 1795, the new Bishop, Señor Doctor Luis Ignacio Maria de Penalver y Cardenas, took possession of the parish church and it became the "Catedral de San Luis."

The stern, Puritan-like Spanish Catholicism never found favor with the French of Louisiana, and the Spanish continually found fault with French religious practices and lack of fervor. The later governors, particularly Carondelet, constantly pleaded with the government for additional grants of money for religious purposes and for more priests who could conduct masses in either French or Spanish. At the end of the period there were only two places of worship in New Orleans, the Cathedral and the Chapel of the Ursulines. Public worship still tended to be exterior and formal, and church attendance was large only during Lent and at Easter. Numerous Protestants had settled throughout the colony, and although prevented from holding services in the more settled areas, openly practiced their faiths in the smaller villages and rural districts.

SOCIAL LIFE AND CUSTOMS. Society and social life flourished in Spanish Louisiana after the American Revolution, the war against the British having ended, so far as Louisianians were concerned, with the fall of Pensacola. Regular soldiers and militiamen returned to New Orleans and the militiamen were mustered out of service; sailors again turned to trading activities, for there was no longer need to patrol the coastal Gulf waters or Lakes Pontchartrain, Maurepas, or Borgne for prowling British frigates or privateers; river boatmen no longer had to travel up the Mississippi in large convoys, for only a few guards were now needed for protection against occasional river pirates. The country settled down to peaceful pursuits, its wealth rapidly increased, and citizens began to enjoy the profits of their labors.

The Creole ball was the social institution of paramount importance in the towns, particularly in New Orleans, and had its counterpart in the parties and dances of the villages and rural districts. The citizens of the capital, according to Berquin du Vallon, took pompous pride in their balls, "comparing them to the brilliant Vauxhall or the Grand Galas of the Paris Opera." Persons of wealth and government officials frequently gave balls for as many as five hundred guests and costing thousands of pesos. Such strict rules of etiquette were enforced that the Abbé Robin complained that "the rigidity of the Grandes Dames" made them "most tiresome."

After 1790 many of the more important balls were given in a wooden hall on Chartres Street, whose sides were lined with boxes arranged in tiers where the *mamans* and their charges sat. The ladies who wished to dance sat in front of the lowest tier, and behind them stood gentlemen awaiting their turn on the dance floor. At one end of the hall was a raised platform for a small orchestra. Du Vallon complained that the hall was "without the glitter and magnificence so necessary to a place of this type—no chandeliers, no mirrors," and that in general it appeared somewhat shabby.

Public balls were held on Sunday and Thursday evenings and were attended by all ranks of white society. Admittance required only the payment of a small entrance fee at the door. Anyone might enter who was decently and suitably dressed and unmasked; the latter requirement had been adopted because of "some scandalous scenes which once ensued as a consequence of their [the Creoles] typical enthusiasm." More than one person had protested "the practice of putting wads of chewing tobacco on the chairs where the ladies sat," the chewing of vanilla sticks and "scattering these wads throughout the building whereby producing an intolerable odor," and other social misdemeanors.

Keeping order was a constant problem, and small detachments of troops were always stationed in the vicinity. On one occasion Governor Salcedo's son attempted to force an English quadrille upon the dancers, who favored a French quadrille. The Creoles drew their swords, and a general fight was averted only by the appearance of the guard with fixed bayonets and by the impassioned speeches of three young Creoles who "eloquently harangued the crowd in the name of peace and the fair sex." The ball continued until early morning under the watchful eye of the old Governor, who permitted the honors to go to the French quadrille.

The exact date of the appearance of Quadroon Balls is unknown, though they most likely did not begin until after large numbers of well-educated and cultured Free Negroes and mulattoes arrived from Santo Domingo during the 1790's. Generally ignored by Louisiana historians, they have become legend and have been given an importance by sensation-seeking writers far beyond their real place in the social life of New Orleans. The customs of polite society were generally more faithfully observed at these events than at the public white balls, the women attending were modestly dressed and even demure in their manners, and the "men who attended both were said to be more considerate in these than in the others." Probably the greatest factor in their rise to notoriety was that white men attended them, not only because they were gay affairs and some of the women beautiful and good dancing partners, but to facilitate the forming of extramarital alliances, a social practice more or less common until recent years in southern European and Latin-American cities.

The only other amusements in New Orleans which approached the popularity of the balls were drinking and gambling, and these pastimes often ended in polite invitations to the dueling field or in rough brawls, which, as Minter Wood wrote, indicated "a scarcity of cultivated minds, natures easily bored, and mental indolence." Consumption of imported wines, cordials, and other liquors was staggering, and Spanish regulations governing drinking and drinking establishments were generally ignored. People of every rank and color gambled at taverns, billiard rooms, and gambling houses; members of officialdom and of high society, at Madame Carondelet's or at the homes of other members of the elite group. Fortunes were won or lost in games of coq, monte, craps, primera, or cané. Punishments for gambling were severe; fines of $50.00 for the players and $100.00 for the proprietor of the houses or ten and twenty days incarceration for the first offense with double the time for second and third offenses, and possible banishment. Slaves were given five to twenty lashes.

Despite their religious severity the Spanish were a pleasure-loving people, and they joined the other nationalities of town or rural Louisiana in enjoying a full social life. They participated in social functions on Sunday afternoons, feast days, Christmas, New Year's, and the various saints' days. A *fiesta*, or party, was *made*, as the Spanish said, whenever possible, and everyone—French, Spanish, Acadian—was invited. In the small towns and rural areas there were fewer excesses in dancing, drinking, or gambling, for whole families participated in social activities. Dances generally were held once a week, and during holiday seasons, twice a week. The merrymakers appeared in simple, homemade costumes, drank freely of tafia, wore themselves out with their lively dancing, and then enjoyed hearty suppers.

Hunting and fishing were enjoyed by both sexes and by children large enough to shoulder a gun or fishing pole. Shooting at a *papegai*, a figure of a bird placed on top of a pole, was popular among the Creoles and Acadians, who also enjoyed bedecking themselves and their horses with gaily-colored ribbons and galloping over the prairies or through the wooded lands. Storytelling was an art, and old and young alike thrilled to the tales of hoary raconteurs. The reading of one's own verses was enjoyed by the Creoles, and at Fort Miró the satirical poetry and Munchausen-like tales of a gay fellow calling himself "De Badinesse," who claimed kinship to the noted Montpelier family of France but whose real name was Babin, made him a widely-sought-after guest.

The correspondence of the upper classes at this time reveal much of the formality of their society, and the letters of Spanish officials, written with quaint, formal phrases, indicate their friendship with many of the Louisiana colonials. Carlos de Grand Pré, when Commandant of the Natchez District, once wrote to Governor Miró: "Permit me to place myself at the feet of your wife, to whom I offer my respect and obedience, and to whom my wife offers her affectionate expressions of love and friendship, as well as Your Lordship. I hope to have the honor of seeing her soon in the company of Your Lordship, whose life I pray the All-Powerful to lengthen the many years I desire. . . . I kiss Your Lordship's hands."

High-level social life, however, did not always run smoothly. In 1783, Margaret Pollock, wife of the American businessman in New Orleans, engaged in a short but sharp written controversy with Governor Miró. When her cook was arrested for some misdemeanor, she immediately wrote the Governor: "Sir, please . . . let reason & Justice take place and Return me my Cook that I Certainle do Mise and Certain it is that you have no Right to detain her upon any protence [sic] whatever." The Governor replied that her letter was "very insulting to the authority of the government" and that her negress was "accused of a crime which must be tried according to the laws." Margaret heatedly replied that "I doubt not but you will order my Servant out of Confinement not that I so much feel the Loss of hir [sic], but humanity obliges me to speak in behalf of the feeble & the Innocent, it is well known that she has been ill treated by those People that dreads not the Laws of God or man. . . . Sir as to Present you with a Petition be assured were I to attempt it, it would only Inflame me to the highest degree, & would of Course parish [sic] in the

Exertion." She closed the communication: "I hope you will not answer this Letter." Existing records do not reveal what happened to the cook.

Courtships were more formal among the Spanish than among the French, and no Spanish girl was left unguarded in the presence of her escort. Even after her engagement a girl's movements were restricted. Betrothals were solemnly pledged before a priest, and a couple who broke the engagement must receive a canonical dispensation before contracting another marriage. Men and women under the age of twenty-five must have the consent of their parents, or if they were dead, that of the nearest senior relative or the local commandant. The penalty for disregarding these regulations was the loss of both maternal and paternal inheritance.

Alliances were ordinarily arranged by parents, usually with the consent of the young couple. During the late years of the Spanish period, however, a daughter of the wealthy planter Marius Bringier was married without her consent to Augustine Tureaud. Before the wedding the young lady wrote numerous entries in her diary listing her dislikes of Tureaud. There is a break in her dairy entries for about two weeks following the wedding; when they are resumed she had completely reversed her opinion of her husband. The marriage was a long and happy one. Occasionally a young lady rebelled. When Marie Louise Pradel, daughter of the richest woman in Louisiana, was informed that she was betrothed to coarse, corpulent, and fortyish Nicolas Foucault, she defied her mother and married a young naval lieutenant.

The practice of signing marriage contracts was universal, just as it had been under the French regime. When the contracting parties were members of wealthy or aristocratic families, the documents were long, explicit as to detail, and signed by numerous witnesses; in the case of common folk they were brief and to the point. A contract signed in the Avoyelles District in 1795 contains less than a dozen lines. It lists as property of the young woman a plot of land valued at $100.00, an "outfitted bed," china dishes valued at $68.00, and forty head of cattle, three mares and colts, and fifteen pigs valued at $300.00; property of the young man was eight head of cattle, eight horses, and "a bed, outfitted," to a total value of about $200.00.

Divorces were not unusual, and judging from the Judicial Records and Notarial Acts, were not difficult to secure, provided both parties agreed to the separation and a division of their property. The payment of alimony was common, and more than one man petitioned the courts to reduce his payments.

EDUCATION AND CULTURE. The state of education of Louisiana colonials is graphically revealed by the oaths of allegiance required by Governor O'Reilly. In most districts the commandants took verbal oaths and then forwarded to the Governor in New Orleans lists of the names of heads of families who had taken them. However, in New Orleans and nearby districts many citizens preferred to personally sign the oaths or to have some friend sign for them, and of these signatures over 60 per cent were not signed by the individuals taking the oath. Men and women who could read and write well, or even who could read and write at all, were comparatively few.

Acting in behalf of his Catholic Majesty, who "resolved to establish schools . . . in the province of Louisiana," on July 17, 1771, Fray Julian de Arriaga, Minister of the Indies, issued regulations concerning education. Instruction was to be publicly given and only high officials would be permitted to employ tutors for their children. The Crown would pay all educational expenses from the general fund until taxes might be arranged for the maintenance of schools. These regulations, according to historian Henry E. Chambers, are the first made for public education and for public-school taxation in Louisiana.

The following year three teachers arrived under the charge of Don Manuel Andrés López de Armesto, who in addition to his duties as secretary of the colony was to act as Director of the Royal Schools. Armesto has the distinction of being the first school superintendent in the United States. Don Francisco de la Colina y Escudero was to teach elementary education, the principles of piety, the practice of virtue, grammar, spelling, penmanship, and arithmetic. Don Manuel Diaz de Lara and Don Pedro de Aragon y Villegas were to give instruction in Latin, religion, and ethics. Each teacher was to receive an annual salary of 700 pesos, while Armesto would be paid 1,000 pesos a year. Armesto would do no teaching but was to have charge of the library, issue regulations for the schools, prescribe the methods of instruction, watch over the progress of the pupils and the piety of both instructors and pupils, and fill vacancies in case of illness or accident.

So vigorous was the public and Church opposition to this attempt at a public-school system, however, that it never achieved any measure of success. Only one public school was in operation throughout the entire Spanish period, and the largest enrollment never reached 150 pupils. In 1788, Governor Miró complained that parents would not send their children to the public school, as they preferred paro-chial schools or private tutors and would not condone the use of the Spanish language. The school building burned during the fire the same year, and the institution led a checkered existence until the end of the Spanish regime, when Father Ubaldo Delgado, *Maestro de Primeras Letras,* and Don Fernando Ybáñez, his assistant, were the only teachers employed.

By 1788 there were eight private schools in New Orleans with a total enrollment of about four hundred pupils, and during the 1790's several refugees from Santo Domingo opened private academies. Probably the best of the private schools was founded in 1800 by Don Luis Francisco Lefort, a naturalized Spaniard who had published English and French grammars in London and Baltimore. Instruction in Lefort's school soon gained the reputation of being "better and more careful than that of the nuns." A military cadet school was maintained in New Orleans, but there is evidence that it was closed from time to time due to "the lack of officers to serve as teachers" and also perhaps for lack of students.

Meanwhile the Ursuline Convent school continued to accept girls and young women on a boarding-school and day-school basis. At the end of the Spanish regime the abbess had eleven nuns under her charge and seventy boarding and one hundred day pupils. The Ursulines, however, would not co-operate with the Spanish government, and Bishop Penalver y Cardenas reported that the nuns were so intensely French that "they refuse to receive Spanish subjects ignorant of French and shed tears for being obliged to make their spiritual exercises in Spanish books." During the 1770's they charged 400 livres a term for boarding pupils, and more than once were forced to sue parents for board and tuition payments.

Numerous tutors were employed in New Orleans and were scattered throughout the rural areas. While a small percentage of them may have been well trained, probably the majority were unable to carry their pupils very far in the fields of learn-ing. They were generally given board, lodging, and a small salary by their employers in return for imparting what little knowledge they possessed to their unruly pupils, and often had to sue to collect their salaries.

At the end of the French regime in 1762 not a single book, pamphlet, or other writing had been published in the colony; indeed, there was no printing press in Louisiana. Before the Spanish took possession, however, Denis Braud, a New Orleans merchant, received permission of the King of France to establish a printing press and began to print "letters of change" (treasury bills, notes, and drafts) in late 1763 or 1764, signing his printed material "Printer of the King." He did some printing for the British of West Florida, and a few of his early broadsides are inscribed as hav-ing been "Published in Mobile." After the arrival of the Spanish he became a *Regidor* and receiver of fines in the first *Cabildo* and changed his name to Dionisio Braud. He disappears from Louisiana history in November, 1773, when he "slipped away from the Province in a foreign boat."

The first colonial attempts at literary art appeared in 1777 when two anonymous poems, one congratulating Gálvez on his recovery from an illness and the second showering upon him "a wealth of florid flattery," appeared. Two years later Julien

Poydras published an epic poem on Gálvez and his Baton Rouge campaign. Because of their internal similarities, Edward Larocque Tinker concludes that Poydras wrote all three poems. Shortly before Louisiana was returned to France in 1803 another poem, an Indian tragedy written by Le Blanc de Villeneuve and titled *Poucha-Houma,* was printed and dedicated to Madame de Laussat.

It is claimed that Louisiana's first newspaper was *La Courier du Vendredi (Friday Courier),* appearing as early as 1785, but no copies exist and some historians have grave doubts that it was ever published. The first newspaper of which copies exist, *Le Moniteur de la Louisiane,* published by Louis Duclot who was probably the editor, appeared in March, 1794. It was a small French-language sheet, composed of four pages, each seven by five inches, with two columns to a page. J. B. L. Fontaine became its editor in 1795, and two years later it became the official government newspaper. The *Moniteur* ceased publication in late 1814 or early 1815.

There were comparatively few private libraries and no public ones in Spanish Louisiana. The royal orders of 1771 providing for public schools included provision for a public or semipublic library in New Orleans, and a collection of books, largely Latin classics, was shipped to the city, but as late as 1780 they lay still unpacked in the Government House. The library was never established and the books finally disappeared. A large number of contemporary inventories of estates list a few books, but large collections were rare. In most cases neither the number nor the titles of the books was listed. Probably the largest book inventory was that of the estate of Jean Prevost, who died only a month before the arrival of O'Reilly. Over 330 volumes were listed, revealing the literary and cultural interests of Prevost; they included works of Montesquieu, Voltaire, Rousseau, Locke, Montaigne, Pasquier, Quintus Curtius, Theophraste, Molière, Racine, Lucien, Euclid, and Virgil, and ranged in subject matter from military tactics to commerce, dictionaries to religious works, Peruvian letters to French memoirs, incubation to law, and from the *Commentaries of Caesar* to William Robertson's *History of America.*

There was little art produced in Spanish Louisiana. Many families, however, brought portraits and other works of art when they migrated to the colony, while others imported various types of art objects. The first record of a music teacher was during the late 1780's or early 1790's, when the wife of the Avoyelles Post Commandant gave lessons on the harp. Military bands played for parades and public events, and smaller bands and orchestras furnished music for banquets and balls. Amateur theatricals continued, aided during the 1790's by the coming of a few former professional actors from Santo Domingo, and were generally given in a building called by the Spanish "El Coliseo" and by the French "La Salle de Comédie." Writers have long credited the first professional theatrical performance in Louisiana to a group of Santo Domingan refugees headed by Louis Tabary in 1791, but this is an impossibility since the Tabary troupe did not arrive in New Orleans until 1804. The first known operatic performance was the production of André Grétry's *Silvain* on May 22, 1796. The Louisiana professional theater had to await the coming of the American regime.

PART FOUR

Early Years of

the American Regime

CHAPTER 14

"THIS NEW, IMMENSE, UNBOUNDED WORLD"

IMPORTANCE OF LOUISIANA TO THE UNITED STATES. During the American Revolution, Richard Henry Lee of Virginia wrote Samuel Adams of Massachusetts that two things were necessary to make the newly born but as yet unemancipated republic strong—the development of New England fisheries and the control of the Mississippi River. In a similar letter to Henry Laurens of South Carolina he emphasized: "These, sir, are the strong legs on which North America can alone walk securely in Independence." A few years later, after Virginia ceded her western lands to the nation, he again wrote to Adams that the cession would "be the means of perfecting our union." Other Americans even then were looking to the west and dreaming of the lands beyond the Appalachians.

Some historians credit Benjamin Franklin with first emphasizing the importance of the Mississippi River and with planting the slowly germinating seeds of the Louisiana Purchase idea. In 1780, while representing the United States in Paris, he wrote John Jay: "Poor as we are, yet I know we shall be rich; and I would rather agree with the Spaniards to buy at a great price the whole of their right in the Mississippi than to sell a drop of its waters." As Virgil Lewis wrote in his *Story of the Louisiana Purchase,* "With prophetic vision the old philosopher then saw that which it would be necessary to do in the future."

After the Revolution, settlers began to push west of the Appalachians to the Ohio, Kentucky, and Tennessee country; by 1790 the more than 100,000 settlers in the area needed to reach world markets with their surplus products. The only practical way to reach these markets, in view of transportation conditions, was to send the goods down the Mississippi to New Orleans, there to deposit and transship them in ocean-going vessels.

The Treaty of 1795 with Spain gave western Americans the use of the Mississippi and the right of deposit at New Orleans. In 1798, when the Spanish threatened to close the port on the Mississippi, the western Americans complained to President John Adams; the Spanish shortly renewed the right of deposit and for the next several years the river trade grew steadily. Finally, in 1802, the lower river and the port were closed. Kentuckians, western Pennsylvanians, Ohioans, and Tennesseans angrily talked of organizing an army and capturing New Orleans, perhaps even the whole of Louisiana. Louis André Pichon, the French Chargé d'Affaires at Washington, wrote to French Foreign Minister Charles Maurice de Talleyrand-Périgord, Prince de Bénévent, that "the people of the west might commit blows of a nature to compromise the [American] government" and that they had a thousand boats on the river, ready to resort to force.

Meanwhile, in June, 1801, American Minister Rufus King in London wrote President Thomas Jefferson that he feared "Spain is ceding Louisiana to France, an inauspicious circumstance to us"; the following month, Jefferson informed William C. C. Claiborne, Governor of Mississippi Territory, that he viewed Spanish possession of Louisiana "as most favorable to our interests, and should see, with extreme pain any other nation substituted for them." Many Americans now began to realize the importance of the Mississippi River and the control of New Orleans to the United States, believing along with Jefferson, that it was to become "the seat of a great and populous empire," and "the mighty mart of the merchandise brought from more than a thousand rivers. . . . With Boston, Baltimore, New York, and Philadelphia on the left; Mexico on the right; Havana in front, and the immense valley of the Mississippi in the rear, no such position for the accumulation and perpetuity of wealth and power ever existed."

AMERICAN PUBLIC OPINION ON LOUISIANA. The United States did not favor France's securing Louisiana, for the peace between France and Great Britain was in reality only a truce; once their struggle was renewed the British would surely capture and occupy the area. American newspapers urged the United States to organize an expedition to capture New Orleans, and Pichon sent Talleyrand newspaper articles reflecting growing American fears of France on the Mississippi and arguing that the United States might be forced to "take possession of New Orleans."

President Jefferson wrote to Robert Livingston, American Minister to France, on April 18, 1802, that the cession of Louisiana to France "works most sorely on the United States," that the possessor of New Orleans "is our natural and habitual enemy," and that "every eye in the United States is now fixed on the affairs of Louisiana. Perhaps nothing since the revolutionary war, has produced more uneasy sensations through the body of the nation." The only way, he continued, that France could reconcile the Americans was by "ceding to us the Island of New Orleans and the Floridas." And one can imagine Jefferson angrily penning these words: "The day that France takes possession of New Orleans fixes the sentence which is to restrain her forever within her low water mark. It seals the union of two countries who in conjunction can maintain exclusive possession of the ocean. From that moment we must marry ourselves to the British fleet and nation."

The spring and summer of 1802 wore on. Claiborne wrote to Secretary of State James Madison: "I wish to God the U. States could possess themselves of East & West Florida, including the Island of Orleans." In December, Jefferson, in his message to Congress, said that "the cession of the Spanish Province of Louisiana to France, . . . will, if carried into effect, make a change in the aspect of our foreign relations."

Meanwhile Frenchmen were excited over regaining the Louisiana colony, and several books were published giving graphic descriptions, and the enormous possibilities, of the West Indian and Louisiana empire Napoleon had restored to France. The First Consul, after considering several others, finally decided to send General Claude Victor to Louisiana as Governor. By the time Victor could reach Louisiana, General Charles Leclerc would have put down the rebellion in Santo Domingo. But Leclerc ran into difficulties; he won no great victories, yellow fever decimated his army, and finally the *Moniteur* of January 7, 1803, announced the general's death. The Spanish royal order authorizing delivery of Louisiana arrived in France in late October, 1802, but Victor had been delayed. The expedition was not yet ready to sail, so Pierre Clement de Laussat, already appointed Colonial Prefect of Louisiana, was ordered to precede Victor, take possession of the colony, and await his arrival. Laussat sailed from La Rochelle on January 10, 1803.

On January 31, 1803, Jefferson emphatically stated, in a memorable interview with British Chargé d'Affaires Edward Thornton in Washington, that he would never abandon his claims to the free navigation of the Mississippi, that the Americans might have "to resort to force," and that if they did "they would throw away the scabbard." Two weeks later Pichon wrote home that hostile sentiments toward France were growing and that at a recent official dinner the toast "peace if peace is honorable, war if war is necessary" had been enthusiastically received. On February 16, Senator James Ross of Pennsylvania introduced a series of resolutions authorizing the President to call out state militia units to occupy "such places on the Isle of Orleans" necessary to guarantee navigation of the Mississippi. The resolutions failed, but another series, offered by Senator John C. Breckenridge of Kentucky, passed, authorizing the President to arm and hold in readiness 80,000 militiamen. Pichon's fears were now realized; the United States was rapidly moving toward war.

LAUSSAT ARRIVES IN LOUISIANA. On March 24, 1803, a vessel arrived at New Orleans from France, bringing the baggage of Colonial Prefect Laussat. His job was to make arrangements for the arrival of General Victor and the French troops, and to establish the new regime in the name of the French Republic in the most effective and dignified fashion. There was an air of expectancy about the Creole city.

Accompanied by his wife (a "handsome woman," according to André Lafargue), his children, and a comparatively small retinue of military and civil officers, a scant household for an official of such importance, the new Prefect had arrived at the Balize about March 22. While proceeding slowly up the river in a government barge, he carefully inspected various installations and at Fort San Felipe was royally entertained by Don Pedro Favrot, the old Spanish Commandant, and his family with "an excellent dinner," after which the party "drank toasts without number to the accompaniment of salvos of artillery." Laussat landed at New Orleans on March 26, and was conducted to the Government House, where Governor Juan Manuel de Salcedo and the other Spanish officials received him. The Marquis de Casa Calvo, who was to serve with Salcedo as a commission for the delivery of Louisiana to France, arrived about two weeks later, and on May 18 the two commissioners issued a proclamation announcing that the province would soon be returned to France. The final preparations had been completed; the arrival of General Victor was hourly expected.

Still in his early forties, Laussat was an intelligent, ambitious, and energetic French civil official, dignified, courteous, and chivalrous, liberal-minded and devoted to the principles of the French Republic. Handsome and commanding in appearance, he radiated force of character, and was, as Lafargue wrote, "an enemy of autocracy and monarchical tyranny, but not a demogogue, a fire brand or a blood thirsty tribune."

He noted that the French Creoles were uneasy, despite the fact that shortly after his arrival they had presented him with a memorial attesting their loyalty. They were disturbed by the new revolutionary ideas of France, worried for fear that good, hard Spanish piastres would soon be exchanged for French paper, fearful of what French trade and taxation policies would be, and, most of all, apprehensive of present French anti-Catholic regulations being applied to Louisiana. The Ursuline nuns left, and though his wife faithfully attended Mass, Laussat was unsuccessful in allaying Catholic fears. French Royalists and émigrés who had come to the colony during the 1790's considered him a revolutionist. He had come to a former French colony now apathetic at the prospect of becoming French again.

Laussat observed that the Americans were the "real danger" in Louisiana. He counted fifty-five American vessels as opposed to ten French and Spanish ships in the harbor, and was insulted when Americans loudly and insolently boasted that they would celebrate the next Fourth of July in New Orleans "on American soil" or that if their government had not acted by that time they would simply take over the colony. If only General Victor would arrive, and with a strong force! But in middle August the fateful news was received; as Laussat reported in a letter, "the courier over land from Washington City brought here the day before yesterday the official news of the cession of Louisiana to the United States April 30, last."

THE PURCHASE OF LOUISIANA. Robert Livingston, American Minister to France, was old, and many considered him a poor diplomat. He had been given the appointment because he was a member of one of New York's wealthy families and was a good friend of President Jefferson. An unspectacular man, he so far had done nothing spectacular in France. In early May, 1802, Secretary of State Madison had ordered Livingston to negotiate with the French government for New Orleans and the Floridas, but Livingston soon replied regarding Napoleon: "There is no people, no legislature, no counsellors. One man is everything. He seldom asks advice, and never hears it unasked. His ministers are mere clerks, and his legislature and coun-sellors are parade officers." Livingston promised to do the best he could, but as late as March, 1803, he wrote Jefferson that "with respect to negotiations for Louisiana, I think nothing will be effected here."

Meanwhile, in January, 1803, Jefferson had appointed young James Monroe special representative of the United States to France and Spain relative to the Louisiana question. He was particularly to assist Livingston in purchasing the Isle of Orleans and securing the right of navigation of the Mississippi. However, shortly before his arrival in Paris startling events occurred with incredible swiftness.

During the early months of 1803, Napoleon began to realize the difficulty of pro-tecting Louisiana from the British, once the war between France and Great Britain was renewed, and it was already rumored that they had completed plans to send a fleet to capture the colony. "I have not a moment to lose," Napoleon told his min-isters, "in putting it out of their reach. They [the Americans] only ask of me one town in Louisiana; but I already consider the colony as entirely lost." He also had another reason to consider the colony lost to France, for on April 8, Livingston had informed him of Senator Ross's resolution urging immediate seizure of at least a portion of the Isle of Orleans.

Many Frenchmen, however, did not wish to relinquish Louisiana so easily, for they had hoped France would rebuild her old colonial empire. Even Napoleon's brothers opposed his fatalism, and one day Joseph and Lucien followed him into the bath and pleaded with him not to sell the colony. Napoleon angrily hurled his snuff box at them. The decision had been made. The matter was closed. On Sunday, April 10, after the Easter service, Napoleon called a few of his ministers together. François Barbé-Marbois, Minister of the Treasury, favored selling the colony, but Denis Decres, Minister of the Navy, and General Louis Alexandre Berthier, Minister of War, were resolutely opposed to the cession as cowardly and entirely unwarranted.

The next morning, however, Napoleon summoned Barbé-Marbois: "They [the British] shall not have the Mississipi which they covet. . . . I renounce Louisiana. It is not only New Orleans that I cede: it is the whole colony without reserve. I know the price of what I abandon. . . . I renounce it with the greatest regret; to attempt obstinately to retain it would be folly. I direct you to negotiate the affair. Have an interview this very day with Mr. Livingston." Almost at the same moment Livingston was writing the President: "Only force can give us New Orleans. . . . Let us first get possession of the country, and negotiate afterwards."

James Monroe arrived in Paris on April 12. That night Livingston gave a dinner party for him to which the French officials were invited, and in the garden discussed purchase plans with Barbé-Marbois. Livingston and Barbé-Marbois met after the party, and the French Minister offered all of Louisiana to the United States for 100,000,000 francs. After considerable jockeying, Barbé-Marbois lowered the price to 60,000,000 francs; but Livingston refused, saying that he had no authority to purchase the whole of Louisiana and that he must first confer with Monroe. He went home and wrote to Secretary of State Madison: "We shall do all we can to cheapen the purchase; but my present sentiment is that we shall buy."

On April 15 the two Americans offered 40,000,000 francs for Louisiana, but the offer was rejected. The next day it was raised to 50,000,000. Negotiations continued for nearly two weeks, and finally, on April 29, Livingston and Monroe agreed to pay 60,000,000 francs and to assume American claims against France to the amount of 20,000,000 francs. The technicalities of the treaty were discussed on May 1, and the purchase agreement was signed the following day; the claims agreement was signed a few days later. The official documents were dated April 30.

The boundaries of the purchase were left indefinite. General Victor's instructions had been to take possession of all of Louisiana, excluding West Florida, but when Livingston asked Talleyrand on May 20 what territory France had received from Spain, he replied that he did not know and added, significantly: "I can give you no direction; you have made a noble bargain for yourselves and I suppose you will make the most of it."

It was well that the negotiations had been concluded with haste, for on the night of May 9, Livingston received a communication from Rufus King in London that a British expedition was ready to sail for Louisiana just as soon as war was renewed between Great Britain and France. The British government, therefore, was immediately notified of the purchase.

Napoleon was well satisfied with the sale, saying: "This accession of territory affirms forever the power of the United States, and I have just given England a maritime rival that sooner or later will lay low her pride." Sometime before, he had remarked that "I shall be useful to the whole universe, if I can prevent their ruling America as they rule Asia." The two Americans were also well pleased with their purchase. After they had signed the final agreements, Livingston said: "We have lived long, but this is the noblest work of our whole lives. . . . From this day the United States will take their place among the powers of the first rank. . . . The instruments which we have just signed will cause no tears to be shed; they prepare ages of happiness for innumerable generations of human creatures."

Who was responsible for the sale and for the purchase of Louisiana? Praise should be given President Thomas Jefferson, Secretary of State James Madison, and James Monroe. Most of the credit for the successful negotiations, however, should be given to Robert Livingston, who had proved himself a discreet and energetic diplomat; one of the French ministers remarked that he was the most persistent negotiator he had ever met. The man really immediately responsible was Napoleon, for his decision alone had made it possible.

News of the purchase reached the United States on July 3, a notable Fourth of July present for the young republic. The next night when French Chargé d'Affaires Pichon attended the holiday celebration at the White House he was accorded unrestrained hospitality. The Jeffersonian Republicans received the news with boisterous enthusiasm; the Federalists with something bordering upon stupefaction, as one critic wrote, over Jefferson's successful diplomacy. The press, on the whole, approved, but the New York *Herald* on July 6 voiced certain reservations: "It may with candor be said, that whether the possession at this time of any territory west of the river Mississippi will be advantageous, is at best extremely problematical." Some critics viewed the cost with alarm—$15,000,000, a sum amounting to over 400 tons of silver, nearly 5½ miles of silver-laden wagons. The interest would amount to over $2,400 a day. If invested the principal would yield an amount sufficient to support 1,800 free schools. Only the South and the West would benefit from the purchase, but would they pay a share of the cost? No, for the whiskey tax had just been removed.

Most men on the street or those who tilled the farms, however, were proud—the United States was now a real nation. Extending from the Atlantic to the Great Stony Mountains, someday it would reach the Pacific. Louisianians viewed the purchase with mixed feelings and although they had not been consulted at any stage of the negotiations, Napoleon counseled them: "Let the Louisianians know that we part from them with regret," let them "recollect that they were Frenchmen, and that France, in ceding them, has secured for them advantages which they could not have obtained from a European nation, however paternal it might have been."

The United States did not have in its treasury the $15,000,000 needed to pay for Louisiana—indeed, there was not a surplus of $15,000,000 in the entire country.

Therefore, it issued bonds, bought by the financial houses of Bering in London and Hope in Amsterdam. The bonds and interest were paid off between 1812 and 1823. The total cost, including interest and the sums paid American citizens who had claims against France, amounted to $23,527,872.57.

TWENTY GLORIOUS DAYS. The sale of Louisiana was a great personal disappointment to French Commissioner Laussat, but he was an adaptable diplomat. He finally received orders to take possession of the province and to officially transfer it to the United States. In a conference with Governor Salcedo and the Marquis de Casa Calvo on November 26 it was agreed that the transfer from Spain to France would take place four days later.

At noon on November 30 the Spanish Governor and Laussat mounted a platform in the council room of the Cabildo, legal documents were read and signed, and the keys of the city and forts were handed to Laussat on a silver platter. Then the official party went to the balcony and watched the Spanish flag hauled down and the tricolor of France take its place. Laussat immediately issued a proclamation to the people which emphasized loyalty to the French flag, for it "recalls your battles and your victories, your loyalty and your valor. . . . it will be preserved and protected in the future by Louisianians, worthy children of our fathers; it will likewise be kept in safety and reverence, through your love, your fidelity and your devotion to the mother country."

The following day Laussat gave an official dinner for seventy-five guests. The first toast, in white champagne, was drunk to Napoleon and the French Republic; the second, in pink champagne, to Charles IV and Spain; and the third, in white champagne, to Jefferson and the United States. A ball, including a larger number of guests, followed. It was opened by the Marquis de Casa Calvo and Madame Almonaster, and the dancing continued until eight o'clock the next morning. Ball followed ball and fete followed fete for the next fortnight, and all was harmony between the Spanish, French, and Americans.

Destroying all traces of Spanish government, Laussat re-established the French governmental system. He abolished the *Cabildo,* and in its place appointed Étienne de Boré Mayor of New Orleans and a city council composed of French Creoles and Americans. He ordered the preservation of judicial and public archives; commissioners were appointed to formulate police regulations; a city fire department was established; the militia was reorganized under the command of Deville de Goutin Bellechasse. While Laussat may have given a mock grandeur to his short regime and have given his new government a semblance of permanency out of keeping with its known temporary nature, his administration of New Orleans was eminently successful. Many of his reforms lasted for years, and some became permanent features of city government. One wonders what his place would have been in Louisiana history had Napoleon not sold the colony.

THE UNITED STATES TAKES POSSESSION OF LOUISIANA. President Jefferson first considered offering the governorship of the new territory to Thomas Sumter, Jr., of South Carolina, son of the old Revolutionary hero, but for some reason abandoned the idea. He then considered the Marquis de Lafayette, who was living quietly at his home at La Grange, near Paris. Lafayette was only forty-six years of age, had lived and fought in America, was very popular with the people, and loved the country and its political ideals. It is not known if Jefferson definitely offered him the appointment, but he wrote Lafayette on November 4, 1803: "I sincerely wish you were here on the spot, that we might avail ourselves of your service as Governor of Louisiana, where the seat of government at New Orleans is among the most interesting spots of our country, and constitutes the most important charge we can confer."

Other men were considered—among them, Andrew Jackson, James Monroe, and Robert Livingston—but the man Jefferson finally selected was William Charles Cole Claiborne. The twenty-eight-year-old Virginian had moved to Nashville during the middle 1790's, had served as Tennessee's lone Representative in Congress from 1797 to 1801, and since that time had been serving as Governor of Mississippi Territory at its capital at Washington. Claiborne was first selected as one of two commissioners, along with General James Wilkinson of the United States Army, to receive the Louisiana territory from Laussat. It was not until the fall of 1804 that Claiborne was officially appointed Governor of the Territory of Orleans, as the area of present-day Louisiana was first called.

Claiborne left Natchez for Fort Adams on December 2, escorted by the Natchez Artillery, the Natchez Rifles, and a company of militia, to meet General Wilkinson and his force of about five hundred regular soldiers and two hundred Mississippi and Tennessee Militia. Moving overland southward from Fort Adams by easy stages, the occupying forces arrived at a designated camp site at Point Marigny, some two or three miles from New Orleans, on the evening of Saturday the seventeenth. When on Monday morning a courier brought news that the two American commissioners had arrived, Laussat immediately set the twentieth as the date for the transfer of the province.

At nine o'clock in the morning the Louisiana militia began to muster at the Place d'Armes and the crowds to gather about the square. A cannon shot signalled that the American force had left their camp, and soon a salute from the twenty guns of Fort St. Charles announced that they were passing through the Tchoupitoulas Gate. About eleven o'clock Claiborne and Wilkinson, followed by a detachment of red-uniformed dragoons, a four-piece battery of artillery, and the other military units, entered the square. The American units formed opposite the French soldiers and local militia.

The commissioners dismounted and marched to the Hôtel de Ville, as the Cabildo was called by the French, where they were met by Laussat and conducted upstairs to the great hall. Laussat seated himself in the center chair on the dais, with Claiborne on his right and Wilkinson on his left. The legal documents were read, Laussat delivered the keys of the city to Claiborne, absolved the Louisianas from their allegiance to France, invited them to become citizens of the United States, and exchanged places with Claiborne. The deed of cession, written in both English and French, was then signed. The three men rose and walked to the balcony overlooking the square. Laussat and Claiborne took positions side by side; according to Vincent Nolte, an Italian living in the city, Laussat was "a man of education and refinement, possessing all the manners of a French courtier," and Claiborne, "exactly the reverse; of fine personal appearance, but in all other respects, a coarse, rude man, and, at the same time, very sharp and knowing, as most Americans are."

The American soldiers fired a volley, a band played "Hail Columbia," the soldiers and hundred-odd American civilians yelled "Hurrah!" as the French flag was slowly lowered and the American emblem as slowly rose. The flags met in their ascent and descent, and stopped; Claiborne and Wilkinson stood stiffly at attention; the band ceased its playing and the crowd grew silent; and Laussat stood rigid, a man of stone, pale and with tightly compressed lips. A French naval ensign received the French flag, bore it through the ranks and handed it to the Sergeant-Major. As Georges Oudard wrote, the Sergeant-Major "wrapped it about his body and thus carried it past the American ranks, who presented arms and saluted the flag to the rolling of drums, amid deep and universal emotion." When an escort of young men carried the flag to Laussat, he silently accepted it and then retired from the balcony, weeping. The purchase of Louisiana had been completed.

Claiborne delivered a brief address, then drafted a proclamation promising that the citizens of Louisiana would be "incorporated into the United States, and admitted as soon as possible according to the Principles of the Federal Constitution to the enjoyment of all the rights, advantages and immunities of citizens of the United States." In the meantime they would be maintained and protected in "the free enjoyment of their Liberty, Property and the Religion which they profess." In a short note he informed Secretary of State Madison that he had officially taken possession of Louisiana. At 3 P.M. the officials of the three nations attended a dinner given by the French Prefect. Then followed a reception and that night a grand ball, at which supper was served at two the following morning. There were reports that some of the guests remained until long after sunrise.

ATTITUDE OF LOUISIANIANS TOWARD THE PURCHASE. When news of the purchase was first received in Louisiana in late summer of 1803, Laussat wrote to Denis Decres that the Anglo-Americans in Louisiana were "extravagantly overjoyed," that the Spanish, "between their delight at seeing this colony escape French domination and their regret at losing it themselves, are for the most part stupid enough to show their satisfaction," and that the French, "that is to say, nine-tenths of the population, are amazed and distressed and talk of selling their property and leaving the country." He may have been correct in his analysis of the Americans and Spanish, but he was incorrect in saying that many of the French were distressed and that they talked of leaving the country. It would be nearer the truth to say that just as many of them had shown little enthusiasm when their colony was returned to France, many were even less enthusiastic when their land was sold to the United States.

It would be difficult to imagine how Louisianians immediately could have become attached to the people who had bought their land, who were for the most part strangers to them, who spoke another language, whose ideas and ideals of government and religion were unknown or unapproved of, whose government was almost destitute of those external evidences and pomp of power then so extravagantly displayed by European nations, whose enterprise and fondness for improvement fretted and annoyed them, who were to them unmannered, unmoraled, and uncouth.

It would take time to make the necessary adjustments; years would pass before the American form of democratic government, American ideals of religious freedom, and American ways of life would become really appreciated in Louisiana. But the Louisianians were an adaptable people. They had lived through one drama, like few in history, which had had a tragic climax—the next drama, yet to be lived by their children and their children's children, would not be tragic, but heroic.

The Americans, in Congress, had spoken of Louisiana as "This new, immense, unbounded world," and were dreaming of a nation which would push to the Pacific. Spain's representative, the Marquis de Casa Calvo, who dreamed of making Louisiana a Spanish colony again, remained in New Orleans until Claiborne gave him his passport in February, 1806, and finally departed, so it was said, "full of wrath and indignation." The French Prefect remained only for about four months, but he, too, had his visions of France regaining the land, when the western Americans severed their allegiance "from the United States Federation." It would not be a wild enterprise, he wrote, "it would on the contrary have innumerable chances in its favor." These Americans, bah! Wilkinson was a drunkard, and impertinent to boot; Claiborne was a fool. But they were only empty dreams. At last on April 21 he bade farewell to Louisiana to assume his new duties as Colonial Prefect of Martinique, and as his ship floated down the Mississippi he was heard to remark: "It is a hard thing for me, having once known this land, to part from it."

CHAPTER 15

FROM TERRITORY
TO STATE

L OUISIANA IN 1803. The purchase of Louisiana almost doubled the land area of the United States. The territory was more than thirteen times larger than New England, nearly three times larger than the thirteen original states of the Union, and roughly a third of the continental area of the present-day nation. It was larger than the combined countries of Great Britain, Germany, Italy, Portugal, and Spain, and nearly one-fourth as large as Europe. Stretching from Canada to the Gulf of Mexico, from the Mississippi to the Rocky Mountains, it was one of the richest areas in the world, with agricultural and ranching lands, large tracts of timberland, and stores of minerals, oil, and natural gas, although most of these natural resources were unknown at that time. Its 830,000 square miles had cost about 4 cents an acre.

Americans had no conception of the territory they had purchased nor could they comprehend its size. The boundaries were undefined and there were no accurate descriptions, only scattered and inaccurate accounts of the settled sections in the south and along the rivers. While exploration would shortly begin, it would be a long time before Americans gained a real comprehension of their purchase—as late as the early 1850's Representative Andrew Johnson of Tennessee predicted that it would take "seven hundred years to dispose of the public lands at the rate we have been disposing of them."

No one knew the total population of Louisiana, for the last Spanish census had been taken fifteen years before the purchase. The settled areas were along the Mississippi, Red, Atchafalaya, and Ouachita rivers and along bayous Teche and Lafourche, generally in the southeast portion of the present state. Southwest Louisiana was thinly sprinkled with scattered farms and ranches, and in the Neutral Ground east of the Sabine River were several hundred squatters, who lived as the Mexican Bishop of Nuevo León wrote, "without a ruler and without laws." The entire northern section of the state, excepting the area of the Ouachita settlements, was "practically a primeval forest," according to Robert Dabney Calhoun, "which had scarcely felt the bite of the settler's axe."

New Orleans had a total population of about 10,000, of whom over a third were Free Negroes or slaves, and was a rectangular-shaped town extending some 1,500 yards along the river and 700 to 800 yards back from it, beyond which lay forest-covered marshy lowlands and swamps. Three or four suburbs were laid out but as yet were unfilled. Four of the five forts had fallen into ruin, only Fort St. Ferdinand was in passable repair, and the ditches outside the palisades had largely been filled. In the severe winter of 1803-1804 firewood-seeking citizens demolished "the palisades, bridges, gates and *chevaux-de-frises* on every side; and . . . dismantled the city of all its apparent military character."

Drainage ditches were partially filled with dirt and rubbish, while the little bridges across them were in bad condition. Streets were unpaved and littered with trash. Wooden buildings and wooden doors and window shutters on brick houses and shops were generally unpainted. The comparatively few business houses included four or five general stores, a trio of Scottish banks, a German business firm, and eight or ten commission houses opened during the Spanish period by Americans from New York, Philadelphia, or Baltimore.

Like all cities of that day, New Orleans was a city of smells; its foul odors so affected French observer Perrin du Lac when he visited the town a few years before the purchase that he wrote: "Nothing equals the filthiness of New Orleans. . . . The city, the filth of which cannot be drained off, is not paved and probably never will be in the hands of the Spaniards. Its markets which are unventilated are reeking with rottenness. Its quay is adorned with fish that rot there for want of purchasers. Its squares are covered with the filth of animals which no one takes the trouble to remove." Despite its appearance and its smells, however, New Orleans compared favorably with most Latin-American, French, or Spanish towns of its size at that time.

The majority of the population were Creoles of French and Spanish descent, but the newly settled Spanish were migrating in sizable numbers to Mexico, Cuba, or other Spanish colonies. Most contemporary descriptions of the French Creoles were not flattering, characterizing them as an indolent, pleasure-loving class, for the most part adventurers and not a few ex-criminals, who lived principally for their balls and their gambling games. Even French Commissioner Laussat referred to them as a "miserable population." Such descriptions, however, did not do the old French Creoles justice; they would have compared rather favorably with French tropical or sub-tropical colonists of that day; many were industrious, had built sizable estates, and as Du Vallon admitted, had "rubbed off the rough corners." The Spanish Creoles were likewise attacked by their contemporaries, one of whom wrote that they were occupied with the "employments of the robe, of the pen, and of the sword," and that most of them were engaged in "feathering their nests at the expense of the King . . . and of the public." The Catalans were excepted, being generally tradesmen.

English, Irish, and Americans who had migrated to Louisiana during Spanish years represented all classes, from the "well reared and entirely honest" to the "coarse and unscrupulous," and to some who were "dregs and scum" and "poor devils or downright rogues." The lowest classes, according to these contemporary writers, were Italians, Gypsies, and *Isleños,* who mostly lived in the swamps as trappers, fishermen, or small gardeners.

Louisiana, then, in 1803 contained a polyglot population, "so diversified as to nations, races and colors," Du Vallon wrote, as to almost defy description, "an original spectacle and one that seems to have been reserved for this little corner of the world." Whatever the sometimes strange, sometimes poor quality, but always colorful and kaleidoscopic ingredients which had been poured into the Louisiana melting pot, they would produce the basic stock of modern Louisiana and the chief source of her present-day heritage.

Because of their religious, political, and social differences, French and Spanish Creoles looked with disfavor upon all Anglo-Saxons who had come to their land since the end of the French and Indian War in 1763. They frequently showed their contempt for the newcomers: when a small earthquake interrupted a New Orleans ball, an old Creole gentleman remarked, glancing at the Americans present, "It was not in Spanish times or the French that the amusements of the ladies were interfered with."

The heritage and the civilization of the Louisiana of 1803 was completely different from that of the United States. A few years afterwards, when young Alexander Porter, who later became a Louisiana Senator, planned to move to Louisiana to practice law, he met General Andrew Jackson, who advised him: "Remember, Alick, you are going to a new country. . . . You will find a different people from those you have grown among, and you must study their natures, and accomodate yourself to them." Not all Americans who came to Louisiana during those early years received such sound advice.

INAUGURATING THE AMERICAN REGIME. From December 20, 1803, until October 2, 1804, William C. C. Claiborne was in charge of civil affairs, while General James Wilkinson was in command of the army units stationed in the colony. They were busy months for the young civil official, for as he wrote to Secretary of State James Madison: "I find myself overwhelmed with business, communications from the different Commandants pour in upon me . . . the Citizens present themselves daily for redress of grievances, and my Court which has hitherto been held once a week is crowded with suits." Claiborne was doing his best, but with some misgivings, for he told Madison that he had "great cause to fear that through want of Judgment, I shall commit many errors, but believe me Sir, I shall do nothing, but with honest intentions, and a Sincere desire to promote the interest of my Country."

His major task was to secure general acceptance of the American regime, and he wrote a continual stream of reports on this subject to Madison. During the first few weeks he proceeded with extreme caution, and nothing occurred to mar his optimism. All seemed to be going well, the commandants had surrendered the posts, the French and Spanish officials were making preparations to depart, and the tranquillity of the people was proved by the fact that "the change in Government has given additional Spirit to Public amusements." It was not long, however, before Claiborne's troubles began.

The first disturbance was a comic-opera episode, which Laussat called the "war of amour-propre." To prevent possible trouble, Claiborne had regulated the order of the dances at public halls—one English quadrille, one waltz, and two French quadrilles. One evening General Wilkinson and his officers began singing "Hail Columbia" at one of these affairs, and the French immediately countered with "Enfants de la Patrie" and shouts of "Vive La République!" A clamor began, the turmoil increased, pandemonium and near-riot ensued before order could be restored. A banquet of Americans and Creoles brought the two factions together, and thereafter there was little trouble at social functions. In middle March, 1804, Claiborne wrote that the people were in "fine Humour."

Meanwhile, Claiborne settled other problems. Realizing that the large numbers of American, Spanish, and French soldiers and sailors in New Orleans, together with "adventurers," "vagabonds," and "various Characters," offered "the materials for a mob," he reorganized several companies of militia and cautiously selected their officers. He improved the mail service to various posts and settlements and instructed militia units to arrest the gabariers cruising along the waterways and selling tafia to the slaves. He recommended that New Orleans city officials take action regarding "the number of dogs, now roaming at large within the City and its environs, and which I consider a great nuisance." When Julien Poydras wrote him expressing some concern regarding religious freedom, Claiborne reassured him that "the inhabitants of Louisiana will be protected in that mode of Divine Worship they may think best," that parishioners might choose their own clergyman, and that he trusted they would be "liberal in their Patronage towards him." About the time Laussat departed the colony, Madison received Claiborne's report that everything was well in Louisiana, that he had been governing with "extreme leniety, and not an individual has yet experienced the severity of the Law."

GOVERNMENT OF THE TERRITORY OF ORLEANS. On March 26, 1804, the President signed a bill making that portion of the Louisiana Purchase south of the thirty-third parallel the Territory of Orleans, the remaining portion becoming the District of Louisiana under the jurisdiction of Indiana Territory. However, the new territorial government did not begin to function until fall of the same year.

In the meantime considerable opposition developed against Claiborne from both Louisianians and Americans, the chief complaint of the Creoles being that he did "not speak the language of the country" and was not acquainted with either the people or their customs. There was also much hostility to the territorial act, which had created an "unorganized" territory generally following the principal of the Northwest Ordinance of 1787, even though the Territory of Orleans had a population of over 5,000, which would entitle it to become an "organized" territory. Étienne de Boré resigned as Mayor of New Orleans in protest in May, 1804, and two months later Congress was petitioned to repeal certain sections of the act.

Claiborne had been informed by President Jefferson that he was serving only in an ad interim capacity as Governor, but in early September the President wrote Henry Dearborn, Secretary of War, that "Claiborne's conduct has on the whole been so prudent & conciliatory that no secondary character could have a better right." Claiborne received his commission later the same month and was inaugurated Governor on October 2.

The new Governor was vested with complete executive powers, including authority to grant pardons and reprieves and to appoint and commission all civil and militia officers, for a three-year term. A secretary was appointed for a four-year term. Legislative powers were given to the Governor and a thirteen-member legislative council to be appointed annually by the President, while judicial authority was vested in a Federal district judge, three judges of a superior court, and justices of the peace, all appointed by the President for a four-year term. The first session of the legislative council convened on December 4, 1804, and adjourned on May 1, 1805, with Julien Poydras serving as president. It is significant that Jefferson seems to have sent the legislative-council commissions to Claiborne in blank and that the Governor appointed men from New Orleans and the southern section of the territory.

Louisianians continued to oppose the form of government provided for them, as well as the fact that Louisiana had been divided into two sections, that they had no representatives in Congress, and that restrictions had been placed on the importation of slaves. A few wanted immediate statehood, but the majority, as legislative-council member John Watkins reported, generally stopped short "at the difficulties of popular representation" and at the higher expenses of statehood.

On March 2, 1805, Congress authorized the President to establish an "organized" territorial government, patterned after that of Mississippi Territory. A bicameral legislature was created, the twenty-five members of the house of representatives to be elected for terms of two years and the five members of the legislative council to be appointed by the President, from a panel of ten men nominated by the house of representatives, to serve for five years. Judges were to serve henceforth during good behavior rather than for a term of four years. This form of territorial government was continued until Louisiana was admitted as a state in 1812.

LOCAL GOVERNMENT. At the first meeting of the legislative council in 1804, Louisiana was divided into twelve counties—Acadia, Atakapas, Concordia, German Coast, Iberville, La Fourche, Natchitoches, Opelousas, Orleans, Ouachita, Pointe Coupée, and Rapides—each to have a county judge, sheriff, coroner, clerk, and treasurer appointed by the Governor. At this time the Spanish offices of commandant and syndic went out of existence.

On July 30, 1805, the Governor called for an election, to be held on the third Monday of the following September, of members to the territorial legislature. To qualify, the voter was required to certify before a notary in the presence of two witnesses that he had been a citizen of the United States for three years and owned at least 200 acres of land; by 1806 it was necessary only to have owned 50 acres for three months. Elections were held at the county seat, extending over a period of three days. Ballot boxes had three locks, to which each of the three commissioners possessed one key, and a county judge presided over the election.

The first act passed at the second session of the first legislature, approved March 31, 1807, divided the territory into nineteen parishes—Ascension, Assumption, Atakapas, Avoyelles, Baton Rouge, Concordia, Iberville, La Fourche Interior, Natchitoches, Orleans, Ouachita, Plaquemines, Pointe Coupée, Rapides, St. Bernard, St. Charles, St. James, St. John the Baptist, and St. Landry—without, however, abolishing the twelve existing counties. The designation "parish" was derived from the French *paroisse* and the Spanish *parroquia,* the ecclesiastical division under the charge of a curate. Exact boundaries of the original parishes have never been accurately determined.

The county system was apparently retained for the purpose of electing representatives and levying taxes, and gradually these functions went out of existence. Counties remained a tenuous, shadowy feature of Louisiana government after the creation of parishes until they were abolished by the Constitution of 1845. The parish in Louisiana has served as practically the same governmental unit as the county in other states.

On April 6, 1807, the territorial legislature provided "that the parish judges, together with the justices of the peace and a jury of twelve inhabitants," should meet once a year "to deliberate upon and make all necessary regulations relative to roads and levees," to regulate other matters of local concern, and that the people should be notified of all regulations. The unique group name, used only in Louisiana, which gradually came into existence for the parish governing body was the "police jury," probably so named because juries ordinarily had twelve members and because the body possessed certain police powers. The parish judge appointed police jurors until 1811, when the office became elective, and by that date the legislature had accepted the police jury as the general parish governmental body.

Appointed for a term of four years, parish judges at first had civil, criminal, and police powers, which were gradually modified as other local offices were created. They executed police-jury regulations relative to levees, roads, and other local matters, generally performing the same administrative duties as county judges in other states. Treasurers kept the parish funds, accounts, and records. Justices of the peace performed the same duties as did Spanish syndics and had jurisdiction over small civil and lesser criminal cases. Sheriffs and coroners performed their accustomed functions. All of these parish officials were appointed by the governor except the constables, who were appointed by the parish judge.

Parish officials assessed property, collected taxes, spent the monies collected, built roads and levees, kept peace and order, and otherwise handled local governmental problems. Assessments were generally low, averaging from $2.00 to $5.00 per acre of land, and the average tax per acre seldom was over 5 cents. Slaves were taxable under territorial law, but the tax was difficult to collect.

During periods of threatened slave disorders or when otherwise necessary, patrols were organized and ordered to such districts "as may be deemed most expedient." Officers of local militia units were elected by company members; when Vincent Nolte was elected captain of a German company in New Orleans, "probably because they every day heard of my money deposits in the bank," he wrote: "Military capacity I did not possess, and my sub-officers, consisting of store-clerks, grocers and trades-apprentices, learned no more of the service than I had picked up the day before."

The municipal government of New Orleans organized by Laussat and consisting of a mayor, a twelve-member council, and a clerk was continued by Claiborne. After his resignation in May, 1804, Mayor Boré was succeeded by James Pitot, who served until the end of July, 1805, when the new city government under the act of incorporation of February 17, 1805, went into effect. In 1811 the charter was amended to provide for an elective mayor, and Nicholas Girod became the first elected mayor of the city.

LAW AND ORDER. Governor Claiborne kept in force most of the old Spanish laws not in conflict with those of the United States, although they were modified by legislation enacted by the Governor and the legislative council. In May, 1805, the legislature passed a law, based largely on English common law, defining crimes and misdemeanors; later attempts to enact a criminal code failed. Three years afterwards Louis Moreau Lislet and James Brown drew up a Civil Code drawn principally from the Napoleonic Code but containing such English, French, and Spanish principles as it was felt were needed in Louisiana.

Under the Federal district court was a superior court, and after 1807 superior-court judges presided over sessions of five district or circuit courts at specified times. Parish courts came into existence with the creation of parishes and had final jurisdiction in cases involving less than $100.00. Jury trials were held upon the application of both parties or at the discretion of the parish judge, and juries were divided as equally as possible between English- and French-speaking jurors, as the maintenance of approximate equality was considered the only guarantee of justice.

Law and order were maintained by sheriffs and constables in the parishes, in New Orleans by the *gens d'armes* until 1806 and after that date by the *garde de ville,* and during emergencies by citizens deputized as police officers. The *gens d'armes,* composed chiefly of former Spanish soldiers and mulattoes, were beaten so frequently by toughs and river roustabouts that Claiborne was forced to order soldiers to patrol the streets at night. The *garde de ville* was composed of three officers and twenty men for the city and of two officers and eight men for outlying districts. At first armed with a sword and a short pike, members of the guard were so badly mauled in a fight with the river ruffians and city bullies that they were disarmed and censured by the city council. It was some years before the guard gained the upper hand, making night patrols of soldiers unnecessary, and even then brawls and fights were commonplace until well after the Civil War. Outside the city there was comparatively little trouble.

A threatened slave revolt in Concordia Parish and an insurrection plot in New Orleans led by a white man in the fall of 1805 influenced the passage of a slave code the following year. The forty-section Slave Code of 1806 was substantially the same as that promulgated by Bienville in 1724 and reenacted by Carondelet in 1792, it generally safeguarded the welfare of slaves, although it regarded them as real estate and subject to mortgage and seizure. The majority of its sections, however, concerned the prevention of Negro uprisings and crimes, and made whites who in any way encouraged "any slave or slaves to insurrection" subject to the death penalty.

The only insurrection of consequence broke out in 1811 in St. John the Baptist Parish, where an estimated number of from 180 to 500 slaves armed themselves and marched down the river road toward New Orleans, killing whites as they went. General Wade Hampton and a detachment of troops moved hurriedly upriver, defeated the Negroes in a pitched battle, killed over fifty of them, and put the rest to flight. Sixteen of the leaders were tried and executed, and their heads were cut off and stuck up on poles at varying intervals along the Mississippi above New Orleans as a warning.

In the summer of 1804 the New Orleans free-mulatto group planned a mass meeting for the purpose of memorializing Congress to give them a greater degree of citizenship, and while the meeting never materialized, for a time feeling ran high in the city. Claiborne met with the colored leaders to work out satisfactory agreements because he feared they would ally with the slaves and cause serious trouble.

Spanish slave regulations in Louisiana had been so leniently administered that it was reported that the slaves were in "a shameful state of Idleness, and want of subordination" and that they wandered about at night "without passports, stealing, drinking and rioting." Enforcement of individual plantation rules and establishment of local patrols after the beginning of the American period gradually brought an end to the disorders. Slaves frequently escaped into Spanish West Florida or into the

Neutral Ground east of the Sabine River during the early years. At first Spanish officials in Texas refused to return runaways, but early in 1809, Governor Don Manuel de Salcedo arranged to extralegally return them to their owners and thereafter there was comparatively little trouble.

MAJOR PROBLEMS OF GOVERNOR CLAIBORNE. Claiborne's most important undertaking as territorial governor was that of making Louisianians into Americans, and, having no background of self-government and no knowledge of American ideals or traditions, many of the French refused to co-operate. When one Creole was requested to vote for a neighbor for Congress, he replied that it was an imposition to send a man so far from home and that he would not assist in inflicting such an unpleasant duty upon any of his neighbors. When J. B. le Roux planned to anglicize his name to "J. B. Lerrocks," a relative taunted him: *"Tiens!* Lerrocks is ver' good Américain, but w'at t'ell you goin' do wid dat 'Jean Baptiste'?"

After the Creoles learned a little about American customs of local government, many became overconfident. Disputing a point of law, one Louisianian said: "How, do you think I don't know, sir? I am a justice of the peace!" Another replied: "I ought to know something about it, I have been twice foreman of the grand jury." But the Governor was optimistic, for he had the able assistance of such influential men as James Brown, Henry Johnson, Edward Livingston, John R. Grymes, Thomas Urquhart, Henry Bry, Evan Jones, and Thomas Bolling Robertson. He wrote to Madison that within a few years Louisianians would be good citizens and "sincere admirers of our Union and government."

Although the western boundary of the Louisiana Purchase had not been definitely fixed, the Spanish in Texas considered it to be east of the Sabine River, probably the line of the Arroyo Hondo and the Calcasieu River. They maintained an army in eastern Texas and held their Louisiana settlements west of Natchitoches. In 1806, after a shooting war had almost broken out, General Wilkinson and the Spanish officials in Texas agreed that the strip of land between the Arroyo Hondo and the Sabine should remain neutral until the matter could be adjusted by the two governments. This no man's land was filled with lawless squatters who robbed and killed until 1810, when a joint expedition of Spanish and Americans drove them out. Robberies and murders were numerous along the San Antonio Trace and Nolan's Trace, however, until 1822, when Colonel Zachary Taylor built Fort Jesup and brought order to the lawless region. The Florida Purchase Treaty in 1819 fixed the boundary, but not until 1826 did the so-called "Free State of Sabine" really become a part of Louisiana.

Throughout the territorial period the Americans of Louisiana and the Spanish of Texas vied with each other for trade with, and control over, the Indians living along the Louisiana-Texas frontier. At San Antonio the Spanish maintained a warehouse for trading goods and presents, which were distributed through English traders stationed at Nacogdoches. In 1805, Dr. John Sibley of Natchitoches was appointed Indian Agent to supervise American relations with the Indians, and the following year, Governor Claiborne met with the Caddo chiefs and secured their promises of friendship and alliance. In his speech to the chiefs, Claiborne said: "Let your people continue to hold the Americans by the hand with sincerity and friendship, and the chain of peace will be bright and strong, our children will smoke together, and the path will never be colored with blood." The great chief of the Caddoes replied that "what I have this day heard will cause me to sleep more in peace." Sibley effectively served both the Indians and Americans until after the War of 1812.

Immediately after the purchase, American land speculators flocked to Louisiana, where they bought land claims at very low prices. The Spanish had followed a liberal policy of granting land, but many titles had never been validated and after the purchase some of the Spanish officials remained in Louisiana, selling predated fraudulent titles to the speculators for a few cents an acre. John Rhea, one of the speculators, purchased eighteen different claims totaling more than 10,000 acres of land, seven of which were later rejected as fraudulent, while another speculator acquired claims, for 120,000 arpents at four cents an arpent, which the government discovered were dated March, 1804.

By act of March 26, 1804, all grants dated after October 1, 1800, date of the Treaty of San Idlefonso whereby Spain returned Louisiana to France, were declared null and void. Three years later boards of land commissioners were appointed to certificate Spanish land grants. It was not until 1837 that a majority of the claims were adjudicated, and as late as 1923 there were over 2,000 confirmed but unpatented claims in the General Land Office.

On July 25, 1805, an "elegant Barge" with "sails, colors and oars," bearing Aaron Burr, former Vice President of the United States, arrived at New Orleans, and for the next several months the city was filled with rumors. An anxious population heard he would either incite a revolution in the western United States or help the Spanish conquer the southern Mississippi Valley area. His shadowy movements intensified the rumors. It was said that General Wilkinson was conspiring with him and that an army was descending the Mississippi.

General Wilkinson arrived in New Orleans near the end of December, and for the next few weeks a sort of "reign of terror" prevailed, with military arrests and conflicts between civil and military authorities. Claiborne summoned Father Antonio de Sedella (Pere Antoine) to the Government House to take the oath of allegiance and in February, 1806, ordered the Marquis de Casa Calvo to leave Louisiana. Burr was arrested near Natchez, but a local court at Washington, Mississippi, dismissed the case for want of jurisdiction. Later arrested in Alabama, Burr was tried for treason at Richmond, Virginia, but was acquitted. The last trace of disorder disappeared when General Wilkinson, who had denounced Burr to Jefferson, left Louisiana to testify in the trial. Historians still disagree as to the real intentions of Burr and his followers.

THE WEST FLORIDA REVOLUTION. During the summer and fall of 1810 in the area presently known as the Florida Parishes there occurred a series of events which must be ranked among the most unique and audacious in all American history—the settlers in that section successfully revolted against Spain and established the short-lived Republic of West Florida.

Begun after the Treaty of Paris of 1763, the Anglo-American settlement of West Florida continued at a greatly accelerated pace after the American Revolution. While acknowledging their allegiance to Spain, the settlers hoped for future annexation to the United States, and their attitude toward Spain left no doubt as to their desires. Spain had considerable trouble in governing the section prior to the purchase of Louisiana and after that date Governor Vicente Folch found it increasingly difficult to enforce Spanish laws and regulations.

The general discontent came to a head in the Bayou Sara–St. Francisville District in the early summer of 1810, when several hundred citizens met at "Egypt" plantation and approved a plan of representative government, which also permitted Don Carlos de Hualt de Lassus, Commandant of the District, and the other Spanish officials to retain their offices. On July 2 a revolutionary congress met at St. John's Plains and continued in session there and at Baton Rouge until August 29. It attempted to work out details of co-operation with the Spanish officials, who left the impression that they were not opposed to the general plan, but De Lassus secretly wrote to Governor Folch for reinforcements.

Upon learning of De Lassus' communication six members of the congress met at "Troy" plantation just outside St. Francisville on September 21 and decided to use force against the Spanish. Philemon Thomas and a small detachment of slightly over seventy mounted men rode for Baton Rouge to capture the fort, which was garrisoned by only thirty-odd men. They launched their successful attack at four o'clock on the morning of September 23 and soon ran up their standard, a blue field bearing a single silver star, which had been made secretly by the women of

Baton Rouge. During the skirmish two men were killed, one of them being valiant young Lieutenant Luis Antonio de Grand Pré, son of former Commandant Carlos de Grand Pré.

Meanwhile, on September 22, the old revolutionary congress met as a convention. On September 26, John Rhea, the presiding officer, proclaimed the declaration of independence of the "State" of West Florida; a short time later the convention drafted a constitution and organized a government closely resembling that of the United States, but also petitioned President James Madison to annex the area to the United States. The congress of the new republic met at St. Francisville on November 19, elected Fulwar Skipwith president, and proceeded to enact legislation. On December 5, Skipwith wrote Madison suggesting that West Florida be united with the Territory of Orleans, "as this arrangement would give to the new State so formed a majority of American over the French Population." However, the President had already, on October 27, issued a proclamation ordering Governor Claiborne to take possession.

On December 10, Claiborne, commanding a small militia force, took possession of West Florida at Baton Rouge and ten days later proclaimed that the area eastward from the Mississippi to the Perdido River "shall constitute one county to be known and called by the name of Feliciana." The county was divided into the four parishes of Feliciana, East Baton Rouge, Saint Helena and Saint Tammany, and in January, 1811, the parishes of "Viloxi" and Pascagoula which lay between the Pearl and Perdido rivers, were added. Both Spain and Great Britain protested the annexation, to no avail. The four western parishes of the County of Feliciana were officially joined to Louisiana by Congressional act approved April 14, 1812.

ECONOMIC PROGRESS. Upon learning that Louisiana would be admitted to the Union when it had sufficient population and the Creoles had accepted the ways of democratic government, speculators of all types, enterprising businessmen, lawyers and doctors eager to secure clients and to build practices, young men, and all those who wished to make a fresh start in life flocked to the new El Dorado of Louisiana. They came from all sections of the United States, particularly from the south and west. Many brought varying amounts of capital; others brought little if any. Some were men, as William Darby wrote, "of candid minds, classical education, and useful professional endowments," while others were "without education or moral principle" and too ignorant or too prejudiced to acquire the language or to appreciate the qualities of the Louisianians.

Whites and Free Negroes from the West Indies continued to arrive in ever increasing numbers, many with their slaves. These included not only Santo Domingans, but Cubans, Jamaicans, and others from the smaller islands. In 1809 it was reported that six vessels alone landed 3,956 persons of color, of whom slightly over half were slaves. Governor Claiborne was skeptical of the quality of these immigrants, writing that some of them were "doubtless worthy men but I fear a majority of them will be useless, if not bad Citizens." But he judged hastily, for as James E. Winston writes, "the degree of sobriety that characterized these refugees is remarkable. . . . they constituted a law abiding and industrious group." Large numbers of slaves were imported prior to 1808 but comparatively few were smuggled into Louisiana thereafter.

Claiborne's estimate in 1809 that there were about 55,000 people in Louisiana was erroneous, for the census of 1810 showed the total population to be slightly over 76,500. New Orleans had grown from a city of 17,000 in 1806 to one of approximately 24,000 in 1810. Other towns were increasing, new towns such as Donaldsonville were being founded, and the countryside was rapidly being settled.

Roads were being rerouted or opened to distant points. Over these roads moved increasing amounts of freight, large numbers of immigrants, mail "expresses" (mail riders), and mail stages. They were, however, little more than traces; more than one traveler condemned them, Fortescue Cuming, who traveled the Bayou Sara–Baton

Rouge Road, writing that much of it was a "complete slough, in some places deep enough to mire my horse to the saddle skirts." In 1810, Nicholas Roosevelt joined Robert Fulton and Robert Livingston in a venture to build and operate steamboats on the southwestern waterways. The group surveyed the route from Pittsburgh to New Orleans, built a 116-foot-long, 20-foot-beam boat, powered by a 34-inch cylinder engine. Christened the *New Orleans,* it left Pittsburgh for New Orleans in late September, 1811, arriving after a series of delays at the capital in early January, 1812. Until she struck a snag and sank during the summer of 1814, the boat operated between New Orleans and Natchez.

Trade mushroomed during the early territorial years. From up the Mississippi came cotton, flour, "rope yarn," lead, whiskey, tobacco, pork, and other products; from the Red and Ouachita river country came furs, hides, and other items; and from American and European ports came manufactured goods. The firm of Barr and Davenport supplied livestock from Texas; John Forbes and Company and other firms imported manufactured goods via Mobile and Pensacola, or directly from Great Britain. Customhouse clearances, however, steadily declined after 1807 due to the war between Great Britain and France, and by 1812 only a few daring captains were slipping in or out of the mouth of the Mississippi in the hope of avoiding the belligerents' prowling warships.

There were few banks and business firms performing banking functions when Louisiana was purchased, and Vincent Nolte wrote that there was not a single house in New Orleans "possessed of any capital worth mentioning." Governor Claiborne realized the necessity for banks, and in 1805 a branch of the First Bank of the United States was opened in New Orleans and the Bank of Louisiana was organized. Six years later the Planters' Bank and the Bank of Orleans were established. These institutions were of great assistance to Louisianians through loans and the extension of credit during the depression years prior to 1812.

SOCIAL AND CULTURAL LIFE. At the end of the territorial period, Louisianians could be divided roughly into three general groups: frontier farmers who lived at a subsistence level; staple farmers and planters who owned land and slaves and who produced cotton, tobacco, and sugar; and people of the towns, particularly of New Orleans, where all economic and social levels could be found. There was generally little ostentation in rural and frontier areas; housing, food, clothing, social customs, and amusements were simple. The planters, of course, lived as did the wealthy of New Orleans, imported clothing and fancy staple foodstuffs, resided in mansions filled with servants, dined at three in the afternoon with numerous guests, and at night dressed and attended balls, dinners, masquerades, or the theater.

Creoles spoke French, much of which had been modified over the years with Spanish, African, and even Indian words and expressions. Americans spoke English, to which had been added localisms from every section of the country—they used such expressions as "I swon," or "gaul durn your picter"; bragged of physical prowess by saying, "bust me wide open if I didn't bulge into the creek in the twinkling of a bedpost, I was so thunderin' savagerous"; or described a slender man as "a fellow so poor and thin he had to lean up agin a saplin' to cuss."

New Orleanians still traveled on unpaved, badly lighted streets, which became quagmires when it rained, for Carondelet's drainage system had yet to be improved. Paved footways, however, now lined some of the more important thoroughfares. Many houses were of wood, although brick buildings were annually increasing. Few public buildings were added during Claiborne's regime as territorial Governor, but a new waterworks system, where slaves pumped water from the Mississippi into "a reservoir from which hollowed cypress logs conducted thin, yellow streams to a few subscribers," had been put into service in 1810, followed by a new market the next year. Plans were being made, however, to add new suburbs and to erect public buildings worthy of decorating a state capital.

New Orleans boasted a theater in 1803, a long, low, cypress building sometimes

[174]

called "Le Spectacle de la Rue St. Pierre," where amateur theatricals were presented. Within a few years "Tessier's Large Room" on St. Philip Street was erected, as was "Moore's Large Building" on Chartres Street, where the first English theatrical performance was given in the spring of 1806. The Spectacle de la Rue St. Pierre was rebuilt in 1807 and renamed the Théâtre St. Pierre; the St. Philip Theatre was opened the following year, and in 1809 the Théâtre Orleans. By this time professionals as well as amateurs were charming audiences with *The Death of Caesar, Don Juan, The Doctor's Courtship,* and *The Battle of the Nile,* which showed "men sinking and swimming and Crokadiles molesting them and Whales, Sharks, Dolphins, Swords, and Flying Fish and Mermaids swimming on the surface of the water."

The *Moniteur de la Louisiane* was the only Louisiana newspaper in existence in 1803, but the same year saw the founding of the *Telegraphe,* printed in both English and French. The *Louisiana Gazette,* the first English-language publication, was established in 1804, and in 1810 became a daily under the new name of the *Louisiana Gazette and New Orleans Daily Advertiser.* The *Lanterne Magique* was begun in 1808, followed the next year by the *Louisiana Courier and the Friend of the Laws* and the *Journal du Soir.* The *Louisiana Planter,* bearing the date line of Alexandria, began publication in 1810. These were all small newspapers, and few copies of them exist today.

A month prior to taking possession of Louisiana, President Jefferson submitted a description of the territory to Congress. Under the heading of "Learning" was one brief paragraph: "There are no colleges, and but one public school, which is in New Orleans. The masters of this are paid by the King. They teach the Spanish language only. There are a few private schools for children. Not more than half the inhabitants are supposed to be able to read and write; of whom not more than two hundred, perhaps, are able to do it well." Scarcely a month had passed before Claiborne appealed to the people for "public schools open and free to all children," but no appropriations were made for the purpose. Education acts were passed in 1805, 1806, and 1811, but little was accomplished in getting schools actually started, despite Claiborne's efforts. By 1812 there were less than half a dozen nondenominational tax-supported public schools in Louisiana. The Governor, however, could not be condemned; the Catholic Creoles believed that education was the province solely of the Church, and Protestant Americans were not yet numerous enough to install the practices of the older states.

The College of Orleans, according to some writers the first institution of higher learning established and supported by a state but in reality a combination primary and secondary school, was incorporated by legislative action in 1805. It ceased to exist in 1826, when the College of Louisiana at Jackson was chartered.

RELIGION. Not understanding American principles of religious freedom, the Roman Catholics were uncertain that they would be allowed to continue their church after the United States took possession. On April 23, 1804, the Ursulines wrote to Jefferson begging that their property be formally confirmed to them so that they might continue their work of charity and education; their fears were allayed by the President's reassuring reply that "the property vested in your institution . . . will be preserved to you sacred and inviolate."

The Catholic faith, however, was at a low ebb in Louisiana. There was only one church of consequence in the entire colony, the Church of St. Louis; only one other chapel in New Orleans, the chapel of the Ursulines; and many of the parishes and villages had only small churches or none at all. Father Gilbert J. Garraghan, a noted modern Catholic authority, admits that "the state of religion in the Louisiana Territory at the period of its acquisition by the United States in 1803 was distressing." In New Orleans the Sabbath was observed in the Continental manner, with stores, markets, barrooms, and theaters kept open and generously patronized, and throughout the colony worship was still "exterior and formal," with regular attendance practiced largely during Lent and Easter.

Bishop Penalver y Cardenas had become discouraged with the lack of response and in 1801 had departed for Guatemala. From 1801 to 1806 the two vicar-generals in authority accomplished little, so the diocese was finally placed under the jurisdiction of Bishop John Carroll of Baltimore. After two priests had turned down the appointment, Abbé Louis Guillaume Dubourg was appointed Administrator Apostolic of Louisiana and the Floridas, and arrived at New Orleans in 1812. A priest later reported that "if Bishop Du Bourg had not come in time to our relief, the last spark of faith would have been extinguished in our country."

There was not a single Protestant church or Jewish synagogue in Louisiana in 1803. There seems little doubt, however, that since the late 1780's itinerant Protestant ministers had been clandestinely and furtively traveling through the central, northern, and Florida Parish sections. The eccentric Methodist minister Lorenzo Dow crossed the Mississippi in the fall of 1804, preached a few sermons, and reported: "I believe there is a Providence in such a vast territory falling to the United States, as liberty of conscience may now prevail as the country populates, which before was prohibited by the inquisition." A Protestant Episcopal Church secured an act of incorporation from the legislature, and began functioning in New Orleans in the fall of 1805. Soon other Protestant denominations began to establish congregations and build churches in Louisiana.

STATEHOOD. Louisianians in general grew impatient for statehood, as Jefferson had promised them equal membership in the American Union. Almost since Claiborne's organization of territorial government, a constant stream of letters had flowed into Washington urging immediate action on the part of Congress. Shortly after the census of 1810 was completed Congress acted, and on February 20, 1811, an act was passed authorizing a constitutional convention, which met "in a large room of Mr. Tremonlet's Coffee House" in New Orleans in November. Julien Poydras, elected chairman, was ably supported by such men as Jacques Villeré, Henry S. Thibodaux, Bernard Marigny, Henry Johnson, Jean Noel Destrehan, Eligius Fromentin, Alexander Porter, Joseph Brown, and others.

The question of a name for the new state created considerable discussion. The story is told that when the name "Jefferson" was suggested, Louis de Blanc de St. Denis, from Atakapas, heatedly declared that if that name had a chance of success he would secure a barrel of gunpowder and blow up the convention. The constitution was drawn up and adopted, and on April 8, 1812, was approved by Congress. The Florida Parishes had not been included, but by supplementary act were added six days later. The new state would be admitted on April 30.

Julien Poydras, as president of the convention, issued writs providing for an election for governor and members of the legislature on June 29. The election was a spirited one, though Claiborne won by a decided majority, 2,757 votes to 947 for Jacques Villeré and 168 for Jean Noel Destrehan. Under the constitution the governor was to be elected by the General Assembly from the two top candidates, and on July 28 Claiborne was elected by a vote of 33 to 6 over Villeré. Governor Claiborne qualified two days later and the same day delivered his gubernatorial message. Louisianians had progressed from Spaniards and Frenchmen with few democratic rights to politically underprivileged territorial Americans to politically equal Americans in a little less than nine years.

CHAPTER 16

LOUISIANA AND THE
WAR OF 1812

THE WAR OF 1812. Thirty-two days after Louisiana was admitted to the Union, President James Madison recommended that the United States Congress declare war against Great Britain. Congress debated the question for a little over two weeks, then on June 18 passed the act declaring war, which was signed the next day by the President.

Great Britain was highhandedly stopping American merchantmen on the high seas and taking American sailors from them; she kept military posts on American soil near the Great Lakes, blockaded American ports, and incited the Indians to war against the western settlers; she hindered American trade with Europe. On the other hand, many Americans, "War Hawks" who were interested in developing western lands and in securing Canada for the United States, wanted a war with Great Britain.

The United States was not prepared for war: the country was not united and large numbers of New Englanders and New Yorkers actively opposed the war, the army was small and ill-equipped, the national treasury had little money. The war on land went against the United States—General Isaac Hull surrendered Detroit; the garrison at Fort Dearborn (Chicago) was massacred; an attempt to invade Canada failed as did a move to capture Montreal; and in late August, 1814, the British captured Washington and burned the capitol, the White House, and other buildings. On the sea, however, it was a far different story. The American navy was small, but the ships were fast and the seamen deadly accurate with their guns. During the early months of the war many individual victories were won, and Oliver Hazard Perry on September 10, 1813, won the decisive Battle of Lake Erie; yet these victories did not prevent the British from effectively blockading American coastal ports.

Soon after the declaration of war, Governor Claiborne reorganized the Louisiana militia and toured the state urging the people to support the government. However, he faced many problems: a hurricane hit the lower Mississippi area, did great damage, and completely wrecked eighteen ships at New Orleans; two British vessels blockaded the mouth of the Mississippi, and trade practically ceased. Furthermore, the people of Louisiana were not united in support of the war. Some of the French Creoles petitioned the French Consul at New Orleans that they were French citizens and not Americans; the loyal element in New Orleans agitated against all aliens; and there were rumors that some Louisianians were actually in correspondence with the British.

Conditions improved early in 1813, and "preparations for a defensive war" proceeded unabated; but during the summer a wave of incendiary conflagrations swept the southern section of the state. It was stopped only after the Governor offered a

$1,000 reward for information leading to the arrest of the persons guilty of starting the fires. In late July the Creek Indians, encouraged by British agents, went on the warpath. On August 30 they captured Fort Mims on the Alabama River and massacred over 250 of the 550 persons in the fort. Jackson marched southward from Tennessee to campaign against them, while Claiborne worked cautiously with the Choctaws of Louisiana. Meeting with a large delegation of Caddo chiefs at Natchitoches in middle October, Claiborne in a rousing speech told them that the British refused to fight the Americans "man to man" and though "a fly you know, brother, may disturb the sleeping lion," the Americans had the power "to punish all their enemies." While Claiborne had done everything possible to put Louisiana in a state of defense, at the end of 1813 she was still not in a position to withstand an invading army.

Jackson continued his campaign against the Creeks in early 1814, fought the decisive Battle of Horseshoe Bend on March 27, and concluded the Treaty of Fort Jackson in early August. Meanwhile, in early April it was rumored that the British planned to attack New Orleans—Napoleon had been defeated and Britain could now throw all her resources against the United States—but the rumor attracted little notice. In late July the British occupied Pensacola and the following month Colonel Edward Nicolls issued a proclamation to the "NATIVES OF LOUISIANA," offering to "liberate" the soil of Louisiana from the "faithless, imbecile government" of the United States and stop the "unnatural and unjust" war being fought by "those brawlers for liberty."

In middle September, Jackson drove off the British attacking Fort Bowyer at Mobile and early the next month moved against Pensacola, which he occupied on November 7, Colonel Nicolls having withdrawn his force. Early in November the Federal government, learning that the British expedition which had attacked Baltimore and burned Washington was concentrating at Jamaica and believing that its next objective would be Louisiana, ordered Jackson to New Orleans. Jackson left Mobile on November 22, just four days before the British expedition sailed from Jamaica.

Meanwhile, in Louisiana the legislature met in extra session, but accomplished little because of mutual distrust and lack of confidence among the members. Claiborne wrote to Jackson at Mobile: "I think with you that the country is filled with traitors and spies." He was partially correct, for spies and a small number of traitors were at work. But at last Louisianians began to rally to the defense of their state; committees were organized to assist the Governor, and in New Orleans a committee of nine prominent citizens urged the people to "Unite! . . . defend to the last extremity your sovereignty, your property; defend your own lives and the dearer existence of your wives and children." Their loyalty and strength would soon be put to the test.

THE BRITISH EXPEDITION. If the British could capture New Orleans, they would hold the key to the entire Lower Mississippi Valley and its rich plunder of cotton, sugar, tobacco, and other products. Furthermore, it would be feasible to move upriver and occupy all of Louisiana. Since the British had never accepted the legality of the Louisiana Purchase, the orders to their officers at Jamaica read, "reduce the Crown Colony of Louisiana." They anticipated little opposition from the Americans and none from the French and Spanish Creoles, who, it was said, would not fight.

During the late summer and early fall of 1814 the British concentrated at Negril Bay, Jamaica, a strong fleet of fifty ships commanded by Vice-Admiral Sir Alexander Cochrane and an army of about ten thousand men commanded by General Sir Edward Pakenham, brother-in-law of the Duke of Wellington. On board the ships were civil officials to take over the government of Louisiana, and their wives as well as wives of naval and army officers. After a final inspection and review, the fleet sailed for Pensacola Bay, then turned westward, anchoring opposite North Chandeleur Island, near the entrance to Lake Borgne, on December 10. Shortly thereafter in London, British Foreign Minister Robert Stewart, Lord Castlereagh, confidently wrote: "I expect at this moment that . . . we are in possession of New Orleans . . . and that the Americans are now little better than prisoners in their own country."

PREPARATIONS FOR THE DEFENSE OF LOUISIANA. Jackson proceeded slowly with a small force along the Gulf Coast, crossed Pearl River near present-day Bogalusa, and continued through Covington to Madisonville, where he embarked across Lake Pontchartrain for New Orleans, arriving early on the morning of December 1.

At this time Jackson was in his late forties, tall, lean, and straight of figure, with a wrinkled and seamed sallow face, bright gray eyes shaded by heavy brows, and iron-gray, bristly hair. Though he was exhausted by exposure and suffering from malaria, his face revealed a restless energy, strong sense of purpose, stern decision, dignity, self-confidence, and intense devotion to duty. He dressed in a small leather cap, a short, blue Spanish coat, well-worn pants, and frayed, high boots. To the immaculately attired and debonair Creoles and well-dressed Americans he looked more like a down-at-the-heels flatboatman than a general who had come to save Louisiana from the invader; soon, however, they came to realize he was a man of iron who commanded their respect.

Jackson's quiet arrival and his immediate and all-consuming attention to the immense problems at hand electrified the Louisianians. He appointed Major Arsene Latour principal engineer, and put the thirty-six-year-old Frenchman to work strengthening the defenses of the city; ordered the scattered army units at Mobile, Baton Rouge, Natchez, and other points to march posthaste; conferred with Mayor Nicolas Girod, who mobilized laborers, carts, and teams to assist in the work on the defenses; ordered Bayou Manchac filled up at its juncture with the Mississippi to prevent use of that waterway by the British; and met with a New Orleans Committee of Public Safety at Maspero's Exchange to advise them in their attempts to weld the citizens into a determined, ready-to-fight unit. He ordered young Captain Henry Miller Shreve, recently arrived from Pittsburgh with the steamboat *Enterprise,* to take his boat up the river to pick up much-needed munitions then en route to the city by flatboat and to take supplies downriver to Fort St. Philip. After a tour of inspection down the Mississippi, Jackson immediately rushed off to inspect the shores of Lake Pontchartrain and Chef Menteur.

Batteries were erected at the Rigolets and at the mouth of Bayou St. John, and earthworks were thrown up along the Gentilly–Chef Menteur Road, Bayou St. John, and both sides of the river below the city. New Orleans became an armed camp where a maelstrom of activity of whites, Free Negroes, and slaves whirled continuously from daybreak to far into the night. Most Louisianians enthusiastically supported the general, the mayor, and the Governor, despite the legislature's dawdling and indecision—it finally did appropriate $17,000 for the war effort on December 13. The contagion of patriotic enthusiasm spread over the state. An old lady wrote Governor Claiborne: "My four sons are at the front with Andrew Jackson. I regret having no others to offer my country; I am bent under the load of years, but, if my services in caring for the wounded should be thought useful, command me, and in spite of age and distance I shall hasten to New Orleans."

But Jackson was on the horns of a dilemma. Which approach to New Orleans would the British use? Would they come from Barataria Bay, by way of the Rigolets and Chef Menteur and along the high ground of the Gentilly–Chef Menteur Road, through Lake Pontchartrain and then along Bayou St. John, or would they come up the Mississippi? Soon the general had his answer.

THE BATTLE OF LAKE BORGNE. A little fleet of six small gunboats, manned by 182 men and commanded by young Lieutenant Thomas Ap Catesby Jones, had observed the British fleet anchor on December 10 and immediately reported to Jackson. On the thirteenth the British sailed into Lake Borgne. The next day Admiral Cochrane transferred about a thousand marines and sailors to sloops of war and heavy landing boats with swivel guns, and with this small armada attacked Jones's little fleet. The American *Sea Horse* was set on fire and blew up; then the wind died and the ships were becalmed. The landing boats, propelled by oarsmen and more maneuverable than the American sailing vessels, soon captured the *Alligator*. The others fought on until they, too, were captured. The British lost about 175 men killed and wounded, including 22 officers, while the American loss was 6 killed and 35 wounded.

The little Battle of Lake Borgne was one of the most significant in American history. While it gave the British undisputed control of the lake, it also informed Jackson of the approximate route the British would use to attack New Orleans, and more important still, it delayed the British landing at the mouth of Bayou Bienvenu thus giving the Americans time to mobilize and concentrate their full strength.

NINE DECISIVE DAYS. Nine days passed between the Battle of Lake Borgne and the Night Battle of December 23, the first of four land engagements fought during the British campaign against New Orleans, nine days critical to the American cause, nine days during which New Orleans witnessed such a frenzy of action and such a panic of many of her citizens as she had never seen before and never would again.

Jackson issued a proclamation to the people of Louisiana on December 16, threatening them with punishment if they failed to unanimously support the cause. When the legislature hesitated to immediately support his recommendation to suspend the writ of habeas corpus, he proclaimed martial law. He ordered Generals John Coffee and William Carroll, en route to New Orleans with their Tennessee militia, to hasten to his relief; Coffee made the last 120 miles in two days and Carroll arrived on December 21. Jackson ordered the garrison of Fort St. Philip to hold the fort as long as a man remained alive to sight a gun. At this time, as Reed Adams writes, "the panic subsided, confidence returned, and cheerfulness was restored. Faction was rendered powerless; treason, on any considerable scale, impossible."

On December 17, Claiborne issued one of the most unusual proclamations ever made by an American governor. After conferences with Judge Dominick A. Hall and legislators Bernard Marigny, Joseph de Roffignac, Louis Louaillier, Jackson's aide Auguste D'Avezac, and the stubborn general himself, in which Jackson strongly opposed, but finally consented to, the proposed action, Governor Claiborne issued a proclamation "To the Barratariors," several hundred privateers headquartered in the vicinity of Barataria Bay, inviting them "to enroll themselves and to march against the Enemy" and "to join the Standards of the United States." He continued that "should their conduct in the Field meet the approbation of Major General Jackson, that officer will unite with the Governor in a request to the President of the United States to extend to each and every Individual as aforesaid so marching and acting a Free and Full pardon."

To the island of Grande Terre, so well described by Lafcadio Hearn as "a wilderness of wind-swept grasses and sinewy reeds waving away from a thin beach, ever speckled with drift and decaying things—wormriddled timbers and dead porpoises," had come about 1808 a band of privateers. They preyed upon French, Spanish, and English ships and needed a location from which to smuggle their captured goods into New Orleans without paying tariff duties. Within a few years young Jean Laffite forged his way to the leadership of the band and became their *capitaine*, or as they expressed his title, their *bos*. Jean Laffite gathered about him strong lieutenants: his brother Pierre, his brother Alexandre Frédéric who signed himself Frédéric Youx but who is better known as Dominique You, the native New Orleanian Renato Beluche, Pierre Sicard, Juan Juanville (better known as François Sapia), Jacinto Lobrano, and Italians Vicente Gambie, Antonio Angelo, and Louis Chighizola. Laffite built a retail warehouse called "The Temple" about halfway between Grande Terre and New Orleans, and here Louisianians purchased imported goods tariff-free at much reduced prices. Good slaves could be bought cheaply at $150 to $200 each, whereas in New Orleans slaves frequently sold at $600 to $700.

The privateers prospered, for Louisianians needed cheap goods and slaves. They made the *Café des Réfugiés* on St. Philip Street their headquarters. Here they rubbed elbows with flatboatmen, filibusters, French *revolutionnaires,* American army and navy deserters—and such leading New Orleans citizens as lawyers Edward Livingston and Pierre Morel, aristocratic Bernard de Marigny de Mandeville, merchant Evan Jones, French nobleman Count Louis Philippe Joseph de Roffignac, legislator Louis Louaillier, painter Jean Baptiste Sel, soldier of fortune Baron de Saint Geme, and others.

But the privateers became too brazen in their violation of American customs duties, and in March, 1813, Governor Claiborne proclaimed the Baratarians "banditti" and ordered them to disperse. This they ignored, and in July, Pierre Laffite was arrested in New Orleans and charged with being "a pirate and notorious smuggler." In late August the British offered Jean Laffite a captaincy and a large cash sum to join their service and to enlist his followers, but he informed Governor Claiborne of the offer and of British movements in the Gulf of Mexico. Pierre mysteriously escaped from jail on the night of September 6, and on September 10, Jean Laffite wrote Claiborne offering his services and explaining his position:

I am the stray sheep wishing to return to the flock. If you were thoroughly acquainted with the nature of my offenses I should appear to you much less guilty and still worthy to discharge the duties of a good citizen. I have never sailed under any flag but that of the republic of Carthagena, and my vessels are perfectly regular in that respect. If I could have brought my lawful prizes into the ports of this state, I should not have employed the illicit means that have caused me to be proscribed.

Claiborne, however, did not trust Laffite. On September 16, Master Commander Daniel T. Patterson, United States naval commander at New Orleans, led an expedition against the settlement on Grande Terre, captured Dominique You and about 80 men, who had already fired the warehouses and the village, while 400 to 500 of the privateers escaped. Patterson brought his prisoners to New Orleans and lodged them in jail. They were still there when Governor Claiborne issued his proclamation of December 17. Jean and Pierre Laffite were in hiding at Alexandre Labranche's plantation in St. Charles Parish, and those who had escaped capture were scattered about near New Orleans.

Jean Laffite immediately went to New Orleans, secured safe conduct from Judge Hall through the services of Edward Livingston and Major Latour, met General Jackson at a store in a building now known as the Old Absinthe House, and offered the services of himself and his men. The offer was accepted, and "Captaine Dominique" organized three artillery units, which were ordered to the old Spanish Fort at the mouth of Bayou St. John.

In nine feverish days everything possible for the defense of New Orleans had been accomplished. The Americans would fight with what they had; militiamen, ill-organized citizenry, free men of color, temporarily paroled privateers, a few regulars, and a handful of Indians would soon face the Royal North Britain Fusiliers, the Old Fighting Third, the Royal Highlanders, and other noted British units which had fought under the Iron Duke of Wellington in the Spanish Peninsula and had stormed the strongholds of Badajoz and Salamanca.

THE NIGHT BATTLE OF DECEMBER 23. After the Battle of Lake Borgne the British reorganized their fleet and army at Pea Island, near the mouth of Pearl River, and on December 22 about 1,600 men, commanded by Colonel William Thornton, rowed across Lake Borgne in barges, landing the next morning at the mouth of Bayou Bienvenu. Thornton sent a detachment up Bayou Mazant and

[181]

thence to the Villeré Canal. The British followed the canal to the Villeré Plantation and quickly occupied the area, but Major Gabriel Villeré had escaped to warn Jackson that the British had landed.

Jackson ordered an immediate mobilization of all available forces at New Orleans. Major J. B. Plauche's Batallion d'Orleans, stationed at Spanish Fort, dashed off for the Place d'Armes, and, according to legend, ran the entire distance. The army units quickly gathered. To quote Grace King:

> As the Cathedral clock was striking three, from every quarter of the city troops were seen coming at a quickstep through the streets, each company with its own vernacular music, Yankee Doodle, La Marseillaise, Le Chant du Depart. The ladies and children crowded the balconies. . . .
>
> Jackson, on horseback, with the regulars drawn up at his right, waited at the gate of Fort St. Charles to review the troops as they passed. The artillery were already below, in possession of the road. The first to march down after them were Beale's rifles . . . in their blue hunting shirts and citizens' hats, their long bores over their shoulders, sharp-shooters and picked shots every one of them, all young, active, intelligent volunteers, from the best in the professional and business circles. . . . At a hard gallop, with a cloud of dust, came Hinds's dragoons, delighting General Jackson by their gallant, dare-devil bearing. After them Jackson's companion in arms, the great Coffee, trotted at the head of his mounted gun-men, with their long hair and unshaved faces, in dingy woolen hunting shirts, copperas dyed trousers, coonskin caps, and leather belts stuck with hunting knives and tomahawks.
>
> "Forward at a gallop!" was Coffee's order, after a word with General Jackson, and so they disappeared.
>
> Through a side street marched a gay, varied mass of colour, men all of a size, but some mere boys in age, with the handsome, regular features, flashing eyes and unmistakable martial bearing of the French. "Ah! Here come the brave Creoles," cried Jackson, and Plauche's battalion, which had come in on a run from Bayou St. John, stepped gallantly by.
>
> And after these, under their white commander, defiled the Freemen of colour, and then passed down the road a band of a hundred Choctaw Indians in their war paint; last of all, the Regulars.
>
> Jackson still waited until a small dark schooner left the opposite bank of the river and slowly moved down the current. This was the "Carolina," under Commodore Patterson. Then Jackson clapped spurs to his horse, and, followed by his aids, galloped after his army.

Some seven miles below New Orleans lay a strip of open ground about 1,500 yards wide, between the Mississippi and the swamp, and across it was an abandoned drainage canal, the boundary of the Chalmette and Rodriguez plantations. Some years before, according to legend, French Marshal Louis Victor Moreau, hero of the Battle of Hohenlinden, pointed out that here was the logical place to force battle on an enemy attacking New Orleans; it is believed that editor J. C. de St. Romes of the *Louisiana Courier* gave the information to Jackson or to Latour. On reaching this point the soldiers threw up a low breastwork on the New Orleans side of the canal.

Jackson decided to attack the weary British, encamped about two miles farther on, that very night. He hit their outposts about eight o'clock, and in a furious charge drove them back. Becoming confused in the darkness, the British gathered in small groups, where the Americans attacked them with gun-butts, knives, tomahawks, and even fists. Jackson withdrew to his line of breastworks about four o'clock the next morning. The British lost over 250, killed, wounded, and missing, while the Americans lost slightly over 200. Major Latour later wrote that this battle saved Louisiana, "for it cannot be doubted but that the enemy, had he not been attacked with such impetuosity, when he had hardly effected his debarkation, would, that very night, or early next morning, have marched against the city, which was not defended by any fortification."

THE GRAND RECONNAISSANCE. For four days the British continued to land troops and bring up supplies and munitions, making no move against Jackson. Meanwhile the armies celebrated Christmas, and British General Sir Edward Pakenham arrived. On the morning of December 28, Pakenham ordered troops forward to feel out the American defensive line, pierce it if possible, turn the flanks, and force a retreat. This accomplished, the British could push the Americans hard and perhaps move on the short distance to New Orleans. The British advanced in solid columns, supported by artillery, but ran into a sheet of shot and shell so terrible that a British historian later wrote that "scarce a ball passed over or fell short of its mark but all striking full into the midst of our ranks occasioned terrible havoc." The attack failed.

The British, however, were not disheartened. After all, they had not attacked in strength nor had they used the full complement of their artillery. The next attack would succeed and New Orleans would fall. When one of the captured British officers was informed that General Jackson had inquired about his personal needs, he replied: "Return my compliments to General Jackson, and say that as my baggage will reach me in a few days I shall be able to dispense with his polite attentions."

THE ARTILLERY BATTLE OF NEW YEAR'S DAY. The morning of New Year's Day was foggy, and believing that the British would not attack, the Creoles asked to have a grand review of the army. Jackson consented, and the bands began to play and the Americans to parade up and down the open field behind their earthworks. Then the fog lifted and a blast from twenty-four British cannon broke over the line. Confusion reigned as the Americans scrambled back to their breastworks to man their fifteen guns, which could fire only about two-thirds of the weight of metal hurled by the British cannon.

The artillery battle began about eight o'clock in the morning and lasted until about one o'clock in the afternoon, by which time the British guns had either been put out of action or abandoned. Throughout the engagement the British infantry waited behind their batteries for a breach to be made in the American breastworks, but they had waited in vain. British Lieutenant George Gleig wrote that "never was any failure more remarkable or unlooked for than this." Admiral Sir Edward Codrington admitted that "not a gun of the enemy appeared to suffer, and our firing [was] too high. . . . Such a failure in this boasted arm was not to be expected, and I think it a blot in the artillery escutcheon." Major C. R. Forrest wrote that "our batteries made little impression upon the enemies parapet."

THE BATTLE OF NEW ORLEANS. For a week the British continued to land and move up reinforcements from their fleet, while Jackson strengthened his line of defenses and welcomed the arrival of 2,000 Kentuckians and other militia units. Three Louisiana militia units were ordered to patrol the area above New Orleans to guard against a flanking attack, and General David Morgan was sent across the Mississippi with 850 men to protect that side of the river.

Jackson had about 3,000 men at his line of earthworks, with 1,000 in reserve; Pakenham had between 5,000 and 6,000 men with which to attack Jackson's line, with 1,200 men in reserve, and another 1,200 to cross the river to attack Morgan. The British had a few more than a dozen usable cannon, while Jackson now had 12 guns behind his line and 9 with Morgan which could be used to help cover the area in front of his line near the river. Jackson's earthworks were irregular in height and width, varying from five to ten feet in height and in some places hardly strong enough to stop a cannon ball. Although the Rodriguez Canal had been a dry ditch, the levee had been cut and it was now partially filled with water; according to

British reports the ditch was about ten to twelve feet wide and three to four feet deep.

The American artillery was divided into eight batteries concentrated in three groups: No. 1, containing four batteries, was near the river and guarded the American right; No. 2, containing two batteries, was in the center; and No. 3, with two batteries, protected the American left. In the coming engagement the British would concentrate their attack almost directly against that section of the line protected by group No. 3.

After some hesitation Pakenham decided to attack Jackson and Morgan at the same time, the main attack being made, of course, against Jackson. Pakenham foresaw the risk of making a frontal attack upon the American line, protected as it was by artillery and by a strong line of earthworks fronted by a water-filled ditch, but was prodded by Admiral Cochrane, who said, sarcastically: "If the army shrinks from the task, I will fetch the sailors and marines from the fleet, and with them storm the American lines and march to the city. The soldiers can then bring up the baggage."

New Orleanians were fearful during the week following the Battle of New Year's Day, for they realized that the British had yet to throw their full strength against Jackson. Jackson and Claiborne had quarreled after the declaration of martial law. It was charged that certain legislators wished to surrender the city without a fight and that a few had actually communicated with the British; it was obvious that some of them supported Jackson in lukewarm fashion. A number of French Creoles had continued to appeal to the French Consul for protection as Frenchmen should the British capture and sack the city. It was known that British spies and American traitors had given Pakenham complete information as to American army strength, equipment, and location of troops. Everyone was apprehensive and many had left the city; Edward Livingston had begged his wife to leave, for he did not dream that raw American troops could possibly prevail against British veterans who had fought Napoleon and sacked Washington. But behind their earthworks Jackson and his men showed little perturbation; they would meet the British assault when it came and fight to the finish.

The morning of January 8 broke with a heavy fog but the Americans were ready, for all night long sounds from the British encampments had indicated that mischief was afoot. About six o'clock the British columns began to advance in solid ranks—the 93rd Highlanders in their bright kilts and tartans, the noted 95th Rifles, the Duchess of York's Light Dragoons, The King's Own, the 21st Royals, the Buck Volunteers commanded by the brilliant Colonel William Thornton, and others. The American batteries opened fire. On the British came, advancing to within 150 yards, then 100 yards, always at a deliberate battle march, the white-webbed bullet- and powder-pouch straps crossed on their chests making them perfect targets.

The American riflemen had not fired a single shot, though the batteries were mowing broad lanes in the British ranks. Then the riflemen opened fire, not in volleys, but with each man firing as he reloaded his gun. The advancing British soldiers fell by the hundreds; only a few reached the American line. The riddled units fell back, re-formed, and advanced again. Battle smoke rose lazily and floated in the fog-laden air. Above the crash of cannon and staccato ping of rifle shot could be heard the yells of soldiers and the martial music of the New Orleans and Plauche bands, pierced by the shrieks of the wounded and the even more hideous screams of mutilated horses. Again the advancing columns were shot to pieces. Once more they re-formed and advanced. The lines wavered as gaping holes suddenly appeared in them, then moved on again. The wounded and dying fell, singly or in groups sometimes five or six men deep, but those behind never broke step; they simply marched over them. At last human endurance was broken; the British halted, turned, and began to run from the field.

General Sir Samuel Gibbs rode up to General Pakenham: "I am sorry to have to report to you, the troops will not obey me, they will not follow me." Pakenham pulled off his hat and rode to the head of the column to cheer his men on, crying out, according to his aide, "for shame, recollect you are British soldiers, this is the road you ought to take." He was carried from his saddle by a mortal bullet, fired so Jackson later wrote, by "a freeman of color, who was a famous rifle shot and came from the Attakapas region of Louisiana," perhaps a certain "Captain" Savary. General Gibbs fell mortally wounded not twenty yards from the earthworks, and General John Keane, shot through the neck, dropped at the edge of the canal.

The soldiers who had faced Napoleon's grenadiers began to panic and flee the field of carnage and death; even the 21st and 44th Regiments, according to Major Sir John Tylden, began "running to the rear, and firing in all directions in the most disorderly manner I ever witnessed." General John Lambert stopped the fighting and ordered a retreat. An American historian thus described this moment: "The proud British army was vanquished; its bugles silenced; its colors trampled in the earth; its guns unable to reply." The British loss was slightly over 2,000 killed, wounded, and missing, nearly 35 per cent of the attacking force; the American casualties totaled 71, including only 6 killed.

Victory assured, the Americans broke into cheers, while Jackson rode along the line and congratulated his men. The bands continued playing, partially drowning out the cries of the wounded British lying in front of the earthworks. Jackson ordered some of his troops to assist in caring for the wounded, some 400 of whom were later brought to New Orleans. The next day an armistice was declared to bury the dead.

What had caused the British defeat, one of the most portentous in all British military history? The destruction of much of their artillery on January 1 left them without sufficient cannon to support the grand attack on the eighth. The failure of a few lesser officers to carry out orders to plant facines and scaling ladders undoubtedly prevented many of the soldiers who reached the canal from crossing it and breaching the line. It was the American rifleman, however, who had won the battle—he had held his fire until the British were within 100 yards; he was an expert in the use of his weapon; he had fired at will and not in volleys, which would have given the advancing army the opportunity to fall with the volley and then advance while the Americans were reloading.

Though decisively beaten the British made no haste to depart the area. It was not until the eighteenth that they withdrew to the mouth of Bayou Bienvenu and not until the twenty-seventh that they boarded the fleet, which had returned after an unsuccessful attempt to silence the guns of Fort St. Philip by bombardment from January 9 to 18.

AFTERMATH. On January 19, Jackson and his army returned to New Orleans, a *Te Deum* was sung at the Cathedral, a triumphal arch was erected in the center of the Place d'Armes, and January 23 was declared a day of prayer and thanksgiving. At the grand ball that evening Mrs. Edward Livingston "with studied enthusiasm" crowned the victorious general with a laurel wreath. Vincent Nolte thus described the general and his wife: "To see these two figures, the general a long, haggard man, with limbs like a skeleton, and Madame la Generale, a short, fat dumpling, bobbing opposite each other like half-drunken Indians, to the wild melody of *Possum up de Gum Tree,* and endeavoring to make a spring into the air, was very remarkable and far more edifying a spectacle than any European ballet could possibly have furnished."

The British fleet still hovered in Louisiana waters, so Jackson kept martial law in effect, over the vehement opposition of New Orleanians. Jackson had Louis Louaillier arrested for publishing a bitter criticism of him, but Judge Hall freed Louaillier on a writ of habeas corpus; Jackson thereupon had the judge and District Attorney John Dick arrested, and mustered the militia out of service. Finally on March 13, Jackson received official notification from Washington that the treaty of peace had been signed and suspended martial law. The British fleet sailed away four days later. Judge Hall resumed his office, and Dick filed charges against Jackson; Hall fined the general $1,000, which Jackson immediately paid, and a group of citizens pulled his carriage to Maspero's Exchange for a celebration. In 1844, Congress voted Jackson the amount of the fine plus interest; the total amounted to $2,732.

Jackson's retention of martial law and his clash with Judge Hall and others caused personal animosities to smolder for years. Although the legislature, which according to Dunbar Rowland had refused to co-operate with him "in the defense of the country," passed a resolution of appreciation to the Tennessee, Kentucky, and Mississippi troops on February 2, its members completely ignored the hardheaded old general who had saved Louisiana. Jackson left New Orleans on April 6.

What happened to the privateers of Barataria? They received their pardons and were thanked by Jackson, who was said to have remarked: "Were I ordered to storm the gates of Hell, with Dominique You as my lieutenant, I would have no misgivings as to the outcome." Many of them went with Jean Lafitte to Galveston, continuing their privateering activities until 1821, when they were driven out by the United States Navy. After that the group scattered.

Renato Beluche became "El Bizarro," the noted admiral of the Venezuelan navy; Vicente Gambie was killed in a naval battle; and Louis Chighizola settled down to domesticity under the name of "Nez Coupe" at Grand Isle. Pierre Sicard, Juan Juanvilles, and Antonio Angelo disappeared. Dominique You moved to New Orleans, where, according to historian Jane Lucas DeGrummond, "he and a busty blond barmaid named Barbette, who came from St. Thomas and stood a head taller than her spouse, ran a tavern." When he died in poor circumstances on November 14, 1830, the city council paid his funeral expenses, business houses closed, flags flew at half-mast, and his old comrades assisted the Masonic order at his burial in St. Louis Cemetery No. 2. Jacinto Lobrano also settled in New Orleans, fought in the Texas War of Independence, had more than one altercation with General Benjamin F. Butler during his occupation of the city in 1862, and died in 1880.

After the breakup of the privateers at Galveston Island, Jean and Pierre Laffite disappeared from history, and until the recent discoveries by New Orleans historian Stanley Arthur there were many legends and unsupported speculations regarding their activities. Arthur has disclosed that Jean and Pierre engaged in trading and other business activities in Charleston and Savannah, that Jean married Emma Mortimore, daughter of a businessman then living in Charleston, and that the two brothers later moved to the vicinity of St. Louis. Pierre died at the age of sixty-five on March 9, 1844, at the small town of Crevecoeur, Missouri.

Meanwhile, according to Arthur, Jean Laffite had changed his name to John Lafflin. He apparently visited New Orleans on several occasions but had grown a beard and was not recognized; it is fairly obvious that certain officials in Washington knew of his new identity. He grew somewhat bitter as the years passed. On March 5, 1832, in a purported letter to his wife he remarked: "Often I ask myself if the service I rendered . . . had been to the contrary the English would have proclaimed a Dominion to the West of the great Mississippi River"; and on July 7, 1833, he allegedly wrote his brother-in-law: "I saved the Union from the Octopus, but the city of Washington remains deaf-and-dumb. I have received eulogies but not recompense—not even a wooden medal." On May 5, 1854, at Alton, Illinois, Jean Laffite died at the age of seventy-two of pneumonia, caused by exposure in aiding a friend. By this time most of his men were already dead; the romantic but shadowy book of the privateers of Barataria was finally closed.

PART FIVE

Ante Bellum Louisiana

CHAPTER 17

ANTE BELLUM POLITICS
AND POLITICIANS

FIRST YEARS OF STATEHOOD. In 1803 many American political leaders thought it would take at least a generation to sufficiently educate the Louisiana Creoles in American political ideals and the everyday functioning of state and local governmental agencies for them to be ready for self government. The Creoles, however, learned much more rapidly than anyone had expected; with their effervescent, voluble character and strength of mind, they took to politics easily and naturally. They might make mistakes, but they had no hesitancy in making political decisions. When the Constitutional Convention of 1811 met at New Orleans in November, twenty-six of the forty-three members were Creoles, and such names as Bellechasse, LeBreton, Marigny, and Villeré outnumbered names like Wells, Johnson, Porter, Thompson, and others of Anglo-Saxon origin. Julien Poydras, who had been serving as territorial delegate to Congress, was brought back to preside over the Convention.

The fundamental law for the new state was drafted swiftly; Convention members simply took one of the latest state constitutions, the 1799 document of Kentucky, made a few minor changes, shortened it a bit, and *voilà*, the work was finished. As most of the Creole delegates were members of aristocratic families and a goodly number of the Americans were well on their way to becoming members of the same group through membership at the bar, extensive landholdings, or advantageous marriages, they approved of the generally aristocratic Kentucky constitution though not of some of its more liberal features.

Executive power was vested in a governor to be selected every four years by the legislature from the two candidates receiving the highest numbr of popular votes. He was required to be thirty-five years of age, a citizen of the United States, a resident of the state for six years, and to own at least $5,000 worth of property. No minister of any religious group was eligible for office. With the consent of the senate, the governor had authority to appoint the secretary of state and the attorney general, and he could name the state treasurer with the consent of both legislative houses. He was required to tour the state once every two years to inform himself of "the general condition of the country."

The two-house legislature was called the General Assembly. Members of the senate were elected for a four-year term and had to own taxable property valued at $1,000; those of the house of representatives served for two years and must possess property valued at least at $500. The judicial power was to be vested in a supreme court which was to have from three to five judges appointed by the governor and confirmed by the senate. The supreme court was required to hold its sessions in New Orleans and Opelousas.

The constitution, which was drafted, according to its preamble, by "we, the representatives of the people," had no bill of rights, restricted the electorate to the landholding class, and was extremely difficult to amend. It had only three sections which might in any way be termed original, two pertaining to law and the other directing the governor's biennial tour of the state. Despite its weaknesses it was a sound but conservative document which was never amended and was not superseded for a third of a century.

Although Claiborne had served as territorial governor, his election as the first governor of the state was unexpected because he was generally unpopular with the Creoles. Furthermore, the period of his territorial governorship had been marked by dissatisfaction and controversy. Claiborne's appointment as territorial governor may have been, as has been charged, a "political accident," but his election as state governor by Creole Louisianians was a vote of confidence for the man who had earned their respect and who had already demonstrated his abilities. The first act of the legislature authorized the annexation of the Florida Parishes; the second fixed the governor's salary at $7,500 per year—at that time the highest in the nation.

Few American governors have had to solve more problems, face more opposition, make more important decisions, or meet more threatening situations than did Governor Claiborne. Distrusted by many of the Creoles, some of whom refused to serve in the legislature or to accept appointments to state or local posts, he was fought at every turn by many of the talented Americans for both political and personal reasons. Complications encountered in putting the new state and local governmental machinery into operation were legion. The Indians of northwest Louisiana were dissatisfied with land-grabbing speculators and mercenary traders. Many citizens could not fully realize that governments needed large sums of money for operation, and it was difficult to collect national, state, and local taxes. The pirates of the Gulf of Mexico and the privateers of Barataria openly smuggled all kinds of goods into the state. After the declaration of war against Great Britain, the enemy blockade of the mouth of the Mississippi created a depression. Many Creoles would not support the state militia; numbers of the newly arrived Americans refused to join the various units if it required leaving Louisiana, and for a time the New Orleans militia refused to be mustered into the service of the United States.

Claiborne tackled these problems with justice and common sense and met the crisis of the British invasion with calm assurance. By the end of his administration Louisiana had passed the critical years, and according to the *Louisiana Courier,* "If we now hold a rank among the most patriotic states of the Union, it is, in a great measure, owing to the example and precepts of Mr. Claiborne." He was elected United States Senator in 1816, but died the following year. Jacques Villeré, his friend and old political opponent, wrote that he was "one of our best patriots. . . . distinguished for his virtues and talents."

NATIONAL PARTY POLITICS. During the first years of statehood native Louisianians were not particularly interested in national politics and the newly arrived Americans were far too busy securing an economic toe hold to seriously care much about national political problems. Many Creoles were still suspicious of the American system and prejudiced against it, while the newcomers were just as suspicious of the political actions of the Creoles. Not until the 1820's did Louisianians begin to take an interest in national politics and not until the 1830's did they formulate their opinions. Before 1850 they sent no outstanding men, excepting possibly Edward Livingston and Alexander Porter, to Congress.

Henry Clay, Andrew Jackson, and John Quincy Adams charmed Louisianians during the 1820's. Clay advocated a protective tariff which benefited the sugar planters, Jackson was the hero of the Battle of New Orleans, but just why the Louisiana delegation supported Adams in the House contest of 1825 and why Adams men won control of the legislature by the middle of his administration no one has ever satisfactorily explained. Jackson carried the state in 1828 (Paul Tulane barbecued a bear in the middle of Jackson Square to celebrate the event) and again in 1832; two years later Louisiana politics began to solidify.

The Whig party was organized in the spring of 1834, and soon National Republicans and deserters from Jackson brought the banner to Louisiana. While the Democrats dominated national elections the rest of the period, the Whigs generally controlled local politics until 1842; often the governor was a member of one party while the legislature was dominated by the other. Although after the death of the Whig party in the early 1850's the American, or Know-Nothing, party was strong for a time, Democrats continued to win the elections.

Louisianians were chiefly concerned with issues affecting their economic interests, such as the bank, the tariff, internal improvements, public lands, levee and drainage-canal construction, and immigration legislation. Slavery provoked little comment until the 1840's, although a few political leaders and citizens had been long aware of the possible seriousness of the problem. In 1838, for example, planter Bennet H. Barrow of West Feliciana Parish wrote in his diary: "Great Excitement in congress. Northern states medling with slavery—first they com'ced by petition—now by openly speaking of the sin of Slavery in the southern states on the floor of congress—must eventually cause a separation of the Union." In the 1850's a few citizens began to read the writings of Abolitionists, but had no intention of following the hope of John Greenleaf Whittier:

> Live, till the Southron, who, with all his faults,
> Has manly instincts, in his pride revolts,
> And lifts, self-prompted, with his own right hand,
> The vile encumbrance from his glorious land!

They agreed with Editor J. D. B. De Bow of New Orleans that the majority of the people of the North were radical and revolutionary and that the South was the only conservative section of the Union.

While most presidential elections were comparatively quiet, a few produced considerable excitement. During the election of 1844, for example, young Robert Patrick wrote in his diary that "there were barbecues, public speeches made by the leaders, torch light processions, glee clubs, and all that sort of thing." Many aspiring rhymesters turned out political doggerel of the following type:

> As I walked out the other day,
> I heard a lovely lady say,
> That if she had a Loco beau
> She soon would tell him, he might go

or, in an even more emphatic vein:

> Git out of the way, you poke root pison,
> You can't hurt Clay & Frelinghuysen.

Ceremonial flag-raisings were common, and in 1856 at one political rally "the American party . . . flung to the breeze the star spangled banner of American independence, inscribed with the glorious names of Fillmore and Donelson! . . . Adolphus Olivier Esq., our great champion of American principles—the young Demosthenes of Louisiana, made one of his most beautiful and telling speeches . . . and for the space of an hour and a half held his audience spellbound by his eloquent appeals."

During the late years of the period three political leaders rose to dominate the Louisiana scene. Native New Yorker John Slidell, a large-statured man with "such silky, snow-white hair that through it the top of his head blushed like the shell of a boiled lobster," a ruthless man of strong mind and will and "some tact and discretion," emerged during the early 1840's to become the dominant Democratic leader

[191]

and a United States Senator. Native-born Frenchman and Pyrennees shepherd boy Pierre Soule, who arrived in New Orleans destitute and with only one shirt, became a Senator and later Minister to Spain. Judah P. Benjamin, born on St. Croix in the West Indies, with his bonhomie air and his dark and expressive eyes and "close reasoning, his acute manner of analysis, his calm self-command, his thorough knowledge of his subject, his fluent and graceful speech," also served in the Senate, and later held three cabinet positions in the government of the Confederate States of America.

STATE CAMPAIGN AND CAMPAIGNERS. Until the election of 1834 the paramount issue in state elections was whether the candidate was "Creole" or "American." During this period the Americans elected Governors William C. C. Claiborne, Thomas Bolling Robertson, and Henry Johnson, while the Creoles elected Jacques Villeré, Pierre Derbigny, and André Bienvenue Roman.

After 1834 party politics became the more important. The Whig party elected governors in 1834 and 1838 when Edward D. White and A. B. Roman won the elections, but subsequent governors were Democrats: Alexandre Mouton, Isaac Johnson, Joseph Walker, Paul O. Herbert, Robert C. Wickliffe, and Thomas O. Moore. Throughout the period many Americans believed the Creoles to be "constitutionally opposed to development and progress," while the Creoles considered the Americans radical in their political ideas. While the great majority of officeholders and legislators were Creoles or Americans, there were a few Italians, Englishmen, and Frenchmen, and, as one commentator wrote, "here and there a Scotchman, with his boat-shaped head and hard common sense."

Many Louisianians had contempt for professional politicians. Alexander Porter once remarked in the Senate that "there is no class of men for whom I have a more thorough contempt. . . . They are a miserable race, generally lost to all honor, truth, and patriotism, who sell themselves for office." Acute observer Cyprien Dufour of New Orleans once wrote: "Elections days are here, as always, I suppose, days of prestige for many men. Unknown the night before, mediocre or superior, they seem to rise suddenly to the pinnacle of human greatness. . . . They go up, up always, and, seeming to pierce the skies, burst forth into a blaze of light, then drop all of a sudden and disappear into obscurity."

But all politicians were not of this breed. Bernard Marigny was a humble man, much loved by friend and foe alike, and as Dufour wrote, "to behold him silently stalking along our streets, one would take him for the peasant of the Danube," never for "a master of laws and of constitutions." Many were brilliant linguists. On one occasion; when Étienne Mazureau was about to deliver a political address, he looked over the audience and said: "I see three nations before me. Americans, I shall speak to you first. Frenchmen, to you next—and to you, my Spanish friends, last. I shall probably occupy two hours with each of you. It will be the same speech; so you who do not understand the English language, need not remain. You who understand French, may return when I shall dismiss these Americans—and you, my Spanish friends, when I am through with these Frenchmen." He then spoke for six hours. Most political leaders served the state well and would have agreed with modest Governor A. B. Roman: "I leave the office with which I have been honored with the painful conviction of having done very little for the good of the state and having often failed in preventing what was injurious."

Campaigns for state offices were usually hard-fought, the candidates attracting much attention as they stumped the state speaking to large audiences at mass meetings or talking with loungers about the parish-courthouse square, the political forum and university of ante bellum Louisianians. Candidates traveled singly or in groups; frequently two candidates for the same office traveled together and took turns in speaking. They joked and played pranks on each other and told stories and sang songs to their audiences. During the campaign of 1849 the opponent of Joseph Walker,

[192]

the Democratic candidate for governor, frequently sang "The Ranger's Lament for Poor Old Joe," the chorus of which ran:

> Take off the saddle from his back,
> Pull down the fodder from his rack;
> There is no more run in poor old Joe—
> Turn him out to grass and let him go.

Legislators often wrote poetry, or what passed for poetry, about opponents in debate. Bernard Marigny was accomplished at this art and one day wrote a witty, satirical verse about several members; W. H. Sparks came back with the following reply:

> Dear Marigny, we're soon to part,
> So let that parting be in peace;
> We've not been angered much in heart,
> But e'en that little soon shall cease.
>
> When you are sleeping with the dead,
> The spars we've had I'll not forget;
> A warmer heart, or weaker head,
> On earth, I'll own, I never met.
>
> And on your tomb inscribed shall be
> In letters of your favorite brass,
> Here lies, O Lord! we grieve to see,
> A man in form, in head an ass.

Sparks later wrote: "He was the aggressor, and, though offended, was too chivalrous to quarrel. He had fought nineteen duels, and I did not want to quarrel either."

CONSTITUTIONS, THE CAPITAL, AND OTHER ISSUES. By the early 1840's the old Constitution of 1812 was out of date. Furthermore, the spirit of democracy was growing, and its conservative provisions regarding the privileges of the land-owner class, the long terms of office, and the extraordinary powers of the governor prompted many political leaders to advocate a new constitution. Therefore, a constitutional convention met in two sessions, one at Jackson during the late summer of 1844 and the other at New Orleans early the next year.

The political spirit of the Constitution of 1845 is well illustrated by the beginning words of the preamble: "We the people of Louisiana." Property qualifications for voting or holding office were abolished and general elections had to be "completed in one day" in contrast to the old custom of allowing several days for an election. The governor lost many of his appointive powers, the office of lieutenant governor was created, parish coroners and sheriffs were to be elected by popular vote, the office of state superintendent of public education was created, and the legislature was directed to "establish free public schools throughout the State." In economic matters the Constitution of 1845 was practically as conservative as its predecessor.

The new organic law did not satisfy all members of the body politic, many of whom believed that it should have been more democratic, and another constitutional convention, therefore, met at Baton Rouge in July, 1852, and drafted a new constitution. While most of the fundamentals of the Constitution of 1845 were retained, numerous liberalizing features were added. Additional state offices were made elective, state aid for public improvements was authorized, and the governor's powers were again reduced. The Constitution of 1852 was a sound and worthy document, laying the foundation for all future constitutions except that of 1868.

The first state capital was located at New Orleans, but in 1825, after considerable debate, the legislature voted to move the capital to Donaldsonville. There had been considerable agitation for some years to move it from New Orleans, which, according to one critic, was a "city so justly compared to a modern Sodom" and a bad influence upon legislators and other officials. The legislature voted $30,000 to build a new "state house," 15 feet wide by 100 feet long, and the five commissioners signed a contract with builder Antoine Peytavin. The building completed, the legislature met in it in 1830. Soon, however, the lawmakers were "thoroughly disgusted" with Donaldsonville and the "unsightly and badly constructed" capitol, and "under the shallow pretext that the roof was leaky, abandoned the place for good and all" and moved back to New Orleans.

The agitation to move the capital from New Orleans continued, however, and in 1846 an act was passed moving it to Baton Rouge and appropriating $100,000 for a new state house. Noted New Orleans architect James H. Dakin drew the plans and became the contractor. The building was completed by 1850 and the seat of government officially moved when Governor Joseph Walker was inaugurated.

The legislators were just as dissatisfied with Baton Rouge as they had been with Donaldsonville. At that time Baton Rouge was an overgrown series of small contiguous villages, known locally as Gras, Devall, Leonard, Hickey, Duncan, Mather, and Beauregard towns. Beauregard Town, elaborately planned by the Spanish, lay between present-day North and South boulevards and between East Boulevard and the river. It had a square in the center with four streets running diagonally from the corners, and on the entire east side was a Place d'Armes. Many streets were named after saints, and one sign painter, who was unacquainted with saints, unwittingly canonized Napoleon, King Maximilian of Bavaria, and King Ferdinand of Spain. A market stood at the river end of North Boulevard about where the Confederate monument is today, and along Front and Lafayette streets were a few stores, several large homes, and the Harney House.

Three years later the New Orleans *Picayune* complained that "at Baton Rouge members find better lodgings in the Penitentiary than elsewhere; a good restaurant would be a blessing; a regular mail from the city or anywhere else would be looked upon as a miracle, and means of speedy transportation so soon as wanted, to any point up or down the coast, would be hailed as a God-send." Not everyone approved of the capitol, whose grounds had been laid out by editor-painter-humorist Thomas Bangs Thorpe and planted with trees, shrubs, and flowers by Thomas Affleck, the noted agriculturist of Washington, Mississippi. Mark Twain later wrote of "this little sham castle," "this architectural falsehood," the "Whitewashed castle, with turrets and things," which never would have been built "in this otherwise honorable place" had it not been for the "medieval romances" of Sir Walter Scott. But the capital remained at Baton Rouge until it was removed to Opelousas during the Civil War.

After Claiborne's administration major governmental problems centered around common, ordinary matters of state government. In 1825, Edward Livingston, Pierre Derbigny, and Louis Moreau Lislet completed the drafting of a civil code. A code of practice was enacted and promulgated the same year, and three years later a code of criminal law was completed by Livingston.

As the years passed, the legislature found it increasingly necessary to pass legislation for economic and cultural improvements or for the specific benefit of parishes, towns, companies, schools, churches, and individuals. As Robert Dabney Calhoun wrote: "Scores of acts were passed empowering the police jury of one parish or another, by name, to do certain things with regard to its police, roads, levees, schools, elections, and other matters which seemed to require deviation from the general laws that had been enacted." The legislature chartered business, municipal, religious, and charitable corporations, gave franchises, authorized lotteries, emancipated minors, and granted divorces. Later in the period it passed legislation regulating railroads and telegraph lines.

Legislators constantly faced the difficulties of language, for some spoke only French, others only English, and a few only Spanish or Italian. While English was the official language of the house of representatives, there was no such rule in the senate. Interpreters were necessary in both houses.

LOUISIANA AND INTERNATIONAL PROBLEMS. Although international matters were the province of the Federal government, during the ante bellum period Louisiana was involved in half a dozen international situations which plagued the government at Washington.

Piracy had almost ceased in Gulf waters at the end of the Spanish period, but with the beginning of the revolutionary era which saw the eventual rise of Latin-American nations, it rapidly increased. It was difficult to draw the line between a pirate and a privateer who sailed under the flag of one of the would-be nations in revolt against Spain; the Baratarians, for example, considered themselves privateers, for the majority of their vessels sailed under the flag of Cartagena. After the War of 1812 the Baratarians reorganized and operated for a time from headquarters at Galveston Island, but Governor Villeré called attention to the problem in his message of 1818, and a Federal-government squadron finally forced the evacuation of the island in 1821. Most of the Latin-American nations had won their independence by 1821, and the day of the buccaneer and privateer soon ended; accounts of piratical seizures on the lower Mississippi or in the Gulf sharply declined in 1825 and 1826 and by 1828 had ceased.

Many Indians still lived in Louisiana at the beginning of statehood, and there was constant trouble between them and the white settlers steadily encroaching on their lands. Those in the state slowly retreated onto less desirable tracts, where they eked out a miserable existence by trapping, fishing, and hunting. By 1830 the Choctaws who lived south of Monroe had moved westward, leaving the Caddo the only large tribe in the state. In June, 1835, in a series of conferences the Federal government offered to purchase all their Louisiana land with the provision that the Caddoes move to Texas. On the night of June 26, Chief Tarshar explained the hoplessness of the Indian situation to his people:

My Children: For what do you mourn? Are you not starving in the midst of this land? And do you not travel far from it in quest of food? The game we live on is going farther off, and the white man is coming near to us; and is not our condition getting worse daily? Then why lament for the loss of that which yields us nothing but misery? Let us be wise then, and get all we can for it, and not wait till the white man steals it away, little by little, and then gives us nothing.

The next day the Caddoes signed the treaty, by which they received $30,000 worth of horses and goods, and shortly thereafter left for Texas. The last Indian lands owned collectively by a tribe, a small plot of seventeen acres, were acquired by the Plaquemine Lumber & Improvement Company in 1889.

Until 1821 numerous Louisianians enlisted in filibustering expeditions to assist Latin Americans in winning their independence; after that date they went to fight in rebellions against existing governments. Prior to the War of 1812 the headquarters of these movements was Turpin's Coffee House on Marigny Street in New Orleans; later leaders plotted at Maspero's Exchange on Chartres Street and by the 1830's were meeting at Banks' Arcade on Magazine Street. Dr. James Long led expeditions to Texas in 1819 and 1821, but each was defeated and Long was eventually captured, taken to the City of Mexico, and executed. At the beginning of the Texas War of Independence a party left New Orleans to capture Tampico, but the attempt failed and most of the men were executed. A small body of men led to Cuba in 1851 by General Narciso López was defeated and the leaders were garroted; in 1855, William Walker invaded Nicaragua and controlled that country for a time.

The Louisiana Purchase Treaty of 1803 had not definitely fixed the western boundary of Louisiana, and after that date both Americans and Spanish claimed eastern Texas and western Louisiana. While the Florida Purchase Treaty of 1819 fixed the boundary at the Sabine, American-Spanish relations were still unsettled, and in 1822, Colonel Zachary Taylor was ordered with four infantry companies to Shields' Spring to build a military post, later named Fort Jesup. For the next twenty years one or more companies of troops were kept at the fort to preserve order in western and southwestern Louisiana and to protect the frontier. In late November, 1845, the Adjutant General ordered the fort abandoned, as it was no longer required for military purposes; the lands of the military reservation were all sold by 1850.

Shortly after the Texas War of Independence began, the New Orleans *Bee* appealed: "Americans to the rescue! Remember the condition of your revolutionary ancestors, when the Indians were united against them. Shall we suffer our colonial friends to be massacred by Indians hired by Mexicans, and have them driven from the colonies which they have honorably purchased and laboriously improved?" Meetings were held at Banks' Arcade and the Rising Sun Tavern, enlistment headquarters were set up, and hundreds of Louisianians volunteered for service in Texas. They marched overland or sailed directly to Texas ports in small groups or as members of organized companies. Loans were floated and ships outfitted for the Texas navy. The Texas fever ran high as William Kean hawked his own poem "Colonel Crockett's Exploits and Adventures in Texas" at the corner of Camp and Common:

> Say what can politicians do,
> When things run riot, plague and vex us,
> But shoulder *flook*, and start anew,
> Cut stick and GO AHEAD to TEXAS!

Ten years later, in 1846, the Mexican War began. Six regiments of ninety-day volunteers were soon enlisted, equipped by the state, and sent to join General Zachary Taylor in southern Texas. Farmers left their plows, lawyers the courtroom, and newsmen their presses—one newspaper editor simply closed his printing shop and put a sign on the door reading: "I voted for Texas. I have gone to help do the fighting." In New Orleans traveler Mary Austin Holley wrote: "The whole city is like a military station. The public squares are occupied with tents, recruiting parties—military bands are playing, flags are flying—streets are filled with soldiers. During the church service parties were marching by with full bands playing."

But disgruntled Louisianians soon began to straggle home. Their enlistments had expired; they had not seen an enemy or fought in a single battle; their pay had been slow in coming and when it finally arrived many found that they owed more than they had coming to them. Many had refused to re-enlist. The Federal government recalled the units, causing a wave of resentment throughout the state. The *Picayune* thundered that the disbanding of the Louisiana volunteers was the result of "the supercilious insolence of an incompetent Secretary of War, the hesitating policy of a weak, scheming and vacillating administration." Many Louisianians later organized or joined military units and fought in Mexico. The war long remained in their memories, as was evidenced by the large number of plantations named after Mexican places or war battlefields.

JUDGES, JAILS, AND JURIES. During the 1850's, Frederick Law Olmstead, the New Yorker who traveled through the South writing a series of articles for the New York press, wrote that "the bar of Louisiana is more talented and respectable than that of any other Southern State, perhaps than that of any State." He added that the "pleadings are oftener in French than the English language; and it is indispensable for a lawyer to have a free command of both languages." A modern authority has written that "perhaps nowhere else in the United States was there then, or has there been since, a more remarkable group of lawyers" than had gathered in New Orleans, where to be a leader of the bar was "an honor as coveted as that of high political office."

The list of noted ante bellum lawyers is endless: François Xavier Martin, with his large head, Roman nose, and thick neck, stern, silent, dogged, without a gleam of humor or sentiment; Pierre Derbigny, high-strung, ambitious, with an idiosyncratic style made necessary by having to transfer French thought to English expression; Louis Moreau Lislet, who had his office at what is now 733 St. Louis Street; George Mathews, short, rotund, and placid, with his humor and good taste; Edward Livingston, who had run afoul of the law in New York and who carved a place for himself in Louisiana legal history; Christian Roselius, who had come to New Orleans as a German indentured servant but whose great house and beautiful gardens now occupied an entire square fronting Broadway.

Other "ornaments" to the Louisiana bar included: Étienne Mazureau, eccentric, the site of whose office at 631 St. Ann has within the recent past been occupied by a macaroni factory; Alfred Hennen, whose mansion was demolished to make room for the Monteleone Hotel; Pierre Soule, who was constantly trying to "separate the inextricable confusion of Roman, Spanish, and English laws—and especially French, the knowledge of which is indispensable"; Henry Adams Bullard, whose opinions were "models of judicial rhetoric, brief, perspicuous, and pointed"; Judah P. Benjamin, who so well served his adopted state and the Confederacy, and who after the War for Southern Independence was admitted to the English bar and became Queen's Counsel; Seargent S. Prentiss, the "golden orator of Mississippi" who had been a tutor in Natchez; Santo Domingan Auguste G. V. D'Avezac who later wrote *Recollections of Livingston;* Swedish Gustavus Schmidt, whose legally precise style "abounded in scholarly touches"; and numerous others whose names should not be omitted from Louisiana legal history.

The laws and legal customs these attorneys worked with were complicated, for they had been inherited with little legal logic from the Corpus Juris Civilis, the Pandects, the Code of Justinian, various laws and codes of France and Spain, criminal and commercial laws and the law of evidence from England, the Code Napoleon, and various Federal and state laws of the United States.

Ordinary cases which reached trial—most were types common to all newly settled, booming agricultural, or rapidly expanding commercial sections—included counterfeiting, arson, river hijacking, robberies, cattle rustling, theft, slave stealing, smuggling, and numerous others, as well as the usual variety of civil suits. The most common crime was assault and battery, and from the number of these cases in the court records it would seem that Louisianians spent a large portion of their time engaged in personal altercations. Admittedly individualistic, strong willed, and opinionated, they frequently went at it with fists, walking canes, rawhide whips, knives, and occasionally with pistols or revolvers. Misunderstandings arose over cards, horse races, or politics, and at balls, political rallies, and anywhere men congregated. On one occasion at Franklin two men sat on opposite sides of the street, yelled contumelies at each other for an hour, then went to work with walking sticks, and finally backed off and shot it out, one of them being killed.

Justice and the courtroom was not without humor, however, even though at times it was necessary to stretch the point. Russell Brooks was charged with shooting a man who stole his horse, "the thief being on the horse when killed," but the jury did not consider the slaying of horse thieves "justifiable homicide." Brooks was the first man hanged in Ouachita Parish, in 1822. When Conrad Keil's wife left him and applied for a divorce in 1826 at Clinton, Keil put a notice in the local newspaper warning citizens not to give the woman credit or harbor her "under pain of subjecting themselves to the law," and urged "my said wife to return to her duty, and conduct herself as a wife ought to do, and the past will be forgiven."

A Shreveport jury retired in 1839 and remained "hung" for six days, when it was discovered that one of the jurors had "absconded," thus making it necessary to discharge the jury. When a thief was caught stealing from passengers on a steamboat in 1844, a court was hastily organized, the man tried by a jury of his peers, sentenced to forty lashes upon the bare back, and the sentence carried out at the next woodyard. In 1846 a South Louisianian sued to recover a cow and produced sixteen witnesses who testified the cow was his, but seventeen witnesses swore that the cow belonged to the defendant. The local barber was called in, the cow was "shaved," and the plaintiff's brand discovered. It was a wild and rollicking period, even in New Orleans, and attorneys frequently depended as much upon their own ingenuity as upon the law.

Free Negroes could not vote or hold office, serve on juries, belong to the militia, or commingle with whites at public places; otherwise they possessed civil rights. They could sue and be sued, serve as witnesses, hold all forms of property, inherit and transmit property, and when charged with crime were tried in the same manner as white persons. The Free Negro in Louisiana had more rights and privileges than he did in most other southern and not a few northern states, and in general the laws enacted against him, even including the act of 1842 prohibiting Free Negroes from entering the state, were not enforced. Many Free Negroes left the state for Cuba and Santo Domingo after the War of 1812, but a rather high percentage of them returned during the 1820's; there was a similar migration northward during the 1850's. Their attitude toward slavery was similar to that of the average white, many of them owned slaves, and observer Frederick Law Olmstead reported that in general they were just about equal, "in all respects, to the white Creoles."

The Black Code of 1806 regulated slavery until 1846, when Act 137 made a few material changes, particularly in the methods of slave trials. In 1855 the legislature enacted a new Black Code embracing the worthwhile features of previous legislation and adding considerable new material, but it was declared unconstitutional by the Federal Supreme Court. Alfred Hennen, in his *Louisiana Digest*, perhaps best characterized the position of slaves: "The slaves' best protection was their value, and the damage due to their master for injuries inflicted upon them."

Some slaves were smuggled into the state throughout the period, the last boatload reaching the Sabine River in 1865, and they were stolen and sold outside the state, particularly in Arkansas and Texas. Patrols were established as much to prevent slave stealing as to regulate the actions of slaves. While state laws and parish police-jury ordinances forbade slaves to possess fire arms or congregate in large groups, owners gave or loaned guns for hunting and permitted slaves to hold dances and other frolics—slave balls were common in New Orleans to the very eve of the Civil War.

Slaves were generally freed through one of three methods: by act of the legislature, by last will and testament, and by so-called "deeds of manumission" or "deeds of emancipation." Manumission laws were tightened in 1830, 1842, and again in 1852, when manumission was forbidden unless the freed slaves were sent out of the United States within twelve months, but masters continued to free slaves until the end of slavery.

The legal rights of slaves were maintained with considerable energy, as numerous legislative acts and court cases testify. Slaves were entitled to "the fruits of their labor on Sundays (1836)); owners could not "abandon" slaves in their old age (1847); agreement with a slave for him to earn his freedom was recognized as a contract (1830); and removal of a master with his slaves to a free state freed the slaves when they were returned to Louisiana (1855). There were numerous court cases in which the master or overseer who cruelly treated or caused the death of a slave was punished in accordance with the law. Free Negroes kidnapped in the North and sold into slavery in Louisiana sued in the local courts and were freed; probably the best example was the suit of Free Negro McPherson *vs.* Robinson in 1832 in Rapides Parish in which McPherson won his freedom and a judgment for the labor he had performed during his enforced slavery.

Despite the efforts of certain northern historians to show that slave insurrections were numerous and that southerners lived in constant fear of them, Louisiana, at least, was remarkably free of such occurrences, only a half-dozen causing much excitement during the entire period. Plots were exposed in Concordia, Madison, and Carroll parishes in 1842, along the river below New Orleans a couple of years later, and in New Orleans in 1853 (inspired by Englishman James Dyson who operated a school for colored boys). In 1837 a well-organized insurrection was broken up in Rapides Parish, nine slaves and three Free Negroes were hanged, and thirty slaves were imprisoned; slave Lewis Cheney, who discovered the conspiracy, was freed by legislative act and given a $500 reward. In the fall of 1840 a quartet of Abolitionists attempted to organize a revolt in Lafayette and St. Landry parishes, but the plot was discovered, three slaves hanged, and the white men severely flogged and escorted from the state.

GOVERNMENT OF PARISH AND TOWN. Town, city, and parish officials faced the usual problems of local government, performed their duties to the best of their abilities, and were constantly subject to criticism from the press and the public. The parish judge was the chief executive officer and had civil, criminal, and police jurisdiction. While the police jury was the parish legislative body, it had some executive functions. Cities and towns had a mayor, a recorder, a council of aldermen, a clerk, a treasurer, and other minor officials. City courts or justices of the peace handled small crimes.

In August, 1813, the Police Jury of St. Helena Parish, to cite one example, drafted a new set of Rules of Order and then got down to the business of ordinances. It regulated taverns and fixed liquor charges. Millers were to keep proper order by "giving every man his proper turn." The poll tax was fixed at $1.00; tax on slaves above the age of ten years, 25 cents; and on horses or mules "above the age of three years," 12½ cents. Every owner of livestock was ordered to file a description of "his ear mark or brand" with the parish clerk and pay him the sum of 50 cents; unmarked cattle, sheep, or hogs over the age of two years were to be considered as strays; strays found in properly fenced fields could be redeemed at 25 cents per day per animal.

All free males in the parish between the ages of sixteen and fifty and all capable male slaves were subject to road-work duty. The ferry over the Natalbany River had to be kept running between daylight and nine in the evening, and the charges were fixed—man and horse, 12½ cents; cart, 25 cents; foot passenger, 6¼ cents; wagon and team, 37½ cents. The charges of the ferry over Bayou Colyell were slightly higher, and the ferry keeper "shall also be compelled to keep a horn on the side of the river opposite his dwelling in some conspicuous place and any person being convicted of taking away or wantonly injuring said horn shall be liable to be fined ten dollars for every such offence for the use of the Parish; and every person making a false alarm by blowing this horn shall be subject to pay a fine of twenty five cents."

Many parish and town regulations of that day now seem odd or out of place. In 1825, East Feliciana Parish contracted for a $2,000 log jail containing a "Debtors Room." In 1828 no one was permitted to have more than three dogs in Marksville Prairie. When the 1829 session of the Washington Parish court was held in the loft of a barn, the judge ordered the sheriff to "confine Col. Connally to his stable as are the remainder of the horses below" because the colonel had imbibed too freely in the courtroom. In 1835 town magistrate James Bradford of St. Francisville offered $20.00 reward for the arrest of "the offenders who broke open the school house of Mr. Palmer last night, and placed the furniture across Ferdinand street."

In 1843 in Sabine Parish anyone "aggrieved" by a wild or ungovernable horse, cow, or hog could make a complaint to the nearest justice of the peace; three years later the police jury declared a bounty of $2.00 on wolves, but repealed it within two years. In 1848 the Methodist and Baptist churches were rented by Sabine Parish for use as a courthouse and as a jury room, three years later in West Felinciana Parish it became unlawful to race horses on the public roads, and the same year the people of Franklin protested to the police jury that at night a person had "to fight his way through a whole legion of dogs." In 1852 the Avoyelles Parish Police Jury prohibited citizens from leaving "dead animals in the bayou in front of one's residence more than 24 hours." Costs of parish government were low throughout the period. Let West Feliciana serve as an example: 1850, $7,219; 1851, $6,575; 1852, $7,130; 1853 (including new courthouse payments), $12,148.32; 1854, $11,365; 1855, $11,034.

New Orleans was divided into three municipalities in 1836, each governed by a council composed of a recorder and elected members. There was one mayoralty, however, and a general council composed of the three municipal councils had power to legislate on matters of common interest. The first municipality comprised the section around the Vieux Carré, the second included Faubourg St. Mary which was above Canal Street, and the third Faubourg Marigny which lay below the Esplanade. The municipalities were reunited in 1852, and the same year the suburb called Lafayette was incorporated into the city.

Until about 1840, according to Herbert Asbury, "politics in New Orleans were probably on a higher plane than ever before or since in any city in the United States"; but "all these virtues vanished with the coming of the American politician." By 1848 politicians had begun to use the newly arrived immigrants, bought their votes, organized them into gangs of thugs, and prevented honest citizens from voting. In 1857, Governor Wickliffe told the legislature that "it is a well-known fact that at the last two general elections many of the streets and approaches to the polls were completely in the hands of organized ruffians" who prevented nearly one-third of the people from voting. The city government was not cleaned up until Federal General Benjamin F. Butler became military governor in 1862.

CHAPTER 18

ECONOMIC LIFE DURING THE
ANTE BELLUM PERIOD

GROWTH OF POPULATION. Louisiana's population grew steadily and rapidly from 1812 to 1860. After the War of 1812 a constant stream of settlers arrived from the older states of the South, the Middle Atlantic states, and even from New England. Irish, Germans, and other nationalities landed at New Orleans, and while the majority moved up the Mississippi to settle in the Middle West, many remained in Louisiana; by 1850 approximately one-fourth of the state's total population was foreign born. Thousands of Negro slaves were brought from the older states of the South and smaller numbers were smuggled from Africa or the West Indies. Free Negroes came from other southern states, a few even from the North, until 1840, but after this date the number materially decreased. By 1860, Louisiana not only contained many nationalities but her citizens could have been classified as capitalists, merchants, planters, landowning farmers, renting farmers, subsistence farmers, "professional" squatters who lived close to the margin of existence, backwoodsmen, laborers, fishermen, trappers, and other groups.

In 1812 the state's total population was slightly over 80,000; in 1820 it totaled over 200,000; by 1840 it had grown to over 250,000; and by 1860 it topped 700,000. Meanwhile the slave population had grown from around 40,000 in 1812, to 69,000 in 1820, to 168,500 in 1840, and to 331,750 in 1860. The Free Negro population increased from about 8,000 in 1812 to 10,500 in 1820 and 25,500 in 1840, but dropped to 17,500 in 1850 and then gained slightly to 18,500 in 1860.

The Irish outnumbered all other foreign immigrants, their heaviest migration occurring during the last twenty years of the period. The Germans came in two waves, the first just after statehood and the second from the early 1840's to 1860. By 1860, New Orleans alone had a German population of between 30,000 and 50,000. In the 1820's a small number of Danes and Scandinavians settled in northern Louisiana, and during the late years of the same decade and in the early 1830's Spanish and Mexicans dissatisfied with the new Mexican republic settled in the western sections of the state.

Many Europeans used the "redemption" system, by which they "bound themselves to service for a period of years after arriving in their new Paradise," to defray the costs of their passage. Contracts were signed in blank before immigrants left European ports and filled out by the purchaser after their arrival at New Orleans. The voyages were nightmares of hunger, disease, and death. Ship captains promised to furnish good food, vinegar (for purposes of cleanliness), beer, and good water, but note the statement of Joseph Elder who made the voyage from Germany in 1854: "This water stinks like the pest, and in the end one could no longer drink it. . . . through the heat and the salted meat we suffered much thirst. . . . Black coffee was served in the morning but it stank so from the water that it nauseated us. For Sunday dinners we had rice and dumplings and beef, which, however, was unpalatable because of all the salt. We threw most of it overboard as a meal for the fish. . . . Every evening we had tea. That was nothing but an emetic. . . . Tuesday we had Sauerkraut and peas, which were so hard that one could shoot birds with them." In March, 1818, three vessels arrived in New Orleans after a five months' voyage; of 1,100 persons who had sailed from Helder (the port of Amsterdam) only 597 were living.

It was estimated that four out of five of the Free Negro group living in New Orleans were mulattoes. The majority of the group lived in the southern sections of the state, though many were scattered along the Mississippi and Red rivers. The leading Free Negro parish in 1859 was Orleans with over 8,000, far outnumbering any other parish; following in order were St. Landry, St. Martin, Natchitoches, Pointe Coupee, and Plaquemines. In 1860 nearly 21,000 Louisianians owned slaves, although over half of this number possessed only five slaves or less. Slightly over 700 slaveowners possessed from 51 to 100 slaves, only 274 from 101 to 200, and only 36 from 201 to 300. Six planters owned between 300 and 500 slaves and 4 planters from 500 to 1,000.

GROWTH OF CITIES AND TOWNS. New Orleans grew at a fantastic rate during the period, from 18,000 in 1812 to 168,675 in 1860. It was the great entrepôt of the Lower Mississippi Valley and vied with New York for first place among American ports. It was not only the business center but the show place of Louisiana, and Louisianians boasted that "there is but one Mississippi River; but one Louisiana, but one New Orleans on the face of the earth." There was criticism, however, from travelers and newcomers, particularly during the summer. Yankee George S. Denison wrote in 1860: "Of all the filthy, damp, hot, and generally uncomfortable and unhappy cities, New Orleans in the summer time is certainly unspeakable."

The city had undergone many changes since those December days of 1803. The city walls and the forts had been demolished and the moats fronting them had been filled and converted into boulevards—the Esplanade, Rampart, and Canal. Bernard Marigny had converted his estate below the Vieux Carré into blocks and streets. On the upriver side of Canal, Jean Gravier's swampland had been taken over by the Americans, the cattle pens demolished, and warehouses, hotels, and public buildings were being built, due chiefly to the efforts of Samuel J. Peters, Edward York, and James H. Caldwell, the theatrical entrepreneur. A new St. Charles Hotel was built in 1851, a hotel which "might be mistaken for a palace if it were in St. Petersburg, a college were it located in Boston, or an exchange if situated in London." The present Garden District was replacing Boré's plantation. The American section gradually developed as the city's business center, with the shopping section along Canal Street, slowly forcing the decline of the old Vieux Carré de la Ville.

Improvements were slowly made over the entire city. The 1810 water works of Louis Gleises were expanded, the first cobblestone pavements were laid on Gravier and Magazine streets in 1817, wooden sidewalks and curbs gave way to brick and stone after 1820, and in 1822, a general paving program was begun. Drainage was improved during the late 1830's. The New Orleans Gas Light and Banking Company was organized by James H. Caldwell in 1834. The thirty fire commissioners of 1816 gave way in 1829 to volunteer companies which rendered good service until 1855, when the Fireman's Charitable Association was given a $70,000 a year contract to protect the city. The Cathedral was rebuilt and the mansard roofs added to the convent and the Cabildo; the Baroness de Pontalba signed contracts for two James Gallier designed apartment buildings; and the Place d'Armes was laid off in trim walks, planted with shrubs and flowers, and honored with the statue to the Hero of Chalmette.

New Orleans in 1860 was a cosmopolitan, metropolitan area representing both the Old and the New. It was actually made up of four cities, New Orleans proper, Lafayette, Jefferson, and Carrollton, while lying immediately across the river was Algiers, which claimed close kinship. Part of the city was quiet and peaceful, part of it noisy and bustling with energy. Its levee, described by J. H. Ingraham as the grandest quay the world had known, surpassing even the quays of Tyre, Carthage, Alexandria, and Genoa, was lined with thousands of ships—ocean steamers representing all nations, Yankee vessels from the Atlantic seaboard, river steamboats, and Gulf coasters—"coming, sweeping, sounding, thundering on, blazing with thousands of lights . . . like Aladdin's palace on fire."

But the old city of French and Spanish days was still the most picturesque in the nation and in 1839, James S. Buckingham wrote lovingly of it. It reminded him of Paris, with the lamps hanging from ropes across the streets, the "noble" old buildings and such new ones as the St. Louis Hotel, which had a ballroom "unequalled in the United States for size and beauty." He enjoyed the operas, concerts, ballets, balls, and masquerades. He appreciated the "frank, warm-hearted and impassioned" Creoles, who believed in enjoying life rather than rushing through it to pile up stacks of dollars, to whom dignity and courtesy and charity were a part of life itself and whose attractive, graceful, lovable women had a "roundness and beauty of shape" quite unlike the "straightness and angularity of American figures." New Orleans was described differently by every traveler, but they all agreed it was the most fabulous and the most interesting city in America.

Excluding Lafayette, Jefferson, and Carrollton, only Algiers and Baton Rouge had more than 5,000 population in 1860. Algiers had nearly 6,000 inhabitants, while the capital had about 5,500. Smaller towns included Shreveport with nearly 2,200, Plaquemine with slightly over 1,600, Donaldsonville, Alexandria, and Homer with nearly 1,500, Thibodaux with nearly 1,400, and Minden with nearly 1,200. All other towns had less than 1,000 inhabitants.

Alexandria had been surveyed and plotted across the Red River from the old site of the Poste du Rapides in 1805 by Alexander Fulton and was named for his daughter. During the early years Timothy Flint described its white houses showing "themselves with their piazzas from under the shade of the beautiful China trees, and Catalpas." Donaldsonville was less well thought of by travelers, and when William H. Russell visited it at the beginning of the Civil War he wrote one could take "the odd, little, retiring, modest houses" which filled the English villages, "cast these broadsown over the surface of the Essex marshes, plant a few trees in front of them, then open a few *cafes billard* of the camp sort long the main street, and you have done a very good Donaldsonville."

By 1819, Fort Miró had been renamed Monroe and was a thriving business center. Shreveport had grown rapidly after the opening of the Red River and was a "flush times" cotton town, lighted in 1860 with rosin gas. By 1860, Baton Rouge, called by J. H. Ingraham the "rural and Franco-American Capital of Louisiana," had its new capitol and the United States military barracks, built in "fine style" and the "most commodious" in the country.

Franklin, to cite an example of a typical village, had been founded about 1800 by Guinea Lewis, a former Pennsylvanian, and was a growing trading center populated by Acadians, Spaniards, Germans, Americans, and Frenchmen, among whom was Louis le Pelletier de la Houssaye, a descendant of one of Louis XV's prime ministers. William Emmer ran the bakery, confectionery, and fruit store; Augustus Knapp sold candies at 12½ cents a pound; two oyster houses offered freshly opened oysters at $1.00 per 100; the "Ice Cream Saloon" at the corner of Main and Commerce sold lemonade, ginger pop, and soda waters in addition to various-flavored ice creams; Levy's Emporium handled fine piece goods; Bloch and Godchaux's imported ball dresses, hats, and ready-made clothing (something new in Louisiana); Miss Bristol fashioned bonnets to order; Erbelding the barber made wigs and toupees and boasted to the ladies that he had had thirty years of hairdressing experience in Paris; Gordy's Hotel took pride in a bathhouse where hot baths of pure cistern water were to be had for 50 cents. As early as 1848 the town contained a carriagesmith, a cabinetmaker, a plowmaker, a gunsmith, three watchmakers, several coopers, a tin shop, a blacksmith shop, a stonecutting establishment, a wallpaper dealer, several brickmaking concerns, and numerous stables which rented sulkies and riding horses.

AGRICULTURE. Rural landholdings ranged from small, frontierlike farms with only a few acres of general food crops to large plantations producing sugar cane, cotton, or tobacco. Most of the holdings were, however, farms rather than plantations. Just before the Civil War in the southern plantation section 11 per cent of the slave-holding landowners held less than 50 acres of land, 15 per cent between 100 and 200 acres, 16 per cent between 500 and 1,000 acres, and 30 per cent between 1,000 and 5,000 acres. Of the nonslaveholding landowners, 44 per cent owned less than 100 acres and 33 per cent between 100 and 200 acres. The large plantations were located chiefly along the Mississippi, the Red River, and the streams and bayous of the southern sections.

Land values varied greatly. Hill lands in the northern and northwestern part of the state could be purchased during the 1850's for from $2.00 to $10.00 per acre. Good plantation land along the Red River varied between $15.00 and $35.00 per acre, while along the Mississippi or one of the major bayous in the southern parishes it averaged from $40.00 to $60.00.

Ordinary farmers lived in plain, comfortable houses, behind which were located barns, granaries, sheds, other outbuildings, and perhaps a slave cabin or two. They produced food crops, raised cattle, hogs, and poultry, grew a little cotton or tobacco as a money crop, and generally lived comfortable, work-filled lives. Pioneer farmers had only a few acres in cultivation, herded livestock over open or timbered land, and lived in poor and sometimes ramshackle houses. In marked contrast, planters had available capital, were generally fair businessmen, and lived in comfort and some-times in luxury.

The Tchoupitoulas Plantation, about twelve miles up the Mississippi from New Orleans, serves as a good example of the large plantation. The Soniat family occupied a large, two-story brick mansion amid gardens of trees, shrubs, and flowers. On one side of the house was a *garconnière* for visiting young men or travelers and on the other side the *pigeonnier* where doves and pigeons were raised. Behind the house was the kitchen, the storehouse, the slave hospital, stables, and other outbuildings. Farther to the rear was the sugarhouse, while below it stood the overseer's house, and beyond that were two long rows of brick slave cabins. Only a man of considerable wealth could acquire, outfit, and stock a large plantation, particularly one which produced sugar. In 1830 an inhabitant of St. Martin Parish reported to *Niles' Weekly Register* that a 1,250-acre, 50-slave, sugar plantation required about $90,000 capital.

Sugar-cane cultivation steadily increased throughout the period, spreading up the Mississippi north of the mouth of the Red River and up that river to the Natchitoches country. After 1830 "ribbon" cane, a very hardy variety, replaced the older "Creole" cane, stream-driven mills were introduced, and improvements in the manufacturing process made. Sugar production increased from 75,000 hogsheads in 1833 to 449,000 hogsheads in 1853, which was the largest amount produced before 1860, when the crop fell to slightly over 220,000 hogsheads.

Cotton was grown over the entire state, the smallest amounts being produced in the low country of South Louisiana. Prices were high until 1837. After a five-year depression there was constant expansion of cotton growing into north and northwest Louisiana, even though prices never returned to their former levels. Production rose from over 375,000 bales in 1840 to nearly 800,000 bales in 1860. Tobacco was raised in large amounts north of the Red River. Frequently farmers and planters raised both tobacco and cotton, for the two crops could be cultivated and harvested at alternating periods. Perique, a strong tobacco used for flavoring purposes, was grown only in St. James Parish. Corn was grown over the entire state for human as well as livestock consumption, and by 1860 production had reached 17,000,000 bushels. The same year over 2,350,000 bushels of potatoes, over 430,000 bushels of beans and peas, nearly 90,000 bushels of oats, and over 50,000 tons of hay were raised on Louisiana farms. While Louisiana was primarily a staple-crop state, it also produced a wide variety of agricultural crops.

Livestock raising was most important in southwest Louisiana. Here there were large ranches, very much like those of a later-day west. Much of this country was open prairie, dotted with patches of trees along the water courses, and one traveler who visited the area in 1816 said that "it is no extravagant declaration to call this one of the meadows of America." By 1860 the state livestock census totaled over 630,000 hogs, nearly 520,000 cattle, over 180,000 sheep, and nearly 170,000 horses.

The vicissitudes of the agriculturalists were many, for there were floods and freezes, insects, plant diseases, levee crevasses, gradual decline of prices as production increased, high cost of machinery, high interest rates, and difficulties in marketing products. Truly could the Trinity *Advocate* editorialize concerning the flood of 1850: "May He who tempers the breeze to the tender condition of incipient life relieve us from the burthen of affliction that now weighs heavily upon us." Planters and farmers generally followed the practice of signing each other's notes and many lost money; some even went bankrupt by their endorsing. On January 1, 1840, West Feliciana planter Bennet H. Barrow wrote in his diary: "I com'ence this year with full determination to attend strictly to my business and to use every economy till I get out of Debt. . . . I borrowed money for other persons 'friend' & now have to pay it over. Mind Who proffesses to be your friend—you see a man working hard & economising help him, but see a fellow dressing fine, using fine language & they are What is called clever fellows—let them pass." He had not, however, learned his lesson, and continued endorsing. Four years later, on May 5, he wrote: ". . . sincerely wish every rascal & persons causing me to be in Debt in Hell *riding a red hot iron.*"

Most ante bellum Louisiana agriculturists were plain "dirt" farmers or planters; few were acquainted with "scientific" agricultural methods. As time passed, however, many subscribed to agricultural publications and some became contributors. Local fairs were organized, the Baton Rouge Agricultural Society was founded in 1827, and the Louisiana State Agricultural Society which came into existence five years later made plans to establish a "model" farm. New agricultural machines and implements came into use: the corn sheller, straw cutter, rice huller, hemp-and-flax breaker, wheat fan, corn-and-cob grinder, as well as new types of plows, harrows, rakes, cotton presses, and sugar mills. Crop rotation increased, as did contour plowing, fertilization, and seed selection. By the end of the period there were over 2,700,000 acres of improved farmland in cultivation. The value of farm machinery had risen to $20,000,000, livestock to nearly $25,000,000, and farm lands to $215,500,000.

TRANSPORTATION. Numerous waterways offered the easiest means of transportation, and during the early years of the period the rivers and bayous were filled with cargo pirogues, arks, broadhorns, keelboats, and numerous other varieties of flatboats propelled by oars and later by horse- or ox-powered paddle wheels. The steamboat made its first appearance in 1812 when the *New Orleans* arrived at New Orleans from Pittsburgh, and although she soon sank from a boiler explosion, earned over $20,000 above her cost carrying passengers and freight between New Orleans and Natchez. Hundreds of flatboats still came down the Mississippi during the 1830's, but by the next decade the day of the flatboat had largely passed. By 1840, Captain Henry Miller Shreve had cleared the Red River above Alexandria of the trees, snags, and drift—generally called the "great raft"—which blocked navigation. The small and ill-equipped steamboats of early years were being replaced during the 1840's by larger and more palatial boats with luxuriously furnished cabins, banquet-serving dining salons, ladies' sitting rooms, orchestras, promenade decks, gambling and drinking rooms, and other features.

Many boats, particularly those of the early years, posted rules and regulations for passengers. When J. G. Flugel journeyed down the Mississippi on the *New Orleans* in 1817, he noted that no gentleman was permitted to enter the lady's cabin on penalty of a $2.00 fine, smoking was forbidden in any of the cabins on penalty of

$1.00 for each offense and "fifty cents for every five minutes the same continued after notice," gentlemen should not lie on berths with their shoes or boots on, and cards and other games were forbidden after 10 P.M. A passenger court of three persons was selected daily to fix fines for all violation of rules and "the amount collected shall be expended in wine for the whole company after dinner." Signs posted at strategic places read: "It is particularly requested that gentlemen will not spit on the cabin floors as boxes are provided for that purpose."

In 1837, Mrs. Mary Austin Holly, journeying to Texas by Gulf steamboat, was elated with the accommodations: "The Captain a gentleman—always at the head of his table—set out in the best style—silver forks, or what looks like silver—large & small, with ivory knives. White waiters, neat & orderly—French Cook . . . & Bedding the finest & whitest linen—water closets—& lady-like chamber maid, every thing nice." During the 1840's British traveler Sir Charles Lyell thought the dinner on board the Mississippi River steamer *Magnolia* "only too sumptuous," for it began "with turtle soup, and two kinds of fish; then followed a variety of dishes, admirably cooked, and then a course of cocoa-nut pies, jellies, preserved bananas, oranges, grapes, and ice-creams, concluding with coffee."

The accommodations on small boats which coursed the smaller rivers and bayous were not as luxurious. In 1840 one traveler complained that the Red River steamboat *Concord* "should be named Discord, for the firemen abused the mate, the cook fought the steward, the mosquitoes waged war on the passengers, and the passengers are not yet done cursing mate, firemen, steward, mosquitoes—in fine, the boat and all connected with her. A more miserable, dirty, slow moving, improvided, chicken thievish craft never walked the waters . . . it excites my spleen to think of her."

While many boats were swift sailers (in 1853 the *Eclipse* steamed from New Orleans to Cairo in three days, three hours, and twenty minutes), others were incredibly slow, not however, quite as slow as Mark Twain made them out to be. He served on the *John J. Roe,* which was so slow that the crew "used to forget what year it was we left port in," "ferry-boats used to lose valuable trips because their passengers grew old and died, waiting for us to get by," and when she finally sank in Madrid Bend "it was five years before the owners heard of it."

Rivers and bayous so completely covered the state that canals were generally unnecessary; in 1860 there were only four canals connecting natural waterways totaling slightly over thirty-six miles, the Barataria Canal with about twenty-two miles being the longest.

When it is considered that George Stephenson built his Stockton and Darlington Railroad in England in 1825, that Belgium's first road was completed in 1833, that France did not even plan a railway until 1833, that Germany's first was opened in 1835, and that Russia did not have a road until 1850, Louisiana's feats in early railroad building become all the more remarkable. During the decade 1828 to 1838 not less than twenty-four railroads were chartered by the state, and ten proposed companies failed to secure charters.

The Pontchartrain Railroad was chartered in 1830, opened its tracks from Elysian Fields to Lake Pontchartrain, about five and one-half miles, with horse-drawn cars the following year, and in 1832 put steam locomotives into service. Incorporated in 1831, some years later the West Feliciana Railroad Company completed its line from St. Francisville to Woodville, Mississippi. The Clinton and Port Hudson Railroad was incorporated in 1833 to build a road from Clinton to the Mississippi River, and later the same year the New Orleans and Carrollton Railroad received its charter to build a line from Tivoli Circle (present-day Lee Circle) along St. Charles Avenue to Carrollton. The Alexandria and Cheneyville Railroad was incorporated in 1833, the New Orleans and Nashville in 1835, the Mexican Gulf in 1837, the New Orleans, Jackson and Great Northern in 1850, the New Orleans, Opelousas and Great Western in 1852, and the Vicksburg, Shreveport and Texas the same year. By 1860, Louisiana had 334¾ miles of track, and the railroads represented a total investment of slightly over $12,000,000.

Early railroads were unbelievably crude. Flat iron bars were nailed to wooden beams about six inches square laid lengthwise across ties about five feet apart. Such crude rails often worked loose and jammed up through the floors of the coaches. Locomotive boilers frequently exploded, livestock wandered onto the tracks, cinders set fire to crops and timberlands, freshets washed out bridges, cars jumped the rails, and train crews occasionally stopped the trains for a short hunt or to fish. As late as 1853 the Carrollton Railroad trains were prohibited from running more than four miles per hour. Cross-country trains never ran on schedules, although those in New Orleans attempted to maintain them.

Land travel was slow and tedious, although by 1860 many roads threaded the state. The Old Texas Road was still a main thoroughfare between Natchez, Mississippi, and Nacogdoches, Texas; the Military Road ran from Fort Jesup northward to Fort Smith, Arkansas, and on to Fort Towson, Oklahoma; the Shreveport-Conway (Arkansas) Road connected those two points; a "blazed" road ran across the northern part of the state roughly following present-day U.S. Highway 80; the Natchez–New Orleans Road passed through Woodville and Baton Rouge; and the St. Francisville–Opelousas Road meandered through the swampy country east and west of the Atchafalaya. Numerous other and shorter roads connected towns and villages. Carts, three-yoke wagons, and stagecoaches cut furrows in the dirt roadbeds, making travel almost impossible in wet weather; more than one parish passed ordinances requiring wheeled vehicles to zigzag along the roads to prevent the cutting of deep ruts.

Mail service was slow and uncertain during the entire period. Carried by post riders, stages, and steamboats, the mail depended for safe delivery upon the trustworthiness of individuals and the luck of travel. Notices from postmasters, like the following in the February 6, 1817, issue of the New Orleans *Louisiana Gazette,* were not uncommon: "I am sorry to inform you that the Mail which probably left New Orleans on Tuesday, has been lost in the Bayou Sarah by the horse drowning, on which it was borne; but as the bags are secured on the horse, and there is little chance of his drifting to the mouth of the creek, I have hopes it may yet be recovered." Small towns were fortunate if they received mail once a week. Improvements gradually were made; adhesive stamps appeared in 1847, envelopes the following year, the stamped envelope in 1852, and registry three years later.

When the telegraph reached New Orleans in July, 1848, the *Daily Crescent* proudly announced that "distance and time are annihilated. We never felt it so completely as at this moment." Less than a month before, the *Crescent* had recounted the story of the old lady who lived along one of the lines then under construction. Upon being told what the telegraph would do, perhaps with some embellishments, the lady became wild with fury and ran to her neighbors: "What do you think?" she exclaimed. "They're setting up that paragraph right agin my door, and now I reckon a body can't spank a child, or scold a hand, or chat with a neighbor, but that plague thing'll be blabbing it all over creation. I won't stand it. I'll move right away where there ain't none of the onnateral fixings."

TRADE AND COMMERCE. Jefferson had written shortly after the purchase of Louisiana that New Orleans was destined to be a "mighty mart of the merchandise brought from more than a thousand rivers" and a great trading city. His prophecy began to manifest itself during the boom years following the War of 1812, for within three years after the Battle of New Orleans most European trading firms of any importance had agents in the city. Thomas Urquhart, for example, represented several Scottish houses, and Vincent Nolte had connections with the English Baring Brothers. In 1818, Nolte began to distribute "printed advice in relation to the eventualities of the cotton market and the crops," a practice soon adopted by other firms. The first New Orleans city directory was published in 1822, listing commission and forwarding agents, commission merchants, factors, importers, over 250 mercantile establishments, over 100 general stores, over 75 grocery firms, some 25 drug houses, over 20 hardware and ship stores, 7 auctioneers, and such specialized operators as salt merchants, molasses brokers, and a dealer in Manila and tarred cordage.

Every visitor to New Orleans commented upon the vast and ever growing commercial activities at the quay, as the river front was commonly called. Colonel James Creecy visited the quay in the middle 1830's and wrote: "With what astonishment did I, for the first time, view the magnificent levee, from one point or horn of the beauteous crescent to the other, covered with active human beings of all nations and colors, and boxes, bales, bags, hogsheads, pipes, barrels, kegs of goods, wares and merchandise from all ends of the earth! Thousands of bales of cotton, tierces of sugar, molasses; quantities of flour, pork, lard, grain and other provisions; leads, furs, &c., from the rich and extensive rivers above; and the wharves lined for miles with ships, steamers, flat-boats, arks, &c. four deep! The business appearance of this city is not surpassed by any other in the wide world: it might be likened to a huge bee-hive, where no drones could find a resting place. I stepped on shore, and my first exclamation was, 'This is the place for a business man!'"

In 1858, Charles Mackay came down the Mississippi and wrote, poetically:

> On the seventh day morning we entered New Orleans,
> The joyous 'Crescent City'—a Queen among the Queens—
> And saw her pleasant harbor alive with tapering spars—
> With 'union-jacks' from England, and flaunting 'stripes and stars,'
> And all her swarming levee, for miles above the shore,
> Buzzing, humming, surging, with Trade's incessant roar;
> With negroes hoisting hogsheads, and casks of poil and oil,
> Or rolling bales of cotton, and singing at their toil. . . .

Mackay's steamboat had brought downriver between 200 and 300 bales of hemp and cotton, 2,000 barrels of flour, 1,990 sacks of corn, 400 barrels of pork, 1,100 sheep, 180 hogs, a "load" of wood and coal, 1,000 chickens, and 400 turkeys.

The value of New Orleans' domestic and foreign trade increased steadily during the years prior to 1860; from 1835 to 1842 it possessed more banking capital than New York. *Hunt's Merchants' Magazine* admitted that it was the "only city in America that can run a close race with New York, and the ratio of its past increase is such that it bids fair to be the empire city of America." The produce it received from the interior increased from slightly over $22,000,000 in 1830 to over $185,200,000 in 1860; its exports rose from $15,500,000 to nearly $108,000,000; and its imports from $7,600,000 to $18,350,000. Some years its exports exceeded those of New York by as much as 25 per cent.

Goods were distributed throughout the state by small steamboats, wagon freighters, small hand-propelled boats, an occasional pack train, and during the later years by the railroads. Livestock was generally driven to markets, of which New Orleans was the most important. In 1860, J. W. Dorr described the drivers as "ranchero looking fellows, with their wide hats, rough attire, bearded faces, and belted armaments of long bowie knives and army revolvers." Outlying farmers and planters went to commercial centers to sell their produce or to make purchases once or twice a year, usually traveling together in sizable groups and camping along the way.

Trading boats thronged the waterways, those from the Ohio River country still flying the "Wabash Coat of Arms"—"a flag-staff with a mammouth Irish potato, a big ear of corn, a golden-hued apple, and a side of bacon pendant, and at the topmost peak a bottle of whiskey." When Sir Charles Lyell entered one of these floating stores in 1846 he found that "it was a shop, containing all kinds of grocery and other provisions. . . . They had a fiddle on board, and were preparing to get up a dance for the negroes. A fellow-traveler told me that these peddlers are commonly called chicken-thieves, and, the day after they move off, the planters not unfrequently miss many of their fowls."

Town and crossroads general stores, as well as specialized stores in the larger towns, grew in number and added to the variety of their stocks. They advertised in the local newspapers and announced new shipments with special "notices"; one West Feliciana storekeeper in the early 1820's informed possible customers that he had just received from Europe "200 CANNISTERS OF THE WELL KNOWN RIFLE POWDER. . . . ALSO—FRESH MACKREL." In the 1850's a northeast Louisiana proprietor announced a consignment of "general merchandise" with more than 140 separate items, including Canton teas, "Red Yankee" plows, eau de Cologne, Russell's shaving cream, Starkey rifle caps, cubeb extract, "lard oil," smoked tongues, cooking stoves, Arkansas saddle trees, oak-tanned russet brogans, walking canes, "fresh" and patent medicines, guava jelly, brooms, rolling pins, tooth brushes, mustang liniment, Scotch snuff, Dutch buckets, curry combs, codfish, egg cups, tobacco and spice jars, ale, whiskey, wines, playing cards, and firecrackers. Louisianians, if they could get to a general store, were well supplied with the world's goods.

MANUFACTURING. Manufacturing was of secondary interest to ante bellum Louisianians, and more than one historian has questioned whether this situation should be attributed to preoccupation with agriculture, domestic and foreign trade, lack of capital, or as Roger Shugg wrote, "to inertia." The census of 1810 revealed that a strong beginning had been made in producing manufactured goods, for there were 29 brick and tile kilns, 14 cotton presses, 17 distilleries, 4 sawmills, several cigar-making establishments, and a total of over 400 cigar makers, over 160 cobblers, nearly 90 blacksmiths, 15 hatters, 10 gunsmiths, several salt works and soapmaking concerns, and over 500 spindles and nearly 1,000 looms in the territory. But the promise of those early years was not fulfilled. By 1840 only 7,500 persons were employed in manufacturing industries, and the total never exceeded 9,000 during the 1850's.

During the 1850's two Louisianians, banker and businessman James Robb and editor J. D. B. De Bow, pleaded with Louisiana and southern businessmen to build up manufacturing and thus free the South of northern control of manufactured products. In an address before a railroad convention at New Orleans in 1851, Robb defended New Orleans businessmen from the charge that they were "too torpid and indifferent to the interests of the city," and tried to awaken the city and the South to the promotion of industry and the mechanical and productive arts. The following year at the New Orleans Southern Commercial Convention, De Bow pleaded that "whatever divisions exist in Southern politics there can be none upon this of Southern Industrial Independence," estimated the annual industrial loss to the North at $100,000,000, and shouted: "Great God! Does Ireland sustain a more degrading relation to Great Britain?"

In 1858, De Bow climaxed his speech to the Montgomery, Alabama, commercial convention by giving an account of the delegates' journey to Montgomery:

They will start in some stage or railroad coach made in the North; an engine of Northern manufacture will take their train or boat along; at every meal they will sit down in Yankee chairs, to a Yankee table, spread with a Yankee cloth. With a Yankee spoon they will take from Yankee dishes sugar, salt, and coffee which have paid tribute to Yankee trade, and with Yankee knives and forks they will put into their mouths the only thing Southern they will get on the trip.

At night they will pull off a pair of Yankee boots with a Yankee boot-jack; and throwing a lot of Yankee toggery on a Yankee chair, lie down to dream of Southern independence, in a Yankee bed, with not even a thread of cotton around them that has not gone through a Yankee loom or come out of a Yankee shop.

In the morning they will get up to fix themselves by a 12x14 Yankee looking-glass, with a Yankee brush and comb, after perhaps washing off a little of the soil of the South from their faces, with water drawn in a Yankee bucket, and put in a Yankee pitcher, on a Yankee wash-stand, the partner in honorable exile with a lot of Yankee wares that make up the sum of the furniture.

In spite of the pleas of Robb, De Bow, and others, however, Louisiana made little progress in manufacturing, and it was estimated that the total capital invested in manufacturing at the end of the period was only slightly more than $7,000,000, chiefly in lumber, flour, cotton, and iron mills, brick and tile kilns, tanneries, distilleries, and sugar refineries.

BANKS AND BANKING. Louisianians needed strong banks to finance their ever growing agricultural and commercial economy. Planters and farmers needed long-term loans to purchase land and slaves and short-term loans to pay running expenses during the few months prior to the sale of their crops. Merchants and other business-men needed capital, and long- and short-term loans to finance increasing inventories and to give credit. Financially, the period was a hectic one in which Louisiana economy in general followed national trends.

The years from 1812 to 1820 were marked by sound, conservative banking, but beginning in the early 1820's the state entered a boom period characterized by rapid expansion in plantation and business operations. The banks handled this expansion without much difficulty, and such losses as they had, according to Louisiana financial historian Stephen Caldwell, "were due to theft, default, and counterfeiting." By 1835 banking capital had risen to approximately $26,500,000 and the number of banks to over forty; five years later there were forty-seven banks (including branch banks) with capital assets of nearly $42,000,000. The Panic of 1837 brought to an end, according to B. R. Curtis, "one of the most extraordinary financial periods" in American history.

The panic did not seriously affect Louisiana at first, but by 1843 the number of banks had dropped to twenty-eight which had a total capitalization of only about $21,000,000. Deposits had meantime dropped from a high of nearly $12,000,000 in 1836 to a low of only slightly over $5,000,000 in 1841. The financial stringency throughout the state became a panic. All but a half-dozen of the principal cotton factors, brokers, and commission merchants of New Orleans failed; nearly 3,000 foreclosure suits were entered in the Parish of Orleans alone; banks ceased to make profits and their bonds were soon in default; public indignation meetings were held and pressure was applied to the Governor to call special sessions of the legislature to enact relief legislation. One North Louisiana critic wrote bitterly that the panic was "all the consequence of fools or knaves in power, who care not who suffer so long as their power is perpetuated."

The legislature responded by passing the banking act of 1842 which placed all financial houses under state control, and the state shortly took over the banks which had defaulted their bonds, assuming the responsibility of repaying some $17,000,000. In 1843 an act further augmented the machinery of state control and permitted debtors to pay off obligations in defaulted bank bonds at par value. A supplementary act in 1855 completed the banking legislation. Collectively, the three acts have been considered by Louisiana historians, as Caldwell remarks, "as the Ark of the Coven-ant." While these acts greatly improved banking operations and were widely imitated by other states, they by no means immediately and completely relieved the state of its financial problems. The general problems of collecting assets continued for the next forty years, and the last of the state bonds were not funded until 1913.

The state slowly recovered from the financial panic, and by the middle 1840's bank deposits began to rise. Internal improvement projects, however, suffered because the Constitution of 1845 prohibited the state from subscribing to improvement companies; the Constitution of 1852 relieved the situation somewhat by permitting 20 per cent of such stock to be held by the state. By 1855 nineteen banks were in operation with a capitalization of over $20,000,000 and had deposits totaling over $11,500,000; five years later the number of banks had been reduced to thirteen, but they had a total capital of nearly $25,000,000 and deposits of nearly $20,000,000.

The back-country farmer or small planter sold his cotton or tobacco to the local merchant at the time of harvesting, meanwhile purchasing his supplies on credit. Large planters channeled most, and in some cases all, of their selling and purchasing operations through large New Orleans commission houses. Many of the towns and villages had no banks at all, the people still used the barter system as much as possible, and everyone scrutinized carefully Arkansas, Mississippi, or Texas bank notes which filtered into the state. No one had paid much attention to the recession of 1857. By 1860, Louisiana was booming again, and more than one writer noted that the entire state was "overflowing with gold."

LABOR. Negro slaves furnished most of the plantation labor, and on the smaller agricultural units the owner often worked in the fields with his slaves. At the end of the period, while there was a large amount of slave labor in the towns and cities beyond that of house servants, much if not most of the hard labor of street-paving, building, and draying was performed by white workers; most of the railroad-building, clearing of land, wood cutting, and especially the digging of drainage ditches was also done by white laborers.

The competition between white and Free Negro labor grew steadily throughout the period, but by 1850 the white laborer's greater productivity was beginning to force the Free Negro out. In 1840 it was estimated that most of the draymen, hotel employees, carpenters, ordinary day laborers, masons, cigar makers, and shoemakers, and a high percentage of the blacksmiths, tanners, plasterers, wheelwrights, cabinetmakers, coopers, barbers, wood dealers, and bakers of New Orleans were colored; twenty years later they had generally lost the battle to the white workers. During the 1850's many skilled white workers were imported by labor contractors from the Middle Atlantic states and New England. The Free Negro laborer was generally as well treated as the white laborer, and his wages, in view of his lesser productivity, were relatively higher than the wages of whites.

Daily wages increased slowly during the period, and by 1860 a day laborer was paid just under $1.00 per day and board, or an average of $1.40 without board. Skilled labor, without board, averaged about $2.75 per day; farm labor could be hired, with board, for an average of about $17.00 per month. Effective unionism did not appear until the 1850's. A Typographical Society, established in 1810, was reorganized in 1835 to procure better wages and on March 16, 1836, the New Orleans *Commercial Bulletin* announced "the prices fixed by the Journeymen Printers at their meeting on the 13th of this month." The Screwmen's Benevolent Association was established in 1850 by about a hundred stevedores who were skilled in the "screwing" of cotton bales aboard ships, and it soon advanced the pay for groups of five men from $13.50 per day to $21.00. Other efforts of union organization made from time to time accomplished little.

Many Free Negroes owned slaves, who labored on their plantations or in their city homes. In 1830 there were approximately 750 Free Negro slaveowners in New Orleans and numerous others were scattered throughout the rural sections. During the period from 1830 to 1860 the successions filed in parish courthouses or other legal records reveal that Cyprian Richard owned ninety-one slaves, Martin Donatto owned eighty-nine, Augustin Metoyer owned forty-six, Marie Metoyer owned fifty, Cecee McCarty owned thirty-two, and Antoine Dubuclet owned twenty. The statement of Negro historian Charles B. Roussève that "most" Free Negroes purchased slaves "for philanthropic reasons, usually to make their lot easier, and often to grant them freedom at a nominal fee" is not borne out by the records; Free Negroes generally owned slaves for the same reason that whites owned them, for their labor. Northern traveler Frederick Law Olmstead was informed by local citizens that the Free Negro planters of the Natchitoches area "were honest, and industrious, and paid their debts quite as punctually as the white planters, and were, so far as they could judge, without an intimate acquaintance, good citizens, in all respects."

Although slaves by law could not own property, there is at least one record of such a case. After the Civil War a correspondent of *Harper's New Monthly Magazine* interviewed Charles Stewart, who had been owned by Senator Alexander Porter of St. Mary Parish and was the manager of his racing stables. Stewart told the reporter that he had purchased his wife Betsy from a Major Puckett for the sum of $350, but that although she had presented him with three children, was a good housekeeper, and could cook "as good biskets, hoecake, baconfry, hominy mush, an' coffee as any gal I seed," she simply would not tell the truth. Stewart said that "I tried 'suasion an' finery, birch rods, split pine, an' a light hickory stick 'bout as thick as my littlest finger, an' I tried makin' her kin an' my kin dat had religion pray fur her at de big camp-meetin'," all to no avail. At last he became completely disgusted: "Dar was a horse-dealer . . . by de name of Jones, what had de finest nag I had seen in a year fur sale at jes' de bery price I paid fur Betsy. De horse . . . was wuf de money, I tell you; so I jes' says to Major Puckett that he could have Betsy back at the same price I paid fur her, and lowin' fur de war an' tar of de four years I had done kep' her, I would throw de boys into de bargain."

New Orleans had become the chief slave-trading center in the lower South by 1830, and remained throughout the period the largest distribution center. The slave-selling season was from late winter through early spring. Slave barracks, auction houses, and showrooms were located in the business district, where the slaves were exhibited and sold, and regular auctions were held on Tuesdays and Saturdays in the rotundas of the St. Louis and St. Charles hotels, the auction rooms of the Masonic Temple, and other places. As early as 1842 there were 185 persons dealing in slaves, while 349 brokers and over two dozen auctioneers sold slaves when the opportunity offered; by 1860 there were 25 slave markets in the city.

Prices varied greatly and were generally considerably lower than those ordinarily listed by historians. Prices, however, gradually rose until the peak was reached just before the outbreak of the Civil War. In 1856 the *Daily Picayune* reported that young prime male laborers were bringing as high as $1,250 to $1,500 and young prime females were being sold at from $1,000 to $1,100. At Baton Rouge, St. Francisville, Alexandria, and other inland markets prices were even higher. Those with special skills, such as cooks, mechanics, carpenters, seamstresses, or sugar makers, brought premium prices.

Despite legislation regulating the life of the slave and protecting him from mistreatment, general conditions of slave life varied with the individual master. Food generally consisted of salt pork, corn meal, and molasses, plus such other items as could be easily and cheaply secured by the owners. There was a lack of variety in slave diet, but this condition also existed among middle-class and poor whites. The slave ordinarily ate about as well as day-laboring whites, and perhaps better than some of them; his clothing and housing would have compared about as favorably.

The slave was whipped for violations of plantation rules and for loafing or doing slipshod work. Some masters were lenient; others brutal. Former slave Charles Stewart reported that Alexander Porter was open-handed and generous but that "he wouldn't stand no foolin' neither. . . . Things had to be jes' so, but dar warn't no naggin' nor scoldin'; it was jes' stiddy management." During the Civil War northern soldier Lawrence Van Alstyne, after seeing a large number of Negroes whose backs were scarred from whippings, wrote that the sight "beat all the anti-slavery sermons ever yet preached." On the other hand there was compassion, kind treatment, and even love. Rachel O'Conner of West Feliciana Parish wrote in her diary in 1830: "Sixteen little Negro children araising . . . all very healthy . . . excepting my little favorite Isaac. He is subject to a cough, but seldom sick enough to lay up. The poor little fellow is lying at my feet sound asleep—I wish I did not love him as I do, but it is so, and I cannot help it."

Bennet H. Barrow of Highland Plantation, West Feliciana Parish, was a typical large planter, owning nearly two hundred slaves, and a few extracts from his diary present the slave-life picture rather graphically:

January 19, 1837: Employed Mr. Bailey as Overseer for $500 & fired him.

September 4 1837: Had a general Whiping frollick. White men sending for some of my women by one of my boys. "one eyed Sam"—a load of buck shot will be the dose if I can see them or find them.

October 7, 1837: George drowned in L. Creek in the field . . . one of the best negros I ever saw or knew to his family as a White person.

November 12, 1837: Atean picked 511   Ben 461—Dave Bartley 511   Dennis 430 Kish 455   Jack 455   [pounds of cotton].

March 26, 1838: Sent Alfred to buy two dozen hoes.

July 25, 1839: I hope the time will come When every Overseer in the country will be compelled to addopt some other mode of making a living—they are a perfect nuisance   cause dissatisfaction among the negroes—being more possessed of more brutal feelings—I make better crops than those Who Employ them.

August 11, 1839: Gave Dave Bartley & Atean a suit. I bought them in N. O. for their fine conduct.

March 30, 1840: Several Sunday Gentleman here yesterday to go a Hunting— nothing provokes me more—Sunday being a day of rest to the negros. I like to be about—allowance day—& they frequently want things not convenient to get any other day—& My orders for every negro to come up every Sunday morning cleaned & head combed—&c.

April 16, 1840: My Hands appear determined to make a crop, if work can do it. never saw hands Work as Well, have never said a word to them—feeling an interest, they look a head & see What is to be done.

October 15, 1840: Am sattisfied the best plan is to give them every thing they require for their comfort and never that they will do without Whipping or some punishment, My negros have their name up in the neighbourhood for making more than any one else & they think Whatever they do is better than any body Else.

December 24, 1840: Gave the negros money last night $700. all went to Town to day.

December 28, 1842: Gave the negros as much of Evry thing to eat & *drink* during the Hollidays as they Wanted   times so hard not able to give any thing more.

January 15, 1843: My Old negro Orange died last night of Old age—Considerable over 100 yrs A more perfect negro never lived, faithful honest & purley religious, never knew him guilty of a wrong.

March 28, 1843: Every thing seems to have gone on well during my absence My negros certainly deserve great credit—or uncom-on good driver "Alfred" [Barrow and his family had just returned from a ten-day trip to New Orleans. He had no overseer at this time.]

January 1, 1846: Negros had a dinner yesterday, some danced all night, those that did not will start to work this morning. . . . finding no Cotton to trash sent for the Fiddle And made them Dance from 12 till dark, other from the Quarter soon joined for the frollic & became quite Lively to the close.

CHAPTER 19

ELEMENTS OF ANTE
BELLUM CULTURE

ELEMENTARY AND SECONDARY EDUCATION. When German traveler Karl Postl visited New Orleans a dozen years after Louisiana statehood, he noted that its educational facilities consisted of only a few private day and boarding schools, an Episcopal and a Roman Catholic secondary school, and the College of Orleans, which offered few college-grade courses. He observed that public education in New Orleans was inferior to "any city of equal extent and less wealth" in the nation. Postl's observation would have applied to the entire state, for little progress had been made since 1812, chiefly because of Catholic opposition and the stigma attached to free schools for indigent children.

The territorial legislature had provided for the founding of free public schools in each county in 1806, but the act was later modified in favor of a system of assistance to local private schools and academies. By 1811 annual grants of $500 were made to such institutions, and the amount rose to $800 by 1821, with the provision that eight free students be admitted. By 1827 the state allowed slightly over $2.60 per month for each student enrolled and the amount was raised in 1833 to $4.00 per month. This principle of limited assistance to schools or their beneficiary students, called "beneficiarism" by some authorities, continued until the adoption of a system of free public schools.

Agitation for a free public-school system continued after statehood. A legislative committee report in 1817 emphasized that public instruction was necessary "in every country where the people are called on to govern themselves." Acting Governor Jacques Dupre in 1831 called attention to the fact that state appropriations to private and parochial schools were largely being wasted. Three years later Governor A. B. Roman stated emphatically that "common schools, wholly free, are the only ones that can succeed under our form of government," because "they break down the odious distinction which exists in those in Louisiana between the children of the poor and those of the rich." This distinction certainly existed; witness the notice which Archibald Palmer published in the *Louisiana Journal* on November 25, 1825: "SLANDER! A report has been circulated by some evil-minded persons, with the intent to injure my character, that my step children . . . have been educated out of the School Charity Fund; I pronounce the author of said report a base liar, and the circulators, calumniators." The legislative committee on education reported in 1836 that the existing system was utterly useless and recommended a free public-school system.

The agitation continued, particularly in the Second Municipality of New Orleans, the newly settled American section above Canal Street, and in 1841 the city was authorized to provide free public education. The Second Municipality council organized a board of directors and school management, which in turn secured the services of A. J. Shaw, a former assistant to Horace Mann in the organization of the Massachusetts public-school system, at that time the best in the United States. Shaw organized free public elementary schools, established a free high school for boys and another for girls, and installed modern methods of instruction. It was not long before the First and Third Municipalities below Canal Street created boards of education and began to organize free public schools. In the First and Third Municipalities instruction was given in French, and historian Alcée Fortier has admitted that "the schools were as distinct, the tastes, aims and aspirations of teachers and pupils as different, as the peoples of England and France." The reputation of the New Orleans Second Municipality school system rapidly filtered out into the rural sections of the state.

The Constitution of 1845 provided that the legislature "establish free public schools throughout the State, and . . . provide means for their support by taxation on property and otherwise," that a state superintendent be elected for a two-year term, and that a seminary of learning be established. Two years later the legislature passed the first state free-school act, which fixed the school age at six to sixteen and provided taxes for educational purposes. Alexander Dimitry became the first state superintendent of public instruction and served until 1851. He urged increased appropriations, consolidation of schools, advanced methods of instruction, and was generally far in advance of his time in his educational ideas.

By 1850, according to the report of Dimitry, the state was spending slightly in excess of $300,000 annually on public elementary education and had built, purchased, or rented nearly 650 schoolhouses, which were attended by approximately 50 per cent of the children of school age an average of six months and thirteen days a year. Dimitry's report gave a false impression of education in the state and was inaccurate in the statement that 50 per cent of the children were attending school an average of six and a half months a year. Large numbers were still taught in private schools or at home by parents or tutors and still larger numbers outside the cities and towns were receiving little if any education.

Despite legislation forbidding their education, some slaves and many Free Negroes received elementary educations, and in 1850 the rate of illiteracy for the Free Negro group was less than that for foreign-born whites. Schools for Free Negroes began to be established shortly after statehood. In 1813, G. Dorfeuille advertised in the *Louisiana Courier* that he intended "to establish a school for the education of colored children" because such an institution was lacking in Louisiana and because "the enlightened persons who heretofore were desirous of having their children educated— I refer to the prudent colored people—were obliged to send them to the North." While records of the so-called "clandestine" Free Negro schools are extremely sparse, several were established in New Orleans prior to 1820.

In 1837 the widow of Bernard Couvent, and a native of Guinea, provided by will that the lot and buildings at the corner of Greatmen and Union streets were to be used as a school for colored orphans. In 1847 ten free men of color formed an organization for the establishment and support of a school for the instruction of indigent Free Negro orphans; this orphanage received endowment grants from Aristide Mary, Thomy Lafon, and other wealthy New Orleans Free Negroes and small appropriations from the state at various times. The same year the École des Orphelins Indigents, sponsored by the Société Catholique pour l'Instruction des Orphelins dans l'Indigence, was established and became the largest Free Negro school in New Orleans. That these New Orleans Free Negro schools performed their functions well is evidenced by the literary and cultural output of the New Orleans Free Negro group during the last three decades of the ante bellum period.

Until 1845 private schools or academies lived a hand-to-mouth existence in spite of state subsidization; the majority were short-lived and existed for only a few terms. In 1860 there were over 150 of these educational institutions scattered over the entire state with a total of nearly 450 teachers and 12,000 students. Many of them were called "colleges" even though their courses of study included only elementary and a few secondary subjects. Tuition for day students ranged from $2.00 to $5.00 per month, according to the school, grade of instruction, and qualifications of the instructors, and special subjects such as dancing and music were subject to extra fees. Boarding pupils paid from $100 to $200 per school year for room, board, laundry, and tuition.

Boys studied reading, writing, arithmetic, grammar, geography, history, and occasionally Latin and Greek. Girls studied geography, French, reading, wrting, calculation, embroidery, design, music, and perhaps orthography, while their "finishing" courses emphasized manners and morals, modern languages, singing, painting, fancy needlework, drawing, and piano playing.

Student life was Spartan, with long hours of study the general rule. Boarding-school boys generally arose before day, as Charles Gayarré recalled, "they then had breakfast, which consisted of a half loaf of dry bread, which each boy procured, on hearing his name called, by going to an aperture whence it was dealt out. From half past 7 until 12 students were engaged with their books and recitations; an hour was then given for dinner, which was a more generous meal than breakfast, and for recess. From 1 o'clock until about 7 they were back again at books. Then came supper, and the evening was devoted to recreation." Robert Patrick remembered the school of Miss Eliza Mills, who was "a strict disciplinarian and very exacting." She taxed Patrick's powers "to the utmost . . . to memorize the long lessons she gave me." Patrick admitted, however, to "learning more than I ever did at any other school in the same length of time."

COLLEGES AND COLLEGE LIFE. In 1860, Louisiana boasted over fifteen colleges with nearly 100 instructors, over 1,500 students, and a total annual state income of nearly $100,000. Few of them were really "colleges," for the majority provided courses at the secondary-school level and compared favorably with the better high schools of the present time. Courses of college level were offered only in classical, scientific, and professional fields.

Ante bellum colleges may be divided into three groups: those supported by the state, those which received limited state support, and those operated by religious denominations and which received little or no state assistance. The first group included the College of Orleans, the College of Louisiana, the University of Louisiana, and the State Seminary of Learning.

The College of Orleans, as originally planned in 1805, was to provide instruction in classical and modern languages, sciences, philosophy, and literature and was to be the capstone of territorial education, for it would also maintain academies and public libraries throughout the territory. It was not until 1811, however, that the territorial legislature appropriated to the institution $15,000 plus an additional $3,500 for the education of 50 indigent students. The college was assisted by small state appropriations until 1825, when these funds were withdrawn in favor of the College of Louisiana.

The College of Orleans never attained real college rank although it provided sound elementary and secondary training. Most of the day students were from poor families who could afford to pay less than one-half of the student's educational expenses. The first head of the school was Jules D'Avezac, a native Santo Domingan, and the last was Joseph Lakanal, a former French priest who had left the priesthood in 1791, was one of the regicides of the French National Convention of 1792, and had later taken a prominent part in subsequent French Republic and Napoleonic activities.

The College of Louisiana, the actual successor of the College of Orleans, was founded at Jackson by legislative act in 1825. By 1831 the college had an enrollment of about eighty students, a faculty of five members, four buildings, and an annual income of $15,000. Twelve years later only forty-six students were enrolled and the faculty included only the president and two professors. In 1845 the state withdrew its support of all higher education in favor of the University of Louisiana.

The University of Louisiana was originally organized as the Medical College of Louisiana in 1834 by several New Orleans physicians. It was chartered the following year, and in 1836 awarded its first degrees, the first given in medicine in the southwest. A pharmacy department was added in 1838. The Constitution of 1845 authorized the establishment of the University of Louisiana with colleges of medicine, law, natural sciences, and literature, but no legislative appropriations were made until two years later. In 1848, J. D. B. De Bow became professor of "Commerce, Public Economy and Statistics," and some writers have called his collective courses the first university "college of commerce" in the United States. While the colleges of medicine and law were successful, those of literature and natural sciences never developed. The "collegiate" or academic department failed to secure appropriations, and in 1855 its property was leased for use as a dance hall, ice-cream parlor, and saloon. Though the University of Louisiana led a precarious existence until the outbreak of the Civil War, it trained many men who became prominent during the years after 1860.

The Louisiana State Seminary of Learning and Military Academy, the ancestor of the present-day state university, grew out of the Federal acts of 1806, 1811, and 1827 which granted lands for the use of a "seminary of learning" in Louisiana. Nothing was done until 1853, when an act was passed authorizing the state superintendent of public education to purchase from Mrs. E. R. Williams a tract of 438 acres of land lying on the northern side of Red River across from Alexandria. Two years later eighty additional acres of land were purchased. The institution opened its doors on January 2, 1860, and by late April the first superintendent, Colonel William T. Sherman, reported that "there were 5 professors, 71 cadets, and 31 beneficiaries." The single building cost nearly $100,000 and the legislature of 1860 appropriated $32,330 for general expenditures and $15,000 for the support of the beneficiary cadets. The institution suspended operations in June, 1861, and did not reopen until the spring of the following year.

The second group of colleges received limited state support. The most important of these were the College of Jefferson at Convent in St. James Parish and the College of Franklin at Opelousas.

The College of Jefferson grew directly out of the dissatisfaction of the Creoles with the establishment of the College of Louisiana at Jackson, which was generally dominated by the Americans. In 1831 a group of Creoles, headed by A. B. Roman, Valcour Aime, Étienne Mazureau, and others, secured a charter for a new college, and its gates were opened three years later. By 1842 the college had five buildings valued at approximately $125,000, land appraised at $10,000, a library of about 7,000 volumes valued at over $8,000, and a considerable amount of laboratory equipment. Annual state appropriations were cut after 1841 from $15,000 to $10,000.

In 1842 the institution had accommodations for three hundred students, was educating a dozen or more beneficiary students, had the best-qualified faculty, and generally was superior to any college in the state. While it was advertised as a non-sectarian college, the Roman Catholic Church was extremely influential in its affairs and it was considered the center of Creole influence. That same year a fire destroyed the main building which housed the library and laboratories; the college never recovered, for the state withdrew its support in 1845. It was forced to close in 1855 and was bought at a sheriff's sale in 1859 by Valcour Aime for $20,000. The college was reorganized and opened in 1861.

The College of Franklin was chartered by the legislature in 1831, largely through the efforts of Americans of the Opelousas region to establish an "American" college in opposition to the College of Jefferson. Its board of trustees, however, included many Creoles from the Teche and Atakapas country. While small legislative appropriations began in 1831, it was not until 1837 that the college was ready to begin operation, when five buildings had been constructed at a cost to the state of approximately $35,000. In 1840 only sixty students were in attendance, and these were not doing work of college level. The College of Franklin lost its state support in 1845 and gradually declined until the Civil War.

The third group of colleges was operated by religious denominations. The most important of these church schools were the College of St. Charles at Grand Coteau, Centenary College of Louisiana at Jackson, the College of the Immaculate Conception at New Orleans, and Mount Lebanon University at Mount Lebanon.

Suppressed by the French government in 1763 and expelled from Louisiana the following year, in 1773 the Jesuit order was suppressed by the Catholic Church. It was restored and vindicated in 1814, and nine years later, at the suggestion of Secretary of War John C. Calhoun, Bishop Louis Dubourg of New Orleans invited the Jesuits to establish Indian missions and schools in upper Louisiana. St. Louis University was one of the institutions established, and by 1834 nearly half of its students were Louisianians. In 1835, Bishop Antoine Blanc asked the Jesuits to found a college in Louisiana. They opened the College of St. Charles at Grand Coteau the same year in a log house and one frame building, with about sixty day and boarding students. Throughout the rest of the period the enrollment averaged about 130 students. The College of St. Charles is said to have been the only college in the Confederacy west of the Mississippi River to remain open during the entire period of the Civil War.

Centenary College had its origin in the College of Louisiana at Jackson, which when it lost state support in 1845 was purchased by Judge Edward McGehee and several other planters of the Feliciana region and given to the Methodist Conference of Louisiana and Mississippi. The Conference had founded a college at Clinton, Mississippi, in 1839, the Centenary of American Methodism, and had later moved it to Brandon. This college was now moved to Jackson, where it remained until 1907. The College of the Immaculate Conception was founded by the Jesuits in New Orleans in 1847, opened two years later, and grew slowly until the outbreak of the Civil War, when the total enrollment was slightly over 250. Sponsored by the Baptists, Mount Lebanon University opened in 1853 and prospered until the Civil War, aided by good endowments and by a $15,000 legislative appropriation in 1855 to purchase library books and laboratory equipment.

While the above four institutions were probably the best of their type, there were numerous other "colleges" established by the various religious denominations. Two schools outside this category should be mentioned, the well-known commercial college established in New Orleans by Colonel George Soulé in 1856 and the first normal school for training teachers, which began operations in the Girls' High School in New Orleans in 1858.

Student life in the colleges of that day was completely regulated. A student was not permitted to leave the college grounds, and was required to remain in his room or in study hall during specified hours and to stand when reciting. He was forbidden to bring animals to school, fight with classmates, or "strike a professor." The Mount Lebanon University regulations of 1860-61 not only prohibited gambling and drinking but decreed that no student "wear upon his person, or have in his possession, while attending in any department of the University, any pistol, dirk, bowie-knife, or dangerous weapons of any kind, under pain of expulsion."

Instructors were kept on tight rein by college presidents, and those in religious institutions were held to conservative interpretations of that faith's religious beliefs and practices. Occasionally they were hailed before boards of trustees, as was young instructor Daniel Martindale of Centenary College in 1850. The board did not sustain the charges of drinking with students in his or their rooms, racing or witnessing horse races "beyond the creek on the Baton Rouge road near Mrs. Kendrick's," but found him an enemy of the Methodist Church for attacking its doctrines and guilty of disturbing the harmony of the faculty by communicating their activities to students. Although he completed the year without incident, he resigned before the beginning of the next session.

College commencements were overly long and boring to some visitors. In 1854,

Dr. Linus Parker, editor of the *New Orleans Christian Advocate* attended the two-day Centenary College commencement exercises. Parker had little comment to make on the Monday night sermon, but he considered the six-speech Tuesday morning literary-society program "rather long." That evening Parker had to listen to six more speeches by members of another literary society. On Wednesday morning "fifteen hundred people at the least were congregated in and around the chapel" to watch the sixteen young men graduate, to hear more student orators speak, and finally to hear the baccalaureate. At the end Dr. Parker grumbled that the "people were too hungry to give the professor's address such a hearing as its merits deserved. Six hours of confinement is too much for the most patient. The conferring of degrees and the baccalaureate should have been kept back until after dinner."

RELIGION. Throughout the ante bellum period Louisiana had the reputation of being one the most vice-ridden and immoral states of the Union. The southern sections and particularly New Orleans were attacked with varying degrees of intensity by most travelers, Protestant and Catholic alike. Catholics attacked their own church for the almost universal lackadaisical attitude of the clergy, while Protestants criticized the superstition and immorality of the people. Episcopal Bishop Leonidas Polk wrote his mother in 1841 that "there is no portion of the whole country so destitute, I presume, as Louisiana" and that New Orleans was a "city of moral darkness and papal superstition," which had "not yet recovered from the evil habits of its early settlers." Frederick Law Olmstead was informed during the 1850's that there was "more morality, and more immorality in Natchitoches than in almost any other place of its size in the United States" and that in Alexandria there was about as much "immorality without any morality at all."

Protestants universally complained about the lax observance of the Holy Sabbath. Bishop Polk once wrote from Central Louisiana that "the Sabbath is no Sabbath here. The stores and shops are kept open just as on other days. . . . At Natchitoches, where I spent a week, the better part of Passion Week . . . I had to defer my Sunday services until twelve o'clock in order to get a congregation." Protestants were still complaining in 1860 that New Orleans' Sundays were days of sports and amusements —horse races, pugilistic contests, cockfights, circuses, balloon ascensions, theatrical plays, minstrel shows, opera, varieties—and open stores and shops doing a thriving business. Catholics countered that the mere fact that persons amused themselves after Mass was no indication of their disregard of religion. Their churches, in addition, were open every day of the week while Protestants kept their places of worship closed and locked except on Sundays.

Itinerant Protestant preachers had begun a clandestine invasion of Catholic Louisiana during the late years of the Spanish regime in spite of strict Spanish regulations against them; their missionary activities greatly increased when the area was opened to all religions after the Louisiana Purchase. The sight of Catholic spires every six or seven miles along the Mississippi from New Roads to New Orleans without "a single Protestant house of worship" was a challenge which they eagerly accepted.

The majority of the preachers who toured the southern sections were met with coolness, a few with hostility. When James Axley went to the Atakapas country in 1806, they knew him by his coat to be a preacher, and told him that they wanted none such in their homes. He asked for food and lodging at one house, but the mistress refused him. Axley thereupon sang several hymns, during which time the woman and her children and slaves crowded around him. Then she shouted: "Pete, put up the gentleman's horse! Girls, have a good supper for the preacher!" Others were not so kindly treated. James Cathcart reported in his diary that when touring the Teche Country in 1819, he waited out a storm at a small town where a little group of Protestants recently had decorated their schoolhouse for the use of one of the itinerant preachers, but "the rabble composed of the lower order of Roman Catholics of French descent . . . decorated the school house with horns & other emblems of derision which prevented the Minister from preaching the next day."

Catholics criticized the general lack of education of Protestant preachers and Protestant heavy drinking and unscrupulous business methods. They undoubtedly spoke with scorn of the preacher who, after reading a text concerning the miracles at the Pool of Bethesda, shouted: "My beloved hearers, I shall in the first place speak to you of the things which you know, and I do not know; second, of what I know, and you do not know; third, of the things that neither of us know." And what of the minister who read his text and then said, "I shall first speak of the chronology of the subject, then its topography, and then its psychology"? While Catholics admitted the "rough piety" of many of the rural Protestants, they charged that piety had not reformed their habits; North and West Louisiana had more "whiskey restaurants" than were needed. They would have read with some self-satisfaction Caroline Poole's 1836 diary entry: "Soon the preacher entered with his large B. under his arm, followed by a little negro boy bearing a tumbler & a glass pitcher of something that looked very like 'water made strong' which he drank during the services."

As Americans continued to settle in the southern sections in ever increasing numbers, direct Catholic opposition was forced to subside and the two groups settled down to real religious competition, which was good for both of them.

Until 1815, Louisiana was a part of the Catholic Diocese of Baltimore, and church affairs were under the control of a resident vicar. In 1815 the area of the Louisiana Purchase became a diocese, with Father Louis Guillaume Dubourg its first bishop, inheriting the old dispute between Father Antoine and Father Patrick Walsh over the pastorate of the Church of St. Louis, a dispute which Father Walsh finally had to win in the civil courts. Bishop Dubourg moved his residence to St. Louis in 1818, and Louisiana affairs were administered by a vicar apostolic until 1827, when the See of New Orleans was established. The office of bishop remained vacant until 1829, when Bishop Leo Raymond de Neckere was appointed.

Upon the death of Bishop Neckere in 1835, Bishop Antoine Blanc was appointed and served until 1850. The wardens of the Church of St. Louis continued to cause trouble, collecting the revenues and claiming the right of electing their own pastor. During the last two months of 1842, Bishop Blanc withdrew all priests and left the church without religious services. The wardens sued in the courts, lost their suit, and peace was finally restored. In 1850, Louisiana was made into an Archdiocese, Bishop Blanc became the first archbishop, and served until his death in 1860. In 1853 the diocese of Natchitoches was created in Louisiana north of the thirty-first parallel.

Under the leadership of Bishop Blanc the Louisiana Catholic Church entered a period of renaissance. The Jesuits were called upon to renew their educational activities, rural parishes were reorganized, a diocesan seminary was established, the St. Louis Cathedral was rebuilt, and publications in both French and English established. Basic cultural differences between Creole and Irish and German Catholics were reconciled.

Organized Protestant activity began immediately after the Louisiana Purchase. During the fall of 1803 four Methodist preachers, headed by the venerable Lorenzo Dow, delivered a few sermons in the area opposite Natchez, Mississippi, and the following year missionary activity began in the Opelousas and Atakapas districts. Meanwhile a group of Protestants had established a church in New Orleans, and in 1805 this congregation voted to select an Episcopalian minister and secured a state charter. The Baptists began their work in 1812 and the Presbyterians five years later. By the 1830's the Protestant denominations had small churches scattered throughout the central, northern and eastern sections, many of them "Union" churches in districts where there were not enough of one denomination to support a single church, and larger churches in the important towns and cities. The Lutherans, Unitarians, Congregationalists, Christians, Universalists, had all established churches by the 1850's. The Jews founded their first synagogue in New Orleans in 1828.

The Protestants produced several important religious leaders prior to the outbreak of the Civil War. New England Congregationalist Theodore Clapp came to New Orleans in 1822 to head a Methodist-Presbyterian group, led an eloquent and stormy career, and finally became a Unitarian more than a decade later. Virginia aristocrat and West Point Graduate Bishop Leonidas Polk came to Louisiana as the Episcopal Missionary Bishop to the Southwest in 1839 and became the first Bishop of Louisiana in 1841. South Carolinian Dr. B. M. Palmer, after a fourteen-year period of service in the Presbyterian Church at Columbia, came to New Orleans in 1856 and immediately became one of the most noted preachers of the city.

By 1860 there were 572 churches in the state with a combined seating capacity of over 200,000, and church property was valued at nearly $3,200,000. The number of churches, capacity, and property valuation of the five leading denominations were as follows:

	Churches	Capacity	Value of Property
Methodist	199	58,181	$ 336,815
Roman Catholic	99	57,600	1,744,700
Baptist	161	47,785	231,945
Episcopal	33	16,525	334,000
Presbyterian	42	15,550	305,500

The moral tone of the state gradually improved, although at the very end of the period the Common Council of New Orleans shocked the nation by passing Ordinance No. 3267, which, according to Herbert Asbury, "marked the first and only attempt by an American municipality to license prostitution." The ordinance went into effect on April 1, 1857, and during the next forty-five days women paid their fees and received "engraved forms appropriately decorated with smiling Cupids." But Mrs. Emma Pickett paid her $250 license fee as the keeper of a *bordello* under protest, filed suit to test the legality of the ordinance, and won her case. The ordinance was revoked in 1859. Many Louisianians throughout the period would have accepted the advice of aged Pedro Favrot, written to his son in 1819, shortly before his death:

My son: Love always without selfishness. Forgive without weakness. If it is necessary to submit, do so without servility. . . . Be sympathetic always with the misfortunes of others. Be tolerant with the faults of others, and be a faithful friend always. . . . Do not be oppressive with your poor debtors. . . . Do not be puffed up with your fortunate talents. . . . It is religion that determines our duties toward God; the civil laws determine our duties toward the state.

And many of them tried to live as did Bennet H. Barrow: "Have never injured any human being to my knowledge."

JOURNALS AND JOURNALISTS. A dozen newspapers began publication during the nine years following the purchase of Louisiana, and by the end of the first decade of statehood many towns had newspapers. During the period more than 150 were published, approximately one-third of them in New Orleans. Small-town newspapers tended to be short-lived, were weeklies rather than dailies, and usually received some financial help from public printing or from political groups. During early years they paid little attention to local news, which was usually well scattered throughout the community before the sheets were lifted from the hand presses, and clipped most of their material from state, out-of-state, or even foreign newspapers. It was not until 1835 that the New Orleans *True American* revolutionized Louisiana journalism by publishing extensive local and state economic, social, and political news.

Newspapers had become fairly well standardized by the 1840's. They devoted space to national and state news, agricultural material, communications from other newspapers, and to tales and poetry copied from American or English magazines. Medical, legal, and local advertisements frequently occupied more than half of the total space. Some of them had specialized "departments" for specific groups of readers. Subscriptions ranged from $1.50 to $2.00 per year. Those in southern Louisiana were usually published in both French and English, and in New Orleans several were published in Spanish or German.

Most of the small-town newspapers pleaded constantly with subscribers to pay their subscription bills. On January 30, 1839, for example, the Clinton *Feliciana Whig* published the following notice: "Wake Snakes!!! Come forward *every one* of ye, and help to lift this great bundle of papers, or they will crush me. They are notes and accounts, of from one to four years standing. . . . I think it is high time they were removed; and if you don't help me, I will get Captain Law, the strong man, to do so and call you out by command, and not by invitation. So you had better take hold now, for I shan't stand it much longer if you don't come on."

The New Orleans *Picayune*, founded in 1837, was the leading newspaper of ante bellum Louisiana. It first sold for a picayune (about 6¼ cents) and during the Mexican War regularly scooped its competitors by having couriers bring the news from the war front by a sort of pony express. Others included the *Delta, Crescent, Bee, Courier, True Delta, True American, Daily Topic, Louisiana Gazette, Commercial Intelligencer,* and *Argus;* at one time the city had nine daily newspapers. Foreign-language newspapers were represented by the *Courier de la Louisiane* and the *L'Ami des Lois et Journal du Soir,* which survived several names and was finally merged with the *L'Abeille de la Nouvelle Orleans* in 1834. The publication of Spanish-language newspapers began during the territorial period with *El Misisipi* in 1808 and *El Mensajero* in 1810, later followed by *La Union.* The Germans published the *Deutsche Zeitung,* founded in 1847.

The Alexandria *Louisiana Planter* (1810), the St. Francisville *Time Piece* (1811), and the Alexandria *Red River Planter* (1813) were three of the earliest newspapers published outside New Orleans, but they were soon followed by other small-town sheets, among the most noted of which were the Baton Rouge *Advocate,* the Alexandria *Red River Republican* and the *Red River Whig,* the Opelousas *Courier,* the Vidalia *Concordia Intelligencer,* the Shreveport *Caddo Gazette,* and the Franklin *Planter's Banner.*

Most editors were strongly partisan, and their campaign battles were often more heated than those of the rival political candidates. During one political campaign, for example, the editor of the *Louisianian* published an editorial attack upon a St. Francisville editor, whom he characterized as "more filthy" than a skunk, more like a "Dog-Face Baboon," and for sale to the highest bidder. Editors accused each other of every sort of misdemeanor, fought on the streets upon occasional meetings, and went to the dueling ground, where they shot it out, punctured each other with rapiers, or slashed with swords.

Ante bellum Louisiana had a long list of noted editors, whom some critics have pronounced the best in the country. James M. Bradford, son of David Bradford, the pioneer printer of Kentucky, founded the St. Francisville *Time Piece* in 1811. George W. Kendall and Francis A. Lumsden, who founded the *Picayune,* made that newspaper one of the most respected in the nation and developed many innovations. Other editors included John Gibson of the *True American,* Francis Delaup of the *Bee,* J. C. de St. Romes of the *Courier,* Colonel H. J. G. Battle of the *Caddo Gazette,* A. C. Bullitt of the *Bee* and *Picayune,* and T. De Valcourt of the *Attakapas Gazette and St. Mary, St. Martin and Lafayette Advertiser* (where probably the first "advice to the lovelorn" column was published).

A majority of the comparatively few periodicals were published in New Orleans. *De Bow's Review,* founded by J. D. B. De Bow in 1846, was dedicated to the promotion of commerce, agriculture, manufacturing, internal improvements, literature, and practically anything that would promote southern welfare. It became one of the best-known and most influential journals of the ante bellum South and published material by such men as Charles Gayarré, Judah P. Benjamin, Joel R. Poinsett, and John W. Monette. The *Southern Quarterly Review* contained articles, fiction, and poetry; *La Propagateur Catholique* and the *Christian Advocate* (Methodist) printed articles of a religious nature; and *L'Album Littéraire* (1843), the first recorded literary magazine published by Free Negroes, published stories, articles, poems, and folklore. Other magazines and journals generally attained only a small circulation and were short-lived.

LITERATURE. The literature of ante bellum Louisiana is possible of many characterizations. In 1826 the *Louisiana Gazette* asserted that "in cultivating Literature and the Arts," Louisiana was "fifty years behind some of our sister states." On the other hand it was the age of poet Theodore O'Hara, of poet Richard Henry Wilde whose *Lament of the Captive* began "My life is like a summer rose," of D. K. Whitaker whom Edgar Allan Poe listed among the cleverest of American essayists, and of historians Charles Gayarré and François Xavier Martin. Some critics have gone so far as to call the period "the golden age of Louisiana literature."

The noted French romanticist François René, Viscount de Chateaubriand, first made Louisianians conscious of the literary possibilities of their land during the first two years of the century with his *Atala* and *René*. French Creoles had long suspected that literary proclivities were the mark of a gentleman, and a large number now turned to drama, poetry, essays, and fiction as a leisure-time activity. "Most of them were occupied chiefly with other pursuits," as Ruby Van Allen Caulfield wrote, "and writing was only a pleasant recreation for them. This no doubt explains the fact that very few of them are known outside of Louisiana."

They wrote on a wide variety of romantic subjects and, according to one authority, produced "an assemblage of works bizarre in character, uninteresting save when presenting pictures of the times wherein they were produced." A few of them, however, achieved signal success in their descriptions of Louisiana and its people, customs, and traditions. Since practically all of their works were published locally, in small editions, and had little sale, the majority of them have disappeared. A score or more of those forgotten works, however, are well worth resurrecting and republishing for modern Louisianians.

While the works of Sir Walter Scott were extremely popular, he had little influence upon the Creole writers, who wrote in French and followed the romantic writers of France. Dominique and Adrien Rouquette wrote poetry; Auguste Lussan, *Les Martyrs de la Louisiane;* Armand Garreau, *Louisiana;* Urbain David, *Les Anglais à la Louisiane en 1814 et 1815;* Alexandre Bardé, *Histoire des comités de vigilance aux Attakapas;* François Xavier Martin, a *History of Louisiana;* and Charles Gayarré another state history in four volumes. Slightly off the beaten track of literature were B. M. Norman's *New Orleans and Environs,* the first guidebook of the city, Vincent Nolte's *Fifty Years in Both Hemispheres,* an account which covers an eight-year residence in New Orleans, and S. S. Hall's *Bliss of Marriage, or How to Get a Rich Wife,* in which the author listed a large number of wealthy young men and women of the area, a book causing half a dozen duels and Hall's hurried departure from town.

Perhaps the most significant and certainly the least known of the literary prose and poetry was the product of a group of French-speaking New Orleans Free Negroes. This group had for some years prior to 1843 been writing poetry, stories, fables, and other short sketches, highly romantic and descriptive of Louisiana life. In 1843 young Armand Lanusse, a locally educated Free Negro, conceived the idea of publishing a literary journal. He secured the aid of J. L. Marciacq, a respected teacher and possibly a Frenchman, who began the publication of *L'Album Littéraire, Journal des Jeunes Gens, Amateurs de la Littérature* (Literary Album, Journal of Young Men, Literary Amateurs), a small, French-language literary monthly containing poems, stories, fables, legends, sketches, and articles. Some contributions were anonymous and some were signed by Armand Lanusse, Joanni Questy, Camille Thierry, Michel Saint-Pierre, Mirtil-Ferdinand Liotau, and others. Although *L'Album Littéraire* soon became a fortnightly magazine, it won only a small circulation and ceased publication within a few years. During its brief career, however, it published considerable material of high quality.

Les Cenelles (The Hawthorns), the first anthology of Negro verse in America, was published in 1845, with Armand Lanusse the editor and promoter. The little

215-page book contained 82 poems from the pens of 17 Free Negro poets, the most important of whom were Lanusse, Mirtil-Ferdinand Liotau, Pierre Dalcour, and Michel Saint-Pierre. Victor Sejour, Louisiana's greatest dramatist, who had over twenty plays produced in Paris, and Camille Thierry, a nondramatic poet, both of whom were living in France, also contributed. The poetry ranged from joyous songs to the hopeless despair of "Le Suicide," the happy humor of "Le Carnaval," the rapturous love of "Chant d'Amour," and the biting irony of the eight-versed "Epigramme," the only poem in the collection which concerned interracial conflict.

On May 9, 1835, a small group of men met in the State Supreme Court room in New Orleans, elected Judge Henry A. Bullard the presiding officer and J. Burton Harrison secretary, and after considerable discussion passed a resolution establishing "The Historical Society of the State of Louisiana" and defining its objectives and the work it hoped to accomplish. A committee composed of Bullard, Harrison, and Senator Alexander Porter drafted a constitution. At a subsequent meeting in January, 1836, Bullard was elected president of the society. The new organization flourished bravely for a short period, then declined, and was reorganized in 1846, with François Xavier Martin as president.

LIBRARIES, PUBLIC AND PRIVATE. After Frederick Law Olmstead had traveled through Louisiana in the 1850's he wrote that in the possession of books and other reading material the New York farmer was ahead of the Louisiana planter, for one "might travel several days, and call on a hundred planters, and hardly see in their houses more than a single newspaper a-piece, in most cases; perhaps none at all; nor any books except a Bible, and some Government publications, that had been franked to them through the post office, and perhaps a few religious tracts or schoolbooks." While Olmstead's statement became the accepted view of the lack of books and other reading material in Louisiana and the South, the New Yorker did not see the inside of enough plantation or farm homes to make such a generalization. Louisianans of that period possessed about the same number of books, in proportion to the white population of the state, as did citizens of other states, excepting perhaps a few small sections of New England and the Middle Atlantic states. In 1820, for example, when New Orleans had a total population of about 27,000, it had nine bookstores, four bookbinders, nine printing offices which published books, and one French and one English circulating library.

The booksellers of the period, who ordinarily sold stationery, magazine subscriptions, and other items in addition to books, sold magnificent editions of the classics of Greek, Latin, French, and English literature, as well as cheaper editions of Scott, Byron, Moore, Cowper, Edgeworth, Austen, Swift, and other popular writers. This writer can testify, after more than twenty-five years of rummaging in old Louisiana houses and their attics, that he has yet to find one in which there were not a few books and in many cases hundreds of volumes dating from this period, volumes which reveal an extremely wide range of interest, in addition to dozens of different French, English, and American magazines.

Newspaper advertisements offer an excellent insight into the number of books sold from time to time, in many cases by the executors of estates. In 1813 the property of Daniel Clark included 700 volumes; three years later B. Lafon sold 450 volumes of encyclopedias, belles-lettres, mathematics, astronomy, geography, voyages, physics, American travels, as well as fiction and poetry. The same year M. Dorfeuille's library included works by Voltaire, Cervantes, Beaumarchais, Le Sage, Boccaccio, and numerous other authors in English, French, and Spanish; and the library of D. Rouquette in 1819 included over 1,300 volumes of "divers good works." The Louisiana Bible Society announced in 1816 that it had just received for distribution over 3,100 Bibles in English, French, and Spanish. Books, in large collections, small groups, or individually, were frequently disposed of by lotteries, the usual price of a ticket being $2.00.

The New Orleans Library Society was organized in 1806 with reading rooms "at the house of the Legislature on Royal Street," but it was shortly moved to a building on Bourbon Street. The society loaned books for varying periods in relation to their size: "Octavos and quartos shall not be lent for more than double the time of duodecimos, nor folios for more than three times that length." The fire of 1810, which destroyed some fifty buildings, consumed the library building although most of the books were saved.

Other libraries were established, not only in New Orleans but in other towns, soon after statehood. The St. Francisville Library Company was organized in 1816, the Library Society of Alexandria in 1824, the Touro Free Library Society of New Orleans the same year, the New Orleans Library Association in 1825, the New Orleans Commercial Library Society in 1831, and the Franklin Circulating Library in 1847, which in a few years had an extensive collection of books and maintained a newspaper reading room containing "upwards of fifty different papers and magazines" from all sections of the country. Meanwhile, public-spirited citizens of New Orleans Judah Touro and B. F. French had opened their collections to the public; in 1833 a legislative library had been opened and in 1838 the State Library, which grew rapidly during the period from 1846 to 1850, when Charles Gayarré was Secretary of State.

DRAMA. While no Louisiana dramatists achieved national success during the period, the people generally loved the theater. Many towns had theaters sponsored by local amateur actors, as for example the Alexandria Amateur Thespian Society. These groups produced plays, occasionally with the assistance of visiting professional stars, and secured engagements for touring professional companies. Showboats and circuses played at bayou and river towns and not infrequently went broke while on tour. In 1838, after a week's engagement in New Orleans, P. T. Barnum's company began a tour of the Atakapas country, but at Opelousas, according to Barnum, "we exchanged the steamer for sugar and molasses; our company was disbanded, and I started for home."

The St. Philip Theater, where plays were given in both French and English, had been built during the territorial period, as was the Orleans Theater, which was completed by John Davis, an *émigré* from Santo Domingo. Noah M. Ludlow arrived in New Orleans in 1817, organized an American company, and thus became the father of the English-language theater in Louisiana. The following year James H. Caldwell, so-called "pioneer of the drama in the South" and one of the nation's first and greatest theater managers, reached the city. Caldwell opened the American Theater in 1823 and twelve years later completed the St. Charles Theater, the largest and most elegant in the South.

Davis, Ludlow, Caldwell, Sol Smith, David Bidwell, Thomas Placide, and Harry Greenwall were the most noted theatrical managers of the New Orleans theater and brought such stars as Junius Brutus Booth, Edwin Forrest, Clara Fisher, James Hackett, Charles Macready, James Wallack, Dan Rice, Tyrone Power, Fanny Elssler, James M. Scott, Charlotte Cushman, Charles Keane and his wife Ellen Tree, and numerous others to the city. Caldwell withdrew from active management in 1843, leaving Ludlow and Smith to dominate New Orleans theatrical life. German-language drama was introduced in the late 1830's, and occasionally amateur groups presented plays in Spanish or Italian. During the ante bellum period more than a score of theaters were built and plays were produced at numerous "halls" and "rooms" as the smaller auditoriums were called.

Theatrical performances began about 6:30, lasted until nearly midnight, and the program usually included a vaudeville, a serious drama, and a comedy or farce, with several song, dance, and skit specialties in between. Seats seldom cost more than $2.00 except for special performances of noted stars, and a section in either the first or second galleries was reserved for Negroes. Disturbances were frequent, although as early as 1804 the city issued theater regulations. Article IV stated that "No one shall express his approval or his disapproval in such a way as to disturb the

calm of the theater, either by noisy clapping if pleased or hissing—if displeased."
Article V forbade the audience to throw oranges "or anything else," start quarrels,
or insult "anybody or come to blows or speak ill of anyone in order to stir up trouble."

MUSIC AND ART. Had a collector of songs and folk music wandered through
Louisiana's rural districts or along the streets of her towns and cities during the late
years of the ante bellum period he would have been amazed at the nationalistic
varieties of music he encountered. He would have heard songs from old France and
old Spain, snatches of liturgical music of Catholic, as well as Methodist, Baptist,
Presbyterian, and other Protestant denominations, themes from world-famous operas
and oratorios, lullabies from the frigid coasts of Nova Scotia or the warm climes of
the Canaries, songs from the mountains of Kentucky and Tennessee, refrains from
mid-seventeenth-century England, wildly rhythmical dances from Cuba or other
West Indian islands, and even voodoo chants from the African Coromantee or Congo
country. Music was an inheritance of all Louisianians, and the songs they sang and
the dances they danced had in many cases been handed down for generations.

A high percentage of the people played some kind of instrument, including accor-
dians, violins, guitars, flutes, pianos, organs, and others, generally for their own
amusement or for the enjoyment of small groups of friends. Home and informal group
singing was an almost universal practice over the entire state, while formal group
singing was extremely popular in the northern sections. Often wealthy families
engaged a small orchestra for a several weeks' private season and invited neighbors
to their nightly concerts.

Blessed with natural musical talents, Negroes played instruments, danced, or sang
at every opportunity. They formed small orchestras and used home-made instruments,
usually of the percussion variety. Drums were made of hollowed-out logs, kegs, barrels,
and even sections of bamboo, the ends of which were covered with cowhide; crude
banjos, violins, and marimbas were fashioned of soft woods; rib bones of animals were
used as castanets and jawbones of asses were dried, which loosened the teeth, and
these were shaken or raked with a stick. These small orchestras improvised "music"
which was the forerunner of modern jazz. Perhaps even more important was the slave
group singing, whose beauty of song numerous travelers and visitors to plantations
have attempted to describe.

It is more than possible that the first opera presented after the Louisiana Purchase
was the one-act *Le Secret,* at the Théâtre St. Pierre on September 14, 1808, and that
it was promoted by John Davis. Several one-act and two-act contemporary French
operas were presented the following winter, and by 1810 three theaters were presenting
operas along with dramas, comedies, and farces. Davis embarked on a long career of
opera presentation in 1818-19 at the new Théâtre d'Orleans, which was to be a
center of opera for many years until it burned in 1866. By 1820 several theaters were
presenting regular or irregular operatic seasons of varying length, whereas the North's
first real opera house was not opened in New York until 1833. By the 1840's the
orchestra of the French Opera was considered the best in the nation, and New Orleans
empresarios had little difficulty in securing the services of established operatic stars for
their seasons. Ante bellum Louisiana opera reached its climax in 1859 with the opening
of the New French Opera House and the great season of 1860-61, when Adelina
Patti charmed audiences from middle December until early March.

Many operas had their American *premières* in New Orleans, including Donizetti's
Lucia di Lammermoor, La Favorita, and *The Daughter of the Regiment;* Massenet's
Herodiade and *Werther;* Saint Saëns's *Samson and Delilah;* Gounod's *La Reine de
Saba;* Meyerbeer's *Les Huguenots* and *Il Profeta;* Verdi's *Rigoletto;* and Lalo's *Le
Roi d'Ys.*

Numerous concert artists visited Louisiana prior to 1860 and all of them appeared
in New Orleans. Ole Bull, the noted violinist, gave concerts between 1844 and 1854.
In 1853, Maurice Strakosch introduced young Adelina Patti, whom the *Picayune*
predicted would "certainly become a vocalist of remarkable power." When Jenny

Lind appeared in New Orleans in 1851, tickets for her first concert were sold at auction, the first bringing $240.

The most noted composer of the time was Louis Moreau Gottschalk, pianist and conductor, who wrote short and melodic piano compositions adapted from Negro and Creole music, along with some less successful serious music. His most noted works included "La Bamboula," "Danse des Ombres," "Ojos Criollos," "Cradle Song," "Danse Nègre," "La Savonne," and his favorite " La Morte." Ernest Guiraud's great reputation was won in France; he composed the opera *Le Roi David*, which was first performed at New Orleans in 1852 when he was only fifteen, and later the operas *Sylvie* and *Piccolino*. In 1875 he wrote the recitatives in Bizet's *Carmen*, which before that time had been spoken dialogue.

The Free Negro group of New Orleans produced a number of accomplished musicians after 1830. In 1838 they incorporated a Philharmonic Society which was empowered to give pay concerts and to employ music teachers to give free lessons to deserving and talented pupils; their orchestra boasted more than a hundred members. Lucien Lambers, a pianist and composer, made a European reputation and later settled in Brazil, while his brother Sidney, a violinist, remained in Europe and was decorated by the King of Portugal. Victor Macarthy was a popular New Orleans pianist; Basile Bares was the leading composer of dance music during the 1850's and a popular performer on the piano; Edmond Dede, a violinist, became popular in Europe and eventually director of the Bordeaux Orchestra; Joseph Beaumont wrote short songs on local and contemporary themes, "Toucoutou" being his best-remembered work.

New Orleans became noted as an art center, particularly for portrait artists, by the third decade of the American period. Rich merchants, planters, and businessmen took pride in having portraits painted of themselves and their families, and also were of the opinion that the possession of a few pictures of quality was a mark of the cultured gentleman. Throughout the period noted artists visited Louisiana, as they did other wealthy sections of the United States, in the hope of finding paying clients, but no native-born artists were produced who made reputations outside the state.

A group of New Orleans citizens organized the National Art Gallery of Painting in 1844, and three years later the noted collection of the Duke of Tuscany was sent to New Orleans in the hope it would be sold in its entirety to the National Art Gallery or some other group, but the venture was unsuccessful and the paintings found their way into the homes of wealthy Louisianians. James Robb was the period's most important collector of paintings, and before his collection was sold in 1859 it was one of the most noted in the nation.

Louisianians never appreciated sculpture as much as they did painting, although many carvings were purchased locally and abroad for home or garden decoration. The most noted single piece of sculpture brought to Louisiana during the period was probably the Clark Mills statue of General Jackson. In 1856 a New Orleans group undertook the rehabilitation of the old Place d'Armes parade ground and laid out a garden in which Mills's 20,000-pound statue, a replica of two others in Washington and Nashville, was placed at a cost of $30,000.

CHAPTER 20

ANTE BELLUM
SOCIAL LIFE

THE LOUISIANIANS. Louisiana and Louisianians were all things to all people who visited the state during those fabulous, and now all but legendary, ante bellum years. Some of the travelers and sojourners rhapsodized and embellished; others minutely examined, studied, and then criticized; still others traveled little or widely but in either case were wholly unable to comprehend the constantly changing kaleidoscope that was Louisiana. A few, like Mrs. Frances Trollope, to quote Mary Austin Holley, "began her tour at the wrong end. Went up the Mississippi when all genteel folks were coming down . . . like going to a watering place in the wrong season."

The citizenry of the state during those years may be divided into several categories —French or Spanish Creoles; Americans; newly arrived Irish, German, and other European immigrants; Free Negroes of all classes; and slaves. The Creoles further divided themselves into social and financial castes or strata, and it is more than probable that none of them agreed as to exactly which category families other than his own belonged. The "Old Creoles" were the top group, and attempted to "creolize" everything and everyone about them; they were *"sorti de la cuisse de Jupiter"* (a piece of Jupiter's thigh) or *de la fine fluer des pois* (of the finest sweet pea blossom). "Countrified" members of their group were labeled *Chacalatas*. Had the New England Cabots who spoke only to the Lowells and the Lowells who spoke only to God migrated to Louisiana, the "Old Creoles" would have snubbed them.

Those of long-time wealth lived in fine houses, were proud of their imported furniture, books, and musical instruments, sent their sons to school in France and their daughters to the convent of the Ursulines, attended the French theater, raced horses, gambled and dueled, and continued to dress in the fashions of a yesteryear. The men could enter only certain occupations or professions without losing social status. They could be bankers, planters, brokers, physicians, priests, or perhaps enter politics, but were barred from any occupation that involved working with the hands or taking off the coat. They treasured the qualities of friendship, kindness, and generosity. W. H. Sparks admitted that they were "more honest and less speculative; more honorable and less litigious; more sincere with less pretension; superior to trickery or low intrigue; more open and less designing; of nobler motives and less hypocrisy; more refined and less presumptuous, . . . of more chivalrous spirit and purer aspirations" than the incoming Americans.

The Creole lady was "a model of refinement—modest, yet free in her manners; chaste in her thoughts and deportment; generous in her opinions, and full of charity," and possessed other qualities which, according to Sparks, "makes them lovely, and to be loved." They were pious and firmly believed in the Church's admonition that the duty of a wife was to produce children at "the regular time." They were treated with a *toujours chapeau bas devant une femme* (always hat off before a woman) attitude, humored their children and their husbands, and passed on the old proverbs of an ancient and rural people—*chacun sait ce qui bouille dans sa chaudière* (each one knows what boils in his own pot)*, on lave son linge sale en famille* (wash your dirty clothes in your own family), and numerous others.

Creole homes were filled with relatives—it was said that a man married not only the Creole girl but her "five hundred relatives," some of whom were called *fainéants* (loafers) because they would not work. They were also filled with children of all sexes, sizes, and colors, for the children of slave house servants also had the run of the house.

The Creoles clung to their individualistic way of life, frowned upon intermarriage with Americans, refused to learn their language, were resentful and contemptuous of them, and considered those who were Protestants irreligious and wicked. In short they attempted to remain a distinct people. While they generally succeeded in the rural sections of South Louisiana, they steadily lost ground in New Orleans; they were seven to one in 1803, three to one in 1820, and two to one in 1830. But they were a tenacious people; the Age of the Creole would be a long time in dying.

Americans swarmed to Louisiana immediately after the purchase, and the tide of migration swelled after the War of 1812. The majority of the newcomers did not agree with the Old Creoles that if riches were worth winning they were also worth enjoying. Most of them were "hell-bent for business," and Sparks admitted that the American's maxim was: "It is honorable and respectable to succeed—dishonorable and disreputable to fail; it is only folly to yield a bold enterprise to nice considerations of moral right. If he can avoid the penalties of the civil law, success obviates those of the moral law." That they succeeded is a matter of record, and a few "grew so rich so rapidly as to mock the fable of Jonah's gourd." Although separated by broad barriers from the Old Creoles, the Americans in the South Louisiana plantation country and in New Orleans soon began to marry their daughters. Both nationalities were improved, as even some of the Creoles admitted.

The Irish, Germans, and other European immigrants settled for the most part in New Orleans or scattered through the state by families or in small groups seeking day labor. While the Germans were fairly well distributed over New Orleans, the Irish settled generally above Canal Street. In 1861 the *Daily Delta* reported that the Irish were for the most part "an intemperate and bloodthirsty set, who are never contented unless engaged in brawls, foreign or domestic—such as breaking of a stranger's pate or the blacking of a loving spouse's eye," but Richard Braniff reported that "the Irish Channel always bore a wonderful reputation because of the splendid class of people who lived there." Perhaps Jennie Green McDonald hit nearer the mark when she said: "Everything was very peaceful. A ship would come in loaded with . . . sailors, and the boys would come into the saloons and of course get into a fight. But our boys would bring 'em right home for a clean shirt and patch up where they'd been cut or hit too hard, and wash all the blood off and all. Everything was done real nice and quiet."

Free Negroes were concentrated in New Orleans, although many lived in small towns along the rivers or owned farms or plantations in various sections of the state, particularly along the south bank of the Red River or the lower Mississippi. In New Orleans, they engaged in business as merchants, money and real-estate brokers, and as barbershop, tailorshop, and other shop proprietors. A few of them, including the Dumas, Clovis, Lacroix, Legoaster, and Lafon families, gained individual fortunes of several hundred thousands of dollars. Some members of this upper financial group, as Charles Gayarré wrote, "educated their children, as they had been educated, in France," and took considerable interest in music, the drama, and literature. The Free Negroes of New Orleans during the ante bellum period attained the highest degree of financial success and the highest level of general culture attained by a similar racial group anywhere in the world.

The slave was everywhere, although he lived in fewer numbers in the northwestern and western sections of the state. He worked the farms and plantations and sometimes learned a trade such as carpentry, blacksmithing, brickmaking and bricklaying, sugar making, or mechanics. Often hired out by his master by the month or year, occasionally he was permitted to keep some of his wages and thus earn his freedom. He cohabited rather than lived with a wife in a married state, generally did not own property, and was seldom taught even the rudiments of reading and writing. On the whole he lived on about the same standard of existence as the common day laborer, and in some cases higher.

He was well treated, even pampered, or he was abused and punished for even slight misdemeanors, according to the temperament of the master. When William H. Russell, the noted English journalist, visited John Burnside's "Houmas" plantation above New Orleans in 1861, he observed slave boys and girls nine, ten, and eleven years old at play and wrote that he was glad to see that they were "exempted from the cruel fate which befalls poor children of their age in the mining and manufacturing districts of England." He might have added that the New England or Middle Atlantic states child was not infrequently forced because of the low wages of his father to begin factory work at an early age.

The American slave's treatment did not greatly differ from that of the European and, in some respects, the American laborer at this time. The European laborer received corporal punishment at the whim of his employer, he was often bound by long-term contract during which he lived under slave conditions, in some countries he was forbidden by law to hold property, and he received no education. American historians have never placed the institution of slavery in its proper time perspective in world history and compared or contrasted it with labor institutions in other nations. The fundamental difference between American Negro slave labor and European serfdom or other labor was that the American slave was always bound for life.

FROM PIONEER CABINS TO PLANTATION MANSIONS. Louisiana's ante bellum homes ranged from the rude cabins of slaves and pioneer and subsistence farmers to the palatial mansions of rich planters and town and country professional men and businessmen. Between the two extremes were ordinary frame houses inhabited by middle-class people of all occupations and varying degrees of economic standing.

Using such rudimentary tools as axes and augers, and sometimes in addition frows, drawing-knives, and crosscut saws, the pioneer or small farmer of the Florida Parishes or western, northern, or northwestern Louisiana built his log cabin with the assistance of his neighbors and lived in it until he could afford a more commodious house of rough-sawed lumber. Generally of British or long-settled American ancestry, he laid the pine logs parallel to the ground, roofed the building with hand-split shakes, tamped down an earthen floor or laid one of hewn, split logs, hung a door made of rough boards split from logs, and constructed a wooden fireplace and chimney well lined with clay. His door was hung on wooden hinges or leather straps and fastened with a wooden latch, and his entire house was mortised and held firmly with wooden pins; there were no nails or other ironwork anywhere in the structure.

Occasionally a double cabin would be built, two separated rooms with a roofed gallery between them, and sometimes with a gallery in front of the whole. If he wanted a large house he built a "double-pen" type, two or more rooms in a row in two separate sections all under one roof with a long and wide hall dividing the two sections.

Home furnishings were few and were handmade with the simple tools available; crudely made beds, tables, chairs, stools, cupboards, and chests and large clothes-presses for the storage of clothing and other items. Cooking kettles, pots, spiders, pans, Dutch ovens and other heavy, cast-iron cooking utensils stood by the fireplace, which might have a swing-out crane for hanging heavy pots and kettles. Crockery, crude china, or tin cups, plates, and dishes were used, as were knives, forks, and spoons made of steel or heavy tin. Skins, homemade quilts, or rough, heavy blankets covered the straw, feather, or grass mattresses.

Farther south, the simple homes of the French and Spanish Creoles were little changed from those of the colonial period. The typical "Acadian" house, as it is still sometimes called today, had a high, steep roof enclosing a front gallery or porch and attic bedrooms, the stairway to which was on the outside, at one end of the gallery. The timbers and rough-sawed boards were vertical, mortised, and wooden-pegged. The space between the outside weatherboarding and the inside boards was usually stuffed with clay and moss daubing. A picket fence enclosed the small yard. The house furnishings were homemade and simply constructed, as in the case of the American farmers.

In contrast to these homes were plantation or city mansions of varying degrees of elegance, built according to French or English architectural styles, with kitchens removed completely or in one wing of the house. The common pattern was two large rooms on either side of the large hall extending through the house and from which an open stairway led upstairs. Sometimes the dining room and kitchen were behind one side, forming an ell. A gallery usually crossed the entire front, frequently extended down the two sides, and occasionally encircled the entire house.

The names of ante bellum Louisiana plantation homes suggested Creole sensibility and American energy. There were "Versailles," "Chateau de Clery," "Fontainebleau," and "Austerlitz"; "Chatsworth," "Belle Grove," and "Highland"; "Ivanhoe," "Rob Roy," "Kenilworth," and "Nottaway"; "White Castle," "Alhambra," and "Rose-down"; "Old Hickory," "Uncle Sam," and "Rattle and Snap," and hundreds of others. One of them, at New Iberia, and now considered one of the finest examples of home architecture in America, was called "The Shadows." While a few of these mansions were designed by architects, the great majority were designed and built by the owners with the assistance of a carpenter or two and the plantation slaves. Slaves were occasionally talented in decorative carving, and some interior and exterior trimming was executed by them, one of the best examples being at "Afton Villa" plantation in West Feliciana Parish. Many of these stout and palatial old mansions, remindful of Louisiana's romantic past, are still standing, and efforts are being made with increased zeal to preserve them.

Numbers of these plantation homes were fronted, flanked, or even surrounded with formal or informal gardens, and practically every traveler who visited Louisiana during this period rhapsodized over their trees, shrubs, and flowers. When Mary Austin Holley visited "Good Hope" plantation on the German Coast in the late 1820's she wrote that the lower river country was a "veritable *Cote d'Or*. . . . We seem to be in the midst of the beauties of nature. . . . If you wish to know what luxurious living is, you must come here. It does not consist of the quantity of things but in their variety and delicacy and exact arrangement. The roses and geraniums are still blooming and the beauty of the orange trees exceeds my imagination. You get no idea of them from the puny yellow things you have seen." Lafcadio Hearn wrote later that the garden of "Le Petit Versailles" was filled with "every known variety of exotic trees, with all species of fantastic shrubs, with the rarest floral products of both hemispheres."

These homes were filled with furniture from the best artisans of America and Europe, and many of them had unusual features. Huge punkah fans (sometimes called *chasses mouches*) were kept in motion by slave boys to stir up a little breeze and/or to keep the flies off dining-room tables. After 1835 many were equipped with gas lights, and the "new patent wash stand with a shower-bath attached" made its appearance in the 1840's. Outside of Bernard Marigny's house was a huge plantation bell which had been cast with more than a thousand silver dollars (many Louisianians returning from the Mexican War brought home Mexican silver dollars for this purpose). "Shady Grove" was completed in 1857 and had a bathroom, while "Walnut

Grove" had running from the dining room to the kitchen a miniature railroad used to bring in the piping-hot food.

COTTONADE AND CRINOLINE. Until late in the period most of the clothing of the common people of frontier or small farms was homemade of cotton, wool, or linsey-woolsey; by the 1840's and 1850's northern domestics had made their appearance, but were "'only worn on extraordinary occasions" by most people. Women wore simple dresses of homespun cloth with tight- or loose-fitting bodices and wide, flowing skirts made by hand without a sewing machine, rough or fashioned shoes made by an itinerant shoemaker, and sunbonnets with the front and sides stiffened with canes. Men wore pants of cottonade with alternating blue and white thread, homemade shirts and shoes, jumpers or rough coats, and straw, split-cane, or reed hats.

By the 1830's stores were beginning to advertise manufactured clothing for men, although the women still patronized the dressmaker or if they were really fashionable, the modiste. The acceptance of ready-made clothing progressed slowly, but, aided by the advertising of the firm of Tulane and Baldwin in New Orleans, was generally accepted by the 1850's. The idea of ready-made clothing appealed to the imagination of the common people; it had democratic implications, and as John S. Kendall wrote, "it placed within the reach even of the remotest wilderness dandy the opportunity to array himself according to the latest mode." The newspapers, even in the small towns, soon began to advertise frock coats and coatees, vests, pantaloons, suspenders, hats, boots, gloves, and other accessories. But for a long time a prejudice continued against the creases, now "regarded as so essential to elegance in masculine attire," creases which were originally caused when ready-made clothing was baled under pressure to be shipped from the factory.

The fashionable gentleman of town and country was an "elegant bird of paradise." He wore fine, "low pressure" beaver hats in a multitude of colors; beaver, horse-skin, and buckskin gloves; frock coats, coatees, vests, pants, and overcoats in widely variant and contrasting colors and materials, even including velvet; socks of cotton, wool, or silk; and shoes from bootmakers of New Orleans, or even London or Paris. Occasionally he became an eccentric in his dress; during the 1850's J. H. Ingraham described an aged and thin French gentleman: "He wore a long nankin blouse (a sort of loose frock-coat) and a yellow vest with bright buttons, gray trowsers [sic] and drab gaiters—altogether a peculiar costume, expecially with his hat, which had a brim so narrow that two flies could not walk arm-in-arm around it, while the gray, weather-worn crown rose upward into the air above him like a rusty stove-pipe."

Fashionable ladies of New Orleans, the smaller towns, and the rich plantation country were, as Sir Charles Lyell wrote during the 1840's, "attired in Parisian fashion, not over dressed, usually not so thin as the generality of American women." They patronized such dressmaking establishments as The Olympic or Scanlan's in New Orleans, frequently paid a quadroon hairdresser by the month, used perfumes and all types of cosmetics, and wore, according to traveler Lillian Foster, "the most superb laces, embroideries and artificial flowers on this side of the Atlantic."

A favored few "ladies of fashion" were able to purchase talented slave seamstresses, and during the early years of the period kept a Negro slave boy "dressing maid"— note the following advertisement: "For sale, a very handsome negro lad, nineteen years old . . . has no fault whatever. His mistress parts with him because, having bought him when a child; she has used him principally as a dressing maid, and he is now too old to do this service for a lady."

The debutante or society matron wore velvet and Marseilles, Irish linen and lawns, Swiss muslins and bobbinets, Carlisle and Cambric ginghams, fringed silk, gauze, and velvet belts and bonnet ribbons, printed and plain Dunstable bonnets, colored bombazines, French and Swiss silks, Spanish shawls, light-colored paper-weight shoes (sometimes actually made of paper), "kiss-me-quick-before-mother-sees-you" bonnets, and late in the period tight-bodiced, hoop-skirted ballroom costumes. She carried herself so exquisitely that one visiting Frenchman was moved to esthetically exclaim: "There is a naivete and simple grace in the ladies that we see not in France, at least not exactly like it. . . . They seem to combine the splendor and haughty bearing of the Spanish women, with the tender loveliness of the Italian, the bonhomie of the French, and the discretion and repose of the English: a noble combination which would constitute a perfect national character."

PLAIN COOKS AND ARTISTS OF CUISINE. The northern author of an ante bellum cookbook who wrote in his preface that "The American stomach has too long suffered from the vile concoctions inflicted on it by untutored cooks. . . . the American kitchen is the worst in the world" was evidently not acquainted with Louisiana Creole cookery. The climate and natural features of Louisiana gave its people a wider variety of foods than most other Americans.

All types of meats and plentiful game and wild fowl, fresh- and salt-water fish, oysters, shrimp, crabs, and turtles (which Governor Paul Hebert raised in Bayou Goula just back of "Home Place") were obtainable for table use. Numerous varieties of vegetables, fruits, and berries were cultivated, as were corn, rice, wheat, and other grains. Common staples were brought from the northern states, while fancier goods were imported from Europe or other sections of the world. Water came from cisterns, dug wells, or from the rivers and bayous and was purified with alum. Ice for cooling drinks and for ice cream was brought from the North during the late winter and stored in icehouses to last through the summer and fall months, until the late 1850's when it began to be manufactured.

South Louisianians continued to label everything "Creole." They raised "Creole" cattle, which produced "Creole" milk, from which was made "Creole" butter. Their "Creole" chickens laid "Creole" eggs; even their vegetables, nuts, and fruits were so named. They prepared gastronomic masterpieces such as bouillabaisse, gumbos, court bouillon, *daube glacée,* jambalaya, and grillades, or such simple dishes as *pain perdu* (lost bread) and hominy grits. Timothy Flint reported during the early 1820's that at one plantation home he had for breakfast "duck-pies, milk, custards, coffee and claret." Their ladies frequently drank iced orange-flower or violet-syrup water on warm summer afternoons when it was too uncomfortable for *café noir.*

In northern, western, and northwestern Louisiana the southern brand of American cooking was the rule, with most of the dishes being comparatively simple, without much seasoning, and of the fried, boiled, or roasted variety. The common people ate corn meal and wheat breads, fried beef, pork, wild game, or fowl, a few staple vegetables, and drank thin coffee. Following his own particular culinary heritage, the North Louisianian ate well, and at Fourth of July celebrations and on other festive days he enjoyed the traditional barbecued beef, lamb, fowl, or pork, to which were added "piles of bread, bowls of Irish potatoes, dishes of tomato sauce, tubs of savory hash," and other dishes.

Any reasonable excuse offered opportunity for a plantation dinner. One group of plantation owners living on Bayou Teche met every Sunday at the home of one or another for dinner, conversation, and card or domino playing. At these feasts as many as fifty guests might enjoy as many courses as there were "billows of the sea," and "each billow was enough to drown a common apetite." At some formal dinners it was a long-established custom for the gentlemen to lead the ladies into the dining room, stand behind them acting as individual waiters until they had finished, then escort them to the ladies' sitting room, after which the men returned to take possession of the table.

On June 6, 1861, William H. Russell breakfasted with John Burnside at "Houmas" plantation. At a reasonable hour Pompey, the Negro manservant, appeared with a "glassful of brandy, sugar, and peppermint beneath an island of ice—an obligatory panacea for all the evils of climate." After a while Pompey returned with the second glass, remarking that "Massa say fever very bad this morning." Then he came back with the third glass, remarking, "Massa says, sir, you had better take this, because it'll be the last he make before breakfast." The breakfast included "grilled fowl, prawns, eggs and ham, fish from New Orleans, potted salmon from England, preserved meats from France, claret, iced water, coffee and tea, varieties of hominy, mush, and African vegetable preparations."

In the larger towns, and particularly in New Orleans, peddlers sold meats, vegetables, fruits, and prepared edibles. Their picturesque chants advertised the specialties of each seller:

> Cantal—ope—ah!
> Fresh and fine,
> Just offa de vine,
> Only a dime!

Or,

> Oyster Man! Oyster Man!
> Get your fresh oysters from the Oyster Man!
> Bring out your pitcher, bring out your can,
> Get your nice fresh oysters from the Oyster Man!

Sometimes the peddler added a bit of humor to his chant:

> The Waffle Man is a fine old man.
> He washes his face in a frying-pan,
> He makes his waffles with his hand,
> Everybody loves the Waffle Man.

Or,

> Icecream, Lemonade,
> Brown Sugar and rotten aig!

Louisianians of that day drank well, and often, even in North Louisiana, although as Fred Williamson has written it was sometimes necessary to offer plausible and implausible pretexts: "One man had the gout, and a stimulating potion would drive it away; a second had a cold, and it would warm him; a third was warm and it would cool him; a fourth was disturbed in spirit, and it would obliterate his care; a fifth was afraid of the foulness of the water, and it would purify it; a sixth was nervous and it would steady his nerve."

In the Creole and American sections farther south planters generally kept an inexhaustible supply of potables, a practice well summarized by Louise Butler, who was perhaps writing particularly of her own "Cottage" plantation in West Feliciana: "Sometimes in one half of the storeroom, but more frequently in a separate cellar, were clarets from Bordeaux, in casks for everyday consumption, in bottles for special occasions; various Chateaux, as Margaux, Lafitte, Y-quem; widows of the irresistible-to-men Cliquot type hobnobbing with Benedictine, Chartreuse and other representatives of a strictly celibate priesthood; port, also in bottles; tokay and Madeira in five-gallon demijohns; Bass' Pale Ale from the land of good ale if not good cakes; labeled rarities in darker bottles and champagne in wicker baskets." New Orleanians and South Louisianians began to drink cocktails, "coolers," and other concoctions during the period: mint juleps of many varieties, cobblers, eggnogs, gin sling, whiskey punch, Tom and Jerry, Tip and Ty, I. O. U., Vox Populi, Silver Top, Virginia Fancy, Smasher, Heater, Knickerbocker, Poor Man's Punch, Moral Suasion, and many, many others.

Guzzle shops and barrel houses had made their appearance along Gallatin, Levee, Peters, and other New Orleans streets by the 1840's, and at such places a man could get a glassful of fiery and potent concoctions for a nickel or a dime. Proprietors not infrequently made their own intoxicants. Port wine was made with burnt sugar, prunes, cherries, alcohol, and water, with a little olive oil added to provide a tawny taste. Ordinary wines were simple mixtures of one part straight alcohol and two or three parts water, slightly colored and flavored to taste. Irish whiskey was made by dumping varying quantities of creosote into a barrel of neutral spirits. Herbert Asbury wrote that "from dawn to dusk the district slept off its debauches behind closed shutters; from dusk to dawn the dives roared full blast," and that the stranger who entered Gallatin Street at Ursuline "with money in his pocket and came out at Barracks with his wealth intact and his skull uncracked had performed a feat which bordered on the miraculous."

The lower orders of Louisiana citizenry ate with speed, noise, and uncouth table manners so well described by Mrs. Trollope: ". . . the voracious rapidity with which the viands were seized and devoured, . . . the loathsome spitting, from the contamination of which is was absolutely impossible to protect our dresses; the frightful manner of feeding with their knives, till the whole blade seemed to enter into the mouth; and the still more frightful manner of cleaning the teeth afterwards with a pocket knife, soon forced us to feel that we were not surrounded by the generals, colonels, and majors of the old world."

In New Orleans more genteel people drank and dined leisurely and well and with proper manners at such popular cafés and coffeehouses as the Café des Améliorations, Café des Exilés, Café des Émigrés (also called the Café des Réfugiés), Café de Ville, Café des Quatre Saisons, Victor's, or at the dining rooms of the St. Charles, St. Louis, or other hotels. The most popular luncheon place for judges, planters, merchants, and other businessmen was Maspero's Exchange (called by the French "La Bourse de Maspero") at the corner of St. Louis and Chartres. Said to have been built in 1788, it was occupied by Pierre Maspero during the first decade of the century. In 1838 he sold out to James Hewlett, who laid a new cypress floor, installed a new bar, and enlarged the café facilities. Maspero's is still in operation (though now only liquid refreshments are served) under the ownership and active management of Arthur Lamazou, the most noted "mixologist" of present-day New Orleans.

MEDICINE AND SOCIAL WELFARE. While the local press and even such out-of-state publications as *Niles' Register* advertised the healthfulness of Louisiana's climate and the longevity of its citizens, they suffered the ordinary ills of mankind in addition to the visits of yellow fever, cholera, small pox, and other less deadly epidemic diseases. Cholera first struck Louisiana in 1832, and it was estimated that almost 6,000 people died of the disease during the following two years. Lesser epidemics hit the state in 1848, 1849, 1850, 1854, and 1855. Yellow fever had first visited the Louisiana colony in 1769, and other epidemics were recorded during later colonial years. After 1810 epidemics grew more serious; fifteen were recorded between that year and 1837, the epidemic of 1833 being the most serious to strike the state. Between 1837 and 1853 it was estimated that over 10,000 lives were lost because of the disease.

The most serious yellow-fever epidemic in the state's history occurred in 1853, when the official death total of New Orleans alone was 7,849, but according to many estimates was nearer 12,000. By late June it was estimated that 20 per cent of the inhabitants had fled the city. Two months later one observer wrote that "Funeral processions crowded every street. No vehicles could be seen except doctors' cabs and coaches, passing to and from the cemeteries, and hearses, often solitary, making their way toward those gloomy destinations. The hum of trade was silent. The levee was a desert. The streets, wont to shine with fashion and beauty, were silent." Desperate prophylactic measures were taken to combat the disease. Cannons were fired, barrels of tar were burned at regular intervals along the streets, bedding and clothing of patients were burned, privies were disinfected with carbolic acid and sulphate of iron, homes were fumigated with sulphuric acid, gutters were flushed. New Orleans was a place of horror and did not recover until 1855.

Most ante bellum doctors were trained by being apprenticed to older physicians. While larger towns and cities had enough doctors to care for the sick, there was a general deficiency in rural areas and small towns, and people largely depended upon home remedies and patent medicines. There were few specialists, although dentists were beginning to operate as a special group. As early as 1825 dentists were insuring teeth for life, at an annual charge of $5.00 per person in family groups or $10.00 per single individual. The most unusual dentist in the state had his chair set up on a platform at the French Market in New Orleans and pulled teeth in full view of curious onlookers; once the victim was seated, the dentist's band struck up loudly and the militant tooth was yanked without benefit of anesthetic.

During the 1830's "Thompsonian" doctors, who believed in "root" medicine as opposed to "mineral" medicines, caused considerable controversy. Leeches were used throughout the period, and giant Hungarian leeches were considered more efficient than their smaller American cousins. Most doctors prescribed large quantities of castor oil and the same drugs, oils, essences, liniments, and other nauseous concoctions used by preceding generations of medical practitioners.

It was the age of the quack and of cure-everything patent medicines. One physician advertised that he could cure "with the greatest ease" a list of over twenty diseases by the use of "direct magnetism." Dr. Christie's galvanic belts, necklaces, and bracelets, together with his magnetic fluids, were guaranteed to cure nervous diseases, convulsions, deafness, and palpitation of the heart. One medical treatise promised to enable the reader to change his "sallow face into one of Beauty," to make his "Wrinkled Skin Smooth," to make his "Brown Teeth as White as Pearls," to preserve his eyesight for life, and to hasten the growth of whiskers and moustachios. Mexican Mustang Liniment had been used by the Aztecs and therefore must be efficacious; it would cure rheumatism, sores, fistula, cracked heels, ulcers, tumors, and spavin. Sutton's Harrodsburg Water, which had been analyzed by Transylvania University, cured every disease or ill from hypochondria to dyspepsia to piles. Manufacturers of bitters and nostrums with a high alcoholic content made fortunes by securing endorsements from temperance leaders and selling their products to those opposed to the drinking of spirituous liquors.

Occasionally editors lashed out at the preposterous claims with biting ridicule. In 1838, for example, the editor of the *Louisianian* wrote that Dr. Brandreth's Universal Pills would not only cure St. Vitus' dance, smallpox, swellings, black jaundice, fevers of all types, and other diseases, but had other and very practical uses: ". . . one Pill . . . worn in each pocket will instantly give ease and plasticity to the tightest pantaloons. A like quantity will create an appetite in the most delicate stomach; or physic a horse. They will also be found to give a rich flavor to apple dumplings, and a peculiar zest to pickled oysters; they will thicken soup, reduce corpulent persons, and are excellent bait for mouse-traps. One pill dissolved in a bucket of rain-water, will be found a perfect water proof lining for canal embankments; placed in steamboat boilers will effectually prevent their bursting, and greatly increase the speed of the boat."

Superstitious cures were numerous. Children wore alligator-tooth necklaces to assist them in cutting teeth; cannon shots killed germs; cobwebs cured open wounds; balsam apples soaked in whiskey cured snakebite; banana leaves cured headaches; Catholic children were vowed to the Virgin and wore white and blue cords around the waist; crushed crab and crawfish eyes were a cure for everything. Colored voodoo doctors and sorcerers did a thriving business, with whites as well as with Negroes.

The practice of medicine, however, made considerable progress. The Medical Society of New Orleans was incorporated in 1818, and two years later the Physico-Medical Society was organized. The Louisiana State Board of Health was first organized in 1821, operated for four years, and was reorganized in 1855. Many physicians studied and experimented and made important contributions to medicine. Dr. François Prevost of Donaldsonville performed the first Caesarean section in the nation during the early 1830's; Dr. Charles Luzenberg was the first to successfully perform intestinal operations and to suture the end of the bowel; Dr. Warren Stone was the first to resect ribs and to compress and ligate arteries; Dr. Charles Faget discovered methods for early diagnosis of yellow fever and was the first to successfully administer chloroform in obstetrical cases; Dr. John L. Riddell invented the binocular microscope and discovered many of the microscopic characteristics of the blood.

The state gave some assistance to Charity Hospital, to other hospitals in the state, to the Howard Association, and to various medical societies. The 24-bed Charity Hospital of Spanish days burned in 1809, and the ground for a new 120-bed hospital was broken in 1815. Another new building was completed in 1839 and an addition nine years later, which enabled 1,000 patients to be accommodated. In 1849 the total hospital income was almost $90,000, and nearly 16,000 patients were admitted.

Until the 1840's parish police juries cared for the deaf, dumb, blind, and insane; after that time the state began to provide institutions for these unfortunates. By 1860 the institution for the deaf, dumb, and blind at Baton Rouge was believed "to be inferior to no establishment of a similar character in our country." Throughout the period orphans were usually cared for by private or religious asylums.

AMUSEMENTS. The Creoles were a gay and festive people, imparting much of their spontaneous and residual zest for living to Louisianians of other nationalistic heritage. Americans who first settled in New Orleans thought the Creoles pleasure-mad, but it was not long before they were, at least in part, agreeing with Bernard Marigny that certain rich men "were born dead, since they never knew how to live." A few would have agreed with the Creole adage, "pleasure and balls when one is young, church and prayer when one is old."

Everyone enjoyed celebrations and rallies, processions and barbecues, fireworks displays and holiday parades. They played billiards, cards, chess, checkers, dominoes, and other indoor games. A Louisiana chess player, Paul Morphy, became one of the best of his generation, successfully touring Europe just before the Civil War. The people attended circuses which traveled about the state in long wagon trains or those which toured in steamboats up and down the rivers and bayous. They went on steamboat parties, chartering a boat for a river cruise, complete with chef, bartender, and band. At Fourth of July celebrations they saw the militia drill, sat down to picnic dinners, heard band concerts, witnessed sports events, listened to speeches by state political leaders, and drank toasts to "the day we celebrate," "the Constitution," and other patriotic institutions, events, or personages.

They heard concerts of all types, as for example those of "Ellene, the Italian Troubadour," who could play at the same time six different instruments—violin, Italian flute, Turkish cymbal, Chinese parasol, drum, and triangle. They attended the cotillions of numerous dancing academies where young ladies and gentlemen demonstrated their newly acquired abilities in dancing quadrilles, *valses un temps, valses à deux temps, valses à trois temps,* polkas, *polasazurkas,* and that newly imported craze, La Moscowiska Polka. They heard lectures on every conceivable subject, from "Electro-Biology" to "Nitrous Oxide Gas" to hypnotism, spiritualism, and birds and animals. And after 1840 ladies might be seen walking or driving along the streets of towns and even villages to newly established ice-cream saloons for refreshment.

In the northern and western sections of the state harvest time was the season for mutual aid, neighborhood feasts, "play parties," candy pullings, and camp meetings. In the Creole country Saturday-night balls and dances were a universal institution. On Saturday morning a youth, carrying a cane pole to which was fastened a red or white flag, rode along the countryside waving the flag. He stopped at the house where the evening's festivities were to be held and tied the pole to the fence, where it would advertise, "This is the place." By sundown families began arriving on horseback and in various wheeled vehicles. The older adults played *vingt-et-un* (twenty-one) or other card games and talked while the young danced and engaged in frivolous or serious flirtations. "The dance was continued until the party was dispersed by the appearance of the sun the following morning," as Thomas C. Nicholls wrote. "Creole girls I found beautiful and fascinating and there was a total absence of all parade and etiquette; each person seemed to come for the purpose of receiving and communicating pleasure and everything was mirth and happiness."

Ordinary "visiting" by entire families might last from a day to a week, or even longer. "Spending the day" involved a huge dinner; riding, hunting, games of various types, or conversation in the afternoon; another huge meal at suppertime; and an evening of games, dancing, and conversation. Group singing around the piano or organ was enjoyed by all, and in 1849, for example, such new sheet music hits as "Dig, Dig, Dig," "The Moonbeam Waltz," "Lonely Rose," "What are the Wild Waves Saying," "Maiden's Dream," and the "Jenny Gray Polka" were popular.

One Friday morning in early January, 1842, according to his diary, Bennet H. Barrow went visiting and after a day of enjoyment brought a group "to my House to dinner, sent & collected the neighbors . . . danced all night by the Piano & Violin." He would not let anyone leave the next day, which was spent in resting and sleeping. "At dark began to dance, at 12 Oclock their consciences made them refuse to dance any Longer, it Being Saturday night, to punish them fastened the doors 'till near two OK   some blew the Lights out   others tried to get out at the windows, Any thing, but dance they would'ent,   retired at 2 OK   all nearly broke down,   never have seen a collection so sudden and so perfectly free   easy & happy for two days & nights, All restraint thrown aside   never enjoyed myself so much." On Sunday he reported that there were "Many Long & weary Looking faces sore feet &c."

People of all ages and sexes hunted and fished, and, particularly in the Florida Parishes, rode to hounds. In South Louisiana the men sometimes killed an ox and then shot at the old Creole *papegai* to win various portions of the animal. By the 1830's boat clubs were popular, and in 1838 the Eagle Boat Club of Bayou Sara challenged the Feliciana Boat Club to race them "to the tune of five hundred dollars." In the early fall of 1841 the first hunting trip of the steamer *Nimrod,* which belonged to the Barrow clan of West Feliciana Parish, was announced. Foot racing was popular during the 1840's. Animal fights had been common during early ante bellum years but had about died out by 1830; in 1817 a series of exhibitions at the New Orleans Amphitheatre featured fights between an Atakapas bull and six dogs, six bulldogs against a Canadian bear, a tiger against a black bear, and an Opelousas bull against twelve dogs.

During the 1830's horseracing became one of Louisiana's most popular sports, and within two decades it was claimed that New Orleans "was the focal point of American horse-racing." During the period the Metairie and Eclipse tracks at New Orleans, the Magnolia course at Baton Rouge, the Fashion course at Clinton, and the St. Francis- ville track, as well as others, became known over the entire United States. In 1838 the *Spirit of the Time,* the nation's foremost sporting magazine, averred that the St. Francisville track was "as well adapted for quick time as the Union Course, Long Island. In location, soil, or beauty, it is not surpassed by any race track we ever saw." Meanwhile Alexander Porter, Alexander Barrow, C. C. S. Farrar, Duncan Kenner, William R. Barrow, Thomas J. Wells, Bennet H. Barrow, Fergus Duplantier, John B. Dawson, and several other Louisiana sportsmen became leaders of the Louisiana turf and won many races with Linnet, Mad Anthony, Josh Bell, Gray Medoc, Lecompte, and other noted horses.

Gambling for high stakes was a passion with many ante bellum Louisianians. Poker, twenty-one or black jack, seven-up or old sledge, and faro were probably the most popular card games, but numerous bets were made on three-card monte, the shell game, and other hand-is-quicker-than-the-eye games of chance. Steamboats usually had a game going for the entire voyage, and such professional gamblers as Jim Miner (also known as Umbrella Jim and the Poet Gambler) and George Devol made and lost fortunes. In one three-day game between wealthy planter Jules Devereaux and three professional gamblers the bar bill was nearly $800, and Devereaux's losses were said to have approximated $100,000. One of gambling's classic anecdotes is said to have originated with gambler Canada Bill, who was marooned for a night in a small river town. He finally found a game, and when his partner discovered the game was crooked and urged him to quit, remarked, "I know it, but it's the only game in town."

Louisianians who could afford it, frequently vacationed at various "watering places" to escape the summer's heat or to improve their health. They went to Pass Christian, Mississippi; White Sulphur Springs or other springs in Virginia; Saratoga, New York; and a few visited Havana, which, according to one traveler, was only the distance of "forty-eight cigars and twelve brandy cocktails" from New Orleans. Many stayed within the state and vacationed at Castor Springs, about thirty-five miles northwest of Harrisonburg; at Buffalo White Sulphur Springs, about the same distance southwest of the same town; or at Last Island off the Gulf Coast until the tragic storm of 1856.

New Orleans was the most popular winter resort in the Lower Mississippi Valley and Louisianians enjoyed its fashionable winter social seasons. Many entries in old diaries or reminiscences are similar to that of R. LeGrand Johnston, who wrote of his kinsman, Colonel Claudius LeGrand of Milliken's Bend, in northeast Louisiana above Vicksburg: "In the opera season in New Orleans, Colonel LeGrand, with his daughters and a train of servants, would go to the St. Charles Hotel and stay until it was over."

The Crescent City was also a pleasure mecca patronized by the wealthy of the nation; witness a British traveler's description of the weekly ball at the St. Charles: "Marvellous collection! The blonde from New England, and the southern planter's son; the brunette from Georgia or Alabama or interior parish of Louisiana; and the male representative of Western trade or Eastern manufactures, or British mercantile snobbishness, dancing vis-a-vis. . . . Here, too, is a modest beauty from Ohio (papa in the pork trade); there a dashing belle, whose altars at Saratoga and the Sulphur-Springs are yet warm with sacrifices of her last summer admirers (her third winter at New Orleans, and no husband yet). . . . Every state with its peculiar beauty in the room. . . . There will be music, dancing, nonsense, eating, and flirting, until three o'clock in the morning, and—the same thing for three or four months thereafter." The winter season in New Orleans, with its Mardi Gras balls, horseracing, sailing on the lake, shopping tours, gambling, dining, and drinking at fashionable hotels and cafés, and other pleasures made that city the most renowned in the country.

Mulattoes of culture and/or wealth gave their own balls at the St. Philip Theater, and later at the Orleans Ballroom. Slaves and low-class Free Negroes danced the calinda, the bamboula, the carabine, the pile chactas, the Congo, or other violent, sensuous, and orgiastic dances at Congo Square. The square was closed to such dances for a few years during the late 1830's and early 1840's but was opened again by the city government in 1845.

The custom of celebrating Mardi Gras originated in southern Europe, was brought to Louisiana by the French, and later was continued by the Spanish. During colonial days, however, it only involved masking and parading along the streets on Shrove Tuesday. Masking was forbidden by the Spanish during the 1790's, was revived after the Louisiana Purchase, but was again forbidden by the Americans in 1806. Masked balls were permitted after 1823, and by 1827 masked marchers were thronging the streets of New Orleans and other South Louisiana towns.

The first formal masked Mardi Gras parade was held in 1838, and according to the *Daily Picayune* featured "several carriages superbly ornamented—bands of music, horses richly caparisoned—personations of knights, cavaliers, heroes, demigods," and other figures, all mounted. The following year it was reported that "a thousand balls" were held during the weeks following Twelfth Night. The Mistick Krew of Comus was organized in the dining rooms above the Gem Saloon on Royal Street in January, 1857, and used Milton's *Paradise Lost* as the theme of their mounted and foot parade.

The fabulous social life of ante bellum Louisiana was never regained after the War for Southern Independence; it died with the booming guns of Fort Sumter. Bernard Marigny, according to Grace King "the last of Creole landed aristocracy, the representative of the strength, the follies, the wealth of a past generation," died in 1868. Many plantation mansions were destroyed during the war, and after 1865 others fell to ruin because their owners could no longer afford to keep them in repair. Many have been restored in recent times, in some cases by northern owners who became enamored of the South, but each year they became fewer in number because of fires, the changing of river courses, or the attacks of industrial progress. The civilization of that era became a legend, passed on to two and perhaps three generations. Today no one lives who remembers the ante bellum years.

Louise Butler of the "Cottage" plantation phrased it well a few years ago, when she wrote of the planter and his home and his civilization: "Ended is the era he made notable. Silent is his old home now, its voice of plaint or pleasure no more heard, its walls fallen or given over to ignoble usages. Here, there, one remains, but

> The grand old house is standing still,
> A stranger's foot is on the sill.

. . . No echo from that vivid, sweet and vanished life? Yes, for the spirit that listens can still hear it, as you of the future will hear it, fainter, sweeter, receding but *never* dying. . . ."

In the office of the Department of History at Louisiana State University hangs a photograph, the work of promising young photographer Roy J. Bailey. It shows only a giant oak and beyond it silent, solitary pillars pointing toward the sky, all that remains of "Belle Grove," one of the most notable of Louisiana's great plantation mansions. Roy Bailey titled his photograph "Faded Glory."

PART SIX

Civil War and
Military Occupation

CHAPTER 21

"THE SWORD OF THE LORD
AND OF GIDEON"

THE GATHERING CLOUDS. Twenty years before the Election of 1860, New Jersey–born, thirty-nine-year-old New Orleans businessman Paul Tulane, son of a French Santo Domingan exile, toured France with his father, and during the tour visited the ports of Nantes and Bordeaux. In Bordeaux, Tulane later wrote, "I saw the gates of warehouses hanging by one hinge, and a cobbler patching old shoes in a room in a noble mansion—a mansion which was almost a palace."

On the journey home Paul asked his father why he had selected such sad places to visit, to which Louis Tulane replied: "For a purpose, my son, Nantes and Bordeaux were built up by the West India trade. The abolition of slavery there destroyed them. You will see New Orleans, which, like them, is dependent on slavery, fall into like circumstances." Subsequently, the old man mentioned the subject again, saying that slavery in the United States would one day be destroyed and that "New Orleans will be ruined," little realizing that within two decades his prophecy would come true. The election of 1860 led to the secession of the southern states and civil war; the following seventeen years were the most tragic in all Louisiana history.

The slavery issue had long troubled the American people. During the colonial period of the Atlantic-seaboard states the people of the North had held slaves, but as slave labor was not profitable there, the northern colonies and states gradually abolished the institution by legislation. By 1820 the North had begun to agitate for the abolition of the institution of slavery in the South; after the founding of William Lloyd Garrison's *Liberator* in 1831, the movement became a crusade led by self-righteous, self-appointed reformers, and within a few years antislavery agitation politically divided the nation.

It was hoped that the Compromise of 1850 had settled the slavery problem permanently, but a series of events occurring during the 1850's further excited and in many cases inflamed the people of both North and South. In 1852, Harriet Beecher Stowe's bitter antislavery novel *Uncle Tom's Cabin* appeared, and within two years over a million copies were sold in the North. Southerners generally did not read the book, but many of them, as did historian Charles Campbell of Virginia, "read enough of it to condemn it" and its one-sided picture of the South. In 1854 the Republican party was organized principally to oppose the extension of slavery in the territories, and shortly afterwards a bloody struggle began between northern and southern settlers for the control of Kansas Territory. In 1857 the Dred Scott Decision of the Supreme Court irritated the North.

The Lincoln-Douglas Debates of 1858 helped crystallize public opinion in both South and North and the next year John Brown's Raid on Harper's Ferry, Virginia, by which Brown hoped to begin a series of Negro insurrections, stirred the South as nothing heretofore had done. In middle December of the same year, newly elected Superintendent of the Louisiana State Seminary of Learning, Colonel William Tecumseh Sherman, wrote to his wife: "As long as the abolitionists and the Republicans seem to threaten the safety of slave property so long will this excitement last, and no one can foresee its result."

In his last message to the legislature on January 17, 1860, Governor Robert C. Wickliffe reviewed past relations between Louisiana and the Federal government and the "quarter-century of sectional warfare waged by the North against the South." The cloud, he said, which was "once a mere speck upon the horizon, has attained such dimensions that it blackens the skies of the majority section" of the American "Confederacy." The fanaticism and fanatics of the North must be "confronted and beaten back." Louisiana should reorganize her state militia for her own protection and stand with the other southern states in protecting "our Constitutional rights."

The day following Governor Wickliffe's address, Henry Watkins Allen of West Baton Rouge Parish, Chairman of the Committee on Foreign Relations of the House of Representatives, introduced a resolution declaring that Brown's attack on Harper's Ferry was a northern attack upon southern rights, that Louisiana should stand with Virginia, and that the choice of a Republican for the presidency in the coming election would be sufficient cause for the secession of the southern states from the Union.

On January 23, Thomas Overton Moore, the new Governor, gave his inaugural address. He spoke of the loyalty of Louisiana to the Union, reminding his audience that "Louisiana has always been moderate and conservative in her sentiments," but stated further that "events seem to be hastening to a crisis the relation which these states bear to the Union in which her duty to herself and to her sister states may be brought into painful conflict with her devotion to the Union." He viewed with "the most serious alarm the condition to which the Southern States will be reduced if a political party, organized in only one section of the country and with followers or sympathizers in the others should obtain possession of the government, when the only foundation on which that party rests is detestation of slavery, and when the minority slave section will be without the power to protect itself through the instrumentality of Federal authority."

Governor Moore revealed the sentiments of the entire South when he pleaded that "every state must be permitted to determine her own social institutions, and left to the enjoyment of them in peace." He closed his short but significant address with the words: "It is my belief as well as my hope that . . . there will yet be allowed to all the states independence and equality, and that harmony and peace will be restored to our people without a sacrifice of interest or loss of honor."

Louisianians agreed with their new Governor. Slavery had been under almost constant attack for three decades—three decades since the founding of the *Liberator*, since tall, homely, sad-faced young Abraham Lincoln had guided his flatboat down the Mississippi to New Orleans. Along with all southerners, Louisianians had long considered the "right" and the "method" of possible secession. Their decision had been made—the Union was a compact between sovereign states and that compact could be broken at any time by the people of a state or their representatives. The problem which would face them during the months immediately ahead was the "expediency" of such a movement. The days when they believed in Louisiana Whig statesman Henry A. Bullard's toast "The Union of the States—it must be preserved" had passed.

THE ELECTION OF 1860. The Democrats were the strongest political group in Louisiana. The old Whig party was dead and its former members could not of course join the Republicans, who were against slavery even though most Republican leaders at this time only opposed its extension into the territories. The Democratic party split over the slavery issue at the national convention, and the Louisiana delegates walked out with the other southerners, formed a southern wing of the party, and nominated John C. Breckinridge of Kentucky for President. Many Louisianians, however, would not support Breckinridge, supporting instead John Bell of Tennessee, standard bearer of the new Constitutional Union party. Only a small group, principally from the sugar parishes of Ascension, Assumption, and Lafourche, supported Stephen A. Douglas of Illinois, candidate of the northern wing of the Democratic party.

The presidential campaign of 1860 in Louisiana was marked in most sections by enthusiastic interest or deadly seriousness, but in a few small areas by almost casual unconcern. There were meetings, barbecues, newspaper editorials, parades, and fireworks, the firing of cannon, banners, and music and flags. "Young Bell Ringers," "Young Men's Douglas Clubs," "Minute Men of '60," and numerous other political clubs were organized. Lincoln was described as "the dirtiest and meanest Abolitionist alive. There is not an emotion of his heart, brain or soul, that is not unutterably filthy." Bell was termed a "quaint, homely, sleepy old gentleman," but gained much support because his followers admitted "of no other platform than the Constitution." Douglas was an "Abolition traitor" who wanted to rule or ruin the South, though many supported him because they admired him for "his bold, consistent and fearless course" and because he represented the "best" citizens of the North.

Senator Judah P. Benjamin, however, probably spoke for most Louisianians when he said: "I have no stomach for a fight in which I am to have the choice between the man who denies me all my rights, openly and fairly [Lincoln], and a man who admits my rights but intends to filch them [Douglas]."

The newspapers backed their favorite candidate; some were fanatic in their denunciations of Lincoln and Douglas, others moderate in their analyses. The New Orleans *Picayune* chartered a dignified, serious course and warned the people of the dangers of seccession: "Every man should understand the position in which this election is likely to place him. . . . There is no possible dismemberment of the Union but by the sword. There is no State secession, peacefully. There is no reorganization of the South but through a baptism of blood." Its editorials were ridiculed by the New Orleans *Delta,* which characterized the *Picayune* as "rivaling the phlegm of old Archimedes studying a mathematical proposition in his tower whilst the enemy was thundering at the gates of Syracuse."

On election day, Louisiana gave Breckinridge 22,681 votes, Bell 20,204, and Douglas 7,625; it is not recorded that Lincoln received a single vote. Douglas carried only three parishes—Ascension, Assumption, and Lafourche; Bell carried nine—East Baton Rouge, Jefferson, St. James, St. John, St. Tammany, Orleans, Ouachita, Tensas, and West Baton Rouge; Breckinridge carried the other thirty-six.

Lincoln had, however, been elected President of the United States. As his future course of action was not clear, public opinion was sharply divided in Louisiana, for many citizens hoped for a compromise solution to the critical problems. One group believed that the South should wait until after Lincoln's inauguration and see what he would do before taking any action; another argued that the time for the secession of Louisiana and the entire south had arrived; yet another group counseled a convention of all the southern states. A few people, believing that they were "facing fact—not theory," declared that "we are doomed if we proclaim not our political independence."

Governor Moore called a special session of the legislature on December 10, 1860. Twenty-three senators and sixty-one representatives were present, and their meetings were marked by general harmony and seriousness of purpose. In his message the Governor said that the time had passed when men hesitated to calculate the value of the Union, and also stated, "I do not think it comports with the honor and respect of Louisiana as a slaveholding state, to live under the government of a Black Republican President." The law had been violated regarding the property of the South, and the questions of the present crisis rose "high above ordinary political considerations," for they involved "our present honor and our future existence as a free and independent people." He recommended an election of members to a convention which would "determine the relations of Louisiana to the Federal government."

Many Louisianians opposed the Governor's recommendations, and the New Orleans *Daily True Delta* two days later reported that "the legislature now in full blast in Baton Rouge will, we have no earthly doubt, do all in its power to second Gov. Moore's suggestion to hasten the secession of Louisiana, right or wrong, cause or no cause, from the Federal Union; and every praise-God-bare-bones in the pulpits of the State, in rivalry of their pious brothers in fanatical and treason loving New England, will bless their endeavors and sanctify their proceedings after their own fashion." Others followed the *Picayune* in counseling deliberative action and in recommending that Louisiana should seek concerted action with the other southern states.

The legislature immediately passed a bill calling for an election on January 7 of delegates to a state convention to meet at Baton Rouge on January 23 to consider Louisiana's position in the Union. Most Louisianians approved of Governor Moore's leadership and the action of the legislature, and would have agreed with the sentiment of the New Orleans *Weekly Delta* that "Governor Moore is not what may be called a 'fast man' in politics; but if he is slower than some others, he is just as sure to come right in the end."

PUBLIC OPINION DURING THE EARLY WINTER OF 1860-61. The winter of 1860-61 in New Orleans promised to be even gayer than usual, for the 1860 crops had been good and prices were satisfactory. The drawing rooms and salons of the principal hotels were crowded with planters and businessmen and their families from all sections of the state. Adelina Patti was headlining an opera season the like of which the old city had never seen, the theaters were crowded, and "the brilliancy" of the audiences had never been excelled. Excitement was in the air. Everyone talked politics—on the street, at public places, even at church.

On November 29, Bishop B. M. Palmer preached a two-hour sermon using a text from Psalms 94:20: "Shall the throne of iniquity have fellowship with thee, which frameth mischief by a law?" He argued that the South should stand against the North, even to the extent of war; that the South had a trust to defend, perhaps with the sword. "Not till the last man has fallen behind the last rampart, shall it drop from our hands; and then only in surrender to the God who gave it." He closed his impassioned sermon: "Whatever be the fortunes of the South, I accept them for my own. Born upon her soil, of a father thus born before me . . . she is in every sense my mother. . . . May the Lord God cover her head in this her day of battle."

W. O. Rogers, a New Orleanian who heard that sermon, wrote: "After the benediction in solemn silence, no man speaking to his neighbor, the great congregation of serious and thoughtful men and women dispersed; but afterwards the drums beat and the bugles sounded." Within a few days the *Daily Delta* had reprinted the sermon three times and had sold 30,000 copies. Shortly thereafter it was distributed in pamphlet form over the entire South. Soon people no longer spoke of *co-operation* with the North; instead, they talked of secession, *and then co-operation* with the United States.

Public opinion, however, was divided. One citizen challenged Palmer: "You would destroy the constitution and the union—this glorious and peerless fabric which has so long and so safely sheltered us, and what, sir, would you rear in its stead?" A large group meeting at Franklin resolved to oppose the "unconstitutional secession of Louisiana"; another group at a St. James Parish meeting decided that the northern states should be expelled from the Union; still another group in St. Charles Parish formed a "company of minute men" to forcibly "secure Southern rights in the Union." At New Orleans, Virginia-born Sallie Holman, member of a theatrical troupe giving shows at the Odd Fellows' Hall, on December 24 sang to a cheering audience the recently written "Southern Marsellaise":

> Sons of the South, awake to glory!
> Hark! hark! what myriads bid you rise. . . .

The majority of the newspapers favored secession, though some argued that the movement toward secession should not be hurried. Of the important newspapers the *True Delta* and the Baton Rouge *Weekly Gazette and Comet* lead the fight against secession. The *Picayune* continued to counsel moderation and argued the possibility of concurrent state action. The *Constitutional* of Alexandria joked about the matter: "If Louisiana secedes from the Union . . . we shall be compelled to advocate the secession of the parish of Rapides from the State. . . . We have a large territory and a numerous population and are perfectly able to take care of ourselves." Perhaps the *Weekly Delta* best summed up the public's attitude when it stated: "We are secessionists because we honestly believe that it is the only possible way in which we can enjoy the rights and privileges which the Union, as originally designed, was intended to bestow upon all the States, according to the just measure of perfect equality."

As the election of January 7 approached, the people divided into two groups—the "Immediate Secessionists," who believed that Louisiana should secede at once, and the "Co-operationists," who believed that the state should co-operate with the other southern states and delay action until President-elect Lincoln had assumed office and announced his policy.

THE SECESSION CONVENTION. The campaign for the election of delegates to the State Convention took on the proportions of a regular political campaign, with rallies, parades, newspaper headlines, decorations, bands, and the constant use of the Pelican Flag and the bust of John C. Calhoun. The news of the secession of South Carolina was received in New Orleans on December 21 and celebrated with great demonstrations and the firing of 800 guns. But by January 7 many people lost interest. Only 37,744 voted, whereas over 50,000 had voted in the preceding presidential election. The voters in 29 parishes were for secession and those of 19 parishes were opposed; the total vote was 20,448 to 17,296. To the State Convention went 80 secessionists, 44 co-operationists, and 6 men who were undecided.

The Convention met at Baton Rouge on Wednesday, January 23, with 127 members present.* It was a middle-aged group, averaging 42.5 years of age; 23 were over 50 and 7 were under 30. Seventy-three-year-old Thomas W. Scott of East Feliciana Parish was the oldest delegate, while 21-year-old David Pierson of Winn Parish was the youngest. Forty-seven members were native-born Louisianians, 9 were foreign born, 11 were born in the North, and the rest were from other southern states. Seventy-five of the members were planters, farmers, or owned agricultural land. There were 39 lawyers, 7 public officials, 5 doctors, and 2 editors. One delegate listed his occupation as "omnibus," while another called himself an "adjuster of averages." Twenty-five produced sugar cane and 41 grew cotton. Their average wealth was almost $130,000. One hundred and seven of them together owned 6,016 slaves, 19 delegates owning 100 or more and 36 owning more than 50.

The body was called to order by Effingham Lawrence, who asked John Perkins, Jr., to take the chair. Former Governor Alexandre Mouton was elected president of the body, several committees were appointed, one of them a fifteen-member committee to report on "an ordinance providing for the withdrawal of the State of Louisiana from the present Federal Union."

The following day Governor Moore reported that during the week after the election he had seized Forts Jackson and St. Philip below New Orleans, the United States Arsenal at Baton Rouge, a Federal revenue cutter, and other Federal property. A motion to approve the Governor's course of action passed by a vote of 119 to 5. The same day, January 24, Chairman John Perkins, Jr., of the Committee of Fifteen, presented the committee's report, " An Ordinance to dissolve the union between the

---

* The original journal of the Convention made up a volume of several hundred pages. It was stolen from the Capitol by a Federal soldier during the occupation of Baton Rouge and was later acquired by a Rhode Island officer, whose son returned it to the state in 1929. It is now in the Louisiana State Museum at New Orleans.

State of Louisiana and the other States, united with her under the compact entitled 'The Constitution of the United States of America.' "† On January 25 the Convention heard speeches of commissioners from Alabama and South Carolina asking for the co-operation of Louisiana in the forming of a Southern Confederacy. A communication from Louisiana's United States Senators John Slidell and Judah P. Benjamin asking for secession was also read.

Several members of the Convention, led by James G. Talliaferro of Catahoula Parish, opposed the Ordinance of Secession when it came up for debate. In a brilliant speech against secession Talliaferro gave the following reasons for his opposition:

1. The acts of aggression against the State could be remedied under the United States Constitution.
2. If the State did secede it would not remedy matters.
3. There was a possibility that the seceded states would not confederate or that the border slave states would secede.
4. Secession was a right not contemplated by the Constitution of the United States.
5. The proper status of Louisiana was with the border states.
6. By secession the State of Louisiana lost any claim it had to the public domain and to all property belonging to the Union.
7. Secession would produce hardships, suffering, and destruction of property.
8. The Ordinance of Secession was drawn up by a convention which did not possess the legal right to sever relations with the Union.

Joseph A. Rozier of Orleans Parish and James O. Fuqua of East Baton Rouge Parish offered substitute ordinances, which were voted down. A motion to submit the matter to the people likewise failed.

The arguments were completed on January 26, and the Ordinance of Secession was adopted by a vote of 113 to 17, President Mouton being permitted to vote "yes" through a suspension of the rules. When the vote was announced Alexandre Mouton proclaimed: "In virtue of the vote just announced, I now declare the connection between the State of Louisiana, and the Federal Union dissolved; and that she is a free, sovereign and independent Power." Then the bar of the House was removed and Governor Thomas O. Moore entered the room, preceded by the Pelican Flag of Louisiana, and took his position on the platform. The Reverend W. E. N. Linfield offered a prayer and Father Darius Hubert blessed the flag. Later, when the Ordinance of Secession was signed by the members of the Convention, eight of the seventeen members who had voted against it signed the document, making the final vote 121 to 9.

PUBLIC REACTION TO THE ORDINANCE OF SECESSION. Most Louisiana newspapers received the news of secession with enthusiasm. The *Picayune* said: "The deed has been done. We breathe deeper and freer for it. The Union is dead. . . . No government ever rose as she did—none has ever so perished. From the cradle to manhood was a single bound. . . . It went through none of the convulsions that marked the decline of other peoples. It was not overthrown by hostile invasion like Greece, nor was it overrun by Vandal hordes as Rome was. Neither did it perish of inanition like Egypt, nor was it conquered as Saxon England was. It was without precedent

---

† During the late 1930's this writer, at that time head of the Department of Archives of Louisiana State University and engaged in collecting state historical, manuscript, and archival material for the Department, found the lost original draft of the secession ordinance with a group of "worthless" papers in the home of Lemuel P. Conner, Jr., of Natchez, Mississippi. Conner's father, who at that time lived in Louisiana and who was a member of the Convention, was a close friend of John Perkins, Jr., and he and Perkins had stayed together at the Palms Hotel. They spent the entire night of January 23 writing and revising a draft of a secession ordinance which Perkins presented to his Committee of Fifteen the following morning. The final draft of the Louisiana Secession Ordinance is essentially the same as Perkins and Conner drafted it. Perkins kept the original draft and sent it to Conner shortly before his death in Baltimore in 1885. The Conner family still has possession of the historic document, and photostats are in the Department of Archives, Louisiana State University.

in its growth, without example in its fall. . . . To the lone star of the State we transfer the duty, affection and allegiance we owed to the congregation of light which spangled the banner of the old Confereracy. . . . The South says to every child of hers, 'Son, give me all your heart'; and the South asks no more than she has a right to, and no more than she will receive."

The New Orleans *Crescent* reported that "by a vote almost unanimous, and with calm dignity and firm purpose, Louisiana resumes her delegated powers, and escapes from a Union in which she could no longer remain with honor to herself or to her sister States of the South. The act was done with no unseemly haste, nor with any exhibition of unnatural passion. The issue of 'immediate secession by separate State action' was distinctly made before the people; and the people decided in favor of immediate secession by electing an overwhelming majority in its favor to the Convention."

A few newspapers, however, took an opposite position or counseled moderation. The *True Delta,* for example, stated that "everything in this city appears to be in rapid progress towards a war establishment," but that local and import-export trade was at a standstill, banks were curtailing their discounts, creditors were calling in loans, business houses were discharging employees to cut expenses, and, "save the office-holders . . . everything looks dubious and bewildered not knowing what to expect or what may happen. . . . thousands are unsure that bread to eat can be obtained for their honest and willing labor from week to week."

Other newspapers expressed sincere regret at leaving the Union. The Shreveport *South-Western* admitted with emotion: "We this day, as orderly citizens, lower the 'stars and stripes' from our masthead! It is with heart-felt emotions, better imagined than portrayed, that we fold the saucy looking 'star spangled banner' that we have always loved, and place the precious memento under our pillow."

The people generally received the news with sincere approval and celebrated Louisiana's independence with enthusiastic spontaneity; guns banged, cannons thundered, state flags were flung to the breeze, and at night public buildings and private homes were brightly lighted. The *Picayune* reported that in New Orleans "every one seemed to breath more freely, every one's heart beat with a more rapid and pleasurable pulsation." Everyone was ready to "defend the sovereignty of Louisiana, come what might, and in the face of every obstacle."

Mayor John T. Monroe of New Orleans ordered "all citizens to illuminate their residences, or places of business" on the night of February 6 in honor of the secession of the state. The *Bee* reported the next day that "the principal display was to be found on Canal, Royal and St. Charles streets, which were thronged with ladies and gentlemen. . . . The Pelican and Boston Clubs on Canal street, and Kittredge's store on St. Charles street, were noticeable in this respect." Fireworks were shot off, speeches were made, and the militia units paraded, their marching formations adding much to the popular demonstration.

The citizenry viewed secession and the possibility of war with the United States with different emotions. One old lady expressed a fervid desire for pieces of "Old Abe's" ear or chunks of his hair. An old man reported that when he saw "the flag of the Union trailed in the dust, and put out of sight" and the flag of Louisiana hung up in its place he cried like a child. Superintendent William T. Sherman of the State Seminary of Learning, realizing that the Convention would vote secession, resigned on January 18 and wrote Governor Moore that "if Louisiana withdraws from the Federal Union, I prefer to maintain my allegiance to the Constitution as long as a fragment of it survives." John Bouligny, a member of the Federal House of Representatives, was the only Louisiana member of Congress to retain his seat after secession, but he soon retired to private life and remained in the North until his death in 1864.

It later remained for young Louisiana Confederate soldier Robert Patrick to go straight to the crux of the causes of all the trouble between North and South; he wrote in his diary: "If I only had the fanatics of the North and the fire eaters of the South, in equal numbers in a pen together, I'd make 'dog eat dog.' I'd *make Rome howl* for once."

THE "REPUBLIC" OF LOUISIANA. For almost two months, from January 26 when the Ordinance of Secession was passed until March 21 when she joined the Confederate States of America, Louisiana was an independent nation. Governor Moore acted as President, the legislature continued in session as a congress, and state courts served in the place of Federal courts.

For nearly three weeks the old state flag was the national flag of Louisiana; then on February 11 the Convention, which had moved to New Orleans, adopted a new one. The emblem had thirteen stripes, six of white, four of blue, and three of red, while in the upper left-hand corner was a red field with a five-pointed yellow star. The flag represented the thirteen stripes of the original Union, the tricolor of France, and the red and yellow colors of Spain. At eleven o'clock the following morning, the members of the Convention, headed by Alexandre Mouton and Lieutenant Governor H. M. Hyams and accompanied by a military escort, marched to Lafayette Square. The flag, made by tentmaker and sailmaker H. Cassidy, was raised over the City Hall, and received a twenty-one-gun salute from the Washington Artillery. Here it flew until pulled down by Federal soldiers after the occupation of New Orleans in April, 1862. Modern critic W. O. Hart has called the flag "the ugliest ever made."

By the middle of February, Governor Moore had appropriated all Federal property in Louisiana; Forts Pike and Macomb had been occupied by the state militia and the United States Mint and Customs House had been secured, along with over $600,000 which was in the Mint. The State legislature and the Secession Convention continued to meet, the legislature passing laws and the Convention adopting ordinances having the effect of laws.

There was some discussion of the legality of the Convention's continuing its activities after the Ordinance of Secession had been passed. A few of its members believed that it should adjourn to meet on call, but the majority were of the opinion that it was only performing functions "imperatively demanded by the withdrawal of the State from the Union." The *Daily True Delta* referred to it as "the Lyceum hall wigwam, jocosely called a state convention." One critic wrote that its members were "in the most oblivious state of incomprehensibility as to what powers they had or had not conferred. They seemed to be in the condition of an antiquated, antideluvian China teapot with a broken spout which was totally inadequate to comprehend whether it had ever given vent to the fumes of Bohea and Souchong!" The people and state government officials, however, offered little if any criticism.

While the work of the Secession Convention, which held two sessions in New Orleans after the Baton Rouge meeting, was of more consequence than that of the legislature, there is little doubt but that it performed functions which were the prerogative of the legislature. It named delegates to the Convention of the Southern States at Montgomery, Alabama; it transferred the powers of the national government to the state government and handled problems of finance, court, and postal affairs; it opened the Mississippi River to all friendly nations; and finally, on March 21 it ratified the Constitution of the Confederate States of America by a vote of 101 to 7 and transferred funds to the new national government of the South. Meanwhile the legislature invited the people of southern Indiana and Illinois to join the Confederacy as a state, appropriated $1,500,000 for the defense of Louisiana, provided for the organization of military units, and outfitted warships at the Algiers shipyard.

The legislature and the Convention adjourned on March 26. During the previous two months Louisiana had been successively a state of the American Union and an independent nation, and was now a member of the Confederate States of America.

The people of Louisiana generally supported the work of the two bodies. The *Daily Crescent* on March 27, 1861, probably voiced the sentiments of most citizens when it said: "The Convention itself was composed of the leading citizens of the state—men eminent for their talents, their virtues and their courage, . . . their proceedings were conducted with dignity and harmony. They have answered to the expectations of the people, and they will receive that welcome at the people's hands which is the highest recognition of a faithful discharge of the representative trust. We extend to each member, at parting, our cordial good wishes." The next day the *True Delta* presented a more critical view when it said the "lampblack aristocracy" had "succeeded in getting all they required of the wigwam convention," and that they had not had the dencency to draw the "drapery of the tomb over the closing scenes of a body which generations yet unborn, as well as those now existing, will long curse as the heaviest and most disastrous affliction that poor Louisiana, always a prey to needy adventurers and broken-down office-hunters, has ever had to support."

Had secession been the proper course of action? A majority of Louisianians would probably have agreed with northern Bishop Thomas M. Clark, who, in a letter to Mrs. Leonidas Polk after the war, discussed the bitter condemnation in the North of her bishop husband for his decision to fight for the South. Bishop Clark wrote: "I was well persuaded that he regarded his course as a sacrifice laid on the altar of truth, and went forth believing himself to be called to wield the sword of the Lord and of Gideon."

LOUISIANA MOBILIZES FOR WAR. Louisiana hurriedly mobilized her military strength during those early months of 1861. The Governor appointed a Military Board, and by February 14 it had issued arms to nearly 1,800 members of volunteer companies; the mobilization continued at an accelerated pace. Military training camps were established in New Orleans and at Camp Moore, north of Amite, where the Crescent Rifles, the Washington Artillery, the Orleans Cadets, the Louisiana Guards, the Louisiana Grays, and other outfits were assembled, given some hurried training, and then held in reserve or sent to Baton Rouge or Forts Jackson and St. Philip.

Everyone tried to join up at once, and there were more volunteers than the state could equip; men "who knew only how to use the yard stick" began to study bayonet exercises; the cadets of the State Seminary of Learning marched off to join the army (except one who joined the United States Navy). In Baton Rouge, out of 1,300 voters over 750 enlisted. In New Orleans, flags flew from the public buildings, bands blared, military companies paraded, and English reporter William H. Russell wrote that "the streets were full of Turcos, Zouaves, Chasseurs . . . there were Pickwick rifles, La Fayette rifles, Beauregard guards, Macmahon guards, and Irish, German, Italian, Spanish and native volunteers. In fact, New Orleans looks like a suburb of the camp at Chalons." Impressment gangs of Irishmen cruised the streets, collaring less-enthusiastic Spaniards and shouting, "For the love of the Virgin and your own sowl's sake, Fernandey, get up and cum along wid us to fight the Yankees."

A hysteria swept Louisiana during those weeks. Those who dared express the opinion that the North might be successful were sent to jail for short sentences in which to rid themselves of such silly ideas. Russell reported that "the moral suasion of the lasso, of tarring and feathering, head-shaving, ducking, and horse-ponds, deportation on rails, and similar ethical processes are highly in favour." The comparatively few men who were "unavailable" were led to enlistment offlces and "encouraged" to take the oath to "bear true allegiance to the state of Louisiana, and serve it honestly and faithfully . . . and obey the orders of the governor and such officers as may be appointed over me." The newspapers admonished, the *Daily Crescent* urging "Get ready for the fight and meet it to the death when it comes."

Long afterwards one man recalled that "I shared the popular delusion that the war would last only a short time, and in common with many other would-be soldiers in New Orleans, I was morally certain that unless I got to the front at once, the fighting would all be over before I had a chance to take part in it." Louisianians, as most southerners during those exciting, pulsating early days of southern nationalism, were ready, with their feet planted firmly in the clouds, to march off to war.

THE WAR BEGINS. At 4:30 on the morning of April 12, 1861, Confederate shore batteries under command of General Pierre G. T. Beauregard at Charleston, South Carolina, opened fire on Fort Sumter, which was on an island in the bay and commanded by Major Robert Anderson. After thirty-four hours of bombardment the fort surrendered at 2:30 P.M., April 13. Two days later President Lincoln called for 75,000 volunteers to force the South back into the Union. The northern press, led by the New York *Times,* labeled the "rebellion" an "embryo tadpole" and urged the North not to mistake "a 'local commotion' for a revolution. A strong, active pull together will do our work effectually in thirty days." On April 19, the 6th Massachusetts Regiment passed through Baltimore on its way southward and in a fight with the citizens killed twelve and wounded a number of them. The next morning the New Orleans *Daily Crescent* screamed the headline, "Northern Troops Moving Southward —They are Attacked by the Baltimoreans." The news spread by river packet and telegraph throughout the state.

Twenty-five-year-old James Ryder Randall, Maryland born but with Louisiana family connections, an English and Latin teacher at Poydras College in Pointe Coupée Parish, was at the Mississippi River wharf about six or seven miles from New Roads when the news arrived. Unable to sleep that night, he arose about midnight, lighted a candle, went to his desk, seized his pen, and wrote the words to one of the most stirring and beloved songs of the Confederacy:

> The despot's heel is on thy shore,
> Maryland!
> His torch is at thy temple door,
> Maryland!
> . . . .
> Thou wilt not yield the vandal toll;
> Thou wilt not crook to his control,
> Better the fire upon thee roll,
> Better the shot, the blade, the bowl,
> Than crucifixion of the soul.
> Maryland! My Maryland!

A few days later the *Constitutional* of Alexandria, a conservative newspaper, gave Louisiana's answer to the challenge: "The Southern states are united as a union. . . . there is but one voice in the land, one purpose, one heart, and one destiny." Donelson Caffery later said in a speech in the United States Senate: "I was a quiet, peaceful citizen, pursuing my calling as a sugar planter in my native state. Suddenly the tocsin of war was sounded throughout the length and breadth of the land. I revered the Union and I honored its flag. But when my state called me to arms, I had to answer the call of the state of my nativity and the state of my love." The conventions and the campaigns and the speechmaking were over. It was time for the work of war.

CHAPTER 22

LOUISIANA AND THE WAR FOR SOUTHERN INDEPENDENCE*

EIGHTEEN HUNDRED SIXTY-ONE. This was the year of preparation. Military supplies of all types were assembled at government warehouses at strategic points throughout the state. Boats collected scrap iron along the rivers and bayous and delivered it to iron foundries at New Orleans. Small industrial plants were enlarged, converted or built to manufacture uniforms, hats, shoes, tents, and other goods needed for the expected war effort. The planting of food crops was encouraged. The state government strengthened Fort Jackson and Fort St. Philip below New Orleans and fitted out gunboats for river-patrol work. The legislature at its November session passed emergency laws and made appropriations for additional military equipment and supplies. It was a year of feverish activity.

The enlistment and training of troops continued, and towns and villages were filled with drilling and parading volunteer companies, many of which had been given such picturesque names as Alligator Rangers, Caddo Lake Boys, Catahoula Guerillas, Knights of the Border, Mounted Wild Cats, Red River Sharpshooters, Sabine Independents, Madison Tipperarys, Yankee Pelters, Franklinton Pumpkin Studs, and numerous others equally individualistic. By the end of June, Louisiana had enlisted, armed, and sent out of the state 16,000 troops, many of which, however, were inadequately supplied and equipped. The state enlisted nearly 20,000 troops during the first nine months of 1861 and during the war organized nearly 1,000 companies containing more than 65,000 men.

The unity of Louisianians, however, was not complete during those stirring months of 1861, and there was evidence of some disloyalty to the state and to the Confederacy. Considerable amounts of cotton shipped to New Orleans were being smuggled through the blockade and sold to the enemy, and in early October, Governor Moore stopped all shipments until the blockade should be lifted. When other evidences of disloyalty came to his attention, he ordered that the city and surrounding parishes be searched for traitors and that they be arrested and their houses burned. Despite the vigilance of the state officials disloyal Louisianians acted as Federal spies throughout the war, keeping the enemy rather well informed as to troop movements and the location of supply depots.

During the early weeks of the war Governor Moore became fearful of an attack on New Orleans and appealed to the Confederate government to stop draining the New Orleans area of military supplies and troops. By middle August, 1861, Major General

---

* Numerous titles have been given to the war fought between the United States of America and the Confederate States of America from the spring of 1861 to the late spring of 1865. When the official records of that conflict were published by the United States government some years after the war it was titled "The War of the Rebellion." Southerners have almost universally called it "The War Between the States." Edward Channing, a New England historian, titled it, "The War for Southern Independence," and this name, in this writer's opinion, is the most accurate and the best. Most present-day authors, in the interest of brevity, simply call it "The Civil War."

David E. Twiggs, commanding general at New Orleans, appealed to the Secretary of War for reinforcements to repel a rumored attack from a fleet of ironclad gunboats. But the Confederate government, completely absorbed with the war in the East, gave little thought to the possibility of an attack on New Orleans or to its strategic consequences if successful. Even Judah P. Benjamin, who should have understood Louisiana's position, was unperturbed; when a group argued the immediate possibility of such an attack, his answer was: "Bah! The truth is, you *are all scared* to death, *down at home!*"

On October 18, Major General Mansfield Lovell, a District of Columbia-born, West Point-educated, retired army officer living in New York City when the war began, became Commander of the Department of Louisiana. Lovell lost little time in writing to Richmond that New Orleans was the city "first in importance in the Confederacy," that it had been completely "drained of arms, ammunition, medical stores, clothing and supplies for other points," and that it would require a great effort to put the city in a proper state of defense. By early December he reported that the forts below New Orleans had been reinforced, two powder mills were producing two tons of powder a day, the fortifications above and below the city were manned by some 8,000 troops, 6,000 armed volunteers were in the city itself, and the cypress-log raft held together by 2½-inch chain cables across the Mississippi at Forts Jackson and St. Philip had been strengthened. Lovell optimistically wrote that he was "fully prepared" and if the enemy attacked he had "no fears about results."

1862. The strategic importance of New Orleans and the Lower Mississippi Valley was obvious to the Federal high command, and by the end of 1861 plans were complete for an attack on New Orleans. The expedition concentrated at Ship Island during March and early April, 1862. Flag Officer David G. Farragut commanded eighteen ships, six mortar steamers, and nineteen mortar boats mounting some two hundred guns, while Major General Benjamin F. Butler accompanied the fleet with a large Federal force.

Commander David Porter, who commanded the mortar flotilla, began to bombard Forts Jackson and St. Philip on the morning of April 18, and continued a furious cannonade for six days. Seeing that the forts could not be reduced by mortar fire, Farragut decided to run past them. About two o'clock on the morning of the twenty-fourth, according to a Federal colonel, "he pipes all hands to quarters, . . . dashes with full head of steam on, right into the teeth of the rebel forts, and gun boats, and rams, and fire-rafts, and floating batteries and all infernal machines of torpedoes and destructives. . . ."

A Confederate, in his description of the battle, wrote that "It was so dark we could see nothing; but as the second rocket faded, in one instant the whole scene was brilliantly illuminated as if by magic. Every gun opened in the forts. The vessels poured broadside after broadside as they rushed past. The mortars filled the air. It was so bright with the glare of the guns' rapid firing, that we could see every yard, every sail, every rope, every man in the rigging, every man at the guns in the Forts, dark against the red sulphurous light. The men working the little howitzers in the rigging of the Hartford looked like black imps or devils clinging and climbing about her ropes. It was the most superb sight I ever witnessed—so flashing, so bewildering, so magnificent, so brief."

The strength of New Orleans had greatly deteriorated during the previous weeks. Lovell had been forced to send all but 3,000 of his troops to South Carolina and Mississippi, the city was close to collapse for want of food (there had been free distribution of food since August, 1861), prices had soared, and martial law had been in effect since the middle of March. On April 1, Governor Moore had telegraphed President Jefferson Davis for troops and munitions: "Now that thirty-seven sail of the enemy are in the river, in God's name, in the name of my State, I ask you to order them to be sent to me immediately." The public, however, was outwardly calm. The Queen Sisters were playing to capacity audiences at the Academy of

Music. George W. Cable later wrote that everyone believed that "nothing afloat could pass the forts. Nothing that walked could get through our swamps." Then came news of the defeat at Shiloh, and when the funeral procession of General Albert Sidney Johnston passed slowly up St. Charles Street past the silent throngs, they began to realize that the war was coming very near.

The news that Farragut had passed the forts reached the city late on the morning of the twenty-fourth, and within an hour "the city was panic-stricken. The firebells were rung twelve times to call out the guards." Men and women ran aimlessly about the streets, despite orders to remain in their homes. The authorities ordered destroyed all supplies which might be of value to the enemy, so warehouses containing over 15,000 bales of cotton and huge stocks of tobacco and other products, coalyards, and lumberyards were set afire; factory machinery was smashed; dry docks were sunk; hogsheads of sugar and molasses were dumped into the streets. General Lovell had no alternative but to evacuate the city, and he advised the naval officer to either move all ships and gunboats up the Mississippi or to attempt to run through the blockade to Mobile. Instead the officer fired the ships, which might later have been used to great advantage in attempting to hold the river.

As the evacuation trains pulled out they left behind a burning city filled with "the wildest confusion." Thousands of people milled about the streets that night watching the fires. By morning they were exhausted and in an ugly mood. They had been betrayed, the newspapers had told them that they were safe. The frightened crowds turned into angry mobs. They looted stores and swung a man who "looked like a stranger and might be a spy" to a lamppost, but a lieutenant of the Foreign Legion cut him down.

Toward noon the Federal ships rounded the bend, exchanging shots with the Chalmette batteries as they slowly sailed upriver avoiding the burning ships floating downstream. Within two hours the "dusky, long, morose, demonlike Yankee steamers" lay "like evil messengers of woe" in front of the city, riding high on the nine-foot river crest so that their guns could rake the streets. Facing them on the levee were thousands "of all nations and various colors, . . . with sombre looks and determined faces," led by a woman who held aloft the Confederate banner and by a fifer who shrilled "Garryowen," "The Bonnie Blue Flag," and "Dixie" under the very guns of Farragut's flagship *Hartford*.

Northern Captain Theodorus Bailey and Lieutenant George Perkins came ashore, walked through the jeering, threatening mob to the City Hall, and demanded the surrender of the city. After a time sixty-year-old Pierre Soule went outside and spoke to the throng while the two Federal officers went out a side door and were driven to the wharf in a closed carriage.

Mayor John T. Monroe would not surrender the city, and for a few days a stalemate existed, the mayor refusing to surrender New Orleans and Farragut threatening to begin a bombardment. On the night of the twenty-seventh about half of the troops at Fort Jackson mutinied, and the next morning it and Fort St. Philip surrendered. Though this changed the situation at New Orleans, Monroe still refused to surrender; so on April 28 Federal Lieutenant Albert Kautz simply cut the halyards above the City Hall with his sword and the Louisiana flag fell, while tears ran down the faces of the hundreds gathered in front of the building. The next day Farragut informed Monroe that there would be no further negotiations and that General Butler would soon land with his troops; New Orleans had not surrendered, it had been captured. On May 1, Butler took formal possession of the city.

Not long after the fall of New Orleans, the Federal fleet took possession of Baton Rouge, and on May 28 a military force arrived at the capital. In late July, Confederate General John C. Breckinridge, former Vice-President of the United States, left Vicksburg, marched southward, and on August 5 attacked the Federals at the capital, driving them to the river, where they were protected by the fleet. Breckinridge withdrew to Port Hudson, and the Federals evacuated Baton Rouge on August 21. Butler ordered the city burned, but at the last moment relented and countermanded the order. A Federal officer wrote, however, that "this place has been nearly completely sacked by the soldiery. . . . Even officer's tents are filled with furniture from deserted houses."

Meanwhile Federal gunboats were cruising up and down the river. At several points between New Orleans and Baton Rouge, particularly at Donaldsonville, small Confederate batteries fired at every Federal boat that passed. Farragut finally ordered Donaldsonville destroyed, and on August 9 the bombardment began; three days later the New Orleans *Delta* reported that "there is nothing left of it now but ruins and rubbish."

Although Louisiana was included in the newly organized Trans-Mississippi Department, Governor Moore realized that little aid could be expected from the Confederacy and began the organization of troops for the defense of the state. Training camps were built at New Iberia, Monroe, and Opelousas. Major General Richard Taylor was given command of the Department of West Louisiana in August, but by October was only able to muster an army of slightly less than 5,000 men, many of whom had no rifles.

In October a strong Federal force under General Godfrey Weitzel marched down Bayou Lafourche, defeated the Confederates at Labadieville, and then continued on to the Bayou Teche country to attack General Alfred Mouton, son of former Governor Mouton, near Franklin. This campaign was still in progress at the year's end. In the middle of December, General Nathaniel P. Banks superseded General Butler in command of the Federal Army in Louisiana, and on December 17 reoccupied Baton Rouge, which he termed "the first rebel position on the river."

The year 1862 was a fateful one for Louisiana. New Orleans was occupied; Baton Rouge was twice captured, the partial burning of the capitol destroying many state records. Southeast and parts of southern Louisiana had been ravaged and sacked by Federal troops, as were parts of the northeastern section of the state. By the end of the year Federal gunboats were in complete possession of the lower Mississippi.

1863. Early in 1863, General U. S. Grant invaded northeast Louisiana as a part of his movement against Vicksburg, marching southward through Carroll, Madison, and Tensas parishes. Although there was little fighting in this area, there was general destruction of property. Clifton Parkhurst, who was with the 16th Iowa Infantry, in the rear of Grant's army, wrote graphically: "We marched for fifteen miles along Lake St. Joseph. . . . The lake was a lovely sylvan flood, and around its fertile shores had been one of the garden spots of Louisiana. Even as we gazed the country to the rear was one vast field of sugar cane and Indian corn. . . . Only the day before, expensive homes, sugar mills, and cotton plants of great cost looked out upon the placid lake in proud serenity. Now, where we marched, were smouldering ruins, and for miles ahead we could see smoke and flames wrapping roofs and walls that towered high." Grant headquartered at Milliken's Bend for a period while his army was strung out for about sixty miles along the river; he finally crossed the Mississippi to invest Vicksburg the last of April.

In March a Federal detachment occupied a considerable portion of the Florida Parishes but was forced to withdraw within a couple of weeks, after, however, rather systematically looting such areas as could be conveniently reached. Early the next month General Banks moved to Brashear City and then up the Teche, which was defended in a series of rear-guard actions by two small Confederate armies commanded by Generals Mouton and Taylor. Banks occupied Opelousas on April 20 and Alexandria on May 7, shortly after Porter arrived there with his river-gunboat fleet. A week later Banks moved down the river, crossing the Atchafalaya at Simmesport and the Mississippi at Bayou Sara on May 23. The campaign had little military signifiicance, for Banks's objectives were to keep the Confederate armies in the area occupied and to destroy "the materials upon which an army could be organized or supported in that country."

His army, however, did not content itself with the seizure or destruction of munitions and military supplies. Frank Flinn, who was with Banks, later wrote that the army did little but gather cotton and other property; Banks himself reported that he had confiscated over 20,000 horses, mules, and cattle, over 5,000 bales of cotton, and "many hogsheads of sugar." Berwick City was the entrepôt for all "confiscated" goods south of Opelousas, and Federal Colonel A. J. H. Duganne wrote: "Contrabands and cottonbales are hurried off upon railway-flats. Shrewd cattlebrokers, after swarming about the quartermaster's doors, drive off their bargains of beeves. Mules are trotted away.... Carts, chaises, family coaches, saddles, harnesses, debris of Attakapas 'confiscation,' are invoiced, via rail, to New Orleans auction blocks." Then the town "caught" fire, and for a day and night "roofs, corridors, galleries, are ignited, and the red element extends and mounts, right and left, in lurid wings," until "the fire becomes exhausted, for lack of materials to feed upon." The Teche country had been left a gutted, blackened waste.

Banks moved southward from Bayou Sara with his army of about 13,000 men to invest Port Hudson, which was held by some 5,500 Confederates. The siege lasted forty-five days, including twenty-one days of hard fighting. The first major attack was made on May 27, and the Federals were repulsed with heavy losses; the second grand assault on June 14 was likewise repulsed. Confederate General Franklin Gardner was content to lie behind his breastworks and await the Federal attacks, which Banks showed little generalship in co-ordinating. One of Banks's officers wrote that "a pair of Turkish pashas would have been quite as enterprising and inventive" as the two army commanders.

A Federal colonel refused to lead his men in a hopeless charge and informed his commanding general: "Tell him that I have formed the column, and that, if he wants it to charge, he may come and lead it. I for my part am not going to take it into that slaughter pen." The Federal soldiers rightly blamed Banks for their heavy losses, and on one occasion when the general spoke to an outfit, according to Captain James H. Croushore, "the officers hurrahed loyally while the men looked on in sullen silence."

At last the Confederates ran out of food supplies—one soldier wrote that a boiled rat was a "better dish than he had expected"—and on July 9, Port Hudson fell. The Mississippi River was now open, and the Trans-Mississippi Department was completely severed from the rest of the Confederacy. As historian Jefferson Davis Bragg wrote: "One marvels now that Appomattox was still twenty-two months away." There was little fighting in Louisiana during the rest of 1863.

1864. Federal military plans called for the occupation of all Louisiana and eastern Texas in 1864. This was to be accomplished by sending a large military and naval expedition up the Red River to capture Shreveport, after which the Federal army would invade Texas. At the same time the central Louisiana area would yield large amounts of cotton, livestock, and other supplies.

In early March, Rear Admiral David Porter of the United States Navy assembled a strong fleet of twenty gunboats and a number of transports at the mouth of the Red River, where he was quietly joined by an army of about ten thousand men under Brigadier General A. J. Smith, which had moved down the Mississippi from the vicinity of Vicksburg. This joint naval-military force moved up the Red River about the same time that Banks's army of nearly twenty thousand men moved northward from Franklin. Fort De Russy, about thirty miles below Alexandria on the Red River, fell on March 14, and two days later Porter occupied Alexandria. The first units of Banks's army arrived eight days later and the movement up the Red River began.

The Confederate army of under nine thousand men, commanded by General Taylor, retreated, fighting rear guard actions to slow up the enemy. Taylor and his staff officers, Generals Alfred Mouton, Camille Polignac, Thomas Green, and John G. Walker, selected a battle site in the hilly, wooded country about three miles southeast of Mansfield and some forty miles south of Shreveport. Here on April 8 was fought the most noted of Louisiana's Civil War battles. After feeling out the enemy with his cavalry, Taylor ordered a general attack. The fighting, marked by headlong charges of Confederate cavalry and infantry, during one of which General Mouton was killed, was as furious as in any battle of the entire war. That night the Federals, the Confederates hard on their heels, retreated twenty-two miles to Pleasant Hill, where the following day another battle was fought, after which Banks retreated down the Red River toward Alexandria.

Banks claimed victory at Mansfield and Pleasant Hill, but the majority of the Federal military and naval officers admitted defeat. Admiral Porter reported to General Sherman on April 14 that "the army has been shamefully beaten by the rebels. There is no disguising the fact, notwithstanding the general commanding and his staff try to make a victory. Armies victorious don't often go back as this one has done."

The retreating Federal army left such destruction in its wake that the area became known as "the burnt district," where the "track of the spoiler was one scene of desolation" and the indiscriminate destruction of property was probably not surpassed at any place or time during the entire Civil War. General Taylor wrote that "The destruction of this country by the enemy exceeds anything in history."

Banks's army entered Alexandria on April 25 in a state of almost complete confusion and demoralization. Admiral Porter testified later that "when I got to Alexandria, I found the army in a great state of stampede. . . . There was the most perfect stampede that I ever saw in an army that was in perfect preparation to go into battle." Colonel Duganne, who wrote that Banks's movement up the Red River had been "like that of a conqueror," admitted that he had been "defeated" in his two engagements with Taylor, and Union soldier Sam Pincus later testified under oath that "after our defeat at Mansfield we retreated in full haste and finally made a halt at Alexandria."

The Federals delayed at Alexandria a little over two weeks because the Red River had fallen so low that it was necessary for Colonel Joseph Bailey, a Federal engineer, to build a dam in order to get Porter's gunboats over the rapids. Before the Federal troops retreated from Alexandria they fired the city, despite the orders of General Banks; other Federal officers were not so considerate, and it was reported that General A. J. Smith said, as he looked back at the burning city, "Boys, this *looks like war!*" A few scalawags rode with the retreating army, including J. Madison Wells, who was to become a Reconstruction governor, William B. Hyman, whom Wells appointed Chief Justice of the Supreme Court, and C. W. Boyce, who would become president pro tem of the state senate of the "occupied" Louisiana government in 1864.

The Confederates closed in after the Federals, who were accompanied by some four thousand Negroes, and the retreat from Alexandria became practically a rout until the protection of the powerful Mississippi River gunboats was secured. A Union captain reported that "'longer and more rapid forced marches than this of ours have been made, but I am glad that I was not called upon to assist at the performance."

Modern writer H. L. Landers has concluded that "no campaign of the Civil War produced so prolific a crop of poisonous quarrels as did this one." The charges and countercharges continued until the deaths of those concerned. Confederate General Taylor condemned General Edmund Kirby Smith for ordering several divisions of his army to Arkansas and always believed that otherwise he might have captured Banks's army and Porter's gunboat fleet. Smith was certainly at odds with Taylor, for in his congratulatory order issued after the two battles he failed to mention Taylor's name. Taylor asked to be relieved from further service under General Smith and was soon ordered to take command of the Department of Alabama, Mississippi and East Louisiana.

The Federal Committee on the Conduct of the War held a full-scale investigation which accomplished little except to bring out the fact that the Federal commanders had been almost completely incompatible, that the expedition had been ordered from Washington, and that, as General T. K. Smith testified, it was "what would be called in military parlance a mercantile expedition." Several civilians had accompanied the expedition, upon the authority of the President, apparently for the purpose of trading in cotton, and the gunboat fleet had confiscated so much cotton that Banks's aide reported that the stamps "C.S.A." and "U.S.N." meant "Cotton Stealing Association of the United States Navy." The Federal government soon incorporated the Department of the Gulf into the Military Division of West Mississippi, under the command of Major General E. R. S. Canby, and Banks was replaced by Major General Stephen A. Hurlbut.

1865. By the beginning of 1865 the South was exhausted, even the army of General Robert E. Lee in Virginia could not be adequately supplied. There was no hope in Louisiana. Federal armies controlled the whole of the southeastern part of the state, and the Confederate forces were not strong enough to attack them. People were dispirited; soldiers had begun to desert and go home, one soldier reporting that from six to twelve of his comrades were deserting every night. The war was almost over.

General Lee surrendered at Appomattox, Virginia, on April 9 and General Joseph E. Johnston in North Carolina a few days later. In Shreveport, Governor Allen went "about his duties as seemingly calm and self-controlled, with as much energy and interest, as if he had been ignorant that a few days would end it all." A Confederate officer wrote that at a Shreveport mass meeting on April 29 the "sun was hot, audience cold and speeches as far as we heard good in their way." A Federal spy reported that "Wholesale desertion" was "openly talked of" and that the spirit of the Confederate soldiers was "crushed." On May 17, Confederate Major David F. Boyd wrote from Alexandria that "all is confusion and demoralization here, nothing like order or discipline remains. . . . We must look the matter square in the face and shape our actions (personally and officially) accordingly."

On May 26, General Simon B. Buckner, acting for General Kirby Smith who had gone to Houston, surrendered the Confederate forces west of the Mississippi; on June 2, General Smith signed the official documents on board the *Fort Jackson*, off Galveston Harbor. That same day Governor Allen issued his last message to the people of Louisiana: "The war is over, the contest is ended, the soldiers are disbanded and gone to their homes, and now there is in Louisiana no opposition whatever to the Constitution and the laws of the United States . . . return to your homes. Repair, improve and plant. Go to work with a hearty good will, and let your actions show that you are able and willing to adapt yourselves to the new order of things. . . . If possible forget the past. Look forward to the future. Act with candor and discretion, and you will live to bless him who in parting gives you this last advice." Then the Governor left for exile in Mexico.

BILLY YANKS AND JOHNNY REBS. The soldiers of both sides generally accepted army life, as do soldiers in all wars, with considerable complaint. The northern soldier, being much better equipped and supplied, complained less than his southern opponent about clothing, food and other necessities. As the war progressed the Confederate supply system gradually failed, and her soldiers had to acquire clothing and rations as best they could and to learn to eat practically anything.

Northern soldiers complained about Louisiana snakes, rains, lice, bugs, and particularly mosquitoes. Lawrence Van Alstyne wrote during the siege of Port Hudson: "I don't suppose there is a spot on earth where there are so many snakes to the acre as right here." One soldier wrote that "rain is good or bad, according to circumstances. In hot weather it cools the skin, invigorates the muscles, and is a positive comfort," but when marching it was "a greater nuisance than people in carriages would imagine." Another Yankee complained: "Every hollow became a puddle before the fellows sleeping in it could get out. . . . We are soaking wet before we know. . . . We stand around and growl for awhile and then settle down and are soon asleep again." Body lice did not cause too much trouble, for "we just boiled our clothes and that's the end of them," but it was different with "a small black bug, just like what we call at home snapping bugs. Their delight is to crawl in someone's ear when asleep. We sleep with cotton in our ears every night. They make a man raving crazy. The doctors pour oil in first, and then syringe them out. Nearly every night there is a bug case." All the soldiers hated mosquitoes, but Van Alstyne thought them so vicious that he remarked, "If I had a brigade of men as determined as these Brashear City mosquitoes, I believe I could sweep the Rebellion off its feet in a month's time."

Most of the Federals were impressed with the stanch and sometimes brash patriotism of the southern girls. One Yankee soldier wondered "if these Southern girls can love as they hate? If they can, it would be well worth one's trying to get one of them." When one young soldier was caught stealing oranges by a pretty girl, who peremptorily ordered him out of her yard, he wrote that "if the Rebels were all like her I would resign and go home at once, for she did actually scare my wits all away from me." Some Louisiana soldiers were extremely critical of the girls of other southern states. Robert Patrick wrote of one Mississippi girl with extreme distaste: "When she straightened up good and unwound herself, she appeared to be fifteen feet long and when she rose from her chair she reminded me of the unfolding of the huge serpents we sometimes see in shows. Her face was thin and sharp and her nose keen enough to split a hair; she was slab-sided and had very large hands. She had very long legs being split up almost to the chin. Her legs looked like straws and were bowed like a pair of hames."

All soldiers complained of army rations. One Yankee explained how hardtack was eaten: "We soak them in our coffee and in that way get off the outside. It takes a long time to soak one through, but repeated soakings and repeating gnawing finally uses them up. Very often they are mouldy, and most always wormy. We knock them together and jar out the worms, and the mould we cut or scrape off. Sometimes we soak them until soft and then fry them in pork grease, but generally we smash them up in pieces and grind away until either the teeth or the hard-tack gives up. I know now why Dr. Cole examined our teeth so carefully when we passed through the medical mill at Hudson." Lieutenant Howell Carter of the 1st Louisiana Cavalry reported that the one way to test the quality of genuine "pure *blue* beef" was to let a rail fence down to four rails and the animal that could not "step or jump over it" was "the genuine article." E. John Ellis of Amite wrote his mother that "when I see dirt in my victuals, I take it out and eat on. If I taste it, I swallow and eat on. If my coffee is not strong, I thank the Lord that it is as strong as it is & drink it."

The citizen soldiers of both sides adapted themselves to war and the constant threat of death as best they could. One Louisiana Confederate wrote that "some of the boys seemed a little frightened under their first fire; as to myself, . . . I did not feel brave at all," while another complained that during his "first personal experience of heavy shelling" if he had been ordered to dismount from his horse he would have been "too weak in the knees to mount again." A northerner scrawled in his diary that the cannon balls "keep coming, and we dodge less and less. If they keep at it long enough I suppose we shall get used to it." Another Yank complained that "the Rebs seem to be getting madder all the time," while a third grumbled, "those cusses jest shot my pipe square out of my trousers' pocket. Look at that hole, now! . . . I wish I was in Massachusetts."

Both northerners and southerners believed strongly in the cause for which they fought. G. L. Alspaugh wrote: "I had rather die fighting the yankees than any other way," while G. M. Lee believed that "our cause is a glorious & holy one and I for one am willing that my bones shall bleach in the sacred soil of Virginia in driving the evading host of tyrants from our soil." Robert Patrick thus expressed his feelings at the grave of a dead enemy: "You were not satisfied to remain at home, and let us alone; you must come to the South to murder our citizens, burn our houses, desolate our homes and lay waste to our country. . . . You for one have met your just reward, which is a grant of land from the Confederates, of three feet by six, in an obscure spot, where your friends, if you have any, will never be able to find your body, for there is nothing to mark the spot except a small hillock of red clay, which a few hard rains will wash away and it will disappear forever."

Most soldiers, North and South, fought bravely, accepted hardships, remained stanchly loyal, and were a credit to their armies. There were exceptions, however. One Louisiana soldier revealed his true character in letters to his wife. Lazy and cowardly, he somehow managed to avoid fighting and continually griped about everything. Finally he was able, through political influence, to secure a soft assignment at Opelousas, where he was stationed during the last year of the war. He spent several days during the first week of April, 1865, near St. Martinville, fishing, visiting, and enjoying "fresh strawberries and cream." Hearing of Lee's surrender, he wrote his wife bitterly: "Gen'l Lee has sold the Confederacy." Later he boasted of his "military record" and rose to a political position of importance in the state.

STATE GOVERNMENT DURING THE WAR. Thomas Overton Moore served as Governor until January 25, 1864, when he was succeeded by Henry Watkins Allen. Both governors were able, conscientious men who did the best they could for a war-torn state.

The state capital was at Baton Rouge when the war began, but with the occupation of that city in May, 1862, it was moved to Opelousas, the executive offices being located in the Lacombe Hotel. Here it remained until January, 1863, when it was moved to Shreveport. The Caddo Parish Courthouse served as the capitol while the governor's office was in an old frame building on the north side of Texas Street adjoining Renfro's Drug Store.

The state government faced many wartime problems. The legislature passed laws, but the presence of the Federal armies made enforcement almost impossible. Raising armies and furnishing supplies were problems of paramount importance; supply depots were established, and numerous small factories were built, including packing houses, cotton-cloth manufactories, and medical laboratories. The raising of war funds and the collection of taxes were difficult. Many governmental and legal records were captured or destroyed, making the trial of suits and other cases difficult. The case of Harp v. Kenner over the payment of a note is an excellent case in point: The man who executed the note was killed, one of the endorsers was in the Confederate Congress, the maker of the note was dead, the holder was a war prisoner in the North, another endorser was in Lee's army in Virginia, and finally, the Ascension parish recorder's office had burned in October, 1862.

Local police juries and town officials had many extraordinary responsibilities. They paid bounties to enlistees, equipped soldiers, furnished relief to needy families, repaired roads, ferries, and bridges, and tried to maintain order. After the occupation of New Orleans in 1862 the maintenance of Confederate local authority was extremely difficult, and General Richard Taylor reported that public sentiment in many localities was "apathetic if not hostile from disaster and neglect."

Not all Louisianians were loyal to their state or to the Confederacy. Outlaws hid in the hills and swamps, while bands of armed men called "jayhawkers" evaded military service, plundered the countryside, burned houses and other buildings, and killed civilians. Fugitives from the draft took refuge in the Catahoula, Pearl River, and other swamps and fired on military details sent in search of them. Deserters and draft dodgers increased after the fall of Port Hudson, and General Taylor was forced to admit that his cavalry could not cope with the lawless elements. Scalawag spies and paid informers followed Confederate armies or haunted troop concentrations and military depots in search of information to forward to Federal military commanders. An independent local government opposed to the state and Confederate governments was organized in Washington Parish. Patrols, Home Guards, and Rangers were organized to defend Louisianians living within the Confederate lines from their own people; two of the most noted companies of Rangers operated in Rapides Parish and were led by David C. Paul and James A. McWaters.

During the spring of 1865 state and local government began to disintegrate, despite efforts of Governor Allen to keep the processes of government in action. State government officially ceased with the surrender of General Kirby Smith's forces, by which time local government was practically nonexistent in most parishes and towns.

LIFE IN THE FEDERAL-OCCUPIED AREAS. While many sections of the state were occupied by Federal armies for short periods, the southeastern section was continuously occupied from the fall of New Orleans to the end of the war. General Benjamin F. Butler, who took formal possession of New Orleans on May 1, 1862, was a Massachusetts Democratic political leader whose father had fought with Andrew Jackson at the Battle of New Orleans. He had voted forty-four times for the nomination of Jefferson Davis at the deadlocked Charleston Democratic Convention of 1860 and had subsequently supported southern Democrat candidate John C. Breckinridge for President. Only forty-four years of age, he was already a successful lawyer, had a large personal fortune, and was a promising politician especially popular with labor for his espousal of a ten-hour day.

A stout man, with a fair complexion and bright but squinting eyes, Butler had a large, half-bald head with heavy features and a "highkeyed, penetrating, tranquil drawl which makes the men titter." He was short of temper, loved controversy, had a brilliant intellect, was certainly no pretender and no hypocrite, but was pompous and tactless. He had social charm when he wished to exert it, but possessed a coarseness well illustrated by his remark when a group of New Orleans women turned their backs to him—they knew which end of them looked best. He was generally popular with his soldiers, largely because they enjoyed making fun of his high-pitched voice and his somewhat grotesque actions; one of them wrote that he "tumbles all to pieces with distress. His body jerks forward; his elbows flap up and down like wings; he seems to trot several feet ahead of his horse; he arrives at the scene of confusion with a face of anguish."

Butler continued martial law in New Orleans because, as he wrote, he was in control of "a city seven miles long by two to four wide, of a hundred and fifty thousand inhabitants, all hostile, bitter, defiant, explosive." He quickly restored order and brought his soldiers under tight discipline; when one group of them plundered a number of houses, four were quickly hanged—after the war Butler's bitterest critics never censured his men for unlawful or unauthorized acts. Butler levied special taxes to feed the poor and relieve their suffering, and by October reported that he was feeding nearly 10,000 families a month at a cost of $70,000, spending $2,000 for the support of five orphanages, and $5,000 for Charity Hospital. He reorganized the public-school system along lines which have lasted to the present time. He fixed food prices in order to curb profiteering. He set a thousand unemployed men to cleaning streets, repairing wharves, enlarging drainage canals, and flushing filthy gutters. He repaired the levee, filled in a portion of the river front with batture sand, and enforced quarantine and fumigation regulations.

Even bitter critic Marion Southwood was impressed and wrote that Butler was "the best scavenger we have ever had." A few years after the war a writer in the New Orleans *Journal of Medicine* admitted that Butler's regime had been characterized by three exceptional facts: the absence of epidemics, a better quarantine than the civil authorities had ever had, and the enforcement of sanitary regulations by an efficient police.

Butler was in a trying position. He was the military commandant of the largest city in the south, one of the proudest and most loyal cities of the Confederacy. The people of New Orleans did everything possible to ridicule, insult, and annoy the soldiers of the occupying army. The women of the upper classes were politely insulting; those of the lower classes not so polite. The *Daily Picayune* on May 9, 1862, commented upon their "shameless conduct," the "shocking nuisance" of their street behavior, and demanded their arrest "whether arrayed in fine clothes or in rags." Something had to be done. Butler found the solution in one of the old London statutes.

He later wrote: "I changed 'London' into 'New Orleans'; that was all. The rest I copied *verbatim et literatim*."

On May 15, he issued General Order No. 28, which stated simply that as the officers and soldiers of the United States Army had been subject to the repeated insults of the women of New Orleans, "in return for the most scrupulous non-interference and courtesy on our part, it is ordered that hereafter when any female shall, by word, gesture, or movement, insult or show contempt for any officer or soldier of the United States, she shall be regarded and held liable to be treated as a woman of the town plying her vocation." This meant that a woman, upon formal complaint, might be arrested, held overnight in the city jail, brought before a magistrate the next morning, and if found guilty, fined $5.00.

"Probably no other action by an American military commander," as Herbert Asbury wrote, "ever aroused such a world-wide storm of resentment and indignation." Southerners believed that the order gave Federal troops permission to insult the women of New Orleans and so advertised the order to the world, and the world answered by condemning Butler as few men have ever been condemned. A northern editor called him "hell's blackest imp; Apollyon's twin brother; the Grand High-priest of Pandaemonium; the unclean, perjured, false-hearted product of Massachusetts civilization; . . . the dirtiest knave God ever gave breath to; total depravity personified; that baggy-faced fruit of perdition, Beast Butler!" But whatever the criticism, the order had the desired effect. New Orleans quieted down.

Three weeks later, on June 5, Butler issued Special Order No. 70, which provided for the execution of forty-one-year-old William B. Mumford on June 7. Mumford had been tried and convicted by a military commission for treason and the "overt act thereof, . . . for the purpose of inciting other evil-minded persons to further resistance" against the United States by pulling down the American flag from the United States Mint two days before formal occupation of the city. The sentence was carried out, and to the people of New Orleans, the state, and the South, Mumford immediately became a hero and Butler his murderer. These two orders made Butler the most hated man in all Louisiana history, not excepting Spanish General O'Reilly, but like O'Reilly he stopped disorder in New Orleans.

In September, 1862, Butler ordered the Federal Confiscation Act of July 17 placed in effect in New Orleans and the areas in Louisiana occupied by his troops. The act stated that the property of all citizens of the Confederacy who had not registered their allegiance to the United States was subject to confiscation. By late October nearly 70,000 persons had registered and those who had not done so suffered greatly.

While the common soldiers were held on tight rein, Butler's officers began to acquire confiscated property of all types at Federal auctions at greatly reduced prices, prices which sometimes were only 10 per cent of the value of the item. In all probability Butler himself acquired no property in this manner, but his brother, A. J. Butler, and numerous others reputedly made fortunes by various forms of extralegal and illegal practices. The word "Butlerize," meaning to steal, came into common use. It should be emphatically stated, however, that Butler's confiscation of property in Louisiana was in conformance with the Confiscation Act, and while Louisiana historians have unanimously blamed Butler, there is no evidence that he at any time went beyond the law. The Congress and the President of the United States should receive the blame, not the commanding general at New Orleans. At no time during his regime was there the wholesale looting and destruction of property permitted by General Banks in the Teche region and during the Red River Campaign and by General Grant in northeast Louisiana. Nevertheless, he received the sobriquet "Silver Spoon" Butler.

General Butler was replaced in December, 1862, by General Banks. One New Orleanian reported Butler's departure from the city: "There was not one hurrah, not one sympathizing cry went up for him from the vast crowd which went to see him off—a silent rebuke. I wonder if he felt it!" Although General Banks eased regulations, the confiscation of property in areas occupied by the Federal armies continued until the end of the war. Most Louisianians never became reconciled to Federal occupation, and when on one occasion someone remarked to General Banks that New Orleans was a Union city, Banks replied: "A Union city? I could carry every Union man in it on a hand-car."

LIFE OF THE PEOPLE DURING WARTIME. Life was difficult for the people at home during the war. The state and local governments were unstable and often powerless to enforce the laws; sugar, cotton, and other crops could not be sold; loans and credit were not available; and ordinary manufactured goods could not be found. Labor was also a problem, for Negroes refused to work or ran away from plantations when Federals were in the area, and many joined the Federal army. By the end of the war over 24,000 Negroes had enlisted in Louisiana, a number exceeded only in Kentucky and Tennessee. In face of the advancing armies many families fled to Texas, in some cases taking their slaves with them. Since the men were in the army, much of the labor had to be performed by women and children.

Prices of the necessities of life constantly rose until it became almost impossible for the poor to provide food, shelter, and clothing. Confederate and state money constantly declined in value. Late in the war butter sold at $5.00 a pound; eggs, $5.00 a dozen; beans, $2.50 a quart; bacon and hams, 75 cents a pound and up; salt, $130.00 a sack; and quinine as high as $150.00 an ounce. One man wrote that before the war he went to market with the money in his pocket and brought back his purchases in a basket; "now, I take the money in the basket, and bring the things home in my pocket."

The word "Confederate" took on a new connotation, for it now meant crude, unfashionable, or obsolete. Sarah Morgan Dawson wrote that "Confederate dresses were old and outmoded; a Confederate bridle was a rope halter; Confederate silver was tin cups and spoons; Confederate flour was unrefined cornmeal." Home manufacturing became common. Hats were made of plaited shucks or of palmetto; "homespun" clothing was dyed with garden-grown indigo, pokeberries, red-oak and other barks; ink was made of magnolia or dogwood bark, pomegranate rinds, or elderberries and green persimmons; shoe blacking was commonly a mixture of soot and molasses, eggwhites and vinegar; coffee substitutes were made of parched potatoes, burned meal, and roasted acorns, the best being made from okra seed.

There was more destruction of property in point of total value in Louisiana than in any southern state. The northeastern section for a hundred miles west of the Mississippi, the Red River Valley south of Natchitoches, the area from Alexandria to Opelousas and down the Teche, the Bayou Lafourche country, were burnt out, looted, and made desolate. Many Federal commanding officers deliberately ordered this devastation or by their actions let their troops know that such destruction would not be punished. Years afterward, General James Tuttle in a speech before the Hayes & Wheeler Club of Des Moines, Iowa, admitted that he had been a "house-burner" and that he was the "General Tuttle whose troops, on the march from Milliken's Bend to Grand Gulf, burned so many fine houses on Lake St. Joseph." One plantation home was "the grandest house I ever saw or read about. The house and furnishings are said to have cost $500,000. . . . [when] I was about two or three miles away, I looked back, attracted by an immense blaze, and the Bowie house was gone. I suppose it was burned by some of my boys."

Federal officers not infrequently protested this wanton and needless destruction. In middle September, 1862, the commander of a United States gunboat addressed his superiors: "I respectfully request instructions if the guns of the *Kathahdin* are to be used for the protection of soldiers upon a maurauding expedition, and if I am to use them in the protection of drunken, undisciplined, and licentious troops in the wanton pillage of a private mansion of wines, plate, silk dresses, the misses and female apparel, to say nothing of the confiscation of sugar, which I believe to be without proper and lawful reasons therefor. . . . I am desirous of encountering enemies and of injuring them in every manly manner, but I cannot further prostitute the dignity of my profession, as I conceive I have done today. . . . It is disgraceful and humiliating to me to be ordered on guard duty of soldiers employed in pillaging ladies' dresses and petticoats, and I respectfully request that I may be relieved from such service."

Most Louisianians accepted hardship and loss of property without complaint. They were proud of their steadfastness during the war years. They were proud of their fathers, brothers, husbands, and sons who served in the Confederate armies, and long afterwards boasted of them. Years later, when a Louisianian was asked something concerning General Robert E. Lee, he might stop, look puzzled for a moment, then reply: "Lee? Ah, yes, I now recall hearing General Beauregard (or it might be General Taylor or some other Louisiana soldier) speaking well of Lee!"

Both North and South deplored the war and each side was glad when it ended. Perhaps northern General E. R. S. Canby, who succeeded General Banks in Louisiana in 1864, summed it up best. "I tell you what it is, Betty," he said to his wife, "this war of brothers has been one of the most terrible things in history. Politicians made it, soldiers fought and deplored it, but it is something to have the Stars and Stripes— the flag of Washington and Jefferson—floating and inviolate over an undivided Union."

CHAPTER 23

"YEARS OF THE LOCUST"

PERIOD OF MILITARY OCCUPATION

EXPLANATION. This era of Louisiana history may be logically organized into two divisions. The first was the war period which began with the fall of New Orleans in April, 1862, and ended with the surrender of General Edmund Kirby Smith in early June, 1865. New Orleans was continuously held by the Federal army, while other sections of the state were occupied and controlled by Federal forces for days, weeks, or even months. The second period began with the end of the war and lasted until the spring of 1877, when President Rutherford B. Hayes withdrew United States Army units from Louisiana.

The era from 1865 to 1877 has generally been called "The Reconstruction Period," a term which implies a period of rebuilding and reconstructing the governmental, economic, cultural, and social life of the South. The name is hardly apt, for little rebuilding or reconstruction was done or even attempted by the Federal government. More accurately, it was a period of peacetime military occupation, for Federal troops remained stationed in the southern states for several years after the war ended; and in Louisiana they remained until April, 1877. During those years army commanders directed and controlled Louisiana's entire political and economic life, and to a certain degree the cultural and social life of her people.

The southern states have the unique distinction of being the only American states to have been "occupied" in peacetime by a military force, and Louisiana holds the dubious honor of having been "occupied" for a longer period than any other southern state.

OVER-ALL VIEW OF THE PERIOD AFTER THE WAR. The soldiers of Louisiana, many of whom like Francis T. Nicholls had "the Yankee mark" on them, returned home during those late spring and early summer days of 1865 to a war-ravaged and desolate state, to humiliation, to unspeakable poverty and despair. They had accepted defeat in battle and had their paroles in their pockets. Their first task was to find work, any kind of work which would support themselves and their families, for they were like former Governor Allen when he wrote: "I am too proud to beg, and too honest, I hope, to steal." They well understood that the state faced the basic problems of restoring government, rebuilding agriculture, developing industry to supply home needs, the practical application and use of free labor, and the definition of the place in society of the newly freed Negro. They expected some material assistance from the Federal government and to be permitted to solve local problems in their own way. But this was not to be.

Years later Charles Marshall of Lee's staff wrote that "no such peace as our peace ever followed immediately upon such a war as our war." It was difficult for Louisianians to grasp the fact that the government of the United States was really not interested in helping to solve the problems faced by the state or the South. Many northern leaders wanted revenge, and a northern historian has recently admitted that "Northern revenge in the guise of the preservation of the dearly won Union was worse for the South than the war." Another described the "outrages, and humiliations worse than outrage, of the period of so-called reconstruction but actual servile domination." George W. Cable called the period "that hideous carnival of political profligacy." Many Louisianians, like the wife of General George A. Custer, who was stationed at Alexandria for a time, wished that "Abraham Lincoln could have been spared to bring his justice and gentle humanity" to the relief of the South.

It was a period of almost constant disorder. Colored and white soldiers of the occupying army insulted and humiliated the people; Negroes roamed about aimlessly, stealing and committing other crimes; Radical white and colored political leaders systematically looted the state. Carpetbaggers flocked to Louisiana from northern states with frenzied desire for power and spoils, and scalawag Louisianians joined forces with them. Newly freed Negroes, illiterate, wholly unprepared for such a transformation, and inflated with their new political and social equality, joined the carpetbaggers, scalawags, and economic speculators. Wise national statesmen might have solved the problems, but there were few such men in Washington and their voices went unheard above the Radical hurricane.

To Lincoln the problem had been simple. In July, 1862, he wrote New York banker August Belmont that "Broken eggs cannot be mended, but Louisiana has nothing to do now but to take her place in the Union as it was, barring the already broken eggs." His "erring sister state" idea was not accepted by the self-righteous leadership now in power, who believed that the South had sinned and therefore should be punished. Ex-Confederates felt like Henry Watkins Allen: "I cannot ask a pardon. A *parole* I would gladly accept. Perhaps a general amnesty may come—if not, I cannot with honor go back and ask pardon for what I don't consider a crime."

So civil strife continued throughout the period, with New Orleans the principal battleground where Conservative and Radical forces struggled to control the government of the state, the Radicals always having the support of the army of occupation. Loyal Louisianians were frequently forced to operate outside the law to preserve a semblance of order. The Ku Klux Klan, the Knights of the White Camelia, Seymour and Blair Societies, the Innocents, and other secret organizations did much good until they came under the control of revengeful leaders and had to be disbanded. Radical leaders organized the Union League to oppose these organizations, and as a result there were race riots in many sections of the state, the worst ones occuring in 1866, 1873, and 1874.

Many of the United States Army officers stationed in towns and villages attempted to prevent disorder. They counseled moderation, urged ex-slaves to return to farms and plantations, and tried to prevent lawlessness. They realized, as Elizabeth Custer wrote, that "the Confederate soldiers had to get their blood down from fever heat," and they did their best to hold in check the insubordinate soldiers under their command. It was the politician, not the army officer, who made Louisiana Reconstruction what it was.

The Negro was the crux of the problem. The former master, as unaccustomed to Negro freedom as the ex-slave, in the majority of cases still treated him as a slave. To the former slave, freedom meant fredom from work. Radical leaders in Washington in no way agreed with Lincoln's statement: "I am not and never have been in favor of bringing about in any form the social and political equality of the black and white races." Numerous Negroes rose to positions of political importance. One became governor for a short period, several were sent to Congress, a half dozen became state officials, over thirty became state senators, and nearly a hundred served in the lower house of the legislature; others were police jurymen, justices of the peace, school-board members, or held other minor offices.

Many were illiterate, or at best could barely sign their names. Witness the statement of one legislator "dat de gen'lm from de parish of St. Quelquechose was developing assertions and expurgating rationcinations clean agin de fust principles of law and equality." Herman Bell, justice of the peace in Ouachita Parish, filled in the blanks of a warrant of arrest as follows: "Whereas, due proof has been made before me by *Some McFarland Sase* that *A case of Salt en battra* did on the *this 9 day of May 1871*, at the Parish aforesaid, commit *Orfence of Salt Anbattra use On Same McFarland by Ben Tolard use a Dangust Weeping with en Temp to kill the weeping was a pocet knife. A Cut the hip er man of this Hip come mighty ner cuting his Tho. . . ."* A Louisiana Negro historian has written that while the Negroes were "illiterate and unprepared for such a transformation in the majority of cases," here and there were men whose background and education fitted them for office.

The Negro Radicals, however, should not be too seriously blamed for the roles they played. The majority of them were only a short time removed from slavery, had little if any education and no experience in politics or government, and were used as tools by unscrupulous white men. The New York *World* admitted that a "White Man's Party" had been forced upon Louisiana through the organization of a "Black Man's Party," through which Radical white leaders ruled the state. Most of the blame must go to the carpetbaggers, the majority of whom were from New England and the Middle Atlantic states, for they formed the largest segment of Louisiana Radical leadership. In 1874 the New York *Tribune* passed judgment upon Louisiana "reconstruction": "They do queer things in Louisiana. . . . and a noble Republican government it is which our administration and the Senate have combined to guarantee them."

RECONSTRUCTION DURING THE WAR. Abraham Lincoln believed that a state could not lawfully or constitutionally leave the Union and as soon as New Orleans was occupied made plans to re-establish civil government in Louisiana. General George F. Shepley was appointed military governor of the state on June 11, 1862, a position under the authority of General Benjamin F. Butler. General Shepley partially restored civil government in southeastern Louisiana, which was under Federal control and which had about two-sevenths of the state's population. He ordered a congregressional election to be held in December in the first and second congressional districts. Bavarian-born Michael Hahn, whose parents had immigrated to Louisiana when he was a child, and New Hampshire-born Benjamin F. Flanders, who had come to Louisiana at the age of twenty-seven, were elected. They were finally admitted to their seats in the House of Representatives and served until March, 1863. No other Louisiana Representatives or Senators were admitted to Congress until after the war.

Two political parties were organized, the Conservative party, generally composed of old-line southern Democrats, and the Free State party, made up of a few Republicans, opponents of secession, and those citizens who had accepted Lincoln's plan of government. In August, 1863, Lincoln asked General Shepley to assist the citizens of the southeastern section in reorganizing a state government. An election was held in February, 1864, and Michael Hahn was elected—the first German-born citizen to become governor of an American state. Hahn was inaugurated at New Orleans the following March 4.

Immediately after the inauguration of Governor Hahn, General Nathaniel P. Banks, who had succeeded General Butler, ordered an election of delegates to a convention to revise the Constitution of 1852. The 97-delegate convention met for 78 days during the early summer of 1864 (during which period it spent $120.78 a day for liquors, cigars, and other sundry items), and adopted the new constitution on July 23. The Constitution of 1864 abolished slavery, extended the suffrage to Negroes who had served in the Federal army, owned taxable property, or who showed intellectual fitness, broadened the powers of the legislature, and extended public education. It was in some ways, as Roger Shugg has stated, "an extraordinary document which contained reforms and innovations of great social import" and would have benefited the state had it been judiciously interpreted.

Governor Hahn resigned on March 4, 1865, after his election to the United States Senate. His governorship and that of General Shepley were generally marked by moderation, good government, and the sincere desire to help the people who lived in the Federal-occupied section of the state. During the same period Thomas Overton Moore and Henry Watkins Allen were the governors of Confederate Louisiana, which contained about five-sevenths of the state's population. Allen had been elected in the regular election held in November, 1863, and took office on January 25, 1864. Thus, from April, 1862, to June, 1865, Louisiana had two governments, the Confederate government and the government supported by the Federal army in the occupied areas.

GOVERNORS WELLS, FLANDERS, AND BAKER. Lieutenant Governor J. Madison Wells of Rapides Parish became Governor of the occupied section of the state upon the resignation of Governor Hahn. The war ended soon after, and the paroled Confederate soldiers, many of whom recovered their citizenship by taking President Andrew Johnson's amnesty oath, returned home. The civil government of Louisiana was recognized, and at the November election Wells was elected Governor for a regular term by a vote of roughly 4 to 1 over Henry Watkins Allen, who was absent in Mexico and did not know that he had been made a candidate. Allen nevertheless carried the parishes of Washington, Rapides, and Bossier. While Wells was a scalawag, he was not typical of the breed for he had been a Unionist from principal and conviction rather than from opportunism. He had remained in Rapides Parish during the war, doing everything possible to obstruct the Confederates until he was forced to flee the area in the fall of 1863. He returned with Banks's army the next year and went to New Orleans after the failure of the Red River Campaign.

During his governorship Wells did much to relieve the shock of Reconstruction in Louisiana by making good appointments to local offices, by many acts of kindness and sympathy to ex-Confederates, by his practical attitude toward the Negro problem, and by his sincere desire to solidly rebuild the state. He did not believe that it was either wise or expedient to clothe the Negro "with the suffrage," for the emancipated slave had "much to learn," and had duties to discharge "which it is incumbent upon us all to instruct him to appreciate and perform." He once told an ex-Federal army officer carpetbagger: "The truth is, sir, that we're very much obliged to you for all you Northern gentlemen have done, but now that you are successful, you had better go home. Louisiana must be governed by Louisianians."

It was not long, however, before accusations that Wells was exceeding his authority as Governor and leaning toward the Radicals cost him the support of many white citizens. A bloody riot occurred in New Orleans on July 30, 1866, in which 34 Negroes were killed and nearly 150 wounded, along with several whites killed and wounded. Meanwhile General Philip H. Sheridan, at that time the army commander in Louisiana, had removed Mayor John T. Monroe of New Orleans from office, along with several other state and local officials. Sheridan so angered the loyal element with his strutting, flourishing of a swagger stick, and imperious manners that the editor of the Alexandria *Louisiana Democrat* wrote, in race horse language, that "he must have been got by a stud tomtit out of a snowbird." The Fourteenth Amendment was rejected by the 1867 legislature and restrictive measures were passed against the Negroes, which caused Congress to fear that they were no longer safe under their former masters. Finally, on June 3, 1867, General Sheridan removed Governor Wells from office.

Benjamin F. Flanders was appointed to succeed Wells. Before the war Flanders had been a successful New Orleans politician and businessman. After brief hitches as New Orleans city treasurer under Butler, as an army captain (he served less than a month), and as a Congressman, he became a special agent of the Treasury Department, a position which enabled him to acquire a sizable fortune. He resigned the governorship in January, 1868. Regarding his governorship Alcée Fortier wrote: "The creature of the military power, he was expected to do its bidding, and he did not disappoint the expectations."

In January, 1868, General Winfield S. Hancock, who had succeeded General Sheridan, appointed Kentucky-born, Louisiana-reared Joshua Baker as Governor. The Constitution of 1868 was ratified in March and went into effect immediately. This constitution was the first such Louisiana document to contain a formal bill of rights and for the most part was a Radical document, chiefly designed to give the Negro the political, civil, and social rights he had been denied by the Constitution of 1864. It was hailed by Louisiana radicaldom, according to the Negro Opelousas *St. Landry Progress,* as "the deathblow of the slave oligarchy in Louisiana." A state election was held at the same time the constitution was ratified, and Illinois-born Henry Clay Warmoth was elected Governor, with Negro Oscar J. Dunn as Lieutenant Governor. Warmoth was to take office on July 13, 1868, but on June 27, General U. S. Grant removed Governor Baker and appointed Warmoth to serve until he was inaugurated for his regular term.

GOVERNORSHIPS OF WARMOTH AND PINCHBACK. Warmoth had first visited Louisiana in 1862 when a lieutenant colonel on detached service and had settled in New Orleans in 1865. He immediately plunged into politics and was extraordinarily successful with Negro voters. At one Negro rally in the fall of 1865, according to the New Orleans *Daily Crescent,* in his speech he oscillated "between the gravity of the owl and the levity of the monkey" and told his audience that the Yankees were inventing machines every day and that when he again went North he would get them "to invent a machine which will pump out your black blood and pump in white blood. There will be no trouble then about your voting, for all you will have to do will be to wash your faces and go to the ballot box."

The worst evils of the entire period began with the administration of Governor Warmoth. Factional politics plagued the state, and each faction stole as much money as possible. In a later interview Warmoth is supposed to have said: " I don't pretend to be honest. . . . I only pretend to be as honest as anybody in politics. . . . Here are these New Orleans bankers making a great outcry against the dishonesty of the Louisiana legislature. . . . Why, damn it, every body is demoralized down here. Corruption is the fashion."

The Radicals secured the election of a legislature in which nearly 50 per cent of the house of representatives and nearly 20 per cent of the senate were Negroes and Warmoth became practically a dictator through his control of the legislature and his extraordinary police powers. He secured the passage of the Metropolitan Police Bill, which organized a police force for Orleans, Jefferson, and St. Bernard parishes under his personal control. The legislature ratified the Fourteenth and Fifteenth Amendments, appropriated huge sums of money, much of which found its way into Radical pockets, and when it finally adjourned, the New Orleans *Times* wrote: "The crime of its life was only equaled by the wickedness of its acts. Its death leaves the State plundered and bankrupted, with a people so shackled, mentally, morally and socially, as to evoke the pity of all more fortunate Americans."

The actions of Warmoth, Dunn, and the legislature brought storms of protest over the entire state. The Ku Klux Klan spread fear and terror among the Negroes, while the Knights of the White Camelia frightened scalawags and carpetbaggers and broke up Radical Negro-white political meetings. The Radicals organized the Union League, and soon Louisiana was practically in a state of civil war, with race riots and other disorders in many sections.

In the election of 1872, Vermont-born William Pitt Kellogg—according to the St. Louis *Republican* a "worn out political bummer from Illinois"—was the candidate of the Radical faction, while the Democrats and Liberal Republicans supported Virginia-born John McEnery of Monroe. Although the election returns proved the election of McEnery, the Radical Returning Board which canvassed election returns declared that all Radical candidates had been elected. But Warmoth and his faction quarreled, and on December 9, 1872, he was impeached by the house of representatives by a vote of 57 to 6. The senate immediately resolved itself into a court of impeachment, which had the effect of suspending the Governor from office. P.B.S. Pinchback, a Georgia-born Negro who had been elected president of the senate after the death of Lieutenant Governor Dunn on November 22, was declared the Governor of Louisiana the same day.

Little of importance occurred during the one-month governorship of Pinchback, who never succeeded in opening the safe containing the records of the governor's office. Denying the legality of the impeachment proceedings, Warmoth refused to appear to answer the charges made against him, and thus matters remained until the inauguration of Kellog on January 14, 1873.

KELLOG AS GOVERNOR. If Warmoth's governorship had been stormy, Kellogg's days in office were tempestuous. It was a period of constant lawlessness and political turmoil. There were bloody riots in Colfax, New Orleans, Coushatta, and other cities in 1873 and 1874. The flood crest was reached with the discovery of a St. Martin Parish Radical and Negro plot in August, 1874, when a Radical revealed the names of the men who were to be killed and the women who were to be kept by the Negro leaders. The discovery of this plot caused a stiffening of white resistance to Radical rule and led many of the more conservative Negro leaders to begin to work with the conservative whites.

White Leagues were organized by loyal citizens over the entire state. In many parishes citizens refused to pay taxes and organized People's Leagues for resisting their collection. Kellogg persuaded the legislature to reorganize the Metropolitan Police into a Metropolitan Brigade on a state-wide basis, subject to the orders of the Governor, and sent a unit of the Brigade to St. Martinville, where the White Leaguers, under the command of Alcibiade De Blanc, defeated it in a pitched battle. In early August, 1874, the New Orleans *Bulletin* estimated the White League strength "now organized and armed" at "fourteen thousand men; over one-half inured to battle and privation," but on August 29 the Minden *Democrat* stated flatly that there were "ten thousand in North Louisiana alone who are ready and willing to march at the first clarion notes of the bugle." Dr. Thomas Cottman, sent by the Federal government to examine conditions in Louisiana, reported that "there must be a change or Civil War is inevitable."

Reaction set in, and large numbers of Negroes, led by those of Natchitoches Parish, began to desert the Radicals and join the liberal Democrats and Republicans. Radical officials were forced to resign in several parishes. A campaign of ridicule against the Governor spread rapidly over the state, usually in the form of songs or jingles like the following:

> The other day in a swampy bog,
> A serpent bit William Pitt Kellogg.
> Who was poisoned, do you say?
> The snake; it died that very day.

President U. S. Grant, who was having enough scandalous troubles of his own at the time, realized that the military occupation of Louisiana must end or a new Civil War would begin. He left the withdrawal of Federal troops, however, to his successor.

The gubernatorial campaign of 1876 began with the organization of political clubs throughout the state. The Radicals organized the Packard Guards, the Councils of Freedom, the Antoine Defenders, the Invincibles, and other units, while the Liberal groups organized the Nicholls-Wiltz Club, the Tilden-Hendricks Club, the Conservative Colored Club, and numerous others. The Radicals nominated Maine-borne Stephen B. Packard, who had been appointed United States Marshal for Louisiana in 1871, for Governor, while the Liberals nominated Francis T. Nicholls, a Louisiana war hero.

The bitter campaign was the final fight for the restoration of Home Rule. Both the Republican presidential candidate, Rutherford B. Hayes, and the Democratic candidate, Samuel J. Tilden, were known to be well-disposed toward the South. Nicholls hammered at paramount issues and jokingly emphasized the loss of his left arm and left foot in Confederate service—he had always wanted to be a judge but that was now impossible, for people would always say that "I was a one-sided judge." The Liberals urged the people to "hold deluded Negroes guiltless . . . let them deal with white villains who are, beyond question urging Negroes into these riotous acts."

The New Orleans *Republican,* a Radical newspaper, threatened Negroes who had joined the Liberals:

> He that from the polls shall stay,
> May live to vote some other day.
> While he that at the polls is slain,
> Can never cast his vote again.

Or with:

> A charge I have
> My God to glorify.
> Mr. Nigger going to vote with us
> Or Nigger going to die.

The Liberals came back in their newspapers with such jingles as "The Reform Song," the chorus of which went:

> Then come, boys, come,
> Make haste to crowd the polls.
> The tide of reform,
> It rises and it rolls.
> The thieves and the rogues
> Will have to hunt their holes.
> When we vote, vote,
> Vote the Democrats in.

Radicalism began to lose ground in the northern states, and the *Nation* admitted that "never again will the North come to the defense of the Negro."

The Radical Returning Board threw out several thousand Liberal votes and declared Packard elected. On inauguration day, January 8, 1877, however, the Liberals marched to St. Patrick's Hall in New Orleans and swore in Nicholls as Governor; at the same time the Radicals inaugurated Packard at the St. Louis Hotel, which was the state capitol at the time. The next day several thousand armed citizens under the leadership of General Frederick N. Ogden quietly took possession of the police stations, the Cabildo, the arsenal, and other public buildings.

The Nicholls legislature immediately went to work. Nicholls appointed a new supreme court which began holding sessions. Taxes poured into his government's treasury. Departments of the state and local governments recognized his authority. Packard's followers began to desert him. President Grant refused to permit the troops to interfere. On March 24, Nicholls proclaimed that his state government was complete in all its branches. A few days later President Hayes dispatched a commission to Louisiana to secure information regarding the election. On April 20, the President directed that the troops be removed from the statehouse, which was done on April 24, and the Nicholls government quietly took possession.

The period of military occupation had ended; Home Rule had finally returned to Louisiana. The *Daily Picayune* exultingly declared the day of the Radical had passed: "His sun has gone down in the gloom of an infamy which will never have a returning dawn in Louisiana"; and in a final burst of editorial oratory: "The years may come and go, the woods decay and wither, but father shall hand the story down to son, how she struggled, suffered, and triumphed, poor, proud, heroic—Louisiana."

COST AND CORRUPTION. The total cost of this corrupt period will never be accurately determined, for much of the corruption was well covered and many of the most damaging records were deliberately destroyed. Moral standards in finance as well as in politics were at the low-water mark of all Louisiana history; if a man could swindle without getting caught he was called a successful businessman or politician. Many of the Radical leaders made fortunes, political and financial gangsters who, as Fred Williamson wrote, "sat in high places and often passed the communion plate on Sunday." A Federal investigating committee in 1873 reported the following figures regarding Governor Warmoth: "He has been governor four years, at an annual salary of $8,000, and he testified that he made far more than $100,000 the first year, and he is now estimated to be worth from $500,000 to $1,000,000." Others may not have done as well as the Governor, but there is little doubt that they did not fare badly.

During the nine-year period from 1868 to 1876 the average annual expenses of the state government were approximately $6,000,000, whereas before the war they had averaged only $600,000. The general appropriation bill for 1870 gives some idea of the cost of government: salaries, $443,719; charities and charitable institutions, $557,600; education, $576,000; printing, $396,000; compensation to tax assessors and collectors, $863,851; interest on the bonded debt, $1,247,000; militia, $75,000; "miscellaneous expenditures," $970,457. The state printer received $125,000 during the legislative session, the senate spent $13,000 for coal and stationery, and Radical country newspapers received some $125,000 for favorable publicity. Neatly tucked away was an appropriation bill for $96,700 for the payment of a judgment against the State, which, according to the *Picayune*, "nobody seems to know anything about." The St. Louis *Missouri Republican* published a detailed list of the monies appropriated and then commented: "These fine figures will give to people in the North some idea of what a gigantic system of spoliation Radical rule is in some of the Southern States."

The convention which drafted the Constitution of 1868 met from November 23, 1867, to March 9, 1868, and spent an average of $1,200 per day, or $240 for each hour it was in session. Its work was actually completed in middle February, 1868, and on the twenty-sixth the *Picayune* complained that there was "no decent pretext for continuing to rob the state." The legislative session of 1871, according to Governor Warmoth, should not have cost more than $100,000, yet its total expenses ran over $900,000. The Governor asked: "What has become of the excess . . . ? It has been squandered by the officers of the Assembly in paying extra mileage and per diem of members for days' service never rendered; for an enormous crop of useless clerks, pages, etc., for publishing the journals of each house in fifteen obscure newspapers, some of which never existed, . . . in paying committees authorized by the House to sit during vacation and to travel throughout the State and into Texas, and in a hundred different ways." Yet the Governor held the legislature under short rein in other ways and as the New Orleans *Times* admitted, never failed "to control the legislature in his own behalf."

Education appropriation bills seldom failed of passage, but most of the monies appropriated never reached the public schools. School funds were apportioned on the basis of the number of educables, and the tax assessors, who made the enumerations, seldom agreed with the census takers. In 1870, Plaquemines Parish had 4,000 educables listed and only 100 pupils in school; New Orleans had 90,000 educables listed and only 19,000 enrolled, and while the 350 teachers were paid an average of only $70 per month the cost of the city's educational system was $374,000. In 1874, Natchitoches Parish had a school fund of nearly $20,000, yet had only one three-teacher Negro school operating; Raford Blunt, an illiterate Negro state senator, was one of the teachers and was also a member of the Parish School Board. In 1871 the State Superintendent of Education reported that most of the $1,193,500 received from the sale of school lands had been stolen by the political machine and diverted to its purposes. In 1877 an investigation of the Department of Education revealed that $2,137,369.02 had been lost to the public schools by mismanagement and corruption.

Tax rates steadily climbed. In 1861 the valuation of all property in Natchitoches Parish, for example, was slightly over $8,000,000. By 1869 it had dropped to under $3,000,000, and by 1873 to only about $1,275,000. In 1861 the parish tax was 1⅔ mills, which yielded approximately $13,500; by 1869 it was 16 mills, which netted nearly $47,000; in 1873 it had risen to 64½ mills, which produced slightly over $82,000. In 1874 one tract of land valued at $3,250.00 was taxed a total of $258.01. On August 1 of the same year the Natchitoches *People's Vindicator* reported 30,000 acres of land "offered at sale for taxes." A few weeks earlier the Shreveport *Times* had cried: "Under the present government of thieves, in God's name, what hope have the people of Louisiana before them?"

Penalties for delinquent taxes rose accordingly. A New Orleans citizen failed to pay his 1874 taxes amounting to $7.25; a year later a bill of $25.26, including a $10.00 charge for "advertising in official journal," was presented to him. Another citizen was billed $237.00 on an overdue tax of $43.50. In 1868, of $2,278,915 collected in taxes $493,324 went to the tax collectors. One of Warmoth's tax-collector appointees in New Orleans received in fees and commissions slightly over $60,000 for the year 1872. "During the ten years preceding 1876," reported historian E. Benjamin Andrews, "New Orleans paid in the form of direct taxes more than the estimated value of all the property within her limits in the year named, and still had a debt of equal amount unpaid."

During the period, the state bonded debt rose from about $6,000,000 to over $50,000,000, and there was little in the spring of 1877 to show how or where the money had been expended. Henry E. Chambers has estimated that the total cost of the four-year period from 1868 to 1872 was in excess of $106,000,000.

SLOW ECONOMIC PROGRESS. Shortly after the end of the war, aged Dr. Sol Smith of Alexandria wrote to a friend that the state was quiet and that the people were displaying great heroism and fortitude in accepting the destruction caused by the war. He said that Louisiana, like the other states of the South, "lies mangled, rent and palpitating in supreme agony of a ruined and trodden down people." His own plantation, which before the war had been valued at about $200,000, was now worth only $10,000 and had a $14,000 mortgage. Because of the Negro labor situation, he did not believe that it could be successfully operated and had decided to move to New Orleans to practice medicine. The majority of the returning soldiers were not as fortunate as Dr. Smith, for they had no profession which would bring in an immediate income.

At the time the Louisiana farmer was returning to his ruined land the northern soldier was returning to a land of prosperity, for northern agriculture had thrived during the war, not only to meet American needs but in addition to help meet food shortages in Europe. Northern industry was flourishing, railroads had expanded operations, capital was plentiful; southern industry had been destroyed, southern railroads had been practically put out of business, there was no capital. In Louisiana, to cite one example, in 1861 the New Orleans, Jackson and Great Northern Railroad had 49 locomotives, 37 passenger coaches, and 550 freight, baggage, and gravel cars; in 1865 the railroad owned 4 locomotives, 4 passenger cars, and 36 freight, baggage, and other cars, and "there was not a dollar of available funds in its treasury."

Farmers still had their land, but much of it had been mortgaged in 1861 and many of the mortgages were due. Their tools and work stock had diminished and in many localities had been stolen or destroyed. Negro labor was disorganized and demoralized. Fred Williamson drew an accurate picture of many sections when he wrote of northeast Louisiana: "Porches sagged, roofs leaked, and walls were cracked in the houses which had not been destroyed. Wherever troops had passed, Yank or Rebel, the rail fences had been burned for camp fires. Field tools and other implements were gone and the boll weevil had come in. Before the war, the cattle of the region had compared favorably with those of the North and West. . . . The breeding cattle were slaughtered with the rest."

A traveler described the areas of almost complete destruction—the Mississippi River section, the Red River Valley south of Natchitoches, areas of southeast Louisiana—and concluded that "the state had been quite well destroyed." The Shreveport *Times* described the water front along Red River, as "a barren waste, over which now and then could be seen probably a sleepy mule with an empty dray." Mark Twain wrote that the "whitewash is gone from the negro cabins now; and many, possibly most, of the big mansions, once so shining white, have worn out their paint and have a decayed, neglected look. It is the blight of war."

Agriculture made slow progress during the years from 1865 to 1877. Despite the good efforts of many Federal military commanders, Negroes did not work well under labor contracts. Planters did not have working capital or credit enough to replace machinery or pay daily wages. In many sections the share-crop system was used, and both planter and Negro farmer did the best they could under difficult circumstances. There were bad crop years, and insects and other pests attacked growing plants; in 1870 and 1872 there were serious floods in several areas of the state. Sugar production, to cite only one example, fell from 459,410 hogsheads for the 1861 crop to 18,000 hogsheads in 1865; by 1867 the crop had reached only 37,364 hogsheads and in 1876 only 169,331 hogsheads. It was several decades before agricultural production equaled that of 1860-61.

Roads had been neglected, railroads had been worn out or abandoned, and steamboats had been destroyed by Federal gunboats during the war years. By 1870, some roads had been repaired, the railroads were partially in operation, and steamboats were again carrying products and goods along the rivers and bayous. While comparatively small amounts of northern capital were invested in Louisiana during those years prior to 1877, some was poured into river and rail transportation facilities, for these were able to show immediate profits; capital for agricultural improvements was almost impossible to secure.

The banks suffered greatly during the war and the period of military occupation. In 1860, Louisiana had had thirteen state-chartered banks with a total capital of nearly $25,000,000, over $26,000,000 in loans and discounts, and nearly $20,000,000 on deposit; at the end of the war there were ten banks with a joint capital of slightly over $7,650,000. Ten years later only five banks were left, with a total capital of $3,725,000 and $4,440,000 in loans and discounts and about $6,150,000 on deposit. The state banks were ill prepared to meet the Panic of 1873, even with the assistance of the nine National banks which had been organized under the National Bank Act of 1863 and which had a total capital of $4,850,000.

Prices for goods and supplies remained high throughout the period. The average Louisianian could afford few if any luxuries, and many could not even afford all of the necessities of life. Home manufacturing of furniture, clothing, tools, and other items in general use was common throughout the state. Little indirect and practically no direct assistance was received from the Federal government in restoring the economic well-being of Louisiana, and it has been stated that during those years considerably more money in the form of taxes was drawn from the state than was returned in the form of economic assistance.

MATTERS OF MIND AND SPIRIT. Public education languished during the war except in New Orleans, where General Butler reorganized the school system under the leadership of northern educators and imported northern teachers. During the last two years of the war the city had over 40 public schools and enrolled over 12,000 children. The Freedmen's Bureau sent teachers to Louisiana and attempted to establish integrated schools in areas occupied by the Federal armies, but the whites refused to permit their children to attend. By the end of the war the Bureau operated nearly 80 schools, with 125 teachers and about 8,000 pupils. These schools were continued after the war ended, and although the Bureau claimed to have taught thousands of Negroes to read and write (50,000 in New Orleans alone), many critics believed that the Bureau schools did more harm than good because of their emphasis upon "the non-essential, fostering race prejudice, and inculcating false political notions."

Robert M. Lusher was elected State Superintendent in the fall of 1865 and started a program of recovery which continued until 1868, when he was ousted and carpet-bagger Thomas W. Conway placed in the position to enforce the educational provisions of the new Constitution of 1868. Under the new constitution "all children . . . between . . . six and twenty-one shall be admitted to the public schools, or other institutions of learning sustained or established by the State in common, without distinction of color, race or previous condition. There shall be no separate school or institution of learning established exclusively for any race by the State of Louisiana." This section was everywhere strongly resisted, was never effectively enforced, and it resulted in the exclusion of the whites from the public schools. Conway apparently did little, and the newspapers of that time labeled him an "ignorant, drunken, incompetent politician."

Negro William G. Brown became the State Superintendent in 1872, holding the position until the end of the period. Little is known of Brown or of his activities, since he apparently had little to do with the schools and employed a northern Baptist minister as his secretary who did the work and wrote his reports. Many New Orleans teachers later testified that they knew nothing about him and only one could recall having ever seen him. In March, 1871, P. B. S. Pinchback was appointed to the New Orleans School Board, which position he held until 1877.

Despite the elaborate school system set up by the Radical government and the monies appropriated to it, little was accomplished, as most of the money was stolen by politicians. Thefts by school boards, superintendents, and principals became common occurrences. The secretary of the Concordia Parish School Board was charged in 1875 with the theft of $34,000. In many schools the teachers were hardly more literate than their illiterate pupils; witness the letter of an applicant for a position in Bienville Parish, who wrote Superintendent Conway inquiring what was "nesessxary or requisit in filling that or gitting the place as a teacher. . . . I was advised to refer to your honor that you was the Right Person and with your appointment on imploying I would be safe in takein a School of that kind I suppose the Reason I have not got a school is from Predudice held on account of Politics in public affairs. . . ." George W. McCranie commented in the *Ouachita Register* in 1875 that "this system has been in operation for nine years, yet not a single scholar has been given to this parish by its operation."

Realizing the educational plight of the South, London businessman George Peabody, who had lived for a time in the United States, established a large fund to assist southern education. The white schools of Louisiana were kept alive mainly by this fund and by individual contributions from 1867 to 1877. The Radicals protested, but the directors of the Peabody Fund understood the situation and refused to give assistance to Negro education. Dr. Barnas Sears became the Louisiana agent of the fund and worked with former State Superintendent R. M. Lusher. Even with the aid of the Peabody Fund, however, many white children received little or no education during the period, and in 1877, out of over 265,000 white children, only 54,390 were in school.

Several Negro colleges or universities were established during the period, the most important of which were Straight University, New Orleans University, and Leland University. Despite private and state assistance, these institutions remained small, but they accomplished something in the way of Negro secondary education and they offered a few courses of college level.

After having been open for only short periods during the war, the State Seminary of Learning was reopened in October, 1865, under the leadership of Major David F. Boyd and four instructors. The Seminary building burned four years later, and the institution was moved to the School for the Deaf, Dumb, and Blind at Baton Rouge. The name was officially changed to Louisiana State University in 1870, during which year the institution received an appropriation of nearly $60,000. The officials consistently refused to admit Negroes, and from 1872 through 1876 the state legislature made only small appropriations or no appropriations at all; normal operation did not become a reality until after 1877.

The great majority of the state's newspapers had suspended publication by the end of the war, and many of them were never revived. Only in the larger towns and cities were the larger and stronger newspapers able to withstand the onslaughts of the troublous times. Never again would the state have the large number of independent, hard-hitting editors it had before 1861. Those papers which did last through the period were necessarily extremely careful of their editorials during the first few years following 1865 but by the early 1870's began a campaign against the evils of the political system and had much to do with the final uprising of the whites in 1876. Throughout those years several colored sheets, like the New Orleans *Louisianian* and *La Tribune de la Nouvelle-Orléans* (published by Dr. Louis Roudanez and the first Negro daily newspaper in the United States), and the Opelousas *St. Landry Progress* (until 1868 when a mob sacked and destroyed the office) reflected the Negro and Radical points of view.

Religious institutions languished because of the lack of money and the poor conditions of travel, but there was much religious activity and Protestant ministers and Catholic priests tried to bring whites and Negroes closer together. The members of the clergy also performed heroic work for the relief of suffering of both races and all creeds. When Father Louis Gergaud of Monroe, for example, died of yellow fever in Shreveport in 1873, everyone remembered how he had labored during the epidemic. The entire population of Monroe marched in the funeral procession, which was headed by a Grand Marshal on horseback and followed by the Monroe Silver Cornet Band, the Monroe Fire Department, and civil and religious organizations.

Revivals became popular among the Protestants, and long after the war and occupation years Grace King recalled Bishop B. M. Palmer thundering "out the matchless eloquence of his sermons to crowded congregations. His big, bare-looking church was stretched to its capacity to hold them. And when the great congregation joined with the choir in singing, 'Guide me, O Thou great Jehovah,' the sound could be heard across the square in front, and the enthusiasm inside the church was such as might well have caused Satan and his minions to hang their heads in shame." "Protracted meetings" were popular among the Protestants of western and northern Louisiana during the late summer and fall seasons.

Before the war Protestant missionary agencies had labored with little success to convert Catholic Negroes. The Catholic Church had depended largely upon the slave-owners to promote their faith with their slaves, and with emancipation this method of securing and holding converts was lost. The result was that Protestant Negroes increased after the war while those who were Catholics tended to decrease; there was little loss, however, from the former Free Negro Catholic group.

The general moral life of the people was at a low ebb throughout the period, and although conditions were generally bad in small-town and rural areas, New Orleans was the most immoral city in the nation, at least to numerous observers. General Benjamin F. Butler and his successors kept the town under control until the end of the war, but after 1865 moral conditions rapidly deteriorated and by 1868, when the worst of the Radical years began, New Orleans was ready to begin her boom years of vice.

The concert saloon, the low-class forerunner of the modern night club, came into existence in 1865, when the St. Nicholas opened its doors on St. Charles Avenue, and within a few years there were a score of such places scattered about the city. It was sometimes difficult to tell the difference between an ordinary saloon and a concert saloon, for both offered music, drink, and food served by female "beer-jerkers," and some of them had a floor show of sorts. In 1869, Wenger's Garden on Bourbon Street advertised a "remarkable machine known as the self-acting organ," a forerunner of the player piano.

The most popular places included the Crescent Hill Saloon at the corner of Canal and St. Charles Avenue, the Royal Palace Beer Saloon and Concert Hall on Royal near Iberville (closed in 1869 when its proprietor was sent to prison for murder), the Canton House on Gallatin (closed in 1867 when Canton "kicked a sailor to death in the barroom"), and the Buffalo Bill House at Franklin and Dryades. The Buffalo Bill House was undoubtedly the most disreputable and toughtest combination concert saloon and dance house, for proprietor Bison Williams employed a large staff of jailbirds, criminals, and toughs, and regaled his customers with suggestive cancan and *clococke* performances, rat and dog fights, wrestling, boxing, and butting matches, and well-acted songs sung by nude singers of both sexes.

The city was filled with *bordellos,* from fifteen-cent Negro cribs on back streets filled with worn-out white and colored hags to twenty-five-dollar "parlor houses" in more respectable sections filled with princess-dressed beauties carefully selected from all the nations of the world. It has been said that after 1866 there was scarcely a single block in New Orleans which did not boast at least one brothel or assignation house of low or high degree. There were no legal difficulties as long as proprietors paid off the police. When the proprietor of the Amsterdam had his place closed and a dozen of his girls fined $10.00 each in 1869, he squawked to a New Orleans *Times* reporter that "if there had been no trouble about paying up regular I would have been allowed to stay there." He had been paying the police captain $80.00 a month along with lesser payments to patrolmen; evidently he had not been paying enough.

SOCIAL LIFE. Social life in New Orleans rapidly resumed its old prewar pace, and the populace enjoyed French and Italian operas, concerts, plays, variety troupes, circuses, Mardi Gras, races, balls, and all varieties of sports. Roller skating was introduced in 1869 and soon became "quite fashionable" for women. The New Orleans Lawn Tennis Club, one of the first in the nation, was founded in 1876. New Orleans social extravagance continued to grow until 1873, when the panic, the burden of taxation, and the turbulent state of politics slowed the pace.

Social life in the parishes was characterized by simplicity, modesty, and a general lack of pretension and extravagance, for the great majority of the people were living in reduced circumstances. Even former Governor Moore was "living in a negro cabin at the head of the quarters," and Mrs. T. L. Raymond later wrote: "I have never forgotten the stately old gentleman with snow white hair and beard, who welcomed us as if we were entering a palace instead of an unpainted negro cabin. Not a word of apology." Many families were still using parched sweet-potato slices for coffee, finely sifted corn meal for flour, and other substitutes. The old days of ante bellum plantation opulence would never return.

Customs of living had not, however fundamentally changed. Women still wore voluminous skirts, capes, and tight-waisted dresses, men trimmed beards, and children dressed like their elders in "made-over" outfits. "Arizona" calico from a small cotton mill in north Louisiana was made into "Dolly Varden polonaises," and ladies were beginning to affect the "Grecian bend" in their posture. Young ladies still used such words as "shucks" or "the dickens" or "dog-gone-it," but never, even under extreme provocation, expletives like "fool" or "the devil."

Entertaining was done by entire families at the home; older folks talked and played cards, younger married and unmarried couples danced, and children played such yard games as "Goosey, goosey gander," "Hide and seek," "King William was King James' son," "Here we go 'round the mulberry tree," "Clap in and clap out," or "Lost my glove yesterday." Everyone sang: "Dixie," "The Bonnie Blue Flag," "Suwanee

River," "Maryland, My Maryland," "Lorena," "Rocked in the Cradle of the Deep," "Home, Sweet Home," and many others. There were great Sunday and festive-day dinners and such light refreshmens as corn-flour cakes and homemade candy.

END OF THE ERA. The period of military occupation finally ended. Louisianians had suffered the presence of Radical political control longer than had the people of any other state in the South. The memories of corrupt government, economic distress, and the many social problems gradually faded as the years of Home Rule passed and as economic, cultural and social conditions improved.

The people of Louisiana had stood the test well, as had all southerners. They had lived through a longer, more troublous era than had any other Americans, before or since that time. In a speech at the end of the period Representative Randall Lee Gibson said: "If it had been foretold sixteen years ago that the white people of Louisiana within eight years would be overcome in a fierce struggle, and that a few strangers from the North, uniting with their slaves, should have complete control of their government; that they would quietly accept a denial of all representation in it, endure a taxation equivalent to confiscation, and witness a carnival of crime and imbecility in which the guarantees for order, life, and property alike well-nigh perished, it would have been regarded as the delusion of a disordered mind."

Historian Charles Gayarré resumed his correspondence with his before-the-war friend Evert A. Duyckinck, a New York editor and publisher, in late May, 1865, and in his letters revealed the attitude of most Louisianians toward secession, the war, and the postwar years. Gayarré made no apology for secession: "We thought that the contumely, the insults, the grievances heaped upon us had become intolerable, and that we could no longer remain in the Union with honor." He stoutly maintained his American patriotism: "We repudiate the idea that we ever ceased to be good Americans." He still argued the right of secession and the justice of the southern cause: "We honestly believed that we were supporting the holiest of all causes, and we still think so. There may be rebellious provinces, but we deny that there can be rebellious states. Washington was a rebel, but not Jefferson Davis." He accepted defeat: "Be it as it may, the question is settled, the South is subjugated, Slavery abolished." He upheld the old civilization of the South: "What we had made of the South, is known to the world. We shall see what the North, with all its isms, will make of it. We fear not the judgment of posterity." He admitted that the South was back in the Union: "In the letter to which I reply, you said: 'The sooner you are all tucked up again under Uncle Sam's coverlet, the better.' Well! We are under it now, but the coverlet covers a living man and a corpse, and an ocean of blood rolls over it."

Seven and a half years later, when the state was in the midst of Radical Reconstruction, he wrote Duyckinck: "We are completely under the rule of ignorant and filthy negroes scarcely superior to the orang outang. The republics of Greece had their Solons, we have Sambo for a legislator. O God!" The people of Louisiana would have written as had Gayarré, had they had the knack, for they generally felt as he felt. It was the bitter, tragic years of military occupation, not the four years of bloody war, which caused the lingering bitterness in the South and in Louisiana.

Time would be the only healer. But the day of understanding and of at least partial forgiveness would not come until the last of those generations who had lived through the period had ended their days on earth. The dawn lights were beginning to flicker during the 1890's, when author Charles Dudley Warner met an old lady at a Confederate Decoration Day service in New Orleans. After a brief conversation concerning the war, she said: "Each side did the best it could; it is all over and done with, and let's have an end of it."

PART SEVEN

Reconstruction

and Slow Progress, 1877-1920

CHAPTER 24

AN AGE OF GOVERNMENTAL CONSERVATISM

AN AGE OF POLITICAL CONSERVATISM. The period from 1877 to 1920 was one of political and governmental conservatism. Liberal leaders who regained control of the state at the end of the period of military occupation well realized the truth of Thomas Carlyle's statement that "the problem of politics is, how out of a multitude of knaves to make an honest people." They had witnessed too many political excesses during those years of military occupation and Radical and Negro rule to take chances with liberal ideas or liberal legislation.

The political leaders of Louisiana for the next forty-three years had either grown to manhood during, or had been reared in the spirit of, what Mark Twain called the "Sir Walter Scott Middle Age sham civilization" of the Old South. Yet that civilization, as Mrs. T. P. O'Connor wrote, generally had "created politicians who were gentlemen of property, distinction, and honour," who did not "put their hands into the pockets of the government and withdraw them contaminated with graft." During the next four decades there would be no such scandals as had plagued the state during the twelve years prior to 1877.

Although the Republican party was active in national and state political campaigns until 1900, it never seriously rivaled the Democratic party, to which Louisiana, like other southern states, had developed a strong allegiance. This one-party system gave rise to factions within that party, and political campaigns were usually struggles between two or more Democratic factions. No single group, however, was able to dominate state politics for very long.

The state ordinarily divided during political campaigns and on political issues into three rather distinctive divisions: North Louisiana, South Louisiana, and Orleans Parish. Until 1900, North and South Louisiana generally united against New Orleans to elect governors and to control legislatures, but after the turn of the century groups from both sections joined with New Orleans to win elections.

Candidates of the various factions called themselves "conservatives" or "liberals," but it made little difference. "Safe" governors were the rule, governors who were in the broader sense conservative in their political beliefs. While changes in the economic life and social patterns of the state caused political machinery to be overhauled from time to time, most successful candidates for office gave only lip service to fundamental and far-reaching reforms. A few governors, of whom Newton C. Blanchard was the outstanding example, undertook such reforms as would fit into the generally conservative, so-called Bourbon-rule pattern of the times. The result was that little political and governmental progress was made; the reforms and liberal legislation which were to make and characterize modern Louisiana had to await a later day.

MAJOR POLITICAL ISSUES. Upon the restoration of Home Rule in 1877 the

Louisiana voter became enthusiastically interested in politics, in which his activities had been so drastically curtailed during the preceding twelve years, and he held that interest until the beginning of the new century. Clear-cut and well-defined issues caused deep concern and led to hard-fought campaigns; by 1900 the majority of these issues had been settled and the average voter lost much of his former enthusiasm for the factional battles of political campaigns.

The immediate and most important political issue was the future position of the carpetbaggers, scalawags, and Negroes in state and local politics. These groups, backed by an army of occupation, had controlled the state for more than a decade, had committed so many excesses, had plunged the state so deeply into debt, and had caused so much governmental, economic, and social disorder that they had no hope of political success once Federal troops were removed. While the carpetbagger and scalawag generally passed quickly and quietly into political oblivion, a few of the better members of these groups were elected to office until the closing years of the century, a phenomenon never adequately explained by those who have written on the political history of the period.

The Negro presented a wholly different problem, for he belonged to another race and existed in such numbers as to make oblivion impossible; in many parishes he outnumbered the whites. Louisiana, like her sister states of the South, immediately began to search for ways to circumvent the Federal constitutional amendments which had elevated the Negro, and the great majority of white voters supported candidates who promised complete co-operation. Until the end of the century two procedures were used to prevent the Negro from taking effective part in politics. The Constitution of 1879 gave the governor unusual appointive powers, and Democratic governors ordinarily appointed white Democrats to office. In time this appointive system was to cause much controversy, but for some years it served its purpose. The second procedure used in keeping the Negro from the ballot box and out of politics was persuasion and if necessary, intimidation. As Melvin Evans wrote: "The South had not yet solved the problem of disfranchising the illiterate, ignorant negro by organic law non-violative of the Fourteenth and Fifteenth amendments to the Constitution of the United States."

The Radical Republicans had used the enfranchised Negro to maintain themselves in office and for the attempted destruction of old southern-white ideals of government. For a time the Democrats in Louisiana attempted to use the Negro as a political ally, but as the years passed the Negro gradually lost ground and was subjected to increased segregation and loss of political influence. P. B. S. Pinchback voiced his bitter disappointment: "For a while we were admitted into the general council chamber, and some little respect was paid to our wishes, but gradually a line of demarkation was drawn between our rulers and ourselves that reached a distinct color line within our party, which took shape and assumed formidable proportions soon thereafter between the two races in the State."

The question of state lotteries created considerable political agitation. Lotteries had long been used in Louisiana by societies and by religious and educational institutions to raise needed funds. The largest of the lotteries was organized as the Louisiana Lottery Company during the corrupt days of military occupation in 1868 and was granted a twenty-five year charter by the legislature. It was not long before antilottery societies were organized and in 1879 the legislature deprived the company of its charter, but the company was victorious in the courts.

The antilottery fight became more heated as the public was made acquainted with actual lottery practices. It was argued that whereas the majority of foreign lotteries kept only about 15 per cent of all monies received for expenses and profits, the Louisiana Lottery Company reserved over 40 per cent. The New Orleans *Democrat* graphically exposed the small chance a ticket purchaser had of winning prizes: "The man who buys a ticket every day at every drawing will have only one chance in 84 years to draw even the $243.35 prize. Old Methusaleh himself had he bucked up against the lottery from his earliest childhood to the day of his death and bought a ticket every day, would have found himself winner of $2,678.85 after having spent about $250,000 on the lottery."

By 1892 the Company was a $28,000,000 business with annual net profits of over $8,000,000 and was an important issue in the political campaign of that year. The antilottery leaders—Murphy J. Foster, Francis T. Nicholls, Edward Douglass White, Donelson Caffery, John C. Wickliffe, Bishop B. M. Palmer, and others—won the election. An antilottery law was passed (despite the company's offer to pay the state $1,250,000 a year), and Paul Conrad, the company president, soon began to advertise that "from and after January 1st [1894] my address will be . . . Puerto Cortez, Honduras, C. A." The company continued to sell lottery tickets until an act was passed in 1894 prohibiting their sale, which ended the lottery business in Louisiana.

Other political issues of the period included the rebalancing of the powers of the governor and the legislature, education, public improvement of roads, bridges, and levees, the offering of economic inducements to out-of-state businesses and agriculturists, and social legislation.

THE GOVERNORS. During the period from 1877 to 1920 nine men served as the state's chief executive. All these governors were Democrats and all of them were generally conservative in their political beliefs. There was little dishonesty in government, for the political leaders were generally men of high purpose. Many of them were Civil War veterans and very popular with the people. Francis T. Nicholls was probably the most beloved, and the fact that he had lost an arm and a foot during the war gave opportunity for some interesting stories about him. Once, when he spoke on Bayou Lafourche, an old Confederate veteran, who was also minus an arm and a leg, came up to him, and said: "Gineral, all what's left of me is going to vote for what's left of you."

As would be expected, there was a general scramble for political appointments after Nicholls became Governor in 1877, and he was reported to have received nearly 350 applications for the position of New Orleans harbormaster alone. In his inaugural address he commented on the "peace and quiet" prevailing throughout the state, was optimistic of the future, and promised rigid economy in state appropriations. His first term was shortened by the Constitution of 1879.

Governor Nicholls was succeeded in 1880 by his Lieutenant Governor, Louis A. Wiltz of New Orleans, who had maintained an untarnished reputation as a legislator and Mayor of New Orleans (1872-74) during the Radical period. Wiltz died the following year, and Lieutenant Governor Samuel D. McEnery of Monroe completed his term of office and was elected in his own right in 1884. McEnery ran against Francis T. Nicholls for the Democratic nomination in 1887, but Nicholls was elected.

Nicholls' second administration was marked by several events which caused intense excitement in the state. In September, 1889, the *Picayune* broke the story that E. A. Burke, a native of Illinois who had become a Confederate in 1861 and an anti-Radical leader after the war, and who had been state treasurer since 1878, had perpetrated a fraud with over $800,000 of state bonds. Burke was in Great Britain at the time raising funds for a gold-development scheme in Honduras. He never returned to Louisiana and practically all of the bonds were later recovered. In the fall of 1890, New Orleans Police Chief David C. Hennessy was murdered, and the same year marked the beginning of the intense drive against the lottery. After completing his second term as Governor in 1892, Nicholls was appointed Chief Justice of the Louisiana Supreme Court and served until his retirement (the first Louisiana judge to be retired on a pension) in 1911. At the time of his death in 1912 the *Picayune* wrote that "he was without doubt the most truly eminent, the most highly esteemed and the most deservedly honored citizen in Louisiana."

Murphy J. Foster of St. Mary Parish served two terms as Governor from 1892 to 1900, but many people did not approve of a governor succeeding himself so this practice was prohibited in the Constitution of 1898. Thereafter, the remaining governors of this period, William W. Heard, Newton C. Blanchard, Jared Y. Sanders, Luther E. Hall, and Ruffin G. Pleasant, each served a single four-year term.

During Governor Heard's administration the mandates of the Constitution of 1898 were enacted, the most important of which were the termination of the penitentiary lease system and minor improvements in education and banking. An oyster commission was created, funds were appropriated for a colored insane asylum at Alexandria, and June 3 was designated as a state legal holiday to be called Confederate Day. President William McKinley visited Louisiana in May, 1901, the first national chief executive to do so while in office.

A four-year reform period began with the administration of Governor Blanchard and would have been even more significant had the Governor commanded the complete support of the legislature. Basic beginnings were made in establishing modern and progressive educational and social welfare institutions. State Superintendent of Schools James B. Aswell led the movement to secure a new teachers licensing system, a state board of teachers examiners, and funds for the construction of new schoolhouses and the purchase of new equipment and additional books. The rate of taxation was reduced following the creation of a state board of equalization. Following the panic of 1907 legislation was enacted at a special session of the legislature which materially strengthened the state banking system. By the end of his administration, Governor Blanchard could point with pride to his achievements in reducing executive patronage, more than doubling appropriations for education, securing the passage of a new primary-election law, and other progressive measures.

Governor Sanders accomplished little. While the Governor was mildly progressive, the legislatures during his administration were lukewarm to fundamental reforms and were severely criticized for their extravagance. Governors Hall and Pleasant were openly conservative. Under Hall there was some taxation reform and the drafting and ratification of the unsatisfactory Constitution of 1913. Pleasant was Governor during the trying period of World War I and no reforms of consequence were even proposed by the state's chief executive.

The Negro question had been settled by the Constitution of 1898 and the economic reconstruction of the state had generally been completed by 1900, so the bitterness caused by the period of military occupation rapidly died away. Although some of the reform ideas of Theodore Roosevelt and Woodrow Wilson filtered into the state, in general the administrations of these governors were marked by caution, and progress was made at a leisurely pace.

CONSTITUTIONS OF 1879, 1898, AND 1913. The constitution of 1868, having been drafted by a Radical convention largely for the benefit of office-seeking carpetbaggers and scalawags and for the immediate political, economic, and social advancement of the Negro, was generally unsatisfactory to the people of the state. A constitutional convention, therefore, was called in 1879. The members, because of the state's recent experiences, had a deep suspicion of legislative bodies and filled the new constitution with inhibitions and limitations against that branch of government. They also sharply defined the duties and activities of various minor officials. The Constitution of 1879 was a long document of 268 articles and covered many subjects which should have been left to legislative action.

Most significant was the granting to the chief executive of extraordinary appointive powers. The governor was given the authority to name all state and local officials whose election was not specifically provided for by the constitution. He had the power to appoint members of police juries, all executive boards, school boards in rural sections, many of the judiciary, and all boards concerned in any way with elections. The capital was returned to Baton Rouge, and the legislature again published laws in the French language, a practice which continued until 1887. The Constitution of 1879, in many ways almost a compilation of laws, remained in effect until 1898.

In 1896 three Negroes were elected to the legislature, Representatives Charles E. Bourgeois of St. Charles, Victor Fauria of St. Tammany, and Henry C. W. Casacalvo of East Baton Rouge. Negro registrations the following year totaled nearly 295,000, approximately 44 per cent of the total. With the potential Negro vote practically equal to the white vote, many whites believed that it was not inconceivable that the Negroes might at some time disregard factional political groups and vote as a unit, thus bringing a return to Radical government. At a special election held on January 11, 1898, the proposition for calling a constitutional convention was passed by a vote of over 36,000 to slightly over 7,500. The convention was empowered not only to draft a new constitution but to adopt it without submission to the people for approval; at the same time its authority was prohibited in many of the fundamental phases of government. Its chief reason to be, according to member Thomas J. Kernan, was "to take away the ballot from almost, if not quite, a majority of the voters of the State."

Kernan's statement was essentially correct, for the Constitution of 1898 reduced Negro registrations by approximately 95 per cent and lowered white registrations by over 23 per cent, generally in the illiterate and lower income brackets. By 1908 only 1,743 Negroes were registered in the state. Section 5 of Article 197, the so-called "Grandfather Clause," read in part: "No male person who was on January 1st, 1867, or at any date prior thereto, entitled to vote . . . shall be denied the right to register and vote in this State by reason of his failing to possess the educational or property qualifications prescribed by this Constitution." Similar "grandfather" clauses were afterward placed in the suffrage regulations in several of the southern states and were not declared unconstitutional by the Federal Supreme Court until 1915.

The Constitution of 1898 was even longer than that of 1879, having 326 articles. In general it limited governmental powers, insofar as possible reserving them to the people. Its limitation on the powers of taxation adversely affected economic progress, public improvements, and the development of adequate educational facilities.

The constitutional convention of 1913 likewise did not have to submit the result of its efforts to the electorate for approval, but was so restricted in the authorization voted by the people that its scope was seriously limited. The Constitution of 1913 contained the same number of articles as its predecessor but was a distinct gain in brevity, for the 1898 document had been amended sixty-five times. Like the constitutions of 1879 and 1898 it contained many provisions which should have been left to the action of the legislature. The convention, however, had ignored the limitations imposed by the act which called it into being, for it drafted a new document in preference to revising the existing constitution. This threw the entire state into confusion and gave rise to considerable doubt as to which constitution was actually in effect. When test cases reached the courts it was decided that the convention of 1913 had no authority to go beyond its call and that the Constitution of 1898 was still in force wherever it was at variance with the Constitution of 1913. A new document was drafted in 1921.

Edward Douglass White was the state's most noted jurist during the period. Son of the former Governor of the same name, White served in the Confederate Army and after the Civil War was a member of the state senate, an Associate Justice of the Supreme Court of Louisiana, and a member of the United States Senate. Appointed to the Federal Supreme Court by President Grover Cleveland in 1894, he served as Associate Justice until 1910 when he became Chief Justice. He died in 1921.

THE SPANISH-AMERICAN WAR AND WORLD WAR I. The United States fought two wars during this period, and Louisiana played her role as a loyal state in both conflicts. Most Louisianians sympathized with the Cubans in their struggle for freedom and in June, 1896, the lower house of the legislature passed a resolution petitioning the Congress and the President to grant full belligerency rights to Cuba. Louisiana's man-power contribution consisted of two regiments of infantry, three batteries of artillery, and several hundred sailors, a total of about five thousand men. The 1st Louisiana Infantry Regiment and the three artillery batteries did not leave the United States, but on January 1, 1899, the 2d Louisiana Infantry Regiment were among the first American troops to enter Havana, where they served for several months.

When the Donaldsonville contingent left for Baton Rouge to join their outfit in late April, 1898, the *Times* wrote that "scenes and recollections of the past were unearthed and brought to view, when fond parents, sisters and brothers, friends and sweethearts, bade farewell to the Southern boys with hearts full of patriotism and pride." When the 2d Louisiana paraded in New Orleans on May 29, 1898, before entraining for Mobile, their colonel, Elmer E. Woods, reported that the previous night had been a typical one for soldiers, for the men had "no mosquito bars, and the little pests of that vicinity had a well whetted appetite for soldiers blood." Louisiana lost only one soldier during the war; Lieutenant J. Numa Augustin, Jr., of the 24th United States Regular Infantry was mortally wounded in the charge at San Juan Hill and died the following day.

Many Louisianians had been eager for the United States to go to the assistance of France for some time before the declaration of war against Germany in 1917, for they were descendants of old French Creole families, and one lady, who lived in New Orleans, reported that the Crescent City "was thrown into a state of wild excitement" when news of the declaration of war arrived. As the troops completed their training and departed, thousands of people assembled at railway stations, the bands playing the "Marseillaise" and patriotic American songs. On one occasion the French Consul General went to the station, waved his hat to the soldiers, and shouted *"Adieu, mes enfants,"* while an old Civil War veteran stood on the curb and muttered that at last he felt that he was a real American again, for his grandson was marching with the soldiers to the aid of France.

Thousands of men joined the military services and several military camps were established in the state, the largest being near Pineville and at the old New Orleans City Park race track. Louisianians bought more than $200,000,000 worth of Liberty Loan bonds, and various local organizations raised money and furnished needed war supplies. The Jennings Cavalry became part of the noted Rainbow Division, the Loyola Medical Unit served on the Italian front, and many nurses were furnished by the Tulane Medical Unit. Marine Major General John A. LeJeune of Pointe Coupée Parish became one of the most famous war heroes and later was named commandant of the Marine Corps.

PARISH AND LOCAL GOVERNMENT. After the withdrawal of the Federal troops in 1877, native whites quickly gained control of parish and local governments. Of first importance was the repair of parish, city, and town buildings which had been allowed to fall into ruin. Many parish and town records, particularly the land records, had been destroyed during the war or the period of Radical government, while those remaining were in complete disorder and had to be reorganized before the various offices of government could function properly. Local governmental agencies were generally heavily in debt. Taxes, which in many parishes had been almost confiscatory, had to be lowered and collected. In view of the poor conditions of the time, local governments economized as much as possible.

Parishes, cities, and towns made slow progress. It was not until 1888, for example, that the Police Jury of Concordia Parish could report the parish out of debt. Sam Block, the president, congratulated the Jury on their wise administration at the regular April 1 meeting and said: "The rate of taxation is now lower, the roads are in better condition, more levees and bridges have been built during your term, and more cash is now in the treasury than at any time since the Civil War. Upon your advent, Parish warrants were selling at .65c on the dollar; there was no money in the treasury and a large outstanding indebtedness for the years 1871-1874. There were also outstanding judgments. This entire debt and interest has been paid and the Parish is now out of debt. . . . Parish warrants are worth dollar for dollar; and there is now $9,941.36 in the treasury. This is the first time since the war that this condition has existed." Other parishes in the state, however, did not match the financial condition of Concordia until after the turn of the new century.

During the period, old parishes were divided and new parishes were created as the population grew and the old governmental units became too large to function effectively. At the beginning of the Civil War there had been forty-eight parishes. Two were added in 1868, nine between 1868 and 1907, and the last five by 1912. The last two parishes were Allen and Jefferson Davis, created out of the parish of Calcasieu on June 12, 1912. Meantime some parishes were created but never established, as was the parish of Troy (from Catahoula) in 1890.

Some parishes relocated their parish seats as towns grew larger and centers of population shifted, a few of them in unusual if not interesting ways. Madison Parish, for example, had been created in 1838, with Richmond (about two miles south of present-day Tallulah) being the first parish seat. Almost completely destroyed by fire in 1859, Richmond was burned again by Grant's army in 1863. The town was never rebuilt, and Delta was made the parish seat in 1868. By the middle 1880's Tallulah was the largest town in the parish and the police jury had "more or less" decided to move the "capital," but delayed in taking action. On the night of March 6, 1885, a group of Tallulah citizens, probably led by Henry Holmes, who was known locally as the "Duke of Rattlesnake Ridge," loaded the parish records in a boxcar and moved them to Tallulah. Here they remained, and a new parish courthouse was built two years later.

Some of the regulations made by police juries and local officials during this period sound a little out of place today. In 1878 the Donaldsonville *Chief* reported that the "jail house has been repaired" and that "horse-racks are being placed in front of the Court-House." Nine years later the Donaldsonville town council adopted resolutions complaining loudly of the "reckless, furious and noisy manner in which plantation carts, etc., are driven through the streets of our quiet city." The ante bellum zigzag regulation was resurrected by many parishes and in 1895 by Ascension Parish, when the police jury adopted an ordinance requiring "three or four-mule carts and wagons to zig-zag on the public roads."

The Avoyelles Police Jury proceedings from 1877 to 1920, to use one parish as an example, yield much information on the conditions, general progress, and customs of the period. The parish had gone into debt $12,800.00 during the eleven years from 1866 to 1876 and $26,924.46 in taxes were delinquent. A. L. Lafargue began a crusade of tax collecting that was so successful he was publicly thanked by the police jury. In 1881 horse racing was prohibited on public roads, and coffeehouse owner George Mayer agreed to purchase the "public privy located on the Courthouse Square." In March, 1885, the jury appropriated $6,000 to build a new courthouse, but repealed the ordinance a month later. In 1889 farmers and planters were prohibited from permitting their hogs to "roam on highways and levees."

Additions and improvements to the old courthouse were made during the early 1890's, including a fireproof vault for the clerk's office. During a smallpox epidemic in 1895, Drs. W. D. Haas and W. G. Branch vaccinated "free of charge," for which service they were later paid $33.00 by the parish. In 1897, $300.00 was appropriated for a new well at Marksville, the well to have a windmill with a 13-foot wheel atop a 40-foot tower, a "sanitary closet" was built in the jail, and a "summer normal school" was authorized for the teachers of the parish. Two years later a new stove was purchased for the West Par-en-haut school, and the Woman's Christian Temperance Union petitioned the police jury to "continue high licenses for selling liquor," for they had "done much good."

The new century brought additional improvements. In 1901 the Avoyelles Telephone Company was granted a franchise to build lines from Bunkie to Marksville, Simmesport, Bordelonville, Plaucheville, Moureauville, and in-between points. Hog killers were appointed for the First Ward, "from Cassandra down as far as levee extends." A brick walk was laid around the courthouse square in 1907. In 1908, the police jury was extremely active. It accepted a new jail, built a "trough for horses" in front of the courthouse, and installed cuspidors for the various parish offices. It forbade the sale of butchered animals "without heads or freshly cut ears" and ordered "Blind Tiger" saloons to be "captured." The 1915 jury ordered dog licenses "levied," appropriated money for "picture slides for agricultural instruction," and built a new "engine house" on the courthouse square.

The Avoyelles Parish Jury began to regulate automobiles in 1910. In May of that year the speed of cars was limited to fifteen miles per hour on straight roads, eight miles per hour on roads with curves, and only four miles per hour while crossing a bridge or passing a buggy, a rider of a horse, a wagon, or in front of a church. Automobiles, when signaled, must stop until a buggy or other horse-drawn vehicle had passed. An eight-inch-square number had to be attached to the rear of every automobile, white on a black car and black on a white car, and each automobile had to be registered with the sheriff, who collected a license fee of $10.00. Eight years later automobiles were permitted to be driven as fast as twenty miles an hour on country roads and twelve miles an hour in towns, but signals must be given when passing other vehicles and headlights must be equipped with "dimmers." Fines for violations of these regulations were from $10.00 to $25.00.

During the 1890's the residents of Plaquemine received a real scare when it was discovered that the original 1782 Spanish land grant to Antoine Rodriguez, on whose land the town was subsequently built, was defective and therefore not valid. During the interim there had been over 12,500 land sales and as many more mortgages passed. Technically at least, title to all land in the city belonged to the Federal government. All titles were validated by special act of Congress in 1897.

In 1870, New Orleans had received a new charter, replacing that of 1836 and inaugurating what was called the "administrative system." The mayor and seven officials met once a week as a legislative body, and each of the seven officials served as the head of a city department—finance, commerce, assessment, improvements, police, public accounts, and waterworks and public buildings. The citizens became dissatisfied with the administrative system after the adoption of the State Constitution of 1879, and in 1882 a new city charter was secured which provided for a mayor, a thirty-member council, a treasurer, a comptroller, a commissioner of public works, and a commissioner of police and public buildings, all of whom were to be elected. The commission type of government was adopted in 1912 with a five-member commission elected on a city-wide basis. An official city flag was first raised in 1918, which had a wide, white middle ground with three yellow or golden fleur-de-lis, a bottom blue stripe, and a top red stripe.

Until 1896 the legislature provided for municipal government by special charter, but in that year provided for a general mayor-alderman government for cities and towns. A new law passed in 1898 classified all municipalities into cities (over 5,000 population, towns (1,000 to 5,000), and villages (150 to 1,000), and continued the mayor-alderman type of government subject to variations for the three classifications. In 1910 the legislature passed a new commission-government law and in 1918 enacted an optional commission-manager plan of municipal government. While legislative control of local government was generally satisfactory, improvement had to await the coming of the modern period.

LAW AND ORDER. The disorder of the period of military occupation slowly subsided in all sections of the state except New Orleans after the restoration of Home Rule in 1877. In New Orleans, however, the change from Radical government brought little improvement despite the efforts of citizens' groups "to suppress crime, to compel the authorities to perform their duties, to watch the city government," and particularly to assist in securing the punishment of dishonest city officials. The police department continued to be a sort of step-child of city government and, as Herbert Asbury wrote, "the focal point of graft and corruption," for "inefficiently organized, underpaid, woefully inadequate in numbers and equipment, and subject to little or no discipline, the police made scarcely any pretense of protecting the lives and property of the citizens." In a memorial sent to the legislature in 1886 it was flatly admitted that "it wants every characteristic, physical, moral and intellectual."

Gangs of so-called "tuffs" or "knockers" roamed the city at night, openly violating the laws and preying on all groups of society without fear of reprisals from the police. At a Basin Street saloon a popular barfly named "Happy Charlie" sang a favorite ditty entitled "Der Nue Orleans Tuff," to the accompaniment of the music of a tin whistle which he blew through his nose,

> I am a man dat most of yer know,
> I'm known as a knocker wherever I go.
> My fame it is fightin'; I kan't get enuff,
> All over de town dey call me a tuff;
> And when I gets roudy I paints de town red.
> I know all de cops; I stan' in wid de roughs,
> Yer kin bet yer sweet life I'm er Nu'Leens tuff.

During the late years of the nineteenth century and the early years of the twentieth the red-light district of New Orleans was sometimes called "Anderson County" because its largest operator and most influential citizen was Thomas C. Anderson. Anderson, whom Asbury called the "big shot of brotheldom," owned saloons, concert saloons, bawdyhouses, and a restaurant and cabaret on Rampart Street which he advertised as "The Real Thing." He became the political boss of the Fourth Ward, was generous to friend and competitor alike, and finally succumbed to the desire to serve in the legislature. His grateful constituents, in recognition of his numerous services to them, rewarded him with two terms shortly after the turn of the new century.

Numerous Italians settled in New Orleans after the Civil War, and some of them belonged to secret societies such as the Mafia and the Camorra, against which the Italian government had been waging a campaign of extirpation. By the 1880's members of the Italian colony, which numbered between 25,000 and 30,000, were living in a reign of terror. The members of the Mafia enforced their control with the stiletto or with the so-called "Mafia gun," a sawed-off, hinged-stock shotgun filled with slugs or buckshot and deadly effective up to about twenty-five or thirty yards. It is claimed that by 1890 there were living in the city some 1,100 Italians who had been forced to leave Italy because of their criminal records.

In 1889, David C. Hennessy was elected superintendent of police preliminary to a general campaign to rid the city of its lawless elements, particularly the Mafia. Hennessy cracked down, and on the night of October 15, 1890, was ambushed and shot. Nineteen Italians were arrested and charged with complicity in the crime. The case came to trial in late February, 1891, during which sixty-seven witnesses appeared for the State and eighty-four for the defense. On March 13 the jury acquitted six of those charged and failed to convict the remainder. The next morning a mob formed at the Clay Statue, then located at the corner of St. Charles and Canal, listened to several speeches, and rushed for the parish prison. They shot or hanged eleven of the nineteen men, then quietly dispersed.

The affair stirred up a storm of controversy throughout the nation and Baron Fava, the Italian Minister to the United States, sailed for home. Newspapers condemned the mob's action. The Nashville *American* called it "one of the bloodiest and most brutal butcheries on record," while the Charleston *News and Courier* termed it the "bloodiest chapter in the history of New Orleans." The New Orleans press generally defended the action taken but devoted comparatively little space to the incident, the *Times-Democrat* asserting briefly that "desperate diseases require desperate remedies. . . . Our justification was—necessity; our defense is—self-preservation, nature's primal law." The remaining eight men were eventually freed, the United States paid the Italian government nearly $25,000 for the families of the slain men, and diplomatic relations were resumed between the two countries. The incident, however, had a salutary effect upon the Mafia and other secret criminal organizations, and no further acts of violence were proved against them.

There were comparatively few crimes of a serious nature committed in the rural sections or in the small towns of the state. In all probability the crime which received the most attention during the period was the murder of Narcisse Arrieux of Donaldsonville in 1878. For this, four men were sentenced to death by hanging. The Donaldsonville *Chief* on August 17 reported that "The dread spectacle of the hanging was witnessed by at least 4000 people, who flocked to town from all directions in a stream that flowed continually from an early hour of the morning until the time fixed for the execution."

Public hangings began to go out of fashion during the 1880's. In New Orleans before the Civil War they usually had been held in Jackson Square or Beauregard Square, and the crowds assumed a somewhat festive air as they turned out to witness the spectacles. John S. Kendall wrote that "everybody attended—solid citizens desirous of seeing the law avenged upon evil-doers; urchins; negroes, nurse maids and their charges, young women and their lovers—a motley but representative throng, curiously indifferent to the horror of these scenes, but fascinated by their drama." After the war, hangings were generally held at the parish prison.

SOCIAL AND PENAL LEGISLATION. There was little state assistance to the indigent aged and infirm during the period, the problem being considered a local one; in 1870 only $98,000 was appropriated to over forty private and sectarian organizations and institutions which cared for such unfortunates. A bill for the relief of the poor failed to pass the legislature in 1870, as its members believed that it was "calculated to encourage laziness," and make "the State of Louisiana a receptacle for the poor of other states." The Constitution of 1879 made it obligatory for each parish to support its own needy persons, and the Act of 1880 ordered police juries to provide for the support of the destitute, with the stipulation that they should not "at public expense, support or aid any persons as paupers except such as are infirm, sick, or disabled." Local taxation provided some assistance to "poor farms," which were partially self-supporting. Subsequent "poor" acts supplemented that of 1880.

Prior to 1852, the blind, deaf, and dumb were cared for by the individual parishes, but in that year the state established an institution for the education of these unfortunates in Baton Rouge. A building completed seven years later housed the institution until 1869, when it was turned over to the State Seminary of Learning, the afflicted students being moved to a nearby building. In 1889 the buildings and grounds of W. H. N. Magruder's Collegiate Institute were purchased by the state, and the blind were moved there the following year. The unfortunate students in both schools were provided with both academic and vocational education.

Prior to 1847 the insane were placed in parish jails or in Charity Hospital at New Orleans if their families would not take care of them, but in that year the Insane Asylum of Louisiana was founded at Jackson. This institution served the state until 1905, when the Central Louisiana State Hospital for the insane was established at Pineville to relieve the overcrowded conditions at Jackson.

In 1877, Charity Hospital had an annual income of less than $100,000 a year, an indebtedness of about $70,000, and spent less than 40 cents per day per patient. Governor Nicholls appointed a new Board of Administrators who immediately began a program of repair and improvement. Horse-drawn ambulances were purchased in 1884, electricity was installed in 1890, and new buildings were constructed, including the new Milliken Building facing Tulane Avenue, between 1898 and 1910. By the latter date patients were being conveyed to the hospital in new ambulances whose "rubber wheels were an innovation, as was the small step at the rear on which the intern stood, clinging precariously to the leather strap provided for this purpose."

In 1904 the hospital cared for nearly 9,000 resident patients, 19,000 nonresident patients, and gave over 73,000 free consultations; five years later it had 52 wards with over 900 beds which were used by nearly 10,000 patients. In 1914 the total annual expenses of the hospital amounted to over $300,000, part of which was paid by the City of New Orleans, part by the state, and part by private contributions. In that year over 17,000 resident patients were treated. But in spite of increased state and city assistance and private contributions and donations, the hospital, along with its smaller sister institution at Shreveport which had been established at the beginning of the period, was not able in 1920 to adequately care for the state's population who could not afford to pay for hospitalization.

Leprosy, now usually called "Hansen's Disease," had existed in Louisiana since colonial times. During the Spanish period those suffering from the disease had been treated at a hospital built by Governor Miró on a ridge of land between the Mississippi River and Bayou St. John near New Orleans, but the number of diseased declined and the hospital was abandoned. Although in 1878 a "pest house" where lepers were cared for was established near New Orleans, little was accomplished until 1892 when the legislature passed an act which provided for a home for those afflicted with the disease, to be administered by the state under contract. In 1894 another act was passed authorizing the governor to appoint a Board of Control. So great was the dread of the disease that the New Orleans City Council refused to permit a building to be constructed in the city, so "Indian Camp" plantation in Iberville Parish was leased; a few years later the Sisters of the Order of St. Vincent de Paul were given charge of the new institution, the plantation was purchased, and additional buildings built. The Leprosarium gained national recognition after the successful introduction of chaulmoogra-oil treatments in 1899. The Federal government took over the institution in 1921.

Construction of a state penitentiary at Baton Rouge begun during the 1830's was finally completed according to the original plan in 1848. It had a ropewalk and machinery for making bagging and other coarse cotton goods and was leased to Ward, McHatton & Company, the state to receive one-fourth of the profits. The penitentiary was taken over by Federal troops in May, 1862, and soon afterwards General Butler ordered the convicts released. After the war the lease system was continued, even though it had been severely criticized for some years; one Louisianian wrote in 1892 that the convicts were "brutalized, many escaped, and the moral influence upon the community was wholly bad." The mortality rate during the 1880's for all prisoners had been approximately 80 per cent, and a ten-year penalty was generally considered a death sentence.

The Constitution of 1898 abolished the lease system, and the state took over the penitentiary and convict labor camps in 1901. Meanwhile, the state had purchased 8,000 acres of plantation land along the Mississippi in West Feliciana Parish and 2,000 acres of sugar land on Bayou Teche in Iberia Parish. In 1908, Governor Blanchard approved an act authorizing the penitentiary at Baton Rouge to be sold, and the same year the convicts were moved to the two plantations. An authority on penal institutions soon wrote that the Louisiana prisoners "were not in the long run as badly off as our convicts in the North, who are contracted out to work in dingy, ill-ventilated and disease-breeding shops, where they are doomed to breathe poisoned air and almost entirely shut out from ever seeing a ray of sunshine." He stated further that Louisiana was "a century ahead of the methods in common practice in the ordinary prisons North and South."

CHAPTER 25

YEARS OF SLOW ECONOMIC
PROGRESS

GROWTH OF POPULATION. Louisiana made slow economic progress during the years from 1877 to 1920. The immediate major objective was the recovery of the ground lost during the war and occupation years, and in some economic fields this was not achieved until after 1900. Years afterward, Edwin L. Stephens, who had become one of the state's educational leaders, reminisced about the period of his boyhood: "Nobody was rich . . . at the time in which my lot was cast—save in the heritage and tradition of the curiosity to know, eagerness to learn, the desire for education, appreciation of culture, and aspiration towards better things. . . . The people were all poor."

But the land was there, the rich earth of Louisiana, about which the editor of the Chicago *Tribune* wrote during the late 1870's: "If, by some supreme effort of nature [it] could be taken up and transported North . . . it would create a commotion that would throw the discovery of gold in California in the shade at the time of the greatest excitement. The people would rush to it in countless thousands." As the years passed, agriculture recovered, while the discovery and exploitation of new raw materials after 1900 aided in the development of industry and speeded up general economic development.

The population increased a total of slightly over 90 per cent from 1880 to 1920, from approximately 940,000 to 1,798,500, while the nation as a whole increased a little over 100 per cent. Meanwhile the rural population decreased from 74.5 per cent to 65 per cent and the Negro population from 51.5 per cent of the state's total citizenry in 1880 to 38.9 per cent in 1920. Foreign-born citizens dropped from nearly 53,000 in 1880 to about 45,000 forty years later. The greatest percentage growth of population was in the northern and western sections of the state. But in national-population rank Louisiana neither gained or lost, for she stood twenty-second at the beginning and twenty-second at the end of the period.

While towns and villages generally grew slowly, a few of them blossomed into cities during the forty-year period. Monroe grew from about 2,000 to over 12,500; Alexandria from 1,800 to 17,500; Baton Rouge from 7,000 to nearly 22,000; Shreveport from 8,000 to nearly 44,000; and Lake Charles from 838 to 13,088. New Orleans made rapid growth as a trade distribution and commercial center, increasing its population from 216,000 to over 387,000. Mrs. T. P. O'Connor wrote that in 1912 "the swampland all around New Orleans is rapidly being reclaimed. Pretty, quaint little houses and bungalows, brilliantly painted, are being built, and the outskirts of the town offer a gay and exotic appearance. . . . The road to Lake Pontchartrain, where there is a club and a tea house and boats of divers kinds for hire, is now lined with motors."

By 1900, cities and towns outside the Crescent metropolis were awakening to the bustling activity of the twentieth century and were beginning to install such modern conveniences as city lighting and water systems, paved streets, and good drainage facilities. A few of them were on the point of laying electric trolley-car tracks along their most important streets. By 1920 city conveniences were commonplace, and in many towns the hitching post was giving way to the marked parking place for automobiles.

New towns were established in the northern and western sections as new agricultural lands were developed. Ruston, for example, was founded in 1884, when the Shreveport, Vicksburg and Pacific Railroad pushed westward from Monroe. The new town, plotted and laid out by the railroad engineers, was named for R. E. Russ, who owned the land on which it was built. After setting aside space for schools, a courthouse, and a cemetery, lots were sold to prospective settlers. Merchants drew lots for the locations of their establishments, and the first business to open its doors was the "eating-house" of Joe Schwab, "who possessed a mockingbird that whistled popular tunes and a wife with a generous disposition but a quick temper."

In 1887 brothers W. W. Duson and C. C. Duson founded Crowley and named it for a Southern Pacific Railroad employee named Patrick Crowley. Plans for the town were drawn, streets were laid out, and drainage ditches were dug. The first sale of lots on February 10-11, 1887, totaled over $25,000. Crowley became the parish seat of newly formed Acadia Parish that same year, and the next year a brick courthouse was completed. In 1890, Crowley had over 400 inhabitants, and two years later New Orleans *Picayune* staff writer M. B. Hillyard compiled a business directory of the new town, in which he wrote: "There is nothing feverish in the spirit of appreciation of Crowley by her citizens. There is no noisy boastfulness, but you will find that people seem to take it as a matter of course that their town lots and prices of land contiguous seem high. They say it is value, not prices. Anyhow, I see nobody anxious to sell, while I have heard a number of offers refused, which, I confess, surprised me." By 1898 the town had a brick and tile factory, an ice plant, rice mills, a broom factory, a good public-school system and several private schools, a half-dozen well-established churches, an opera house, and "seven secret societies."

Not all Louisiana towns were so active or progressive. In 1890, Louisiana historian Alcée Fortier visited St. Martinville, and afterward described it as a quaint "old Creole town" where there was not much activity in business, but "order and decency prevailed everywhere and the people were uniformly affable and polite." The town had but one hotel, which had a wide gallery and massive brick columns, where "everything is as in ante-bellum days; no register awaits the names of the guests, and the owner seems to have implicit confidence in the honesty of his boarders." Many towns and villages retained their ante bellum physical characteristics until the end of the period, and since that time a few communities, villages, towns and cities have initiated well-organized programs to retain at least some of the evidences of old Creole and ante bellum heritages.

AGRICULTURE. During the first half of the period, M. B. Hillyard, Daniel Dennett, Dr. W. C. Stubbs, Dr. Seaman A. Knapp, and other scientific agriculturalists, journalists, and parish and local political leaders enthusiastically propagandized the opportunities in Louisiana agriculture. At a state-wide agricultural fair during the late 1880's one speaker made a strong plea for exploiting the "wonderful resources" of the state and for exhibiting the best products in order to stimulate quality production: ". . . the oranges and bananas of Plaquemine will mingle beautifully with the apples and pears and peaches of Claiborne; the wheat of Union can be interwoven with the rice of Jefferson, while the sugar of St. Mary will vie in whiteness with the fleecy staple of Caddo; the market gardeners of Tangipahoa and St. Bernard can exchange congratulations with the haymakers and stock-growers of Calcasieu and St. Landry."

It was not until after 1900, however, that agriculture and agricultural production generally recovered the ground lost during the years from 1861 to 1877. In 1860 farm lands had been valued at approximately $215,000,000; in 1890 their value was only $110,500,000. Farm equipment had declined from $20,000,000 to about $7,000,000 and livestock from nearly $25,000,000 to $18,000,000. Of the important staples of 1860, only tobacco, sugar, and rice showed a gain in the crop of 1890 over that of the former year—tobacco from nearly 40,000 pounds to nearly 49,000, sugar from 266,000,000 pounds to 292,000,000, and rice from 6,330,000 pounds to nearly 75,650,000. Cotton and corn still had not caught up with the 1860 production, rye had dropped to only 374 bushels, and wheat had declined to 257 bushels.

Despite the fact that the number of large farms and plantations of over 1,000 acres increased from 381 in 1860 to 1,277 thirty years later, the total number of farm establishments increased from 17,328 in 1860 to 69,294 in 1890 and in average acreage decreased from 537 acres to 138 acres. While there are no statistics for tenancy in 1860, by 1890 a little over 55 per cent of the farm units were cultivated by owners, over 27 per cent by share croppers, and nearly 17 per cent by those who rented for a fixed yearly cash payment.

The increasing use of scientific agricultural methods gained momentum as the years passed. The World's Industrial and Cotton Centennial Exposition, which was held in New Orleans in late 1884 and early 1885, greatly stimulated the farmers. The first agricultural experiment station was established at Kenner in 1885, the second at Baton Rouge at the State University the following year, and the third at Calhoun two years afterward, all under the directorship of Dr. W. C. Stubbs. At these experiment stations demonstrations were given in the terracing of land, in the use of new farm machinery, in the treatment of animal and plant diseases, and in numerous other areas of agricultural activity. Many farmers, however, were slow in adopting the new discoveries and methods, and one northeast Louisiana farmer refused to admit that farming could be taught by a "college professor," saying: "Why, I've worn out two farms; you can't tell me how I ought to farm."

The Louisiana State Agricultural Society was organized in 1886 to promote "the collection and diffusion of agricultural information and . . . progressive, profitable agriculture." Within a few years farmers were listening to professional agriculturists speak on such subjects as "Good Roads," "Truck Growing in Louisiana," "Grasses and Forage Crops," and the "Relation of L.S.U. and A.&M. College to the Development of the State."

In 1885, Dr. Seaman A. Knapp, after a distinguished career at Iowa State College, became associated with a group developing a tract of land in southwest Louisiana, moved to Lake Charles, began aiding farmers in the development of better farming methods, and worked out a demonstration system for training of individual farmers. His "Ten Commandments of Agriculture" were widely adopted in Louisiana and in the South—preparation of well-drained, well-pulverized seedbed, seed of best variety, giving plants plenty of space in which to grow, intense tillage during the growing season, scientific use of fertilizers, systematic crop rotation, use of better implements and more horsepower, utilization of all waste products and idle lands with livestock, production of all food of men and animals, and keeping a complete accounting system. In 1904, Dr. Knapp became associated with the Federal Department of Agriculture to help fight the boll weevil. He died in 1911. Charles W. Dabney wrote that "he brought knowledge, hope and prosperity to a stricken people at a time when they were almost hopeless," while Walter Hines Page called him "the greatest schoolmaster of the age."

The home, blue ribbon, or Noble varieties of sugar cane were most cultivated during the early 1900's, but they became subject to various diseases and the D-74 and D-95 varieties were then introduced from Cuba. These canes were soon attacked by root rot, the mosaic disease, and insect pests of several types. About 1920, D. W. Pipes, Jr., and Elliott Jones of Houma introduced POJ seed canes from Java, and the new type was widely accepted.

The most progress was in the production of rice. At the beginning of the period small plots were grown in South Louisiana in low places where standing water reduced irrigation to the simplest process. It was called the "Providence Crop," for it generally depended upon rainfall and families leaned heavily upon it for subsistence. During the 1880's middle-western grain farmers began to settle on the fertile lands of south-west Louisiana and the development of modern rice production began.

A revolution in rice production was accomplished within a twelve-year period; twine binders were introduced in 1884, steam-vacuum irrigation pumps in 1885, Engellery hullers and polishers in 1891, Randolph rice headers and combines in 1892, the canal system of irrigation near Jennings in 1893 by C. L. Shaw and A. D. McFar-land, improved harvesters in 1894, centrifugal pumps in 1895, and well irrigation by Jean Costex of Mermentau the same year. Meanwhile steam plows and cultivation machinery had been developed, along with elevators for loading railroad cars with bulk rice. The Rice Association of America was organized at Crowley in December, 1901, to help increase production and promote the sale and consumption of rice.

At the beginning of the period the Carolina, Honduras, and Japan varieties were most commonly used, but by 1911, Sol Wright, a former Indiana wheat farmer and the "Burbank of the rice industry," had developed the superior Blue Rose variety. Wright later developed other popular varieties, including the Early Prolific, the Lady Wright, and the Edith. By 1936 the *United States Agricultural Year Book* reported that "roughly 73% of the rice produced in the United States in 1934 consisted of varieties developed by the late S. L. Wright."

Agricultural clubs had been organized in the parish schools after 1910, and in 1913 these groups affiliated with the national 4-H Club. In 1914, Mamie Miller, a rural schoolteacher in Ouachita Parish, began the organization of home-canning clubs. The same year farmers' co-operative demonstration work was merged with the Agri-cultural Extension Service at the State University, and Dr. W. R. Dodson, Head of the Agricultural College and Director of State Experiment Stations, was named the first director.

Meanwhile, numerous agricultural journals were being established, over forty of them during the period from 1877 to 1920. Most lived only a few years, but they accomplished many services for the farmer. These publications included the Crowley *Louisiana Farmer and Rice Journal,* the Franklin *Planter's Home Journal,* the Morgan City *Rural Topics,* the New Orleans *Cotton Trade Journal,* the New Orleans *Louisiana Planter and Sugar Manufacturer,* and the Winnfield *Farmers' Union Banner.*

In spite of the many improvements in Louisiana agriculture after 1877, numerous small farmers lived on a bare margin of existence, many of them squatters on sub-marginal land. They owned a few cattle and hogs, a horse or two, hunted and fished, and cultivated a little patch of ground on which they raised sweet and Irish potatoes, tomatoes, onions, and a few other vegetables. As late as 1920 some of them could be found who fitted Elizabeth Custer's description of 1865: "Small, low, log huts, consist-ing of one room each, entirely separated and having a floored open space between them. . . . The men and women slouched and skulked around the cabins out of sight, and every sign of abject, loathsome poverty was visible, even in the gaunt and famished pigs that rooted around the doorway." The decrease in submarginal agriculture had to await coming decades.

INDUSTRY AND THE EXPLOITATION OF NATURAL RESOURCES. There was comparatively little progress in industry until 1900, but after that date Louisiana began to develop new industries of many types. Not only were additional natural resources of great commercial value discovered in many sections of the state, including natural gas, sulphur, oil, and new beds of salt, but the older known resources, such as fur-bearing animals, fish and seafoods, and lumber, also entered a new period of development. Industrial plants began locating in Louisiana because of newly discovered raw materials and, in addition, because of the mild climate, abund-ant water resources, low-cost fuel, labor supply, and new transportation facilities.

Large-scale lumbering began during the middle 1870's, the Pharr and Williams' Sawmill at Patterson, operated by John N. Pharr and F. B. Williams, being among the first. Joseph Norgess, who operated several early mills in the Teche country, and Joseph Rathborne, who built one of the first large sawmills in the state at Harvey, were also among the early operators. During the 1890's, after the completion of the Kansas City Southern Railroad, the western section of the state rapidly developed its lumber industry. Large-scale lumbering started in the Bogalusa district in 1907, when Colonel William H. Sullivan began operations for the Great Southern Lumber Company interests, and within a year the town had a population of over 1,500.

The early Louisiana lumber mills produced railroad ties, telephone and telegraph poles, shingles, barrel and hogshead staves, boards for cypress cisterns which had an average longevity of half a century, rough-sawed lumber for ordinary building purposes, and high-quality curly and gnarled cypress for fine finishing work. Most of the South Louisiana lumber was cypress, while that of the Bogalusa and western sections was varieties of pine.

The timber workers of no other state, with the possible exception of Maine, had so many stirring adventures and faced so many varied and unusual working conditions as did the "swampers" of southern and south central Louisiana. Armed with axes and saws they went into the swamps in boats, cut down the trees, and snaked them along the swamp waterways and bayous to the small mills. The first "swampers" were natives of the section; later recruits, generally called "bummers," came from the forest sections of the North, along with skilled lumbermen and woodworkers from Pennsylvania and Wisconsin. Many of the northern laborers worked only for the season and then returned home for a vacation with little in their pockets. Unskilled workers were generally paid from twelve to thirty cents per hour for a ten- to twelve-hour day and were furnished with housing at a nominal rental. It was a rough and hard life—the felling of the trees, the dangers of unskillfully wielded axes, the treacherous drifts of the rivers, and the perils of malaria and other diseases.

By 1906 the cypress industry had come of age, with fifteen large producers selling their products through the Southern Cypress Lumber Selling Company of New Orleans. The R. H. Downman Cypress Mills, one of the largest manufacturers of cypress lumber in the world, with several mills in South Louisiana, advertised that "we always have in stock from 40 million to 50 million feet of band sawn Louisiana Red Cypress." In 1906, Louisiana produced over 7 per cent of the lumber milled in the nation and ranked second among the states; it held this position throughout the rest of the period, except for 1914 when it ranked first and produced nearly 11 per cent of the nation's lumber, approximately 4 billion feet.

The Louisiana oil industry began in 1901, when wells were drilled near White Castle and Jennings. The White Castle well encountered pockets of oil, but not in paying quantities, while the Jennings well gushed oil for nearly a day and then clogged up. Within a year several wells had been drilled in the Jennings area, and the first really successful well was brought in during the early summer of 1902. The Mamou Field (later called the Evangeline Field) produced 500,000 barrels in 1903 and had a total of thirty-three producing wells by the end of 1904. Oil production began in the Caddo Parish region in 1904 but did not become really successful until two years later when over 4,500 barrels were produced.

Gas seepages had been known in colonial Louisiana, but the first well which produced gas used for lighting purposes was not drilled until 1870 at Shreveport. Although no efforts to develop this industry were made until the early 1900's, by 1906 there were eleven producing gas wells in the Caddo area. The enormous pressures of the Caddo field gas caused considerable difficulty, and it was not for some years that methods were discovered to properly control the wells. Soon after gas was found near Monroe in 1916, the North Louisiana oil and gas fields were booming. By 1910, the Standard Oil Company had completed its Oklahoma to Baton Rouge pipeline, which also carried northern and northwestern Louisiana oil, and was the largest processer of oil and oil products.

Louisiana's first sulphur deposit was discovered in 1869 in Calcasieu Parish, but commercial production did not begin until 1895, when the Frasch method of mining was introduced. Between that date and 1914 the Calcasieu field supplied about 75 per cent of the nation's sulphur. With the discovery of other fields in southern and southeastern Louisiana the importance of this field began to decline and was generally exhausted by 1924.

Rock salt had been discovered at Avery Island early in the Civil War but did not become commercially important until 1879, when the American Rock Salt Mining Company began operations. By 1913, Louisiana ranked second among the states in the production of salt, and by the end of the period was producing approximately 350,000 tons per year.

The Spanish-moss industry became commercially important during the 1880's when steam-driven gins, presses, and cleaning machinery began to replace old hand methods. At first the product was used mainly in the manufacture of mattresses and pillows, but in later years its use was gradually applied to many industries, especially in the making of all types of padding and stuffing materials. The national fur industry was supplied with Louisiana opossum, mink, skunk, raccoon, and muskrat pelts. The state's more than 7,000 square miles of tidewaters supplied abundant amounts of shrimp and oysters, and fresh-water and salt-water fisheries furnished many varieties of fish, as well as turtles, frogs, and crawfish, for out-of-state as well as domestic consumption.

A commission on natural resources was created in 1908, and Governor Sanders appointed Henry E. Hardtner, a prominent North Louisiana lumberman, its first president. As a result of Hardtner's report of 1910 the Conservation Commission was established by law in 1912 to make rules and regulations for the preservation of the state's natural resources. The Constitution of 1921 established a Department of Conservation.

By 1920 the leading natural-resource industries were petroleum refining, lumbering, sugar refining, paper manufacturing, and rice cleaning and polishing. General manufacturing plants produced lumber products, boots and shoes, brick, cigars and cigarettes, barrels, soda, packaged foods, fertilizers, and hundreds of other products. While Louisiana was still a rural, agricultural state in 1920, she was rapidly developing a balanced economy in all the economic fields.

TRANSPORTATION. At the beginning of the period water transportation was the most important method of travel and all of the larger Louisiana rivers and bayous were highways of trade and commerce. By the end of the century railroads had been built throughout the state and the smaller lines were being consolidated into the major systems. Roads were greatly improved during the years after 1900, although the paving of highways had to await the modern era.

Albert L. Grace has written that "the most glorious days of steamboating were those between 1880 and 1898, when there were more packet boats and larger and more palatial steamers than in any other decade." Regularly scheduled river boats ran from New Orleans, Baton Rouge, and other Mississippi River towns to Natchez, Vicksburg, Memphis, St. Louis, Louisville, Pittsburgh, and other upriver cities, while smaller scheduled and unscheduled boats threaded the more winding and shallower waters of the state carrying both passengers and cargoes.

On the Mississippi the late winter and spring months saw the coming of numerous timber rafts, coal barges from Pittsburgh, trading scows and broadhorns from middle-western states loaded with "fruit and furniture" as the saying went, but actually filled with every kind of produce. The river-boat pilots hated these powerless craft, for their pilots simply would not obey the law which required them to have lights burning, making it difficult for steamboat pilots to see them in the darkness. Accidents were frequent and it was a common occurrence for steamboat pilots to suddenly hear a voice come from the darkness: "Whar'n the hell you goin' to! Cain't you see nothin', you dash-dashed aig-suckin', sheep-stealin', one-eyed son of a stuffed monkey!" And if the pilot so much as "brushed" the scow, barge, or raft a lawsuit would be awaiting him when he next returned to New Orleans.

[299]

The River steamboats carried the farmer's products to market, and brought him farm tools, supplies for his family, and the luxury goods he desired. Some of the boats carried large numbers of passengers and many tons of freight; in 1897, for example, the *Natchez*, captained by Blanche Douglas who was the wife of noted steamboat captain T. P. Leathers, reached New Orleans with 500 passengers and 4,247 bales of cotton. Such gigantic boats as the *Grand Republic* were on the St. Louis-New Orleans run; the *Natchez*, the *J. M. White*, and the *Pargoud* were in the New Orleans-Vicksburg trade; the *Paul Tulane*, the *Edward J. Gay*, and the *Jesse K. Bell* carried passengers and goods between New Orleans and Bayou Sara; the *Ouachita*, the *La Belle*, the *John D. Grace*, and the *Trudeau* were on the Red River. Smaller trading boats, such as the *Teche* and the *Lafourche* which served the regions of those two bayous, plied the lesser rivers and bayous, carrying a small tonnage of freight and only a few passengers.

Steamboats still had to contend with the usual river problems of snags, shallow water, crevasses, boiler explosions, scarcity of wood and coal for fuel at given points, and trouble with roustabout crews. The Red River had been cleared of its obstructions during the 1830's by Henry M. Shreve, but the smaller streams and bayous still caused steamboat captains considerable worry. Congress passed an act in 1879 providing for the appointment of a Mississippi River Commission to "improve and give safety and ease to the navigation thereof," and in 1890 the act was amended to include the construction and repair of levees. Between 1865 and 1903 the state spent nearly $23,500,000 on levees and after the later date received increased assistance from the Federal government. Bayou Plaquemine became unnavigable in the 1880's, but work was started in 1895, and the bayou was cleared and a new lock at Plaquemine completed in 1909. Boats could then pass from the Mississippi into Bayou Plaquemine and continue by way of Grand River to the Atchafalaya and Bayou Teche.

Larger steamboats had become "floating palaces" by the 1880's. Steam hoists replaced man power, coal replaced wood for fuel, and electric lights took the place of kerosene lamps and wood torches. Cabins were fitted with elaborate furnishings, dining-room chefs prepared banquets, and passengers lived in complete comfort. But the old boat songs were still sung and they amused many a passenger:

> We'll give her a little more rosin,
> And open her blower wide,
> To show them the way to Natchez,
> Runnin' against the tide.
> Oh, a little more rosin,
> A little more pitch and pine!
> Throw in a can of glycerine
> And a barrel of turpentine.

The verses of another song went this way:

> Late in de fall de ribber mos' dry,
> Water lie low and de banks lie high,
> Bullfrog roll up his pants jes' so,
> An' he wade acrost from sho' to sho'.

> Water so shaller dat de eel can't swim
> 'Dout kickin' up de dus' in de middle o' de stream;
> Sun shine hot, an' de catfish say,
> We'se gettin' right freckly-faced down our way!

Men long remembered the steamboat lore. They remembered the great race in 1870 between the *Natchez* and the *Robert E. Lee* from New Orleans to St. Louis, a distance of 1,278 miles. The *Lee* won in 3 days, 18 hours, and 14 minutes. They remembered the nicknames of various boats. The *Twelfth Era* was called *Era No. 12;* the *Bryarly,* the *Joe;* the *John D. Scully,* the *One-Arm John* (because she had but one chimney) ; the *La Belle,* the *Dirty Belle* (because she used so much fuel that clouds of smoke belched constantly from her stacks) ; and the *Independent,* the *Fourth of July.* They remembered them for their whistles, each of which had an individual sound. Albert L. Grace wrote fondly of the "melodious" whistle of the *Edward J. Gay,* which was sunk in 1889, and of how the whistle was later recovered. He wrote that the *Jesse K. Bell* had the "loudest whistle," and that the *Paris C. Brown* had "the frekiest [*sic*] of all river whistles; it was of the 'wild cat' variety, up and down, tending to startle one out of two nights sleep." They told of how the rats ran off the *Paris C. Brown* at Plaquemine, how three Negro roustabouts refused to continue the trip, and how the boat sank a few hours later.

The old steamboat days came to an end shortly after 1900 when the railroad lines and networks were completed, and the number of steamboats rapidly declined on the rivers and bayous of Louisiana. Frederick Way, Jr., wrote sadly in his *The Log of Betsy Ann* that the "stately steamboats with mellow whistles" had "no place in the modern hurly-burly of reeking gas fumes, nerve-shattering shrieks of freight locomotives and the buzz-saw drones of airplane motors." A colorful period in transportation had passed from the American scene.

In 1861 there were only a little over 300 miles of railroad track in the entire state and the longest line was only 88 miles in length. The many miles of track abandoned during the Civil War were reclaimed between 1865 and 1877, and a few new lines were built. The New Orleans, Mobile and Chattanooga Railroad reached Donaldsonville and began to run trains to New Orleans in 1871. The Donaldsonville *Chief* of October 14 proudly announced that the train arrived at noon each day and departed on its return trip at one o'clock, and that city papers not six hours old could now be purchased. The trains had some disadvantages, however: "A man might find a lucrative business in traveling up and down the railroad and picking up the hats that blow from the heads of the passengers. . . . We are of the opinion that there have been enough hats scattered along the road since it has been opened to fill a small size hat store."

Other railroads were organized or reorganized, including the New Orleans, Opelousas and Great Western; the New Orleans and Pacific; the St. Louis, Avoyelles and Southwestern; and the Vicksburg, Shreveport and Pacific. Baton Rouge was reached in 1881, and it was proclaimed that "trains will run through from New Orleans to Baton Rouge, and return every day." So many New Orleans and downriver people wished to visit the capital of the state that the railroad soon organized excursion trains. The great period of railroad building was from 1880 to 1910, by which date the state had nearly 5,600 miles of track.

There were many amusing and interesting anecdotes connected with Louisiana railroad building. When the railroad came through the region of what is now Bunkie, it wanted a right of way across R. B. Marshall's land. His little daughter had a pet monkey but she pronounced the word "bunkie," so Marshall stipulated that the new railroad station must be called Bunkie. When Samuel H. Lockett first traveled from Tallulah to Delhi he protested to the public: "I wish to record as a warning to all travelers that that run of eighteen miles cost me nine dollars." Out in the western part of the state when stage driver "Captain" Kelly heard they were going to build a railroad to Texas he remarked: "I don't believe they will ever do it, because thar ain't any use in it. I can carry all the mail and all the passengers that ever will want to go between here and Shreveport. But if they do build their railroad I shall quit driving a stage, for I'll be durned if I'll go to Texas."

Most people still traveled to small towns and parish seats over ungraded dirt roads, which were dusty when the weather was dry and filled with ruts and mudholes when it was wet. There was no system of state highways, individual parishes building and maintaining the roads within their boundaries. Every male citizen between the ages of fifteen and sixty could be forced to donate twelve days of labor per year to the parish roads, serving at the will of a road overseer who was appointed by the police jury and served without pay. E. B. Cottingham of Caldwell Parish some years ago told of road repair in that parish: "The roads were all washed out in ruts, the axmen would cut brush; some of the boys would drag the brush to the ruts and place it, then the shovels and hoes would get to work and cover it with two or three inches of dirt— we were then ready for another rut after we swapped chews of tobacco or lit our pipes."

During the early years of the period caravans of wagons hauled goods into the country areas from the river towns. The wagoneers usually stopped at night at "wagon yards," where stalls and feed were provided for their horses or oxen. The men slept either in their wagons or in nearby rooming houses. One of the last wagon yards in Louisiana was owned and operated by E. G. Calvery at West Monroe.

Louisiana's most unusual road during the period was the Bossier Parish "Shed Road," which ran from the hills southward to within about two miles of Bossier City. The brown, sticky mud of the Red River Valley was without bottom when it rained, so the planters and farmers tried to make a satisfactory "corduroy" road of logs laid crosswise. They failed, however, for the mud would not hold the logs firmly in place. Finally Judge John W. Watkins of Minden secured a special charter from Congress to build an entirely different type of road; a nine-mile shed was constructed, with ditches on either side, and the road was built under the shed. A four-yoke ox team and wagon was charged $1.50, a four-mule team and wagon $1.00, and a person afoot 5 cents. The road was profitably operated for a number of years, until the railroad reached that section during the late 1880's.

Prior to 1900 there were comparatively few bridges over major streams or bayous. In some localities railroads permitted the use of railroad bridges for wagon and other road traffic. The bridge between Monroe and West Monroe was opened to such traffic in 1889, after the city had provided planking to cover the rails (which had to be removed for trains). The new "free" bridge, it was announced, would cause the old ferry to "fall into a Rip Van Winkle sleep now. . . . Hurrah for the Free Bridge."

Main roads gradually developed into intrastate highways, and their maintenance by adjoining landowners was recognized as both unfair and unsatisfactory. Police juries were authorized by the Constitution of 1898 to create road districts and to issue bonds for road construction and maintenance; twelve years later, Act 49 of 1910 marked the beginning of state control and maintenance.

COMMERCE AND THE DISTRIBUTION OF EVERYDAY COMMODITIES. The total capital invested in all Louisiana manufacturing concerns at the end of the period of military occupation was less than $12,000,000. Several factors were responsible: ante bellum agricultural economy, depredations of the Civil War, lack of available capital, poor railway transportation facilities throughout the state, lack of or high cost of manufacturing fuels, and the shallow channel at the mouth of the Mississippi. Within two decades these disadvantages were about overcome and the state was beginning to increase the production of manufactured goods. By 1900 there were in the state 4,350 manufacturing establishments, the great majority of which were small, employing approximately 42,000 workers and producing in excess of $121,000,000 worth of products.

Within the next twenty years, owing largely to the rapid development of the extractive industries of oil, gas, sulphur, and salt, the state began to emerge as one of the important manufacturing areas of the South. In the last year of the period the state had nearly 2,500 plants, factories, and other manufacturing establishments, many of which compared favorably in size with those of the North, employing nearly 110,000 workers who produced nearly $224,000,000 worth of goods. The chief manufacturing cities were New Orleans, Shreveport, and Baton Rouge; the manufactured goods produced included sugar and molasses, lumber and timber products, cottonseed oil and cottonseed cakes, oil products, and such miscellaneous goods as boots and shoes, brick and tile, wagons, clothing, flour, furniture, cigars, naval stores, and packaged food products.

Foreign import and export commerce developed slowly after 1880, ranging between $70,000,000 and $100,000,000 during the next two decades. By 1910 the total value of this trade had reached nearly $200,000,000 and by 1920 nearly one billion dollars a year, with New Orleans the second port in the nation, doing an import-export business of more than $250,000,000 a year above Philadelphia, its closest competitor. Of the total American exports in 1920, New Orleans handled one-half of the rice and shellfish; approximately one-third of the barley, harness and saddlery, unrefined paraffin, and staves; and one-quarter of the wheat, resin, carbon black, hogsheads and barrels, and zinc. Other leading exports included cotton, sugar, lumber, oil, rice and other grains, iron and steel, foodstuffs, barrel and cask staves, soap, and tobacco. Leading imports were coffee, bananas and other tropical fruits, sisal, nitrates, oil, mahogany, sugar, and molasses. At the end of the period over 80 steamship lines were operating from the port of New Orleans and over 4,100 ships were entering and clearing the port annually.

The rapid growth of New Orleans as a foreign port was the result of the work of Captain James B. Eads, who completed the first successful jetty system at the mouth of the Mississippi in 1879, after surmounting innumerable physical handicaps and governmental red tape. Eads had guaranteed a 30-foot-deep and 350-foot-wide channel and had promised New Orleans, "If I am permitted to proceed, I shall certainly open the mouth of your river, and will double the value of every foot of ground in your city." By December, 1877, he had a 22-foot-deep channel from South Pass over the Gulf bar and a year and a half later had deepened it to 30 feet, sufficient to handle any ship then afloat. Ead's success was hailed over the entire nation, and a New York journalist wrote that "genius, persistence and practical skill have seldom won so great a triumph over the forces of nature and the prejudices of men."

Meanwhile, owing to the gradual improvement of her river wharfage and river and rail transportation facilities, New Orleans had emerged as the leading goods-distribution center of the South, and at the end of the period the organization of river barge lines and the building of the Industrial Canal promised further development. Goods in everyday use were distributed throughout the state in several ways. General stores in New Orleans and the larger towns sold all types of merchandise, while stores specializing in one particular commodity sold shoes, men's or women's clothing, or hardware. In the smaller towns and villages the general store, usually the only type found, carried everything that was needed by farmers, planters, and townspeople— clothing, shoes, foodstuffs of all sorts, tools, agricultural machinery, harness, patent drugs, notions, saddles, hats, bolts of cloth, spices, and many other goods.

The floating store, or trading boat, another distributive agent, still cruised the rivers and bayous, particularly in the southern sections of the state, throughout the period. The trading boat resembled an ordinary ferryboat, except that its large cabin was filled with groceries, dry goods, hardware, notions, and other goods. The boat was frequently operated by a man and his wife, the man running the engine while his wife acted as pilot. It stopped at small towns or at the wharves of planters, where the whistle was blown and the owners waited for customers. The floating storekeeper sometimes accepted poultry, cured meat, vegetables, and other farm products in payment for his goods.

The peddler operated in much the same way except that he carried his goods in a covered wagon or hack, camped each night by the roadside near a stream, and sold his goods from house to house. He traded for his food supplies and supplemented his meat supply by hunting or fishing. While the majority of peddlers carried general stocks, some of them specialized in a particular commodity. A few were Gypsies, who usually carried only cheap jewelry, trinkets of various sorts, and what would today be called ten-cent-store items. Many of the peddlers saved their money and later established stores in the smaller towns; they had about disappeared by 1920.

In the larger towns, particularly in New Orleans, there was a different type of peddler. He walked the streets with his goods on his back or in a cart or hack, or set up a small stall at the side of the street. He sold coffee, pastries, fruits, meats, vegetables, notions of all types, and other things. The majority of these town peddlers were Negroes, who used special chants, songs, or cries in French or English to advertise their goods. One of the best known coffee women of New Orleans was named Zabette, and Lyle Saxon fondly wrote that "her coffee was the essence of the fragrant bean, and since her death the lovers of that divine beverage wander listlessly around the stalls on Sunday mornings with a pining at the bosom which cannot be satisfied."

BANKS AND BANKING. Finances in Louisiana were at a low ebb when the state was returned to Home Rule in 1877. The state debt was enormous and taxes were high, agriculture was in bad condition and farmers had little money, business was generally poor. During the business and financial panic of 1879 banks closed throughout the state; even the three largest banks of New Orleans could pay their depositors only 15 to 50 per cent of their deposits. While some recovery had been made by 1882, the total banking capital of the state amounted to only $5,158,000. In 1882 the legislature passed a new banking act which permitted the organization of banks with small amounts of capital, from $10,000 in towns with a minimum population of 2,000 to $100,000 in cities of over 25,000. While the act did much to aid small towns it did not completely relieve the general financial situation, and until late in the period many of them were without banks. Marksville, for example, did not have a permanent bank until 1897.

The financial strength of the state slowly improved. In 1881 there were less than twenty banks with total resources of about $23,500,000; by the end of the century the number had increased to over seventy-five with resources of over $54,000,000. In 1898 the new constitution created the office of bank examiner, the Act of 1902 established required state bank reserves, the Act of 1916 ordered the bank examiner to report to the legislature every two years, and the Act of 1918 required a strengthening of state bank reserves. By 1920, Louisiana had a total of 265 state and national banks with resources of nearly $520,000,000. Throughout the period, however, many city workers and small rural agriculturists did not trust banks to keep their money, hiding it instead under bricks in the fireplace, burying it in the yard, or concealing it in other places. It was said that one Marksville citizen concealed his savings by boring a deep hole in the leg of a chair, inserting the money and then putting a carefully fitted stopper in the hole. Many small-town banks made slow progress until the people learned to trust them.

As the state was in debt to the amount of over $50,000,000 in 1878, public officials economized in every way possible and by 1906 had reduced the bonded debt to slightly over $11,000,000. The state debt began to slowly climb after 1906 as additional funds were needed for public improvements of various types. That the state was in good financial condition in 1920 is indicated by a total valuation of all property of practically $1,700,000,000 and total taxes for all purposes of nearly $40,000,000.

LABOR. Early in 1879 many Negroes in the South began an exodus to Indiana and Kansas, those of Louisiana largely going to the latter state. While it is not known exactly what caused the movement to begin, it was not long before the Colored Colonization Society of Topeka, Kansas, began to send circulars to the Negroes of Louisiana promising 160 acres of land to each family. Meetings were held at several places in southern and southeastern Louisiana, some under the leadership of Negro Henry Adams, at which groups of families made plans to move to a "promised land" in Kansas. Within a year many of the Negroes were ready to return, but were completely without funds and some were destitute. Numerous planters sent funds to enable their former plantation workers to return home. Adams claimed that he led

98,000 persons from Louisiana and Mississippi; a more accurate estimate indicated that only about 800 Louisiana familes migrated. While Negro leader Carter G. Woodson called those who left the South during this period the "talented tenth," the simple fact was that the poor and ignorant Negroes were victimized by northern promises of lands and political and social equality.

After 1880 there was much competition between white and Negro labor, particularly in the urban centers, and it was not long before the leaders of both races began to form labor organizations. While the majority of these unions lasted only a short time, others continued for a number of years. By the late 1880's the Knights of Labor claimed to have over forty "assemblies" in the state, and in 1887 called a strike of Negro sugar-cane plantation workers at the height of the grinding season. There was so much disorder that eight companies of the state militia were called out to police the violence-ridden sections in the sugar region.

New Orleans witnessed numerous small strikes between 1880 and 1892, but it was not until the fall of the latter year that a general strike of major importance was called. An easy victory of the streetcar drivers in the spring of 1892 led to a series of labor demands by the other unions, and when these were not met, a general strike was called on November 8. Over 20,000 men from 42 unions stopped work. The labor organizations refused to arbitrate and the capital interests were arrogant and blind to everything except their own concerns. The strike failed and New Orleans became a closed-shop city, a condition which led to irregular labor troubles during the rest of the decade. After a series of labor disputes in New Orleans involving railway freight workers had stirred up public opinion, the legislature of 1908 passed a series of labor-regulatory acts which provided for enlarging the powers of the state labor commissioner, protection of workers, child-labor regulations, and others. The state witnessed comparatively few serious labor-capital disputes outside of New Orleans during the rest of the period.

One of the most important labor developments during the period was the tremendous increase of women workers. By the 1880's approximately one-fifth of the women of the state were gainfully employed, slightly less than one-half of whom were engaged in professional or personal services while most of the others were employed in agriculture. There were also numerous teachers, nurses, boardinghouse keepers, waitresses, restaurant proprietors, factory workers, and even a few barbers and professional musicians. These workers generally made comparatively few attempts to establish unions.

CHAPTER 26

EDUCATIONAL PROGRESS AND
THE GROWTH OF CULTURE

GENERAL PROGRESS IN PUBLIC EDUCATION. The story of public education in Louisiana from 1877 to 1920 may be divided into two rather distinct periods. From the end of the period of military occupation to the beginning of Governor Newton C. Blanchard's administration in 1904 educational advancement was extremely slow, despite the diligent work of dedicated educational leaders. After the election of Blanchard and State Superintendent James B. Aswell the idea of strengthening the entire education program was spread so forcibly throughout the state that the public began to take more interest in the work, and by the period's end public education was beginning to emerge into the present era of rapid and noteworthy progress.

The general school act of 1877 reorganized the state board of education, provided for parish and district boards, for state financial assistance on the basis of the number of educables, for the certification of teachers by the parish boards, for a state school tax of two mills, and issued new regulations for the New Orleans public-school system. Governor Francis T. Nicholls appointed two Negroes to the state board of education and appointed Negroes to many parish boards. Soon the local complications which had arisen between whites and Negroes during previous years were effectively removed as seperate schools were provided for the two races. In 1877, Robert M. Lusher became superintendent again and began to develop a permanent school system.

There were many basic problems and much work to be done. Less than 20 per cent of the state's nearly 270,000 white children of school age were enrolled in school, conditions were deplorable in the rural parishes, the Peabody Education Fund had withdrawn its support two years previously, and in some parishes the school funds were still under the control of Radical politicians. The stigma of public education was still present, not to be generally removed until after the end of the century. Qualified parish superintendents were few. Local and parish school boards were highly politicalized, and while this situation has considerably improved since 1904, it has never been completely alleviated. South Louisiana Catholics were still antagonistic to public education, and it was not until sizable numbers of Protestants moved into those districts and the better education of public schoolteachers became obvious that this antagonism began to disappear slowly and the people to realize that education was more than the mere learning of the Credo and the Ave Maria and the preparation of children for confirmation in the Church. The general poverty of the state made the raising of educational funds difficult.

The first period saw the rise of active, noteworthy educational leaders in addition to Robert M. Lusher and President David French Boyd of Louisiana State University —Thomas Duckett Boyd of Louisiana State University, William Preston Johnston, President of Louisiana State University and first President of Tulane, Tulane Professor Henry E. Chambers, State Superintendent W. H. Jack, Calcasieu Parish Superintendent John McNeese, New Orleans Superintendent William O. Rogers, and teachers Mrs. Mattie H. Williams of Shreveport, T. S. Sligh of Homer, George D. Alexander of Minden, to mention just a few.

In 1887, Professor Chambers addressed a convention of parish superintendents at Baton Rouge, stating forcibly that an efficient public-school system must be characterized by adequate, permanent educational funds, by authority to vote special school taxes, and by educated, professionally trained parish superintendents and teachers. Chambers was ahead of his time, but he made such a profound impression upon his listeners that they carried his message home and began to work for his program. By 1891, State Superintendent W. H. Jack could say that "the people, black and white, throughout the State, are thoroughly alive to the importance of public education."

The Louisiana State Educational Association was organized at Minden in 1883, largely through the efforts of George D. Alexander, T. S. Sligh, and Mrs. Mattie H. Williams, but comparatively little is known of its activities during the first years. The Association met annually in different towns and attracted a growing membership which included laymen as well as public-school leaders. It was reorganized in the 1890's, renamed the Louisiana Teachers' Association, and entered upon a new period of active growth and development.

Meanwhile, education magazines and journals were being established. The *Louisiana Journal of Education,* the second educational journal south of the Ohio River, was founded by Robert M. Lusher and W. O. Rogers in 1879 and was published until 1888 under the editorships of Lusher, Rogers, William Preston Johnston, and Richard Henry Jesse. The *Progressive Teacher,* under the editorship of Professor Chambers, was published from 1885 to 1889, when it was merged with the *Southwest Journal of Education* of Nashville. About this time G. D. Pickels of Mansfield established *Looking Ahead,* which lived a hand-to-mouth existence for two or three years, and for nearly a year versatile editor-educator Colonel T. Sambola Jones of Baton Rouge edited and published the *Louisiana Educator.* The *Louisiana School Review* was founded in 1895 with Professor Chambers as the first editor. These educational publications did much to lead and consolidate educational opinion but none of them became economically sound; firmly established educational publications would have to await the modern era.

In 1889 at a state convention of the Louisiana State Educational Association, Mrs. Mattie H. Williams proposed the organization of a state chautauqua, challenging the people of Louisiana to "arise and shake off the incubus of illiteracy, and undertake measures which would stimulate a new sense of responsibility in affording educational opportunities to the young people of this state." Judge A. A. Gunby afterwards wrote that "she impressed the gathering like an electric thrill." Mrs. Williams became "the mother of the Louisiana Chautauqua," and the following year it was officially organized at Ruston. By 1892 special buildings had to be constructed in order to accommodate the numbers of teachers attending the lectures of such nationally known public leaders as Reverend T. DeWitt Talmage, Reverend Thomas Dixon, Tom Watson of Georgia, William Jennings Bryan, and General John B. Gordon. In 1897 a Peabody Institute was held at the Ruston Chautauqua, and teachers were given credit for attending it; this was the beginning of college and university summer schools in Louisiana. The Chautauqua made numerous contributions to Louisiana education and culture for about fifteen years, then began to decline because of the withdrawal of state support.

Parish Institutes, financed largely by the Peabody Board and directed by the President of the State Normal School and the State Superintendent of Education, during the early 1900's began to instruct teachers in educational methods and to educate laymen to the need of increasing state support of public education and in 1906, J. E. Kenny became full-time institute conductor, which position he held until he resigned to accept the presidency of the Louisiana Polytechnic Institute at Ruston in 1908.

[307]

During the years after 1877 parish superintendents administered teachers' examinations and certified teachers with the local school boards. In 1904 a legislative act gave the state superintendent authority to issue state teaching certificates and to require parish superintendents to earn professional certification; eight years later the state department of education took over the work of giving examinations and issuing certificates in three classes, depending upon the grade made in the examinations. By 1916 the requirements for high-school-teacher certification were raised to thirty-six hours of college work.

Enrollment in public schools gradually increased. It totaled slightly over 54,000 in 1880, 210,000 in 1905, and over 354,000 in 1920, when, however, only about 70 per cent of school-age children were actually in attendance. Meanwhile the average length of the school term for white schools had increased from about four and one-half months in 1880 to over eight months at the end of the period. During the same period salaries for white teachers had increased from between $30.00 and $50.00 per month to an average of nearly $100.00. Between 1900 and 1920 the illiteracy of the native white population ten years of age and over was cut from 17.3 per cent to 10.5 per cent. Negro education lagged during the entire period; less than half the Negro educables attended school in 1920, Negro schools operated an average of four and one-third months per year, and Negro teachers received an average annual salary of about $425. Despite the lack of educational advantages for the state's Negro population as a whole, illiteracy for all Negroes over the age of ten was cut from 61.1 per cent in 1900 to 38.5 per cent in 1920.

James B. Aswell was the father of modern education in Louisiana. A native of Jackson Parish, he attended the Peabody Normal College, the University of Nashville, the University of Chicago, was a country- and high-school teacher, and from 1900 to 1904 served as the President of the Louisiana Polytechnic Institute. Upon his election as State Superintendent of Education in 1904, Louisiana had for the first time a professionally trained educator at the head of its educational system. Aswell was State Superintendent until 1908 and later served several terms in Congress.

Aswell stimulated a great awakening in public education throughout the state. He imported out-of-state parish superintendents, supervisors, and teachers because of their ability and educational qualifications, strengthened school institutes, inaugurated a basically sound high-school system, consolidated country schools, and built hundreds of schoolhouses which accommodated thousands of additional children. He crystallized public sentiment in favor of tax-supported schools and was largely responsible for greatly increasing school revenues principally through the passage of special school-tax laws. Aswell was ably succeeded by T. H. Harris who served during the rest of the period.

Practically every legislature after 1906 passed educational measures. In that year the School Library Act provided funds for the establishment of school libraries. The Burke Act of 1912, named after its author, Senator Walter J. Burke of New Iberia, was a general educational act which reorganized the entire state educational system. The Johnson Act of 1916, fathered by Senator Delos R. Johnson of Washington Parish, repaired the weaknesses of the Burke Act and added improvements. In 1918 the Hamley and Byrne amendments to the constitution provided for additional state and parish school taxes. State appropriations had increased slowly from about $500,000 in 1880 to slightly over $1,000,000 in 1904; after the latter date they began to rapidly increase. They reached a total of $5,870,000 in 1912 and by 1920 had jumped to nearly $16,500,000. Louisiana was ready to move into the modern period of educational development and progress.

CHARACTERISTICS OF ELEMENTARY AND SECONDARY SCHOOLS. Public schools made more rapid progress in New Orleans and in the northern and western parts of the state than in South Louisiana. Plaquemine, for example, did not have a public school until 1887, when a two-room schoolhouse was built; its first high school was not erected until 1911. Monroe, on the other hand, had public schools prior to 1880 and began high-school work in 1885. One of the rules of the Monroe High School during those early years read: "Neatness of clothing and person will be exacted. A child cannot fulfill his destiny unless he is cleanly. Soap and water are a means of grace. It is impossible to conceive of a pure mind and godly presence clad in unclean vestments."

Schoolhouses were poorly built, frequently were only abandoned buildings, and had little equipment. Louisiana educator V. L. Roy, a former superintendent of Avoyelles Parish, in recalling his school days in Avoyelles, wrote that the first school he attended had a dirt floor and "we sat at tables and ordinary store counters on hard wooden benches. There were no blackboards, maps, globes, or charts. The only desks were those some of the boys had made themselves for their own use. My achievements during the session, as I remember it, were learning the alphabet—something which teachers of today would deplore, at best." There was little improvement during subsequent years for "the best teachers were paid $50 a month. The annual session ran two to five months. Few communities had actual schoolhouses, and in most cases a vacant store or an abandoned saloon served the purpose. I believe our little school in Mansura moved to new quarters every year of each of the nine years I attended, and five of the buildings we occupied were one-time saloons." As late as 1896 a Cottonport teacher complained that he was compelled "to rent an old dilapidated building in a field," for which he had to pay "the sum of $5.00 a month." He reported that "with two exceptions, the parents of the children refused to send wood," so that during winter weather he "was compelled to teach in the cold."

The first high schools were for students of the eighth through the eleventh grades and their subjects included languages, grammar and composition, mathematics, history, literature, music, and science. Recitations were generally for forty minutes, and there were frequent examinations. Outside activities included literary societies, typewritten school newspapers, military training, and athletic contests in football, basketball, and baseball. Only about 10 per cent of the students who started high school finished the course, while less than 30 per cent of the graduates entered college.

Public schools and high schools began to improve after 1900. Better buildings and equipment were provided, teachers were better trained, and school libraries were enlarged. Supervisors were appointed to help improve the quality of instruction. Superintendent L. J. Alleman of Lafayette Parish conceived the idea of consolidating small schools, and in 1904 the schools of the Evergreen District were consolidated by the school board, the first such consolidation in the state. In Avoyelles Parish, V. L. Roy developed a library program in 1905 and a few years later founded an organization which developed into the 4-H Club movement.

In addition to public elementary schools and high schools were the many private or religious academies and institutes scattered throughout the state, some of which were called colleges, and these institutions generally accepted boarding as well as day students. The Cadeville Normal School and Commercial Institute was a good example of this class of educational institution. Opened in the middle 1880's, it was located in the hill country of Ouachita Parish about seven miles south of Calhoun. Here students could "get board, including fuel, lights, washing, etc., at the boarding hall at $8 a month." The school advertised that telegrams could be received via Calhoun in care of the principal and that mail was delivered three times a week by Mrs. M. P. Henry, the mail carrier. At Cadeville, according to the 1889-90 bulletin, "there is no saloon nearer than 15 miles and students are free from the evils and distracting influences that corrupt their morals. There are no loafers, roughs or 'dudes' to entice the unsuspecting boy into sin and disgrace."

COLLEGES AND UNIVERSITIES. Numerous educational institutions dignified with the names of colleges, universities, institutes, or seminaries had been founded during the ante bellum period. The great majority, after flourishing for a few years, declined and finally closed their doors. There were a number of these institutions scattered throughout the state in 1860, but most of them went out of existence during the years from 1861 to 1877. After the end of military occupation higher education began a period of steady growth both in the number of institutions and in the quality of instruction.

The legislature established the Louisiana State Agricultural and Mechanical College in 1873, providing that "no race nor color" should be excluded, and the following year the college opened its doors at the Chalmette Battle Ground. In 1877 the State University and the Agricultural and Mechanical College were united under the title of Louisiana State University and Agricultural and Mechanical College. In 1886 the Federal government granted the University use of the extensive grounds and buildings of the military garrison and arsenal at the northern end of Baton Rouge, and full title was given to this property by Act of Congress in 1902. By 1910 new buildings had been constructed on the fifty-two-acre campus; the University organization included the colleges of arts and sciences, agriculture, and engineering, the Audubon Sugar School, the law school, the teachers' college, the graduate department, and the summer school. The total enrollment was over 1,300 students.

Other state colleges were founded after 1880, principally for the purpose of training teachers for the public schools or providing academic and vocational education for Negroes. The State Normal School of Louisiana, now Northwestern State College, was founded at Natchitoches in 1885, Louisiana Polytechnic Institute at Ruston in 1895, and Southwestern Louisiana Institute at Lafayette in 1901. Southern University, for Negroes, organized in New Orleans in 1880, was moved to Scotlandville, its present location, in 1914.

Several endowed or religious colleges and universities were also founded. Tulane University was established in 1884 through the financial support of wealthy businessman Paul Tulane, who gave all his New Orleans real estate "for the promotion and encouragement of intellectual, moral and industrial education among the white young persons in the City of New Orleans" and "for the advancement of learning and letters, the arts and sciences." Two years later Mrs. Simon Newcomb donated $100,000 to the Tulane Educational Fund to be used in establishing the H. Sophie Newcomb Memorial College for Women as a co-ordinate college of the University. At her death in 1901 the college received an additional bequest of about $2,700,000. Other private institutions at the end of the period included Loyola University of the South (1904), St. Mary's Dominican College (1861), Dillard University (Negro—1869), Xavier University (the only Catholic college for Negroes in the nation—1915), New Orleans Baptist Theological Seminary (1917), Louisiana College (1906), Leland College (Negro—1870), and Centenary College (moved from Jackson to Shreveport in 1907).

LIBRARIES. In addition to the extensive libraries of Louisiana State University and Tulane University, there were sizable collections of books at the various other state and private educational institutions. In 1897 the Fisk Free Library was opened to the public and shortly thereafter was joined with the Lyceum Library; a gift of $50,000 from the estate of Simon Hernsheim specified that the name should be changed to the New Orleans Public Library, while in 1908 a financial grant from Andrew Carnegie enabled a new building to be constructed at Lee Circle. The Howard Memorial Library, erected in New Orleans in 1889 by Miss Annie T. Howard as a memorial to her father, soon became an important historical-research library because of the collecting activities of Librarian William Beer. The Carnegie Library of Lake Charles was opened in 1904, after A. V. Eastman and others had taken the initiative in organizing a city library. Meanwhile, Alexandria, Shreveport, Baton Rouge, and other cities had established libraries.

A State Library had been authorized as early as 1833, but little was accomplished until after the Civil War despite the efforts of Charles Gayarré and others. By the end of the century a valuable collection of some 40,000 volumes was housed in a building at the corner of Union and Baronne streets in New Orleans. Catalogs were published in 1877, 1886, and 1905.

During the late years of the century James S. Zacharie began to agitate for the establishment of a State Museum, which was finally accomplished through legislative enactment in 1900, but the act was never carried into effect. In 1906 the legislature authorized the State Museum to accept the exhibit which had been prepared for the Louisiana Purchase Exposition at St. Louis and to permanently house the collection at the Washington Artillery Hall in New Orleans. Robert Glenk, custodian and later director of the Museum, developed a large collection of museum-type relics, manuscripts, and archives of Louisiana's historical past. The Museum moved to the Cabildo and the Presbytère in 1911, and utilized part of the lower Pontalba Building for its library.

During the entire period, however, despite the establishment of the State Museum, the state did little to assist in preserving its archives and other historical records. Although the neighboring states of Arkansas and Mississippi established departments of history and archives early in the century, nothing comparable was done in Louisiana. This work was not finally accomplished until recent years.

NEWSPAPERS AND MAGAZINES. Only a small number of newspapers and magazines continued publication during the Civil War and military-occupation periods; the *Picayune* being the only English-language, ante bellum newspaper in New Orleans to survive. After 1877 newspapers recovered their former prestige through the editing, reporting and writing of such journalists as James L. Freaner, Lafcadio Hearn, Henry J. Hearsey, Dominic O'Malley, George W. Cable, Henry Castellanos, Jose Quintero, Henry Rightor, Catherine Cole (Mrs. Martha R. Field), Dorothy Dix (Mrs. Elizabeth M. Gilmer), and others. The New Orleans *Item* was founded in 1877 and the *States* three years later. The *Times,* which had been founded in 1863, joined with the more prosperous *Democrat* (1875) in 1881 to become the *Times-Democrat* and was for a number of years one of the most brilliantly edited of American newspapers, until it became the *Times-Picayune* in 1914. Until the end of the century New Orleans journalism was almost as individualistic and colorful as it had been during ante bellum years. The New Orleans *Crusader,* a Negro newspaper dedicated to waging a battle against post-Reconstruction discriminations, was founded in 1889 by Louis A. Martinet and was active for nearly a decade.

The leading newspapers of the state published outside New Orleans during the period included the Alexandria *Town Talk,* the Baton Rouge *State-Times,* the Baton Rouge *Advocate,* the Monroe *Bulletin,* the Monroe *News-Star,* the Natchitoches *Enterprise,* the Lake Charles *American Press,* the Lafayette *Advertiser,* the Shreveport *Journal,* and the Shreveport *Times.* The New Orleans *Deutsche Zeitung* (1848), the most noted of the German-language newspapers, was succeeded in 1907 by the *Neue Deutsche Zeitung,* which continued publication until August, 1917. The several French-, Italian-, and Spanish-language newspapers established did not rise above mediocrity and generally lasted but a few years.

The most representative and best-edited magazine was *De Bow's Review,* which had been founded before the Civil War and which stopped publication in 1880; it continued to urge the industrialization of the South and advancement in all economic and cultural activities. In all, over a hundred magazines were established but usually continued publication only a few years. The *Comptes-Rendus de L'Athénée Louisianais,* an outstanding literary magazine, appeared irregularly and is still being published. Humorous publications included *Gas,* the *Jolly Joker,* and the *Lantern,* while the *New Citizen* was especially for women. None of the Louisiana magazines achieved a national circulation.

LITERATURE AND HISTORICAL WRITING. Literature flourished during the entire period, and Lafcadio Hearn, George W. Cable, Charles Gayarré, Grace King, and a few other writers achieved national reputations. Since there were no publishers of consequence in the South, it was difficult for writers to keep in close contact with publishers' needs and with national trends in various literary forms;

consequently, many Louisiana writers wrote for their own amusement and enjoyment and for the local public on subjects of local color.

During the 1890's and early 1900's a Bohemian group of young writers, reporters, musicians, artists, and professional men met irregularly at Walter Parker's apartment in the French Quarter of New Orleans and haunted the old Royal Street bookstores. According to Parker, the historian of the group, "they wrote plays, which sometimes were produced; several light operas; articles which occasionally sold for money . . . read Shakespeare, Cellini, Balzac as a regular diet." Dominique You, Jean Laffite's chief lieutenant, was the hero of many of their writings. While they produced nothing of lasting value, they set the pattern for a later group which inhabited the Vieux Carré during the 1920's. Much of their work was sheer, delightful nonsense of the quality of Henry Rightor's jingle:

> Adele, Adele, I wish you well.
> Oh, may I kiss your toe?
> No, no, Monsieur, my lips are here—
> You need not stoop so low!

Native-born George Washington Cable was the first important post-Civil War author to appear on the Louisiana literary scene, with his stories of "supposed" Creole life published in *Scribner's Monthly*. Book rapidly followed book—*Old Creole Days, The Grandissimes, Madame Dalphine, Dr. Sevier, The Creoles of Louisiana, Bonaventure, Strange True Stories of Louisiana*. One American literary critic wrote that upon finishing *Madame Delphine* "a glow passed over me from head to foot and back from foot to head, and I said to myself, with profound feeling: 'It has come at last!' I meant the day of the South's finding her expression in literature. . . . I realized then that the South had the material in her old past, and that we had the writers with the art to portray it." Another critic wrote that while Cable had "a marvelously acute ear, a sympathetic heart," he came very near "caricaturing" Creole life, for "his feeling for African slaves, octoroons, quadroons, ran away with him." Grace King later characterized him: "Of course I understood even then that he was a genius, but he did not understand the Creoles." Critics, especially Louisiana critics, have been arguing over the work of Cable ever since.

Humble journalist Lafcadio Hearn arrived in New Orleans in 1878 and settled down in a house on Bourbon Street. A native of the Ionian Isle of Santa Maura, Hearn was what Edward Larocque Tinker called "a queer sort of human cocktail, having a little dash of everything—English, Gypsy, Irish, Greek, Arab, and Moor." He had lost the sight of one eye completely and the other was strangely myopic, allowing him hardly more than 30 per cent vision. Along with his journalistic work he soaked up the legend and lore of New Orleans and Old Louisiana as a blotter and then began writing his stories of local genre in the *Times-Democrat*. Hearn published *Gumbo Zhebes; Little Dictionary of Creole Proverbs* (1885) and in 1890 *Chita; A Memory of Last Island*, an account of the hurricane of 1856. His style was oriental in its richness and beauty, his descriptions of nature among the most beautiful in our language, and, as historian Allen Nevins wrote, "he enameled and polished each paragraph with meticulous care. Over each essay the near-sighted word-jeweler toiled like a lapidary over his precious gems." He later went to Japan, married there, and one of his grandsons even today keeps close contact with Louisiana and her literature.

Other writers gained at least passing notice on the national literary scene. Dr. Alfred Mercier described ante bellum life; Ruth McEnery Stuart (of whom Joel Chandler Harris said: "You have gotten nearer the heart of the negro than any of us!") and Kate Chopin wrote stories and tales; Eliza Ripley recreated the old social life of New Orleans. Mary Ashley Townsend, whose pen name was Xariffa, wrote poetry, as did Elizabeth Nicholson, who signed herself "Pearl Rivers," and Mollie Evelyn Davis and Helen Pitkin Schertz. Albert Delpit went to Paris, where he attracted much attention with his dramas. Frank McGloin wrote highly colored romances. Father Adrien Rouquette, noted missionary to the Choctaw Indians of Bayou Lacombe, wrote poetry of high quality. After completing her *Recollections of Henry Watkins Allen* in 1866, Sarah A. Dorsey wrote stories and novels of an older Louisiana.

Charles Colton wrote humorous and delightful little poems, one of which, "A Kitchen Free-For-All," began:

> The fork said the corkscrew was crooked;
>   The remark made the flatiron sad;
> The steel knife at once lost its temper,
>   And called the tea-holder a cad.
> The tablespoon stood on its mettle;
>   The kettle exhibited bile;
> The stove grew hot at the discussion,
>   But the ice remained cool all the while.

And after giving other details in four stanzas, the poem ended:

> You'd not think a thing that's so holey
>   As the sieve would have mixed in the fuss,
> But it did, for it said that the butter
>   Was a slippery sort of a cuss.
> No one knows how the row would have ended,
>   Had not the cook, Maggie O'Dowd,
> Her work being done, closed the kitchen,
>   And thusly shut up the whole crowd.

Negro literature declined during the period from the high quality of Free Negro writing of ante bellum years. Many of the old, cultured Negro group of New Orleans lost their wealth or moved from the state, and most Negroes at this time were more interested in journalistic writing and in political advancement. The last important work in French published by a Negro was *Nos Hommes et Notre Histoire* (Our Men and Our History), written by Rodolphe L. Desdunes and published in 1911, which recounted Negro contributions to Louisiana literature, art, and other fields, and which was of high quality.

Although Charles Gayarré was over seventy years of age at the beginning of the period, he lived to the age of ninety, and until his death in 1895, bestrode the Louisiana literary field like a colossus. He carried on a constant correspondence with friends in the North, much of it in a humorous vein. When his autobiographical *Fernando de Lemos* appeared, he wrote to Evert A. Duyckinck that "the protestants are delighted, and the catholics are in an ecstacy. . . . Confederates and Federals approve, Southern and Northern men compliment . . . and the negroes are so flattered in my representation of their race that they are disposed to think that I am a greater man than Massa Lincoln. I fear that I am in danger of being run by them for the presidency. . . ."

Gayarré wrote numerous newspaper and magazine articles during his last years on such widely variant subjects as "An Old Street in New Orleans," "Financial Condition of Louisiana," "Hurricanes in Colonial Louisiana," "On the Establishment of Paper Mills in Louisiana," and even one "On the Advantages of Manufacturing Porcelain in Louisiana." He reissued his *History of Louisiana* in four volumes in 1879 and engaged in controversy with Cable after his "The Creoles of History and the Creoles of Romance" had rather completely demolished Cable's Louisiana French and Spanish Creoles. Near the end he wrote: "My same old friends. You know them— will never leave me. . . . the Archbishop comes around once a month and gives me much good advice. Then, too, Dr. Palmer [Bishop B. M. Palmer of the First Presbyterian Church] calls to see Mrs. Gayarré about as often, so between the two we have very pleasant evenings." After his death his friend Frank D. Richardson wrote: "In time the State may perpetuate his memory but will hardly honor him as he has honored her."

Grace Elizabeth King succeeded to the position held by Gayarré in Louisiana letters. A native New Orleanian, Miss King published her first story, "Monsieur Motte," in the *New Princeton Review* in 1886, and for the next three decades wrote numerous novels, articles, histories, and sketches about Louisiana and New Orleans. She is chiefly remembered today for her historical and descriptive works rather than for her fiction. Her chief books include: *Balcony Stories; La Dame de Sainte Hermine; Creole Families of New Orleans; Jean Baptiste Le Moyne, Sieur de Bienville; The Pleasant Ways of St. Medard;* and her most noted work, *New Orleans, The Place and the People.* Her last book, *Memories of a Southern Woman of Letters,* was published in 1932, the year of her death. At a memorial service given at a meeting of Le Petit Salon, a half-literary, half-social organization over which she presided for a number of years, Lyle Saxon said that "in her work she has truly transcribed the spirit of the great days of the past 'in old New Orleans.'"

Louisiana veterans of the Civil War, like those in other states North and South, wrote reminiscences and recollections during the years following that conflict. The most significant works by Louisianians included William Miller Owen's *In Camp and Battle with the Washington Artillery,* P. G. T. Beauregard's *A Commentary on the Campaign and Battle of Manassas,* Howell Carter's *A Cavalryman's Reminiscences of the Civil War,* and Richard Taylor's *Destruction and Reconstruction,* which is one of the very best of all Civil War reminiscences. Eliza Ripley's *From Flag to Flag* tells the story of one family's exile from Louisiana during the war period.

Despite the fact that the state took no official interest in preserving its historical records, many Louisianians discovered and wrote about its past. William Preston Johnston wrote a life of Albert Sidney Johnston and Judge Alfred Roman described the military operations of General Beauregard. John Dimitry, Albert Phelps, Grace King, and John R. Ficklen wrote short histories of the state, while Alcée Fortier wrote widely in the Louisiana historical field and in 1904 published his four-volume state history. John G. Belisle wrote a *History of Sabine Parish.* Newspaper-editor Napier Bartlett penned *Stories of the Crescent City.*

Henry Rightor edited the *Standard History of New Orleans* in 1900 under rather peculiar circumstances. A publisher had contracted with a New Orleans historian for a history and had sold the work by subscription, but the historian failed to write it. The publisher called upon Rightor for help, so Rightor drafted several of his friends, assigned the chapters, and they went to work. Thirty days later A. G. Durno, B. R. Forman, Jr., John R. Ficklen, Alcée Fortier, Walter Parker, Norman Walker, and the others turned in their copy. Rightor's work was the standard history of the city for the next twenty years and is still widely used as a reference book.

PAINTING AND SCULPTURE. The war-ravaged 1860's and the radical and disordered 1870's gave little encouragement to painting, sculpture, and the allied arts. A revival of art, however, began during the late 1870's, and painting in particular has flourished until the present day. Enoch Perry painted portraits; Samuel Walker became noted as a portrayer of Louisiana people; George Sullivan and Achille Peretti painted after the style of the old masters. Erasme Humbrecht painted murals for the St. Louis Cathedral and other churches, while Alexander Alaux painted a large panorama of "De Soto's Discovery of the Mississippi." After 1914, Luis Graner gained a reputation for his scenes of rural Louisiana.

The most noted painting of the entire post-Civil War period was E. D. B. Fabrino Julio's "Last Meeting of Lee and Jackson," the two originals of which now hang in the Louisiana State Museum at New Orleans and in the library at Louisiana State University. Mark Twain, as was his habit, had a few humorous remarks to make. It was a fine painting, he said, but like all historical paintings was meaningless without its title, and many names would fit just as well as the one chosen: "Jackson Accepting

Lee's Invitation to Dinner," "Jackson Declining Lee's Invitation to Dinner," "Jackson Asking Lee for a Match," and others. The painting became immensely popular, and large and small lithographic reproductions were widely sold.

While Alexander J. Drysdale gained little fame during his lifetime, today he is generally considered to have been the best artist of the period. At his studio in the Board of Trade Building in New Orleans he operated a sort of one-man picture "factory," turning out paintings of Louisiana lowlands and swamps by the dozen, and selling them for bargain prices. It is said that he lined up his boards and canvases and painted all the skies, followed by the grasses, the trees, and the water of lakes or bayous. His misty landscapes look as though they were seen during a light rainfall or in the haze of early morning. During the last twenty years his works have become collector's items and now sell for high prices.

Comparatively few sculptors made noteworthy reputations. Achille Parelli made head studies; Joseph Domenget and Romeo Celli lived and worked for many years in the New Orleans French Quarter, as did Florville Foy and Eugene and Daniel Warburg. Other forms of art included wax figures, finely decorated pottery and china, wood carving, cast and wrought ironwork, and ornamented plantation bells. Several art associations or leagues which encouraged art and displayed various of its forms to the public were founded in the state, particularly in New Orleans. The Art Union, the Southern Artist's League, and the Arts and Exhibition Club were among those founded in the 1880's. The Art Association of New Orleans was organized in 1905, and a short time later the Louisiana State Museum began to gather together the artistic work of the entire state. In 1911 the Delgado Museum was completed in New Orleans through the generosity of Isaac Delgado, a wealthy sugar broker. Meanwhile, the colleges and universities in the state began to offer art courses.

THE DRAMA. New Orleans had been a noted theatrical city during ante bellum years, and other cities and towns in the state had witnessed performances of both permanent groups and traveling companies. Interest was rapidly revived after the war. During the late sixties and early seventies Negro actors performed at the Orleans Theater in plays by Negro writers such as Victor Sejour, Adolphe Duhart, and others, many of their performances being benefits to help the needy of the city. After 1880 among the city's best were the Tulane and Crescent theaters, where Julia Marlowe, George Arliss, Richard Mansfield, Minnie Maddern Fiske, Otis Skinner, Walter Hampden, the Barrymores, and other noted actors of the day could be seen. New Orleanians "idolized" theatrical stars, and when Sarah Bernhardt gave nine performances at the Grand Opera House, ticket scalper Edgard Bouligny of the "R. E. Lee Hat Store" at the corner of Canal and Bourbon sold "season" boxes at from $160.00 to $270.00, and single seats at from $18.00 to $30.00; despite the fact that he was "exposed" by the press, the theater was sold out before Mme. Bernhardt arrived in the city.

At the beginning of the new century the Baldwin, Lyric, Elysium, and other theaters were flourishing centers of dramatic entertainment. At Welch's Hippodrome, later called the Winter Garden, and at the Schubert, musical comedies, dramas, and vaudeville were presented, these popular theaters sometimes charging only ten cents for an ordinary evening's entertainment. The first amateur nights were given at the Winter Garden, where, if acts did not satisfy the audience, the people yelled, "Get the Hook," and the actors were pulled off the stage. Shakespearean dramas were popular with whites and Negroes alike, and early in the 1900's a Negro theatrical troupe brought all-Negro-performed drama to the Pythian Hall, the Lyric, and the Palace. Meantime other towns in the state welcomed troupes of traveling players. The minstrel show had been popular as early as the 1820's, and after the war the entire state swarmed with professional and amateur minstrel performers. New Orleans was the center of this type of entertainment; a success in the Crescent City meant a successful tour of the state.

[315]

Showboats still cruised the rivers and bayous, giving plays, minstrel shows, and other forms of entertainment, and reached their peak of popularity during the years between 1870 and 1890. Many of these floating theaters had pleasing, romantic names, such as the *Cotton Blossom,* the *River Maid,* or the *Daisy Bell;* the *Golden Rod* had a large 24-by-40-foot stage, a 40-by-162-foot auditorium, and was considered one of the finest ever built. Newspapers usually carried advertisements announcing the coming of a showboat; then, a few hours before it came to the river landing, a messenger rode through the streets announcing the exact time of its arrival. The landing was heralded by the music of the steam calliope, and when the boat docked, the showboat band crashed into a fast march and a parade of performers left the boat and marched through the town. That night the troupe usually played to a full house.

MUSIC. The Creoles of Louisiana, being a musical people, enjoyed attending concerts and the opera as well as singing and playing instruments at home. Before the war New Orleans had been one of the great opera centers of the nation, but afterwards there was a sharp decline in professional music performances throughout the state; music theaters closed their doors, music societies disbanded, and even the French Opera Company could support only infrequent performances. This condition lasted until after 1900, when there was a revival of interest in music.

German singing clubs became active in New Orleans after 1880, community singing became immensely popular in the northern and western sections of the state, and brass bands were organized in many towns and communities. The New Orleans Great Louisiana Field Artillery Brass and Reed Band, one of the most popular aggregations, frequently gave concerts in other towns. The Werlein, Grunewald, and Blackmar music companies were the most important publishers of songs and instrumental music. Ernest Guiraud continued his composition of serious music in France, and his last opera, *Frédégonde,* which had been completed by Saint-Saëns, was produced in 1895, three years after the composer's death. After 1900 several Louisiana composers added new vitality and new Louisiana folk themes to the world of music. The New Orleans Philharmonic Society was organized in 1906, and a few years later Dr. Leon Ryder Maxwell became the director of the Newcomb School of Music.

But it was the Creole who dominated Louisiana music; it was his songs and dances that helped to keep alive the old customs and habits, and when the Creole Louisiana soldiers marched through French towns during World War I, they astonished the inhabitants by singing nineteenth-century and even eighteenth-century French songs.

RELIGION. While Louisiana remained sharply divided between Protestant and Catholic throughout the period, there was a growing tendency for Catholics to invade the northern sections and for Protestants to invade the southern areas. Despite this tendency, however, at the end of the period there were several southern parishes which listed but a few Protestants and six northern parishes which did not list a single Catholic.

Several religious characteristics and developments of the period are noteworthy. There was a growing tendency for South Louisiana Negroes to leave the Catholic Church and join Protestant denominations, particularly the Baptists and Methodists. Many Negroes still clung to primitive religious practices regardless of the creed to which they belonged and indulged in voodoo rites and rituals. The Catholics strengthened their organization and organized the Diocese of Lafayette in 1918 with Jules Jeanmard as bishop. Pulpit oratory declined from its high ante bellum position, despite the work of many priests and ministers, including such men as Father Emmanuel De La Morinere and Bishop B. M. Palmer. Father Adrien Rouquette continued his missionary work among the Choctaw Indians of the Bayou Lacombe area until a year before his death in 1887. The St. Louis Cathedral had been rebuilt in the 1850's but by 1881 was beginning to need repair; in that year lightning damaged the structure considerably, leading to the complete rebuilding of the exterior and interior, under the general direction of Father Hyacinthe Mignot.

About this time Angelo Fontini became the sacristan of the Cathedral, the last and most picturesque of a long line of beadles. John S. Kendall lovingly described him a few years ago: "By his post Frontini was authorized to wear at all services in the Cathedral a long cut-away coat of scarlet garnished with galloons of gold cord, with a wide scarf of black velvet also bordered with gold braid, across the body from the left shoulder to the right hip. On his breast he displayed a large silver plaque engraved with the arms of the diocese. He had, too, a sword which flapped arrogantly against the broad red stripe that ran down the side of his black silk trousers. Finally, there was a huge black gold-embroidered plumed hat, as big as that of a Napoleonic marshall, and a long ebony staff with a bulbous silver head. Doubtless this costume was as much of an anachronism in New Orleans as that which the Papal Guardsmen wear at the Vatican, but that never troubled Frontini. When he paraded in all of his finery he was as proud as the proverbial peacock, which, in fact, he greatly resembled." When he died in 1914 he was one of the most universally known and best-beloved men in New Orleans.

During the 1880's there was a revival of camp meetings in northern and western Louisiana. To the brush arbors erected during the late summer and early fall, hundreds flocked to sing rousing religious songs and hymns, to hear strongly emotional sermons, to repent of their sins, and as one man wrote, "to let the Lord reign in their hearts in order that their souls might live." Frederick Williamson wrote that "the old-time camp meeting was a gathering place for the people of the entire region. Families came in wagons, bringing food supplies and remaining day after day until their stock of provisions was exhausted. When darkness fell and the camp fires blazed to the accompaniment of songs and hymns, rising and falling with gradually increasing crescendo, spirits ran high and men and women fell prostrate before the emotional tide that engulfed them." Grace Ulmer wrote that the sermons were simple, that there was "no higher criticism, no new-fangled theology—Heaven was glorious and Hell was hot." Not a few Baptists and Methodists believed that Episcopalians and Catholics could have but little real religious feeling because they conducted no camp meetings to renew their faith and to give satisfaction to the emotional outpourings of the spirit.

CHAPTER 27

EVERYDAY LIFE IN "OLD LOUISIANA"

SLOW PASSING OF THE OLD WAYS. The interim years from the end of the period of military occupation to the advent of the modern era have been fondly called by romantic and tradition-minded members of the older generation "The Days of Old Louisiana." Dean Pierce Butler of Newcomb College rather aptly named the period "The Unhurried Years," because it was a serene, leisurely time and no one was in much of a hurry. People seldom traveled, and when they did it was generally for short distances, either in a buggy, hack, wagon, or on horseback. They retained their old customs and living habits, for modern conveniences did not begin to come into everyday use until the later years.

Older Louisianians remembered the days before the War for Southern Independence. They strongly believed that life then was just a little bit better than it had been since, and they impressed this upon their children and their children's children. Even today the oldest generation in many parts of the South speak of that conflict simply as "The War." As the years passed, every Confederate veteran became an officer; there were generals, hosts of colonels, numerous majors, and lesser numbers of captains and lieutenants. One British traveler wrote with rare understanding that "everybody is either a general, colonel, or major; and the best rule perhaps, if you don't know exactly what a man is, to call him 'General.' If he is a general, you are right; and if he isn't, he will excuse the mistake."

Mrs. T. P. O'Connor rather accurately described the older lady of the period—she was a person of "unassailable dignity and rigorous habits. Never on the warmest summer's day did she take off her 'stays' and put on a loose muslin wrapper; no matter how high the temperature, she was always scrupulously dressed, with not a hair out of place. A ruffled cap of beautiful lace with strings was tied under her chin; an embroidered collar of sheer muslin was fastened at the neck with the miniature of a young man in a uniform." Ladies of this group retained their pre-Victorian literary tastes, blushingly read *Tristram Shandy* and *Roderick Random* even though they preferred Scott, Byron, Bulwer, and Miss Edgeworth, and indignantly refused to have anything to do with that "immoral" George Eliot. They lovingly held to the perfection of ante bellum years—when the visiting young woman from New York remarked, "What a wonderful moon you have down here," the old grandmother softly reminded her, "Ah, bless yo' heart, honey. But you ought to have seen that moon befo' the Waw!"

It was a common sight during those years to see old men wearing suits of "Confederate Grey," with the little buttons of the "Southern Cross of the Confederacy" on their lapels. When a visitor to New Orleans remarked to the body servant of an aged "major" that he was "getting on, you know, in years," the old-time Negro replied: "De Major is jes' as full of ambition as he kin be. . . . he is got a gallant young heart. . . . When I sends him out in de mornin' dere ain't no young blade in New Orleans what is any better turned out, den what de Major is. . . . when he is walkin' down de street even right young girls turns dere heads to look at de Major . . . sometimes he's right hard to manage."

The veterans of the War for Southern Independence retained their loyalty to the Confederacy, and it took the war with Spain to turn them into real Americans again. One wrote at the time that when he learned that Fitzhugh Lee and Joe Wheeler had been made generals in the United States Army and placed in command of United States troops he realized once again "that the Stars and Stripes was my flag, and that the Stars and Bars was only a flag of memory."

During the first half of the period, town, village, and countryside kept their old appearance; not until after 1900 did they begin to show unmistakable signs of material progress. "And far down on the Gulf the ancient beldam, New Orleans," according to historian W. F. Cash, "was rubbing the dream of her old-time glory from out her eyes and turning proudly to her new role as mistress to a swelling host of stout, black, rusty, prosaic ships panting upon the Spanish Main or breasting the Atlantic." But the change did not occur overnight, for the old city still clung to its gay habits remindful of a Viennese operetta and to melodic sounds recalling a Johann Strauss.

Frances and Edward Larocque Tinker captured the feeling of New Orleans during those years when they described the nursemaids with their charges dotting "the streets everywhere, and the gay-colored dresses and ribbons of the women, and the white and blue linen clothes of the men," which gave "the appearance of a huge garden party with ice cream wagons on the side streets and balloonmen and organ grinders at every corner: a brilliant kaleidoscope of constantly changing beauty." Mary Ashley Townsend, the Louisiana poet, perhaps even better captured its spirit in her "Down the Bayou":

> Its red-tiled roofs, its stucco walls;
> Its belfries, with their sweet bell-calls;
> The Bishop's Palace, which enshrines
> Such memories of the Ursulines;
> Past balconies where maidens dreamed
> Behind the shelter of cool vines;
> Past open doors where parrots screamed;
> Past courts where mingled shade and glare
> Fell through pomegranate boughs, to where
> The turbaned negress, drowsy grown,
> Sat nodding in her ample chair. . . .

"Duty" and "loyalty" and "honor" were still in observance, and that which was impossible was frequently made possible through the magic power of the three words. There was the young lawyer and judge who sat on the balcony of a vacation resort with his two mothers-in-law, two sets of children, and one wife: "After the death of his first wife, his mother-in-law came to live with him and take care of his children. He married again, an only daughter, and her mother couldn't live alone, so she too joined the family circle. Then came more babies and there they all were, quite united and happy together."

While the Civil War marked the beginning of the end of the Old Creoles' civilization, it was a long time in the dying. The structure of their aged and high culture crumbled very slowly. Little by little they became poorer. Their homes had to go. Family records were lost or destroyed. Treasured heirlooms were sold as financial desperation drove them to antique dealers or to Americans with cash in pocket. But for many years they set the standard, gave tone, and exercised general control over society and social life.

Those Creoles of a generation ago possessed friendliness, cordiality, and a captivating naïveté. They had sentiment, a charm of manner, candor, gaiety, spirit combined with a certain languor, and, as Charles Dudley Warner wrote, "either simplicity or the art of it." They were law abiding and quiet, generally conservative, and slow to change their habits and customs. The family was the center of life, and families were large. One Creole who had a musical ear named his five sons Valmir, Valmore, Valsin, Valcour, and Valerien. Another family did even better: Perpetuée and Lastie Broussard had sixteen children, all of whose names began with an "O." There was Odile, Odelia, Ovide, Onesia, Otta, Omea, and so on, until the last baby, whom they named Opta. They still spoke of "Creole cabbages," "Creole horses," "Creole lilies," and retained numerous "inbred habits, superstitions, proverbs, all with derivations springing from that past that belonged to the Creoles."

They firmly believed that life should be lived to the fullest, that it should be enjoyed, and that much of it should be spent with one's family or in other social intercourse. When Samuel Lockett toured the state just before the period began, he needed his horse shod and was quite impatient at the delay. The Creole blacksmith remarked to him: "Sir, you are not a Louisianian or, at least, not a Creole—they all like to wait. . . . a Creole will come here in the morning to get a horse shod, or a plow pointed, and when the job is done he will sit down and wait until another comes along for company; the second will have his little job and before it is over, maybe a third will call for a small piece of work, and the two first will wait for him; and then they all come and eat dinner at my table, and after dinner they must wait until they have a smoke, and then till the cool of the evening, and so they wait and wait."

But Americans from other states began settling in Creole Louisiana in increasing numbers after 1880; they were aggressive and many refused to learn the French language. Creole children began to refuse to speak French because other children taunted them with "Kiskee-dee" (Qu'est-ce que dit? What did you say?) and other unflattering phrases. In 1886 the Creoles organized the Creole Association to help preserve their old ways of life, but it was not effective and soon passed out of existence. The old Creole houses of New Orleans, with their balconies of iron, winding stairs, and flower-filled patios, as did the old homes of Creoles over the entire state, began to show signs of age. The Day of the Creole was almost over. Of late years, however, interest has reawakened. Louisianians are now reviving many of the old Creole ways, and St. Martinville is once more the Creole capital of Louisiana.

While the relics of the Old Southern and Old Creole civilization generally disappeared, in spite of sporadic and inefficient attempts to preserve them, some remained as mute but eloquent testimony of days and institutions and ways of life which had passed. In 1912, John Galsworthy, the noted English writer, visited New Orleans and one night was guided through the ruins of the St. Louis Hotel. He later wrote, in his "Inn of Tranquility": "Trying to pierce that darkness we became conscious, as it seemed, of innumerable eyes gazing, not at us, but through the archway where we stood; innumerable white eyeballs gleaming out of blackness. From behind us came a little laugh. It floated past through the archway, toward those eyes. Who was that? Who laughed in there? The old South itself—that incredible, fine, lost soul! That 'old-time' thing of old ideals, blindfolded by its own history. . . . And rather quickly we passed away, out of that 'old-time place'; where something had laughed, and the drip, drip, drip of water down the walls was as the sound of a spirit grieving."

The scene changed, as the New South and the New Louisiana gradually developed. Justo Sierra, the noted Mexican statesman and writer, wrote after his visit to New Orleans in his *En Tierra Yankee* that the old elegant and aristocratic civilization of Louisiana was falling before the brutal civilization of coal and iron. Louisianians, who were aware of the change, agreed with historian Alcée Fortier when he wrote: "Let us not scorn . . . the Old South, for the New South . . . is but the continuation of the Old South; the New is possible only because the Old has existed."

IMPROVEMENT OF EVERYDAY LIVING CONDITIONS. Modern conveniences of living which are accepted as a matter of course today were unheard of at the beginning and for many years of the period. During the 1880's, typical plantation boy William Edwards Clement learned to read by the light of coal-oil (then called "insurance" oil) lamps. His home had no plumbing: "The first bathroom, too, was quite a curiosity. Somehow I at first looked upon that new innovation as 'sissy,' encouraging softness." Drinking water, which generally came from an unscreened cistern or shallow well, sometimes contained wiggle tails and small snakes. As there were no door or window screens to keep out flies and mosquitoes, mosquito bars of fine gauze were placed over the beds. The first screened porch, or "gallery mosquito house" as they were first called along the lower Mississippi, was supposedly built by Jacob McWilliams at Plaquemine during the late 1880's. People either stayed hot during the summer or cooled themselves with palmetto fans; in winter, rooms were warmed by huge fireplaces or cast iron stoves. On Saturday night "we did not turn on the hot and cold water. Instead we luxuriated in the embrace of a big tin bathtub, carried into the bathroom for that purpose—the portable kind, with a raised, roundish back and curved arm rests."

There was little to choose between Creole New Orleans and American New Orleans during those years, for as John S. Kendall wrote: "In all New Orleans there were only a few dozen telephones, no electric lights, few or no private heating systems, no sewerage worthy of the name, no protection against mosquitoes and other annoying and sometimes dangerous insects, no municipal water supply accessible to house-holders, no effective drainage. Not every street was paved; most of them in the French quarter, some in the American Quarter near Canal street, but elsewhere they were dirt roads, liable in the frequent torrential rains to degenerate into quagmires. The streets, where they were illuminated at all, were lighted by gas-jets that shed a flickering yellow glow at the street corners but left the intervening distances in darkness."

At the beginning of the period none of the Louisiana cities had underground sewage systems, the first such system being installed in New Orleans in 1880 when that city had a population of more than 200,000 people. The water supply of city and town was still provided by scattered public or private wells and private cisterns. In Plaque-mine, for example, the first city water system did not come into existence until 1892, when the Plaquemine Water Works Company was organized, secured a ten-year franchise, sunk several wells, and erected tanks. "Fire-wells," public wells from which water could be drawn in case of fires, were common in most towns. In 1886, Napoleon-ville had six fire-wells and was about to dig a seventh, whereupon the Donaldsonville *Chief* announced: "Donaldsonville has none and ought to be ashamed of herself." By that date a large town like Carrollton, now a part of New Orleans, had over two dozen fire-wells. By the early 1900's many towns were beginning to drill deep wells, erect water towers, and lay underground water pipes in their more thickly populated areas.

New Orleans had railways for horse-drawn street cars at the beginning of the period, but other cities did not make such improvements until after some years had passed. Though gentlemen paid before taking their seats, ladies sat down and gave their fare to the nearest man, who passed it forward to the coin box or to the driver. Along the ceiling was a cord, attached to a bell, one stroke of which meant "stop at the first crossing," while two strokes ordered the driver to "stop at once."

The New Orleans and Carrollton Railroad was the first to run its cars with electricity, in 1893. The *Daily Picayune* headlined the event: "Yesterday, for the first time, New Orleans rode by wire. The experience proved delightful, safe and successful. . . . Promptly at 10, the gay, spic and span green cars were drawn up on Carrollton Avenue for the trip to the foot of Baronne, the present terminal of the road. The street was filled with spectators, and ladies in private carriages drove up to see the start. . . . Mr. Haile gave the signal to start, and as gently as a leaf drifting on a summer river, the car rolled along . . . and pompously as any Carnival king made its triumphant way to Canal Street."

Although New Orleans was lighted by gas, most towns still used coal-oil lamps. Both coal-oil lamps and gaslights had to be regularly cleaned and had to be lighted every night by a lamplighter. By the late 1880's Donaldsonville had fifty coal-oil street lamps and spent $180.00 per year for the coal oil used. In 1896 the one lamplighter still cared for all the city's lights and the *Times* complained: "Through what is supposed to have been the carelessness of James Jones, the lamp at the corner of Mississippi street and Railroad avenue caught on fire last evening at about 9:30 o'clock. . . . There is a complaint that the lamplighter fails to properly trim the wicks." Two months later the same newspaper urged the installation of electric lights: "Here as soon as darkness spreads over us we seem dead. . . . We are too big to remain in the dark any longer." Shortly after this it was announced that the Electric Light and Power Company would soon be formally organized and that the company by economical management "could lower the price so that they would soon have its lights in every store and in a great number of our private buildings."

While some towns jumped from coal-oil lights to electric lights, many followed their coal-oil lights first with artificial-gas lights, then with natural-gas lights after 1916, and finally with electric lights. New Orleans began to install electric lights in the first, second, third, and fourth municipal districts in 1887; by 1900 the entire city was lighted by electricity. Crowley and Opelousas erected electric-light plants during the middle 1890's, while the Donaldsonville *Times* continued its complaints about the city's lighting system: "In the meantime Donaldsonville . . . has to grope along with oil lamps." By early May, 1898, however, the newspaper could brag: "The Lights in Operation. Yesterday a portion of the city's electric plant was tested and found to work all right, and last night the principal streets were lighted by electricity. . . . to-night every light in the city will be in operation."

Most towns still depended upon volunteer companies of firemen to fight fires. These companies took great pride in their organizations, and each company was a sort of social club. The men wore bright uniforms, kept their fire engines shining, and paraded their equipment at every opportunity. One such organization, the Hope Hook and Ladder Company of Plaquemine, organized in 1882, built a large hall, the upper floor to be used for dances, social gatherings, and theatricals, and the lower floor to house the company's fire truck. Until 1885 the bells of the Catholic church were used to sound the alarm of fire; after this the fire companies installed bells at their individual headquarters. By 1894, Plaquemine had six fire companies, the members of which manned hand-pump engines that were effective if the fire was near enough to a good well, a water-filled drainage ditch, or the river, and one Babcock chemical engine effective only during the early stages of a fire. Until 1891 fire fighting in New Orleans remained in the hands of the Firemen's Charitable Association; in that year its contract expired and the city organized a municipal fire department under the control of the city's Board of Fire Control and the Fire and Lighting Committee of the city council.

Sidewalks went through four stages of development, starting with a low, leveelike banquette, which was afterward topped with wooden planks, usually laid lengthwise. The third stage was the brick sidewalk. Modern concrete sidewalks did not appear in most towns until after 1920.

Although the commercial ice plant had made its appearance in Louisiana before the beginning of the period, Louisiana in general still depended upon winter shipments of northern ice. Ice was shipped by ocean vessels from the New England area to New Orleans or by great river barges from the upper Mississippi and Ohio rivers to river towns. At these points it was repacked in sawdust-filled barrels and distributed throughout the state. Frequently the supply was exhausted before the first shipments were received the following year. "Ice factories" which used filtered pure water were built in most sizable towns during the 1890's, although Monroe and a few others had established ice plants which made their product from unfiltered well or river water during the preceding decade.

Mail service improved with the inauguration of special-delivery service in towns in 1885; the first rural free delivery mail route in Louisiana and the second in the United States was established in the vicinity of Thibodaux in 1896, and the first air-mail flight in 1912, when George Mestach made the second successful, official flight in the United States, from New Orleans to Baton Rouge in one hour and thirty-two seconds.

A telephone line from New Orleans to Donaldsonville, built by the Great Southern Telephone Company, was completed in the early fall of 1883. William Edwards Clement recalled the coming of telephones to Iberville Parish about three years later: "I remember the erection of the first poles in front of our plantation and the stringing of the wires. All this was quite a curiosity, of course, and we—in our immaturity— greeted it with the doubt and contempt any such fool enterprise should properly merit. People like us, with swift horses always ready, could send messages, or visit around at will. We were getting along fine, saw no use for crazy innovations such as telephones. It was just a fad and would soon die out." Within twenty years, however, there were "speaking telegraphs" and "talking telegraphs" over the entire state; the telephone had become a part of the pattern of ordinary life.

While it is not known when the first automobile was brought into the state, Louisianians began to purchase cars early in the century. In 1909, Ralph DePalma set a world's record at New Orleans with a speed of sixty miles per hour, an event which aided in popularizing the new vehicles. By 1916 there were nearly 9,000 automobiles on the assessment rolls of the various parishes, and thereafter the increase was rapid. Parish regulations for cars may seem somewhat out of place today, but at the time the newfangled contraptions were taken seriously and owners of riding and driving horses looked upon them with considerable skepticism. The hard-surfaced road had been developed by 1920, but few miles of the new-type roads had been completed.

Airplanes made their appearance only a short time after automobiles, and in 1910 an "international aviation tournament" was held at New Orleans. One of the planes rose to over 7,000 feet and recorded a mile in 57 seconds. The featured event of the tournament was a race between an automobile and an airplane. The Packard car defeated the plane, which was piloted by John Moisant, for whom present-day Moisant Airport was named. By the end of the period a few Louisiana cow pastures had been converted into air fields.

Motion pictures were introduced about the time of World War I. In Marksville, for example, "the pictures" or "picture slides" were first shown in a tent pitched on a vacant lot near Jules Coco's store in 1918. A short time later an old building facing the courthouse square was converted into a "picture house" and was so used until "The Palace" theater was built in 1920.

Patent medicines were still in general use, and great numbers of "cure-alls" were sold. Stanch members of the Woman's Christian Temperance Union were in many cases enthusiastic purchasers, even though the only therapeutic value of the nostrum was in the stimulating action of the alcohol it contained. It has been said that the most successful druggists were those who carried the largest stocks of these magic elixirs and who first built soda fountains and began to push a new drink called "Coca-Cola."

It was the age of the country doctor and the general practitioner in the towns and cities, and Louisiana seems to have had a fair share of highly individualistic medical men. Old Doctor Charles Luzenberg was extremely fond of medical experimentation. One of his fondest dreams was to find a man with no nose who would permit him to furnish a new one made out of the flesh and skin of a Negro, the object being to ascertain if, in time, the black nose would become white. Doctor John L. Jones of the New Orleans Irish Channel, a forgetful man who treated white and colored alike regardless of their infectious diseases, consistently forgot to carry his prescription pad; therefore, he simply tore off his shirt cuffs and wrote the prescriptions on them. On one occasion he wrote the prescription on a door, whereupon the huge Irishman for whose wife it had been written yanked the door from its hinges and carried it to the drugstore.

It was Dr. Armand Mercier who recounted the following incident to Dr. Rudolph Matas: "We are not infallible; we are physicians, not popes. Listen: you are aware that sometime ago I was as thin as a lath." Mercier recounted how he went to three doctors and "the first found fault with my heart; the second with my spine, and the third with my liver, each of these vital organs being fatally affected." What did he do? He took an entire cask of rich Burgundy and "kept drinking a bottle of Chamber-tin at my breakfast and another bottle at my dinner, until the three hundred bottles which the cask contained had been absorbed. And now, 'look at me,' tapping on his abdomen, 'I am as rotund as a hogshead.'"

But Louisiana's physicians made many contributions to American medical science. Dr. Albert Miles improved the techniques of artery surgery, Dr. Joseph Holt was the first to successfully disinfect ships with the fumes of sulphurous acid, Dr. Edmond Souchon was the first to preserve anatomic dissections with permanent color of muscles, vessels, and organs. The first ear, eye, nose, and throat hospital in the South was founded by Dr. Arthur Washington de Roaldes; the first use of warm ether without heating by flame (which reduces the danger of pneumonia) was accomplished by Dr. Ansel Caine; and the first health train in the South was equipped and operated by Dr. Oscar Dowling when President of the Louisiana State Board of Health.

The state suffered yellow-fever epidemics in 1878, 1879, 1880, 1883, 1897, and 1899. The last important epidemic occurred in 1905, when 452 persons died out of a total of nearly 3,500 who had contracted the disease; a sharp contrast to the epidemic of 1878 which cost the lives of over 4,000 persons. The last epidemic was in 1909, but because of the work of Dr. Quitman Kohnke in leading the fight against the mosquito and in promoting the screening and "oiling" of cisterns, comparatively few lives were lost. Educating the public, however, was a slow process, as evidenced by the case of the old Irishwoman of New Orleans who at first refused to allow her cistern to be oiled: "Well, come in and do it, if yez is bound to, but I don't believe yez can keep the Lord from gettin' those He wants by puttin' a little ile on the cistherns." Even the chills, which Mark Twain said was the "merciful provision of an all-wise Providence" to enable lazy folks "to take exercise without exertion," passed from the realm of human miseries.

COURTSHIP, MARRIAGE, AND FUNERAL CUSTOMS. Courtship was not as easy and simple as it is today. If a young man wished to formally call upon a young lady he sent a friend to ask permission of her father; if he was simply looking around he was very careful to be completely impartial in his visits to various homes where there were young ladies of marriageable age. If he began to concentrate on one home he immediately became a source of much-talked-of speculation throughout the entire neighborhood. Parents, and particularly the mothers, as Lyle Saxon wrote, "boasted of the calls of a suitor on their daughter and discussed frankly his morals, manners, breeding, background and financial condition. When he started making engagements for the balls or cotillions, it was considered that romance had bloomed, and woe betide the insincere young man not thoroughly aware of the delicate implications attached to showing a Creole girl such attention without the proper and expected intention." Newly arrived Americans frequently had to be rather pointedly told by brothers or cousins of the young lady just what was expected of them.

Marriage was the entire aim of life of young Creole girls, and they were well trained in all the feminine arts attractive to men. They moved with dignity and without noise, gliding from place to place, as one observer wrote, "without apparent effort, gracefully and silently." They early learned the art of make-up and of wearing their clothing with simple and appealing artlessness. They could converse easily and discuss many of the major issues of the day through the obvious medium of asking the opinions of others; it was currently said that "she didn't graduate from a college, my dear, but she can entertain a whole parlor full of people."

Newly arrived Americans and foreigners in Louisiana generally thought Creole girls extremely beautiful, though some New Englanders considered some of them a bit plump. And they did make dainty pictures, sitting in the parlor, quiet, gracious, neatly dressed and coiffured, daintily munching "sweet crackers" and sipping lemonade, thinned Grenadine, or *Biere Creole*. One completely enamored Yankee wrote: "In entering a sanctuary the soul bows down. The pen feels moved when it touches upon a sacred subject. . . . One finds in the traits of the Creole a distinction perfect in harmony and form. Pure profiles, patrician lines, oval and delicate chiseling . . . a a little aerial—the ethereal dominating the material, the ideal combating reality."

Couples were seldom left alone, and many a young man spent the entire evening playing riotous games of dominoes with the girl's father, while her mother and all her aunts cautiously questioned him about his family and his financial and social assets. If he continued to call, Papa asked him what his intentions were. This was to save the young lady's time, which she could ill afford to waste on a young man who "had a heart like an artichoke" (meaning a leaf for everyone), for she would be considered an "old maid" at the age of twenty-five and might as well throw her corsets in the armoire and begin to wear hooded bonnets with ribbons that tied under the chin.

The Creole formal engagement was a serious and ritualistic affair. The young man, and if possible his father, called on the young lady's father. The young lady was not consulted, though probably in the majority of cases she had already indicated to her father that she was just as enthusiastic about the business as the young man. All the family skeletons and trees were properly examined and explained; material wealth meant but little, it was *la famille* that counted. Were they *gens du commun?* What was their ancestry? And eventually there came the indirect, carefully worded, but well-understood question—was there even a minute trace of *café au lait?* When everyone was satisfied, the formal marriage contract, listing the financial assets of each party, was drawn up and signed by the young couple and a host of witnesses.

The engagement breakfast was attended by all the aunts, uncles, cousins, and other relatives of the betrothed couple. The engagement ring, presented to the young lady after the breakfast, was usually a ruby in a yellow-gold setting. The groom-to-be presented her with a "wedding basket," filled with articles of lace, shawls, gloves, and pieces of jewelry. She could not wear or use any of these things, of course, before the wedding. Mondays and Tuesdays were considered the best days for weddings; Saturdays and Sundays were "common" days on which no one would consider being married, and Friday was "Hangman's Day," when criminals were executed, and naturally out of the question.

Catholic couples who wanted a really fashionable wedding went to New Orleans and were married in the St. Louis Cathedral; otherwise the wedding was in the local church. The ceremony was usually in the late afternoon or early evening, until 1910 when the Archbishop forbade marriages in the afternoon. Protestant weddings usually caused considerably less fuss and bother than those of Catholics. The groom simply went to the courthouse, got the license, and the wedding was performed, either at the church of the couple's choice or at the home of the bride. On one occasion at Delhi, however, a young Irishman had considerable trouble. He rode sixteen miles to Rayville, got the license and returned to his waiting bride-to-be. But the license did not have the last name of the young lady on it, only her first name, so back he went to the parish seat. While he was gone the news leaked out, and he returned to find the whole town gathered to witness his wedding.

Wedding rings, called "alliance" rings, were generally worn by the bride and groom and were usually engraved with their initials and the date of the wedding. After the ceremony Catholic couples signed the register, while Protestants signed their names in the family Bible. Rice was never thrown, nor did the bride try to toss her bouquet to her best unmarried friend. The flowers were sent to the cemetery, or, if the bride were a Catholic, to the convent where she had been educated.

Funerals involved much more preparation and formality than at the present time and certain traditional customs were rigidly followed. All clocks were stopped at the hour of death, mirrors were covered, and black crape was hung on the front door. Twigs of orange leaves were frequently sewn to the clean sheet spread on top of the "cooling board," where the body lay until it was placed in the coffin. Older people were usually buried in black coffins, while lavender or gray coffins were used for the middle-aged, and white for children. Everyone dressed in black mourning costumes, and if persons did not own the appropriate types they were rented for the funeral.

Wakes were commonplace, particularly with the Irish of New Orleans, and were held the night before the funeral. The women of the family, assisted by neighbors and friends, prepared huge platters of cold meats, salads, cakes, cookies, and brewed pots of coffee; the men dug deep into their pockets to buy quarts of good whiskey and wine. After paying their respects to the grieving family and to the dead person, guests adjourned to the dining room for food and drink. As James McGooey recalled New Orleans Irish Channel wakes some years ago: "Everybody'd go into the parlor and look at the corpse and say fine things, though some of 'em had never seen the man when he was alive. Then they'd go out in the backyard, get drunk and fill their bellies with food."

A black hearse, drawn by black horses draped with black and decorated with black plumes, was used for adults, while white horses and decorations were used for children. Burials were from the home of the deceased. If the family was in poor or even moderate financial circumstances, the undertaker redecorated the parlor with carpets, and coverings for the chairs and sofas, and hung black or white curtains and drapes. Sometimes a band playing funeral music went with the procession to the graveyard, and occasionally horses drawing the hearse were trained to keep step with the music.

Throughout the period the home was the center of life. In it people were born and perhaps married, in it they died, and from it their remains were carried to the cemetery. Not long ago an old Louisianian said: "Nowadays people are born in hospitals, get married in hotels, buried from the undertaker's. All they use their homes for is a place to change clothes."

SUPERSTITIONS. Superstitions were common, and although not everyone believed in all of those currently in use, most people usually practiced a few private superstitious beliefs. The future state of the weather could be determined by certain signs: bad weather was coming if gulls flew excitedly in circles; fogs were on the way if the light of the moon and stars reflected clearly in water; bad weather was predicted if horses ran or jumped about the levees. Along the lower Mississippi, heavy rains were thought to come from the vicinity of Morgan City, so the appearance of a cloud in the southwest caused steamboatmen to cry, "Morgan's gonna take the lid off the well. Batten down the hatches."

There were superstitious cures for every kind of human ill: babies were given mud-dauber's-nest tea to make them strong and healthy; aching joints were treated with an ointment made from mashed lightning bugs; sassafras tea taken in the spring was supposed to thin the blood which had become thick and sluggish during the winter months; weakly children slept on mattresses of moss gathered from cypress trees, in order that the strength of the trees might flow into them. Boils were healed with mixtures of sugar and egg yolks or charcoal and lard, while snake bites could be cured if the wound were immediately dipped in water, which also caused the snake to die. Persons tormented with asthma wore muskrat skins over the chest; those who suffered from kidney disorders drank huge quantities of swamp-lily tea.

Bad luck or death was foretold by many signs. Getting a haircut on Friday would certainly bring on some sort of illness, while sneezing at the table meant that someone would soon die. To prevent losing money, a person burned onion peelings or carried a sprig of verbena in his pocketbook, and burned clothing was never patched or repaired for to do so meant death in the family. Coffin lids were frequently left unnailed so the spirit could get out on Judgment Day. Though dreams warned of approaching bad luck, it could be warded off by carrying the ninth bone of a black cat's tail in the pocket or by tying butterfly wings to the right leg.

In South Louisiana lived numerous evil spirits, many of which inhabited the bodies of living persons and animals, especially wolves, snakes, or bats. There were *loup-garous* and zombis, and children were constantly warned to be careful or "the *loup-garous* will get you." As one old man explained it some years ago: *"Loup-garous* is them people what wants to do bad work, and changes themselves into wolves. They got plenty of them, yes. And you sure know them when you see them. They got big red eyes, pointed noses and everything just like a wolf has, even hair all over, and long pointed nails. They rub themselves with some voodoo grease and come out just like wolves is. You keep away you see any of them things, hein? They make you one of them yes, quick like hell. They hold balls on Bayou Goula all the time, mens and womens, both together. They dance and carry on just like animals, then." However, all a person had to do to frighten away a *loup-garou* or a zombi was to throw a frog at him, for they were very much afraid of frogs.

The Devil also roamed South Louisiana, assuming many disguises in order to fool and trap people. When on earth, he was called the Evil One and was assisted by evil spirits such as *letiches,* the souls of unbaptized babies, which haunted little children at night. Mermaids and sirens haunted the Gulf shores to entice and trap fishermen. It was necessary to be constantly vigilant, for the Devil used many wiles and even the most appealing and beautiful things to ensnare his victims.

The Louisiana Negro not infrequently grafted African and West Indian sorcery, magic, and primitive religious practices onto his superficial Christianity, and practiced serpent worship, followed implicitly the ministrations of voodoo doctors, and indulged in wild emotional incantations, rites, processions, and dances. Numerous writers have described the Sundays at Congo Square in New Orleans, where "whites stared at the spectacle of hundreds of Negroes of all ages leaping, swinging, and gliding to African rhythms, modified by French steps and tunes set to the measured beat of the drum." Many superstitious Negroes, as well as unlettered and impressionable whites, bought voodoo amulets, charms, love philters, and even poisons. Negro voodoo priests and priestesses in New Orleans and the more thickly Negro-populated rural areas held regular or irregular voodoo conclaves, some of which were simply unrestrained orgies.

Voodooism gradually disappeared from New Orleans after the death of the noted voodoo queen Marie Laveau during the late 1880's, but has not yet completely passed from the Louisiana scene. In certain sections of the state *gris-gris* powders and charms are still sold; in these areas it is not uncommon to find chicken bones lying on the doorstep, red powder sprinkled on the sidewalk, or a black cross mark on the front of a house. Clandestine meetings are still occasionally held, chiefly in the rural areas, and one may still hear on Saturday nights the boom-boom-boom of the orgiastic and demoniac primitive drums.

AMUSEMENTS AND SPORTS. Rural and small-town Louisianians enjoyed a wide variety of amusements during the years of Old Louisiana. In the country areas there were hay rides, watermelon and bee-tree cuttings, sugar-cane peelings, family dinners, "preachings" and camp meetings, logrollings and chimney daubings, boating, ice-cream and singing parties, dances, amateur theatricals and musicals, or other forms of entertainment. Rural upstate dances started at sundown and continued until daybreak, and as Grace Ulmer wrote, included "Contra dances, cotillions, waltzes, and cross-the-corner reels swept steadily on to the music of 'Turkey-in-the Straw,' 'Cotton-Eyed Joe,' 'The Old Gray Horse Came Tearing Through the Wilderness,' 'Dinah,' 'Get Along, Liza Jane.'" The prompter called the dances and saw to it that the fire did not burn low: "Swing your corners, now your partners, promenade around and put on another piece of pine."

New Orleanians enjoyed balls and dances, plays, operas, concerts, picnics at Lake Pontchartrain, and numerous other activities. Aged Gus Laurer recalled a few years ago how the citizenry took rides on the "horse-cars," danced at Hopper's Garden, Delachies' Picnic Grounds, or at the Washington Artillery Hall, walked along the levees to watch the ships, or rode "Old Smoky Mary," the railroad train, out to Spanish Fort.

Circuses, animal shows, trapeze and sleight-of-hand performers toured the state by railroad, boat, and wagon. Medicine shows, some of which were called "Kickapoo Indian Shows," presented Indian dances and tomahawk-throwing exhibitions before selling their cure-alls. Organ grinders walked along the streets of New Orleans and other towns, cranking their hurdy-gurdies for a few coins. In the Crescent City probably the most noted cynosure was the circus which was always found playing in the vacant lot where the old Orleans Theater had stood.

The South Louisiana *fais-do-do* still was usually given on Saturday nights. During the morning young men rode through the villages and along the countryside calling out that the dance that night would be at so-and-so's house or at the village dance pavilion. At sundown everyone climbed on horses or into buggies, carts, or wagons and went to the dance, put the small children to bed in the *parc aux petits,* and the evening's entertainment began. The older people played cards or talked, and some of them danced. Everyone made frequent trips to the wine, beer, lemonade, and coffee tables. Supper was served at midnight and was usually a fish gumbo or bisque. The dancing continued until the musicians got up, went out into the yard, and fired several pistol shots into the air, yelling, *"Le bal est fini."*

City and town balls were much more formal, whether in New Orleans or in an upstate town like Tallulah. The *Madison Parish Journal* in 1884 gave a lengthy and complete description of one elaborate affair in the typical phraseology of the small-town journalist. The delicious foods which "graced" the supper table were the subject of detailed comment, as were the ladies in attendance. One young lady, much "admired for her graceful carriage and modest demeanor, wore a charming white dress with pink trimmings," while another, "a brilliant brunette, whose sparkling black eyes played havoc with many hearts, was dressed in a rich pink dress." The hostess, "in an exquisite costume of embroidered red mull . . . contributed largely to the success of the ball by her charming manners and pleasant attention to all of the guests."

While the public Quadroon Ball of New Orleans had generally gone out of fashion, there were private, invitation balls where the women present were quadroons and octoroons of light coloring. Shortly after the beginning of the period a correspondent of the Chicago *Times* visited the city and attended one of these functions. After describing the young quadroon women with a rhapsodic and ecstatic pen, he got around to the men in attendance: "Most of them were Democrats, several were statesmen. . . . Judges and journalists, senators and generals, doctors and merchants, each acting as the oak to some octoroon ivy. . . . It was like the scene from some novel of the Orient—an Arabian Night entertainment in the capital of Louisiana." Toward the close of his account, he wrote: "From personal observation, I saw nothing even approaching indecency at the quadroon ball." Negro dances were much as they had been during slavery days, when many of the plantations had slave dance halls. The calinda and the bamboula were still danced, though with considerably less lasciviousness than formerly, and such violent and primitive dances were plainly going out of fashion.

During the 1880's wandering groups of Negro musicians, many of whom were boys and youths, began to wander the streets of New Orleans playing for whatever coins they could collect from passers-by. They used violins, kettles, cowbells, gourds filled with pebbles, harmonicas, banjoes, guitars, all sorts of drums, whistles, and anything else that would make a noise. In the middle 1890's a group of boys calling themselves "The Spasm Band" began to find engagements at West End and other resorts. Their fame grew, and their outfit was soon advertised as "The Razzy Dazzy Spasm Band." Then about 1900 the owner of the Haymarket Dance Hall on Customhouse Street hired a group of adults and billed them under the same name. When the boys of the original band protested, the adult group was renamed "The Razzy Dazzy Jazzy Band." The name caught the public fancy and was used by other musical combinations, which used no written music and played their syncopated music by ear and emotion. These bands spread over the Lower Mississippi Valley, slowly developed a new type of American music, and eventually introduced it to Chicago under the name of "jazz" about 1915.

The custom of celebrating the Mardi Gras season had been discontinued during the Civil War years, but was revived in 1866, and by 1870 the various organizations were again giving balls and sponsoring parades. By 1900 the festivities had assumed their modern pattern. While New Orleans was the center of interest and activity, there were celebrations in numerous other towns and cities in the southern part of the state.

One of the most unusual amusements was the ring tournament, where mounted men, dressed as knights of old, rode along a course at breakneck speed and with the point of a lance stabbed suspended rings. The champion named the queen of the grand ball which followed the tournament. Ring tournaments began before 1860, were revived after the end of the Civil War, and lasted until about 1900, when they went out of fashion. During the last two decades of the nineteenth century the Louisiana centers of the sport were Lake Providence, Tallulah, Shreveport, Mansfield, Natchitoches, Alexandria, New Iberia, and particularly Opelousas and vicinity. At the 1891 Opelousas tournament occurred the noted "Sir Godfrey de Bouillon" incident, which kept the area laughing for years. Sir Godfrey's horse, unaccustomed to carrying a lanced, shielded, and spurred knight dressed in flashing colors and flowing capes, bolted, whirled around, and ran down the course in the wrong direction, whereupon a diminutive colored boy rushed to the betting shed and yelled, "Sir Gumbo de Bouillon is in the soup."

There was much home and community singing, and song festivals were common in the northern sections. Many of the old Creole, river, and water-front songs and Negro spirituals and work songs have become a part of the folklore of Louisiana. In South Louisiana the Creoles faithfully went to Mass each Sunday, then devoted the rest of the day to pleasure, one observer noting that "guests came for breakfast and remained until past midnight." The same writer wrote that "New Orleans is a dreadful place in the eyes of a New England man. They keep Sunday as we in Boston keep the Fourth of July."

Drinking was a part of the convivial pattern of Louisiana social life, although it was frequently frowned upon in certain northern sections. A Chicago *Times* correspondent wrote: "Let not the member of any temperance society visit New Orleans. They have more saloons to the square inch here than any place I know of and they have no midnight closing ordinance. . . . For steady drinking give me New Orleans. None of your northern hog-wash either, but the fiery liquids, such as brandy and absinthe. . . . Yet these Southerners drink like gentlemen. They seldom, if ever, stagger under their loads; but walk square up, like Charley Lever's bold dragoons, with three bottles inside their belts. . . . Evaporation does much for a man in this climate, which explains why, with drinking so common, intoxication is so rare."

Sports of all sorts were enjoyed by men and boys of all ages. Boys learned to fish and hunt as soon as they were strong enough to shoulder a fishing pole or a gun. Men hunted bear, bobcats, deer, small game, and all kinds of wild fowl. Wild-hog hunting became so popular in the swamp areas west of the Mississippi that the "hog dogs of Catahoula" were developed, one of the finest breeds of hunting dogs in the world. Theodore Roosevelt hunted in the Catahoula country and wrote vividly of one of the guides: "Holt Collier could not read or write, but he had all the dignity of an African chief, and for half a century he had been a bear hunter, having killed, or assisted in killing, over three thousand bears."

In 1890, Louisiana became one of the first states to legalize prize fighting, and New Orleans immediately became a center for the sport. A "round" lasted until one of the fighters was knocked down. In 1893, Andy Bowen and Jack Burke fought a 110-round fight lasting 7 hours and 19 minutes, the fight ending in a draw. After 1877 baseball fever hit the state; soon every village and town had its team. Rules were considerably different from those in effect today, and huge scores of twenty, thirty, and even forty runs were not uncommon.

Since special diets and dieting were practically unheard of during the entire period, Louisianians continued their old custom of eating well. The easy acquisition of game animals and birds and all varieties of fish offered culinary opportunities denied the people of other states. While American Louisiana featured good southern cooking, it was the Creole who still gave opportunity for gastronomic surfeiting with jambalaya, *daube glacée,* grillade, fricassee, brochette, gumbo, bisque, and court bouillon. Sunday dinners and banquets took much time because of the endless procession of dishes, which caused an English visitor to write that one would have to have the stomach of one of the old Greek gods in order to enjoy all of them.

PART EIGHT

Modern Louisiana

CHAPTER 28

POLITICS IN THE MODERN ERA

INTRODUCTION TO THE PERIOD. In a speech delivered before the United States Senate on January 22, 1936, Senator John H. Overton stated that for a quarter of a century prior to 1928, Louisiana had been "controlled by Governors elected from the upper stratum of society and subservient largely to the interests of the wealthy classes. . . . The politicians of this regime did nothing toward a constructive development of the State or a recognition of the rights, necessities, and hopes of the humbler classes."

There was considerable truth in Senator Overton's statement. During the years after 1877, Louisiana politics, like state politics in general throughout the South, were generally controlled by conservative doctors, lawyers, merchants, bankers, and the representatives of manufacturing and industrial interests. These men decided who would run for local and state public offices and after their candidates had been elected, forced them to comply with their dictates. They usually followed a laissez-faire attitude toward industry, encouraged capital investments, but gave comparatively little attention to legislation which would have helped the great masses of rural folk and townspeople.

By the turn of the century many of the Bourbons, or Confederate Brigadiers, as southern political leaders were sometimes called, were passing from the political scene, but their places were being taken by men just as conservative and just as responsive to vested interests. In 1897 the Choctaw Club of New Orleans, a group of professional and semiprofessional politicians dedicated to the control of city and parish politics, was organized and from 1900 to 1924 supported the successful gubernatorial campaigns of Heard, Blanchard, Sanders, Pleasant, and Fuqua. During their campaigns these men promised liberal reforms but, with the exception of Blanchard, after the election accomplished little beyond economy in government, the maintenance of white supremacy and the retention of the political control by the upper economic groups. Louisiana, like some of her sister southern states, continued to lag behind the rest of the Union.

During this era there began to arise in the South a group of political leaders generally known as "Dixie Demagogues," who, as historian Francis Butler Simkins wrote, led "the great masses of the poorer whites who had nothing to ship by classified rates and no insurance policies to bother about," but who also possessed the ballot and who "in a blind sort of way wished to express their grievances against the rich man above them and the Negro below them. They turned to leaders who were willing to pander to their pride and their prejudices." These leaders realized that they represented a much wider cross section of the body politic than did those leaders then in power. This movement found its culmination in Louisiana in the rise of Huey P. Long, who has been credited by some historians as "the most famous of the group."

After 1920 the people of Louisiana became intensely interested in political issues, joined political factions, and actively campaigned for their chosen candidates. Candidates for office promised more and more reforms, the great majority of which would improve the living standards and general welfare of the farmer and the working classes of society. Voters began to forget the old heroes of Civil War days, as political leaders found new causes for political revolutions every four years and promised additional largesses. Many of their proposed reforms became realities; there were better roads and bridges, better elementary schools, high schools, and colleges, better hospitals, better institutions for the deaf, dumb, and blind, and improved mental and penal institutions. Great sums were poured into public health and welfare and pensions for the aged. The movement which began in 1920 with John M. Parker and which was continued after 1928 by Huey P. Long is still in active progress, and the state is performing services never dreamed of by political leaders a generation ago. And more and more the people of Louisiana have come to expect and even to demand additional appropriations for these services with each new governor.

The political issues were obvious: roads, education, social welfare, labor, taxes, the proper use of natural resources, and the relative power and authority of the governor, the legislature, and local government officials. Political factions and their leaders have disagreed about these issues. Over them, bitter battles have been fought; because of them, political leaders have risen to positions of influence which not all of them were able to retain. The Louisiana Negro, unlike the Negro of other southern states, was not used as a political issue and although he benefited from the extensive social legislation took little interest in politics. As late as 1940, when there were over 700,000 white registrants, there were fewer than 1,000 Negroes registered to vote; the Negro in Louisiana politics has become an important issue only since that time. During the years after 1920, Louisiana became one of the most politically conscious states of the Union and its government one of the most highly politicalized. Politics has been a constant, ever-present force in modern Louisiana life.

GOVERNORS PARKER, FUQUA, AND SIMPSON. The progressive pattern of the modern era had begun to manifest itself during the late years of the preceding period and fundamental beginnings were made during the first eight years after 1920. By 1928 the political kaleidoscope of the past thirty years had achieved maturity.

John M. Parker emerged as a political leader during the campaign of 1912, was defeated for the governorship in 1916, and was elected after a bitter campaign in 1920 against the Old Regular candidate Colonel Frank P. Stubbs. A so-called "gentlemanly reformer," Parker and his leaders made plans for a constitutional convention, a new state university, a state highway system, new Civil Service and social legislation, and other much-needed reforms. But the Governor disagreed with several of the factional leaders who had supported him, particularly over the highway program and Civil Service proposals, mishandled the natural-gas-production problems, and failed in his campaign promise to furnish New Orleans with cheap supplies of natural gas. Though only a part of his over-all legislative program succeeded, tremendous progress was made. However, Parker had seemingly not been aware of some of the fundamental issues which had only recently emerged, and the vested interests had generally been successful in opposing his program for larger appropriations for state institutions and for severance taxation.

One of Parker's 1920-campaign platform planks had been the calling of a constitutional convention; such a convention met at Baton Rouge in March, 1921. The 146 delegates represented a fair cross section of state political leadership; included were 2 former governors—Pleasant and Sanders—and 3 women. The new constitution was generally statutory in nature, so much so that twenty-four delegates protested that it was "a long and cumbersome constitution containing matter legislative in character." Others charged that it had been dictated in part by special and vested interests. It completely satisfied only a few members of the convention, and some refused to sign the completed document. It was Louisiana's tenth constitution and presently is the longest state constitution in the nation. In 1954 it ran to over 550 pages, with over 125 pages of index, and included over 325 amendments.

The constitution's most significant sections dealt with the reorganization of the judiciary, the creation of an improved roads system, a revision of the suffrage, some reorganization of secondary and higher education, and the addition of three executive officials—the commissioner of agriculture and immigration, the register of the land office, and the commissioner of conservation. It also provided for a severance tax and for a state income tax. Some Louisianians believed that the Constitution of 1921 was too conservative, others that it was too progressive. Regardless of these extreme opinions, its liberal features indicated the growth of liberal political tendencies and made possible much of the legislation which has been enacted since its adoption. Many present-day political leaders believe that it has outlived its usefulness and that a new constitution should be drafted.

Despite the fact that many modern Louisianians, because of the later and more spectacular gains of Huey P. Long, have overlooked the work of John M. Parker, it must not be forgotten that he was the real "trail-blazer," the "pathfinder," the "father" of modern Louisiana, for it was Parker who made plans for a new State University, hauled agriculture out of its doldrums of half a century, began to lift Louisiana out of the mud through the foundation of a state highway system, conceived the idea of securing larger state revenues to finance greater services to the people from severance, income and gasoline taxation and other untapped income-producing sources, and led the first fight in the reform of the civil service, the executive branch, and other divisions of state government. A Louisiana statesman has recently written that "the foundations he laid, and advocated, remain today. They are his monuments."

The gubernatorial campaign of 1924 was a rousing one. Three candidates entered the first primary-election campaign: Henry L. Fuqua, manager of the state penitentiary and the personal selection of former Governor Sanders and the Old Regular organization of New Orleans; Lieutenant Governor Hewitt Bouanchaud, who had the support of Governor Parker and the so-called "New Regulars"; and young Huey Pierce Long, Chairman of the Public Service Commission. Long attacked the corporate interests; pointed to his record against the gas, oil, and utility companies; pledged good roads, free textbooks for secondary schools, free fishing, and free trapping; and made other tangible appeals to the common people. He ran third in the primary but received the majority vote in twenty-one parishes and a plurality in seven. In the runoff, with Long remaining silent, Fuqua won by over 30,000 votes.

Henry L. Fuqua served until his death on October 1, 1926, and was succeeded by Lieutenant Governor Oramel H. Simpson. During their administrations the legislature enacted anti-Ku Klux Klan measures which outlawed all types of hoods, masks, or robes, excepting only those worn at Mardi Gras time or at masked balls or parties. A toll bridge east of New Orleans across Lake Pontchartrain was authorized, as was the construction of the first buildings at the new State University south of Baton Rouge. However, little fundamental legislation for the benefit of the working classes was passed. Late in 1926, Simpson, who had strong ambitions to be elected Governor in his own right, began to create a patronage organization in preparation for the campaign of 1928.

The campaign of 1928 was the most significant in Louisiana history after that of 1876 and was far-reaching in both its immediate and long-term results. The New Regulars of New Orleans and widely scattered groups throughout the state supported Governor Simpson. The New Orleans Choctaws and other conservatives backed Congressman Riley J. Wilson. Huey Long, meanwhile, had mended his political fences, had completed a loosely knit organization, and had grown into a master politician. While he generally conducted an "anti-campaign" against his opponents and the corporate interests, he renewed his active support of those individual benefits to the common man for which he had fought during the campaign of 1924.

Long was the most active of the candidates. He constantly toured the state, speaking and organizing the farmer and working classes against the wealthy and politically powerful groups which had formerly controlled the state government, against what Hodding Carter has called "the political and economic ducks which were not only sitting but anchored in a bayou of special privilege." He spoke the language of the country people when in country precincts and the language of town and city dwellers when speaking in their communities. He spoke in hamlets where a speech by a candidate for governor had never been heard. His most noted speech of the entire campaign was supposedly given at St. Martinville, at the Evangeline Oak, where he bitterly attacked the old conservative and nonprogressive governing interests:

> Evangeline is not the only one who has waited here in disappointment. Where are the schools that you have waited for your children to have that have never come? Where are the roads and the highways that you spent your money to build, that are no nearer now than ever before? Where are the institutions to care for the sick and the disabled? Evangeline wept bitter tears in her disappointment. But they lasted through only one lifetime. Your tears in this country, around this oak, have lasted for generations. Give me the chance to dry the tears of those who still weep here.

Historian Allan P. Sindler has written that the Evangeline Oak speech "served to fix the campaign of 1928 as the culmination of the class struggle in Louisiana."

As the days and weeks passed, Long further matured as a hard-hitting, crowd-pleasing campaigner. He called people by their first names. He paused during his speeches to recognize old friends and acquaintances whom he spotted in the audience. He buttressed arguments for his social- and public-welfare program with well-chosen Biblical quotations and with excerpts from the speeches of American statesmen. He developed an art of speechmaking which delighted the people by its humorous attacks on his opponents. Everyone laughed with him when he walked mincingly across crudely built platforms, explaining that he had finally saved enough money to buy a new pair of shoes, and that his feet hurt. Parish and local leaders began to join him. He led in the first primary election with nearly 127,000 votes to Wilson's nearly 82,000 and Simpson's slightly over 80,000. When Wilson found that he could not secure the unified support of the Simpson faction, he withdrew from the second primary and Long became the Democratic candidate, which was equivalent to election, without the necessity of a runoff campaign.

Sindler suggests that "the fact that Simpson later accepted a $5,000 per year state attorneyship from Governor Long provides the best explanation" for the failure of the Simpson faction to promise support to Wilson in the second primary campaign. It must be remembered, therefore, that Long secured the governorship through a first primary vote of 126,842 against the combined vote given Wilson and Simpson of 162,073.

HUEY LONG. In his inaugural address, Governor Long pleaded for harmony and progress: "I know that there is honor, valor, energy, capacity and wealth in our great state which, properly co-ordinated, guarantees prosperity to our commonwealth, and then, through them, we may be a happy and contented people, all blessed with the comforts, conveniences and with some of the luxuries of this life, in a land where there can be every cause for friendliness and good fellowship to abound." The heritage of Louisiana's past offered the political opportunity; the man and the hour had met.

Long had carried with him into state office only Lieutenant Governor Paul Cyr and Treasurer H. B. Conner. Only eighteen members of the house of representatives and nine members of the senate had supported his candidacy for governor. Undaunted, he plunged into his legislative program and secured cheaper gas for New Orleans, the enactment of a free-textbook law for elementary and high schools whether private, parochial, or public, the passage of a constitutional amendment authorizing a

$30,000,000 bond issue for roads and bridges, the reduction of property assessments, free night schools for adult illiterates, the right to vote without payment of poll taxes, increased appropriations for the State University, and other progressive measures.

The people of Louisiana may have expected, as southern historian Francis Butler Simkins wrote, " an unconventional regime, but the reality which evolved was beyond all expectations. The Kingfish—as Long was dubbed—administered shock after shock, adding discomfort to confusion, and flouting the traditions of an ordinarily dignified office." He soon gained control of the patronage and as Senator Overton later admitted: ". . . ousted and kept out of power and continued until his death to keep out of power the political lords of the old regime."

Long called a special session of the legislature in December, 1928, to enact highway legislation made possible by the ratification of a constitutional amendment. Made unduly overconfident by his extraordinary success in gaining complete control of this session, he broke with Lieutenant Governor Cyr and Colonel John P. Sullivan of the New Orleans Choctaw faction. Forces began to unite against him at the special session of March, 1929, which Long had called to enact a tax on refined crude oil. The Governor was expelled from the house of representatives because of his personal lobbying tactics, he was accused by Lieutenant Governor Cyr of signing oil leases which were disadvantageous to the state, his attempted intimidation of Baton Rouge newspaper editor Charles Manship was exposed, and on March 22 the Shreveport *Journal* called for an investigation and possible impeachment.

The clamor for impeachment grew. On March 27 the *Times-Picayune* argued that "he is temperamentally and otherwise unfit to hold the office. His tactics and methods reveal him to be a cruel political tyrant, willing to resort to almost any expedience to carry out his own wishes and purposes." Nineteen general articles of impeachment were brought against him, of which a few less than half were voted by the house and sent to the senate. In the senate fifteen of the thirty-nine members soon signed the celebrated round robin, which simply stated that because "of the unconstitutionality and invalidity of all impeachment charges against Huey P. Long, Governor," they would not vote for conviction. In view of the fact that a two-thirds vote was required in the senate, the movement against the Governor had failed. Long had won the most significant victory of his career—a victory which had been won because fifteen members of the senate had refused even to "hear" the evidence which had prompted the charges voted by the house of representatives.

He now shifted his political machine into high gear. The Governor rapidly gained control of one state agency after another. John H. Overton charged that there "then began that ruthless warfare against Governor Long that is perhaps without a parallel in the history of our Government. Almost every conceivable attempt was made to discredit him and his administration." On the other hand, the Governor was not at all averse to using whatever tactics he might think necessary to beat down state-level or local opposition or to keep in line officeholders, appointees, and legislators who developed weak spines or hides or who might even be considering joining the opposition. The bitterest period in Louisiana personal politics since the days of the Radicals of 1868 to 1877 existed from this time to the day of Long's death.

Long became a candidate for the United States Senate in 1930 and defeated incumbent Joseph E. Ransdell by 38,000 votes, carrying 53 parishes. Lieutenant Governor Cyr now insisted that Long's position as Governor and Senator-elect was illegal and had himself sworn in as Governor by a Shreveport notary in October, 1930. Long promptly informed him that by this action he had forfeited his own position, and had the president pro tempore of the senate, Alvin King, sworn in as Governor. The State Supreme Court, in what Cortez Ewing called "one of the most bizarre decisions in American Judicial history," declared that it lacked jurisdiction in the matter, the case was dropped, and King completed Long's term as Governor. Long did not take his senatorial oath until January 26, 1932.

Oscar K. Allen, supported by Long, South Louisiana politician Dudley J. LeBlanc,

George S. Guion (with Long's younger brother Earl K. Long as his running mate), William C. Boone, and William L. Clark, Jr., were the gubernatorial candidates in 1932 and Allen won the election with 56.5 per cent of the total votes cast. He served until his death on January 29, 1936, and was succeeded by president pro tempore of the senate James A. Noe, Lieutenant Governor John B. Fournet having been elected to the State Supreme Court.

Long soon acquired a national reputation in the United States Senate through his independent actions and skill as a debater, although his friend John H. Overton later admitted that he "put through to final passage no bill or measure." He had supported Franklin D. Roosevelt in 1932, but it was impossible for two such politically ambitious men to long remain in agreement over basic issues or even to remain compatible. In the spring of 1932, Long had initiated his "Share-Our-Wealth" program, which brought him thousands of supporting letters from the poorer elements of American society and subscriptions for his *American Progress,* and by February, 1935, claimed to have organized Share-Our-Wealth clubs over the entire nation.* The Roosevelt regime began its attacks on Long in late 1933 and appropriated many of Long's social-welfare programs; Long retaliated by dubbing the President "Prince Franklin, Knight of the *Nourmahal*" (the private yacht of millionaire Vincent Astor), and by withdrawing his support of New Deal banking, agricultural, and economy measures.

But "The Kingfish," as he liked to term himself, kept close watch and a tight control over Louisiana. His enemies said: "L'état, c'est Huey," and with justification, for by this time he was the acknowledged dictator of the state. The members of the state militia and the Bureau of Identification were called "Huey's Cossacks." One critic charged that at this time he had the "highest degree of state control ever recorded under America's democratic form of government." He rode herd on each session of the legislature, alternately sitting on the steps in front of the two chambers, speaking quietly with members as they came forward for orders and smilingly nodding here and there to his floor leaders.

Material progress throughout the state continued. By 1935 there were 2,446 miles of concrete highways, 1,308 miles of asphalt roads, and nearly 10,000 miles of graveled roads under state maintenance, in sharp contrast to the 296; 35; and 5,728 miles in 1928. A 34-storied, 450-foot-high state capitol had been built to replace the old structure so ridiculed by Mark Twain. A new executive mansion, which Francis Simkins described as "a cross between a museum and a post office," had been completed. New life had been pumped into the State University. Plans were complete for a new Charity Hospital. Welfare institutions of every sort were appearing over the entire state.

To his followers Long was a dedicated leader of the "forgotten man"; he was idolized by the "Have-nots"; and as Allen Sindler wrote, he was "unofficially canonized" by devoted Catholic followers—after his death they included in the personal columns of the *Times-Picayune* such notices as "thanks to St. Peter, St. Joseph . . . St. Huey." It may be, as John Temple Graves has written, that "the King's English was for him something to be killed in the presence of those sweating masses whom he promised to make kings." The fact remains, however, that to these "sweating masses" he was one of their very own, when on March 5, 1935, he said in the United States Senate:

---

* Long's "Share-Our-Wealth" program was first announced in the *Times-Picayune* of February 22, 1928. Some critics claim that the genesis of the idea came from a booklet titled *Issues of the Day—Free Speech—Financial Slavery,* published by State Senator S. J. Harper in 1918. The *Louisiana Progress* first appeared on March 27, 1930, featuring the acid and effective cartoons of Trist Wood, and was published irregularly until on August 24, 1933, it became the *American Progress,* which finally suspended publication in February, 1940. It is significant that Long never attempted to establish the "Share-Our-Wealth" program in Louisiana, the one state over which he held dictatorial control.

Mr. President, I am not undertaking to answer the charge that I am ignorant. It is true. I am an ignorant man. I have had no college education. I have not even had a highschool education. But the thing that takes me far in politics is that I do not have to color what comes into my mind and into my heart. I say it unvarnished. I say it without veneer. I know the hearts of the people because I have not colored my own. I know when I am right in my own conscience. I do not talk one way in the cloakroom and another way out here. I do not talk one way back there in the hills of Louisiana and another way here in the Senate. I have one language. Ignorant as it is, it is the universal language of the sphere in which I operate. Its simplicity gains pardon for my lack of letters and education.

Nevertheless my voice will be the same as it has been. Patronage will not change it. Fear will not change it. Persecution will not change it. It cannot be changed while people suffer. The only way it can be changed is to make the lives of these people decent and respectable. No one will ever hear political opposition out of me when that is done.

Contrary to Long's protestations, however, that he was "an ignorant man," that he had "had no college education," that he had "not even had a high school education," the fact remains that he was not an ignorant nor an uneducated man. He had attended Winnfield and Shreveport high schools, for a year had been a student at the University of Oklahoma, and frequently boasted that he had completed a three-year law course at Tulane University in one year, after which he was admitted to the Louisiana bar.

LONG'S ASSASSINATION AND PLACE IN LOUISIANA HISTORY. But Huey Long's course was about run. Back in Louisiana his attempt to secure control of poll commissioners brought forth a prophetic statement from Mason Spencer, a northeast Louisiana legislator: "I am not gifted with second sight. Nor did I see a spot of blood on the moon last night. But I can see blood on the polished floor of this Capitol. For if you ride this thing through, you will travel with the white horse of death. White men have ever made poor slaves."

In early September, 1935, Long hurried home from Washington to be on hand for the year's fourth special session of the legislature, and on Friday night, September 6, scattered a broadside over the entire state. The heading read: "They Must Come To The Mark. . . . In the land of plenty there can be no justification for starvation, nakedness or homelessness"; on the reverse side of the one-page sheet was the bold-face line: "What Is It They Want To Undo?" On Sunday night, September 8, Long was assassinated in a corridor of the State Capitol. His alleged assassin, Dr. Carl A. Weiss, Jr., of Baton Rouge, was riddled with over sixty bullets by Long's bodyguards.

The political leader was given five blood transfusions but steadily lost ground. Shortly before midnight on September 9, he roused, murmured softly, "I wonder what will happen to my poor university boys," and lapsed into unconsciousness. He died a few minutes after 4 A.M. on September 10, and moments later Governor Allen issued the statement: "This marks with the death of Huey P. Long the passing of the greatest builder of economics in the history of Louisiana in 225 years. It also marks the passing of the greatest hero for the common right of all the people of America."

To those who had opposed his dictatorship, no such sentiments were possible. One of his opponents later wrote: "If I were to say now, or if I had written then, that Long's death distressed me, I'd be lying. As an abstract political or moral principle, assassination cannot be defended. But if ever a tyrant invited death, Huey Long did." There is no doubt but that the personal traits which had led to his meteoric career were in the end responsible for his death.

The Senator was buried on September 12. That night a young history instructor at Louisiana State University wrote to his family: "Late this afternoon as the sun was dipping low on the western horizon across the placid, muddy ripples of the Father of Waters, Huey Pierce Long, United States Senator, Dictator Extraordinary, and self-styled 'Kingfish' of Louisiana, was lowered slowly into his grave in the beautiful sunken garden in front of his greatest building achievement, the thirty-four storied state capitol of his empire. His beloved Louisiana State University cadet band played with muffled drum beat and in funeral march time his own composition 'Every Man a King,' while the Reverend Gerald L. K. Smith, the leader of his 'Share-Our-Wealth' movement, preached a brief, eloquent sermon. Countless thousands of people, most of whom were his followers, stood with bared heads, many with tear-moistened eyes, as they watched their fallen leader return to earth. Overhead, airplanes looked down upon a spectacle unique in the annals of American history."

The anti-Long press wrote that the city of Baton Rouge "took on a holiday attire," that "people were dressed as if for a gala occasion," and that there was little sign of "deep feeling." However, there was little basis for such statements, although the young instructor noticed "only two flags at half-mast" in the city. He continued that most of the thousands who attended the funeral were from rural and small-town areas "and their actions told a mute story of their affections for their fallen leader." He overheard a little boy say: "What are we going to do for school books now?"

His observations reveal the intense drama of that September day: ". . . the capitol building pointing upward into a cloudless sky; the people, many of whom have waited all night that they might have the opportunity of seeing their leader buried; an old man, standing with bared head just as the casket came out the capitol door, saying in no uncertain terms to a middle-aged country yokel, 'Take off your hat'; a young mother snatching a blossom from a funeral wreath and saying, 'I'm going to put this in my baby's memory book'; two fellows talking, one of whom was remarking, 'I'm damn glad he's planted'; . . . a twelve year old boy selling coca-cola and doing a nice business; a family of negroes, the mother silently weeping; a tall, ruddy-faced state policeman with tears rolling down his cheeks; . . . a woman remarking to her husband, 'I know a lot of people who would have liked to have come but who had no transportation.' Upon which the man replied, 'If Huey had been living he would have got them here!'; a chartered bus driver remarking 'Why they're all here I don't know'; . . . the flowers that covered the sunken garden, a space about 60 to 75 by 200 feet; . . . the face of Long composed and natural but shaded too white from the tint of the powder used; the casket, plain and simple; . . . a man with a half-empty beer bottle in each hand."

Near the end of his description he wrote, significantly: "It is impossible to predict just what the political reaction will be. The Long machine is now firmly entrenched but with four or five leaders, coming from different parts of the state, clamouring for power it is to be doubted that the machine will hold up under fire for any great length of time. Already some are backing away and are making overtures to the Roosevelt government. . . . The Long job-holders are fighting for those jobs and the 'outs' are fighting to dislodge the 'ins.' . . . The editorial tonight . . . made perfectly plain that the Long regime must be wiped out."

Huey Long had fostered much liberal legislation, and under his leadership Louisiana had emerged a progressive state. It must be realized, however, that other leaders would also have forged ahead, for progress was a sign of the times. Was Long's program, either in whole or in part, the outgrowth of his personal political philosophy or was it the practical application of shrewd political leadership in a state during the early years of the Great Depression? How much of his program would have succeeded had it not been for the fact that many Louisianians were sorely beset by the want and uncertainty of depression years? Did his program assist in mitigating the effects of the depression in Louisiana and, if so, to what extent? Future research will do much in answering these and other questions pertinent to his regime.

Was Long's over-all leadership of Louisiana good or bad? A historian recently wrote that "he may have done a lot to jerk the state into the 20th century." A critic admitted that "he gave the people what he had promised them and this was unique in

Louisiana history." Allen Ellender wrote that "if dictatorship in Louisiana, such as was charged to Huey Long, will give to the people of our nation what it gave to the people of my native state, then I am for such a dictatorship." Liberal Hodding Carter later admitted that "I know now that part of our failure arose from an unwillingness to approve any Long-sponsored proposal for change, regardless of its merits."

On May 28, 1959, Sam H. Jones, the reform governor of 1940 to 1944, speaking at a New Orleans Junior Chamber of Commerce–Louisiana Civil Service League memorial luncheon honoring the late civil service crusader Charles E. Dunbar, Jr., summarized the Long era:

> We had spawned a weird, governmental monstrosity. . . . It grew, thrived on the most bizarre methods and the wildest propaganda, had a wild and hectic career, and finally was halted and brought down in its tracks by an aroused and courageous citizenship. . . .
> The right of free elections was wiped out and the absolute control thereof was given to the leader of one political faction. Freedom of the press was attacked by a law that had to be declared unconstitutional by the United States Supreme Court. Freedom of assembly vanished. And laws were passed that were never read by the Legislature and many of which were revised, if not entirely written, after the adjournment of the law-making body. . . .
> Public records were closed to the public. The State Police became the law of the land, with authority to supersede any and all local enforcement officers; to arrest citizens on political charges and transport them to distant jails beyond the reach of friends . . . without benefit of bail by any court, and subject only to release by the head of the State Police. Martial law was imposed on the state capitol for six months at one time, when there was no disaster, no riot, no rebellion and no strife . . . and hence no justification.
> It was a reign of tyranny. Political opponents in many cases had to meet, clandestinely, under the cover of darkness to exercise their rights as American citizens. We lived under a government which had the power to make and break banks . . . or by spite and vengeance, to drive industry out of the state . . . or catapult it to fabulous wealth as it chose. This was a government which, by whim and caprice, denied men and women the right to practice their trades and professions . . . or by favoritism granted such rights without regard to qualification or ability.
> It was a government which held the destinies of private citizens in its hands, with no less power than that exercised by the totalitarian states in the days prior to World War II. . . .
> The State, itself, fell to the lowest depths in public esteem it has ever occupied in all history. And when the end finally came, it came with defeats and debacles and bankruptcies and indictments and suicides and scandals.

To many national leaders, as to Jonathan Daniels, Huey Long's Louisiana was simply "a Caribbean republic"; to William A. Percy of Mississippi, he was "a moral idiot of genius." Others thrilled to his political daredevilry and forgave "his bad manners as irrelevant in the face of many constructive achievements." A few laughed at his antics, and it was Will Rogers who wrote after Long's all-night filibuster in the Senate that "he pulled the biggest and most educational novelty ever introduced into the Senate. He read 'em the Constitution of the United States. A lot of 'em thought he was reviewing a new book." Long once wrote his wife: "I wonder if the people will ever realize and appreciate what I am trying to do?" A recent appraisal is that "probably the best evaluation of him is to say he was not half as good as his friends would have you believe, and not half as bad as his enemies would want you to believe."

Whatever the individual contemporary or present-day judgments of Huey Long, had a majority of Louisianians actually accepted, in the words of one political writer, "the strong man who promises the filled stomach and vengeance, bread and circuses and a top place for the bottom rail?" Late in 1939 a Gallup poll asked the question of Louisianians: "Taking everything into consideration, do you think that Huey P. Long was a bad or good influence in Louisiana?" And of those who replied 55 per cent said that Long had been a "good influence."

It is still too early for the historian or political scientist to accurately evaluate the man or his age. The passions are still too deeply fixed in Louisiana, where men either hate or revere his memory. The generation who fought with him or who fought against him, and their children, and possibly their children's children, must pass from the scene before anything approaching an impartial, critical appraisal can be written. Any biography before such time shall pass may be well filled with anecdotes, and they are innumerable, and may give an excellent running narrative of day-by-day events, but the biographer can never properly appraise the man or the good or bad over-all influence he had upon Louisiana. The final judgments can only be made by the long, merciless tests of history.

GOVERNOR LECHE AND THE "LOUISIANA SCANDALS." A Texas legislator once remarked that Huey Long was like a mule—"without pride of ancestry or hope of posterity." A more incorrect political evaluation was never made, for at Long's death in 1935 he left a numerous and politically active progeny; many of his descendants were already occupying important political offices, and they and others would be a vital and important force in Louisiana politics for the next quarter of a century. These men soon divided into two warring camps. One group, headed by Acting Lieutenant Governor James A. Noe, favored carrying on the late Senator's Share-Our-Wealth, anti-New Deal, and economic programs; the other, dominated by Seymour Weiss, Robert Maestri, Abe Shushan, and a few others, favored the swift restoration of harmony with the Roosevelt government, Louisiana business interests, and many of Senator Long's former political enemies.

The election of 1936 saw the beginning of the period in Louisiana politics which has continued to the present day, for in second-primary campaigns the factions have generally lined up on two sides, one group composed of former followers of Huey Long and the other of those who opposed him or his principles or his methods. These two factions have campaigned in each election since 1936; in many first-primary elections, however, they have split into smaller groups.

Richard W. Leche, a minor member of the top echelon of Long leaders, became the standard bearer in 1936, with Earl K. Long as his running mate, and was elected over Cleveland Dear by slightly more than 67 per cent of the votes cast. Leche soon made peace with Roosevelt, and the Justice Department shortly thereafter abandoned its tax prosecution of Abe Shushan, Seymour Weiss, Jules Fisher, and other Long leaders. In return for the new "hands-off" policy of the Federal government toward Louisiana, Leche and his group co-operated with Roosevelt's highly politicalized manipulation of construction and relief funds in the state.

The Leche group soon began an orgy of political malfeasance and governmental graft in office which more than faintly resembled the administration of Warmoth and Kellogg. Huey Long was reputed to have once said that "if those fellows ever try to use the powers I've given them without me to hold them down, they'll all land in the penitentiary." Legislators were placed on governmental payrolls, small percentages were deducted from the checks of state and local government departmental workers, and the Director of Charity Hospital began to deduct $2.00 from hospital employees' checks to pay for subscriptions to the *American Progress*. Building supplies disappeared, as did state-owned livestock.

Leche held the legislature under tight control, and the senate once completely reversed a vote of 24 to 9 on a measure to 25 to 2 when it accidently discovered that the first vote had been contrary to the Governor's wishes. The *Times-Picayune* reported that St. Mary Parish Representative C. R. Brownell admitted that "our present policy seems to be to raise salaries, add taxes, increase appropriations, entertain endowments and memorials and buy real estate. Let's ride high, wide and handsome—on with the dance. Who pays?"

The storm broke on June 25, 1939, when Louisiana State University President James Monroe Smith resigned and disappeared. It was found that he had misused several hundred thousands of dollars of University funds. Governor Leche resigned the next day, the first Louisiana Governor to resign from office, and was succeeded by Lieutenant Governor Earl K. Long. Four suicides followed the exposures, and between July, 1939, and November, 1940, there were almost 50 indictments involving nearly 150 persons and more than 40 organizations and business firms on charges of the use of WPA labor and theft of material, income-tax evasion, mail fraud, "hot oil," violations of the antitrust laws, "kick-backs," and conspiracy to defraud. Nearly 50 years of imprisonment and a total of over $60,000 in fines were pronounced and imposed against 51 persons and 17 firms. Governor Leche, President Smith, and several others were given prison sentences.

The "Louisiana Scandals" of 1939 shocked the entire nation and led Allan Sindler to write later: "The seeds of Huey Long thus bore bitter fruit in the Scandals of Dick Leche. The heirs of the Kingfish, inheriting his power and class support, solidified factional control by making peace with federal and state opposition, and then proceeded to conduct the affairs of government as a plunderbund."

The candidates in the first-primary election of 1940 were Earl K. Long, anti-Long reformer and Lake Charles lawyer Sam H. Jones, former Long leader James A. Noe, and minor candidates James H. Morrison and Henry V. Moseley. Earl Long castigated "High Hat Sam, the High Society Kid, the High-Kickin', High and Mighty Snide Sam, the guy that pumps perfume under his arms." Noe claimed to be a reformer who had hoped to clean up the post-Huey Long mess and that he had fought Leche in 1936. Morrison toured the state with a monkey which he called "Earl Long" and a "convict" parade, violently attacking Leche and Earl Long as men of the same stamp. Jones promised to clean house and argued that he was "not running against a dead man, I am running against a gang of rascals as live as any gang that that ever lived."

Earl Long led in the first primary with nearly 41 per cent of the votes to 28 per cent for Jones and 21 per cent for Noe. In the second primary Jones won over Long by 19,000 votes, gaining almost 52 per cent of the total votes cast. Strangely enough, while Long received a majority of the New Orleans vote, he failed to win a majority in rural areas.

YEARS OF REFORM AND "HARMONY," 1940-48. The legislature passed most of the Jones reform program, and House Speaker Norman Bauer praised the new order when he wrote: "There is a vast distinction between receiving the recommendations of the governor with an open mind . . . and servilely accepting, without due consideration, a legislative program inimical to the interests of a free people we are sworn to serve." Many phases of government were returned to local governmental units. More than a hundred state agencies were removed from the control of the governor. A Civil Service system was adopted for state employees. Legislation restricted payroll padding, deductions, dual jobholding, and other such practices.

The Long faction immediately began a counterattack, much of it through the courts, and steadily chopped away at the Jones program. By 1942, the prosecution of Long faction political malefactors by the attorney general had slowed up, and the New Orleans *States* was protesting that the promises "to prosecute all thieves are not being kept." By that time, too, the United States had entered World War II and people had become more interested in the progress of the war than in state politics. During the rest of his term Jones "held the line," while the Long forces continued to harry the administration at every opportunity.

Jones failed to build a strong anti-Long reform political organization, for he was not a natural politician and could never have become a political hero to the masses of the people. This he admitted when he said that he was not Governor because he wanted "hooray and applause. I'm Governor because someone had to clean up the mess that Huey and his successors left." But the mess had not been completely cleaned up and many local political situations could have been favorably compared with those of Plaquemines and St. Bernard parishes, where the reformers said: *"Le Politique . . . She Stink, She Stink!"* The Governor, however, had done his best in this area of reform and critics of the administration were overlooking the traditional American separation of authority between state and local government, the sometimes "brazen defiance of state authority," and the judicial rulings of certain local courts.

In the late fall of 1943 Jones was ready to make his "Report to the People." In a series of ten radio talks, he reviewed his campaign pledges and his accomplishments. He emphasized benefits and services to the citizenry, public construction, business, agricultural and educational improvements, natural resources and efficient governmental practices. The statehouse dictatorship had been abolished, the legislative branch of the government again occupied its proper place in an American democratic state, and the general reform movement had been projected for the future. The Governor pointed with pride to the fulfillment of practically all of his campaign pledges and closed his last address with the words: "I have kept the faith. I have fought the good fight." Despite the criticism of opponents and arguments of detractors, a modern historian of the period has called him "The Liberator of Louisiana."

Had it not been for World War II, everyone would have enjoyed the campaign of 1944. It would have been a rousing one, but because of the war it was one of the quietest campaigns in recent times, even though eight candidates were seeking the office of governor. James H. Davis, Public Service Commission member and recent City Commissioner of Shreveport, received the blessing of a majority of the reformers. He conducted a "happy" campaign, complete with satisfying speeches, music and song, for he "just wasn't mad at anybody" and stood on a platform with which few voters could find fault. Other "reform" candidates were Henry Vincent Mosley, Amite newspaper editor Lee Lanier, and Mayor of Shreveport Sam Caldwell. A large group of the Long faction supported Lewis Morgan of St. Tammany Parish, who had the blessing of Robert S. Maestri and Earl K. Long for his running mate. Congressman James H. Morrison adopted a "reform" platform which contained many of Morgan's planks, and claimed to be an independent independent. Former Conservation Commissioner Ernest Clements claimed to be the only true follower of Huey Long, but like Morrison added little to Morgan's platform, while Dudley J. LeBlanc guaranteed the voter a full life from cradle to grave without cost or physical effort.

After the votes were counted the anti-Long forces had little reason to relax, for although Davis polled nearly 35 per cent of the votes, Morgan had received 27.5 per cent and Morrison almost 16 per cent. During the runoff campaign between Davis and Morgan, the Long faction was joined by several of the "independent" groups and even by a few "reformers." Davis won the runoff election by only a few more than 30,000 votes, or 53.6 per cent to 46.4 per cent of the votes cast.

The reformers hailed the election as "a great victory for clean government," and Jones bragged with considerable truth that it marked "the first time in forty years that an independent governor has been succeeded in office by an independent governor." But a reaction to "reformism" set in during the following four years, greatly encouraged by the irresponsibility of the legislature and by the rise and effectiveness of pressure groups. Davis was accused of exerting too little executive leadership in state government activities, particularly in the legislature, and "legislative irresponsibility apparently increased in direct proportion to the availability of surplus funds" as annual treasury surpluses helped in part to lead to well-planned and well-organized raids by the education and other pressure groups. But the intense bifactional politics of former years gradually subsided, and at the close of one legislative session Davis left the chamber to the accompaniment of accolades and cheers.

There were few attempts at further extensive reforms, but Davis kept those which had been initiated by his predecessor. His 1944-46 biennial budget exceeded that of 1942-44 by $16,000,000 and totaled nearly $200,000,000. Owing to the war there was a lack of labor and material, which prevented a building program. Despite the sniping of political opponents, "there were elements of strength in the Davis performance never clearly realized" by even the reformers or by the citizenry of the state. His plan to create a sort of "trust fund" with the surplus was defeated in the house of representatives and only through the occasional use of the veto power was he able to keep a balanced budget and at the same time increase teachers' salaries, extend state payments to education, allocate additional highway funds to parishes, raise salaries of state officials, extend the statewide drainage system, establish a state retirement system, and again provide tax exemptions for new industry entering the state. The administration of penal and health institutions was separated and his defense of labor caused a labor leader in 1952 to call him "the best Governor Louisiana labor ever had." The most important of his proposed constitutional amendments in 1944 and 1946 were ratified. The Governor, along with ex-Governor Sam Jones, supported the New Orleans Independence Citizens Committee, which, during the mayoralty campaign of 1946, secured the election of reform candidate deLesseps S. Morrison over Mayor Robert S. Maestri and the Regulars.

REACTION AND AGAIN REFORM. The gubernatorial election of 1948 was in many ways one of the most befuddling in recent Louisiana history. The one-man government practices of the Huey Long period and the scandals of his immediate successors had led in 1940 to an eight-year period of reform and return to somewhat normal government. A rapidly increasing state-taxation program had provided increased funds for all state departments, for the pressure groups, and for public welfare in general. With almost every Louisianian enjoying the benefits of war and postwar prosperity, why kick the "rascals" out? Politics, however, is almost completely unpredictable at times, and the body politic indeed has a short memory.

Sam Jones again entered the lists, reviewed the scandals of 1939, pointed with pride to the accomplishments of 1940-48, and insisted that the major issue was "progress or depravity." James H. Morrison attempted to become the leading Longite candidate and secured considerable support from the Old Regulars. Judge Robert F. Kennon believed that he was the only true leader of reform, attacked all his opponents, including Jones, and did much to divide the anti-Long faction.

It was Earl K. Long, however, who touched the match to the campaign. He charged Jones and Davis with "do-nothingism" and pledged what his opponents called "do-everythingism," for he guaranteed $50-per-month old-age pensions, twelve-month salaries for school bus drivers, $5,000 homestead-tax exemptions, $2,400-minimum teachers' salaries, improved welfare institutions, a greatly increased road-building program, a trade school in every parish, a state bonus for all World War II veterans, improved port facilities for New Orleans, and restrictions on the export of natural gas from the state. He apparently had few political friends at the beginning of the campaign but soon gained the support of members of the old Huey Long group—Clements, LeBlanc, Leander Perez, Maestri, William Feazel (who was supposed to have kicked in heavily to the campaign budget), and most important of all, Huey Long's widow and son Russell.

Long ran far ahead of his opponents in the first primary. He received over 267,000 votes, Jones over 147,000, Kennon 127,500, and Morrison 101,750. In the runoff he won over Jones by 432,528 to 223,971 votes. While, according to Allan Sindler, Jones' defeat could be at least partially explained "in terms of his personal unpopularity, his campaign tactics, and the resentments created by his Crime Commission investigations and his natural gas policy," there is little question but that Long had implanted in the minds of many people the idea that the preceding eight years had been years of old-fashioned Bourbonism. The entire Long ticket went into office, as well as a majority of the candidates for the legislature who had given him their support or who had received his blessing.

Long inherited a state-treasury surplus of nearly $50,000,000 and a continually rising state income. New taxes were levied which resulted in an increase of total state revenue from almost $200,000,000 for the fiscal year 1947-48 to over $322,500,000 in 1948-49, and much of the increase was used to carry out the Governor's campaign promises relating to public-welfare programs. Civil Service was effectively crippled in the regular legislative session of 1948 and repealed at a special session a few months later, which echoed Representative Charles Anzalone's retort: "Let's feed the horse that brought in the feed and the fodder during the campaign." Resentment began to grow as the charge was made that Long had returned to the old Huey practices of tax and spend and politicalize.

This resentment became obvious at the August, 1948, senatorial primary election. Senator John H. Overton had died in May and Governor Long had appointed William Feazel to the position in order that Russell Long might qualify in the fall election to complete the remaining two years of Overton's term. Campaigning with the support of the Long faction and generally on purely state issues, Russell Long was elected over Judge Robert F. Kennon by a majority of less than 11,000 votes. The Governor now called a halt to many of his past tactics and began to preach and practice "sweetness and light." When Russell Long ran for a full term of office in the Senate against Malcolm LaFargue in 1950, he campaigned on his two-year senatorial record, on his support of southern issues, and on mild liberalistic issues pleasing to both factions. That he secured many anti-Long faction votes was obvious, for he was elected by a 68.5 per cent majority of the votes cast.

Governor Long, encouraged by Russell Long's smashing victory, returned to old tactics in bidding for personal power. He proposed calling a convention to draft a new constitution, which would not be submitted to the people for final approval. Dissension arose within the ranks, and despite the fact that the Governor retained control of the legislature, many of the Longite leaders began to pull away or to warn that the Governor had gone too far and that the faction was in serious danger of repudiation.

Nine candidates entered the gubernatorial race of 1952: hand-picked Long candidate Carlos Spaht; Lieutenant Governor William J. Dodd; Register of the Land Office Lucille May Grace who had broken with Long; Dudley J. LeBlanc, now noted as the manufacturer of the cure-all Hadacol; James M. McLemore; T. Hale Boggs; Judge Robert F. Kennon; Cliff Liles, a former legislature sergeant-at-arms; and Kermit Parker, the first Negro since the days of military occupation to run for governor. After a rousing but somewhat politically cloudy campaign, Spaht and Kennon entered the second-primary campaign, in which all the other candidates pledged support to Kennon. He won by nearly 180,000 votes, gaining 53 of the 64 parishes, and carried with him into office a majority legislature.

Kennon's term of office brought many state governmental reforms. The highway, institutions, and welfare departments were placed under the control of citizen boards. The Budget Office was reorganized. A constitutional amendment was ratified requiring a two-thirds majority for the passage of bills increasing taxes or levying new ones. Voting machines were required for all precincts. Civil Service was made a part of the constitution. A Legislative Council was established. Numerous other changes were made, generally along the line of reducing the powers of the governor, and there was no question but that the people in general approved of the governmental reforms made by the administration.

The Governor conducted the activities of his office on a high-level governmental plane in keeping with traditional American separation of powers. He encouraged members of the legislature to renewed independence, handled troublesome political problems with patience and tact, and was moderate in spite of pressures for an increased program of governmental spending. He will be remembered for the progress which was made during his administration in behalf of responsible, constiutional government.

During the years from 1952 to 1956, however, Governor Kennon lost favor with many of those who had supported his campaign. His appropriation bills were higher than those of his predecessor. He was charged with having violated campaign pledges. He failed to keep friendly contact with many local political leaders who had so diligently worked for his election. State Auditor Allison R. Kolb gave undue publicity to his exposés of sometimes minute irregularities in local governmental offices, even when they were simply the result of poor bookkeeping methods and not through any criminal intent. Superintendent of State Police Francis C. Grevemberg was accused of violating law-enforcement agreements with local officials, and not infrequently, in the opinion of many citizens, high-handedly ignored them in traditionally local law-enforcement matters. The Governor apparently did not keep harmony within his faction nor retain the organization which had elected him. These factors boded ill for the election of 1956.

The campaign of 1956 was one of the longest and most bitterly fought in recent Louisiana history. Ex-Governor Earl K. Long had campaigned during the entire Kennon administration, and he was joined in 1955 by Francis Grevemberg, Mayor deLesseps Morrison of New Orleans, James McLemore, and member of the Board of Highways Fred T. Preaus. Long, materially aided by his candidate for lieutenant governor, educator and ex-legislator Lether E. Frazar, was swept back into office in the first primary by receiving slightly over 50 per cent of the total votes cast.

TAXATION AND THE COST OF GOVERNMENT. In 1921 the total income of the state was a little over $17,000,000; in 1954-55 it was almost $500,000,000. By 1954-55 nearly 23 percent of the state's income came from mineral leases and royalties and a little over 12 per cent from taxes on natural resources taken from on or under the ground. The sales tax brought in over 12 per cent; other taxes, including those on gasoline, tobacco, incomes, beverages, licenses, and fees of various types, made up the balance of the state's income. In 1954-55 the state spent nearly $450,000,000, of which $91,000,000 had been received from the Federal government. Of this amount over 32 per cent went for education, 24 per cent for public welfare, and 16 per cent for highways. The rest of the general appropriation was spent for hospitals and institutions, homestead exemptions, payments and interest on the state debt, the ordinary costs of government, and other services.

Government and the operation of governmental services cost a great deal of money and, as Louisiana governmental services have been greatly extended since 1920, their costs have greatly increased. In 1955 state governmental agencies employed nearly 35,000 persons and municipal and parish governments an additional 60,000. Of the state employees nearly 10,000 served in the health, hospital, and welfare divisions, over 9,000 in education, and over 5,000 in the Highway Department.

By 1949, Louisiana ranked thirty-ninth in the nation in average income per citizen, but at the same time ranked first in per-citizen state taxes, second in per-citizen state debt, and third in per-citizen cost of government. Total state expenses (not including distributions to parishes and municipalities) during the Jones administration were slightly over $369,000,000; the Davis administration, nearly $528,000,000; the Long administration, slightly over $1,367,000,000; and the Kennon administration, nearly $1,735,000,000.

The state debt rose from $169,000,000 when Davis left office, to $215,000,000 when Long left office, to $231,000,000 when Kennon left the governorship in 1956. Meanwhile Davis, Long, and Kennon left surpluses to their successors averaging about $40,000,000. The per capita expenses for three state budgetary items for the fiscal year 1957-58, as compared with the adjoining states and the national average, were as follows:

	Education	Welfare	Health & Hospitals
Louisiana	$64.68	$46.50	$14.19
Arkansas	30.30	19.05	6.75
Mississippi	35.19	17.44	5.77
Texas	41.61	16.83	6.02
National Average	39.37	16.64	11.46

During the fiscal year 1956-57 the state spent for old-age assistance, aid to needy blind, aid to dependent children, disability assistance, and general assistance a total of $128,000,000 through approval of over 33,000 applications.

No one could deny the fact that Louisiana has become a "high-spending" state. Many critics have charged that Louisiana has become a "welfare state" and that it performs too many services for the individual members of its citizenry. One such critic recently expressed the hope that "responsible individualism, and the dignity of man may again become the militant faith of our people so that they will successfully challenge the advocates of collectivism and the irresponsibility of the 'welfare state.' " Comparatively few voices have been raised during the past three and a half decades in stanch support of good business and sound economy practices. During the 1960 session of the legislature, however, Senator A. C. Clemons, Jr., of Jennings, in a speech before the senate, pointedly told his colleagues:

> As a member of the Finance Committee, I thought this group of men was to study and attempt to seriously consider this 800 million dollar budget. This is what happened. 850 million dollars was spent in 12 hours. This is spending tax dollars at the rate of 71 million per hour and to go further 1 million dollars a minute. This is in my opinion ridiculous. . . . Time after time when the Finance Committee was meeting I questioned why it took so much money to run the different departments and I was told not once, but several times, there was no need for me to worry about what it costs because there was nothing I could do to stop this crazy spending anyway. On one occasion I succeeded in cutting 70 thousand dollars from one of the department heads budget and the committee okayed it. The very next day the department head appeared before the committee and the 70 thousand dollars was put right back on. In other words, you are not supposed to ask questions and try to protect the taxpayers interest by asking and demanding where all this money is being spent. . . . Let me assure you that I am not discouraged. I am going to continue to ask questions and I am going to attempt to get the right answers as long as I represent the people of my senatorial district.

The senators listened politely but casually to Senator Clemons. There were no questions, no discussions, no debate. The Lieutenant Governor rapped with his gavel and the legislative body proceeded with the order of the day.

SUMMARY OF THE PERIOD. The period from 1920 to the present day has variously been titled "The Progressive Age of Louisiana," "The Age of Huey Long," "The Age of the Development of the Louisiana Welfare State," and numerous others. Huey Long was the dominant figure in Louisiana politics from the time of his election to the governorship in 1928 until his death in 1935. Since that time Long and anti-Long factions have battled for leadership in, and control of, state political affairs, and many state officials have held their offices for short periods as the tides of factional battles have shifted. It is significant, however, that since 1940 the anti-Long forces have won four of six gubernatorial elections and since 1942 have carried four of five mayoralty elections in New Orleans. In spite of political and personal disagreements between the anti-Long leaders there has been a sustained continuity in the battles for reform in Louisiana.

Louisiana's Congressional Representatives and Senators have generally taken little part in state politics and have represented the people of their districts and the entire state rather than a single political faction. Senator Allen J. Ellender has served continuously since his election in 1936, drawing support from all political groups, and Senator Russell Long, despite the charge of his critics that *"stat magni nominis umbra"* (he stands, the shadow of a great name), has developed into a liberal statesman who has won interfactional loyalty.

Elected officials at the state level have generally not been able to cross factional lines; one of the exceptions, however, is Wade O. Martin, Jr., who has been Secretary of State since 1944. Martin drew primarily Longite support in his first campaign, received wide support from other factions in the election of 1948, was unopposed in 1952, and received the endorsement of all factions in 1956, winning over his independent opponent in that election by gaining an unprecedented 93 per cent of the total ballots cast. Appointive officials have in most cases gone out of office with the governor who appointed them. Probably the most notable exception was George Wallace, who served as counsel to most of the governors from 1928 to 1956.

Much liberal legislation has been passed by the legislatures since 1920, and if the claim is true that Huey Long jerked the state into the twentieth century, it must also be admitted that opposition governors have continued to assist in making Louisiana a progressive state. Just how much of this progress can be credited to Huey Long no one can say, but progress has been a characteristic of the years since the beginning of John M. Parker's administration.

The chief governmental trends of the period are more or less obvious. The executive branch of the government has steadily grown in power and influence, despite the recessions of the Jones and Kennon governorships. The legislative branch has, during many sessions of the legislature, almost completely abdicated its role in ordinary democratic government, subserviently bowing to the will of the governor. Although Louisiana is now an urban state, legislative districts remain much as they were a half century ago, which gives the rural areas far greater power in state government than their population warrants. The gradual assumption of state-government power at the expense of local governmental units has been "viewed with alarm" by many members of the body politic.

While many Louisianians feel that they cannot point with pride to their state government of the past thirty years, others give their stamp of approval. Both Huey Long and his brother Earl have been called dictators, but during their administrations there was always an active and articulate minority opposition. Huey Long had more supporters in 1930 in his campaign for the United States Senate than he had in his gubernatorial race in 1928, and Earl Long won nearly 10 per cent more votes of all those cast in the first primary of 1956 than he did in the first primary of 1948. There seems to be little doubt but that strong and intense bifactional rather than two-party politics will continue in Louisiana.

CHAPTER 29

ECONOMIC PROGRESS

GROWTH OF POPULATION. The story of Louisiana's progressive economic life since 1920 can be divided into four distinct periods. The state made slow but steady growth until 1929, when a depression hit the entire United States and much of the civilized world; during the years which followed, Louisiana suffered considerably less than many other states. After the nation entered World War II in 1941, Louisiana's entire economy was geared to meeting wartime emergencies in the production of foodstuffs, munitions, and various categories of supplies. Since 1946 the state has witnessed what can only be termed a fantastic agricultural, manufacturing, industrial, and commercial boom.

The population of the state and its cities grew rapidly after 1920. In that year the population was approximately 1,800,000; in 1930 it was slightly over 2,100,000; by 1940 almost 2,364,000; by 1950 it had grown to nearly 2,700,000; and in 1958 it was over the 3,000,000 mark. The density of population had grown from 39.6 per square mile in 1920 to almost 70 per square mile. It is estimated that by 1965, Louisiana's population will exceed 3,500,000. In 1920 slightly over 65 per cent of the population of the state was rural; at the present time over 55 per cent of the people live in urban centers and less than 45 per cent in rural sections. Cities and towns grew steadily until World War II, and since that time have greatly accelerated their rate of growth; New Orleans, for example, has doubled its population since 1920 and Baton Rouge has increased by more than 600 per cent. During the ten-year period from 1940 to 1950, Baton Rouge increased 261.8 per cent; Lake Charles, 94.6; Lafayette, 74.6; and Shreveport, 29.6.

Despite constant total population growth, the percentage of Negroes has been steadily declining. In 1920, nearly 40 per cent of the total citizenry of the state was Negro; at the present time only 31 per cent is colored. The Negro population is centered chiefly in 22 parishes, which border the Mississippi, Red, and Atchafalaya rivers, where 40 per cent or more of the population is colored. West Feliciana leads all other parishes with about 70 per cent.

There have been several distinct population tendencies in modern Louisiana, and there is every reason to believe that these tendencies will continue. People are deserting the farms. Louisiana is a "gainer" state, as contrasted with neighboring Arkansas and Mississippi which are "loser" states. Small towns have grown proportionally in population along with New Orleans, Shreveport, Baton Rouge, and other larger cities. There has been considerable shifting of population from town to town. The proportion of citizens over the age of sixty-five in Louisiana is increasing about 12½ per cent more than the national average.

AGRICULTURE. While Louisiana is developing industry at a rapid rate, agriculture is still the most important economic activity. Over 500,000 people live on farms and produce field crops, livestock, and poultry which in 1954 were valued at over $360,000,000. These farms occupy almost 40 per cent of the total land area of the state, the average farm having slightly over 100 acres, and more than half of them are operated by families who own the land. The number of farm units has steadily decreased since 1920; according to Federal census records there were over 160,000 farms in the state in 1920, 150,000 in 1930, slightly more than 124,000 in 1950, and a few over 110,000 in 1954.

Louisiana's mild climate, abundant rainfall, and unusually fertile soils make possible the growing of many different crops, ranging from cotton, sugar cane, and tobacco to rice, sweet potatoes, strawberries, pecans, and truck-garden products, and including even lily bulbs and vetiver, a grass whose roots are used in making perfume. Some crops, particularly rice, have to be irrigated, but the great majority depend upon natural rainfall. The southern sections of the state have particularly long growing seasons, which makes possible the growing of two or more crops a year. The state ranks first in the nation in the production of sugar cane, sweet potatoes, and early-spring strawberries, second in rice and tung nuts, sixth in cotton and velvet beans, and eighth in cowpeas.

Despite the fact that the number of cotton farmers and the total cotton acreage have been cut by more than half during the last twenty-five years, cotton is still the most important agricultural crop. Cotton production declined from almost 800,000 bales in 1930 to 555,000 bales in 1954, valued at nearly $100,000,000. Franklin, Richland, Caddo, St. Landry, and Morehouse are leading cotton-producing parishes, each producing more than 25,000 bales. Rice is the second-ranking crop and is grown principally in southwest Louisiana, where the growing plants are irrigated from bayous or wells. Production has steadily increased from a total of 16,000,000 bushels in 1920 to over 33,000,000 bushels in 1954, valued at nearly $66,000,000. Jefferson Davis, Acadia, Calcasieu, Evangeline, and Vermilion are ranking parishes, Vermilion leading with a total in 1955 of over 8,650,000 bushels. While Louisiana ranks first among the states in the production of sugar cane, this crop ranks third in the state. The 1954 crop ran over 5,500,000 tons and was valued at nearly $35,000,000. The leading parishes include Assumption, Iberia, Iberville, Lafourche, St. James, St. Mary, and Terrebonne, Assumption holding first place with more than 750,000 tons.

Minor crops include sweet potatoes from St. Landry, Lafayette, Acadia, St. Martin, and Evangeline parishes, strawberries from the Florida Parishes, and truck crops from the lower Red River and lower Mississippi River valleys. Corn is grown over the entire state and is used chiefly for the production of corn meal and cereals and for the feeding of livestock; hay and forage crops for livestock are also grown on a state-wide basis. Perique tobacco is grown in St. James Parish, while general varieties are grown in scattered areas throughout most of the state. Vetiver is grown in Tangipahoa Parish and Creole Easter-lily bulbs in Plaquemines Parish. Comparatively small quantities of oats, peanuts, soybeans, peas, and other crops are produced by farmers engaged in general farming.

The pecan is the principal orchard tree, though peaches, oranges, and other fruits are grown. The area surrounding New Orleans is an immense truck-gardening district which supplies the markets of the north and east during the winter and early spring months, as well as the cities of the state. Scattered truck-garden areas are found throughout the southeastern, south central, and southern sections. Truck crops produced include cabbage, cauliflower, broccoli, turnips, onions, lettuce, spinach, okra, snap beans, watermelons, sweet peppers, pimentos, tomatoes, and cucumbers. In 1954, for example, over 3,300 acres were planted in snap beans, principally in St. Helena, Livingston, Tangipahoa, and Plaquemines parishes; the same year over 3,500 acres were planted in watermelons, chiefly in Lincoln, Bienville, Union, Ouachita, and Washington parishes, and over 1,850 acres in sweet peppers and pimentos, the two leading parishes being St. James and Tangipahoa.

Since 1940, Louisiana has developed into an important livestock-producing state, and at the present time over two-thirds of the farmers raise cattle, hogs, and sheep for sale to city markets and packing houses. Dairy sales ranked third in 1954 in total value among the important agricultural products when the total income reached nearly $42,000,000. The 1955 livestock census revealed that the cattle population was nearly 1,800,000; hogs, 410,000; and sheep, 132,000. These animals, together with poultry, were valued at over $115,000,000.

Many factors have aided in the improvement of Louisiana agriculture since 1920. There have been inventions and improvements in agricultural machinery, as for example the cotton-picker and the sugar-cane harvester. The State Department of Agriculture and Immigration, together with the United States Department of Agriculture, has greatly aided agriculture through various livestock, poultry, plant, and other improvement programs. An all-out attack has been made against pests and diseases. The Louisiana Agricultural Extension Service now operates in all parishes, and farmers are taught how to operate their farms more efficiently. Agricultural fairs and festivals have encouraged farmers to take greater pride in their plant and animal production.

Since the beginning of the depression of 1929, Louisiana farmers have learned to become more self-sufficient and to increase production through co-operative enterprises. In 1934, for example, nearly one-half of the farm families were on relief, simply because they did not produce enough of their needed food supplies; the following year over 132,000 out of 170,000 farms had farm gardens and most farmers no longer needed relief assistance. In 1938 they produced and stored for future use nearly 2,575,000 containers of canned vegetables and fruits and over 925,000 containers of canned preserves and jellies.

The various governmental farm services have materially aided the farmer to improve, not only his land and his crops and livestock, but also his general business and living conditions. A few years ago Bicniar Prioux of Iberia Parish testified that "the Extension Service is the best thing that ever happened for the farmer who has to make a living from his farm." S. J. Colvin of Lincoln Parish wrote that the farmers of his section had been taught the proper methods of terracing; "if we had known at the beginning what we know now, we could have saved ourselves a heap of trouble." J. C. Vines of Tensas Parish proudly said that "when I get into trouble I talk it over with the county agent, and he usually shows me the way out. We couldn't get along without him." From July to September, 1956, to give only one example, nearly 122,000 farm animals were vaccinated against Brucellosis at no cost to their owners. In 1955 there were nearly 1,100 Home Demonstration Clubs in the state with a membership of over 31,000 and over 1,450 4-H Clubs having nearly 80,000 members. The modern Louisiana farmer is a businessman who uses modern methods in the operation of his agricultural unit, regardless of whether he operates a large plantation or a small truck farm.

It was not until after the flood of 1927, when over one-fourth of Louisiana's farm lands were flooded, according to Sam Mims, that "the National Congress quit splitting hairs under the doctrine that so long as the water of the Mississippi remains within its banks it's ours but when it breaks over, it's yours." Prior to that time, continued Mims, Uncle Sam "had only dallied flirtatiously around the river's edge. Now he dived in, body and breeches, and started a war to end wars." At the present time there are over 2,900 miles of levees in Louisiana, chiefly along the Mississippi, Red, Atchafalaya, and Ouachita-Black rivers.

LUMBERING AND FOREST PRODUCTS. Louisiana has over 16,000,000 acres of forested land, practically all of which is of commercial value. On about two-thirds of this total acreage grow oak, ash, hickory, and other hardwoods, while the remaining third produces several varieties of pine and other softwoods. About 75 per cent of the forest lands are privately owned, and almost 18.5 per cent is in planted tree farms. The timber inventory of 1955 revealed that Louisiana is growing over 700,000,000 cubic feet of timber annually and that there were over 6,325,000 hardwood trees and over 1,555,000 softwood trees in the state.

The Louisiana lumbering industry gradually declined during the early years of the period as the old and natural stands of trees were cut by great lumber companies which made little attempt to reforest the cutover areas. Production declined from approximately 3 billion board feet in 1925 to slightly more than one billion board feet in 1945, and to almost 775 million board feet in 1954. When the last of the large lumber mills closed at Bogalusa in the spring of 1938, the *Enterprise* reported that the Great Southern Lumber Company's "wildcat siren whistle, which for years called hundreds of men to work, became a dirge Saturday when its sounding signified the cutting of the last log by the one-time greatest sawmill of the world. . . . A few officials and friends watched the final operation of the saws as people watch at a funeral ceremony." Only fifteen years before, it had been predicted that Louisiana's stand of timber could never be completely exhausted, when Colonel A. C. Goodyear wrote long-time sawyer Ben Sellers: "I hope you may be with us to saw the last log but I'm afraid you won't be for if you are you will make Methusalah look like a baby."

The first commercial pulpwood produced in the state was cut near Bogalusa in 1917 and converted into paper by the Bogalusa Paper Company, a subsidiary of the Great Southern Lumber Company. Within the next ten years several plants began to use pulpwood for the manufacture of various paper products. By 1954 pulpwood production had reached 13,500,000 cubic feet, the state had nearly 10 per cent of the national pulp-production capacity, and ranked third behind Washington and Florida.

Wood products include lumber of all types, shingles, barrels and hogsheads, veneers and plywoods, boxes, railroad ties, telephone and telegraph poles, furniture, wooden fixtures, pulp for paperboard, container board, paper, and other articles. By 1954 the paper and paper-allied products industries were producing nearly $300,000,000 worth of goods annually, while the lumber manufacturing output was over $175,000,000. That same year the total number of persons engaged in the many phases of the forest-products industries totaled nearly 50,000.

OIL, GAS, AND MINERALS. Louisiana has been blessed with tremendous deposits of oil, gas, and nonmetallic minerals; there are no metallic-mineral deposits of economic consequence within the state. By 1955 these underground resources were valued at more than a billion dollars by the United States Bureau of Mines.

There are oil or gas wells in practically all of the state's sixty-four parishes. While several fields were already in production in 1920, really large-scale drilling did not begin until after this time. By 1926 the state had over thirty oil fields, and production of oil had more than tripled, having passed 23 million barrels, while gas production was well over 150 billion cubic feet. The production of both oil and gas tripled during the following ten years, and doubled during the succeeding decade. Drilling was begun in 1947 in the offshore, or tidelands, areas off the southern coast of the state by the Kerr-McGee Oil Company, and the bringing in of their well marked the beginning of production in the Gulf of Mexico. During the next eight years about 50 oil and/or gas fields were discovered; by 1955 nearly 400 wells were producing over 22,000 barrels of hydrocarbons a day. Gulf of Mexico production has led to a controversy with the Federal government over the ownership of offshore water and land, which has not yet been brought to final settlement. This dispute has resulted in a comparatively sharp decline of exploratory activity in the Gulf of Mexico since 1950.

By 1955 there were almost 700 proven oil and/or gas fields in the state with more than 21,000 wells capable of producing gas or oil. During that year over 4,300 new wells were drilled and over one-half of them were productive wells. Also during that year Louisiana had the highest average among the states for production from wildcat wells, slightly over 28 per cent of them being productive. Louisiana's deepest oil well, in Plaquemines Parish, has a depth of over 22,500 feet, more than four miles. In 1955 oil production topped 260 million barrels, while gas production reached nearly 2 billion million cubic feet.

During the period from 1948 to 1958 state-owned oil-and-gas lands have produced a surplus revenue of approximately $541,000,000. While few people criticized the state's immediate use of these extra funds, there was sharp criticism during the early months of 1958. B. L. Krebs, writing in the *Times-Picayune,* said bluntly: "Of this sum $72 million was used for highways, $19 million for debt service. The balance of $450 million could have been used to wipe out the state debt; to drain the rich over-flowed lowlands; to build a chain of dams, reservoirs and outlet canals to supply ample fresh water in times of drouth to every city, town and parish in the state; to conserve its fisheries and fur industries, to assist in bringing back to full production the depleted forest lands. But it wasn't. It has been used, is being used today, and from all indications will be used next year and in succeeding years unless stopped by the voters, to maintain a program of 'benefits' to the people that is so out of proportion to the amounts spent by other states for the same purposes as to border on the fantastic." It must be admitted that neither executive nor legislative departments of the state government have made serious attempts to halt the ever growing demands of the various strong pressure groups for increased benefits from this temporary largess.

While salt in commercial quantities was discovered in south Louisiana over a hundred years ago, it did not become industrially important until after 1920. It is now mined in twenty-five sections of the state, but principally in Iberia, St. Mary, and Winn parishes, Iberia Parish being the largest producer. Louisiana salt is of high commercial value because most of it is over 98 per cent pure and is found in large, easily mined deposits. In 1955 production exceeded 3 million tons valued at over $10,000,000.

The old Calcasieu sulphur field was exhausted in 1924, but eight years later the Jefferson Island field was opened, followed the next year by a field at Grande Écaille. By 1940-41 the state produced slightly over a million long tons of sulphur. There has been considerable sulphur exploration since those years, and over 200 salt domes have thus far been discovered, but only 19 of them have sulphur in commercial quantities. The 1955 production was nearly 2,100,000 long tons, most of which came from five mines in four parishes—Grande Écaille and Garden Island Bay in Plaquemines Parish, Bay Ste. Elaine in Terrebonne, Chacahoula in Lafourche, and Starks in Calcasieu. A new mine is under development at Lake Pelto in Terrebonne Parish.

The state has well-distributed deposits of clay, gravel, sand, and limestone, particularly in the hill sections, large supplies of shells, and some gypsum and stone. Clay production, which reached nearly 1,600,000 tons in 1955, is used chiefly for heavy clay products, brick, and light-weight aggregates. Over 8 million tons of gravel and sand are annually used for structural and paving purposes. Oyster shells are dredged chiefly in Cameron Parish. Winn Parish is the heaviest producer of gypsum, while the largest producers of limestone are Winn and Bienville parishes. In 1955 the value of these miscellaneous minerals was estimated at over $25,000,000.

MANUFACTURING. Although Louisiana has made gigantic strides in the field of manufacturing since World War II and is one of the leaders in the South, its percentage increase, while above the national average, is somewhat below that of the other southern states. The number of manufacturing plants in the state increased 100 per cent from 1939 to 1953, but increased 110 per cent in the entire South. During the same period manufacturing employment increased 92 per cent in Louisiana, but 151 per cent in all of the southern states; manufacturing-plant wages and salaries increased 905 per cent in Louisiana, but jumped 982 per cent in the south as a whole. The percentage of persons in Louisiana engaged in nonagricultural activities has actually dropped one-tenth of one per cent during the past twenty years, from 21.9 to 21.8 per cent.

In certain industrial fields, however, Louisiana has exceeded the southern rate of advancement. The petroleum increase between 1939 and 1953 was 526 per cent in the South and 933 per cent in Louisiana. Chemical industries expanded 544 per cent in the South and 574 per cent in Louisiana. Total mineral production increased 411 per cent in the South and 550 per cent in Louisiana. These favorable percentages seem to indicate that Louisiana's industrial future lies in the petroleum and chemical fields, and this is further made obvious by the knowledge that Louisiana's chief mineral resources are oil, gas, sulphur, and salt, fundamental necessities in the production of many chemicals.

Another factor in Louisiana's industrial growth is the fact that since 1936 the state has permitted new industries to apply for tax exemptions for the first ten years of plant operation; in 1954 plants valued at more than $200,000,000 were constructed under this plan. Credit should also be given to the State Department of Commerce and Industry in advertising Louisiana's natural resources and in encouraging manufacturers to locate and build plants in the state. Many modern industrialists and political leaders are seriously worried, however, over the fact that Louisiana has become such a high-taxing, high-spending, constantly expanding welfare state and also by the fact that its government has shown little effectiveness in protecting the treasury from the raids of pressure groups. There seems little question but that Louisiana is presently losing ground in the southern race for industrialization to states practicing a more conservative attitude toward state spending.

In 1954 the manufactured products of Louisiana were valued at nearly one and one-fifth billion dollars. Chemicals and chemical products ranked first; foods and foodstuffs, second; petroleum and coal products, third; and pulp, paper, and wood products, fourth. Other classifications of goods produced included transportation equipment, metal products, stone, clay, and glass products, machinery, furniture, leather goods, and many others of lesser importance—candies, fertilizers, soda, boxes, mattresses, boats, vinegar, perfume, chocolate, wigs, sails, beer, tombstones, oil tanks, and yeast products. The 1954 report of the Department of Commerce and Industry breaks down Louisiana manufacturing activities into nearly a thousand categories. Among the southern states, Louisiana ranks first in the production of paper pulp, second in petroleum-coal products, fifth in food manufacturing, and sixth in chemicals and lumber and wood products.

The industrial use of Louisiana's greatest single resource—raw water—has apparently just begun, and the state's supply is the most abundant in the nation. This water resource is based on Louisiana's heavy rainfall, the flow of enormous supplies of water through underground water-bearing formations, and the tremendous amounts carried by the Mississippi, Red, Sabine, Ouchita, Pearl, and other rivers. An average of 650,000,000,000 gallons of water flow daily from Louisiana's streams into the Gulf of Mexico, and there are sections in the state where wells pumping as high as 3,000 gallons a minute could be continuously operated without seriously lowering the underground water table. The industrial use of water increased from over 1,900,000,000 gallons a day in 1950 to approximately 3,750,000,000 gallons a day in 1955.

During the past several years new Louisiana industries have tended to concentrate along the Mississippi River south of Baton Rouge and in the area of Lake Charles, with minor development in the Monroe, Shreveport, and New Iberia-Lafayette sections. Years ago historian John Finley predicted that the Mississippi would some day lose its "titanic ambition for quiet flowing" and would begin to minister to human needs. This statement was re-echoed recently by Grace de la Croix Daigre: "A hundred faces he has, dat Ol' Man Ribber. Some of them dark with violence and dumb with terror we hope never to see. But among his fairer countenances is the oft-unrecognized aspect of generosity. Like so much of Nature's benevolence, the Ol' Man's legacy goes to those enterprising souls who are willing to sweat a bit for it."

WILDLIFE AND FISHERIES. The wild bird and animal life and the fish of Louisiana's bayous, streams, and Gulf waters are of much economic importance, and the State Department of Wild Life and Fisheries regulates, aids, and helps preserve these natural resources. Louisiana's wildlife preserves, among the world's largest, may be divided into three categories. Five migratory-waterfowl refuges totaling 250,000 acres are located along the Gulf Coast; three upland game-bird refuges have a total of 133,000 acres; over a dozen game refuges, ranging in size from 5,000 to 46,000 acres and having a total of 226,000 acres, are scattered about the state. The first state and nationally owned migratory-waterfowl sanctuaries in the world were established in Louisiana and were the result of a movement led by Edward Avery McIlhenny of Avery Island. The Louisiana Wild Life Federation, a nonprofit, nonpolitical organization, was organized in 1940 to assist in preserving the wildlife of the state.

Among the fur-bearing animals are nutria (brought from South America in 1938), raccoon, squirrel, muskrat, mink, opossum, otter, fox, and wildcat. The muskrat ranked first in commercial importance during the 1954-55 season, and over 1,380,000 pelts, valued at more than $1,520,000, were taken. Nutria was second with approximately 375,000 pelts, raccoon third with nearly 85,000 pelts, and mink fourth with 65,000 pelts. In all nearly 2,000,000 pelts of various animals were sold, and they were valued at nearly $3,500,000. More than 11,000 alligators were killed for their hides and meat in 1954-55, although only 38 of them were over 10 feet in length.

The catching and processing of fresh- and salt-water commercial fish is an important present-day industry. Commercial fresh-water fish include catfish, buffalo, gaspergou, garfish, and other varieties, while the salt-water fisheries catch shrimp, oyster, turtle, crab, Gulf menhaden, trout, redfish, flounder, pompano, red snapper, sheepshead, and mullet. The first commercial canning of shrimp was done in 1867 by the Dunbar family at Grande Terre Island, but the shrimp-packing industry did not really begin until 1918. At that time seines were discarded in favor of huge nets called "trawls," which were handled by motors on board large shrimp boats. The marketing of headless shrimp began in 1934; today shrimp are packed in many ways, and in 1955 the production totaled over 365,000 barrels valued at over $20,000,000. In 1955 oyster production reached almost 740,000 barrels; hard-shell crab, over 10,000,000 pounds; and soft-shell crab, 1,500,000 pounds. Louisiana produces about 80 per cent of the crawfish sold in the United States, over 775,000 pounds in 1955; the same year 125,000 pounds of frogs and over 130,000 pounds of turtle meat were sold. Fresh- and salt-water fishing brought Louisiana fishermen an income of over $25,000,000 in 1955.

In addition to direct state income, Louisiana's wildlife and fishing lands, streams, and Gulf waters offer fine sport to thousands of citizens and provide many a zestful meal for their tables. The most common game animals include deer, squirrel, rabbit, and bear, although the bear is almost extinct. During a normal winter season an estimated 2,000,000 ducks, 450,000 geese, and 100,000 coots winter in the state, while an additional 2,000,000 of these migratory birds stop over in Louisiana for varying periods. There are thousands of acres of private game preserves and nearly a thousand hunting clubs scattered throughout the state. Nearly half a million hunting and fishing licenses of all categories were sold in Louisiana in 1955.

TRANSPORTATION. There were nearly 50,000 miles of highways, roads, and streets in Louisiana in 1955. Almost 16,000 miles were under state control; approximately 28,000 miles were under the control of parishes; and about 5,000 miles of streets were under the supervision of cities and towns. These highways, roads, and streets were used by 750,000 automobiles, nearly 200,000 trucks, and nearly 75,000 buses, trailers, and other types of licensed vehicles. There were over 300,000 traffic signs on the state-maintained highways in 1955.

The State Highway Department spent nearly $83,000,000 during the fiscal year 1954-55 on the construction, maintenance, and administration of state highways. Louisiana's highways cost relatively more than do highways in other states due to the presence of swamplands and lowlands, and the large number of rivers and bayous in the state. Not only are construction costs high in swampland and lowland areas but the maintenance of highways is considerably higher than in upland regions where road foundations are more solid. Since 1930 the state has built over thirty major bridges, eight of which cost more than one million dollars. Altogether there are more than 6,000 bridges on the state-maintained highways, 125 feet of bridging for every 2.5 miles of highway.

In the state there are more than 4,000 miles of railroad track used by over thirty different railroad lines. The largest lines include the Southern Pacific (709 miles), Texas and Pacific (611 miles), Missouri Pacific (574 miles), Louisiana and Arkansas

(423 miles), and Yazoo and Mississippi Valley (387 miles). But all of Louisiana's railroads are not large lines or systems. The Tangipahoa and Eastern Railway Company's track from Fluker to Ogden is only 3.5 miles in length, and the shortest railroad, the Washington Western Railway Company, from Jenkins to Green, has only one mile of track.

Serving the people of Louisiana are more than a dozen airlines, most of which are interstate or international lines. Louisianians can now fly to practically any town or city within the borders of the state and, through the use of connecting lines, to the major cities of the world. The state has over 175 airports and airstrips of various classifications, more than 20 seaplane bases, and a half-dozen heliports. The Louisiana Aeronautics Commission was created by the legislature in 1936 to regulate the location, construction, and maintenance of airports, and in 1941 this governmental function was transferred to the State Department of Public Works.

The navigable waters of Louisiana, on which boats or barges may operate during all or part of the year, total nearly 5,000 miles. Some of these streams, bayous, and rivers are long and carry heavy boat and barge traffic, the Mississippi River, for example, flowing over 550 miles within the state or along its boundary. On the other hand, some rivers, streams, and bayous are very short; the Tangipahoa River can be navigated for only fifteen miles, Petite Anse Bayou for only eight miles, and Dorchite Bayou for only a half-dozen miles. The Intracoastal Waterway provides a 12-foot-deep and 125-foot-wide minimum channel across the southern part of the state and connects with the Mississippi River system, the Great Lakes, and various Louisiana waterways. The Mississippi River is nontidal above the mouth of the Red River, and the Mississippi River Commission (established by the Federal government in 1879) attempts to maintain a thirty-five-foot channel south of Baton Rouge for ocean-going ships and a nine-foot channel above Baton Rouge for barges and other river craft.

COMMERCE. Louisiana has throughout the period of its statehood been a leading commercial state, both for interstate commerce as well as for the importing and exporting of commodities. Several factors have greatly aided the development of interstate and foreign trade during the modern period, including the easy availability of water, rail, and air transportation, the rising industry of the state, the increasing development of the facilities of its three major seaports, and its location with relation to the other states of the Union.

The chief imports are sugar, molasses, bananas, bauxite, coffee, petroleum, minerals and metals, phosphates and fertilizers, rubber, burlap, and bagging. Sugar, molasses, petroleum, and bauxite are imported chiefly for manufacturing purposes. The most important exports are wheat, corn, flour, cotton, oils and greases, sulphur, feeds, and steel products. These imports and exports in 1954 had a gross weight of over 10 million tons and were valued at nearly 2 billion dollars.

New Orleans is Louisiana's largest port. It is the second-ranking port in the nation in dollar value of foreign-trade cargoes and the fourth ranking port in weight of cargoes. During the twelve months preceding July 1, 1955, nearly 3,700 vessels and nearly 2,300 inland-waterway and river boats and barges docked at New Orleans and handled nearly 50 million tons of cargo. While the majority of the vessels doing business at New Orleans were American, 419 Norwegian, 301 Dutch, 246 British, and 207 German ships used the port.

One reason for the growth of New Orleans as a shipping center is that it has a Foreign Trade Zone, which was created in 1947 and is one of four such zones in the United States. This zone is a fenced-in area where foreign goods may be stored, processed, and repackaged without payment of American customs, duties, excise, or other taxes. These goods may then be shipped to other countries or imported into the United States. New Orleans also has International House, a world-wide businessmen's organization with over 2,400 members, which is a trade and commercial friendship center where world businessmen may gather to transact their business. It also has the International Trade Mart, a five-story exhibit building, where sellers from the entire world display and take orders for their goods.

The New Orleans Traffic and Transportation Bureau is a nonprofit, nontrading corporation whose activities include the furnishing of transportation and other trade information to shippers. The port has over thirteen miles of deep water terminals and operational facilities with an average depth of thirty-five feet and has the fastest turn-around time for ships of any port in the nation. The Board of Commissioners of the Port of New Orleans, a state agency, has general jurisdiction over the wharfing and berthing facilities, which have a capacity of 105 ships. In 1955 the total export and import cars switched in New Orleans totaled nearly 110,000, while the total carloadings numbered almost 470,000. Air-express shipments averaged about 6,000 per month.

Baton Rouge is Louisiana's second port, the thirteenth port in the nation, and the farthest inland deep-water port with a thirty-five-foot channel. It has over 150 industries manufacturing chiefly petroleum, chemical, and aluminum products. In 1955 its port handled slightly over 16.5 million tons of cargo, its railways 125,000 carloadings and its air facilities over 10,000 air-express shipments. Lake Charles is the third-ranking port in the state and has a deep-water channel to the Gulf of Mexico. In 1955 the port handled nearly 15.5 million tons of export-import goods.

Not all of Louisiana's commercial business is the handling of manufactured goods. One of its most important businesses is the entertaining of tourists. In 1954 over 3,000,000 tourists visited Louisiana, and it was estimated that they spent nearly $300,000,000 while in the state. The three most important tourist attractions are New Orleans, Baton Rouge (the state capital and the home of the State University), and the Acadian Country. The state maintains several tourist-welcoming stations at highway entrances, where assistance and advice in arranging sight-seeing trips are given.

BANKS AND BANKING. Prior to the present era, Louisiana frequently had to borrow money from outside the state to promote its agricultural and other resources. While business firms still borrow huge sums from outside the state, most of their financial transactions are now with local banks.

The state began to modernize its banking system in 1902, and in 1918 additional legislation helped place Louisiana banks on a sounder financial basis. These and subsequent laws, aided by Federal legislation, have greatly strengthened the banks. By 1946 there were in Louisiana 122 state and 33 national banks with a total capital of more than $27,500,000 and total assets exceeding $1,600,000,000. Bank deposits the same year reached nearly $1,200,000,000. Nine years later the number of banks had slightly increased, their capital and assets had been multiplied several times, and deposits had reached nearly $2,500,000,000. In 1955, Louisianians also owned more than $50,000,000 worth of United States Savings Bonds and had more than $400,000,000 of savings in various homestead associations.

LABOR. Although Louisiana had many labor unions prior to 1920, it was generally considered to be a nonunion state. Labor Day was not officially recognized until 1928. The modern organization of labor unions began during the years from 1910 to 1914, when the Brotherhood of Timber Workers succeeded in securing higher wages and a nine-hour day. The State Federation of Labor made its appearance in 1916, and the organization movement continued until 1929, when the number of labor unions began to decline. Since 1938, however, hundreds of unions representing the different labor groups have been organized.

The legislature has passed numerous laws regulating labor. Women's and children's labor laws regulate the labor of these two groups, although the basic Child Labor Law of 1908, even after considerable amendment, was condemned in 1957 by Commissioner of Labor Sidney J. Caldwell as being inadequate. The Workmen's Compensation Law protects those who are injured on the job, and employers must furnish reasonable medical, surgical, and hospital service, most of which services are provided through workmen's compensation insurance. The Department of Labor was created in 1936, replacing the Division of Labor and Industrial Statistics which had been established in 1908. The department is headed by a commissioner appointed by the governor and is composed of divisions which are responsible for specific functions. The state maintains local employment offices in its major cities and in 1954 obtained jobs for nearly 210,000 persons, almost 125,000 of whom were agricultural workers. The same year nearly $20,000,000 was paid in unemployment benefits, representing a total of 892,000 weeks.

Working conditions and wages have been generally good since the close of World War II. In 1954, over 140,000 Louisiana manufacturing laborers worked an average of 41.4 hours per week and received an average weekly wage of $75.35. In the same period, Class A accountants averaged $79.50; printing and publishing workers, $84.05; chemical workers, $85.46; petroleum-refining laborers, $98.25; and sugar industrial laborers, $60.35. Despite good pay, however, many workers were dissatisfied with wages, with working conditions, or had other complaints. During the five-year period from 1950 through 1954 there were 244 strikes involving nearly 102,000 workers, and during the fiscal year 1956-57 the Department of Labor received 3,491 wage disputes, of which only 755 were dismissed without action.

CHAPTER 30

EDUCATIONAL AND CULTURAL DEVELOPMENT

GENERAL EDUCATIONAL PROGRESS. The progress made by public education in Louisiana since 1920 is rather graphically demonstrated by the steady increase in total amounts expended. The amount spent for the fiscal year 1920-21 was $13,750,000, ten years later it had increased to $20,902,000, and in 1940-41 to $27,533,000. The increase thereafter was considerably more rapid—$60,744,000 in 1947-48; $106,435,000 in 1950-51; $135,145,000 in 1953-54; and $199,000,000 in 1957-58. During the 1955-56 fiscal year, 38.2 per cent of all state revenues went to education. Of the 1957-58 educational dollar 60.29 per cent went to public schools, 9.38 per cent to state colleges, 8.13 per cent to the teachers' retirement system, 8.03 per cent to the State University, 7.4 per cent to the public-school lunch program, and the balance to special and trade schools, for textbooks and supplies, and for miscellaneous expenses. During the past twenty years there has been a steady decline in the percentage of educational funds allocated to the State University, a situation which bodes ill for the progress of that institution.

In 1921 there were 336,000 white and 229,000 colored children of school age in the state, only about 70 per cent of whom were actually attending school; by 1954 these numbers had risen to 484,000 and 288,000 respectively, and over 95 per cent of the children were enrolled in school. At the beginning of the 1950's nearly 18.0 per cent of all citizens over the age of twenty-five years had received seven years of elementary education, nearly 11.5 per cent had completed four years of high school, and nearly 5.0 per cent had finished four years of college.

In 1921 there were slightly less than 10,000 schoolteachers; thirty-five years later the number of teachers in the public schools had more than doubled. In 1921-22 only slightly more than 13 per cent of the teachers had received four years of college training or held a bachelor's degree; by 1952-53, 81 per cent of the white teachers and 78 per cent of the colored teachers held the bachelor's degree and over 13 per cent of all teachers held the master's degree. In 1920-21 the average white teacher received a salary of $1,036, and the average colored teacher $429; in 1952-53 white teachers received an average salary of $3,494, and colored teachers $3,000. By 1957-58 slightly over 90 per cent of all teachers had received a minimum of four years of college training and received an average salary of $4,459, with principals receiving an average salary of $6,638.

Despite these gains public education in Louisiana, as well as in the other states, has been widely attacked during the past several years. Most of the criticism has been directed at teacher-certification methods, the college or university professional education courses required at the expense of content courses, the growing number of fringe or noncontent courses offered in secondary schools, the lunch program, the cost of school transportation, the practice of automatic promotions, the uneconomical continuance of small high schools, the lack of needed special school for physically handicapped children, and the public educational system's inability to weed out weak teachers.

One educator recently charged that many teachers would be better trained if a high percentage of the education courses were eliminated from university or college education curricula, for they made the "teachers more banal-minded" because they were "stuffed with religiosity—which is not religion." He closed his blast: "God pity your pupils; don't blame them for not being educated. What a teacher needs, aside from having sense and character, is basic knowledge in history, science, languages, literature, the fundamentals. All a would-be teacher gets out of education is palaver." These blistering attacks have in no way adversely affected Louisiana public education, however, for the educators and the State Department of Education are acutely aware of educational problems affecting the state and are constantly working toward improvement.

ELEMENTARY AND SECONDARY EDUCATION. The State Department of Education, headed by an elected state superintendent, is responsible for primary and secondary education in Louisiana. This department is under the policy supervision of a State Board of Education, which consists of eleven members elected by the voters of the state, and is organized into six divisions: Elementary and Secondary Education, Higher Education, Vocational Education, School Administration, Special Services, and Vocational Rehabilitation and Veterans' Education. The department makes an annual report to the governor and to the legislature on educational conditions, progress, and anticipated improvements. Educational progress implies improvement in each aspect of education—various courses of study, teacher training, supervision of teaching processes, teacher-benefit laws, consolidation of schools, transportation of pupils, school attendance, school finance, libraries, textbooks, and lunch programs, all of which come under the authority of the State Department of Education.

The voters in each of the sixty-four parishes elect a Parish Board of Education and the cities of Bogalusa, Lake Charles, and Monroe also have independent city school systems. The parish boards and the city boards of these three cities appoint a parish or city superintendent of education and direct elementary and high-school education in their districts. Local boards are, however, supervised and generally controlled in regard to textbooks, the certification of teachers, courses of study, and other matters by the state department.

Much has been done during the past two decades to improve the elementary- and secondary-school system of the state. Courses of study have been broadened; at the beginning of the period many students studied only arithmetic, reading, and writing, but today they are taught additional courses which help fit them for modern life. In the past prospective teachers had to pass qualifying examinations; today they receive training in the theories of education and in advanced teaching methods. Not many years ago the state provided no classroom supervision of instruction; today classroom supervisors, especially trained in teaching methods and in definite fields of subject matter, assist teachers to give the most effective possible instruction to their students.

In 1921 there were more than 3,400 public schools in the state. Through consolidation and school-bus transportation, this number was reduced until in 1948 there were only approximately 2,250 schools and in 1954 less than 1,600 schools. Prior to 1928, pupils furnished their own textbooks and other school materials. In that year the legislature passed the first Free Textbook Law and additional legislation has been passed since then, so that today the pupil is furnished free textbooks, books and other library materials, paper and pencils, audiovisual aids, and much more special equipment. The first public-supported school-lunch program was initiated at the Charenton Indian School in St. Mary Parish in 1932; the first legislative appropriations were made in 1939; and the free lunch regardless of need program initiated in 1948. By 1954 there were more than 1,400 lunch programs serving an average of over 400,000 pupils daily.

By 1957, Louisiana supported over twenty-five trade schools located at strategic points throughout the state, as well as schools for the handicapped—State School for the Blind, State School for Blind Negroes, State School for the Deaf, State School for Deaf Negroes, and State School for Spastic Children. Since 1920 three progressive educational leaders have held the office of state superintendent: T. H. Harris (1908-40), John E. Coxe (1940-48), and Shelby M. Jackson (since 1948).

HIGHER EDUCATION. There are twenty-three colleges and universities in Louisiana, ten of which are supported by the state and thirteen by funds from private endowments and religious institutions. In 1954-55 over 35,000 students were enrolled in these colleges and universities, and by 1957-58 over 30,000 students were enrolled in the ten state-supported institutions alone.

Louisiana State University is the state's largest institution of higher learning. It is governed by a fifteen-member Board of Supervisors, of which the governor is an ex-officio member and appoints the other members for overlapping terms of fourteen years. Prior to 1925 the university was a comparatively small institution, but in that year it was moved from its old campus on the present-day capitol grounds to its new 4,700 acre campus, although some classes were still held on the old campus until 1932. During its first 87 years, from 1860 to 1946, the university awarded approximately 12,000 degrees; since 1946 more than 15,000 students from all parts of the world as well as from Louisiana have been awarded degrees. Its buildings and equipment are presently valued at nearly $95,000,000 and its library, containing over 800,000 books and ranking third in the South in total expenditures for 1958-59, is the largest research library in Louisiana. The University had a total enrollment, including its summer term, in 1958-59 of nearly 18,000 students. In September, 1958, a branch of the University was opened at New Orleans.

The modern University has a threefold mission of serving the state through teaching, research, and extension. Courses in practically every field of learning are offered at the undergraduate level at less cost per undergraduate-student class hour than is possible at the state colleges. Research in such practical fields as sugar chemistry, agriculture, geology, animal industry, agricultural economics, and others earns millions of dollars for the people of Louisiana every year. Medical research at the School of Medicine at New Orleans saves Louisiana lives and relieves much suffering of those who are ill. The Agricultural Extension Service annually reaches more than 250,000 Louisiana families, conveying to them the latest information and techniques developed in agriculture. The General Extension Division links learning and living; approximately 150,000 persons annually attend the over 850 conferences and meetings covering everyday working and living activities sponsored by this division. As Louisiana State University President General Troy H. Middleton recently said, "Louisiana and LSU have grown together, each contributing to the strength of the other in a partnership which has produced much in the past. The future of both is inseparable."

The other nine state colleges are governed by the State Board of Education and are: Francis T. Nicholls at Thibodaux, Louisiana Polytechnic Institute at Ruston, McNeese State College at Lake Charles, Northeast State College at Monroe, Northwestern State College at Natchitoches, Southeastern State College at Hammond, University of Southwestern Louisiana at Lafayette, and two Negro institutions, Southern University at Scotlandville (the colored state university and the largest Negro college in the United States), and Grambling College at Grambling. In 1955-56 these nine institutions had a total enrollment of over 10,000 students.

Three recent trends in higher education have caused some concern among practical educators during the past decade. Despite increased appropriations the State University has not been granted sufficient funds to keep pace with other such institutions in the nation, particularly in the fields of graduate instruction, research, and applied practical services to the people of the state offered by the General Extension, Agricultural Extension, and other divisions. The action by the legislature in making senior colleges out of former junior colleges is spreading the higher education dollar extremely thin. Some of the state colleges have been authorized to give graduate instruction and advanced degrees despite their lack of requisite instructional, library, laboratory, and other research facilities.

Tulane University (including Sophie Newcomb College for women) and Loyola University of the South at New Orleans are the largest private institutions of higher learning. The Tulane University 100-acre campus, buildings, and equipment are valued at more than $30,000,000, its endowment is more than $35,000,000, and its 1954-55 budget was in excess of $8,600,000. Its library, including the recently acquired Howard Memorial Library, is particularly strong in the fields of law, medicine, and commerce, and ranks fifteenth among university libraries in the South. Its 1958-59 enrollment approached 10,000 students. Loyola University's campus and plant are valued at more than $10,000,000 and its total enrollment exceeds 6,000 students. During the years since 1920 the other private institutions have kept pace with general higher educational advancement and have increased their plants, endowments, and student enrollments.

LIBRARIES AND MUSEUMS. The Louisiana State Library, which provides information and book services to the people of the state, to state and local officials, and through book loans to other libraries, was founded in 1925 in one room of the Old State Capitol, with Essae M. Culver as director. At that time Louisiana was considered one of the nation's most "bookless" states. A modern state library building was completed in 1958, a fitting monument to Miss Culver's years of dedicated service. The State Library now has branches over the entire state and works in close cooperation with parish and city public libraries.

The library's collections total over 400,000 books and other library materials, and it annually mails over 50,000 packages of books and makes over 2,000,000 book loans. It has a large collection of films on various subjects and over 3,000 talking books for the blind, which are loaned to other libraries, groups, and individuals. It annually supplies various types of information to over 50,000 people in the state. That it has a practical, everyday value to the people of Louisiana is well illustrated by two letters written its officials. One borrower wrote: "Again I want to thank you for lending me books which have enabled me to establish a growing typist and mimeographing business." A new American citizen from southwest Louisiana wrote: "I passed the examination for citizenship, thanks to you for sending the right kinds of books for me to read."

Most of the parishes have their own libraries, located at the parish seats, the East Baton Rouge Parish Library being the largest with over 360,000 books, followed by Ouachita and Calcasieu parishes. Some of the city libraries also have large collections of books. The New Orleans Public Library is by far the largest general library in the state with well over one million books in its collections. It annually loans over a million volumes to readers, and its holdings include many valuable magazines and newspaper files.

Louisiana's libraries have been fortunate in having had some noted librarians who were much interested in collecting material on the history of the state. James A. McMillen, Librarian at Louisiana State University for a number of years, was largely responsible for the acquisition of the University's great collection of books, pamphlets, newspapers, magazines, and government documents pertaining to the history of Louisiana. William Beer was the head of the Howard Memorial Library of New Orleans from 1891 until his death in 1927 and was one of the nation's greatest book collectors. A friend once wrote that he "collected everything from sugar reports to rare Louisiana imprints, and plenty of both. Quite right he was, too, for there was no branch of knowledge upon which he was not called upon, at some time or other, to furnish books."

The Louisiana State Museum is the official state museum. Dr. Robert Glenk served as its director for over thirty years and during that period accumulated a sizable collection of museum materials on Louisiana history. During recent years, however, the Museum has lost stature among institutions of its type because it has not been professionally operated. It also administers and maintains the Huey P. Long residence in New Orleans.

There was comparatively little and no organized activity throughout the state in the collection and preservation of the private and official records of the state's historical past until the 1930's. In 1933, Edwin Adams Davis, a member of the Louisiana State University Department of History, began to collect private manuscript records on a part-time basis for the University Library. Two years later he organized the University's Department of Archives and in 1936 secured the passage of a law permitting this department to receive the noncurrent official state, parish, and city records and archives which were no longer needed in government. During the next ten years he traveled over the entire state, collecting over 980,000 state and over 88,000 parish archives, and over 175,000 manuscripts of over 700 Louisiana families and business concerns. Today the Department of Archives at Louisiana State University is one of the major university departments of the South engaged in this type of work.

The most important art museums are the Isaac Delgado Museum of Art in New Orleans, which contains a noteworthy collection of paintings and sculpture, the Louisiana State Museum at the Cabildo, and the State Exhibits Building at Shreveport. The Acadian House at the Longfellow-Evangeline Memorial Park near St. Martinville exhibits furniture, utensils, and other home furnishings used by the Acadians, while the Victor C. Barringer House in Monroe contains a good collection of Indian cooking vessels, pottery, and other relics. Noteworthy medical collections are owned by Louisiana State University and Tulane University medical schools. The largest historical museum collections are at the Louisiana State Museum, which also exhibits extensive groups of family relics and other items of Louisiana historical importance, and at the Louisiana Historical Association's Confederate Historical Museum also at New Orleans, which receives negligible state support and which houses a noteworthy collection of relics, portraits, weapons, and other items pertaining to Louisiana history and particularly to the War for Southern Independence. Less important historical museums are found at Louisiana State University and at Tulane University.

NEWSPAPERS, MAGAZINES, RADIO, AND TELEVISION. Modern Louisiana is well equipped with news- and information-dispensing agencies in the fields of newspapers, magazines, trade publications, government departmental organs, journals of organized groups, radio and television.

Nearly a score of daily newspapers are strategically located among the major towns and cities of the state. The most important New Orleans newspapers are the *Times-Picayune* and the *States and Item;* in Baton Rouge are published the *Morning Advocate* and the *State-Times,* and in Shreveport the *Journal* and the *Times.* Other leading newspapers include the Alexandria *Town Talk,* the Lake Charles *American Press,* the Lafayette *Advertiser,* the Monroe *News Star* and *World,* and the Ruston *Daily Leader. The Federationist* is a publication of the Louisiana Federation of Labor. The *Louisiana Weekly,* published in New Orleans, is one of the leading Negro newspapers of the South.

Since 1920, New Orleans, and to a lesser extent the state at large, has had a group of newspaper reporters who attracted national attention, not only because of their reporting but because many of them published literary or historical books of New Orleans or Louisiana. These journalists include John McClure, Lyle Saxon, Bruce Manning, Hamilton Basso, Hermann B. Deutsch, Meigs O. Frost, John Chase, Robert Tallant, Louise Guyol, Louis Hennessey, Charles L. Dufour, Stuart Landry,

Harnett Kane, Merlin ("Scoop") Kennedy, Doris Kent LeBlanc, Flannery Lewis, David Stern, and several others.

Numerous magazines and journals of various types are published in the Spanish, Italian, French, and German languages as well as in English, and include labor, trade, commercial, and professional publications such as the *American Cotton Grower,* the *Daily Journal of Commerce,* the *New Orleans Medical and Surgical Journal,* and rice, sugar, and coffee journals, all published in the interest of their special fields.

In 1922, shortly after the first radio programs were broadcast from KDKA in Pittsburgh, Pennsylvania, WAAB, owned by the Coliseum Place Baptist Church, and WWL, of Loyola University, began broadcasting in New Orleans. During the 1920's newspapers started to operate radio stations in conjunction with their publications. KWKH of Shreveport became the first Louisiana radio station to attract national attention when W. K. Henderson, a retired businessman, publicized his fight against chain stores. WDSU of New Orleans was the first station to make direct broadcasts from ships and airplanes and to broadcast Southern League baseball games. There are presently more than sixty radio stations in the state. Several hundred Louisianians have amateur transmitting and receiving stations and communicate with other radio amateurs all over the world; many have short-wave receiving sets and hear programs from Havana, the City of Mexico, and other foreign cities. Louisiana television made its appearance in 1948 when station WDSU-TV began broadcasting in New Orleans. By 1956 over 51 per cent of Louisiana's households contained television sets. The more than 400,000 sets were receiving programs from eleven Louisiana stations.

LITERATURE. Although Louisiana had occupied a high place in literature during the last twenty-five years of the nineteenth century, from 1900 to 1920 comparatively little was written in or about Louisiana. Beginning in the early twenties, however, there came a "reawakening," when writers discovered that the fabulous and romantic history of Louisiana offered many themes and plots for novels, short stories, plays, biographies, historical fiction, and other forms of writing.

This literary movement began in New Orleans, where a group of young writers, some of whom were later to gain national recognition, lived and labored in the Vieux Carré, studying Louisiana's colorful past and present and from it drawing inspiration and material for their creative work. Sherwood Anderson, William Faulkner, Ernest Hemingway, and others contributed to a little magazine called the *Double Dealer,* as well as to other publications, and began to make reputations. The *Double Dealer* was published monthly in editions of from 15,000 to 18,000 copies; subscriptions were modestly priced at $2.50 a year. Forty-three issues in all were printed from January, 1921, to May, 1926. It was edited and published by Julius Weis Friend and his sister, Lillian Marcus, aided and abetted by Albert Goldstein, Basil Thompson, and John McClure. Members of this group and others who closely followed them made notable contributions to the Louisiana theme. Walter Coquille became known for his dialect "Bayou Pom Pom" tales and James J. McLoughlin wrote fascinating newspaper stories, also in dialect, under the name of "Jack LaFaience."

Before long the renaissance literary movement spread over the entire state. At Louisiana State University two English faculty members, Robert Penn Warren and Cleanth Brooks, Jr., began the publication of the *Southern Review,* which gained international fame. There also historian Wendell H. Stephenson edited the *Journal of Southern History,* first assisted by Edwin Adams Davis and later by Fred C. Cole, who succeeded Stephenson as editor. These two journals were sponsored by the University and continued publication for some years until the university withdrew its sponsorship.

Meanwhile Lyle Saxon had developed as Louisiana's most articulate and best-loved writer. After a newspaper apprenticeship with Baton Rouge and Chicago newspapers and with the *Times-Picayune,* he published his first short story, "Cane River," in the *Dial* magazine in 1926. His first book, *Father Mississippi,* resulted from his coverage of the 1927 flood for the *Century* magazine. Thereafter he wrote *Fabulous New*

Orleans (probably the most noted of all modern Louisiana books), *Old Louisiana,* and *Lafitte the Pirate.* As State Director of the Federal Writers' Project of Louisiana he edited *Louisiana, A Guide to the State; New Orleans City Guide;* and *Gumbo Ya-Ya,* with the assistance of Robert Tallant and Edward Dreyer. His *Children of Strangers* is one of the most sensitive novels ever written about the modern Negro. The *Friends of Joe Gilmore* was published in 1948, two years after his death.

Perhaps the tribute most pleasing to Saxon's friends appeared in the "Personals" column of the New Orleans newspapers on April 17, 1946. Inserted by George Sessions Perry, it read: "Since it is an old New Orleans custom to print one's feelings in religious matters and since Lyle Saxon so deeply favored each of these old customs, I'd like to burn this one small candle of congratulations to God Almighty, who now has the rich, the easy, yet exquisite pleasure of the company of this lonely, generous man."

Robert Tallant took Saxon's place as Louisiana's most beloved author and her best writer on the Louisiana theme. He wrote more than a dozen novels and other works on Louisiana, of which *The Romantic New Orleanians, Mardi Gras, Mrs. Candy and Saturday Night,* and *Mr. Preen's Salon* are probably the most widely known. Tallant died suddenly in the spring of 1957, and his death was a great loss to Louisiana literature. Robert Ruark once pleased Louisianians in his column when he wrote regarding Tallant: "Now here is a guy who gives you all the New Orleans atmosphere and the New Orleans feeling . . . good dialogue and some sharp, clean satire and a lot of sound and smell."

During the same period, Gwen Bristow and her husband Bruce Manning, E. P. O'Donnell, and others were writing Louisiana novels which earned national approval. Roark Bradford wrote penetrating and humorous stories and books on the plantation Negro, his most noted works including *This Side of Jordan, John Henry, Kingdom Coming,* and *Ol' Man Adam an' His Chillun.* Hewitt L. Ballowe, a retired doctor who lived all his life near the mouth of the Mississippi, wrote *The Lawd Sayin' the Same* and *Creole Folk Tales,* which have become famous in the field of American folk literature.

John Smith Kendall published a *History of New Orleans* in 1922, and shortly thereafter Stanley C. Arthur began to write and publish works on New Orleans and Louisiana history, including *Old New Orleans* and his most noted work *Jean Laffite; Gentleman Rover,* which partially clears up the mystery of what happened to the pirate after the Battle of New Orleans. William Spratling and Natalie Scott published their *Old Plantation Houses in Louisiana,* Herman Boehm de Bachelle Seebold completed his two-volume *Old Louisiana Plantation Homes and Family Trees,* and George C. H. Kernion brought out his *Old Families of Louisiana.* Sidney A. Marchand, Corinne L. Saucier, and William Edwards Clement contributed to local history with *The Flight of a Century in Ascension Parish; History of Avoyelles Parish, Louisiana;* and *Plantation Life on the Mississippi.* Thomas Ewing Dabney discussed the first hundred years of the New Orleans *Times-Picayune,* while John S. Kendall published *The Golden Age of the New Orleans Theater.*

Other historians were active. Frederick W. Williamson completed *A Narrative History of Northeast Louisiana* and *Yesterday and Today in Louisiana Agriculture.* Henry Plauche Dart specialized in Louisiana law, Louise Butler in the Feliciana country, J. Fair Hardin in the Red River Valley and northwest Louisiana, G. P. Whittington in central Louisiana, William A. Read in Louisiana Indians and place names, Robert Dabney Calhoun in Concordia Parish and the vicinity. Henry E. Chambers published *A History of Louisiana* in 1925, which many historians consider to be the best general history of the state yet written. Harnett Kane's *Louisiana Hayride* presented a strong anti-Long picture of recent Louisiana politics, while *The Bayous of Louisiana* and *Deep Delta Country* beautifully described the country and people of southern Louisiana, but his subsequent work has not measured up to his earlier promise.

[366]

Charles B. Roussève's *The Negro in Louisiana* was the first work covering the Negro in Louisiana. Hodding Carter's *Lower Mississippi* presented a well-written and scholarly account of the area. Wendell H. Stephenson wrote biographies of slave trader Isaac Franklin and ante bellum Senator Alexander Porter, Edwin Adams Davis edited the diary of ante bellum Feliciana planter Bennet H. Barrow, Charles Roland wrote the definitive study of the sugar planters during the Civil War. F. Jay Taylor edited the Civil War diary of Robert Patrick, and Ross Phares wrote a popular biography of Louis Juchereau de Saint-Denis.

Garnie W. McGinty wrote a critical account of the overthrow of the carpetbag regime from 1876 to 1880 and the first modern one-volume history of the state. W. Darrell Overdyke completed his *History of the American Party in Louisiana;* T. Harry Williams published *P. G. T. Beauregard: Napoleon in Gray* in 1954 and two years later edited the Mexican War reminiscences of the same general. New Orleans newspaperman Charles L. ("Pie") Dufour temporarily left his press activities in 1957 to publish *Gentle Tiger: The Gallant Life of Roberdeau Wheat.* John Duffy published the first volume of his monumental two-volume *Rudolph Matas History of Medicine in Louisiana* in 1958; in 1959 John L. Loos brought out his scholarly *Oil on Stream! A History of the Interstate Oil Pipe Line Company, 1909-1959* and Edwin Adams Davis his *Louisiana: The Pelican State.*

Modern Louisianians who were writing fictional works included John C. Chase, Pierre Paul Ebeyer, Mrs. Alice W. Graham, Mrs. Sue Brown Hays, whose *Go Down, Death* sold more than 100,000 copies, Stuart Landry, Father Edward Murphy, whose first novel, *Scarlet Lily,* reached the 200,000 mark in sales, mystery writer W. Shepard Pleasants, David Stern, creator of the talking mule Francis who became a movie hero, and numerous others.

While as yet the great authors of a few years ago—Lyle Saxon, Roark Bradford, Hewitt L. Ballowe, E. P. O'Donnell, Robert Tallant—have not been challenged, the romantic and drama-packed Teche country, the Barataria area, the Vieux Carré of New Orleans, the Delta country, and the Natchitoches area offer challenging themes, plots, and characters to the more than a hundred Louisianians who are actively engaged in some form of writing. The literary future of Louisiana is extremely promising.

THE ARTS. Since 1920, both New Orleans and other sections of the state have attracted numerous painters and artists in other fields, some of whom have been natives of the state. Though Alexander J. Drysdale, the painter of misty Louisiana swamp scenes, continued his work for a short time after 1920, it declined considerably in quality and did not measure up to his earlier work. P. M. Westfeldt was a noted water-colorist, and Robert B. Mayfield is remembered for his sketches of New Orleans. Ronald Hargrave spent several years in New Orleans, painting portraits and making notable etchings of Vieux Carré scenes. Weeks Hall of "The Shadows" at New Iberia, who died during the summer of 1958, will long be remembered for his paintings and artistic photographs. E. H. Suydam sketched throughout the state, and illustrated the books of Lyle Saxon.

Conrad Albrizio and Duncan Ferguson have executed murals for many public buildings, and Mrs. Olive Leonhardt has published a book of drawings called *New Orleans, Drawn and Quartered.* Architect Nathaniel C. Curtis, Sr., published *New Orleans, Its Old Houses, Shops, and Public Buildings,* which is already a collector's item, and Clarence J. Laughlin brought out his *Ghosts Along the Mississippi,* a new and original commentary on the Louisiana scene in pictures. William Spratling, who now lives in Mexico, taught art at Tulane University for a number of years and became a noted painter of Louisiana houses and people, while Charles W. Bein, a water-colorist, for a time headed the New Orleans Art School. The Baroness Lucienne de St. Mart, a miniature painter, had a studio for a number of years in one of the Pontalba Buildings on Jackson Square, where she was frequently bothered by tourists who believed she was the original Baroness de Pontalba, who had the buildings constructed in 1848.

Louisiana's most noted present-day artist is Caroline Wogan Durieux, a member of the Department of Fine Arts at Louisiana State University. She has worked with all known media of painting and has recently developed new processes for the atomic reproduction of paintings and drawings. She is best known as a humorous and satirical painter, and her work has attracted national and even international recognition.

The most noted cartoonist during the first two decades of the period was Trist Wood. Until the advent of Huey Long's *Louisiana Progress* he drew sharp and critical political cartoons for the New Orleans newspapers; after the establishment of the *Progress* he helped shape Louisiana political history in that publication. W. V. Hall, Roy Aymond, and Keith Temple of the *Times-Picayune,* John C. Chase of the *States,* and Jack Sparling of the *Item* also made reputations in this field.

There has been considerable activity in photography. Arnold Genthe published *Impressions of Old New Orleans.* Grace de la Croix Daigre of Plaquemine took notable pictures of places and people along the lower Mississippi, gave one-man shows throughout the state, and exhibited her work in the United States, Europe, and even in South America and Asia. Elemore Morgan, of Baton Rouge, has perhaps the best present-day collection of photographs on the Louisiana scene.

Arthur Morgan is the state's most important modern sculptor and the first native-born Louisianian to make an international reputation in this field. Born in Ascension Parish in 1904, he achieved his first success at the age of twenty, when he was hailed by the New York press as a boy prodigy. Perhaps his most noted work is his statue of Chief Justice Edward Douglass White now in the national capitol at Washington, D.C. Early in his career critic Edward Eckland wrote that "not only does he dream, but like the naive child, must take his dreams apart, piece by piece, to find what they are made of. He has learned how to take them apart and also how to put them together, and his works are his fancies wrought in bronze and marble. . . . with his chisel he alternately hammers, beguiles and coaxes the yielding stone to the gradual unfolding into life, so that the world may look and say,—This is Nature—this is Life."

Enrique Alferez is another well-known sculptor who has done figures for several of the state's public buildings. Juanita Gonzales, until her death in 1935, was thought to be a young sculptress of great promise; her heads of Francis T. Nicholls and General Richard Taylor at the State Capitol are considered excellent work. Richmond Barthé, a Negro sculptor, has shown remarkable ability in depicting Negro character, and his "The African Dancer," "The Boy with a Broom," "The Crab Man," and "Toussaint l'Ouverture," have received acclaim in both the United States and Europe.

Art leagues and guilds have been established in many of Louisiana's major cities, as for example the Arts and Crafts Club of New Orleans, the Art Association of New Orleans, the Baton Rouge Art League, and the Shreveport Art Club. The Art Commission, a branch of the state government, maintains headquarters at the Old State Capitol and is headed by Jay R. Broussard. State-wide organizations, like the Louisiana Art and Artists Guild, assist in promoting exhibitions and in encouraging young artists in the several fields.

DRAMA. While professional drama has declined in importance throughout the state since the appearance of motion pictures, radio, and television, the major cities are occasionally visited by traveling companies of players, and New Orleans regularly offers plays during the winter season. Showboat performances continued to be given until recent years; the last Mississippi River showboat gave performances at New Orleans in 1931, and the last showboat presented a season of plays at the New Orleans New Basin Canal in 1940.

The amateur or little-theater movement has made rapid progress. Le Petit Théâtre du Vieux Carré of New Orleans was founded originally under the name of the Drawing Room Players in 1916 and became one of the best-known little theaters in the nation. Le Petit Théâtre du Réveil Française was established in 1930 for the purpose of reviving the French language in New Orleans, and four years later the Group Theater came into existence. Civic theaters, Town and Gown Players, Players' Guilds, Little Theaters, and other similar organizations have been established in many towns and communities, and though the actors of these groups are all amateurs, they usually employ professional directors for their productions. All the colleges and universities have speech departments which sponsor dramatic performances of various types. *The Cajun,* written by Ada Jack Carver of Natchitoches, won second place in the 1926 National Theater Competition, Le Petit Théâtre du Terrebonne of Houma attracted considerable attention, and Mrs. Bessie Alexander Ficklen of New Orleans authored her excellent *Handbook of Fist Puppets* in 1935.

Louisiana novels and stories have furnished the plots for many Hollywood motion pictures during the past three decades, and in addition the state has had several sons and daughters who have achieved success on the legitimate stage or in motion-picture, radio, or television work.

MUSIC. Music declined after the Civil War, but revived strongly after 1900. The New Orleans Philharmonic Society was founded in 1906, and by the 1920's was giving concerts and bringing noted vocal and instrumental artists to the city. The New Orleans Civic Symphony, organized in 1936, a few years ago was merged with the Philharmonic Society to become the New Orleans Philharmonic Symphony. Dr. Henry W. Stopher achieved nationwide recognition for the State University's department of music during the 1930's when he brought ex-Metropolitan baritone Pasquale Amato and the noted conductor Louis Hasselmans to the institution to produce operas.

Two days after a brilliant performance of Meyerbeer's *Les Huguenots,* on the evening of December 2, 1919, the old French Opera House of New Orleans, one of the most cherished buildings in Louisiana, was destroyed by fire. Thereafter for ten years New Orleans was without opera. In 1930 the Chicago Civic Opera troupe enjoyed a short season, and was followed in 1935 and 1936 by longer engagements of the San Carlo Opera Company. The Metropolitan Opera Association enjoyed brief but brilliant seasons in 1939, 1940, and 1941, and a few years later the New Orleans Opera House Association began to promote music dramas. Agitation has been strong in New Orleans for a number of years for the construction of a new opera house, while André Lafargue urged that its "home must be a resurrection, architecturally and otherwise, of the old-time and never-to-be forgotten French Opera House, standing again at the corner of Bourbon and Toulouse streets, as a guiding light, a beacon of operatic endeavor and New Orleans musical fervor."

The college and university departments of music throughout the state have made many contributions to serious music through their orchestras, bands, and other music organizations. John Morriessy, Director of the Tulane University band, has become a band-music composer of national recognition through his compositions on Louisiana and Latin-American themes, while band director Dwight Greever Davis of Northwestern State College has gained a wide reputation as a conductor, band-music arranger, and organizer of a central music organization for the states of Arkansas, Louisiana, and Texas. Dillard University sponsors the Lower Mississippi Valley Musical Festival, and when the program was inaugurated in 1937 more than three hundred singers participated in the concerts. In more recent years music has become highly developed in the public junior-high schools and high schools, and annual contests are held between the various bands and orchestras.

Musical compositions by Louisianians or about Louisiana have aroused considerable public interest since 1920. Mortimer Wilson's *New Orleans,* based on the New Orleans Mardi Gras, won the 1920 prize for the best original American overture. Ferde Grofé caught the rich coloring of the Old Louisiana in his *Mississippi Suite,* as did Virgil Thompson in the *Louisiana Story*. Jacque Wolfe's *Swamp River Suite* and his musical score for Roark Bradford's immortal *John Henry* are highly descriptive of Louisiana.

CHAPTER 31

LIFE IN THE MODERN
STATE

An OLD CULTURE AND A MODERN CIVILIZATION. Louisiana has made rapid progress during the past four decades, and many features of the "Old Louisiana" are now but memories of a past generation. Louisianians live in better houses equipped with once-undreamed-of household conveniences and with radio and television sets to bring the outside world into their living rooms. Their work has been made easier by the labor-saving devices of the industrial age. Improved schools, colleges, universities, and libraries offer the opportunity for better educations. They have more and better automobiles, travel over superior hard-surfaced roads, use bridges instead of ferries to cross bayous and rivers, and have all but forgotten the breakdowns, flat tires, and "boggings-up" of only a few years ago. The many inconveniences of the "old days" håve disappeared, and the younger generation is accepting the new conveniences as a matter of course.

Until recent years many towns and villages of South Louisiana were more European than American in appearance, and those of the northern and western sections of the state were old fashioned and unprogressive. During the last few decades these towns have shaken off the lethargic past and are beginning to look like those of other states. The 1920's brought so many changes in the Vieux Carré of New Orleans that civic-minded citizens organized an association for the preservation of its historic buildings and old Spanish appearance. In more recent years Abbeville, St. Martinville, Thibodaux, Natchitoches, and a few other towns have taken steps to preserve some of their Old-World atmosphere.

Country life has become more attractive because of the installation of rural electrical systems, indoor plumbing, and natural or bottled gas. Farmers have built new homes, new barns, and other farm buildings. In 1930 only 1½ per cent of the Louisiana farms used electricity; in 1954 over 92 per cent were electrified. Over 50,000 farms have electric washing machines, over 30,000 have electric water pumps, over 15,000 have electric freezers, and many have electrical cooling systems. The day of the walking plow and the palm-leaf fan has passed.

The old civilization of Louisiana is rapidly disappearing, except in more remote villages and rural areas. The older Negroes, however still say that "when you'se young you heats from the inside out, when you gits old you heats from the outside in"; grandmothers and grandfathers still tell their grandchildren "when the cat's away the rats give a ball" or "grab for too much and it slips away from you" or "when we come close to a giant, he often turns out to be only a common man on stilts." To many South Louisianians a modern clothes closet is still an "armoire"; they still drink "café noir," strong and black and hot, or "café au lait," with hot milk. And occasionally when you make a purchase at a store or pay your monthly bill the proprietor will still give you a little gift as "lagniappe." The Louisiana Folklore Society, the

Louisiana Historical Association, and other organizations are trying to preserve many of the old customs, traditions, folkways, buildings, and historic landmarks.

Louisianians no longer live in the past and talk about the "good old days before the war" as their grandfathers did, for the generations who lived during the periods of the War for Southern Independence and military occupation have passed from the scene. Louisianians live in the present and look forward to the future, and if they occasionally talk of "Yankees" and Yankee ways, it is usually in jest and in the pride of the state and of the South. The heroic years from 1861 to 1865 and the tragic years of Radical rule are now a part of the Louisiana heritage.

The modern Louisianian will perhaps be pardoned if he takes great pride in his old civilization and cultural heritage. Some years ago Colonel James M. Morgan, who was born and reared in New Orleans, returned home for a visit and was standing on the Esplanade looking across the street at the old house where he had been born and where he had spent his youth. A tourist guide walked up behind him and in well-staged, somewhat broken English of the South Louisiana bayou country offered to show him about the city for a dollar. Indignantly the colonel turned on him, and with the gestures of the country shouted in his native patois, *"Mo pas oule que to fait ça!"* The prospective guide gasped and said, *"Mais Monsieur, vous êtes de nous autres?"* And the colonel replied, "Yes, I am a Cajun just like you and the next fellow who mistakes me for a Yankee will either have to take a thrashing or give me one."

The romantic and historic past, the bustling, industrial present, and the boundless future are happily combined in Modern Louisiana. The speech, customs, and other heritages of many nationalities give extra color to a land where the old rubs shoulders with the new. Its varied resources bring new citizens every year, while the relics of the old civilization, warm climate, and many recreational opportunities are an attraction to numerous tourists. Louisiana *is* an interesting state. Between Opelousas and Morgan City lies the heart of the romantic Bayou Teche and Creole country, while in the Feliciana parishes and along the lower Mississippi are many ante bellum homes. Grand Isle is a picturesque fishing, trapping, and resort village, and others are found in the Delta country of the Mississippi and scattered about the southern part of the state. Examples of early French architecture and plantations once held by slaveowning Free Negroes are found in the Natchitoches section.

New Orleans is the most "different" city in the nation, its modern Canal Street shopping center just a stone's throw away from the aged and historic buildings of the Vieux Carré. Perhaps one of the best characterizations of the city came recently from a writer in the *Louisiana Municipal Review,* for he catches her spirit as few writers have done: "New Orleans is the tinkle of a piano in the Vieux Carré and the smoke-filled atmosphere of an off-the-sidewalk bar. It is superb creole food prepared and served with the elegance of dinner in an Old World palace . . . it's the whisper of voodoo and gris-gris and the noise of slave auctions that lingers, like the voice of a ghost. . . . It is the fleeting glimpse of a Vieux Carré patio with palms and sub-tropical plants speckled with sunshine and shadow . . . Basin Street . . . and above-the-ground cemeteries. . . . It's the smell of fish at the historic French Market . . . it's the old man dreaming away the hours on a bench in Jackson Square and the inspired move of an artist's pencil . . . it's the spires of St. Louis Cathedral against a blue sky."

THE PEOPLE OF MODERN LOUISIANA. A few years ago Gilbert L. Dupre of St. Landry Parish wrote of Louisiana and its people: "I love its soil. I love its people. We are cosmopolitan to the core. Originally of French and Acadian descent, the American is now with us. My children are descended from a Connecticut Yankee on the mother's side. That's a good cross. Creole on one side, Yankee on the other."

Modern Louisianians are bred from many nationalities and races: Indians, Frenchmen, Spaniards, Canary Islanders, West Indians, English, Germans, Italians, Acadians, Free Negroes from Santo Domingo, Negro slaves from Africa or the other slave-holding states, Irish, Chinese, Sicilians, Hungarians, Slavonians, and probably others too. Each of these national and racial groups contributed to Louisiana's culture and civilization. In most communities these nationalities and races are well mixed, but in others one group may remain almost intact, thereby preserving many of its native or nationalistic customs; these communities, called "culture islands," are fairly well geographically scattered about the state. Pure Spanish, for example, is still spoken on Delacroix Island in St. Bernard Parish, many Slavonians live in Plaquemines Parish and speak their native Slav language, and a sizeable group of Hungarians is found in Livingston Parish.

It has been suggested that three statues in the state represent the basic national and racial energies which lifted Louisiana from the Mississippi swamps. The statue of Bienville, the "Father of Louisiana," in front of the new railroad station in New Orleans, typifies her French heritage. Overlooking Cane River at Natchitoches is the bronze figure of an old Negro, who might stand as deputy for his people. A third statue, that of Huey Long, looks from the formal sunken garden toward the State Capitol and might well represent the energy and drive of the Anglo-Saxon. Other statues should be erected to other representatives of peoples who have worked to make a great and interesting state.

Many of the French, Spanish, Italian, German, and other nationalities have continued to teach their native tongue to their children. It is not unusual today to hear two languages mixed in the same sentence, and such phrases as *"beaucoup* persimmons," meaning many persimmons, are frequently heard. Many Modern Louisianians of French descent deliberately mix up their English as a joke among themselves or for the benefit of newcomers or wide-eyed tourists. They will say "he lives in that house which is white, him," or will end the sentence with "Yes?" or "No?" or *"Hein?"* If you tell a South Louisiana girl that she is pretty she may reply, "You is tell me something what I is know." And if you talk of leaving the state, the Cajun may ask you, as one did his friend some years ago, "For why you want to go to She-cow-go, you? See how the sun she shine on the bayou, *hein?* If you was in She-cow-go you would not see the sun like those, no? In She-cow-go when the sun come up, the smoke from Pittsburgh he pass all over She-cow-go." And he will laugh with you at his little joke.

Fun-loving Creoles not infrequently dress up their speech with exaggerations or inversions. Witness the old Cajun who said: "You see ma cow down by de bayou you push heem home, yes. He been gone tree day now—yesterday, today, and tomorrow." Or the old lady, as she looked with loving eyes at her husband of nearly half a century: "It ain't much fun being married twice as old as yourself to a man, no."

Louisianians are proud of their nationalistic and racial heritages. Not long ago an aged Creole pointedly told this writer: "General Jackson? Certainly I have heard of him. He fought at Chalmette. He helped Jean Laffite and the Creoles lick the British." Even first-and second-generation citizens brag of the fact that they are Louisianians. Not too many years ago an old man who lived south of Lafayette boasted that he was a Louisianian, even though he had been born outside the state and his father had been a politically prominent carpetbagger during the Radical years of military occupation. Today many citizens who have no French ancestors at all are learning to speak French, and some of them even say, *"Je suis Français, Français de la Louisiane,"* (I am French, Louisiana French).

AMUSEMENTS AND SPORTS. Modern Louisiana has more numerous and more varied types of fairs and festivals than any other state in the Union. These fairs and festivals are generally staged for educational purposes, to advertise a particular natural resource or product, and to provide recreation. The entire state participates in the State Fair, while area fairs are primarily for particular sections. Joint-parish fairs are sponsored by two or more parishes, parish fairs by individual parishes, community fairs by individual towns or communities, and product fairs by those interested in the production of rice, oranges, peaches, yams, or other products.

There are held yearly more than a hundred fairs and festivals, including over fifty parish or joint-parish fairs, nearly twenty product festivals, over a dozen area fairs, and several community fairs. As late as 1910 the legislature made no appropriations for the benefit of these institutions, in 1920 slightly less than $50,000 was appropriated, but in 1955 the legislature appropriated nearly $3,500,000 for the biennium 1955-56. During recent years there has been mounting criticism of the large sums given by the legislature to these fairs and festivals, some citizens believing that the various communities should finance their own projects.

In 1956 the state celebrated the two hundredth anniversary of the coming of the Acadians to Louisiana. A group of citizens from all sections of the state organized a program of activities for the entire year, which closed with a colorful festival at St. Martinville, the Acadian capital of Louisiana. One of the most interesting of Louisiana festivals is the Natchitoches Christmas Festival, which is completely supported by that community. It originated in 1927, when Max Burgdorf suggested that the city sponsor a lighting and fireworks display, and has developed until today the entire city is decorated and lighted at Christmas time. The business section of Natchitoches receives special attention with over $75,000 worth of lighting equipment, including over 125,000 light bulbs. People from many states, as well as thousands of Louisianians, visit Natchitoches each year to see the display of lights and the fireworks exhibition.

Even more widely known outside the state is the Louisiana carnival season which ends on Mardi Gras day. The center of carnival activities is New Orleans, where there are numerous regularly scheduled day or night parades and dozens of balls held by the various carnival organizations. The King of the Carnival on Mardi Gras day is Rex, the Lord of Misrule, while Comus is the Lord of Mirth and Laughter. New Orleans is jammed with masked revelers from the entire state and nation, but the police have little trouble with the vast crowds and join in the merrymaking. At six in the evening masks are removed but the funmaking continues until midnight ushers in Ash Wednesday, the beginning of the Lenten Season, and the revelry must cease.

Some years ago a visitor to Louisiana wrote: "Though New Orleans can strike a serious note, it is a gay-hearted city. New York is too hurried even to smile, London on a sunny day can only look complacent and cheerful, but New Orleans can riotously laugh. During the carnival, Rex, its king, is the merriest, maddest, gayest of all living monarchs. Mardi Gras makes even the most melancholy citizen cheerful. The people love the carnival and never grow tired of it, for it means colour, light, music and movement." John Temple Graves believed that New Orleans "would be gay until the heavens fell," and that the Crescent City's gaiety was "in the blood, a relic of history . . . a Latin touch that will have no commerce with Anglo-Saxon heaviness." Although New Orleans has the most important carnival in Louisiana, many other towns, cities, and communities celebrate the season with balls and parades.

In addition to modern commercialized entertainment, Louisianians still enjoy many of the old amusements. Families and friends still gather for dinners, parties, and visiting. *Gumbo ya-ya,* where people get together and just talk, is still enjoyed; and on Saturday nights, particularly in southern bayou country, the old *fais-do-do* is still held in much the same manner as it was in a yesteryear.

Some of the state's greatest assets are its mild climate, numerous streams, bayous, and lakes, rolling hill country, broad prairies, and extensive forests which offer outdoor sporting opportunities possessed by few sister states. Hunting is universally enjoyed, the coastal marshes, streams, and lakes being combed for ducks, geese, and other wild fowl, the upland areas for quail, squirrels, and rabbits, and the interior ridgelands and swamps for deer, wild hog, and even bear. The sportsman can fish in fresh-water bayous and streams for bass, crappie, and perch, in the Gulf of Mexico for shark, king mackerel, or tarpon, and in the coastal lagoons and bays for trout, sheepshead, pompano, flounder, red snapper, and redfish.

The state maintains more than a dozen state parks, including Lake Bistineau State Park in Webster Parish, Chicot State Park in Evangeline Parish, Fontainebleau

[374]

State Park in St. Tammany Parish, and Sam Houston State Park in Calcasieu Parish. These parks have vacation cabins, picnic shelters, beaches, small game courts, and group camp buildings, and everywhere in the state are opportunities for camping, swimming, boating, and hiking.

Louisianians love competition in their sports. Horse racing, and power-boat, pirogue and sailboat racing are popular, and racing meets and regattas are held annually at various race tracks and on Gulf, lake, bayou, and river waters. Scholastic and college competitive sports, such as football, basketball, baseball, and track, attract many thousands of spectators annually. The Mid-Winter Sports Carnival is held annually at New Orleans in the last week in December and ends with the Sugar Bowl football game on January 1. Cities and towns have recreational parks, golf courses, tennis courts, and picnic grounds.

Creole and Negro folk music is still a part of Louisiana social life but is disappearing as members of the older generation pass from the scene. Some Louisiana Creole infants, however, are still put to sleep with the old, traditional cradle songs. The fortunate child still hears "Comper Lapin" (Gossip Rabbit), "O Mi Sieu Banjo" (O Mister Banjo), and "Cher, Mo L'Aime Toi" (Dear, I Love You So), and other songs; as he grows older he learns game songs, songs of love, war, and joy, and the old tunes played and sung for generations at *fais-do-dos*.

Negroes still sing spirituals, although those in the French language are rapidly passing, and no one knows where or when the old music or lyrics were written, perhaps, as Rosemary and Stephen Vincent Benét wrote,

> Out of stolen Africa,
> The singing river rolled,
> And David's hands were dusky hands,
> But David's harp was gold.

One of the most poignant spirituals runs:

> Tell yuh 'bout a man wot live be-fo Chris'—
> His name was Adam, Eve was his wife.
> Tell yuh how dat man he lead a rugged life,
> All be-cause he tak-en de 'ooman's ad-vice.
> She made his Trou-ble so hard—
> She made his trou-ble so hard—
> Lawd, Lawd, she made his trou-ble so hard.
> Yas, indeed—his trou-ble was hard.

Negro river and roustabout chants are sometimes heard in more remote sections and even along the New Orleans water front:

> They ain't but a thousand mo'—
> My knee bones is achin',
> My shoulder is so'—
> When I make this trip
> Ain't gonna make no mo'.
> Coonjine, nigger, coonjine.

or,

> What makes me lak my Baby so?
> She does my washin', she pays my bo'd;
> She pays my bo'd, she pays it right,
> I'm goin' to git on the big boat next Sad-day night.

"Oh, Babe" was popular nearly a hundred years ago and has not yet completely disappeared. A few of its many stanzas include:

> Told my women when I lef' town,
> I been a good ole wagon, but I mos' broke down,
> Oh, Babe. . . .
>
> I bucked dem dice, an' ma point wuz fo',
> Ella's in jail an' ma money don't go,
> Oh, Babe.
>
> That ole dame got mad at me,
> I won ten dolluhs, wouldn't give her but three,
> Oh, Babe.
>
> I'll be dogged ef I kin see,
> How dat money got away frum me,
> Oh, Babe. . . .

It is only natural that New Orleans, where modern jazz originated, is still one of the jazz capitals of the nation. During past years many musicians who later gained national reputations started their careers in Vieux Carré bars and nightclubs or in smaller barrel houses. Included in the group are Jelly-Roll Morton, Sidney Bechet, Louis Armstrong, King Oliver, Louis Prima, Pete Fountain and numerous others.

RELIGION. In 1956 a survey of the National Council of Churches revealed that Louisiana had the highest percentage of churchgoing citizens in the nation, with over 80 per cent of the white population attending Protestant, Catholic, or Jewish churches. Slightly over 50 per cent of these people are Protestant, a little more than 47 per cent Catholic, and the rest are either Jewish or belong to some other faith. About 80 per cent of the colored population are Protestants, a majority of them being Baptists. There are over 2,500 churches in the state, New Orleans alone having over 750. The largest religious denominations in point of number of churches are the Baptist with over 1,200, the Methodist with more than 600, and the Catholic with over 350.

Many old religious customs are still observed, though others are passing from common use. In New Orleans, in particular, the custom of offering public thanks to some saint by way of a newspaper advertisement is still practiced. The celebration of All Saints' Day, with the gathering of people in candlelighted cemeteries, may yet be witnessed in South Louisiana. Fishing boats and fleets are still blessed, the most important of these ceremonies being the annual blessing of the shrimp fleet. Funerals are still sometimes announced on a black-bordered poster giving the name of the deceased and the time and place of the funeral. The little Catholic Chapel of the Madonna, located about nine miles south of Plaquemine, has the distinction of being the smallest church in Louisiana; the building is only eight by eight feet and just large enough for a small altar, a priest and his assistant.

Three important fraternal orders are allied with religion, the Masonic Order, the Knights of Columbus, and B'Nai B'Rith. The Masonic Order is open to all persons who believe in God and the immortality of the soul, regardless of faith; the Knights of Columbus is a Catholic organization; and B'Nai B'Rith is for Jews. The colored branch of the Knights of Columbus is called the Knights of Peter Claver. These organizations all have women's auxiliaries. In 1955 there were almost 50,000 Masons in Louisiana, nearly 20,000 members of the Knights of Columbus, and about 6,000 members of B'Nai B'Rith.

FOODS AND FASHIONS IN COOKERY. An English visitor to New Orleans once wrote that it was the one city in the world "where you can eat and drink the most and suffer the least"; another traveler said that New Orleans was the "only city in America where street quarrels may be heard over the respective merits of certain restaurants and dishes." These comments need not have been restricted to the Crescent City, for the entire state, particularly the southern sections, is renowned for its excellent, and to other Americans exotic, food.

Louisiana cookery still is basically of two types: the cookery of the northern and northwestern sections of the state, which was inherited from English-speaking ancestors from the eastern southern states, and the Creole or southern Louisiana cookery, which combines the French love of delicacies with the Spanish taste for poignant seasonings. The members of every national group living in colonial, ante bellum, old, or modern Louisiana, however, have contributed to the great variety of Louisiana dishes. Today the Louisianian eats French and Spanish bisques, gumbos, and jambalayas, American corn pone, chitterlings and pie, Southern fried chicken and hushpuppies, and even Hungarian kapostas and goulashes.

Roy Alciatore, the proprietor of Antoine's Restaurant in New Orleans, has given a good explanation of Louisiana's Creole foods: "I consider myself most fortunate in having been born in that most extraordinary heaven of natural resources, encompassing in its borders all that could possibly be desired for a full and happy existence. Native Louisianians are in a class by themselves because their environment and unsurpassed opportunities have made them acutely appreciative of the better things of life." He continued that "Louisiana cooks are past masters in the art of seasoning and therein lies the secret of their success in imparting flavor to their cuisine." In support of Alciatore's statement that "where else in the world will one find such a variety of seafood," one visitor appreciatively described the New Orleans French Market, where "the fish stalls were shimmering mounds of silver, purple and blue, with strings of red snappers hanging above, seemingly carved out of pink coral. Grey trout, speckled with orange and scarlet, were flanked with enormous lobsters and greenish grey crabs."

A few of the old-time dishes are still prepared by cooks in the Creole sections. *Maquechou* is a dish made of corn cut from the cob and smothered with onions; *jambalaya au congri* is a combination of kidney beans or cowpeas and rice cooked with a little onion, salt meat and/or ham, and still sometimes called *moros y Cristianos* (Moors and Christians); and *daube glacée* is a jellied veal made with calves' and pigs' feet by old cooks who refuse to use modern short-cut methods of preparation. *Riz au lait* is a dessert made of rice boiled in milk; *pain-patate* is a small cake made of sweet potatoes, while *calas tout chaud* are rice cakes fried in deep fat, liberally sprinkled with sugar, and served hot. *La cuite* is a heavy cane syrup filled with pecans, and *bière douce,* which is almost unobtainable today, is a wonderful combination of pineapple peelings, brown sugar, cloves, and rice.

Coush-coush (sometimes spelled "kush-kush" and sometimes called "kush"), corn meal soaked with milk and fried in a little fat, is still eaten for breakfast. Bouillabaisse, which British novelist William Makepeace Thackery called "a sort of soup, or broth, or stew, or hotchpotch of all sorts of fishes," is yet found on many Louisiana tables. Gumbo is still a prime favorite, and one occasionally hears the old jingle which used to be recited by the irreverent:

> Poor crawfish ain't got no sho,
> Frenchmen catch 'em and make gumbo.
> Go all 'round the Frenchmen's beds,
> Don't find nothin' but crawfish heads.

"Pot liquor and corn pone" is a universal favorite, pot liquor being the water in which any variety or combination of varieties of greens have been cooked with a piece of salt meat or ham. Huey Long once took time out in the United States Senate to explain to the uninitiated how to prepare the dish properly.

Some Louisianians, particularly the Negroes, have given nicknames to some of their

[377]

dishes. The "Sunday breakdown" is fried chicken and grits, "flat cars" are pork chops, while "red and white" is red beans and rice, and a "coal yard" is a cup of strong, black coffee. They have also composed songs and written verses and jingles about them, like the one in which the narrator delivers the admonishment,

> When I dies, do bury me deep,
> Put a jug of 'lasses at my feet.
> Put a chunk of corn bread in my hand,
> So I can sop my way to the Promised Land.

While many of the intricately fashioned dishes are disappearing from everyday tables, numerous restaurants in the southern section of the state keep alive the grand tradition of Creole cookery. New Orleans is the gourmet's capital, and has several restaurants which have achieved national and even international fame with their culinary creations. Although Antoine's has been in existence since the 1840's and is the most noted restaurant, Kolb's, La Louisiane, Manale's, Maylie's, Tujague's, Commander's Palace, and several others have built noteworthy reputations over the years. Galatoire's is a distinctly French epicurean Mecca and has stanchly refused to yield to the lures of overcommercialization. Occupying an entire early-nineteenth-century mansion on Royal Street is Brennan's, owned and managed by members of the Brennan family, the newest, most picturesque, and hard-pressing Antoine's as the city's most distinctive restaurant, where a leisurely dinner on the second-floor gallery overlooking the dimly lit, fountained patio is both a gastronomic and esthetic experience not soon forgotten.

FLAGS AND OFFICIAL EMBLEMS OF LOUISIANA. Many flags have flown over Louisiana or over various sections of the state. From the days of early French settlement until the Spanish officially took possession of the colony the golden lilies of the French kings, the yellow fleur-de-lis flecked on a white shield, waved from the several capitals in southern Mississippi and Alabama and finally from the Government House at New Orleans. It was followed by the red, white, and yellow flag of Spain, with golden castles and rampant red lions on a red and white quartered field; in 1785 the flag of Spain was changed and the bars of Aragon were added. From 1763 to the time of the successful campaigns of Governor Bernardo de Gálvez the present-day Florida Parishes belonged to Great Britain, and this section flew the crosses of St. George and St. Andrew.

During the first twenty days of December, 1803, the tricolor of Revolutionary France was Louisiana's flag and was succeeded by the flag of the United States. In 1810, when the people of the Florida Parishes revolted against Spain and organized an independent republic, they raised a flag bearing a large white star on a blue field. The western boundary of the Louisiana Purchase had not been fixed in 1812 when the state entered the Union, and Spain claimed the southwestern section east of the Sabine River. Before the boundary was officially fixed by the Florida Purchase Treaty, which was proclaimed in 1821, Mexico had won her independence from Spain, and some historians claim therefore that the flag of Mexico flew over the narrow section of land just east of the Sabine River called the Sabine Strip.

After Louisiana seceded in 1861 and before she joined the Confederate States of America, she was, technically at least, an independent nation, and her flag had red, white, and blue stripes and a single yellow star in a red field. This flag was followed by the Stars and Bars of the Southern Confederacy, and after the end of the Civil War, by the flag of the United States again.

Louisiana did not officially adopt a State Seal until 1902. The official description is as follows: "A pelican, with its head turned to the left, in a nest with three young, the pelican, following the tradition, in the act of tearing its breast to feed its young; around the edge of the Seal to be inscribed 'State of Louisiana.' Over the head of the pelican to be inscribed 'Union, Justice'; under the nest of the pelican to be inscribed 'Confidence.' " There was continued argument for many years over this seal and the exact meaning of the words "with its head turned to the left." Did this mean to the bird's left or to the left of the person looking at the picture of the seal? Only recently the Secretary of State decided that it meant to the pelican's left and to the right of the person looking at it.

The official State Flag, adopted in 1912, has a blue field, on which is a white pelican, feeding its young as in the State Seal. Below the pelican is a white ribbon on which is written in blue the State Motto, "Union, Justice, Confidence." The State Bird is the Eastern Brown Pelican. The State Flower is the white blossom of the magnolia tree, and though many people consider the magnolia as the State Tree, it has never officially been so designated. The State Song, adopted in 1932, is the "Song of Louisiana," with both music and words by Vashti Robertson Stopher. The State March Song, "Louisiana, My Home Sweet Home," was adopted in 1952, and the words are by Sammie McKenzie and Lou Levoy, the music by Castro Carazo.

Louisiana has several nicknames of which "The Pelican State" seems to be the most popular; less common are "The Bayou State," "The Sugar State," and "The Creole State." Louisianians themselves also have nicknames, being called "Pelicans," "Creoles," and sometimes "Tigers," which originated with the noted Louisiana military unit that fought in the Civil War.

A MODERN LAND OF TALES AND LEGENDS. Louisiana is a modern and progressive state, but is filled with folklore and tales and legends, a few of which have been deliberately fashioned by Louisianians for their own amusement or for more credulous tourists and sojourners. Anyone will tell you that Louisiana was named for Louis XIV of France and his mother, who was Anna of Austria; in fact, however, La Salle named the country "Louisiane," which meant literally the "land of Louis." The Spanish kept the same name but naturally used their own spelling, "Luisiana." After the area was purchased by the United States, Americans combined the two words using the French spelling of "Louis" and the Spanish ending "iana."

One of the oldest of Louisiana legends concerns a supposed visit by French Prince Louis Philippe to Valcour Aime, a wealthy planter who lived just above New Orleans, in 1798. According to the legend the dishes of gold which were used at a banquet for the prince were afterwards tossed into the Mississippi. Only two things are wrong with this romantic story: first, Valcour Aime was a very sound businessman and would never have thrown away the golden dishes; second, he was not born until 1798 and would scarcely have been old enough to have entertained the prince. Citizens of New Orleans enjoy telling tourists about the house in which Louis Philippe, Lafayette, and Marshal Ney, one of Napoleon's generals, are supposed to have visited on one occasion. It is a wonderful story, but, in fact, Louis Philippe visited Louisiana in 1798, Lafayette in 1825, Marshal Ney was never in Louisiana at all, and the house was not built until 1832.

Louisianians still repeat legends of the noted slave outlaw, Bras Coupe, who had superhuman strength, or the true tale of Coulon de Villiers, who captured George Washington at Fort Necessity. There are tales of Jean Laffite and of numerous treasures buried throughout the state. There are strange legends about birds and animals and fish, such as the one about the choupique which is able to live out of water. There are tales about that fabulous riverman Mike Fink and Northern statesman John Hay once wrote a poem about the noted Jim Bludso, whose steamboat exploded, a poem which ends:

> The fires bust out as she clar'd the bar,
> And burnt a hole in the night,
>   And quick as a flash she turned and made
> For that willer-bank on the right.
>   There was runnin' and cursin', but Jim yelled out

[379]

Over all the infernal roar,
    "I'll hold her nozzle again the bank
Till the last galoot's ashore."

    Through the hot, black wreath of the burnin' boat,
Jim Bludso's voice was heard,
    And they all had trust in his cussedness
And knowed he would keep his word.
    And, sure's you're born, they all got off
Afore the smokestacks fell,
    And Bludso's ghost went up alone
In the smoke of the *Prairie Belle*.

    He weren't no saint but at jedgment
I'd run my chance with Jim,
    'Longside of some pious gentleman
That wouldn't a-shook hands with him.

There are hundreds of mosquito and bug descriptions and stories, many of which were first written or told by travelers and later adopted by Louisianians. British Reverend David Macrae protested that the mosquitoes ". . . which have no moral right to appear before the month of May, were already beginning to sound their piobrach in the bedroom. I got no sleep the first night with these little winged tormentors. The second night the mosquito-curtains were up." French traveler Berquin Du Vallon wrote that "From the beginning of spring to the beginning of autumn these diabolical creatures provoke you, harass you, torment you unceasingly with their sharp bills." It was poet Joaquin Miller who made the acquaintance of ". . . a lot of jet-black bugs as big as mice," at the Canal Street wharf. "I never saw such creatures in my life," he wrote. "Now and then they would dive off into the water. One of these bugs finally elbowed around and lifting upon his hind legs looked me squarely in the eyes. He had a mustache like the King of Italy."

The best and most beloved of all Louisiana legends was "invented" one afternoon by those two joke-loving, strongly pro-Louisiana authors, Lyle Saxon and Roark Bradford. Inventing the tale as they went along, they straight-facedly told it to northern writer Carl Carmer, who was in Louisiana at the time gathering material for a book. Carmer swallowed the tale and put it in his book, from which it has been copied and recopied by numerous writers. Ben Botkin even put it in his *Treasury of Southern Folklore* as an authentic Louisiana legend. Louisianians have eagerly claimed it as such.

Saxon and Bradford, amid chuckles and occasional laughter, told this writer the circumstances under which the legend of Annie Christmas was "invented." Late one afternoon the two men were in a Vieux Carré bar having a quiet and sociable drink, when in walked the "northern nuisance," who it was charged, was noted for "picking other people's brains" and then not giving them proper credit in his published work. One of the two men suddenly had the inspiration—they would never admit which one it was—and started right off. "By the way, Carmer, I suppose that you're going to include the Legend of Annie Christmas in your book?" Carmer had never heard of it. "What, you've never heard of Annie Christmas? Why that's the most noted of all Louisiana legends." Carmer shook his head. "Good Lord, man, you've never—" Whichever one it was began the tale, went as far as he could and stopped, and the other, who during the period had been "inventing" furiously, picked up the story.

Annie Christmas was a gigantic Negress, (although in some later versions she is white) nearly seven feet tall and weighing over 250 pounds, and had a huge handlebar mustache. She was a river woman who could outfight, outdrink, outwork, outsmoke, outrun, and outlove any riverman who ever lived. She was as strong as Paul

Bunyan, perhaps even a mite stronger. John Henry would have been like a little boy compared to her, and Pecos Bill would have been bested in lassoing lightning or riding tornadoes had they been permitted to contest hand-to-hand in such a rodeo. She once bent over and kissed the Mississippi in a moment of gratitude, and the Old Man completely dried up from bank to bank for fourteen miles. She had a voice as loud and deep as a foghorn, could whip a dozen river boatmen with one hand tied behind her back, and had no difficulty in carrying a hogshead of sugar under each arm and another on top of her head. She once towed a barge up the Mississippi from New Orleans to Natchez so fast that the boat skipped over the water like a swallow, and she never once got out of breath.

While Annie usually dressed as a man, she sometimes wore red satin gowns and scarlet plumes. Her necklace was over thirty feet long, each bead representing eyes she had gouged out or noses and ears she had bitten off in her fights. New Orleans toughs were afraid to enter saloons when she was so decked out, for at such times she was a lovin' woman; they remembered that occasion when she, in a fit of pent-up emotion, grabbed that Wisconsin lumberjack, kissed him, and had left nothing but a grotesque piece of charred cinder. Annie finally fell in love with a little shrimp of a gamblin' man named Charlie, and instead of having twins or triplets, Annie and Charlie had twelve sons who were over seven feet tall by the time they were six years old. Finally Charlie died and Annie gave him a fine funeral. Then she and her twelve sons placed his body on a river barge, and together they floated down the Mississippi and out to sea, never to be seen or heard of again.

A STATE WITH A FABULOUS HISTORY. Other states have interesting, romantic histories; that of Louisiana has been truly fabulous, for it incorporates all of the attributes which make up a fast-moving, action-packed, strong-charactered drama. Much of what has occurred has not yet been told by the historian and much of that which has been written has been inaccurately presented. Grace King wrote that Louisiana had been the "spoiled child of American historians, who have treated her more as some charming character of fiction than as a sister in the sedate family of states." A critic wrote of one author's work: "She has not only given us back our past, but has stuck a rose in its teeth, and a pomegranate bloom behind its ear!"

Louisiana history needs no added glamour. The names of her parishes, for example, indicate their own romantic story. Some, like Avoyelles, Natchitoches, Ouachita, or Caddo were named for Indian tribes, while Calcasieu (crying eagle), Catahoula (beloved lake), and Tangipahoa (ear of corn) were Indian words. Others, such as Baton Rouge (red stick), Terrebonne (good earth), or Plaquemines (persimmons), recall the French period. La Salle, De Soto, Iberville, and Bienville were named after explorers or colonial leaders, while Iberia, Concordia, East Feliciana and West Feliciana reflect the Spanish regime. St. James, St. John the Baptist, and St. Martin have a religious origin. Some were named for American statesmen like Washington, Franklin, or Jefferson, others for such Confederate leaders as Jefferson Davis or General P. G. T. Beauregard.

The names given the old plantations reveal a historic or romantic past—"Kenilworth," "Ivanhoe," "Palo Alto," "Afton Villa," "Waverley," and numerous others. Streets of towns, particularly those of the older sections, perpetuate the past. In New Orleans the Spanish period is represented by Galvez, Gayoso, and Salcedo; the French Revolutionary neoclassicism by Apollo, Bacchus, and Dryades; the age of the Corsican by Napoleon Avenue, Austerlitz, Jena, and Marengo. The American period after 1803 brought names of American heroes.

Louisiana's past is liberally sprinkled with gallant and romantic incidents, as for example the romantic story of the casket girls or the gallant stand of Jackson and his men at Chalmette. A stanch young Civil War soldier's humor is revealed by a section in one of Wylie Micajah Barrow's letters: "This morning I was up early as there was no use to attempt to sleep. We had nothing to eat until nine o'clock when they brought us a barrel of crackers and some bacon. We fried the bacon on sticks. Lord deliver me from such such hard ships [sic]; sitting on the ground, trying to keep warm, our eyes filled with smoke, and no handkerchief to blow my nose on. Sky cloudy." One young Louisiana student just before the outbreak of the Civil War showed his strong sense of duty when he wrote to his father: "I intend to remain & study until my Country calls me home; & if she does, I will lay aside my law books, and shoulder my musket." Young James Stubbs inadvertently revealed his code of personal conduct when he wrote: "I have tried hard all the time to conduct myself soberly & quietly; I have not had a cross word with any one at all. I have treated everybody as politely as possible."

Despite Louisiana's colorful and dramatic past, she has done less than any other state to preserve the private records of her people and the official records and archives of various governmental divisions. The French were careless in the keeping of records, but the Spanish, realizing their historical importance, kept and preserved carefully the records of their government. The archives of French and Spanish Louisiana were sealed by Laussat, the French Commissioner, in 1803 and were later acquired by Governor Claiborne. After some time Claiborne turned them over to the Municipal Council of New Orleans. Still later they came under the custody of Peter Pedesclaux, who had been appointed custodian of notarial records by Governor Claiborne. They remained intact for many years, but without proper care and without ever being indexed or even inventoried.

Some time before the Civil War the state archives were removed to the capitol at Baton Rouge by order of the legislature, and the Louisiana Historical Society was made official custodian. Before the capitol was burned in 1862 they were plundered and many of the documents carried off by Federal soldiers. Others were destroyed or seriously damaged by fire and water. After the Civil War numerous documents were found in other states, particularly in Wisconsin, and some of these were returned to the state. The archives were again placed under the control of the historical society, which filed them for safekeeping in the Cabildo. Since that time, despite the tremendous progress of archival science, Louisiana's priceless records and archives have been carelessly handled and many have been destroyed. Others have been stolen and have found their way into the hands of collectors or into archival depositories and libraries in other states.

While the Department of Archives at Louisiana State University has done much since its founding in 1935 to collect and preserve the archives and private manuscripts of Louisiana's past, it is not an official state agency and its work has therefore been limited. By 1956, Louisiana was the only state in the Union which did not maintain an agency for the collection, preservation, and better organization of its state, county, and local archives and historical records.

Such an agency, the State Archives and Records Service, was created by the legislature in 1956 after a two-year, state-wide survey, sponsored by Secretary of State Wade O. Martin, Jr. and generally supervised by Edwin Adams Davis, had been completed by John C. L. Andreassen, but received no appropriation with which to function. The 1958 legislature made a small appropriation to the Service and under Andreassen's directorship it began limited operations. It is hoped that the Service will soon secure modern facilities for the proper processing and storage of these important documents and that it will be granted sufficient funds to at least match the work done by such southern states as North Carolina, South Carolina, Georgia, Virginia, Tennessee, and Mississippi. Henry Plauche Dart's eloquent and almost pathetic plea— "Let us put our archives in shape for the children who will soon take our places, that they may study the past and plan for the future"—may in the near future be possible of realization.

A few years ago historian Wendell H. Stephenson wrote that "the history of Louisiana is practically virgin soil. . . . There is . . . no satisfactory comprehensive history of Louisiana." Stephenson's statement is true. Despite the historical writing of the more remote past and even that of recent years, much remains unwritten. The state badly needs a new generation of dedicated Louisiana historians who will diligently research and then write scholarly monographs on the multiple phases of Louisiana history, for only after this enormous job of spadework is done will it be possible for a historian or historians to produce that definitive history for which the state has so long been waiting.

The two historical associations in the state have not provided the proper leadership for such work. The Louisiana Historical Society, which had active and inactive periods after its original organization in 1835, was reorganized in 1893, began to issue annual *Publications,* and to hold meetings where Louisiana's history was discussed. During the past thirty years, however, the Society has become chiefly a New Orleans organization and, despite generous direct legislative grants until recent years, has taken little interest in stimulating historical activity throughout the state. From 1917 until a few years ago it published the *Louisiana Historical Quarterly,* the printing of which was paid for by the state, its editors during the years until 1948 being John Dymond (1917-21), Henry P. Dart (1922-34), and Walter Prichard (1935-48). From 1948 until it ceased publication, the *Quarterly* led a hand-to-mouth existence; during several of those years, however, Joseph Tregle of Loyola University performed outstanding service as editor and made heroic personal efforts to keep it alive without financial assistance from the society.

The Louisiana Historical Association was organized in New Orleans by a group of Civil War veterans in 1889 for the purpose of preserving the records and relics of that conflict. It established the Confederate Museum in that city and for a number of years was very active in its work, then went into a period of decline. In 1958 the Association was reorganized at Louisiana College, Pineville, on a state-wide and broader historical basis, amended its charter, and made plans to achieve the objectives of a really functioning state historical organization. By January, 1960, it had increased its membership to over 500 and had brought out the first issue of its quarterly journal, *Louisiana History,* sponsored by Louisiana State University and edited by Edwin Adams Davis and A. Otis Hebert, Jr. It is hoped that the legislature will provide sufficient funds to enable the Association to modernize and adequately maintain the Confederate Museum, continue the publication of *Louisiana History,* and sponsor the publication of secondary and source books relative to the history of the state.

A FINAL WORD. Louisianians have always loved their land; they agree with the words of French Commisioner Laussat as he left Louisiana in 1804: "It is a hard thing for me, having once known this land, to part from it." They recall its history, the old days when their ancestors, in the words of N. H. Herrin, "lived in the grand manner, with a pure Gallic touch for comfort and gaity, and died slowly, for their ghosts still remain." They agree with Lafcadio Hearn's words about New Orleans, applying them to the entire state: "Rest with me. I am old, but thou hast never met with a younger more beautiful than I. . . . My charms are not the charms of much gold and great riches, but thou mayst feel with me such hope and content as thou hast never felt before . . . if thou leavest me, thou must forever remember me with regret."

They love their homes and the opportunities for enjoyable living which the present state offers them. They agree with the words of former big-league baseball pitcher Bill Lee, when he retired and returned home: "Baseball doesn't give you much of a chance for home. Man, nothing can beat the feeling when you walk in your own backyard after supper, and the dogs come jumping up on you with rabbits in their eyes."

Modern Louisianians are trying to preserve the old values of life, among which one historian lists pride, bravery, honor, courtesy, generosity, and loyalty. They agree with the statement President William Howard Taft made in New Orleans in 1909, "one of the advantages of living in a State like Louisiana is that we get a proper sense of proportion with reference to the place we occupy in history." A recent author, expressing it somewhat differently, mentioned six senses which would apply to Louisianians—the sense of place: the strong feeling for the land and community where one lives; the sense of family: respect for ancestors and for what they accomplished; the sense of unity: the closeness which Louisianians feel when they meet away from home; the sense of proportion: the combination of courtesy, leisure, and hard work; the sense of humor: the love of legends and tall tales and the ability to sometimes laugh at ourselves; and the sense of religion: the deep religious feeling which has caused Louisianians to be the most churchgoing people in the nation.

Will future citizens of Louisiana be able to retain the real and worthwhile values of their old civilizations while continuing to keep in step with scientific, industrial, and cultural progress? The answer will be up to each new generation. Louisianians of the present and those of the future might well heed the words of Daniel Webster: "Our proper business is improvement. Let us cultivate the resources of our land, build up its institutions, promote all its great interests, and see whether we also, in our day and generation, may not perform something to be remembered."

BIBLIOGRAPHY

The following list of books in no way forms a complete or comprehensive bibliography of Louisiana history nor does it include all the materials used in the preparation of this historical study; it only comprises what this writer considers to be a representative group of more or less fundamental works dealing with the state's history in general or with various topical subjects, phases, or chronological periods.

Specific monographs printed from 1895 to 1917 in the *Publications* of the Louisiana Historical Society or in the *Louisiana Historical Quarterly* (1917-1957), as well as those on Louisiana history published in other historical journals, have not been cited. Travelers' accounts and the descriptions of those who sojourned in the state for varying periods have been generally omitted. Only a few of the mimeographed publications of the Federal Archives Survey and the Historical Records Survey have been included. No attempt has been made to identify or list the different editions and/or translations of various older works, many of which have appeared under changed titles—the works of Gayarré, for example, have been printed in both French and English and in several editions.

It is hoped that the list will be of service as a general guide to those who are seriously interested in learning more about the events and the personalities of Louisiana's fabulous and frequently highly dramatic past.

ABERNETHY, THOMAS PERKINS, *The Burr Conspiracy* (New York, 1954).

ADAMS, HENRY, *History of the United States*, 9 vols. (New York, 1889-1891). [See proper volumes for British Invasion of 1814-1815.]

ANDERSON, JOHN Q., ed., *Brokenburn; The Journal of Kate Stone, 1861-1868* (Baton Rouge, 1955).

ANDREASSEN, JOHN C. L., *Louisiana Archives Survey. Report No. 1: Survey of Public Records* (Baton Rouge, 1956).

ANDRY, LAURE, *Histoire de la Louisiane* (New Orleans, 1882).

ARTHUR, STANLEY CLISBY, *Audubon; An Intimate Life of the American Woodsman* (New Orleans, 1937).

ARTHUR, STANLEY CLISBY, *Jean Laffite, Gentleman Rover* (New Orleans, 1952).

ARTHUR, STANLEY CLISBY, *Louisiana Tours; A Guide to Places of Historic and General Interest* (New Orleans, 1950).

ARTHUR, STANLEY CLISBY, *Old New Orleans; A History of the Vieux Carre, its Ancient and Historical Buildings* (New Orleans, 1937).

ARTHUR, STANLEY CLISBY, *The Story of the Battle of New Orleans* (New Orleans, 1915).

ARTHUR, STANLEY CLISBY, *The Story of the West Florida Rebellion* (St. Francisville, 1938).

ARTHUR, STANLEY CLISBY, and KERNION, G. C. HUCHET DE, *Old Families of Louisiana* (New Orleans, 1931).

ASBURY, HERBERT, *The French Quarter* (New York, 1936).

BAILLARDEL, A., and PRIOULT, A., *Le Chevalier de Pradel; Vie d'Un Colon Français en Louisiane au XVIII Siecle* (Paris, 1928).

BALLOWE, HEWITT LEONARD, *Creole Folk Tales; Stories of the Louisiana Marsh Country* (Baton Rouge, 1948).

BALLOWE, HEWITT LEONARD, *The Lawd Sayin' The Same; Negro Folk Tales of the Creole Country* (Baton Rouge, 1947).

BANKSTON, MARIE LOUISE BENTON, *Camp-fire Stories of the Mississippi Valley Campaign* (New Orleans, 1914).

BARBÉ-MARBOIS, FRANÇFIS, *Historie de la Louisiane* (Paris, 1829).

BARDÉ, ALEXANDRE, *Historie des Comités de Vigilance aux Attakapas* (Saint-Jean-Baptiste, Louisiane, 1861).

BARNWELL, ROBERT GIBBES, ed., *The New-Orleans Book* (New Orleans, 1850).

BARROW, C. J., *Biographical Sketches of Louisiana's Governors* (Baton Rouge, 1893).

BARTLETT, NAPIER, *Military Record of Louisiana: Including Biographical and Historical Papers Relating to the Military Organization of the State* (New Orleans, 1875).

BARTLETT, NAPIER, *A Soldier's Story of the War, Including the Marches and Battles of the Washington Artillery, and of Other Louisiana Troops* (New York, 1874).

BASSO, ETOLIA S., ed., *The World from Jackson Square, A New Orleans Reader* (New York, 1948).

BASSO, HAMILTON, *Beauregard, The Great Creole* (New York, 1933).

BAUDIER, ROGER, *The Catholic Church in Louisiana* (New Orleans, 1931).

BAUDRY DES LOZIÈRES, LOUIS NARCISSE, *Second Voyage à la Louisiane, Faisant suite au Premier de l'Auteur de 1794 à 1798* (Paris, 1803).

BAUGHN, WILLIAM, *The Changing Structure of the Louisiana Economy* (Baton Rouge, 1954).

BEALS, CARLETON, *The Story of Huey P. Long* (Philadelphia, 1935).

BEERS, HENRY PUTNEY, *The French in North America. A Bibliographical Guide to French Archives, Reproductions, and Research Missions* (Baton Rouge, 1958).

BELISLE, JOHN G., *History of Sabine Parish, Louisiana* (Many, 1912).

BELL, AMOS W., *The State Register* (Baton Rouge, 1855).

BERNARD, ANTOINE, *Histoire de la Louisiane* (Quebec, 1953).

BERTRAND, ALVIN L., *Agricultural Mechanization and Social Change in Rural Louisiana* (Baton Rouge, 1951).

BICKLE, LUCY LEFFINGWELL, *George W. Cable; His Life and Letters, by His Daughter* (New York, 1929).

BIEVER, ALBERT HUBERT, *The Jesuits in New Orleans and the Mississippi Valley* (New Orleans, 1924).

Biographical and Historical Memoirs of Louisiana, 2 vols (Chicago, Goodspeed Publishing Co., 1892).

Biographical and Historical Memoirs of Northwest Louisiana (Chicago, 1890).

Biographical Sketches of Louisiana Governors from D'Iberville to McEnery, by a Louisianaise (New Orleans, 1883).

BLAIN, HUGH MERCER, ed., *Favorite Huey Long Stories* (Baton Rouge, 1937).

BLESSINGTON, JOSEPH P., *The Campaigns of Walker's Texas Division* (New York, 1875).

BOLTON, HERBERT EUGENE, ed., *Athanese de Mezieres and the Louisiana-Texas Frontier, 1768-1780*, 2 vols. (Cleveland, 1913-14).

BOOTH, ANDREW B., *Records of Louisiana Confederate Soldiers and Louisiana Confederate Commands*, 3 vols. in 4 (New Orleans, 1920).

BOSSU, JEAN BERNARD, *Travels Through that Part of North America Formerly Called Louisiana*, 2 vols. (London, 1771).

BOTKIN, B. A., ed., *A Treasury of Mississippi River Folklore* (New York, 1955).

BOTKIN, B. A., ed., *A Treasury of Southern Folklore* (New York, 1949).

BOURGEOIS, LILLIAN C., *Cabanocey; The History, Customs and Folklore of St. James Parish* (New Orleans, 1957).

BRAGG, JEFFERSON DAVIS, *Louisiana in the Confederacy* (Baton Rouge, 1941).

BRASHER, MABEL, *Louisiana, A Study of the State* (Richmond, 1929).

BRUNN, H. O., *The Story of the Original Dixieland Jazz Band* (Baton Rouge, 1960).

BUCHANAN, W. C., *Louisiana Geography* (Oklahoma City, 1957).

BUNNER, E., *History of Louisiana from its First Discovery and Settlement to the Present Time* (New York, 1841).

BURSON, CAROLINE MAUDE, *The Stewardship of Don Esteban Miro, 1782-1792* (New Orleans, 1940).

BUSHNELL, DAVID I., *The Choctaw of Bayou Lacomb, St. Tammany Parish, Louisiana* (Washington, 1909).

BUTLER, BENJAMIN FRANKLIN, *Autobiography and Personal Reminiscences of Major-General Benj. F. Butler; Butler's Book* (Boston, 1892).

BUTLER, BENJAMIN FRANKLIN, *Private and Official Correspondence of Gen. Benjamin F. Butler During the Period of the Civil War*, 5 vols. (Norwood, Mass., 1917).

BUTLER, PIERCE, *Judah P. Benjamin* (Philadelphia, 1907).

BUTLER, RUTH LAPHAM, ed. and trans., *Journal of Paul du Ru* (Chicago, 1934).

CABLE, GEORGE WASHINGTON, *The Creoles of Louisiana* (New York, 1884).

CABLE, GEORGE WASHINGTON, *Strange Stories of Louisiana* (New York, 1888).

CALDWELL, NORMAN WARD, *The French in the Mississippi Valley, 1740-1750* (Urbana, Ill., 1941).

CALDWELL, STEPHEN A., *A Banking History of Louisiana* (Baton Rouge, 1935).

CARAYON, P. AUGUSTE, *Bannissement des Jésuites de la Louisiane* (Paris, 1865).

CARLETON, RODERICK L., *Local Government and Administration in Louisiana* (Baton Rouge, 1935).

CARLETON, RODERICK L., *The Reorganization and Consolidation of State Administration in Louisiana* (Baton Rouge, 1937).

CARPENTER, M. H., *Counting the Electorial Votes of Louisiana, 1877* (Washington, D. C., 1877).

CARPENTER, W. M., *Sketches from the History of Yellow Fever* (New Orleans, 1844).

CARTER, CLARENCE EDWIN, ed., *The Territorial Papers of the United States*, Vol. IX: *The Territory of Orleans, 1803-1812* (Washington, 1940).

CARTER, HODDING, *John Law Wasn't So Wrong* (Baton Rouge, 1952).

CARTER, HODDING, *Lower Mississippi* (New York, 1942).

CARTER, HODDING, *Where Main Street Meets the River* (New York, 1952).

CARTER, HODDING, and CARTER, BETTY W., *So Great a Good, A History of the Episcopal Church in Louisiana and of Christ Cathedral, 1905-1955* (Sewanee, Tenn., 1955).

CARTER, HOWELL, *A Cavalryman's Reminiscences of the Civil War* (New Orleans, n.d.).

CASADO, VICENTE RODREGUEZ, *Primeros Años de Dominación Española en la Luisiana* (Madrid, 1942).

CASKEY, WILLIE MALVIN, *Secession and Restoration of Louisiana* (University, La., 1938).

CASTELLANOS, HENRY C., *New Orleans As It Was* (New Orleans, 1895).

CASTONNET DES FOSSES, *La Louisiane sous la Domination Française* (Nantes, 1887).

CAUGHEY, JOHN WALTON, *Bernardo de Galvez in Louisiana, 1776-1783* (Berkeley, Calif., 1934).

CHAMBERS, HENRY E., *A History of Louisiana*, 3 vols. (New York, 1925).

CHAMBERS, HENRY E., *Mississippi Valley Beginnings* (New York, 1922).

CHAMBERS, HENRY E., *West Florida and Its Relation to the Historical Cartography of the United States* (Baltimore, 1898).

CHAMBON, CELESTIN M., *In and Around the Old St. Louis Cathedral of New Orleans* (New Orleans, 1908).

CHAMPIGNY, JEAN BOCHART, *État-Present de la Louisiane, avec toutes les particularités de cette Province d'Amérique* (LaHaye, 1776).

CHAMPIGNY, JEAN BOCHART, *La Louisiane Ensanglantée* (Londres, 1773).

CHAPIN, ADELLE (Le Bourgeois), *"Their Trackless Way"; A Book of Memories* (New York, 1932).

CHARLEVOIX, PIERRE FRANÇOIS XAVIER DE, *History and General Description of New France*, 6 vols. (New York, 1900).

CHARLEVOIX, PIERRE FRANÇOIS XAVIER DE, *A Voyage to North America: Undertaken by Command of the present King of France, Containing the Geographical Description and Natural History of Canada and Louisiana*, 2 vols. (Dublin, 1766).

CHARNLEY, MITCHELL VAUGHN, *Jean Lafitte, Gentleman Smuggler* (New York, 1934).

CHILDS, WILLIAM TALBOTT, *John McDonogh, His Life and Work* (Baltimore, 1939).

CHRISTIAN, J. T., *A History of the Baptists of Louisiana* (Nashville, 1923).

Chronological List of Constitutional Provisions, Acts and Joint Resolutions of the State of Louisiana Relating to Her Public Lands from 1817 to 1886 (Baton Rouge, 1889).

CLAPP, THEODORE, *Autobiographical Sketches and Recollections, During a Thirty-five Years' Residence in New Orleans* (Boston, 1857).

CLEMENT, WILLIAM EDWARDS, *Plantation Life on the Mississippi* (New Orleans, 1952).

CLINE, RODNEY, *The Life and Work of Seaman A. Knapp* (Nashville, 1936).

[COCHUT, ANDRÉ], *The Financier, Law; His Scheme and Times* (London, 1856).

COMTE DE PARIS, LOUIS PHILIPPE ALBERT D'ORLÉANS, *History of the Civil War in America*, 4 vols. (Philadelphia, 1875-1888).

Condition of Affairs in Louisiana (House Document No. 91, 42 Cong., 3 Sess., Washington, 1873).

CONDON, J. F., *Annals of Louisiana, 1815-1861* (New Orleans, 1882).

[CORCORAN, D.], *Pickings from the Portfolio of the Reporter of the New Orleans "Picayune"* (Philadelphia, 1846).

CORTHELL, ELMER LAWRENCE, *A History of the Jetties at the Mouth of the Mississippi River* (New York, 1880).

COULTER, E. MERTON, ed., *The Other Half of Old New Orleans* (Baton Rouge, 1939).

County-Parish Boundaries in Louisiana (Historical Records Survey. New Orleans, 1939).

COX, ISAAC JOSLIN, ed., *The Journeys of René Robert Cavelier Sieur de la Salle*, 2 vols. (New York, 1905).

COX, ISAAC JOSLIN, *The West Florida Controversy, 1793-1813* (Baltimore, 1918).

COXE, DANIEL, *Description of the English Provinces of Carolina by the Spaniards called Florida, and by the French, Louisiane* (London, 1741).

CRAMER, ZADOK, *The Navigator . . . to which is added an appendix containing an account of Louisiana* (Pittsburgh, 1811).

The Creole Tourist's Guide and Sketch Book to the City of New Orleans (New Orleans, 1910).

CROSS, ROBERT ALAN, *The History of Southern Methodism in New Orleans* (New Orleans, 1931).

CROUSE, NELLIS M., *Lemoyne d'Iberville: Soldier of New France* (Ithaca, 1954).

CRUCHET, RENÉ, *En Louisiane* (Bordeaux, 1937)

CRUCHET, RENÉ, *France et Louisiane* (University, La., 1939).

CURTIS, NATHANIEL CORTLANDT, *New Orleans, Its Old Houses, Shops and Public Buildings* (Philadelphia, 1933).

CUSHMAN, HORATIO BARDWELL, *History of the Choctaw, Chickasaw and Natchez Indians* (Greenville, Texas, 1899).

DABNEY, THOMAS EWING, *One Hundred Great Years; The Story of the Times-Picayune from its Founding to 1940* (Baton Rouge, 1944).

DARBY, WILLIAM, *A Geographical Description of the State of Louisiana* (New York, 1817).

DART, BENJAMIN WALL, *Constitutions of the State of Louisiana and Selected Federal Laws* (Indianapolis, 1932).

DAVID, URBAIN, *Les Anglais à la Louisiane* (New Orleans, 1845).

DAVIS, EDWIN ADAMS, *Louisiana: The Pelican State* (Baton Rouge, 1959).

DAVIS, EDWIN ADAMS, ed., *Plantation Life in the Florida Parishes of Louisiana, 1836-1846; As Reflected in the Diary of Bennet H. Barrow* (New York, 1943).

DAVIS, FORREST, *Huey Long; A Candid Biography* (New York, 1935).

DAWSON, SARAH MORGAN, *A Confederate Girl's Diary* (Boston, 1913).

DEBOUCHEL, VICTOR, *Histoire de la Louisiane, Depuis les Premiéres Découvertes jusqu'en 1840* (Nouvelle-Orléans, 1841).

DEILER, JOHN HANNO, *The Settlement of the German Coast of Louisiana and the Creoles of German Descent* (Philadelphia, 1909).

DELANGLEZ, JEAN, *The French Jesuits in Lower Louisiana, 1700-1763* (Washington, 1935).

DENNETT, DANIEL, *Louisiana As It Is* (New Orleans, 1876).

DESDUNES, RODOLPHE L., *Nos Hommes et Notre Histoire* (Montreal, 1911).

DESMAZURES, ADAM C. G., *Histoire du Chevalier d'Iberville* (Montreal, 1890).

DEVOL, GEORGE H., *Forty Years a Gambler on the Mississippi* (New York, 1887).

DEVRON, GUSTAVE, *The Story of Medicine in Louisiana* (New Orleans, 1895).

DIDIMUS, HENRY, *New Orleans as I Found it* (New York, 1845).

DIMITRY, JOHN, *School History of Louisiana* (New York, 1877).

DITCHY, JAY K., *Les Acadiens Louisianais et Leur Parler* (Baltimore, 1932).

DORSEY, FLORENCE L., *Master of the Mississippi; Henry Shreve and the Conquest of the Mississippi* (Boston, 1941).

DORSEY, SARAH A., *Recollections of Henry Watkins Allen* (New York, 1866).

DUBROCA, LOUIS, *L'Itinéraire des Français dans la Louisiane* (Paris, 1802).

DUFFY, JOHN, ed., *Parson Clapp of the Strangers' Church of New Orleans* (Baton Rouge, 1957).

DUFFY, JOHN, *Rudoph Matas History of Medicine in Louisiana*, (Volume I, Baton Rouge, 1958).

DUFOUR, CHARLES L., *Gentle Tiger; The Gallant Life of Roberdeau Wheat* (Baton Rouge, 1957).

DUGANNE, AUGUSTINE JOSEPH HICKEY, *Camps and Prisons; Twenty Months in the Department of the Gulf* (New York, 1865).

DUMONT DE MONTIGNY, BUTEL, *Mémoires historiques sur la Louisiane*, 2 vols. (Paris, 1753).

DUNCAN, HERMAN COPE, *The Diocese of Louisiana: Some of its History* (New Orleans, 1882).

DUNN, T. C., *Morehouse Parish* (New Orleans, 1885).

DUNN, WILLIAM EDWARD, *Spanish and French Rivalry in the Gulf Region of the United States, 1678-1702* (Austin, Texas, 1917).

DU PRATZ, ANTOINE SIMON LE PAGE, *Histoire de la Louisiane*, 3 vols. (Paris, 1758).

DUPRE, GILBERT L., *Political Reminiscences* (Baton Rouge, 1917).

DURHAM, JOHN P., and RAMOND, JOHN S., *Baptist Builders in Louisiana* (Shreveport, 1934).

DYER, BRAINERD, *Zachary Taylor* (Baton Rouge, 1946).

ENGELHARDT, GEORGE WASHINGTON, *New Orleans, Louisiana, The Crescent City* (New Orleans, 1903).

EVANS, MELVIN, *A Study in the State Government of Louisiana* (Baton Rouge, 1931).

EWER, JAMES K., *The Third Massachusetts Cavalry in the War for the Union* (Maplewood, Mass., 1903).

EYRAUD, JEAN M., and MILET, DONALD J., *A History of St. John the Baptist Parish, With Biographical Sketches* (Marrero, La., 1939).

FAIRALL, HERBERT S., *The World's Industrial and Cotton Centennial Exposition, New Orleans, 1884-85* (Iowa City, Iowa, 1885).

FAY, EDWIN WHITFIELD, *The History of Education in Louisiana* (Washington, 1898).

FEIBELMAN, JULIAN B., *A Social and Economic Study of the New Orleans Jewish Community* (Philadelphia, 1941).

FICKLEN, JOHN ROSE, *History and Civil Government of Louisiana* (Chicago, 1901).

FICKLEN, JOHN ROSE, *History of Reconstruction in Louisiana* (Through 1868) (Baltimore, 1910).

FINERAN, JOHN KINGSTON, *The Career of a Tinpot Napoleon; A Political Biography of Huey P. Long* (New Orleans, 1932).

FLEMING, WALTER L., *General W. T. Sherman as College President* (Cleveland, 1912).

FLEMING, WALTER L., *Louisiana State University, 1860-1896* (Baton Rouge, 1936).

FLETCHER, JOEL L., *Louisiana Education Since Colonial Days* (Lafayette, 1948).

FLINN, FRANK M., *Campaigning with Banks in Louisiana* (Lynn, Mass., 1887).

FLINT, TIMOTHY, *Recollections of the Last Ten Years* (Boston, 1826).

FLYNN, DENIS, *Why? Huey P. Long was Murdered. The True Story Told* (New Orleans, 1936).

FOOTE, HENRY STUART, *The Bench and Bar of the South and Southwest* (St. Louis, 1876).

FOOTE, LUCY B., *Bibliography of the Official Publications of Louisiana, 1803-1934* (Historical Records Survey. Baton Rouge, 1942). [See continuation of Official Publications by Lucy B. Foote (1935-1948) and Margaret T. Lane (1948-1953).]

FOOTE, LUCY B., *Bibliography of the Official Publications of Louisiana, 1935-1948* (State of Louisiana, Official Publications, Volume I. Baton Rouge, 1954).

FORD, JAMES A., *Analysis of Indian Village Site Collections From Louisiana and Mississippi* (New Orleans, 1936).

FORTIER, ALCÉE, *A History of Louisiana*, 4 vols. (New York, 1904).

FORTIER, ALCÉE, ed., *Louisiana: Comprising Sketches of Counties, Towns, Events, Institutions, and Persons, Arranged in Cyclopedic Form*, 3 vols. (Atlanta, 1909).

FORTIER, ALCÉE, *Louisiana Folk-Tales in French Dialect and English Translation* (Boston, 1895).

FORTIER, ALCÉE, *Louisiana Studies; Literature, Customs, and Dialects, History and Education* (New Orleans, 1894).

FOSSAT, GUY SONIAT DU, *Synopsis of the History of Louisiana* (to 1791). Translated by Charles T. Soniat. (New-Orléans, 1903.)

FRANZ, ALEXANDER, *Die Kolonization des Mississippitales bis zum Ausgange der Franzosischen Herrschaft* (Leipzig, 1906).

FRÉGAULT, GUY, *Le Grand Marquis, Pierre de Rigaud de Vaudreuil et la Louisiane* (Montreal, 1952).

FRÉGAULT, GUY, *Iberville le Conquérant* (Montreal, 1944).

FRENCH, B. F., *Historical Collections of Louisiana* [Title varies], 7 vols. (New York, 1846-1875).

GAYARRÉ, CHARLES ÉTIENNE ARTHUR, *History of Louisiana*, 4 vols. (New Orleans, 1903).

GIRAUD, MARCEL, *Histoire de la Louisiane Française*. Tome Premier: *Le Régne de Louis XIV, 1698-1715* (Paris, 1953).

GIRAUD, MARCEL, *Histoire de la Louisiane Française*. Tome Second: *Années de Transition, 1715-1717* (Paris, 1958).

[GLASS, J. S.], *St. Martin Parish, The Richest Sugar Lands in the State* (St. Martinville, 1898).

[GLEIG, GEORGE ROBERT], *The Narrative of the Campaigns of the British Army at Washington and New Orleans* (London, 1821).

GOODMAN, WILLIAM DAVIS, *Gilbert Academy and Agricultural College, Winsted, Louisiana. Sketches and Incidents* (New York, 1892).

GOSSELIN, AUGUSTE, *Journal d'Iberville* (Évreux, France, 1900).

GOULD, EMERSON W., *Fifty Years on the Mississippi, or Gould's History of River Navigation* (St. Louis, 1889).

GRACE, ALBERT L., *The Heart of the Sugar Bowl; The Story of Iberville* (Plaquemine, 1946).

GRAHAM, KATHLEEN, *Notes On A History of Lincoln Parish, Louisiana* (Ruston, 1934).

GRAVIER, GABRIEL, ed., *Relation du Voyage des Dames Religieuses Ursulines de Rouen à la Nouvelle-Orléans* (Paris, 1872).

GRAVIER, HENRI, *La Colonisation de la Louisiane à l'Epoque de Law, 1717-1721* (Paris, 1904).

GRIFFIN, HARRY LEWIS, *The Attakapas Country; A History of Lafayette Parish, Louisiana* (New Orleans, 1959).

GUÉNIN, EUGÈNE, *La Louisiane* (Paris, 1904).

GUÉRIN, LÉON, *Les Navigateurs Français; Histoire des Navigations, découvertes et colonisations françaises* (Paris, 1847).

HALL, ABRAHAM OAKEY, *The Manhattaner in New Orleans; or, Phases of "Crescent City" Life* (New York, 1851).

HALL, WINCHESTER, *The Story of the 26th Louisiana Infantry, in the Service of the Confederate States* (n.p., 1891).

HAMILTON, HOLMAN, *Zachary Taylor, Soldier of the Republic* (Indianapolis, 1941).

HAMILTON, PETER JOSEPH, *Colonial Mobile* (Boston, 1910).

HAMMOND, HILDA P., *Let Freedom Ring* (New York, 1936).

HARDIN, J. FAIR, *Northwestern Louisiana; A History of the Watershed of the Red River, 1714-1937*, 3 vols. (Louisville, 1937).

HARMON, NOLAN B., *The Famous Case of Myra Clark Gaines* (Baton Rouge, 1946).

HARRINGTON, FRED HARVEY, *Fighting Politician: Major General N. P. Banks* (Philadelphia, 1948).

HARRIS, D. W., and HULSE, B. M., *The History of Claiborne Parish, Louisiana* (New Orleans, 1886).

HARRIS, THOMAS H., *The Story of Public Education in Louisiana* (New Orleans, 1924).

HARRIS, THOMAS O., *The Kingfish, Huey P. Long, Dictator* (New Orleans, 1938).

HARRISSE, HENRI, *Histoire Critique de la Découverte du Mississipi, 1669-1673* (Paris, 1872).

HATCHER, WILLIAM B., *Edward Livingston, Jeffersonian Republican and Jacksonian Democrat* (Baton Rouge, 1940).

HAVARD, WILLIAM C., *The Government of Louisiana* (Baton Rouge, 1958).

HEARN, LAFCADIO, *Chita: A Memory of Last Island* (New York, 1889).

HEARN, LAFCADIO, *Creole Sketches* (Boston, 1924).

HEARN, LAFCADIO, *"Gombo Zhebes," A Little Dictionary of Creole Proverbs* (New York, 1885).

HEARN, LAFCADIO, *La Cuisine Creole* (New York, 1885).

HEINRICH, PIERRE, *La Louisiane sous la Compagnie des Indes, 1717-1731* (Paris, 1908).

HENNEPIN, LOUIS, *A Description of Louisiana*. Translated by John Gilmary Shea. (New York, 1880).

HENRY, A., and GERODIAS, V., *The Louisiana Coast Directory* (New Orleans, 1857).

HEPWORTH, GEORGE H., *The Whip, Hoe, and Sword; or, The Gulf Department in '63* (Boston, 1864).

Historical Epitome of the State of Louisiana (New Orleans, 1840).

Historical Sketch Book and Guide to New Orleans and Environs . . . edited and Compiled by Several Leading Writers of the New Orleans Press (New York, 1885).

HODGE, FREDERICK W., *Handbook of American Indians* (Washington, 1912).

HOSMER, JAMES K., *The Color-Guard: Being a Corporal's Notes of Military Service in the Nineteenth Army Corps* (Boston, 1864).

HOSMER, JAMES K., *The History of the Louisiana Purchase* (New York, 1902).

HOWARD, PERRY H., *Political Tendencies in Louisiana, 1812-1952* (Baton Rouge, 1957).

HUBERT-ROBERT, RÉGINE, *L'historie Merveilleuse de la Louisiane Français* (New York, 1941).

HUHNER, LEON, *The Life of Judah Touro (1775-1854)* (Philadelphia, 1946).

HULSE, B. M., *History of Claiborne Parish, Louisiana* (New Orleans, 1886).

HUTCHINS, THOMAS, *An Historical Narrative and Topographical Description of Louisiana and West Florida* (Philadelphia, 1784).

[389]

IRBY, SAM, *Kidnaped by the Kingfish, by Sam Irby, the Victim* (New Orleans, 1932).

IRWIN, RICHARD B., *History of the Nineteenth Army Corps* (New York, 1892).

JAMES, JAMES ALTON, *Oliver Pollock; The Life and Times of an Unknown Patriot* (New York, 1937).

JEWELL, EDWIN L., ed., *Jewell's Crescent City, Illustrated* (New Orleans, 1873).

JOHNSON, LUDWELL H., *Red River Campaign; Politics and Cotton in the Civil War* (Baltimore, 1958).

JOHNSON, THOMAS CARY, *The Life and Letters of Benjamin Morgan Palmer* (Richmond, 1906).

JONES, DR. JOSEPH, *Medical and Surgical Memoirs*, 3 vols. in 4 (New Orleans, 1876-1890).

Journal de la Guerre du Micissippi contre les Chicachas, en 1739 et finie en 1740. . . . Par un officer de l'armee de M. de Nouaille (Nouvelle York, 1859).

The Journal of Jean Laffite; The Privateer-Patriot's Own Story (New York, 1958).

KANE, HARNETT T., *The Bayous of Louisiana* (New York, 1943).

KANE, HARNETT T., *Deep Delta Country* (New York, 1944).

KANE, HARNETT T., *Louisiana Hayride: The American Rehearsal for Dictatorship, 1928-1940.* (New York, 1941).

KENDALL, JOHN SMITH, *The Golden Age of the New Orleans Theater* (Baton Rouge, 1952).

KENDALL, JOHN SMITH, *History of New Orleans*, 3 vols. (Chicago, 1922).

KEYES, FRANCES PARKINSON, *All This is Louisiana; An Illustrated Story Book* (New York, 1950).

KING, GRACE ELIZABETH, *Creole Families of New Orleans* (New York, 1921).

KING, GRACE ELIZABETH, *Jean Baptiste Le Moyne, Sieur de Bienville* (New York, 1892).

KING, GRACE ELIZABETH, *Memories of A Southern Woman of Letters* (New York, 1932).

KING, GRACE ELIZABETH, *New Orleans; The Place and the People* (New York, 1895).

KING, GRACE ELIZABETH, and FICKLEN, JOHN ROSE, *A History of Louisiana* (New York, 1893).

KING, GRACE ELIZABETH, and FICKLEN, JOHN ROSE, *Stories from Louisiana History* (New Orleans, 1905).

KINNAIRD, LAWRENCE, ed., *Spain in the Mississippi Valley, 1765-1794*, 3 vols. (*Annual Report of the American Historical Association for the year 1945*, Washington, 1949).

KNIFFEN, FRED B., *The Indians of Louisiana* (Baton Rouge, 1945).

KNOX, THOMAS WALLACE, *Camp-Fire and Cotton-Field: Southern Adventure in Time of War* (New York, 1865).

LaCOUR, ARTHUR BURTON, and LANDRY, STUART OMER, *New Orleans Masquerade; Chronicles of Carnival* (New Orleans, 1952).

LAFON, BERNARD, *L'Annuaire Louisianais pour l'Anee 1809* (New Orleans, 1808).

LA HARPE, BERNARD DE, *Journal historique de l'Établissement des Français à la Louisiane* (Nouvelle-Orléans, 1831).

LAND, MARY, *Louisiana Cookery* (Baton Rouge, 1954).

LANDRY, STUART OMER, *The Battle of Liberty Place; The Overthrow of Carpet-Bag Rule in New Orleans, September 14, 1874* (New Orleans, 1955).

LANDRY, STUART OMER, *History of the Boston Club* (New Orleans, 1938).

LANDRY, STUART OMER, ed., *Louisiana Almanac and Fact Book* (New Orleans, 1949 ff).

LANE, MARGARET T., *List of the Public Documents of Louisiana, 1948-1953* (State of Louisiana, Official Publications, Volume II. Baton Rouge, 1954).

LA SALLE, NICHOLAS DE, *Relation of the Discovery of the Mississippi River.* Translated by M. B. Anderson. (Chicago, 1898).

LATOUR, ARSÈNE LACARRIÈRE, *Historical Memoir of the War in West Florida and Louisiana in 1814-15* (Philadelphia, 1816).

LATROBE, B. H. B., *Impressions Respecting New Orleans, 1818-1820* (New York, 1951).

LAUSSAT, PIERRE-CLÉMENT DE, *Mémoires sur Ma Vie* (Paris, 1831).

LAUVRIÈRE, EMILE, *Histoire de la Louisiane Française, 1673-1939* (Paris, 1940).

LAVAL, ANTOINE FRANÇOIS, *Voyage de la Louisiane, fait par ordre du roy en l'année mil sept cent vingt* (Paris, 1728).

LEBRETON, DAGMAR RENSHAW, *Chahta-Ima; The Life of Adrien-Emmanuel Rouquette* (Baton Rouge, 1947).

LECONTE, RENÉ, *Les Allemands à la Louisiane au XVIIIe Siecle* (Paris, 1924).

LE JEUNE, LOUIS, *Le Chevalier Pierre Le Moyne, Sieur d'Iberville* (Ottawa, 1937).

LEWIS, VIRGIL, *The Story of the Louisiana Purchase* (St. Louis, 1903).

LOGGINS, VERNON, *Where the Word Ends; The Life of Louis Moreau Gottschalk* (Baton Rouge, 1958).

LONG, HUEY, *Every Man A King* (New Orleans, 1933).

LONG, HUEY P., *My First Days in the White House* (Harrisburg, Penn., 1935).

LONGINO, LUTHER, *Thoughts, Visions, and Sketches of North Louisiana* (Minden, 1930).

LONGSTREET, STEPHEN, *The Real Jazz Old and New* (Baton Rouge, 1956).

LONN, ELLA, *Reconstruction in Louisiana After 1868* (New York, 1918).

LOOS, JOHN L., *Oil on Stream! A History of Interstate Oil Pipe Line Company, 1909-1959* (Baton Rouge, 1959).

Louisiana, A Guide to the State (American Guide Series, New York, 1941).

Louisiana: Its History, People, Government and Economy (Louisiana Legislative Council, Research Study No. 7. Baton Rouge, 1955).

Louisiana Newspapers, 1794-1940; A Union List of Louisiana Newspaper Files Available in

Offices of Publishers, Libraries, and Private Collections in Louisiana (Historical Records Survey. University, La., 1941).

Louisianians and Their State. A Historical and Biographical Text Book of Louisiana (New Orleans, 1919).

LYON, E. WILSON, *Louisiana in French Diplomacy, 1759-1804* (Norman, Okla., 1934).

M'CALEB, THOMAS, ed., *The Louisiana Book: Selections from the Literature of the State* (New Orleans, 1894).

McGINTY, GARNIE WILLIAM, *A History of Louisiana* (New York, 1949).

McGINTY, GARNIE WILLIAM, *Louisiana Redeemed; The Overthrow of Carpet-Bag Rule, 1876-1880* (New Orleans, 1941).

McHATTON, P. E., *From Flag to Flag* (New Orleans, 1889).

McINTIRE, WILLIAM G., *Prehistoric Indian Settlements of the Changing Mississippi River Delta* (Baton Rouge, 1958).

McLOUGHLIN, JAMES JOSEPH, *The Jack Lafaience Book* (New Orleans, 1922).

McLURE, MARY LILLA, *Louisiana Leaders, 1830-1860* (Shreveport, 1937).

McLURE, MARY LILLA, and HOWE, J. ED., *History of Shreveport and Shreveport Builders* (Shreveport, 1937).

McMURTRIE, DOUGLAS C., *Early Printing in New Orleans, 1764-1810, with a Bibliography of the Issues of the Louisiana Press* (New Orleans, 1929).

McNEIL, EVERETT HENRY, *Tonty of the Iron Hand* (New York, 1926).

McVOY, LIZZIE CARTER, and CAMPBELL, RUTH BATES, *A Bibliography of Fiction by Louisianians and on Louisiana Subjects* (Baton Rouge, 1935).

McWILLIAMS, RICHEBOURG GAILLARD, ed., *Fleur de Lys and Calumet; Being the Pénicaut Narrative of French Adventure in Louisiana* (Baton Rouge, 1953).

MAGRUDER, HARRIET, *A History of Louisiana* (Boston, 1909).

MARCHAND, SIDNEY A., *Acadian Exiles in the Golden Coast of Louisiana* (Donaldsonville, 1943).

MARCHAND, SIDNEY A., *The Flight of a Century (1800-1900); In Ascension Parish, Louisiana* (Donaldsonville, 1936).

MARCHAND, SIDNEY A., *The Story of Ascension Parish* (Baton Rouge, 1931).

MARGRY, PIERRE, ed., *Découvertes et Établissements des Français dans l'ouest et dans le sud de l'Amérique Septentrionale, 1614-1754*, 6 vols. (Paris, 1879-88).

MARTIN, FRANÇOIS XAVIER, *The History of Louisiana. From the Earliest Period* (New Orleans, 1882). [Contains also W. W. Howe's Memoir of the Author and J. F. Condon's Annals of Louisiana (1815-1861).]

MERCIER, ALFRED, *Biographie de Pierre Soulé, Sénateur à Washington* (Paris, 1848).

MERCIER, ALFRED, *L'habitation Saint-Ybers; ou Maitres et Esclaves en Louisiana* (Nouvelle-Orléans, 1881).

MONETTE, JOHN WESLEY, *History of the Discovery and Settlement of the Valley of the Mississippi*, 2 vols. (New York, 1848).

MONTAGNE, CHARLES, *Histoire de la Compagnie des Indes* (Paris, 1899).

MOODY, V. ALTON, *Slavery on Louisiana Sugar Plantations* (A reprint from the *Louisiana Historical Quarterly, 1924*. New Orleans, 1924.)

MOREAU, LISLET LOUIS, *Digeste Général des Actes de la Législature de la Louisiane, Passés depuis l'anée 1804 jusqu'en 1827*, 2 vols. (Nouvelle-Orléans, 1828).

MOREAU LISLET, LOUIS, and CARLETON, HENRY, *The Laws of Las Siete Partidas which are still in Force in the State of Louisiana* (New Orleans, 1820).

[MORRISON, ANDREW, compiler], *New Orleans and the New South* (New Orleans, 1888).

MOUNT, MAY W., *Some Notables of New Orleans. Biographical and Descriptive Sketches of the Artists of New Orleans and Their Work* (New Orleans, 1896).

MURPHY, EDMUND ROBERT, *Henry de Tonty; Fur Trader of the Mississippi* (Baltimore, 1941).

MURPHY, WILLIAM M., *Notes from the History of Madison Parish, Louisiana* (Ruston, 1927).

The New Orleans Guide, or General Directory for 1837 (New Orleans, 1837).

New Orleans City Guide (American Guide Series, Boston, 1938).

NOLTE, VINCENT OTTO, *Fifty Years in Both Hemispheres* (New York, 1854).

NORMAN, BENJAMIN MOORE, *Norman's New Orleans and Environs* (New Orleans, 1845).

NORTHUP, SOLOMON, *Twelve Years a Slave* (Auburn, N.Y., 1853).

O'CONNOR, THOMAS, *History of the Fire Department of New Orleans from the Earliest Days to the Present Time* (New Orleans, 1895).

Official Records of the Union and Confederate Navies in the War of the Rebellion, 31 vols. (Washington, 1895-1927).

Official Report Relative to the Conduct of Federal Troops in Western Louisiana During the Invasions of 1863 and 1864; Compiled from Sworn Testimony Under Direction of Governor Henry W. Allen (Shreveport, 1865).

OPOTOWSKY, STAN, *The Longs of Louisiana* (New York, 1960).

O'PRY, MAUDE HEARN, *Chronicles of Shreveport* (Shreveport, 1928).

Ordinances Passed by the Convention of the State of Louisiana (New Orleans, 1861).

OSTERWEIS, R., *Judah P. Benjamin* (New York, 1933).

OUDARD, GEORGES, *The Amazing Life of John Law: The Man behind the Mississippi Bubble* (New York, 1928).

OUDARD, GEORGES, *Four Cents an Acre; The Story of Louisiana Under the French* (New York, 1931).

OUDARD, GEORGES, *La Louisiane au Temps des Français* (Paris, 1931).

OWEN, WILLIAM MILLER, *In Camp and Battle with the Washington Artillery of New Orleans* (Boston, 1885).

PARKS, JOSEPH HOWARD, *General Edmund Kirby Smith, C. S. A.* (Baton Rouge, 1954).

PARTON, JAMES, *General Butler in New Orleans* (New York, 1864).

PAXTON, W. E., *A History of the Baptists of Louisiana* (St. Louis, 1888).

PEABODY, CHARLES A., *The United States Provisional Court for the State of Louisiana, 1862-1865 (Annual Report* of the American Historical Association for the year 1892, Washington, 1893).

[PEDRICK, WILLIAM E.], *New Orleans As It Is* (Cleveland, 1885).

PERRIN DU LAC, F. M., *Voyage dans les Deux Louisianes et chez les Nations Sauvages du Missouri* (Paris, 1805).

PERRIN, WILLIAM HENRY, *Southwest Louisiana, Biographical and Historical* (New Orleans, 1891).

PHARES, ROSS, *Cavalier in the Wilderness; The Story of the Explorer and Trader Louis Juchereau de St. Denis* (Baton Rouge, 1952).

PHELPS, ALBERT, *Louisiana; A Record of Expansion* (Boston, 1905).

Picayune's Guide to New Orleans (New Orleans, 1904).

PITTMAN, PHILIP, *The Present State of the European Settlements on the Mississippi* (London, 1770).

Plantation Diary of the Late Mr. Valcour Aime (New Orleans, 1878).

POLK, W. M., *Leonidas Polk, Bishop and General*, 2 vols. (New York, 1915).

POOLE, THOMAS W., *Some Late Words About Louisiana* (New Orleans, 1889).

PORTRE-BOBINSKI, GERMAINE, *French Civilization and Culture in Natchitoches* (New Orleans, 1934).

PORTRE-BOBINSKI, GERMAINE, and SMITH, CLARA MILDRED, *Natchitoches; The Up-To-Date Oldest Town in Louisiana* (New Orleans, 1936).

POSEY, WALTER BROWNLOW, *The Baptist Church in the Lower Mississippi Valley, 1776-1845* (Lexington, 1957).

POSEY, WALTER BROWNLOW, *The Development of Methodism in the Old Southwest, 1783-1824* (Nashville, 1933).

POWELL, ALDEN L., *A Primer on Government in Louisiana* (Baton Rouge, 1946).

The Present State of the Country and Inhabitants, European and Indians of Louisiana on the North Continent of America, by an Officer at New Orleans to His Friend at Paris (London, 1744).

RANKIN, DANIEL S., *Kate Chopin and Her Creole Stories* (Philadelphia, 1932).

READ, WILLIAM A., *Louisiana-French* (Baton Rouge, 1931).

READ, WILLIAM A., *Louisiana Place Names of Indian Origin* (Baton Rouge, 1927).

REED, EMILY HAZEN, *Life of A. P. Dostie; or, The Conflict of New Orleans* (New York, 1868).

RENAUT, F. P., *La Question de la Louisiane, 1796-1806* (Paris, 1918).

Report on the Louisiana Election of 1876 (Senate Document No. 701, 44 Cong., 2 Sess., Washington, 1877).

Report of the Select Committee on Condition of the South (House Document No. 261, 43 Cong., 2 Sess., Washington, 1875).

Report of the Select Committee on the New Orleans Riots (House Document No. 16, 39 Cong., 2 Sess., Washington, 1867).

REYNOLDS, GEORGE M., *Machine Politics in New Orleans, 1897-1926* (New York, 1936).

RIGHTOR, HENRY, ed., *Standard History of New Orleans* (Chicago, 1900).

RIPLEY, ELIZA, *Social Life in Old New Orleans* (New York, 1912).

ROBERTSON, JAMES A., *Louisiana Under Spain, France and the United States, 1785-1807*, 2 vols. (Cleveland, 1911).

ROBERTSON, MINNS SLEDGE, *Public Education in Louisiana After 1898* (Baton Rouge, 1952).

ROBIN, CLAUDE C., *Voyages dans l'intérieur de la Louisiane*, 3 vols. (Paris, 1807).

ROBINSON, ELRIE, *Biographical Sketches of James M. Bradford, Pioneer Printer* (St. Francisville, 1938).

ROBINSON, ELRIE, *Early Feliciana Politics* (St. Francisville, 1936).

[ROBINSON, WILLIAM L.], *The Diary of a Samaritan, by a Member of the Howard Association of New Orleans* (New York, 1859).

ROLAND, CHARLES P., *Louisiana Sugar Plantations During the American Civil War* (Leiden, Holland, 1957).

ROURKE, CONSTANCE MAYFIELD, *Audubon* (New York, 1936).

ROUSSÈVE, CHARLES B., *The Negro in Louisiana: Aspects of His Culture and Literature* (New Orleans, 1937).

ROWLAND, DUNBAR, *Encyclopedia of Mississippi History*, 2 vols. (Madison, Wis., 1907).

ROWLAND, DUNBAR, *History of Mississippi, The Heart of the South*, 2 vols. (Chicago, 1925).

ROWLAND, DUNBAR, ed., *Mississippi Provincial Archives, 1763-1766* (Nashville, Tenn., 1911).

ROWLAND, DUNBAR, ed., *The Mississippi Territorial Archives, 1798-1803* (Nashville, Tenn., 1905).

ROWLAND, DUNBAR, ed., *Official Letter Books of W. C. C. Claiborne, 1801-1816*, 6 vols. (Jackson, Miss., 1917).

ROWLAND, DUNBAR, and SANDERS, ALBERT G., eds., *Mississippi Provincial Archives*, 3 vols. (Jackson, Miss., 1927-1932).

ROWLAND, KATE MASON, and CROXALL, MRS. MORRIS L., eds., *The Journal of Julia Le Grand* (Richmond, 1911).

SAINT-MÉRY, MOREAU DE, *Lois et Constitutions des Colonies Françaises de l'Amérique Sous-le-Vent, de 1550 à 1785*, 6 vols. (Paris, 1784-1790).

[392]

SAUCIER, CORINNE L., *History of Avoyelles Parish, Louisiana* (New Orleans, 1943).
SAXON, LYLE, *Fabulous New Orleans* (New York, 1928).
SAXON, LYLE, *Father Mississippi* (New York, 1927).
SAXON, LYLE, *The Friends of Joe Gilmore* (New York, 1948).
SAXON, LYLE, *Lafitte the Pirate* (New York, 1930).
SAXON, LYLE, *Old Louisiana* (New York, 1929).
SAXON, LYLE, and others, eds., *Gumbo Ya-Ya* (New York, 1945).
SCHLARMAN, J. H., *From Quebec to New Orleans* (Belleville, Ill., 1929).
SCOTT, JOHN, *Story of the Thirty Second Iowa Infantry Volunteers* (Navada, Iowa, 1896).
[SEALSFIELD, CHARLES], *Les Émigrés Français dans la Louisiane (1800-1804)* (Paris, 1853).
SEARS, LOUIS MARTIN, *John Slidell* (Durham, N. Car., 1925).
SEEBOLD, HERMAN DE BACHELLE, *Old Louisiana Plantation Homes and Family Trees*, 2 vols. (New Orleans, 1941).
SEMPLE, HENRY CHURCHILL, *The Ursulines in New Orleans . . . 1725-1925* (New York, 1925).
SERRANO Y SANZ, MANUEL, ed., *Documentos Históricos de la Florida y la Luisiana, Siglos XVI al XVIII* (Madrid, 1912).
SHEA, JOHN GILMARY, *Discovery and Exploration of the Mississippi Valley* (Albany, N. Y., 1903).
SHEA, JOHN GILMARY, *Early Voyages up and down the Mississippi by Cavelier, St. Gosme, Le Sueur, Gravier and Guignas* (Albany, N.Y., 1861).
SHERTZ, HELEN PITKIN, *Legends of Louisiana* (New Orleans, 1922).
SHUGG, ROGER W., *Origins of Class Struggle in Louisiana; A Social History of White Farmers and Laborers during Slavery and After, 1840-1875* (Baton Rouge, 1939).
SINCLAIR, HAROLD, *The Port of New Orleans* (New York, 1942).
SINDLER, ALLAN P., *Huey Long's Louisiana; State Politics, 1920-1952* (Baltimore, 1956).
SITTERSON, J. CARLYLE, *Sugar Country: The Cane Sugar Industry in the South, 1753-1950* (Lexington, Ky., 1953).
SKIPPER, OTTIS CLARK, *J. D. B. DeBow; Magazinist of the Old South* (Athens, Ga., 1958).
SKIPWITH, HENRY, *East Feliciana, Louisiana, Past and Present; Sketches of the Pioneers* (New Orleans, 1892).
SMITH, T. LYNN, and HITT, HOMER L., *The People of Louisiana* (Baton Rouge, 1952).
SMITH, WEBSTER (pseud.), *The Kingfish; A Biography of Huey P. Long* (New York, 1933).
Soard's Blue Book of New Orleans, for 1890-91 (New Orleans, 1890).
[SONIAT DU FOSSAT, MRS. EUGENE], *Biographical Sketches of Louisiana's Governors from D'Iberville to Foster* (Baton Rouge, 1893).
SOUTHWOOD, MARION, *"Beauty and Booty"; The Watchword of New Orleans* (New York, 1867).
SPARKS, W. H., *Memories of Fifty Years* (Philadelphia, 1870).
SPEARS, JOHN R., and CLARK, A. H., *A History of the Mississippi Valley From its Discovery to the End of Foreign Domination* (New York, 1903).
SPRATLING, WILLIAM A., and SCOTT, NATALIE, *Old Plantation Houses in Louisiana* (New York, 1927).
State Papers and Correspondence bearing upon the Purchase of the Territory of Louisiana (House Document No. 431, 57 Cong., 2 Sess., Washington, 1903).
STEPHENSON, WENDELL HOLMES, *Alexander Porter, Whig Planter of Old Louisiana* (Baton Rouge, 1934).
STEPHENSON, WENDELL HOLMES, *Isaac Franklin; Slave Trader and Planter of the Old South* (University, La., 1938).
STERN, JACQUES, *Les Colonies Françaises, Passe et Avenir* (New York, 1943).
STODDARD, AMOS, *Sketches, Historical and Descriptive, of Louisiana* (Philadelphia, 1812).
STUBBS, WILLIAM C., *A Handbook of Louisiana* (New Orleans, 1895).
SURREY, N. M. MILLER, ed., *Calendar of Manuscripts in Paris for the History of the Mississippi Valley*, 2 vols. (Washington, D. C., 1928).
SURREY, N. M. MILLER, *The Commerce of Louisiana During the French Regime, 1699-1763* (New York, 1916).
SWANTON, JOHN R., *Indian Tribes of the Lower Mississippi Valley and the Adjacent Coast of the Gulf of Mexico* (Washington, 1911).
TALLANT, ROBERT, *Mardis Gras* (New York, 1948).
TALLANT, ROBERT, *The Romantic New Orleanians* (New York, 1950).
TAYLOR, F. JAY, ed., *Reluctant Rebel: The Secret Diary of Robert Patrick, 1861-1865* (Baton Rouge, 1959).
TAYLOR, RICHARD, *Destruction and Reconstruction; Personal Experiences of the Late War* (New edition edited by Richard B. Harwell. New York, 1955).
TESTUT, CHARLES, *Portraits Litteraires de la Nouvelle-Orléans* (Nouvelle-Orléans, 1850).
THOMPSON, MAURICE, *The Story of Louisiana* (Boston, 1888).
THOMPSON, THOMAS PAYNE, *Louisiana Writers Native and Resident* (New Orleans, 1904).
TINKER, EDWARD LAROCQUE, *Gombo, The Creole Dialect of Louisiana* (Worcester, Mass., 1936).
TINKER, EDWARD LAROCQUE, *Lafcadio Hearn's American Days* (New York, 1924).
TISCH, JOSEPH LASAGE, *French in Louisiana; A Study of the Historical Development of the French Language of Louisiana* (New Orleans, 1959).
TOMPKINS, F. H., *North Louisiana, Its Soil, Climate, Productions, Health, Schools, etc.* (Cincinnati, 1886).
TONTI, HENRI DE, *Dernières découvertes dans l'Amérique Septentrionale de M. de la Sale* (Paris, 1697).

TRANCHEPAIN, ST. AUGUSTIN DE, *Relation du Voyage des Premières Ursulines à la Nouvelle-Orléans et de leur Établissement en cette ville* (Nouvelle-York, 1859).

TREFOUSSE, HANS L., *Ben Butler: The South Called Him Beast!* (New York, 1957).

TUNNARD, WILLIAM H., *A Southern Record. The History of the Third Regiment, Louisiana Infantry* (Baton Rouge, 1866).

TURNER, ARLIN, *George W. Cable: A Biography* (Durham, N. Car., 1956).

[VALETTE LANDUN, M. DE], *Journal d'un voyage à la Louisiane, fait en 1720* (La Haye, 1768).

VALLON, BERQUIN DU (Berquin Duvallon), *Vue de la Colonie Espagnole du Mississipi, ou des Provinces de Louisiane et Floride Occidentale, en l'année 1802* (Paris, 1803).

VAN ALSTYNE, LAWRENCE, *Diary of an Enlisted Man* (New Haven, Conn., 1910).

VERGENNES, CHARLES GRAVIER DE, *Mémoire historique et politique sur Louisiane* (Paris, 1802).

VETTER, ERNEST G., *Fabulous Frenchtown* (Washington, 1955).

VILLERS DU TERRAGE, MARC DE, *Les Dernières années de la Louisiane Française* (Paris, 1905).

VILLIERS DU TERRAGE, MARC DE, *Documents Concernant l'Histoire des Indiens de la Région Orientale de la Louisiane* (Paris, 1922).

VILLIERS DU TERRAGE, MARC DE, *Histoire de la Fondation de la Nouvelle-Orléans, 1717-1722* (Paris, 1917).

VILLIERS DU TERRAGE, MARC DE, *La Louisiane de Chateaubriand* (Paris, 1924).

VOGEL, CLAUDE L., *The Capuchins in French Louisiana, 1722-1766* (Washington, D. C., 1928).

VOORHIES, FELIX, *Acadian Reminiscences* (Opelousas, 1907).

VOSS, LOUIS, *History of the German Society of New Orleans* (New Orleans, 1927).

VOSS, LOUIS, *Presbyterianism in New Orleans and Adjacent Parishes* (New Orleans, 1931).

WALKER, NORMAN McF., *Historical Sketch Book and Guide to New Orleans* (New York, 1885).

WALLACE, JOSEPH, *The History of Illinois and Louisiana Under the French Rule* (Cincinnati, 1893).

WALLACH, KATE, *Research, in Louisiana Law* (Baton Rouge, 1958).

The War of the Rebellion: A Compilation of the Official Records of the Union and Confederate Armies, 128 vols. & index vol. (Washington, 1880-1902).

WARMOTH, HENRY CLAY, *War, Politics and Reconstruction; Stormy Days in Louisiana* (New York, 1930).

WARREN, HARRIS GAYLORD, *The Sword was Their Passport; A History of American Filibustering in the Mexican Revolution* (Baton Rouge, 1943).

WATSON, WILLIAM, *Life in the Confederate Army* (New York, 1888).

WHITAKER, ARTHUR P., ed., *Documents Relating to the Commercial Policy of Spain in the Floridas, with Incidential Reference to Louisiana* (Deland, Fla., 1931).

WHITAKER, J. S., *Sketches of Life and Character in Louisiana, The Portraits Selected Principally from the Bench and Bar* (New Orleans, 1847).

WHITFIELD, IRENE THERESE, *Louisiana French Folk Songs* (Baton Rouge, 1939).

WHITTINGTON, G. P., *Rapides Parish, Louisiana; A History* (A reprint from the *Louisiana Historical Quarterly*, 1932, 1933, 1934, 1935. Alexandria, n.d.).

Who's Who in Louisiana and Mississippi; Biographical Sketches of Prominent Men and Women of Louisiana and Mississippi (New Orleans, 1918).

WILEY, BELL IRVIN, and FAY, LUCY E., eds., *This Infernal War; The Confederate Letters of Sgt. Edwin H. Fay* (Austin, 1958).

WILKERSON, MARCUS M., *Thomas Duckett Boyd; The Story of a Southern Educator* (Baton Rouge, 1935).

WILKINSON, ANDREWS, *Plantation Stories of Old Louisiana* (Boston, 1914).

WILLIAMS, T. HARRY, *P. G. T. Beauregard, Napoleon in Gray* (Baton Rouge, 1955).

WILLIAMSON, FREDERICK W., *Yesterday and Today in Louisiana Agriculture* (Baton Rouge, 1940).

WILLIAMSON, FREDERICK W., and WILLIAMSON, LILLIAN H., *Northeast Louisiana; A Narrative History of the Ouachita River Valley and the Concordia Country* (Monroe, 1939).

WILSON, DONALD V., *Public Social Services in Louisiana* (Monroe, 1943).

WINSOR, JUSTIN, *The Mississippi Basin, The Struggle in America Between England and France, 1697-1763* (Boston, 1895).

WINZERLING, OSCAR WILLIAM, *Acadian Odyssey* (Baton Rouge, 1955).

WISNER, ELIZABETH, *Public Welfare Administration in Louisiana* (Chicago, 1930).

Woods Directory, Being a Colored Business, Professional and Trades Directory of New Orleans (New Orleans, 1913).

ZACHARIE, JAMES S., *New Orleans Guide* (New Orleans, 1902).

A PICTORIAL
PORTFOLIO

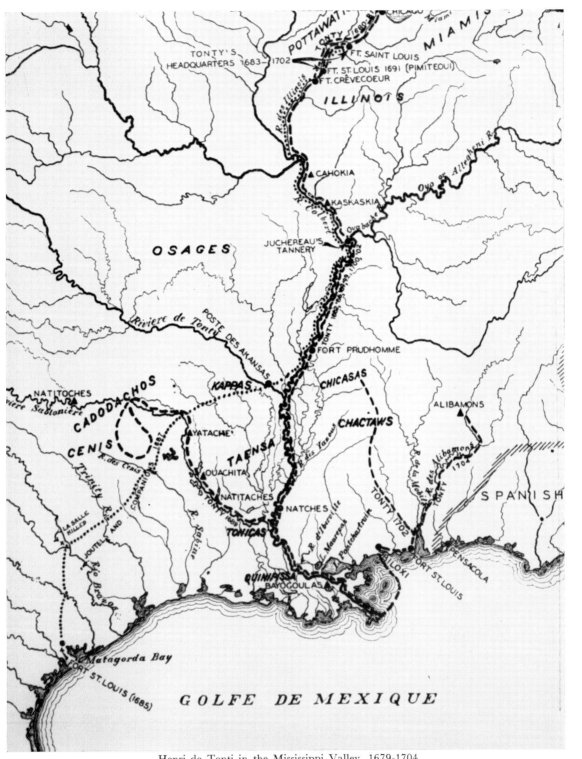

Henri de Tonti in the Mississippi Valley, 1679-1704

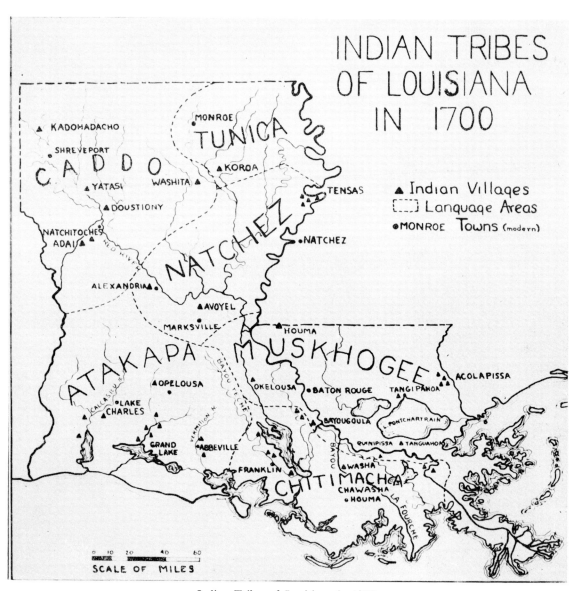

Indian Tribes of Louisiana in 1700

Reproduction of painting of Bienville, in Louisiana State Museum

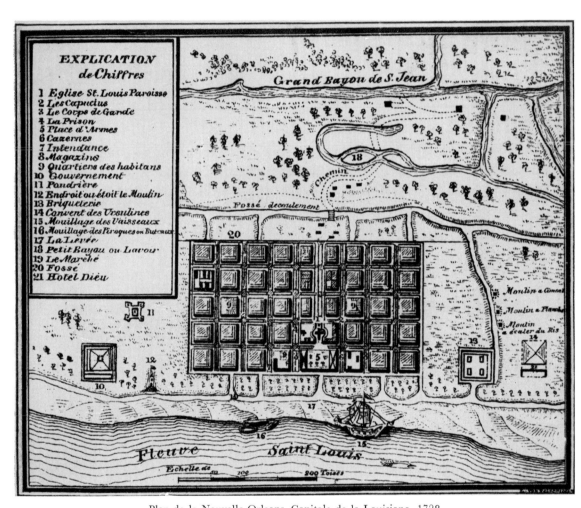

Plan de la Nouvelle Orleans, Capitale de la Louisiane, 1728

(Courtesy of Department of Commerce and Industry)

Display of Flags

(Courtesy of Department of Commerce and Industry)
Medallions on Lamp Posts, New Orleans

(Courtesy of Department of Commerce and Industry)
Medallions on Lamp Posts, New Orleans

(Courtesy of Department of Commerce and Industry)
Medallions on lamp posts, New Orleans

(Courtesy of Department of Commerce and Industry)
Medallions on Lamp Posts, New Orleans

Signing of Louisiana Purchase

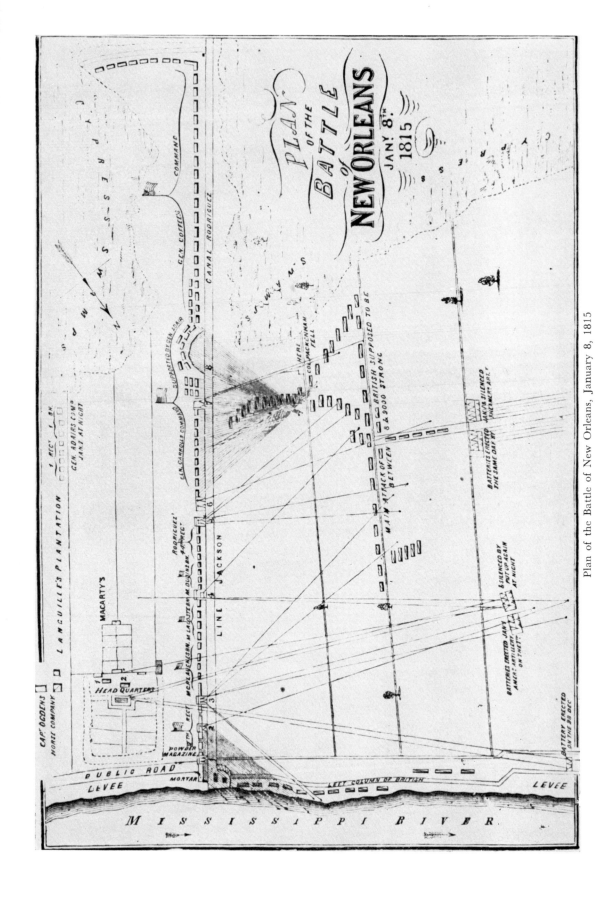

Plan of the Battle of New Orleans, January 8, 1815

Mississippi River Scene

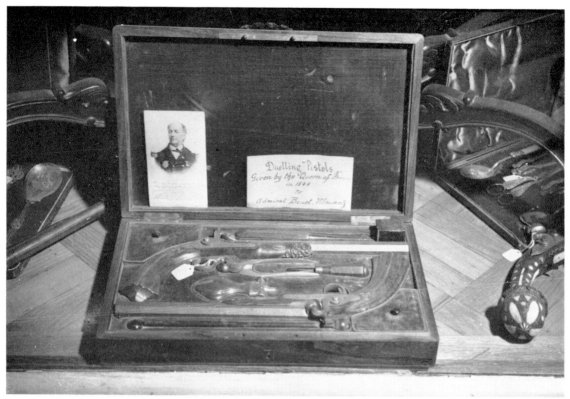

(Courtesy of Department of Commerce and Industry)

Duelling Pistols (Given by Queen of France)

From Davis, *Louisiana, The Pelican State*

Old Scene on the Mississippi

Early View of Baton Rouge

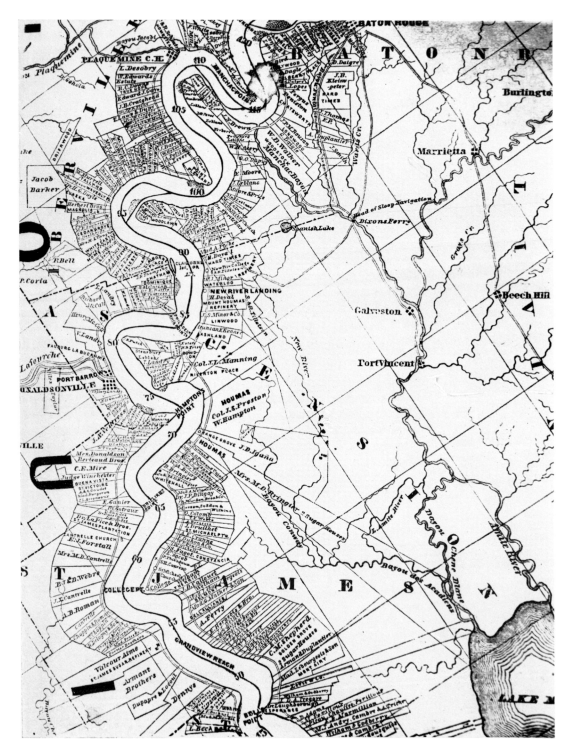

Map of the Mississippi River Plantations, between Baton Rouge and New Orleans

Madewood Plantation, Bayou Lafourche

Napoleon House, New Orleans

Louisiana Parishes
1860

From Davis, *Louisiana, The Pelican State*

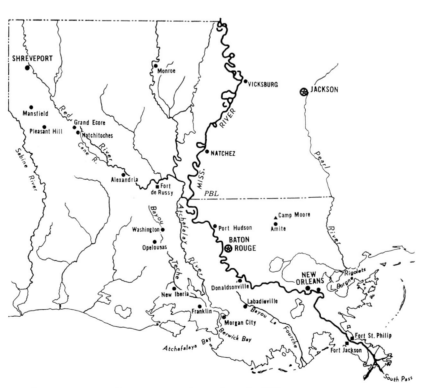

Louisiana During the Civil War

From Davis, *Louisiana, The Pelican State*

Arrival of Captain Bailey, at New Orleans, to demand the surrender of the City

Capture of Baton Rouge, December 17, 1862

Return of a Foraging Party of the 24th Reg. Conn. Volunteers

Burning the Capitol at Baton Rouge, December 30, 1862

Headquarters, General McPherson, Lake Providence

Battle of Grand Coteau, November 3, 1863

Banks' Army crossing Cane River, March 31, 1864

Admiral Porter's fleet passing through Col. Bailey's Dam, May, 1864

Canal Street, New Orleans, 1902

(Courtesy of Chamber of Commerce, New Orleans)

Richardson Hall, Tulane University, New Orleans

Charity Hospital, New Orleans, about 1873

Charity Hospital, New Orleans

Canal Street Fountain, New Orleans, about 1873

(Courtesy of Department of Commerce and Industry)

St. John's Cathedral, Lafeyette

(Courtesy of Department of Commerce and Industry)

Vermilion Parish Court House, Abbeville

First Successful Oil Well, September 21, 1901 near Jennings

State Capitol, Baton Rouge

Statue of Evangeline

The Shadows, New Iberia

Greenwood, beautiful Plantation Home

Acadian House Museum at Longfellow-Evangeline
State Park

Huey P. Long Grave

Aerial View, downtown Shreveport

L.S.U. Memorial Tower

Jackson Square, in front of St. Louis Cathedral

Cabildo, New Orleans

Evangeline Oak

INDEX

INDEX